Essential
Public
Health

Essential Public Health

L J Donaldson
QHP, MSc(Anatomy), MD, FRCS(Ed), FFPHM, FRCP, FRCP(Ed), FMedSci
Honorary Professor of Applied Epidemiology
University of Newcastle upon Tyne

R J Donaldson
OBE, CStJ, DPH, FFPHM
Consultant in Public Health Medicine
Lately Director of the South Eastern Consortium for training in
Public Health Medicine, St George's Hospital Medical School, London

SECOND EDITION

 PETROC PRESS

Petroc Press, an imprint of LibraPharm Limited

Distributors

Plymbridge Distributors Limited
Plymbridge House
Estover Road
Plymouth
PL6 7PZ
UK

Published in the United Kingdom by LibraPharm Limited, Gemini House, 162 Craven Road, Newbury, Berkshire, RG14 5NR.

A catalogue record for this book is available from the British Library

ISBN 1 900603 32 2

Typeset by ReadyText, Bath, UK.
Printed and bound in the United Kingdom by MPG Books, Bodmin, Cornwall.

Contents

About the Authors

Professor Liam Donaldson has held senior executive posts in public health and management within the National Health Service. In the mid-1990s he was Regional Director and Director of Public Health for one of the eight NHS regions in England serving a population of about seven million. He has also held a number of senior academic posts in epidemiology and public health. His responsibilities have included health-policy making, management, research and teaching. He has lectured extensively to staff and students in all health care disciplines and has published widely in medical journals on topics arising from his research and on health policy matters generally. He holds an Honorary Chair at the University of Newcastle-upon-Tyne and has been awarded honorary degrees by the universities of Huddersfield and Bristol. In 1998 Professor Donaldson was appointed as the Government's Chief Medical Officer for England.

Dr R. J. 'Paddy' Donaldson OBE has had a long and distinguished career in Public Health. As a Medical Officer of Health he dealt with the wide range of problems of large urban populations. Later, he held senior academic appointments in London University Medical Schools where his responsibilities included designing and running major training programmes in public health. He has been a major figure in post-war public health in Britain. Dr Donaldson has written extensively on health topics and spoken to health professionals in Britain and many other countries. He has served on many committees which advise government.

Publishing Acknowledgements

We are grateful to individual publishers, institutions, editors and authors for permission to reproduce material as tables, figures or illustrations. In most cases the source is acknowledged in full as a footnote to the presentation but we also take this opportunity to use the more detailed form of words requested by some copyright holders and to make the following additional acknowledgements.

The Association of the British Pharmaceutical Industry (ABPI): Table 4.11. Professor Adrian Davis: Figure 5.5. *American Journal of Epidemiology*: Figure 9.3. BBC Books: The extract [Table 10.3] from *Where on Earth are we Going?* by Jonathon Porritt reprinted on page 430 is reproduced with the permission of BBC Worldwide Limited. Copyright ©Jonathon Porritt 1990. BMJ Publishing Group: Figures 2.11, 2.12, 2.16 and Tables 2.17, 2.18 were first published in the *Journal of Epidemiology and Community Health*. Figures 2.3, 4.10, 4.11, 8.8 and Tables 2.9, 2.10, 2.12, 2.13, 2.14, 4.1 and 4.5 were first published in the BMJ and are reproduced by kind permission of the BMJ. Bradford Health Authority and Dr Dee Kyle: Table 3.12. *Canadian Medical Association Journal*: Table 4.7. No magic bullets: a systematic review of 102 trials of interventions to improve professional practice. Adapted from, by permission of the publisher, CMAJ, 1995; 153 (10), pp. 1423–31. The Carnegie United Kingdom Trust: Table 8.1. Columbia University Press: Figure 3.6. *Community Organising* by George Brager and Harry Specht. Copyright © 1973 Columbia Unversity Press. Reprinted with the permission of the publisher. *Diabetologia*: Figure 2.5. *Effective Health Care Bulletin*: Figure 2.2 and Tables 6.9, 8.8. *Epidemiologic Reviews*: Tables 2.6 and 7.3. Family Planning Association: Table 6.7. Health Education Authority: Figures 3.2, 3.17, 3.21 and Tables 3.8, 3.19 are copyright of the HEA and are reproduced with permission. Healthcare Computing & Communications Canada Inc: Figure 1.11. *Health Policy*: Table 1.6 reproduced with permission from Elsevier Science. *Health Trends*: Table 1.4. *Hospital Medicine*: Tables 2.1 and 2.11. *Journal of Otolaryngology*: Table 4.6. *Journal of the Royal Society of Health*: Table 1.1. King's Fund Publishing: Tables 3.11 and 10.6 reproduced by kind permission of King's Fund Publishing. *The Lancet*: Figure 2.4 and Table 2.19 © by the Lancet Ltd. Macmillan Press Ltd: Table 2.4 reprinted by permission of Macmillan Press Ltd and Klim McPherson. Manchester University: Table 7.6 reproduced by courtesy of the Director and Librarian, the John Rylands University Library of Manchester. *Medical Care*: Figure 6.7 reproduced by kind permission of Lippincott, Williams & Wilkins. Merseyside Health Impact Assessment Steering Group: Figure 10.3. Scott-Samuel A, Birley M, Ardern K. The Merseyside Guidelines for Health Impact Assessment. Liverpool: Merseyside Health Impact Assessment Steering Group/Liverpool Public Health Observatory, 1998. Professor R Balarajan and The National Institute for Ethnic Studies in Health and Social Policy: Figure 1.1. The National Radiological Protection Board (NRPB): Figure 10.6 and Table 10.8. OECD: Figure 4.12 © OECD. Office for National Statistics (ONS): for permission to reproduce Figures 1.4, 1.5, 2.7, 2.13, 2.15, 3.7, 3.8, 6.1, 6.5, 6.6, 6.9, 6.12, 6.15, 7.2, 7.4, 7.5, 8.1, 8.2, 8.3, 8.7, 8.11, and Tables 6.2, 6.3, 6.5, 6.6, 8.4, 8.7, 8.6 © Crown Copyright 2000. Oxford University Press: Figures 2.1, 3.16, 8.5 and Tables 2.2, 2.3, 5.4, 8.9 are reproduced by permission of Oxford University Press. *Paediatric and Perinatal Epidemiology*: Table 7.10 reproduced by kind permission of Blackwell Science Ltd. Public Health Laboratory Service: Table 9.2. *Public Health Reports*: Figure 3.14. Royal College of Psychiatrists: Tables 2.22, 2.23, 2.24, 7.4, 7.7, 7.12. Royal Society of Medicine: Figure 8.9. David Sackett: Table 4.4. The Sainsbury Centre for Mental Health: Figures 7.3, 7.6 and Tables 7.8, 7.9. The Stationery Office (TSO) for permission to present various analyses of official statistics throughout the book. The Wellcome Institute Library for supplying the historical pictures in Chapters 3 and 7. WHO Regional Office for Europe: Figure 10.5, Table 3.10. WHO Geneva: Figures 1.10, 3.9, 3.10, 3.12, 6.10, 8.4, 8.6, 10.4 and Table 3.4.

Our apologies to any individual, organisation, institution or publication we may have omitted from the above list. In addition, the publisher has attempted to contact all of the holders of copyrighted figures, tables and data. If any has been inadvertently overlooked, the publisher will be only too happy to make the necessary arrangements at the earliest opportunity.

Introduction

As a new century begins, our book has been in continuous print for 17 years, first as *Essential Community Medicine*, then as *Essential Public Health Medicine*, now as *Essential Public Health*. We are heartened that we have been able to meet the needs of so many readers for so long.

The text aims to bring together, in one volume, the principles and applications of epidemiology, the main health problems experienced by populations and by the main groups within them, the strategies for intervention to promote health and prevent disease, the main themes underlying health policy formulation and a description of the provision of health services.

The fact that *Essential Public Health Medicine* became a standard text in so many institutions of learning and training as well as the large and very positive response we have had from students and practitioners in a variety of disciplines, emboldens us to claim that we largely fulfil these aims. Students, both undergraduate and postgraduate, in a number of disciplines have even written to us to say that they were successful in examinations through reading the book and receiving no other teaching. As experienced teachers we would not encourage nor would we condone such an approach. Nevertheless, we are pleased that the book provided the breadth and depth of knowledge required.

In building upon these foundations, why, then, have we seen the need so radically to revise what has become *Essential Public Health*? Firstly, the 1990s has been a decade of major change, not just in the understanding of the epidemiology of diseases but in the concepts and philosophy of public health and in the structure and functioning of health care services. Secondly, we have benefited from the constructive comments of students and colleagues on the previous edition.

Each chapter has been revised. Many new themes have been introduced and many new subjects dealt with in the earlier book have been brought up-to-date. We have also introduced much new material of direct practical relevance.

Chapter 1 of *Essential Public Health* describes the ways in which an assessment can be made of the health and health needs of a population. The main sources of information on health and health services are reviewed with examples of their uses. The common measures of morbidity and mortality are described together with illustrations about how they are used to describe health problems in populations. Throughout this first chapter, we have placed special emphasis on providing simple descriptions and definitions of the concepts involved and on explaining the origins of the common types of routinely available and specially-collected data.

Chapter 2 draws together the main approaches of public health investigation starting with the ways in which descriptive epidemiological data can be used to examine the frequency of diseases within and between populations and over time. The main study methods of epidemiology – cross-sectional or prevalence studies, cohort studies, case-control studies and randomised controlled trials are described. Emphasis is placed not just not on the conceptual basis of these important methods of investigation but on their strengths and weaknesses and their applicability in particular situations. The final section of Chapter 2 gives examples of practical investigations in public health. Each is described from our own experience so that we are able to draw attention to the reality of carrying out such investigations as well as how to interpret and act upon the findings which emerge from them. The field of study is sometimes referred to as 'quick and dirty' investigation. We do not subscribe to this philosophy and our emphasis is on the need for rigour even when a pragmatic approach needs to be taken in deciding the scope of the study and the speed with which it is carried out.

Chapter 3 discusses the concept of health and deals with the subject of health promotion encompassing health education, disease prevention and health protection. The main strategies in health promotion are described in this chapter and the main health problems amenable to intervention in this way are discussed. There are strengthened sections on drug and alcohol abuse, infection with the Human Immune Deficiency Virus (HIV) which causes the Acquired Immune Deficiency Syndrome (AIDS), and public health policy. The previous sections on coronary heart disease, stroke, accidents and presymptomatic screening have been expanded and brought up-to-date.

Special emphasis is given in Chapter 3 to the promotion of health in the younger age-groups where the foundations of healthy living can be laid. Many young people become involved in different types of risk-taking behaviour during their teenage years. In the case of smoking, drinking, drug or solvent misuse, such behaviour has considerable impact on current as well as future health. Unhealthy patterns of behaviour can be developed during adolescence which are carried through into maturity and adulthood. Not only must young people be informed and educated, they must be encouraged to practise and adopt a range of lifestyles. Chapter 3 discusses these issues and the challenges of, and strategies for, achieving behaviour change in all age-groups, particularly young people. Chapter 3 also discusses inequalities in health and the powerful underlying influence of social and economic determinants on health.

In the first three chapters, many of the scientific foundations of public health are laid down. Throughout the reader is made aware of the strengths and limitations of the data, of how data are turned into information and of the challenges in changing human behaviour and designing programmes to promote health and prevent disease.

The modern welfare state is a large and complex structure with diverse origins and traditions. The late 1990s saw it undergo major reform with the introduction of fundamental changes to the National Health Service.

Chapter 4 brings together in one place a description of the present structure, organisational framework and method of functioning of this wide range of services. New sections deal with quality in health care, including a description of the concept of clinical governance and the structure and processes which support it. The sections on the planning, management and funding of the health service have also been substantially expanded.

Early life is the time when the foundations of health are laid when some of the risks are greatest. Chapter 6 deals with the health of mothers and children. The main epidemiological features of health and disease in infancy and childhood are described as are the risks to fetal and maternal health. The main measures of fertility in a population are described, so too are the main trends over time in fertility and the factors which can influence the number of completed pregnancies in a population. The causes of death at different periods of infancy are also discussed and the various mortality rates in early life are defined. The range of approaches which can be taken to promote health in pregnancy and childhood are described as are the maternity and child health services themselves.

Increasingly, more and more people in many countries of the world are living into late old age. They will have needs which must be met not just by those services which diagnose and treat illness but also those which enhance their capacity for independent living and provide appropriate support where this is not possible. There are other groups within the population with special needs: adults and children with physical disability, people with mental illness and those with learning disability. All these groups need services which are broad-based and delivered by a wide range of agencies within the community which are working towards a common purpose. They also need services which are based upon a clear assessment of their needs. This means being familiar with all relevant sources of data and the ways in which they can be used to describe the needs of a group within the population. Chapters 5 (*Physical Disability*), 7 (*Mental Health and Learning Disability*) and 8 (*Health in Later Life*) are concerned with these groups. In these chapters greater emphasis has been placed on defining the needs as well as describing the framework of service provision required. The development of care in the community and the need for coordination of the work of different care agencies and the professional staff working within them is particularly emphasised. The importance of taking account of, and meeting, the needs of family members and other informal carers is also stressed.

Chapter 9 deals with communicable diseases. We have retained the approach of describing individual diseases which we used in the earlier book but have also introduced a new classification of these important health problems. We have described more diseases. In *Essential Public Health* there is also a new emphasis on practical approaches to the introduction and surveillance of communicable diseases – especially the handling of outbreaks and untoward incidents.

The importance of the relationship between the quality of the environment and people's health has long been recognized. Moreover, there have been a number of major incidents around the world which have all too dramatically highlighted some of the contemporary threats and hazards, both to the well-being of individuals and to the planet itself. There is still an enormous amount to be learned about the influence of the environment on health. The growth in interest and rapidly rising concerns about wider environmental issues make it certain that there will be an increasing focus on the links between environmental and health issues. In Chapter 10, we describe the impact of the environment on health as well as strategies for promoting health through the creation of sustainable development, and we discuss risk and its communication.

In introducing *Essential Public Health* to our readers both old and new, we believe we have built upon the successful formula of its predecessor. However, looking at it afresh, revising and introducing much new material, we have been able to encompass the entire scope of modern public health as well as describing and discussing the range of services required to provide a comprehensive system of care. We look forward to continuing to receive the views of our readers in providing the kinds of constructive comments which we have found so valuable in the past.

We would like to acknowledge our special thanks to a large number of colleagues who have so generously provided their specialist expertise in commenting on the book. We have not named them all here but our gratitude to them is deep nonetheless. We would like to thank in particular: Raj Bhopal, Sarah O'Brien, Tricia Cresswell, Jim Smith, Mike Barnes, Ian Dalton, Tom Fryers, Bill Kirkup, Cliff Bailey, Judy Wilson, Jackie Sutherland, Anne Dart, Jim Farrell, John Reid. In addition, Liam Donaldson would like to thank his colleagues in the Department of Health for the checks and suggestions they made to the final drafts of the chapters. We owe a deep debt of gratitude to Eileen Smith. Any omissions or errors of fact and interpretation are our own. Any opinions expressed are our own and not those of any body we represent or may have represented in the past.

Chapter 1

Assessing the Health of the Population

Introduction

One of the great strengths of the National Health Service, and one which has endured since its inception in 1948, is the concept of responsibility for the health of geographically-defined populations, not just the patients who seek help from the service.

This is in contrast to the health care systems of some other countries where the population for which health care is provided is not so readily identifiable or comprises, for example, those subscribing to a health insurance plan. In Britain, a framework of service provision helps to ensure that a comprehensive range of care, based in primary care in hospital and in the community, is made available to local populations on the basis of their health needs.

The assessment of a population's health needs is not, however, a straightforward process. Health is not easily defined, other than in broad terms, and it certainly cannot be measured with precision. Instead, a wide range of sources of data are available, some used as proxies, to illustrate, with appropriate analysis, different aspects of the health of a population living in a particular place: its size and composition; the people's lifestyles; the illnesses and diseases which are experienced; and those of its numbers who are born or who die. By piecing together information from different sources, of different types and to which different levels of importance are attached, it is possible to begin to develop an understanding of the health of a population.

This first chapter describes the main ways of obtaining data which can contribute to the assessment of a population's health. In looking at all of the sources of data relevant to population health and health care, it is useful to consider three distinct groups. Firstly, there are data which describe populations. Without a knowledge of the numbers and characteristics of people at risk of ill-health or death, it is impossible to make sense of morbidity or mortality data. Secondly, there are what may be termed health event data, triggered by occurrences related to an individual's health which are then recorded. The starkest of these is death certification, which provides relatively accurate and complete information on the last illness of all individuals, but says little about previous health. This category also includes the recording of contact with the hospital services and with primary care. The third group comprises a variety of population-based health information, including lifestyle and other aspects of health status. In theory, this is often what is most wanted in order to study population health, but in practice the data tend to be patchy, incomplete and irregularly available.

All sources of health data, to a varying degree, are subject to quantitative and qualitative deficiencies which limit the conclusions which can be drawn from them. These drawbacks are best appreciated by being familiar with the way in which the data are gathered.

Population Description

Fundamental to any consideration of population is a periodic count of the number and characteristics of people in a given area. This is known as the population census.

The Census

A census has been carried out every ten years in Great Britain since 1801, except in 1941 during World War II. Authority for the census is enshrined in an Act of Parliament. Before each census there is extensive public consultation on conduct and content.

The law requires that all people alive on the night of the census are enumerated, traditionally, in the household or establishment where they spent that night. A household is defined as one person living alone or a group of people, not necessarily related, living at the same address, with common housekeeping – sharing at least one meal a day or a living room, temporary residents being included. In 1991 the country was divided into some 130,000 enumeration districts, each containing on average 200 households. An enumerator for each district ensures that the head of the household completes a form giving details of every person in that household.

In the 1991 census, data were collected about the household as well as about individuals. The former comprise postcode, type of building, number of rooms, tenure, the presence of certain amenities (bath, shower, toilet, central heating) and the number of cars or vans. The head of household then lists the names of people in the household, in each case stating their: sex; date of birth; marital status; usual address; relationship to head (for example, wife, daughter); whereabouts on the night of the census (if absent); address one year previously; country of birth; ethnic group; the presence of long term illness, health problem or handicap which limits daily activities; whether they are working and details of occupation and employment; higher education; the address of students and school children; and, usual means of transport to work. Similar information is required for members of the household absent on census night. People aged 18 years or over are asked also about higher qualifications. In Scotland and Wales, questions are asked about people's ability to speak, read or write Gaelic or Welsh.

The census in England and Wales is coordinated by the Office for National Statistics (ONS), formerly the Office of Population Censuses and Surveys (OPCS), which collates and processes all of the census data, under conditions where strict confidentiality is observed. The General Register Office for Scotland and the General Register Office for Northern Ireland carry out similar functions for their respective countries. Names are not entered into computers for processing but used only for internal checking of completeness and accuracy of forms. In analysis, great care is taken not to differentiate very small communities in which an individual person might be identified.

Publication of results takes three forms. Firstly, in published reports, secondly, in analyses made available on request and thirdly, advances in computer technology have greatly improved the facility to handle census data so that relatively inexpensive packages are available to enable handling of analyses (including mapping) down to small areas, on micro computers.

The completeness of the census is difficult to estimate. Clearly, enumeration of 100% of the population is the aim. Problems in underestimation include the tendency to underenumerate very young children, the homeless, young adults (especially young men), armed forces staff and their dependants Accuracy is also difficult to assess. Statements on age and marital status are sometimes inaccurate, and particular problems arise with vague and imprecise statements of occupation, on which social class analysis is based. Nevertheless, and notwithstanding these difficulties, the decennial census represents a most valuable periodic count of the population, for use as a baseline in further analyses.

Ethnic Minority Populations

The 1991 census was the first to include a question on ethnic groups and therefore enabled the analysis of local populations in these terms. Ethnic minority people have special needs which are important to the provision of health services (Table 1.1).

Table 1.1 Ethnic minority populations: areas where cultural differences have implications for health or the provision of services

- Uptake of services
- Presentation of illness
- Perceptions of health and disease
- Life-style and cultural practices
- Encounters with services
- Patterns of disease
- Use of alternative medicine

Source: Donaldson LJ, Odell A. Planning and providing services for the Asian population: a survey of District Health Authorities. Journal of the Royal Society of Health 1984; 6:199–202.

The non-white population makes up approximately 6% of the population of Britain (Figure 1.1). The largest proportion of this population lives in London with relatively high proportions also living in the West Midlands, East Midlands, West and South Yorkshire, and the North West.

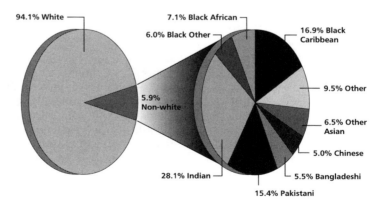

Figure 1.1 Distribution of ethnic minority populations in Britain.

94.1% White
7.1% Black African
6.0% Black Other
16.9% Black Caribbean
5.9% Non-white
9.5% Other
6.5% Other Asian
5.0% Chinese
5.5% Bangladeshi
15.4% Pakistani
28.1% Indian

Source: Balarajan R. Ethnic Diversity in England and Wales, 1997. National Institute for Ethnic Studies in Health and Social Policy.

The ethnic minority population is not a homogenous group. The main groups are those of Afro-Caribbean or of Asian (Indian, Pakistani or Bangladeshi) origin. Nor is the ethnic minority population evenly distributed within the population of Britain.

The populations of Bradford, Birmingham, Southall, Tower Hamlets and Leicester all contain substantial numbers of 'Asians' but these same populations are very differently composed. Whether an Asian man or woman is a Hindu, a Muslim or a Sikh, whether he or she came to Britain directly from India, Pakistan, Bangladesh or had lived or been brought up in East Africa, may all be important influences on the kinds of health problems to be expected, and the appropriate approach required for the planning and provision of services.

Generally, the age structure of people belonging to ethnic groups is younger than the indigenous population but as the population ages the special problems of their elder members will pose challenges for services in the future.

Birth and Death Registration

Populations do not remain constant. Over time, individuals die, and new ones are born, and it is important to track both processes to understand how populations are changing. This is primarily done through the registration of births and of deaths.

In Britain, and most developed countries, the registration of births and deaths is a legal requirement, placed on an individual known as the qualified informant – usually the nearest available relative. In England and Wales the process is organised by the Office for National Statistics (ONS), through a network of local registration and sub-registration districts throughout the country, administered by Superintendent Registrars and local registrars of births and deaths.

In the case of death registration, there is a degree of overlap with death certification, which is considered below. The certificate of cause of death, issued by a doctor or coroner, is used by the Registrar to register the death along with information from the informant. He or she then gives the informant a certified copy of the death register entry ('death certificate'), which is used for a variety of legal and administrative purposes.

Population Estimates and Projections

Whilst the population census takes place usually every ten years, there is clearly the need to produce statements of population size, and details of characteristics such as age and sex, for periods between census points. Such statements are produced annually and are called population estimates. Population estimates are derived by taking the census as a baseline, adding births, subtracting deaths and making an allowance for migration. Since births and deaths are events which have to be registered as a legal requirement, these components of estimation are reasonably sound. The weakness in the process is the allowance made for migration. Information on external migration (that is in and out of Britain) is reasonably accurate, but an understanding of internal migration has to be based on an accumulation of local knowledge, including things such as new housing development, clearance of old housing estates and the mass movement of population to other areas.

Population estimates become less reliable as time moves away from the census baseline, but they are nevertheless valuable and for many uses they are quite adequate.

Population estimates deal with populations between census points. In contrast, population projections are attempts to project the characteristics and size of populations into the future, making assumptions about fertility, mortality and migration. Population projections can be quite accurate in the short term. For example, a projection of the number of people aged 65–74 years in 20 years' time will be quite accurate, as the number of people now aged 45–54 years is known, as is the expected mortality of this age-group. On the other hand, a projection of the number of school children in 30 years' time will be less accurate because current fertility experience may not be maintained for the next 15 to 25 years. For this reason, population projections are often produced as a series, giving alternative figures based on whether low, intermediate or high levels of fertility are assumed.

Population Location

Classification by geographical location of residence is of increasing importance in health care, both for epidemiological and health service purposes. For example, locating the homes of individuals with a particular disease permits exploration of that disease's relationship with specific geographical features or it can allow calculation of disease rates for specific communities. The precision of geographical location needed will depend on the particular analysis being performed. It makes sense, therefore, to use a building block from which appropriately-sized 'patches' can be assembled. Ideally, one would wish to use the precise grid reference of each home but this is not routinely collected.

Census data are collected on the basis of enumeration districts (EDs), areas which were the responsibility of a single enumerator who distributed and collected the census forms on census night. As a way of breaking the population down by area, however, this is not particularly useful, not least because it is never used by individuals themselves, who do not know their own enumeration district, and so it is not generally recorded (for example when a person attends hospital). Although it is possible to convert addresses into enumeration districts, this is a laborious process which has to be done by looking them up manually. Until recently, populations were more commonly broken down into local authority wards, which could be done automatically for census data by the Office for National Statistics, but was still laborious to derive from addresses at local level. Postcodes, however, are readily available and are now the primary geographical unit of all mortality, fertility and health service recording in England. It is likely that data for the 2001 census will be analysed using advanced computer software in such a way as to allow much greater flexibility in the geographical aggregation and mapping of data.

Postcodes

The postcode is based on an eight-character designation which always includes one or two central 'blanks'; for example, NE30 4ET. In this example, 'NE' denotes the postcode area, of which there are about 120 in the country. The '30' represents a postcode district, and the '4' the postcode sector within a district. Finally, the 'ET' identifies a small geographical area (commonly about 15 households) within a sector which is known as the unit postcode. There were two million unit postcodes in the United Kingdom at the end of the 1990s. There are problems with the use of postcodes. For example, not all people know or remember them accurately and, inevitably, there are delays in the issuing of new postcodes to cover housing development. In a partnership between the Royal Mail, the Office for National Statistics and the Department of Health, postcodes are made available to the NHS, updated every six months, and are becoming increasingly reliable in their translation to other area-based classifications.

All birth, death and most patient-based service data are now postcoded. This fact and the availability of computer programs to assign postcodes to local or health authority areas and approximate grid references means that postcodes are a very powerful tool for geographical analysis of health data (Figure 1.2).

Deprivation Measures

Exploration of health differences between population groups whose social and economic circumstances differ may be based on classifications derived from occupation, such as social class or other socio-economic groupings (see Chapter 2). However, these classifications have come under increasing criticism from social scientists as reflecting too rigidly a particular hierarchical view of society which has become outmoded in other contexts. Increasingly, inequalities in health (see Chapter 3) are examined through analyses based on measures of material and social deprivation which are unrelated to occupation. A variety of indicators of the deprivation status of populations have been proposed, generally based on variables recorded in population censuses. They differ according to the nature of the concept of deprivation that underlies them (for example, encompassing wealth, income, social isolation, environment), and which factors are selected to differentiate groups on this basis (such as employment status, overcrowding or car ownership). Both because these factors are generally restricted to census variables, and because the underlying concepts of deprivation are often quite complex (and sometimes not made explicit), it must be remembered that all of the various indices and scores are more or less indirect indicators rather than direct measures.

Two deprivation indicators have come to be frequently used in public health research in Britain and in the surveillance of local population health. These are the Townsend Material Deprivation Score[1] and the Jarman Underprivileged Area Score[2] (both named after the researchers who first put them forward). The Townsend Material Deprivation Score is based on four census variables – the percentage of private households with more than one person per room; the percentage of private households with no car; the percentage of private households which are not owner-occupied, and the percentage of residents eligible for employment who are unemployed. These four factors were explicitly selected to reflect different aspects of material deprivation, and are combined into a single overall deprivation index. The Jarman Underprivileged Area Score was not actually constructed as a measure of deprivation but as a measure of General Practice workload. The variant of the Jarman Underprivileged Area Score in common use is based on eight variables, which were derived from a study of general practitioners' subjective expressions of social factors amongst their patients which most affected the need for primary care services, and therefore their workload. Figure 1.3 shows the strong association between one of these deprivation measures (the Townsend Score) and an important cause of death.

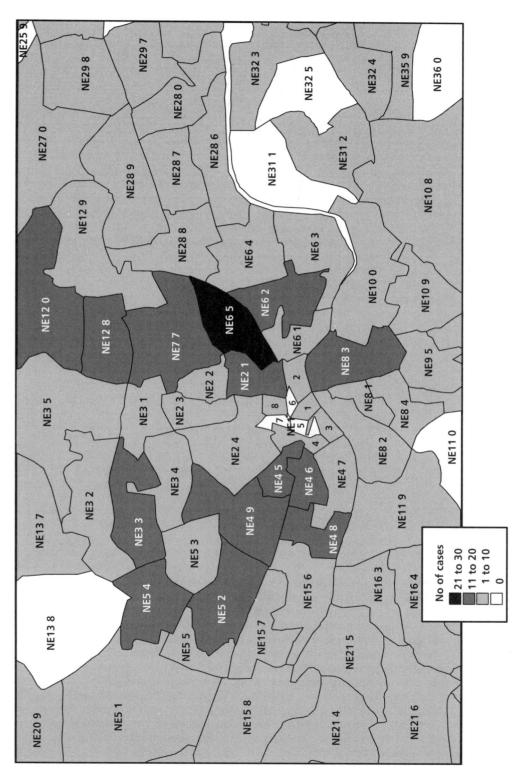

Figure 1.2 Distribution of Chlamydia cases in an urban conurbation by postcode sector.

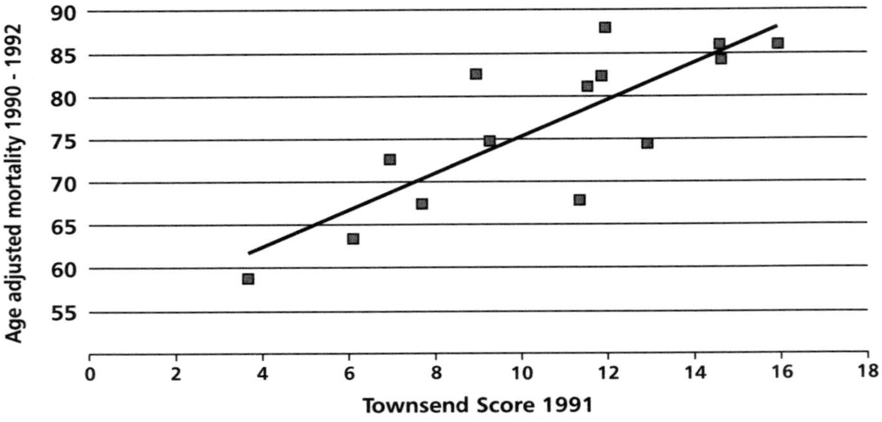

Figure 1.3 Ischaemic heart disease deaths and Townsend Score for health authorities in northern England.

Health Events

There are a number of routes through which data triggered by health events are collected. A major one is the certification of cause of death when an individual dies. Although it may seem a strange starting point when considering population health, there are good reasons to suppose that mortality data are amongst the most reliable indicators of the extent and nature of ill-health in a population, although clearly suffering from limitations in considering chronic and non-fatal illness. A second route is the recording of data relating to episodes of hospital care, which continues to grow in accuracy and completeness, but still relates to only a minority of ill-health, most of which does not involve hospital referral. A third route is the recording of primary care data, which should cover a much greater proportion of ill-health (over 90% of episodes of illness that result in contact with general practitioners are dealt with entirely in the primary care setting). However, data collection is still markedly less well-developed and complete in primary care.

Mortality

Reference has already been made to the legal requirement that all deaths be registered within five days of the date of death. In addition, when a death occurs, the registered medical practitioner who attended the patient during their last illness is required by law to issue a medical certificate of the cause of death (Figure 1.4).

This statement must indicate the date the deceased was last seen alive, whether the body was seen after death, as well as whether the certified cause of death is based on post-mortem evidence. The certifier is asked, if possible, to state the length of time between onset of any disease and death, and does so in about 30% of deaths. This certificate may be sent by post to the local Registrar of Deaths, although it is commonly given to the so-called qualified informant (usually a close relative) who must attend the Registrar's office to give, orally, details of place and date of death, name, sex, date and place of birth of the deceased, and the deceased person's occupation and place of residence. Normally, the Registrar is then able to complete a local death register and issue an order permitting disposal of the body. Virtually all deaths in England and Wales are registered electronically, using Registration Service software, and copies sent on floppy disc weekly to the Office for National Statistics (ONS) for processing. Causes of death are coded according to the International Classification of Diseases. The ONS sends to Directors of Public Health of subscribing health authorities a monthly electronic extract of deaths of district residents and other deaths which occurred in the district (the 'public health mortality file').

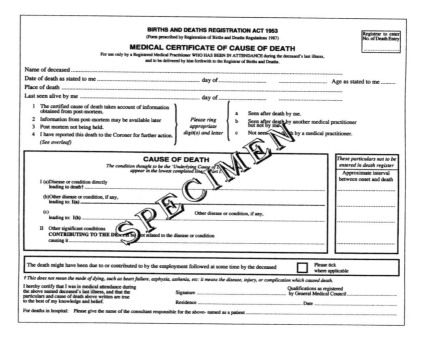

Figure 1.4 Medical certificate of cause of death.

Certification of Cause of Death

The medical certificate of cause of death requires the certifier to list the condition or, sequence of conditions or events, leading to the person's death. The cause of death certification falls into two sections. Part 1 asks for the direct cause of death (1a) together with conditions (if any) leading to the direct cause of death. For example:

1a Uraemia
1b Acute retention of urine
1c Benign prostatic hypertrophy

or

1a Acute myocardial infarction
1b
1c

Part II asks for the significant condition contributing to death, but not part of the direct sequence, if any, as for example:

II Diabetes mellitus

A common problem with medical certification is the use of mode of dying (cardiac arrest, asystole) as cause of death. This is of no value. If no other details are obtained, such cases would normally be referred to the coroner, as would all cases where the cause is unknown or where there are suspicious circumstances. Just under a quarter of all deaths are certified by the coroner, usually following a post-mortem examination by a pathologist appointed by the coroner. The coroner must enquire into deaths associated with accidental, violent, unnatural, sudden causes and deaths due to occupational diseases.

The certifier must distinguish direct causes of death from other contributory causes and must show the underlying cause of death in the lowest completed line of Part I of the certificate. Coding at the Office for National Statistics make the assumption that the certifier has followed this practice. In which case the so-called 'general rule' in coding underlying cause of death applies. In guidelines issued by the World Health Organization, this general rule must be overridden in certain circumstances, most commonly when the completion of Part I of the certificate does not follow a proper clinical sequence of events. Under these or similar circumstances, coding follows rules which determine selection of the underlying cause of death. These issues concerning certification of cause of death and its coding are important because they ultimately determine the content of population-level mortality statistics, which are normally based on this underlying cause of death. In the early 1990s ONS introduced automated coding of cause of death, incorporating software developed in the USA to select underlying cause. This has improved consistency and comparability with other countries also using this software. It has also made it possible to code all conditions mentioned on the certificate routinely ('multiple cause coding of deaths') and to make these data available for analysis.

Mortality notification has the advantage that it is legally required, and refers to an event which is unlikely to be missed. Even so, some data may be unreliable. If the qualified informant is a close relative, then clearly data are likely to be more accurate than if details are given by someone more remote. However, the qualified informant may be vague about the deceased person's actual occupation, or may give the most senior occupation held during life, even though they should be asked to give the last gainful occupation of the deceased. Even the medical reason given for death may be subject to uncertainty, being based largely on clinical opinion in many cases. Deaths in the elderly are often ascribed to terminal conditions such as 'bronchopneumonia', when the certifier is unsure of the precise cause, whereas a death in a young person may be investigated more fully.

Measures of Mortality

The basic unit of measurement used in studying mortality in populations is the rate. The rate consists of three components: a numerator, which is the number of people in the population who have died; a denominator which is the total number of people in the population and the time period during which deaths took place.

The use of a rate allows a comparison between different populations, different subgroups within the same population, or populations, at different times. A statement of absolute numbers, such as '100 deaths from coronary heart disease occurred last year in District A compared with 700 in District B' may be of value to the local undertakers in helping to assess their likely workload, but does not tell us whether mortality from coronary heart disease is a greater health problem amongst the inhabitants of District A compared to District B, since the relative sizes of the two populations are not given.

Crude Death Rate

The simplest form of mortality measure is the crude death rate, which takes the number of deaths in a period, usually a year, and expresses that number per 1000 population at risk of dying in the middle of the year, using the mid-year population estimate described earlier.

Use of crude death rates has the advantage that mortality can be expressed in a single figure. This is helpful in comparing mortality within an area over a period of time, so long as the age and sex structure of the population does not change too much. The disadvantage of crude death rates is that they cannot be used to compare mortality experience between areas because of possible differences in age and sex structures of the populations in those areas. A new town, for example, is likely to have a lower crude death rate than a seaside retirement resort. This is because in the former, there will be fewer people in age-groups at risk of dying compared to the latter.

Specific Mortality Rates

The need to look beyond crude death rates leads to the use of specific rates. A specific mortality rate refers to the number of deaths occurring in a subgroup of the population. Age and sex together with cause are the most commonly described subgroups. Occupation, social class and the ethnic group are others. Thus, the annual age-specific death rate for 15–24 year-old males would be expressed as: number of deaths in the year amongst men aged 15–24 years divided by the number of men of that age in the population. If this value is multiplied by 1000 then it gives the rate per 1000.

In practice, age-specific rates are nearly always also sex-specific since important differences exist between males and females in their risk of dying from or developing certain diseases.

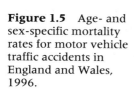 **Figure 1.5** Age- and sex-specific mortality rates for motor vehicle traffic accidents in England and Wales, 1996.

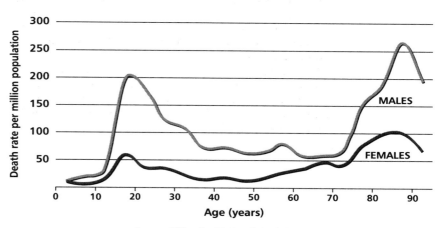

Source: Office for National Statistics.

Death rates may be expressed for individual causes of death rather than the all cause rates that have been described thus far. Most health problems show an effect of some kind with age, as shown in Figure 1.5, so that crude death rates are inadequate to describe conditions which are heavily loaded at the extremes of life. The study of age/sex and other specific rates is by far the best way of examining how mortality or other measures vary between different populations. However, by moving away from the crude death rate in order to observe such detailed measures, an attractive feature of the crude rate is lost, namely, its ability to convey an impression in a single figure.

Standardised Rates

A more useful summary measure, which takes account of the different age structures of two populations so that their mortality experience can be compared directly, is provided by standardisation. In age standardisation, a single standardised death rate is calculated in which allowance has been made for the age (and usually also sex) structure of the population in question.

There are two methods of standardisation: indirect and direct. Both involve choosing a standard population (for example, the population of England and Wales in 1999 or the European Standard Population), which is broken down into specific age (and usually sex) groups.

In the *indirect method* of standardisation, the death rates experienced by each age-group of the standard population (for example, females aged 15–24 years in England and Wales) are applied to the population of the same age-groups in the study area. This shows how many females aged 15–24 years in the study area would have died if the standard population's death rate had prevailed. After the calculation has been performed for all age-groups the resulting total number of deaths is added up. These deaths did not actually occur, but are those which would have occurred if the study population had experienced the same mortality as the standard population, and hence they are referred to as 'expected' deaths. The 'expected' number of deaths can then be compared to the actual, or 'observed', number of deaths. The most common means of comparison is the Standardised Mortality Ratio (SMR). This is the ratio of observed deaths to expected deaths and is usually expressed as a percentage. By definition, the standard population has an SMR of 100% (i.e., observed and expected deaths are the same). SMRs over 100 (the % sign is usually not used) represent unfavourable mortality experience, and SMRs below 100 show relatively favourable mortality experience; the effect of differences in the age and sex profile of each population having been taken into account.

Table 1.2 illustrates the process of calculating the SMR for deaths in females aged 15–64 years, in one part of the country, compared to the standard female population of England and Wales. The SMR of 106 for the area in question indicates that the mortality rate was 6% higher than if the specific rates for the England and Wales population had applied.

Table 1.2   Indirect standardisation: worked example of the calculation of a standardised mortality ratio (SMR)

The aim is to compare the mortality experience of women (aged 15–64 years) in one part of the country (the study population) with that of all women of the same age-group in England and Wales (the standard population).

Age-specific death rates for all females in England and Wales (standard population)

Deaths per 100,000 population

15–24 years	29.7
25–34 years	44.2
35–44 years	110.7
45–54 years	290.2
55–64 years	855.4

Population of females in the study population

Population

15–24 years	70,100
25–34 years	72,000
35–44 years	65,000
45–54 years	57,200
55–64 years	59,400

'Expected' number of deaths of females living in the study population if their experience was the same as all females in England and Wales

'Expected' deaths

15–24 years	$29.7 \times (70,100/100,000)$	=	21
25–34 years	$44.2 \times (72,000/100,000)$	=	32
35–44 years	$110.7 \times (65,000/100,000)$	=	72
45–54 years	$290.2 \times (57,200/100,000)$	=	166
55–64 years	$855.4 \times (59,400/100,000)$	=	508
			799

'Observed' (actual) deaths of study population
females aged 15–64 years   849

SMR (as a percentage)(England and Wales = 100)

$$\text{SMR} = \frac{\text{observed deaths}}{\text{expected deaths}} \times 100$$

$$= \frac{849}{799} \times 100$$

$$= 106$$

Table 1.3   Worked example of direct standardisation

The aim is to produce an age standardisation death rate for females (aged 15–64 years) in one part of the country (the study population) standardised to the England and Wales population.

Age-specific death rates for females in the study population

	Deaths per 100,000 population
15–24 years	25.7
25–34 years	36.1
35–44 years	103.1
45–54 years	304.2
55–64 years	949.5

Population of females in England and Wales (standard population)

	Population
15–24 years	3,631,600
25–34 years	3,852,300
35–44 years	3,500,400
45–54 years	2,873,200
55–64 years	2,631,500
Total population	16,489,000

'Expected' number of deaths of England and Wales females if their experience was the same as females in the study population

		'Expected' deaths
15–24 years	$25.7 \times (3,631,600/100,000) =$	933
25–34 years	$36.1 \times (3,852,300/100,000) =$	1,391
35–44 years	$103.1 \times (3,500,400/100,000) =$	3,609
45–54 years	$304.2 \times (2,873,200/100,000) =$	8,740
55–64 years	$949.5 \times (2,631,500/100,000) =$	24,986
Total expected deaths		39,659

Age standardised death rate of the study population
females aged 15–64 years

Deaths per 100,000 population

$$= \frac{\text{expected deaths}}{\text{standard population}} \times 100,000$$

$$= \frac{39,659}{16,489,000} \times 100,000$$

$$= 241 \text{ per } 100,000$$

In indirect standardisation, the death rates occurring in the standard population are applied to the study population. In the *direct method* of standardisation the reverse process is used (Table 1.3). The age-specific death rates of the study population are applied in turn to the numbers in each corresponding age-group of the standard population, to give the number of deaths which would have occurred in the standard population if the death rates in each study population had applied. This number of deaths is divided by the total standard population to give an age standardised death rate for the population under study.

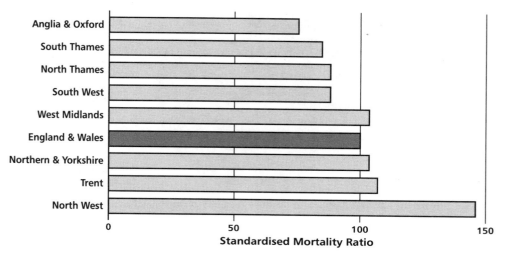

Figure 1.6 Standardised mortality ratios for cervical cancer in English health regions, 1996.
Source: Public Health Common Data Set, 1997.

In these examples, standardisation has been used to examine mortality in different areas. The process can be applied to any subgroups of the population where suitable data are available; for example, social class or occupational group. Although most commonly used to take account of age and sex, standardisation can also be used to adjust for differences in other characteristics. For example, perinatal mortality rates may be standardised for birth weight. The essence of standardisation is that it holds constant, and therefore eliminates the effect of, the characteristic being standardised (for example, age, sex) so that the effect of other factors can be examined. Once a factor has been used in standardisation, it cannot be used to explain variation between rates. Figure 1.6 shows Standardised Mortality Ratios for cervical cancer in parts of England. The differences cannot be explained by the fact that different regions had different age structures, since it is age which has been standardised.

Avoidable Deaths

Avoidable death is a concept which addresses deaths from those causes and in those age-groups where preventive measures or better clinical management might have avoided deaths (Figure 1.7). There are difficulties with this approach when comparing different parts of the country, particularly in taking account of different disease severity, which may account for the variation observed. Nevertheless, the avoidable deaths concept has proved valuable in providing a focus for further investigation or for targeted action.

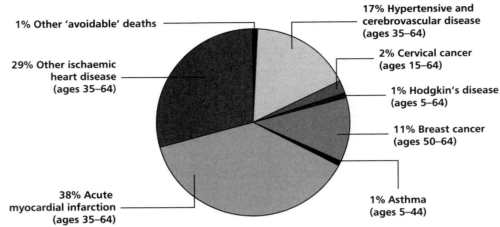

1% Other 'avoidable' deaths

17% Hypertensive and cerebrovascular disease (ages 35–64)

29% Other ischaemic heart disease (ages 35–64)

2% Cervical cancer (ages 15–64)

1% Hodgkin's disease (ages 5–64)

11% Breast cancer (ages 50–64)

38% Acute myocardial infarction (ages 35–64)

1% Asthma (ages 5–44)

Figure 1.7   'Avoidable' and other potentially reducible causes of deaths, England and Wales, 1994–96.
Source: Public Health Common Data Set, 1997.

Another approach to assessing the scope for improvement in population mortality is the examination of deaths according to years of life lost prematurely. In a typical calculation, the number of deaths under 75 years are multiplied by the number of years of life lost (at zero age, an average of 74.5 years; at 74 years, an average of 0.5 years) to give total years of life lost. This total figure can then be expressed both absolutely, and as a rate relative to the population at risk (Figure 1.8).

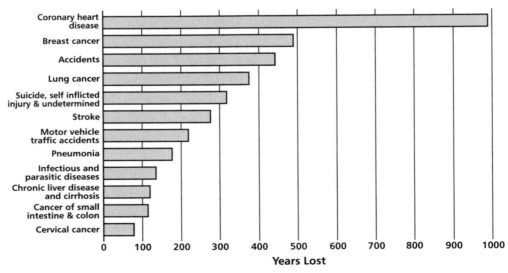

Figure 1.8   Average years of life lost per 100,000 population aged under 75 years in England and Wales, 1994–96.
Source: Public Health Common Data Set, 1997.

Hospital Systems

Morbidity

The lessening reliability of mortality data as a window on illness and disease makes it important to establish and maintain systems of information which describe, more directly, the size of the pool of such morbidity in the population. Yet, no single source of routinely collected health data will provide a comprehensive picture of the range of illnesses and diseases from which people suffer. Moreover, much of the information which is available is incomplete, largely because a substantial number of cases may not be counted.

It is difficult to imagine a service industry in the non-health sector functioning without a clear idea of the size of various groups of customers within the population who will require, or benefit from, its services. Yet, this is just the position the health service has been in during the past.

Mortality more or less defines itself, death being so clear cut, whereas morbidity does not always do so. Whilst there may be a relatively common understanding of what represents a strangulated hernia, there may be less of an understanding, even amongst doctors, about what threshold of blood pressure represents hypertension. Self-reporting of illness is also enormously variable. Patients do not have common thresholds in presenting illness to a general practitioner. One person's problem may not be perceived as such if experienced by another. Similarly, changes over time may reflect changes in people's expectations of their own health, as well as changes in the incidence and duration of sickness.

A wide diversity of data about illness or disease (morbidity data) are collected, some nationally, others only locally, some routinely, others on an *ad hoc* basis for a specific purpose, some as a statutory requirement, others on a voluntary basis. In considering the value of such data, it is important to be fully aware of their limitations. These are best appreciated by understanding the source and method of collection of the data.

Mostly, those using morbidity data will be concerned with two issues. Firstly, they will want to understand how complete a coverage of the disease problem the data provide, and secondly, to decide how valid was the method of ascertaining whether disease was present or absent. Many routinely available sources of morbidity data are deficient in both these respects. If they are based upon the collection of information about patients who have made contact with services (and many are) they will not comprehensively give information about all cases of the disease which exist in the population.

In considering how completely a particular source of morbidity data described the disease problem in the population, it is helpful to bear in mind the 'iceberg' concept depicted in Figure 1.9. The phenomenon whereby only a proportion of patients make contact with health services and, in particular with the hospital services, is often referred to as the tip of the iceberg. The process which leads people into the tip of this iceberg is complex and depends on many factors such as: the patient's perceptions of their ill-health; their own attitude and that of their family, friends and society in general to illness; and the availability of medical services and the quality of previous consultations.

A number of types of morbidity data are collected, analysed and presented on a routine basis. Examples include notifications of communicable diseases (described in detail in Chapter 9), data on hospital inpatients, notifications of fetal anomalies (described in detail in Chapter 6), abortion statistics and cancer registration. Many other types of morbidity data are available routinely or on an *ad hoc* basis but are less useful in assessing the health of a population on a day-to-day basis.

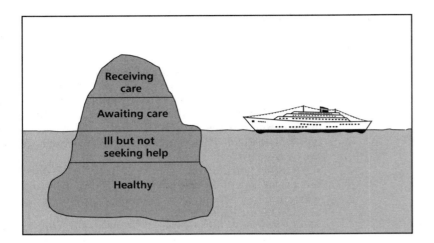

Figure 1.9 The iceberg concept of health care.

Hospital-based Data

Traditionally, many countries have used hospital inpatient data as an indicator of morbidity. However, such data can only take account of those conditions for which inpatient care is required. Diseases for which the patients do not require hospitalisation will not be revealed by examining hospital inpatient statistics only. Many 'important' health problems (for example, the common cold, migraine, backache), at least as judged by the proportion of the population affected by them and the economic impact of working days lost, will seldom lead their sufferers to require hospital inpatient care.

For relatively serious conditions, such as asthma, hernia or arthritis, a proportion of people afflicted will not make the decision to seek health care (even though they may recognize themselves as ill). A further proportion will visit their general practitioners only. Others will come to the attention of hospital services as outpatients or inpatients. Only the very last group will be recorded in a system of morbidity data based on hospital inpatients. In some disorders where hospitalisation is virtually mandatory, such as a fractured neck of femur or a perforated duodenal ulcer, hospital rates may approximate to the total size of the disease problem in the population. These situations are so few, that conclusions about incidence of disease based on hospital inpatient data should be interpreted with great caution (see also Chapter 2).

Hospital Episode Statistics (HES)

The Hospital Episode Statistics (HES) system of data recording seeks to capture every episode of inpatient care which takes place within a National Health Service hospital in England. An 'episode' is defined as a period of treatment under the care of a particular hospital consultant. Patient-based inpatient and day case events are recorded daily in every hospital through a computerised Patient Administration System (PAS). The data are transferred using the NHS-wide Clearing Service (NWCS) to IBM services who construct the dataset on behalf of the Department of Health.

The range of data collected covers items such as: hospital of treatment; health authority of residence; patient administrative details (for example, birthdate, sex, postcode of usual address, new NHS number); admission details (for example, referring general practitioner, admission/discharge details, method/source of admission); consultant episode details (for example, consultant code, specialty); and clinical details (primary and subsidiary diagnoses, operations and procedures undertaken). For maternity admissions details of the delivery record are entered as are details about the baby itself. For people with mental illness, additional information is collected annually on long-stay patients (those over one year) and on patients detained under one of the sections of the Mental Health Act.

Whilst Hospital Episode Statistics provide a useful potential source of information on illnesses treated in hospital, in the authors' experience their value is limited for this purpose by the quality of clinical information recorded as well as the completeness of returns made by some hospitals – although coverage and data quality improved during the late 1990s. The quality of clinical information will continue to improve with the increased use of Hospital Episode Statistics data to measure hospital, and in particular clinical performance.

Korner Data

The main system for recording health service activity is the Korner aggregate returns (named after the chairman of a Steering Group which reviewed health information requirements in the early 1980s). Information is collected on patient activity in the hospital and community health services in England and includes categories such as: accident and emergency attendances; ambulatory care attendances; hospital inpatient and day case admissions; activity in radiological, laboratory and other diagnostic departments; clinic activity; activity associated with paramedical services; and activity associated with health visiting and community nursing. Information dealing with other aspects of the health service (for example, the estate, transport, manpower, finance) are also routinely gathered and analysed.

Korner returns are made at different intervals. Some are made quarterly, some annually. They provide aggregated returns which enable patient activity data to be compared between localities or over time and which allow such data to be linked to manpower and finance data. They are usually presented for broad clinical specialty groupings and do not enable clinical or demographic variables to be analysed. Returns are classified by a particular code number. For example, KH07 is a quarterly return recording the number of people waiting for hospital inpatient admission. Return KH08 collects data on National Health Service operating theatre use and availability and allows, for example, the efficient use of such theatres to be reviewed.

Systems for Aggregation of Data

The relatively systematic recording of morbidity data in hospitals has raised issues of how to classify the conditions that people present with and the treatment that is carried out. Statistical classifications aggregate data into a defined number of categories according to a documented framework of rules, conventions and index; for example, the International Statistical Classification of Diseases and related Health Problems 10th revision (ICD-10) and the OPCS classification of surgical procedures 4th revision (OPCS-4). Groupers such as Healthcare Resource Groups (HRGs) aggregate date into larger categories for the purpose of higher-level analysis; for example, resource management, needs assessment and performance monitoring.

International Statistical Classification of Diseases and Related Health Problems 10th revision (ICD-10)

The World Health Organization, by international agreement, produces 'The International Statistical Classification of Diseases and Health Related Problems' or 'ICD' as it is commonly known, and this is used in many countries as the principal means of classifying and coding both mortality and morbidity experience.

The latest revision of the ICD, known as ICD-10, was published by the World Health Organization in the early 1990s, and is replacing its predecessor, ICD-9, as the standard coding system. The existence and widespread use of such an internationally agreed disease classification is of vital importance. Without it, comparisons of statistics over time and between different places would not be possible in any valid or meaningful form. Through the years, the classification has moved from being disease-orientated, and primarily a means of assigning causes of death, to include a wider framework of illness and other health problems.

The tenth revision groups diagnoses, signs and symptoms, causes and other factors into 21 chapters, starting with those relating to infectious and parasitic diseases and ending with codes for factors influencing health status and contact with health services (Table 1.4).

Table 1.4 Composition of chapters in the tenth revision of the International Classification of Diseases (ICD-10)

Chapter number and designation		Range of codes
I	Certain infectious and parasitic diseases	A00–B99
II	Neoplasms	C00–D48
III	Diseases of the blood and blood-forming organs and certain disorders involving the immune mechanism	D50–D89
IV	Endocrine, nutritional and metabolic diseases	E00–E90
V	Mental and behavioural disorders	F00–F99
VI	Diseases of the nervous system	G00–G99
VII	Diseases of the eye and adnexa	H00–H59
VIII	Diseases of the ear and mastoid process	H60–H95
IX	Diseases of the circulatory system	I00–I99
X	Diseases of the respiratory system	J00–J99
XI	Diseases of the digestive system	K00–K93
XII	Diseases of the skin and subcutaneous tissue	L00–L99
XIII	Diseases of the musculo-skeletal system and connective tissue	M00–M99
XIV	Diseases of the genito-urinary system	N00–N99
XV	Pregnancy, childbirth and the puerperium	O00–O99
XVI	Certain conditions originating in the perinatal period	P00–P95
XVII	Congenital malformations, deformations and chromosomal abnormalities	Q00–Q99
XVIII	Symptoms, signs and abnormal clinical and laboratory findings, not elsewhere classified	R00–R99
XIX	Injury, poisoning and certain other consequences of external causes	S00–T98
XX	External causes of morbidity and mortality	V01–Y98
XXI	Factors influencing health status and contact with health services	Z00–Z99

Source: Ashley, J. The international classification of diseases: the structure and content of the 10th revision. Health Trends 1990–91; 4:135–7.

The codes are alphanumeric, and run from A00.0 to Z99.9, excluding the letter U, which is reserved for additional codes and changes arising between revisions of the classification. The first three characters of a code define a category, with the fourth character supplying extra detail. Hence K26 is the category 'Duodenal ulcer' and K26.1 is 'Duodenal ulcer – acute with perforation'. Figure 1.10 shows a short extract from the chapter on diseases of the digestive system to illustrate the range of code numbers available for a common surgical condition. The classification is stable over time and has a fixed number of mutually exclusive, all-encompassing categories. Conditions are assigned to the categories according to defined rules, conventions and an index. In order to ensure that all conditions can be classified, a number of special-ised categories exist – most notably the 'other specified' notation. These latter codes provide the stability of the classification over time allowing new conditions a slot in which to be placed.

Figure 1.10 Extract from the chapter on diseases of the digestive system within the tenth revision of the International Classification of Diseases (ICD-10).

K35 **Acute Appendicitis**
K35.0 **Acute appendicitis generalised peritonitis**
Appendicitis (acute) with:
- perforation
- peritonitis (generalized)
- rupture

K35.1 **Acute appendicitis with peritoneal abscess**
Abscess of appendix

K35.9 **Acute appendicitis, unspecified**
Acute appendicitis without:
- perforation
- peritoneal abscess
- peritonitis
- rupture

K36 **Other appendicitis**
Appendicitis:
- chronic
- recurrent

K37 **Unspecified appendicitis**

Source: Reproduced, by permission, from ICD-10 International statistical classification of diseases and related health problems. Tenth revision, volume 1. Geneva, World Health Organization, 1992, p569.

Classification of Surgical Operations and Procedures (OPCS-4)

In England, the primary classification of operative procedures and other interventions is the Fourth Revision of the Classification of Surgical Operations and Procedures, known as OPCS-4. The codes use a similar format to those in ICD-10 and cover pro-cedures within anatomical systems as well as subsidiary codes for methods (laser therapy for example) and specific sites of operation (such as upper inner quadrant of the breast). The classification was designed specifically for theatre-based surgery. Recent advances allowing operative procedures to be carried out in ambulatory or pri-mary care settings have meant that the system is outliving its usefulness.

Healthcare Resource Groups (HRGs)

Codings of diagnoses and operations using the classification systems described in this section are essentially primary, in that they represent the finest level of detail routinely available. Increasingly, classification systems at a secondary level are being used. These take one or more of these, or other, primary classifications together with factors such as age and sex, to produce broader groupings that describe clinical activity called measures of case mix. Diagnosis Related Groups (DRGs) were originally used by the Medicare system in the United States for reimbursement of health service charges. The most widely used version of this system had 467 groups, each defined by one or more of: diagnosis, surgical procedure, comorbidities and complications, age, sex and discharge disposition. Each case-mix group was intended to cover a clinically coherent set of conditions that carried approximately the same cost implication (so-called iso-resource groups). Healthcare Resource Groups (HRGs) are the specific British evolution of DRGs, both for use within hospitals, and more widely in other health settings.

Clinical Terminologies

A relatively recent development (certainly in contrast to the long-standing diagnostic and surgical systems described above) are schemes in which terms are used to describe concepts which are arranged formally according to their meaning to produce an electronic thesaurus. These terminologies seek to cover most of the information included in a medical record (symptoms, physical signs, diagnosis, treatments, clinical procedures).

At the end of the 1990s two such systems were in use: SNOMED International (developed in the United States) and Clinical Terms Version 3 (Read Codes) developed in the UK. The former contains over 144,000 terms and term codes and the latter approximately 230,000 codes and 270,000 terms (including synonyms).

These clinical terminologies are intended to allow doctors to use their preferred clinical terms which can then be converted automatically by computer software into codes. In this way the detailed clinical information required to support patient care and the electronic healthcare record can also be aggregated into statistical classification and groupings (Figure 1.11).

Figure 1.11 The relationship between terminologies, classifications and groupings.

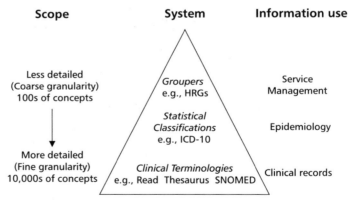

Source: Adapted from Read JD, Sanderson HF, Drennan YM. Terming, Encoding, Grouping: The Language of Health. Proceedings International Medical Information Association's 8th World Congress on Medical Informatics. Vancouver: 1995.

General Practice Systems

The primary care setting is a very important source of data. A high proportion of the population is registered with a general practitioner. A wide range of health problems are dealt with in primary care. Knowledge of the health experience of this population allows greater insight into the early stages of the natural history of illnesses and, in the majority of cases, it is the point of entry into the health-care system. It does not, of course, tell us anything about illnesses which are unrecognized by the patient or for which the patient undertakes self-medication.

In many parts of the country, practices, groups of practices or whole areas have established systems to record data on the contact patients make with primary care. An example of the kind of analysis which can be provided is shown in Figure 1.12 in which general practitioner referral patterns to a specialist service are compared. Exploring such variation with the primary care teams concerned can help to improve the process of referral to hospital for patients.

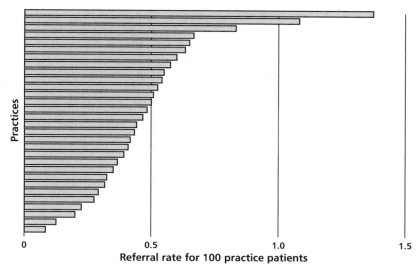

Figure 1.12 Variation in practices referring patients to hospital for ear, nose and throat treatment.

Source: Northumberland Health Authority, 1996.

Following an initial study in the mid-1950s, a national study of morbidity statistics from general practice now organised jointly by the Royal College of General Practitioners (RCGP), the Office for National Statistics (formerly OPCS) and the Department of Health has, since the early 1970s, been continued at approximately ten-year intervals. It uses a sample of volunteer general practices in England and Wales.

Most general practices file records alphabetically by the surname of the patient. This is essential to allow the receptionist to retrieve the correct case notes when a particular patient attends for consultation. It does not, however, enable the general practitioner to identify particular groups (for example, all schoolchildren) within the practice population. The general practice age-sex register is a file of the practice population arranged by age and sex. Such registers began as systems using small index cards bearing the name, sex, date of birth and address of each patient, possibly together with other details (for example, National Health Service number). These cards were then filed in age bands for males and females separately. With the growing availability of relatively cheap computers, many practices now have computerised age-sex registers. This enables other data to be added on each patient (for example, the need for repeat prescriptions or the presence of chronic illness such as diabetes).

The age-sex register is a relatively simple device. It can give the modern general practitioner invaluable assistance in a number of ways. It can provide a list of the names of patients in particular age-sex groups for which special preventive or surveillance measures can then be organised. For example: the very elderly (who may be visited regularly at home); pre-school children (who are given a full course of immunisation and vaccination); middle-aged men (who may be offered blood pressure checks).

In addition, the register can serve as a denominator for the calculation of age-sex specific rates or be used as a sampling frame for research studies.

Registration of Disease

A register has four main characteristics:

(a)   it identifies individuals;
(b)   these individuals each have the same particular feature in common, which is the focus of interest for the register;
(c)   it is longitudinal in that the information held about individuals is updated in a defined systematic manner;
(d)   it is based on a geographically-defined population.

A number of registers are currently maintained in the health field and serve a range of different purposes.

Cancer Registration

The National Cancer Registration scheme has been operating since the end of World War II, although a system was in operation in some parts of the country in the 1920s when radium treatment commenced. It is organised on the basis of health regions and information is also processed nationally by the Office for National Statistics which maintains a National Cancer Registry for England and Wales. Each Regional Cancer Registry holds details of the identity and of the type of neoplasm for each person resident or treated in the region who has been diagnosed as having cancer (certain premalignant tumours are also included).

The National Cancer Registry at the Office for National Statistics, through notification by each region, assembles a minimum data set. This includes: patient identification details (name, previous surname, address, postcode, sex, date of birth, marital status, NHS number, date of first diagnosis, date of death); details of the tumour: site of primary growth, type of growth, basis upon which the diagnosis was made and grade and stage (the latter two items for some cancers only). Also included are certain other details relating to the tumour and its treatment. Regional cancer registries may also collect as optional other data (for example, ethnic origin, occupation, industry of the patient and head of household) which can also be notified nationally. Such data enable the incidence of cancer to be examined geographically, within subgroups of the population and over time. They also enable survival to be compared for cancer at different sites. Such analyses can reveal the improving survival for cancer at some sites due to more effective treatment (Figure 1.13).

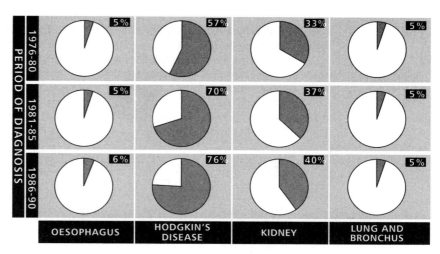

Figure 1.13 Five-year survival rates for certain cancers: recent trends.

Source: Northern and Yorkshire Cancer Registry and Information Service, 1998.

Other Case Registers

Registers have been established to study other conditions such as psychiatric illness, child abuse, ischaemic heart disease, stroke and trauma. It has been argued that the proliferation of such registers, accumulating large amounts of data, must incorporate checks to ensure high quality or their cost will not be justified. The availability of cheap, small computers and the growing interest of clinicians in automating records increases the risk of unplanned growth of registers.

Establishing and Running a Register

Before a register is established, consideration must be given to why the register is required; what disease is being registered; how cases are to be identified and reported; what information will be recorded on each case; how information will be stored and communicated; who will be responsible for producing analyses and servicing requests; who will produce reports; what the financial implications will be, and how patient confidentiality, ethical and data protection requirements will be satisfied. To be of any real value, a disease register, once established, must be maintained to a high quality. This means addressing at least two fundamental issues: completeness of case ascertainment and validity. Unfortunately, this is not always recognized and the resources set aside to run the register may be insufficient to allow quality control issues to be tackled. The day-to-day problems of running a case register are formidable and include: searching for missing records; making good of incomplete or inaccurate records; the elimination of duplicate entries; resolving coding queries; ironing out computing difficulties, and responding to requests for analyses.

One of the main problems of any registration system is achieving comparability of diagnosis. Wherever possible, strict rules should be laid down so that there are well-defined criteria which must be present before a particular diagnosis is made. Variations in diagnostic and classification practices can give rise to problems when comparing data for different countries, different parts of the same country, or the same population over time. Duplication sometimes occurs, but with proper organisation it is usually possible to identify whether an incoming record belongs to an existing registration or not. However, undercoverage (cases eluding registration) is an almost intractable problem with all registers. Most registers rely on some agreed procedure of notification of cases by health workers, with varying degrees of success.

The decision to establish a register should not be undertaken lightly. It requires proper justification, skilled organisation, adequate resources and, above all, dedicated and imaginative leadership.

Uses of Registers

Whilst in practice, many disease registers have a single disease focus, they also have the potential for multiple uses. In addition to measuring the amount of disease in the population, they can monitor temporal trends; they can be used in patient follow-up; they can enable comparisons of treatment outcomes; they can facilitate service evaluation; they can be used as the basis for studies of disease causation; they can be used for research and clinical audit, and they can be used to organise services for patients.

Measures of Morbidity

There are two types of measure of illness or morbidity. They are *incidence* and *prevalence*. It is important to be able to distinguish between them (Table 1.5).

Table 1.5   Measures of morbidity

$$\bullet \quad \text{Incidence rate} \quad = \quad \frac{\text{number of new cases of disease in specified time}}{\text{number of person-years at risk during period*}}$$

*average number at risk during period × length of period

$$\bullet \quad \text{Point prevalence} \quad = \quad \frac{\text{number of persons with disease at a point in time}}{\text{total population}}$$

$$\bullet \quad \text{Period prevalence} \quad = \quad \frac{\text{number of persons with disease during specified period}}{\text{total population at mid-point of interval}}$$

Incidence and Prevalence

The incidence rate measures the number of new cases of a particular disease arising in a population at risk in a certain time period. In contrast, prevalence measures all cases of the disease existing at a point in time (point prevalence) or over a period in time (period prevalence). Although one often speaks of the prevalence rate of a particular disease, strictly speaking it is not correct to refer to prevalence as a rate. More correctly it is a ratio, since it is a static measure and does not incorporate the idea of cases arising through time. The point prevalence measure is often compared to a snapshot of the population. It states the position at a single point in time. In measuring a particular disease, prevalence counts individuals within the whole spectrum of that disease from people who have newly developed the disease to those in its terminal phases; whereas incidence just counts new cases. Thus, prevalence results from two factors: the size of the previous incidence (occurrence of new cases of the disease) and the duration of the condition from its onset to its conclusion (either as recovery or death).

In most chronic diseases complete recovery does not occur. Many people develop diseases (for example, chronic bronchitis, peripheral vascular disease, stroke) in middle-age which they may carry until their death. The incidence of a condition is an estimate of the risk of developing the disease and hence is of value mainly to those concerned with searching for the causes or determinants of the disease. Knowledge of the prevalence of a condition is of particular value in planning health services or work-load, since it indicates the amount of illness requiring care. Relatively uncommon conditions (i.e., those with a low incidence) may become important health problems if people with the disease are kept alive for a long period of time (producing a rela-tively high prevalence figure). An example of such a condition is chronic renal failure which is rare, yet because dialysis and transplantation can keep sufferers alive, it becomes an important health problem which consumes considerable resources.

Population-based Health Information

Data which describe lifestyle and other underlying factors which influence a popu-lation's health are important in improving the public health.

General Household Survey

One way of obtaining information on illness which does not present to the health service at all, is to choose people from the general population and obtain information about their health directly. The General Household Survey (GHS) includes the collec-tion of such information.

The General Household Survey began in 1971 and has been running ever since. It is a continuous survey based upon a representative sample of around 12,000 private households in Britain. Interviews are conducted throughout the year with the adult members of these households and, in addition, parents are asked for some details of each child in the household under 16 years of age. The information collected is not restricted to health. Indeed, the survey serves many government departments and includes questions on housing, economic activity, pensions, leisure activities, educa-tion and the family. The questions on health relate to acute illness in the last two weeks; health during the previous year; presence of chronic illness; consultations with a doctor; visits to hospital (as an inpatient or outpatient); wearing of glasses or contact lenses, as well as smoking and drinking habits.

The General Household Survey gathers data on self-reported morbidity and disability. Questions are asked about both acute and long-standing illness and, if present, whether they limit or restrict activity in any way. Figure 1.14 illustrates the use of such data and shows a steadily increasing trend for self-reported long-standing illness. However, such changes should be interpreted with caution in view of the subjective nature of the reported information and their possible susceptibility to rising expectation.

The main limitation of the General Household Survey is that, since it relies on the evidence of the individual, errors may be introduced due to forgetfulness, differing perceptions of illness, or withholding certain information. Moreover, in some cases diagnostic labels are attached to the illness by the patient. Although the interviewers, who are not medically qualified, are trained to probe for as much clarifying detail as possible, they are unlikely to conform with the terminology or accuracy of a medical practitioner's diagnosis.

Despite these disadvantages, the General Household Survey enables major and minor illness to be described in the population as a whole. It avoids the disadvantages of data systems which monitor contact with health services in that it seeks to count both declared and undeclared illness. Data are collected along with information on a wide range of other subjects, thus allowing associations between such variables and health indices to be explored in a preliminary fashion.

Figure 1.14
Percentage of men
and women
reporting long-
standing illness and
restricted activity.

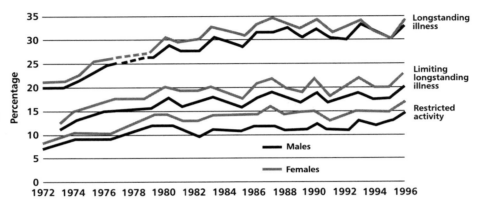

Source: General Household Survey for 1996. London: Stationery Office, 1998.

Data on Lifestyle and Risk Factors

Determining the extent of particular lifestyles or risk factors within a population is an important aspect of assessing its health need. As with morbidity data, the sources of data on lifestyle are very disparate. In many cases, such data are collected for purposes not directly connected with health. For example, the National Food Survey, conducted on behalf of the Ministry of Agriculture, Fisheries and Food, began in 1940 and is based on a random sample of private households in Great Britain. It provides information on food consumption and expenditure. Information on smoking and alcohol consumption, collected through the General Household Survey, also has wider applications.

From time-to-time, major surveys are carried out on behalf of government to establish lifestyle or risk factor prevalence.

National Health Survey

The Health Survey for England has been run annually since 1991. The survey is based on a random sample of some 16,000 adults aged 16 years and over living in private households in England. Since 1995 children aged 2–15 years have also been included. The survey is described in more detail in Chapter 2 as an example of a prevalence study. It has three main components: a health and socio-economic questionnaire, physical measurements (e.g., height, weight, demi-span, waist/hip ratio and blood pressure) and a blood sample (e.g., tested for haemoglobin, ferritin and cholesterol). Key topics are repeated each year to enable comparison over time, but in addition there are modules on specific disease areas and health problems that are covered at periodic intervals (e.g., cardiovascular disease, respiratory disease, accidents, disability).

Furthermore, in individual years, specific population groups (e.g., children and ethnic minorities) may be over-sampled, and there are plans to extend the survey to cover those living in private institutions.

Local Health Surveys

Although information from sources like these provides valuable insights into health-related lifestyles and risk factors on a national basis, it cannot readily be extrapolated to populations at local level. Increasingly, local health programmes are seeking to promote health and prevent illness and premature death. Information on the prevalence of risk factors and health-related behaviours is required for this purpose. The gap in public health information at local level can be addressed by commissioning or conducting lifestyle assessments involving postal or face-to-face interview questionnaire surveys of the population. It is essential that such local surveys seek to adopt valid survey instruments and survey methods. Comparisons over time and with other populations are then possible. It is also important that local surveys are properly resourced so that there can be comprehensive data capture and control of quality as well as effective analysis and communication of the findings.

Other Health Status Measures

A separate set of measures seek to go beyond the more clear-cut health events which have been described so far. Many such measures have been developed because many existing indicators do not fully measure the effects that disease has on people's physical, social and emotional well-being. There is a need to address issues such as quality of life and the concept of health itself.

Health and Disease Rating Scales

Measures which attempt to do this fall into two main categories. Disease-specific measures focus on the aspects of health which are considered to be especially important in determining the quality of life for patients suffering from particular conditions. For example, some rating scales have been developed for arthritic patients which provide summary measures of symptoms including pain, function, range of motion of joints and the absence of deformity.

In contrast, general health scales attempt to measure the aspects of quality of life which are important to everybody, irrespective of their health status. Very few such measures are in regular use but they have been widely developed in a research context. One example is the Nottingham Health Profile[3] which asks people a series of questions and assigns a score for each of six categories (physical mobility, pain, sleep, energy, social isolation, emotional reactions). Each category is scored 0 to 100, and rather than combining the scores to derive a summary health status measure, the score in each category is presented separately. Other measures which are more suitable than the Nottingham Health Profile for use in general population samples, include the Short Form 36 (SF36) and the EuroQol. Even a simple question on self-rated health has been shown to predict the likelihood of subsequent death.

Quality Adjusted Life Years (QALYs)

The Quality Adjusted Life Year, or QALY, is a health measure of a different kind. The concept arises from the wish to compare the effect of different interventions across the spectrum of health care. Such comparisons are needed, for instance, to assess priorities for the use of limited resources, or to identify the effectiveness of different programmes to improve health (such as, say, coronary artery surgery and smoking cessation). One obvious measure would be the number of years of life that each intervention would, on average, be expected to add, compared with the average expectation of what would happen without treatment. Thus, for example, treatment of a particular cancer might be known from follow-up studies to result in an average survival of ten years, compared with untreated average survival of two years, resulting in an estimated gain of eight years of life per person treated.

There are two problems with this approach. Firstly, it is known that individuals do not value all years of life equally. For example, a year of life spent suffering the side-effects of repeated chemotherapy would be regarded by most people as decidedly inferior to a year spent symptom-free, and survival under these conditions should not be assessed as such a gain. Secondly, many conditions do not markedly shorten life, but they reduce its quality, and many treatments are aimed at improving quality of life rather than increasing survival, which could not be assessed simply by estimating expected additional life-years.

Some mechanism therefore needs to be found to adjust life-years for quality of life, and this is the objective of the QALY. Quality of life is usually measured by assessing two or more aspects of people's health, such as pain, disability, mood or capacity to perform self-care, social activities or main activities like housework or paid employment. These assessments are then reduced to a single measure of changes in quality of life relative to a state of perfect well-being which is valued at unity. Combining this measure with information on life expectancy, by multiplying each year by its corresponding quality adjuster, gives an estimate of health improvement as QALYs gained.

Because the capacity to improve the population's health is inevitably constrained by the resources available to health care, the increase in QALYs arising from the use of health services is usually compared to the cost of treatment.

Table 1.6 Cost per quality adjusted life year (QALY) league table

Treatment	Service cost per QALY gained (£)
Special chiropody at home, 75 years and over	229
GP's advice to give up smoking	274
Chiropody in a clinic for ages 60–75 years	694
Pacemaker implantation	957
Hip replacement	1,025
Valve replacement for aortic stenosis	1,260
CABG:* severe angina, left main disease	1,416
CABG: severe angina, triple disease	1,731
CABG: moderate angina, left main disease	1,822
Kidney transplantation	4,099
Heart transplantation	6,983
Haemodialysis at home	15,029
Haemodialysis in hospital	19,129

*CABG = coronary artery by-pass graft. *Source*: Bryan S, Parkin D, Donaldson C. Chiropody and the QALY: a case study in assigning categories of disability and distress to patients. Health Policy, 1991; 18:169–185.

QALYs are an appropriate measure to focus on the predominant modern health problem – chronic disease. Table 1.6 shows how QALYs can be used to compare all kinds of health care, from preventive services to acute and rehabilitative care.

However, whilst QALYs continue to be developed in a research context, their routine use in the health service is limited by the practical and theoretical difficulties of deriving valid single indices of quality of life, and by reservations regarding the fairness and appropriateness of QALYs as a basis for assessing the need for different health services.

Access to Information

Access to health and health-related information was revolutionised by the growth of electronic media during the 1990s. It is now possible for those working in health services and public health researchers to retrieve and analyse data on local populations which is up-to-date and reasonably accurate in a way which was not possible earlier in the twentieth century. Thus, for example, ten years' population health data can be obtained on a CD and loaded on to an individual personal computer and a trend can be plotted (say) for cervical cancer mortality. Such sources are very diverse and constantly being updated and added to.

Public Health Common Data Set

Data on local populations in England covering demography, fertility, morbidity, mortality and the provision of healthcare have been produced as the Public Health Common Data Set since the late 1980s and are now released in computer-readable format. Data are presented as numbers, standardised rates and ratios (with statistical confidence limits) by different geographical areas. Although the data are generated from the traditional sources already described, particularly population, mortality and vital statistics and hospital activity data, its production in such a conveniently accessible form (with statistical derivations such as rates and confidence intervals already calculated) represents a major step forward.

Information Strategy

In the 1970s and 1980s one goal of health information systems was to enhance medical record linkage. This is the process whereby health records from two or more different sources and containing different types of information are brought together to provide a single file for an individual. Such a process when achieved in the past greatly enhanced the usefulness of the information collected. For example, the linkage of cancer registration statistics with mortality data enables survival rates to be compared between different groups of people with different types of cancer.

The advent of advanced information technology in the 1990s transformed thinking about health service information needs in the future. New proposals to modernise the National Health Service's use of information through advanced information technology were presented in the Information for Health strategy in the late 1990s (Table 1.7).

A long-term goal of the strategy is creating the Electronic Health Record (Figure 1.15) which will provide a continuing log of information over a patient's lifetime of contacts with the health and social care services. It will be developed within primary care where patients' contacts with the health service are most numerous. It will take information from electronic patient records, which will collect information on the episodes of care received by a patient in a particular institution (for example, a hospital). A unique NHS number acts as the basis for linking different records and drawing them into the Electronic Health Record. By 2005 the first generation of Electronic Health Records (based on Electronic Patient Records) should have been achieved.

Table 1.7 Key components of the NHS Information Strategy in the period 1998–2005

- Lifelong electronic health records for every person in the country
- Round-the-clock on-line access to patient records and information about best clinical practice, for all NHS clinicians
- Genuinely seamless care for patients through general practitoners, hospitals and community services sharing information across the NHS information highway
- Fast and convenient public access to information and care through on-line information services and telemedicine
- The effective use of NHS resources by providing health planners and managers with the information they need

Source: Information for Health, London: NHS Executive, 1998.

Such a record, once created, has the potential to fulfil a wide variety of uses, including supporting the process of care; evaluating health services; giving access to vital clinical information round-the-clock, and providing anonymised summaries of data for processing population health need, research and planning services. High standards of confidentiality and protection of data will be needed in such a system.

The planned connection of all computerised general practices to a computer network (NHSnet) during the year 2000 should improve communications within the NHS. This will enable Primary Care Groups, and NHS Trusts, to send and retrieve an increasingly large range of information.

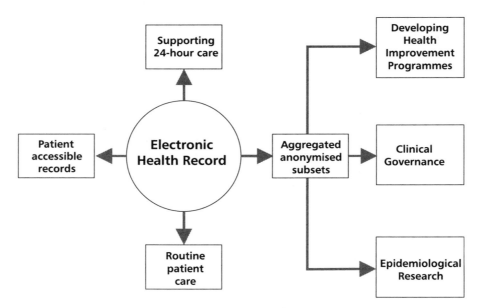

Figure 1.15 Using the Electronic Patient Record.
Source: Information for Health, London: NHS Executive, 1998.

Conclusions

All the sources of data covered in this chapter (and others not described) can be of value in assessing the health needs of a population. In practice, however, the needs-assessment process involves a variety of approaches, including the use of routinely available data to provide continuous surveillance of health patterns or trends; *ad hoc* analysis of routinely available data to answer a particular question or throw light on a particular problem, and the gathering of data which are not available routinely. The form of the needs assessment will differ according to the purpose for which the information is required. Figure 1.16 shows the main categories of information which are required to make an assessment of a population's health needs.

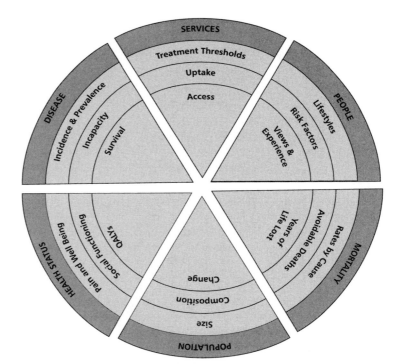

Figure 1.16 The scope of health needs assessment.

Chapter 2

Approaches to Investigation

Introduction

The investigation of health problems in populations, and of the health services which provide care to them, is a key function of public health.

Anyone leading, or participating in, such investigative work should have a good knowledge of the range of routinely available data about health and health services, some of which are described in Chapter 1. It is equally important to have an understanding of their strengths and weaknesses because there are enormous dangers in the uncritical use of routinely available health data. Indeed, it is all too common to see analytical reports written for bodies responsible for taking major policy, or resource-allocation decisions which contain conclusions far more sweeping than should be drawn given the limitations of the data.

Those involved in public health investigative work must also be familiar with, and skilled in, the methods and techniques of epidemiology. Epidemiology is one of the population sciences basic to public health. The techniques and methods of epidemiology and its general approach of a population perspective on health, disease, and health services leads it to have a very widespread application throughout the field of public health. The epidemiological perspective is a key component in identifying health needs; examining the pattern of disease problems within and between populations; searching for the causes of disease; formulating health promotion and disease prevention strategies; studying the natural history of disease; and planning and evaluating health services.

This chapter deals with the way in which epidemiological techniques and methods can be used to investigate the health problems of, and the health services provided for, a population (Table 2.1).

Table 2.1 Some reasons for carrying out a public health investigation

- Defining the characteristics of a population
- Assessing health needs
- Describing a problem
- Searching for causes
- Identifying areas for improvement
- Evaluating new and existing services
- Planning service responses
- Pointing to scope for prevention
- Assisting resource allocation decisions

Source: Adapted from Donaldson LJ, Kirkup W. Hospital Medicine, 1998; 59:1–5.

Comparing Disease Patterns Between and Within Populations: Descriptive Epidemiology

Chapter 1 described the range of information which could be used to describe the health of a population. Having assembled the necessary information to be able to examine a particular indicator (for example, mortality under the age of 65 years from coronary heart disease or the incidence of fractured neck of femur), the next questions which inevitably will occur to the investigator will involve comparisons. How does the population under study compare with other populations? How does the occurrence of the problem in the population currently, compare with earlier time periods? Are different subgroups within the population affected by the health problem to a greater or lesser degree? Comparisons of this kind are the basis of hypothesis formulation and problem solving.

The use of health information in this way, whether derived from routinely available data or assembled by special surveys, is usually referred to as *descriptive epidemiology*.

When using the technique of descriptive epidemiology, it is particularly important to take a cautious and stepwise approach to interpreting the findings and before drawing conclusions, no matter how tentative. This is not just good scientific practice, it is the duty of the responsible investigator to the population which he or she is studying.

For example, to present information showing that the incidence of childhood leukaemia in one part of a region is higher than another without first carrying out some checks on the data in the cancer register (and other data sources) would be wrong. Comprehensiveness of ascertainment of cases, the validity of the recorded diagnoses on individual children, and the accuracy of the places of residence attributed to the cases, are all potential sources of misleading conclusions as well as unnecessary public disquiet and anxiety.

It is essential that before conclusions are drawn about differences in the occurrence of health problems between different populations, or over time, consideration is given to whether the differences may not be real.

Are Differences Real? Three Important Questions

In determining whether differences between populations or over time truly reflect different levels of a particular disease, it is helpful to address three questions.

What are the Criteria for Defining the Disease?

It is well known that there are variations in medical practice (between different time periods, different places and even individual doctors on different occasions) which influence the way in which a particular diagnostic label is applied to a particular condition.

An illustration of apparent variations in the occurrence of psychiatric illness which can be partly explained by variations in the diagnostic process, is provided by considering a cross-national study carried out in the mid-1960s. At that time it had been recognized that there were apparent differences in the frequency of certain psychiatric illnesses in the United States of America compared with the United Kingdom. If such differences were real, then valuable clues to the causes of certain psychiatric illnesses might be available. These considerations gave rise to an investigation into the differences.

Table 2.2 shows the results of an analysis of two samples of patients in psychiatric hospitals in London and in New York. There appeared to be a much higher percentage of schizophrenics and alcoholics in the New York sample than in the London sample. In contrast, patients with depression and mania were much more common in the London sample. Using a standardised interviewing technique, each patient in the sample was examined by a member of a team of project psychiatrists as soon as possible after admission, and independently of the hospital staff.

Table 2.2   The hospital diagnoses of the London and the New York samples

	New York percentage (n = 192)	London percentage (n = 174)
Schizophrenia	61.5	33.9**
Depressive psychoses	4.7	24.1**
Mania	0.5	6.9**
Depressive neuroses	1.6	8.0**
Other neuroses	2.6	5.7
Personality disorders	1.0	4.6*
Alcoholic disorders	19.8	3.4**
Drug dependence	0.0	0.6
Organic psychoses	5.2	1.7
Other diagnoses	3.1	10.9**

*Difference significant at 5% level **Difference significant at 1% level. *Source:* Cooper JE *et al.* Psychiatric Diagnosis in New York and London: a comparative study of mental hospital admissions. London: Oxford University Press, 1972.

Table 2.3 shows the results of comparing the original hospital diagnoses with the subsequent project diagnoses in the two samples. Once alcoholics and drug addicts had been excluded, the comparison of the two sets of project diagnoses showed no significant difference for schizophrenia, personality disorders, neurosis (other than depressive) and organic psychosis. This suggests that the original differences – in the hospital diagnoses – between the two centres were largely the result of variation in the diagnostic criteria used by the psychiatrists.

Table 2.3   The project diagnoses of the London and the New York samples after the exclusion of alcoholics and drug addicts

	New York percentage (n = 192)	London percentage (n = 174)
Schizophrenia	39.4	37.0
Depressive psychoses	26.8	24.2
Mania	7.7	6.7
Depressive neuroses	9.2	15.2
Other neuroses	2.1	4.2
Personality disorders	5.6	3.6
Organic disorders	3.5	3.6
Other diagnoses	5.6	5.5

Source: Cooper JE *et al.* Psychiatric Diagnosis in New York and London: a comparative study of mental hospital admissions. London: Oxford University Press, 1972.

The report concluded that the most important of these differences was that the New York concept of schizophrenia, at that time, was much broader than that used in London, and included cases which many British psychiatrists would have called depressive illnesses, neurotic illnesses or personality disorders (see Figure 2.1).

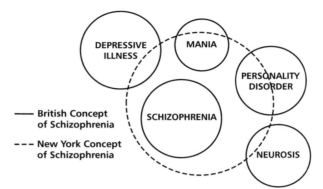

Figure 2.1 The difference between the New York and British concepts of schizophrenia.

Source: Cooper JE *et al.* Psychiatric Diagnosis in New York and London: a comparative study of mental hospital admissions. London: Oxford University Press, 1972.

Although this study is many years old it illustrates a principle which can be a pitfall for any comparison of disease frequency. Variation amongst doctors in the choice of labels for particular clinical problems or causes of death is quite commonplace. While it may not be of paramount importance as far as the individual doctor and patient are concerned, it becomes central when data are aggregated for the purpose of producing a population count of the number of cases of a disease or the number of deaths from a particular cause. It is even more important to establish the diagnostic criteria which have been used to count cases of the disease when comparisons are made between different populations or when a disease trend over time is observed. Otherwise, spurious conclusions about apparently major differences may be made (just as in the psychiatry example described above). This potential problem is applicable to all diseases, no matter how objectively the diagnosis is made.

Have all Cases of the Disease Been Identified?

False impressions about the amount of disease in one population compared to another may also be gained through a failure to take account of differences in the efficiency of case detection.

For example, the observation that a particular cancer is commoner in a Western country than in a developing country may lead to speculation about risk factors in the two countries. Such a line of thought would be unwise without first examining the efficiency of the two cancer registration systems. The apparently higher occurrence of the cancer in the Western country may simply reflect the fact that it has an efficient, well-maintained cancer registry which detects and records most cases of cancer which occur. The cancer registry of a developing country, perhaps covering a rural population which does not readily have access to medical services, may not be so efficient at detecting cases of the cancer. But this does not necessarily mean that they are not occurring as often as in the Western country, merely that they are not being recorded.

This is a rather obvious example to illustrate the importance of being aware of possible differences in disease detection rates when making comparisons. It should be remembered that this pitfall can be encountered when comparing disease frequency from region-to-region, city-to-city, and hospital to hospital and not just between developing and developed countries.

Table 2.4 Possible reasons for variations in surgical operation rates between populations

- Demographic differences
- Different rates of underlying illness
- Random fluctuation
- Availability of resources or supply
- Clinical judgement varies
- Different patient expectation or demand
- Prevailing clinical traditions vary
- Inaccuracies in data sources

Source: McPherson K. In Anderson TF, Mooney G. The challenges of medical practice variations. London: Macmillan, 1989.

A particularly common source of fallacious reasoning about disease differences between populations is when studies use hospital inpatient data. This is also an issue of differential case ascertainment. Because the true incidence of the condition in the population is seldom known, it must be remembered that hospital cases of the disease can only approximate incidence in diseases where a high proportion of people who develop them are hospitalised. Since there are relatively few diseases which fall into this category, it follows that differences between populations in the occurrence of a particular disease based upon studies of hospital admission rates should be treated with great caution because they are likely to reflect differential admission rates for the condition rather than differences in the true incidence of the disease in the population (Table 2.4).

An example is the analysis depicted in Figure 2.2. This shows the rate of hip joint replacement for planned (i.e., non-emergency) episodes of care in different parts of England. Thus, it is describing the treatment of patients who mainly have osteoarthrosis of the hip joint causing pain and limitation of movement. Geographical variation between services would be seen for many surgical operations.

Figure 2.2 Age-standardised rate of planned hip joint replacement in regions and districts of England for people aged over 45 years.

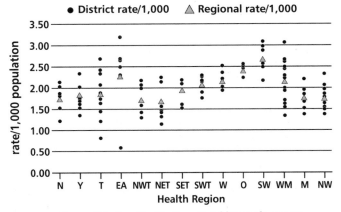

Source: Effective Health Care. Total hip replacement. Leeds: Universities of Leeds and York, 1996.

However, the error in interpreting this variation would be to regard operation rate as a proxy for disease incidence. Someone drawing such a conclusion might start to explore theories as to why osteoarthrosis of the hip joint was more common in some parts of the country than others. There may indeed be genuine geographical variation in its incidence but a study based on admission rates for hospital treatment is not the way to establish it.

Is the Population at Risk Accurately Defined?

In any measure of disease frequency, it will be necessary to relate the number of cases of the disease to the population from which they arose. A difference between two populations in the incidence of a disease or in mortality from a particular cause may be related to differences in the characteristics of the populations (such as age and sex) which affect the rate of disease. Once such characteristics are corrected for, an example being through standardisation (see Chapter 1), the differences in disease experience are no longer apparent. It is important to recognize this possibility at an early stage before too much interest is shown in apparent major variations in disease frequency.

It is also important to be sure that all cases of the disease or deaths are related to an identifiable (ideally) geographically-defined population upon which accurate estimates are available of its size and structure. Hospital catchment populations which can change rapidly over time, and may vary according to the type of diseases being examined, are notoriously unreliable in this respect.

The Approach of Descriptive Epidemiology

Provided these limitations are always borne in mind when comparisons of disease frequency are being made, important observations may result from examining the pattern of diseases within populations.

Beyond simply the interest which is engendered by studying any population health problem, the process of descriptive epidemiology has three specific purposes. Firstly, to identify the scope for research into the causation of diseases or other health problems which might lead ultimately to their prevention; secondly, to help plan services for the whole population; and, thirdly, to highlight populations or groups within the population which are in special need of health service initiatives.

Example of a Descriptive Epidemiological Approach Yielding Clues to Causation

Figure 2.3 shows the findings of a study which used routinely available data to describe the trend over time in mortality from asthma.

The most striking observation from this trend was the rapid increase in the mortality rate from the disease which occurred in boys aged 10 to 14 years over the period from the mid-1950s to the mid-1960s.

This led the investigators to seek an explanation for this tragic apparent increase in loss of life and to discover whether the trend might be reversible. However, before going further it was important for them to bear in mind such a change may be artefactual rather than real.

For example, was it possible that asthma was being more frequently used as an underlying cause of death by doctors completing death certificates in circumstances where previously some other terminology had been used? This was excluded by the investigators who found no downward trend in deaths from other respiratory disease diagnoses to coincide with the apparent increase in asthma deaths.

Having excluded this and other artefactual possibilities for the increase in asthma mortality, two other explanations were considered. Firstly, that the disease (asthma) had become more common (the incidence had increased) but that the proportion of asthmatic children who died from their disease remained static (i.e., that the case fatality rate remained stable) or, alternatively, that the disease had not become more common (the incidence was stable) but that the children who developed the disease died more often from it (the case fatality rate had risen).

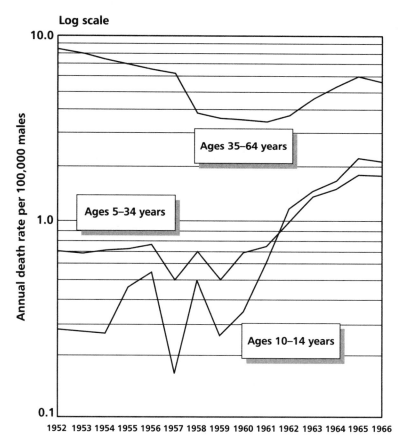

Figure 2.3 Asthma mortality in males in England and Wales from 1952 to 1966.

Source: Speizer FE, Doll R, Heaf P. Observations on recent increase in mortality from asthma. BMJ, 1968; i:335–9.

The investigators in this study could find no evidence from other data sources to suggest an increase in the incidence of asthma and therefore concluded that the rise in mortality shown in Figure 2.3 was due to an increase in case fatality. There was a strong suspicion that the change was due to medications used to treat childhood asthma at that time and the next phase of the study was to seek information from the general practitioners of the children who had died of asthma about the drugs which had been used to treat them prior to death.

At the time, corticosteroids had been recently introduced into clinical practice and one of the known side-effects was suppression of the adrenal gland and therefore there was a suspicion on the part of the investigators that this group of drugs may be implicated in causing the deaths of asthmatic children. However, the survey of general practitioners revealed that this was not the case but that bronchodilators in the form of pressurised inhalers had been used in a high proportion of cases. A high dosage form of isoprenaline, administered in the form of an inhaler, was the drug most commonly involved. This drug can, amongst other side-effects, produce abnormal heart rhythms when taken to excess and there was clearly a possibility that children self-administering the drug to relieve acute bronchospasm might have used it indiscriminately and excessively when symptoms were severe.

At the time this drug had been available without prescription. As a result of the findings of the study it was subsequently made available only on prescription. Warnings were circulated to all doctors about these side-effects and printed warnings were also included in the instructional material for patients using these pressurised inhalers. As a result of these measures mortality from asthma declined. Similar epidemics of asthma deaths occurred in Scotland, Ireland, Australia and New Zealand. The drug was not sold in the Netherlands (a point that becomes relevant in the description that follows).

This is a classic example of descriptive epidemiological investigation leading to successful preventive action. Usually, however, it would first be necessary to move from the suggestion of causation created by the descriptive approach to investigate the presumed causal factors using more specialised epidemiological methods before drawing firm conclusions and taking definitive action. In this case, however, the findings were of sufficient importance and the public health problem was of such great concern that immediate action was justified.

The subject of preventable deaths in asthma has continued to be controversial. While the trend in Britain, and in some other Western countries, declined following the 1960s, a further increase has occurred in New Zealand whose cause has not been fully elucidated. However, studies strongly suggested that another drug – fenoterol – may have been associated and a health warning was issued in New Zealand. Unlike England and the Netherlands, this drug was available without prescription in New Zealand.

Figure 2.4 Time trends in asthma mortality (aged 5–34 years) in three countries in relation to introduction of inhalation therapies.

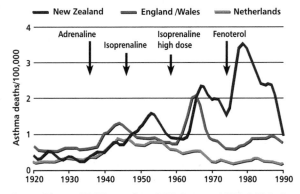

Source: Blauw GJ, Westendorp RGJ. Lancet, 1995; 345:2–3.

Other experts have disagreed with the fact that these trends in asthma mortality are treatment related. This shows that descriptive epidemiology does not provide proof of causation only pointers to further investigation. Nevertheless, the time trends represent a fascinating epidemiological story and a challenge to public health in identifying a source of potentially preventable death (Figure 2.4).

Patterns of Disease: Time, Place, Person

The technique of descriptive epidemiology traditionally examines disease patterns across three main dimensions: in relation to *time*, in relation to *place*, and in relation to *person*.

Describing Disease in Relation to Time

When describing the way in which the occurrence of a disease varies with time there are three common methods of examining the relationship: seasonal variation; epidemic curves; and long-term (secular) trends. However, any temporal cyclicity may be studied (for example, diurnal rhythms or patterns).

Seasonal Variation

Many diseases exhibit seasonal variations in their occurrence: peaks in the frequency of these diseases occur regularly at particular times of the year. Respiratory infections, for example, are more common in the colder months. In some non-infectious conditions seasonal variations have been clearly demonstrated, but no satisfactory explanation has, as yet, indicated why they should occur. For example, Figure 2.5 shows apparent seasonal variation in the onset of insulin-dependent diabetes mellitus in children. The data are derived from a 26-centre European study in which standardisded methods of case definition and ascertainment were used. It can be seen that there was a peak occurrence in the winter or early spring (December through March). Data were published in the early 1960s which showed a greater incidence of childhood acute lymphoblastic leukaemia in the summer months. When put together (in the light of a more modern understanding), data of these kinds derived from older studies have led to suggestions that these diseases in children may be caused or precipitated in genetically susceptible individuals, by an infectious agent, possibly a virus.

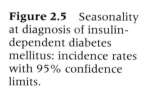

Figure 2.5 Seasonality at diagnosis of insulin-dependent diabetes mellitus: incidence rates with 95% confidence limits.

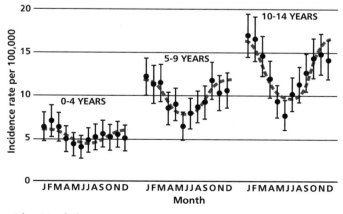

Source: Lévy-Marchal C, Patterson C, Green A. Diabetologia, 1995; 38:823–830.

Such findings must be interpreted cautiously because they raise questions about the extent of detection of cases and the way in which the onset of the disease is determined. Even if such a seasonal pattern is established, this is not proof of a causal link between any particular infectious agent and the disease. However, it is a further example of how examination of the pattern of disease can provide a clue which may prompt further investigation of the relationship between genetic and environmental factors which in turn may lead to a greater understanding of its causal mechanism.

Epidemic Curves

The increase in the frequency of a disease over a relatively short period of time above its baseline level of occurrence is termed an epidemic.

Sometimes the term is also used to describe increase in frequency, over a period of years, of diseases which have had a stable (and lower) level of occurrence for decades. Coronary heart disease and lung cancer are often referred to as the modern epidemics. Trends over years, or decades and longer, however, are usually described as secular trends.

Secular Trends

The study of the pattern of diseases over long periods of time, years, decades, or even centuries, highlights many changes. Major diseases of the past have faded from importance, while others have become increasingly prominent.

As will be clear from the discussion earlier in the chapter (particularly the asthma mortality example), there are many pitfalls in interpreting secular trends in the frequency of a disease. Its true frequency may not have changed over time but improvements in methods of detection and diagnosis, fashions in diagnosis, changes in the criteria used to define or classify it, may suggest that it has.

Some of the most spectacular secular changes in the pattern of disease in industrialised countries have involved the decline in the importance of the infectious diseases as major health problems and causes of death. The decline in infant and childhood mortality, largely as a result of general measures (sanitary reforms, improvements in living standards and nutrition) which reduced the impact of the infectious diseases, improved life expectation for modern Britons compared to their Victorian counterparts. These changes are discussed in detail in Chapter 8 in relation to population ageing. This secular change in mortality from infectious diseases in turn, therefore, had wider implications beyond its immediate impact for the size and structure of the population.

Tuberculosis was one of the great scourges of the recent past, often referred to as the 'white man's plague'. Bunyan, in his writings, gave it the chilling and evocative title 'Captain of the men of death'. In 1855, for example, 13% of deaths from all causes were attributed to tuberculosis. By the end of the 1990s the figure had fallen to 0.1%. Although the disease is now a much less common cause of mortality and morbidity, it is becoming an important health problem again world-wide – particularly in ethnic minorities in the United Kingdom.

The decline in mortality from tuberculosis (Figure 2.6) had begun before the advent of specific medical measures. This highlights another principle in interpreting secular trends. If the frequency of a disease is already declining it must not be assumed automatically that the introduction of a specific measure has brought it about.

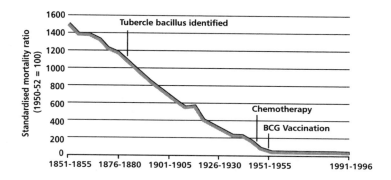

Figure 2.6 Death rates for tuberculosis in England and Wales 1851–1996.

Describing Disease in Relation to Place

Description of the pattern of disease in geographical terms can be undertaken in a number of ways, although there are three main aspects: national variation (within a country); international variation (between countries); smaller area variation (for example, urban/rural).

National Variation

For many diseases in Britain, there is variation in morbidity and mortality rates between different geographical areas. Chronic bronchitis, for example, is more common in the urban industrial areas of northern England than in the rural areas of the south. Other diseases are also distributed in a similar way. The overall result is that general mortality within Britain is lower for the population of southern England and East Anglia and higher for parts of northern and north-western England, Wales and Scotland (Figure 2.7). The reasons for this are multifactorial and complex.

Figure 2.7 Standardised mortality ratios for all causes of death amongst men in the United Kingdom, 1996.

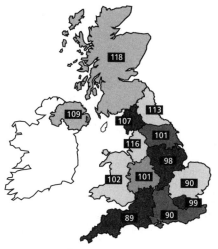

Source: Office for National Statistics.

International Variation

Many diseases vary in frequency between different countries and on occasions this may give clues to causation. Table 2.5 shows the variation in the prevalence of neural tube defects (spina bifida, anencephaly and encephalocele) between populations in European countries. Registers of congenital malformations had been established to monitor the occurrence of such birth defects and enable comparisons to be made.

As Table 2.5 shows, considerable variation was seen between the different populations. Moreover, rates were generally higher amongst births occurring in the British and Irish centres than those in other European countries.

The reasons why some countries show a higher prevalence of neural tube defects than others is not known but the observation emphasises the need for studies to elucidate causation. Until it becomes possible to prevent all cases of neural tube defect, reducing its impact requires folate supplementation preconceptually and successful antenatal detection programmes coupled with the offer of termination of affected pregnancies (see also Chapter 6).

Table 2.5 Total reported prevalence (number and rate per 10,000 births) of neural tube defects (including livebirths, fetal deaths from 20 weeks gestation and induced abortions following prenatal diagnosis) in 16 EUROCAT registries, 1980–1994

	All neural tube defects	
Registry	*Number*	*Rate per 10,000*
Glasgow	519	27.2
Dublin	820	25.6
Belfast	967	23.9
Galway	79	19.0
Asturias	51	13.9
Northern Netherlands	229	12.0
Odense	90	11.6
Paris	588	11.5
Bouches-du-Rhône	261	11.3
Basque Country	88	11.0
Hainaut-Namur	168	10.9
Malta	51	10.6
Antwerp	33	10.0
Strasbourg	170	9.8
Tuscany	156	8.6
Switzerland	197	5.5

Source: EUROCAT Working Group. Prevalence of neural tube defects – see:
www.iph.fgov.be/eurocat/eurocat.htm

Small Areas

An example of the analysis of health data in relation to smaller geographical areas is illustrated by early work carried out in north-east England. Teesside was a County Borough formed in 1968 and disbanded in 1974 with the reorganisation of local government. The Borough covered 49,000 acres and had a population of almost 400,000. Lying close to an industrial belt of large chemical and steel complexes on the banks of the estuary of the River Tees was a collection of old urban centres with a high proportion of poor housing. Moving away from the river, pollution lessened and the countryside opened up. The objective of the work was to identify the deprived sections of the population and to bring services to support them. Small area analysis of health differences are now commonly undertaken but they were not at that time.

From census data three housing characteristics were used for all the separate small enumeration districts in Teesside. These were: (a) proportion of houses lacking one or more basic amenities (wc, bath, hot and cold water); (b) proportion of houses with more than 1.5 people per room; (c) proportion of houses which were privately rented. Using predetermined criteria, the enumeration districts with poor housing characteristics were categorised as 'downtown'. The population was approximately a fifth of the total. The remainder of Teesside was referred to as 'the rest'.

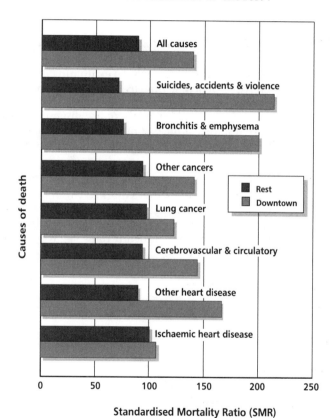

Figure 2.8 Standardised mortality ratios (SMRs) for various causes in 'downtown' areas compared with 'the rest' of Teesside County Borough.

Source: Adapted from Donaldson RJ. Urban and suburban differentials.
In: Carter CO and Peel J (Eds), Equalities and Inequalities in Health.
London: Academic Press, 1976.

A number of health indices were then compared in order to examine differences between these two types of area. When compared for standardised mortality ratios (SMRs) for various causes of death, infant mortality or illegitimacy rates, the 'downtown' areas persistently fared worse than 'the rest' of Teesside. The cause of death analysis is shown in Figure 2.8 and demonstrates the unfavourable mortality experience of people living in the 'downtown' areas, particularly with respect to respiratory disease and suicides, accidents and violence. This study thus identified the multiple deprivation of the inner urban area: poor housing, high unemployment, poor health, and low uptake of services. Through these findings action was taken to deploy services to meet these problems, although it must be appreciated that such problems, rooted in social, economic, cultural and environmental factors, will not be resolved by action within the health service alone. Indeed, even in the 1990s, active research programmes were still underway in the Teesside area to try and explain the reasons for the poor health of people living in some small communities and to assess the respective contributions of deprivation, environment and lifestyle to poor health and premature death. This illustrates the enduring nature of many geographical inequalities in health and the complexity in pursuing them to a successful public health conclusion.

Describing Disease in Relation to Person

There are many more ways of examining the pattern of disease in relation to the characteristics of people than by either time or place.

Most diseases show a distinct pattern when looked at by age, sex, occupation and social class. In addition, there are diseases which vary with ethnic origin and with marital status. Some examples of patterns of disease in relation to some of these variables are described in this section, though there are many others.

Age and Sex

Almost all diseases show a marked variation with age. Indeed, mortality rates from all causes show a distinctive pattern (Figure 2.9). Once the first few years of life have been passed, there are relatively few deaths per unit of population until the age of about 35 years, when death rates begin to increase sharply with each successively higher age-group.

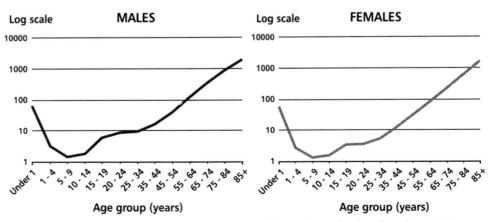

Figure 2.9   Mortality rates per 10,000 population in England and Wales, 1998.
Source: Office for National Statistics.

There are differences, too, in the importance of various causes of death at each age. Figure 2.10 shows that in the younger age-groups, accidents and violence are a more important cause of death than diseases, while in the older age-group, diseases of the respiratory and circulatory systems and cancer come to the fore.

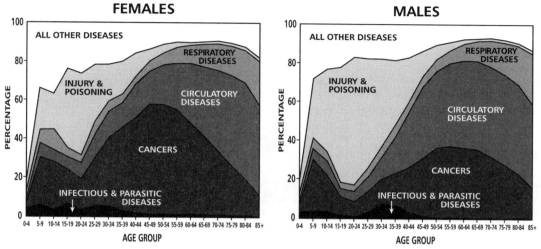

Figure 2.10   Selected causes of death by age and sex in England and Wales, 1995.

Not all disease shows a straightforward increase in occurrence with age. Figure 2.11 shows that even within a disease category, for example, fractures, there can be very different age patterns according to the fracture site. Fractures of the neck of the femur (Graph A, Figure 2.11) show a very low incidence in childhood and early adult life, with a steadily increasing rate for both sexes from middle age upwards. Apart from a small peak in childhood, fractures of the upper end of the humerus (Graph B, Figure 2.11) show a similar pattern. The tibial and fibular fractures (Graph C, Figure 2.11), show a peak occurrence in young men, largely as a result of sporting and road traffic accidents while fractures of the lower end of the radius and ulna (Graph D, Figure 2.11), where a common mechanism is a fall on the outstretched hand, show a peak in both sexes in the younger age-group as well as in older women.

Figure 2.12 is derived from the same study of fracture incidence in a geographically-defined population but this time compares the size of the male and the female incidence rate at each site in two broad age-groups: people over 55 years of age and people under 55 years of age. The incidence rate for males and females in each age-group is compared by means of their ratio. The purpose of analysing these data in this way was to try to throw light on the possible influence of menopausal changes on fracture incidence.

There were interesting differences between the sexes at different ages according to the site of fracture. These fell into two broad patterns. In the first pattern of fracture sites (Graph A, Figure 2.12), there was a male excess in both younger and older age-groups. In the second pattern (Graph B, Figure 2.12) female incidence began to predominate over male after the age of 55 years.

This sex pattern in fracture incidence at different sites points to a number of possible explanations: osteoporotic fall in bone mass around the time of the menopause; a greater propensity to falls amongst older women, and neuromuscular deterioration with age which may reduce the degree of skeletal protection when trauma occurs.

As with any descriptive epidemiological data, these interesting sex differences in the incidence of a disease do not provide direct evidence of causal association but do point the way for further epidemiological studies aimed at elucidating causation and possibly scope for prevention of an important public health problem.

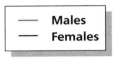

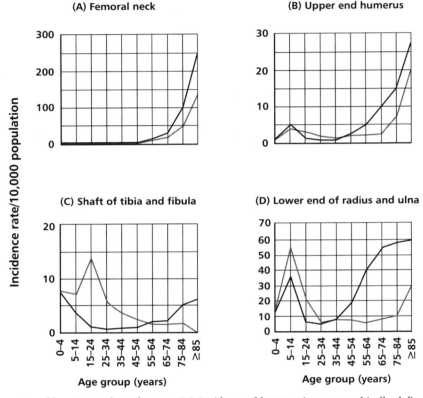

Figure 2.11: Age- and sex-specific average annual fracture incidence rates (per 10,000 population) at selected sites.

Source: Donaldson LJ, Cook A, Thomson RG. Incidence of fractures in a geographically-defined population. Journal of Epidemiology and Community Health, 1990; 44:241–5.

Occupation and Social Class

The study of mortality in groups of workers in particular occupations or industries has a long tradition, and through the years has uncovered particular risk factors for particular diseases which have arisen in the working environment.

In 1911, the Registrar General in Britain first used a hierarchical classification of social class based on occupation. The move to collect and present data in this way was prompted by the concern expressed by many of the social reformers of the time – such as Charles Booth (1840–1916) and Seebohm Rowntree (1871–1954) – about the high rates of mortality amongst the poor; in particular, infant mortality. The classification grouped people according to the skill required for, and the social standing carried by, their particular occupation.

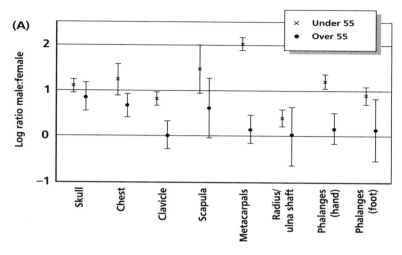

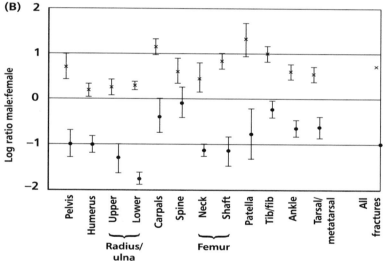

Figure 2.12 Log ratio of male: female fracture incidence rates (per 10,000 population) for those aged under 55 years (×) compared to those aged 55 years and over (●) for specific fracture sites.

Source: Donaldson LJ, Cook A, Thomson RG. Incidence of fractures in a geographically-defined population. Journal of Epidemiology and Community Health, 1990; 44:241–5.

Data on occupation continue to be used to produce various methods of social and economic classification. Broadly, the assumption underlying this approach is that someone's occupation is a good guide to his or her position within society.

A very wide range of approaches to defining social class have been used by governmental agencies in different countries or by research workers. Most measures take, either singly or as a composite measure, three aspects about the person: occupation, education and income.

In Britain, occupation remains the main basis for such social and economic classifications and detailed data about occupation are collected at birth, marriage, death, at the time of the census, and in responses given to government social surveys.

Classification of Occupation

Two widely used classifications are derived from such occupational data by grouping of occupations. Social class based on occupation (also called the Registrar General's social class or simply social class) and socio-economic groups.

The basis of the collection of occupational data for these official purposes (and hence their aggregation to produce social class and socio-economic group measures) is the Standard Occupational Classification. This classification is intended to be applicable to all paid jobs. On the basis of the typical work activities associated with the job, occupational groups have been created. The grouping is on the basis of occupations which are similar in terms of the level of skills (experience or qualifications) needed to carry them out and the nature of the work activities.

At the first level, the Standard Occupational Classification comprises approximately 3800 detailed occupational titles (for example, bank-note engraver, mussel gatherer, member of the Stock Exchange). These are aggregated into 371 unit occupational groups (for example, caretakers, nursery nurses, glass product and ceramics makers) which in turn are further aggregated into 77 minor occupational groups (for example, woodworking trades, filing and records clerks, catering occupations). Finally, there are 22 sub-major groups and the highest level of aggregation which is called major occupational groups (for example, clerical and secretarial occupations, managers and administrators, plant and machine operators) of which there are nine.

Social Class Based on Occupation

Strict rules are in existence to ensure that occupational groups are correctly assigned to their social class. In addition, there are a number of more complex issues surrounding the usage of the system generally and in specific circumstances. For example, when considering the position of an unemployed or retired person, should their last occupation be chosen as representative or the main occupation followed during their work career? In practice, for people in work, the current occupation is used and for those not in work it is their last main paid occupation which is used.

Another example of the potential complexity of assigning a social class to someone relates to the position of women and children. Traditionally, the occupation of the (usually male) head of household has been used to assign a social class to other household members viewed as dependent. This is still the case for many purposes. However, as the position of women in society, at work and in the home has changed and as household structures have become more varied, the appropriateness of assigning social class to household members using the head of household's occupation has increasingly been debated. There is no easy way round the difficulty when trying to characterise a household. However, for some statistical purposes, married women who are employed are classified by their own occupations.

In general, each occupational group is given a basic social class, although certain groups (for example, managers or foremen) are allocated to a higher social class than others in their occupational group on the basis of their level of responsibility.

The present social class categories are as follows:

I	Professional
II	Managerial and technical
IIIN	Non-manual skilled
IIIM	Manual skilled
IV	Partly skilled
V	Unskilled

Figure 2.13 shows data comparing mortality in younger men by social class. A familiar gradient of increasing mortality with lower social class is evident. The pattern of increasing mortality on moving down the social-class scale is a feature of all age-groups from birth, through childhood into adult life and is present for almost all major causes of death.

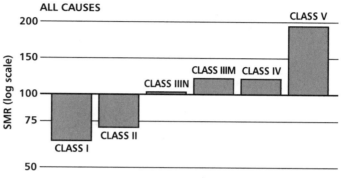

Figure 2.13 Standardised mortality ratios by social class: men aged 20–64 in England and Wales (1991–93).

Source: Drever F, Whitehead M (Eds), Health Inequalities. London: Office for National Statistics, 1997.

Socio-economic Groups

This is an alternative way of classifying the population on the basis of employment status and occupation. It was introduced in 1951 and has been extensively amended since then. There are 17 categories; for example, 'agricultural workers' or 'professional workers, self-employed'. Unlike social class the numbering of the groups is not hierarchical. The groups are sometimes combined into six 'collapsed categories', as used in Figure 2.14. This analysis shows the proportion of cigarette smokers in each socio-economic group and allows the factors which might contribute to differential smoking rates to be explored.

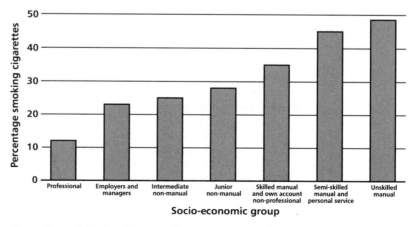

Figure 2.14 Prevalence of cigarette smoking in economically active men by socio-economic group.

Source: General Household Survey for 1996. London: The Stationery Office, 1998.

Ethnic Origin

The pattern of health of migrant groups in Britain became clearer during the 1980s and 1990s when ethnicity was a more commonly recorded variable. However, most studies of mortality still rely heavily on country of birth and therefore second generation migrants are excluded.

In relation to all adult men, all-cause mortality is higher for people born outside England and Wales except for Caribbean men (who have a lower than average all-cause mortality).

When specific causes of death are examined, particularly striking is the relatively high rate of death from ischaemic heart disease amongst men born in the Indian sub-continent and the relatively high mortality from stroke amongst men born in the Caribbean and West African countries (Figure 2.15).

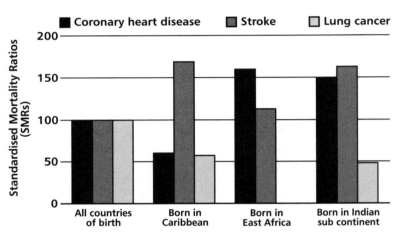

Figure 2.15 Standardised mortality ratios by country of birth for men aged 20–64 years in England and Wales.

Source: Adapted from Health Inequalities. Drever F, Whitehead M (Eds). London: Office for National Statistics, 1997.

The study of disease and mortality in populations of different ethnic origin can provide important clues to disease causation. There is a particular tradition in descriptive epidemiology of studying the disease and mortality experience of migrant populations to see whether their disease experience remains as in their country of origin or changes to their new country of residence.

The study of an ethnic minority population which retains distinct cultural traditions and practices in comparison to a long-standing indigenous population can also yield clues to disease causation. Figure 2.16 compares the occurrence of cancer at different sites for Asians (defined as people not of United Kingdom descent who originate from India, Pakistan or Bangladesh or people of Indian or Pakistani descent who originate from East Africa) and non-Asians living in Leicestershire, England.

A relatively complex statistical approach was necessary to compare the incidence of cancer in the two populations because, at the time of the study, concurrent denominator data on the Asian population were not available (the study was before the time of the 1991 census when ethnic origin questions enabled much more reliable information on the size and structure of the ethnic minority populations to be made available).

It is not necessary to understand the details of the methodology for the purpose of this illustration, merely to note (as is shown in Figure 2.16) the apparent excess (over the 'expected' occurrence) amongst Asians of cancers of the tongue, oral cavity, pharynx, oesophagus, and of some other sites.

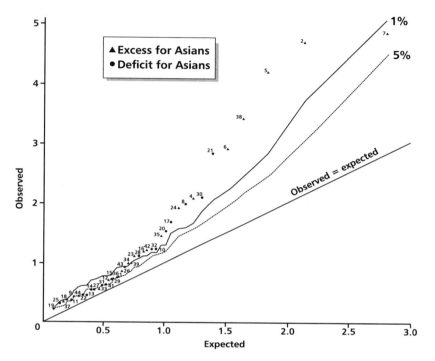

Figure 2.16 Contributions of each cancer site to the overall chi-squared test with simulation envelopes for 1% and 5% levels of significance (log units).

Site of cancer: 1 Lip, 2 tongue, 3 salivary glands, 4 gum, floor of mouth, other mouth, 5 oro-, naso-, hypopharynx, 6 other oral cavity, 7 oesophagus, 8 stomach, 9 small intestine, 10 colon, rectum, 11 liver, bile ducts, gallbladder, extrahepatic bile ducts, 12 pancreas, 13 peritoneum, 14 other and ill-defined (digestive organs, and peritoneum), 15 nasal cavities, etc, 16 larynx, 17 trachea, bronchus, lung, 18 pleura, thymus, heart, 19 bone and cartilage, connective tissue, 20 malignant melanoma, 21 other skin, 22 breast, 23 uterus unspecified, 24 cervix, 25 placenta, 26 body of uterus, 27 ovary and tubes, 28 other female genital, 29 prostate, 30 testis, 31 penis and other male genital, 32 bladder, kidney, ureter, 33 eye, 34 brain, other nervous system, 35 thyroid, 36 other endocrine, 37 other ill-defined sites, 38 lymph nodes, other and unspecified, 39 secondary of respiratory and digestive system and other site, unspecified site, 40 lymphosarcoma and reticulosarcoma, 41 Hodgkin's disease, 42 other lympoid, 43 multiple myeloma, and 44 leukaemia.

Source: Donaldson LJ, Clayton DG. Occurrence of Cancer in Asians and non-Asians. Journal of Epidemiology and Community Health, 1984; 38:203–207.

It is, of course, important to exclude spurious explanations of the kind discussed earlier and particularly to consider the possibility that the findings might be due to selective immigration. In this case could Asian people have come to Britain because they were already suffering from cancer (for example, to obtain treatment)? This is always an important potential explanation to consider in studies of immigrant populations. However, it was considered implausible in this particular example.

Of particular relevance to the excess of Asian cancer cases at the particular sites found in the study shown in Figure 2.16 is the habit of betel chewing. In countries where betel is chewed, its common accompaniment in the chew, tobacco, has been implicated in the causation of cancerous and precancerous lesions of the oral cavity. It has further been suggested that elements in the betel chewing habit other than tobacco – that is, the areca nut, the betel leaf, or the lime additive – may be causally linked to oral cancer as well as pharyngeal and oesophageal cancer.

The Asian population, one of the main ethnic minority populations of present-day Britain, is still relatively young in its age structure. Chronic diseases such as cancer are uncommon. This will not always be so. As the population ages, there will be a need to be able to anticipate the main health problems of this community. Observational studies, such as the one illustrated here, can never prove cause and effect but do provide important pointers to areas where further epidemiological inquiry is required. They also indicate a need to establish the prevalence within the ethnic minority population of traditional practices and behaviours which may be of public health importance.

Cross-sectional or Prevalence Studies

The previous section has dealt with the techniques of descriptive epidemiology in which comparisons are made, in mortality or the occurrence of disease between populations, within groups of the same population, and over time. Most of the examples given derived the information for making such comparisons from routinely available health data.

Quite often, it will be important to describe the size of a health problem within a population but it will be found that routinely available data are not adequate to fulfil this task. For example, a health authority wishing to establish the prevalence of dementia within its population would not readily be able to do so from available sources of data. Leaving aside problems with the quality of death certification in the elderly, mortality statistics would completely underestimate the problem because only a relatively small proportion of people with the disease at any one time are dying from it. Similarly, statistics derived from hospital admissions (whether to psychiatric or general wards) would also underestimate the problem because a high proportion of people with dementia might be expected to reside within the community and not be in contact with hospital services.

It is in such circumstances that consideration may be given to carrying out a survey to gather data directly about members of the population to gain a more accurate estimate of the prevalence of the disease in question.

If such a special study is to be carried out, it will also usually be widened to include the gathering of other relevant information on the population under study, other than purely the disease of interest. Thus, a prevalence study of the extent of dementia in the population would be unlikely to limit itself to assessing elderly people for the presence or absence of dementia but would also gather data on factors such as their domestic circumstances, their capacity for self-care and their physical status.

Surveys in which information is gathered directly from members of a population can be carried out for reasons other than to establish the prevalence of a disease and this section describes the general approach to such surveys and why they may be carried out. Notwithstanding the precise purpose of a particular population survey, two general terms are often used to describe them: prevalence studies and cross-sectional studies. Both terms emphasise a key feature of such surveys, that they describe the population at a point in time – like a snapshot.

Aims of Cross-sectional Surveys

As has already been described, one purpose in carrying out a cross-sectional survey is to establish the prevalence of a disease in the population. Another purpose is to describe the characteristics of the population when there are no routinely available data to do this. This may be to establish a particular aspect of the population's need for health or social services or to establish the prevalence of risk factors (for example, intravenous drug abuse, cigarette smoking, obesity) which can be the basis of health promotion programmes. A population may also be surveyed to establish people's views on health or health services, thereby yielding information not otherwise available and which may also be of major importance in planning and developing services. Whatever the aims of a cross-sectional study, many of the aspects of the methodology will be broadly similar.

Outline of Methodology

The cross-sectional study is a type of epidemiological investigation which seeks to gather data on one or more aspects or characteristics of individuals resident in that population at a particular point in time. Because it will seldom be feasible or necessary to gather such data about every member of the population, usually a sample is chosen to be studied. On the basis of the findings within the sample, general conclusions are drawn about the population.

Choosing the Study Population

Assembling the population for this kind of study involves gaining access to a representative list of members of the population and then applying the technique of sampling to this list.

Sampling

A number of important considerations should be borne in mind when choosing a sample. Uppermost is the need to appreciate that, in taking a sample, the underlying objective is to make true statements about the population itself.

The technique of drawing a sample has an important bearing on this process. There are two main ways of obtaining a sample of people: firstly, by the quota method and secondly, randomly.

Quota Sampling

The quota sample is often employed by market research organisations. This method involves the interviewer seeking a specified number of people to fit into a pre-agreed sample configuration. Men or women of particular ages or social backgrounds may be sought out, for example, by approaching people in the street. This type of sampling is generally unsatisfactory because it is unlikely to result in a sample which is representative of the whole population. For instance, a sample of middle-aged men, drawn by quota sampling in a shopping centre in mid-morning, would be unlikely to be truly representative of all middle-aged men in the particular town. Groups such as the unemployed or shift workers would tend to be over-represented.

Random Sampling

The basic and most commonly used sampling method in survey research is the random sample. There are a number of different ways of obtaining a random sample, but all have the following in common: the results can be generalised to the total population from which the random sample was drawn and the precision of the estimate derived from the sample can be calculated statistically.

Choice of a Sampling Frame

The first step in drawing a random sample is to construct a suitable sampling frame. A sampling frame is merely a list (actual or notional) of the population. The nature of the sampling frame will vary according to the purposes of the survey. A sample for a survey of infant feeding practices might be drawn from all birth registrations in a particular area. In a survey of occupational diseases, the sampling frame might be the employment records of particular firms.

Many population surveys in public health will aim to conduct an investigation in a sample of the population of a geographically-defined area: say a health authority. Obtaining a suitable sampling frame, (i.e., a list of the residents of that authority), from which to draw a suitably-sized sample survey is not a straightforward proposition. A traditional approach is to use the electoral roll, which supplies a list of people qualified to vote listed by the street within the different electoral wards of a town or city. As a sampling frame representative of the general population, however, this has serious limitations. The most obvious is that people below voting age are excluded. In addition, the rolls are often out of date as people move into or out of the area.

As more general practitioners have combined into large group practices, the potential for the use of age-sex registers as representative sampling frames has increased. The computerised central registers of patients registered with family practitioner services also have extremely important potential in this respect. It is important here, too, to realise that the register may be inflated by people who have died or left the area but whose names have not yet been removed from it.

Having obtained a suitable sampling frame, there are a number of different approaches to obtaining the random sample. The most direct is to choose people at random from the sampling frame until the required sample size is achieved (simple random sample).

A simple 10% random sample of a population of 1000 people would involve picking at random 100 names from amongst the 1000 listed. It is absolutely essential however that each time a name is chosen, every individual has an equal chance of being picked. One technique for ensuring that this is the case is through the use of a table of random numbers. In the example above, the people in the population are numbered from 000 to 999. Using a special table of random numbers, 100 numbers are then picked and the people corresponding to the numbers listed become the sample. Modern computer technology can be used to generate a random sample if the sampling frame is held on a computer database.

Another approach is to draw a systematic random sample in which individuals are picked from the sampling frame in sequence. A 10% random sample drawn in this way would involve choosing every tenth name on the list (a 1-in-10 sample), only the first selection being made from the table of random numbers.

This is often a much more convenient way of drawing a sample. Systematic sampling is usually a perfectly satisfactory method, but it depends on people or items listed on a sampling frame being arranged in a way that does not introduce bias. For example, a 1-in-10 systematic sample drawn from a list of married people in which the husband's name always came first would result in either every person chosen being female or every person being male.

Stratification

This may be used to ensure adequate representation of different sections of the population. The population is divided into sections or strata, for example social classes, age-groups, or places of residence. A random sample is then drawn from within each stratum. Stratified sampling has the additional advantage that it allows a different size of sample to be taken from each stratum to reflect the varying size or importance of the different strata.

Multistage Sampling

This is often a convenient technique in large surveys. For example, a survey of lung disease in steel workers might take as its first-stage sampling frame a list of all towns with steel works. Having chosen an appropriate number of towns randomly, a second-stage sampling frame consisting of the names of employees could be drawn from the towns which had initially been chosen. The workers for examination would then be drawn at random from the second frame. The advantage of having adopted a two-stage sampling technique is clearly that the need to draw up a named list of steel workers in the whole country was by-passed, thus saving time and avoiding difficulty and cost to the investigators.

Gathering Data on the Sample

The information to be gathered on members of the sample, once it has been drawn, will depend on the aims of the population survey. However, a number of general principles apply.

Definition of What to Collect

At the outset, decisions need to be taken about the information which is required to address the aims of the study and how it is to be collected. There will be some types of information which address the central research question (for example, a person's blood pressure in a population survey of hypertension) while other information will be gathered because it provides important background on the characteristics of the sample or because it may be relevant to the analysis of the main factors under study.

Consideration must next be given as to how best to obtain the data in order to provide the required information. This may sound like a simple matter but it seldom is. Consider a seemingly straightforward variable such as social class which might be collected as an important piece of information in a population survey of mothers' infant feeding practice. Interviewers questioning members of the sample could not simply ask the mothers: 'What is your social class?'. The responses to such a general question by a population, with varying perceptions of what was meant by the concept of social class, would yield data from which no valid conclusions could be drawn about the social class of the respondents in relation to the Registrar General's definitions. A proper approach would involve the construction of a question which would provide the elements necessary to categorise the respondent by social class. Ideally, such a question should be derived from established survey work in the field and be of proven validity.

There are two general groundrules which are helpful to bear in mind when addressing these issues about information gathering. The first is always to take a pedantic approach to considering the way in which each piece of information, even the simplest, is to be derived. For example, to derive age, should respondents be asked their precise age, to place their age in a banding or age-group, or should they be asked their precise date of birth? This needs to be discussed in the planning stage of the survey and a decision taken on what seems appropriate, bearing in mind the aims of the study and the method of data collection. The second groundrule is to use, wherever possible, established and validated measures or questions. For example, in a questionnaire survey of lifestyle which seeks to establish levels of alcohol intake in the population, rather than the investigators thinking up their own question to elicit information they should make use of the format of questions used in well-respected previous studies in this field.

Table 2.6 1987 Revised American College of Rheumatology criteria for rheumatoid arthritis

Criterion no.	Criterion description
1	Morning stiffness of at least one hour's duration
2	Arthritis of at least three joint groups with soft-tissue swelling or fluid observed by a physician
3	Arthritis involving at least one of the following joint groups: proximal interphalangeal, metacarpophalangeal, and wrists
4	Symmetrical arthritis
5	Subcutaneous nodules
6	Positive rheumatoid factor test
7	Radiographic changes typical of rheumatoid arthritis

Source: Hochberg MC, Spector TD. Epidemiology of Rheumatoid Arthritis: update. Epidemiologic Reviews, 1990; 12:247–51.

Special and more difficult judgements have to be made when gathering data to provide information about the prevalence of a disease. The first step is to agree on an operational definition of the disease under study and the method by which it is to be measured or detected. Even a formally stated definition of a disease may be of little practical value in conducting a survey to determine its prevalence. It is necessary to agree and lay down strict criteria which must be fulfilled in order that a person is counted as having the disease. Table 2.6 shows an approach which has been used in obtaining a list of criteria to define a chronic disease. It illustrates the contrast with the clinical situation, where the features of an illness which are taken as the basis for attaching a particular diagnostic label, may vary markedly between different doctors. The reasons underlying those decisions may not always be apparent. In planning a population study to determine the prevalence of a disease it is essential to resolve and adhere to a working definition or the results collected will have no meaning outside the context in which they are collected.

Method of Data Collection: The Survey Instrument

The choice of the method through which the data necessary to address the aims of the study will be derived is another important decision in planning a population survey. To a certain extent, this will also depend on the aims of the investigation.

The term used to describe the method of data collection is the *survey instrument* and sometimes it can literally be an 'instrument' (for example, a sphygmomanometer used to measure blood pressure in a population survey of hypertension). More often, however, the survey instrument is the document in which survey data are recorded: for example, a questionnaire to be administered by trained interviewers or a proforma used to extract data in a standardised format from various clinical records.

A detailed consideration of questionnaire design is beyond the scope of this book but there are a number of important aspects to be considered, for example: the structuring of questions (including the relative merits of closed versus open); the order in which questions should be asked; the avoidance of questions likely to lead to ambiguous or biased answers; the layout of the questionnaire; the coding of responses to facilitate analysis.

Questionnaires are of two broad kinds: those which will be administered face-to-face by an interviewer and postal questionnaires. Although postal questionnaires have the advantage that they allow a much larger sample size, they can have serious disadvantages because of the restricted range of topics which can be covered and in the generally higher levels of non-response which tend to occur with this method of questionnaire administration.

Whatever survey instrument is chosen, it is important that before the full-scale survey is undertaken, a *pilot study* is carried out on a small number of people within the sample. This allows difficulties with the questionnaire or other aspects of the survey to be ironed out or corrected before the survey proper is commenced.

Standardisation of Measurement and Interview Technique

Variation between measurements is another important consideration in a population survey and as the example of the measurement of blood pressure shows (Figure 2.17), it can have a wide variety of sources. The main concern is with systematic variation or bias.

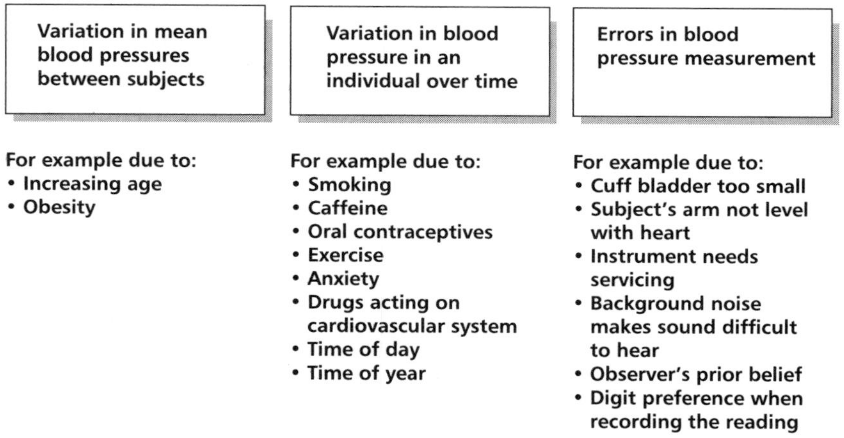

Variation in mean blood pressures between subjects	Variation in blood pressure in an individual over time	Errors in blood pressure measurement
For example due to: • Increasing age • Obesity	For example due to: • Smoking • Caffeine • Oral contraceptives • Exercise • Anxiety • Drugs acting on cardiovascular system • Time of day • Time of year	For example due to: • Cuff bladder too small • Subject's arm not level with heart • Instrument needs servicing • Background noise makes sound difficult to hear • Observer's prior belief • Digit preference when recording the reading

Figure 2.17 Sources of variation in blood pressure measurement.

Some variation can be reduced by standardising the procedures in the study as, for example, when physical examinations are being carried out. This will best be ensured by training examiners and checking their technique (for departure from the standard) at intervals during the conduct of the study.

If interviewers are being used to elicit information from members of the study population by questionnaire, they must be trained. This can be done by recording pilot interviews on videotape. Thus the interviewers and the study organisers can assess the results together and correct any faults in technique.

These are only some aspects of the process of preparing and monitoring interviewers who are responsible for gathering the survey data. There are many others, including: agreeing rules to be adopted when the respondents are reluctant to answer the questions posed; what to do when other family members seek to participate in answering questions on the respondent's behalf, and the extent to which interviewers should react to (or make observations on) responses made to the questions.

A lack of clarity on these and many other aspects of interviewing can risk the results obtained being invalid or biased in ways which may be impossible to detect or eliminate from the analysis. This is why the choice of interviewers is particularly important, as is their training and experience in both the general techniques of interviewing and the issues which are specific to the particular investigation.

Variation arising from scientific instruments used in surveys can be reduced by introducing strict quality control. In studies using laboratory measurements, test solutions or reagents can be employed to ensure standardisation.

The Problem of Non-response

A major difficulty when gathering data in population surveys, is the problem of non-response or non-cooperation.

The planning and organisation of the study should be geared to obtaining the highest possible recruitment of the sample under investigation. Key factors for success in minimising non-response will include: the nature of the initial approach made to members of the sample; the wording of a letter of introduction; the institution on the notepaper heading and, who the signatory is. These are factors which can make the difference between a very high rate of participation in the subsequent interview and a disastrous level of refusals or non-response.

It is inevitable, however, that some degree of non-response will remain, even after the most careful planning and the most strenuous efforts to reduce it. The main concern with non-response is that the non-responders are unlikely to be typical of the remainder of the sample. Depending on the circumstances, they may be more (or less) likely to suffer the disease or other subject of the investigation and hence their omission is likely to lead to bias when drawing conclusions from the results of the sample. Aside from initial attempts to keep non-response to a minimum, when it does occur the first approach is to make extra efforts on this group to gain their cooperation. Where this fails, a second strategy is to obtain as much indirect evidence as possible about the non-responders so as to make an estimate of the kind of bias which may be introduced by their omission.

Sometimes it is asked what level of response rate is acceptable? This question is almost impossible to answer in general terms because it depends on the nature and aims of the study. The concept to be borne in mind, however, is a simple one. Unless data on the sample (originally chosen) are fully captured, then the findings will not be truly representative of the whole population from which the sample was drawn. This is after all the purpose of the prevalence survey.

Some degree of non-response is, however, a feature of nearly all population surveys. The aim should be to achieve a response rate in the 95 to 100 per cent range. Some surveys do manage to do this although it would seldom be expected in postal surveys. However, it is more common to see reports of surveys with response rates in the mid to upper 70 per cent range. This is far less satisfactory but can still yield valuable findings, particularly if some data are available on the non-responders and if conclusions are drawn more cautiously than would be the case with higher response rates.

A further problem in interpreting data from population surveys to establish disease prevalence is the need to be fully aware that the population being dealt with is a survivor population. If the disease has an appreciable mortality the most severe cases will have died and any cross-sectional study will not include the entire spectrum of disease.

Example of a Prevalence Study: The Health Survey for England

A health survey of private households in England is carried out annually and includes interviews and some examinations and tests of children (over two years old) and adults in each household surveyed.

The sampling frame for the health survey for England is the Postcode Addresses File (PAD) which contains 720 postcode sectors (a description of the components of the postcode in Britain is given in Chapter 1). The method of sampling is a multistage stratified technique – a number of stratification factors are used to ensure that the eventual sample is broadly representative of the whole population of England. Sampled addresses are then sent an introductory letter which is then followed by initial contact with an interviewer. At each household which agrees to cooperate an interviewer administered questionnaire is first completed with the head of household or partner and then an individual questionnaire interview is carried out with each household member. Height and weight are also recorded at this first interview. Interviewees are then asked to agree to a second-stage visit when a nurse visits to carry out certain measurements and take a blood sample.

Detailed sampling rules govern which members of the household (particularly children) are to be included. Explanatory leaflets describe the purpose of the survey and help to gain compliance. Quality control measures include: training of interviewers and nurses; checking of interview and measurement quality, and protocols for interviewing and measuring children. There are rules to govern what to tell people if abnormalities are found and what action needs to be taken. Some information is gathered on non-responders and reasons for non-response.

The health survey's methods are worthy of careful study as an example of how a well conducted prevalence study is planned, executed and analysed. Valuable information about the health of the population can be derived from it including: general health, long-standing and acute illness, limitation of function, respiratory disease and certain other specific illnesses, experience of major and minor accidents, smoking and drinking, obesity, blood pressure, lung function, blood haemoglobin, and use of health services.

An example of the kind of information which is yielded by this prevalence study is shown in Figure 2.18. The public health importance of this finding is striking: high blood pressure is a risk factor for coronary heart disease and stroke. Yet, just under half of the people with high blood pressure were not being treated and 40% of those who were being treated did not have their blood pressure under control.

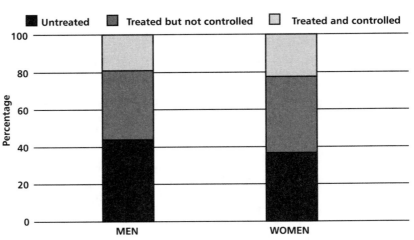

Figure 2.18 Control of high blood pressure in adults.

High blood pressure = Systolic ≥ 160 mmHg or Diastolic ≥ 95 mmHg

Source: DoH Health Survey for England, 1996.

Studies to Investigate Disease Causation

One of the most important areas of investigation in public health is the exploration of hypotheses involving factors which may be responsible for causing disease. It is of particular importance because, if such links can be established, then there may be scope for prevention by intervening against causal agents.

A causal hypothesis may spring from clinical impression, from laboratory observations, or from examining descriptive data in populations in relation to time, place or person as was described in the first section of this chapter (Table 2.7).

Table 2.7 Common ways in which ideas about causation emerge

- Laboratory study
- Clinical impression
- Clusters of rare disease
- Descriptive epidemiological studies
- Cohort and case-control studies

Thereafter, the testing of the hypothesis that the factor, or factors under examination may be responsible for causing the disease is a matter for carefully designed studies using epidemiological methods, each of which has its own special characteristics governing its use.

The previous section of this chapter has demonstrated that the techniques of descriptive epidemiology require a clear understanding of the sources of available data, the ways in which they can be used to make comparisons and, particularly, the limits which must be placed on any conclusions which can be drawn. This is even more important when using the more specialised study methods of epidemiology, two of which (cohort and case-control studies) are described in detail in this section.

One of the principal reasons for the existence of such study methods, and their complexity, is the fact that the investigator of causal relationships in human populations is denied the experimental approach.

If the laboratory scientist wishes to investigate whether or not a suspected cause results in a particular outcome or effect, he frequently does have at his disposal the experimental approach. Suppose, for example, that a particular chemical is suspected of causing breast cancer in white mice. The investigator could take a strain of white mice and allocate them at random into two groups. One group would receive the presumed causal chemical, the other group would be treated identically in all ways, except that the mice would not receive the chemical. The investigator would then observe the occurrence of breast cancer in the two groups of animals and draw conclusions. In the laboratory experiment, the investigator is in control of the events and as a result has an extremely powerful and direct method at his disposal. Similar experiments to test the effect of a suspected causal factor in groups of humans are usually quite unacceptable. Thus, if the same chemical which caused breast cancer in the white mice was suspected of causing breast cancer in human females, an experiment could not be carried out in which one group of women was given the chemical and the other was not. Experiments may, sometimes, be performed on groups of people where removal of a suspected causal factor or addition of a supposed beneficial factor could result in an improvement in health, although the ethical aspects of such studies needs the most careful consideration. The most usual experiment carried out in human subjects is the controlled clinical trial in which new therapies are tested out on people with particular diseases.

Sometimes, fortuitously for the investigator but often to the great misfortune of the population concerned, natural experiments take place which allow conclusions to be drawn about causation. Examples of this are the observations on the incidence of cancer following the exposure to radiation from Hiroshima bomb and the Chernobyl nuclear accident, the observation of the association between Burkitts lymphoma and Epstein-Barr virus infection and the observation of the incidence of vaginal tumours in the female offspring of women treated during pregnancy with diethylstilboestrol.

Usually, however, the experimental approach is ruled out for ethical reasons when investigating the effects of causes in human populations.

Instead, the search concentrates on associations between the factor, or set of factors, and a disease. This 'observational' approach (to distinguish it from the 'experimental') involves comparing the disease experience of two or more groups of people in relation to their possession of certain characteristics of exposure to a suspected factor or factors.

There are two main approaches to investigating causal hypotheses: cohort and case-control studies (Figure 2.19). Each has its own specific design features. Both involve comparisons being made between different groups of people but the basis of this comparison is entirely different in the two types of study.

In the cohort study, the comparison is being made between people who have been exposed to the hypothesised risk factor and people who have not been exposed to it; each group is then studied to see whether they develop the disease. In the case-control study, the disease is already present in one group (the 'cases') and absent in another (the 'controls'); the two groups' previous exposure to the hypothesised risk factor is then compared.

Before each of these methods is described in more detail, two important points should be borne in mind. Firstly, most health professionals, managers and students, even those specialising in the public health field, will never themselves carry out a cohort study or a case-control study (except when investigating outbreaks of communicable disease). However, some of the decisions which they take will be based upon the evidence of such studies undertaken by others. This is why it is important to have a good understanding of each methodology, when it is appropriate to apply it, what its potential limitations are, and where the possible sources of bias lie. Whole texts have been written on these study methods, particularly dealing with the statistical analysis of the data which are produced, but it is not essential to have an understanding of these matters to an advanced level. It is much more important to grasp the basic principles of both cohort studies and case-control studies.

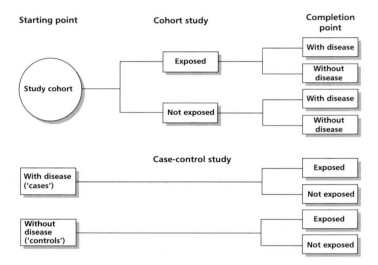

Figure 2.19 The main features of cohort and case-control studies.

The second point to be borne in mind is that the decision to make use of these specialised methods cannot be undertaken lightly. Their use is a matter for careful deliberation and would usually only be undertaken by a team of researchers or investigators, including (or with the advice of) a statistician skilled in the design and analysis of such studies. The next sections describe the main features of the two methods.

Cohort Studies

Outline of Methodology

The cohort study is a type of epidemiological investigation in which a population apparently free of the disease under study (or sample of such a population) is assembled and each individual is categorised according to whether they have been exposed to the risk factor(s) of interest. The cohort is then followed-up to see whether individual members of it develop the disease under study (or other diseases). Comparisons are then made between the occurrence of the disease in the 'exposed' compared to the 'non-exposed' groups within the cohort. If the intention is to test the hypothesis that smoking causes lung cancer, the initial step is to classify the study cohort into smokers and non-smokers. The cohort is then followed-up over time and cases of lung cancer are detected as they occur. The results would then be analysed to show what proportion of the smokers developed lung cancer compared to the proportion of non-smokers.

A cohort study may be conducted prospectively or retrospectively. In a prospectively conducted cohort study, the initial exposure data are collected on the members of the cohort and the investigators then wait for cases of the disease to crop up over time. This is the commonest type of cohort study, so much so that the terms 'cohort study' and 'prospective study' are sometimes used synonymously.

It is possible, however, to conduct a retrospective cohort study where data on the cohort's exposure, as well as its disease experience, are already available. This can only really be contemplated where good past records exist to define a historical cohort. For example, suppose that a very large general practice had maintained very comprehensive records on medications prescribed to the practice population over a long period of time. If in the present day, a particular drug became suspected of causing a type of cancer, the records of such a practice may allow a retrospective cohort study to be carried out. In such a study, a cohort would be assembled at some notional past date from the old practice population records and the people within it would be classified according to whether they had been prescribed the drug of interest or not. Their past and present medical records would then also be examined to record their disease history and particularly whether they developed the cancer which was under study.

This is a simplified description of a complex methodology but in the relatively unusual situation where past data are available comprehensively on a large population, the retrospective cohort study has advantages of speed and lower cost compared to the more common prospective approach.

Choice of a Study Population

A cohort is a group of people who share a similar experience at a point in time. A birth cohort is people born on a particular day or in a particular year and a marriage cohort, those married in a given year. People residing in a particular geographical area or workers in an industry at a certain time also constitute a cohort.

In a cohort study investigating a causal hypothesis, the precise choice of cohort will depend on the nature of the disease under investigation. The cohort might be a group of people who have been exposed to a particular hazard (for example, a serious water pollution incident); a large workforce in a particular industry (for example, asbestos workers), or the population of a geographically-defined area (for example, a small town).

Characterising the Cohort

The way in which data are assembled to characterise the initial cohort of people to be followed-up will very much depend on the aims of the study. In a cohort study examining the risk of cancer arising from an industrial hazard, it is likely that quite detailed information would be gathered on the employment history of the workers concerned, their likely exposure in the workplace to quantified levels of the presumed risk factor, as well as whether they had other habits or characteristics which might influence the possibility of them developing the disease (for example, cigarette smoking). In a cohort study examining the risk of development of heart disease in a population, a sample of the population might form the study cohort and each member might be assessed by questionnaire, as well as by clinical and biochemical examination to determine their baseline status in terms of the risk factors under investigation.

The Follow-up Phase

The follow-up phase of a cohort study, conducted prospectively, requires very careful planning and preparation. Particularly in studies where a long follow-up period is required, the difficulties in keeping track of members of the cohort who move away from the area can be very great and the process can be expensive. Considerable stability is also required in the investigative team, particularly amongst its leaders, if the study is to be brought to a successful conclusion.

A number of decisions need to be made when this phase of the cohort study is being designed. One important decision is how, and at what intervals, re-assessments of the original members of the cohort will be made. This decision is somewhat easier when the outcome under study is a clear end point such as death. In such circumstances sources of mortality data can be kept under constant review and the records of members of the original cohort can be flagged as the deaths occur to denote the outcome. Where the study is examining less dramatic outcomes, such as the progress of children whose mothers were exposed (and not exposed) to a particular hazard in pregnancy, it would be necessary (in this example) to decide on the time periods at which the children in the original cohort would be given further developmental assessments. Clearly, it would be quite impractical to undertake this with great regularity on the very large numbers of children who would be involved.

Case-control Studies

The main attraction of a case-control study, especially when compared to a cohort study, is that it is relatively quick and cheap to undertake. Gathering data does not involve a long period of follow-up of the study population. That is not to say that the methodology is free of problems and these along with its main features are described in this section.

Outline of Methodology

The case-control study is a type of epidemiological investigation in which an assessment is made of the extent to which people with an established disease ('cases') and a comparable group who do not have the disease ('controls') have been exposed to a risk factor believed to be responsible for causing the disease.

For example, if it is the intention to investigate the hypothesis that smoking causes lung cancer, the investigation begins by taking people with lung cancer and suitable controls who do not have lung cancer. Enquiries are then made to discover how many of the lung cancer patients were smokers and how many of the control patients were smokers. The method of investigation in a case-control study is, almost without exception, retrospective. The investigator looks back in time on the past exposure history of present day cases of the disease and of the controls.

Choice of a Study Population

In practice, the design of a case-control study is much more difficult than this broad outline of the methodology implies. One of the key initial decisions for the investigator is to decide on the way in which the cases and controls which make up the study population will be chosen. If wrong decisions are made at this stage of the investigation, then the sources of bias which are introduced could render the results of the study invalid and useless.

Selection of 'Cases'

The choice of 'cases' should start with the formulation of a clear operational definition of what constitutes a 'case' of the disease under study. Decisions will need to be taken on whether to study a broad diagnostic category (for example, adult acute leukaemia) or a more homogenous diagnostic grouping (adult acute myeloid leukaemia). This decision depends on the nature of the investigation but, in general, the more heterogeneity in the diagnostic group, the less likelihood of being able to link a specific risk factor to the disease causation. On the other hand, the narrower the category of disease for inclusion of 'cases' in the study, the less general applicability will the findings have. For example, a case-control study to investigate possible risk factors in osteoarthrosis which took as 'cases' people with disease of the metacarpal joints and which yielded a finding of an apparently new risk factor for the disease would have thrown light on the causation of osteoarthrosis. However, general conclusions could not necessarily be drawn about osteoarthrosis of other joints in the body because the 'cases' were limited to people with disease at one particular site.

Having established a 'case' definition, it is most important to identify a source of all cases so that all eligible cases can be recruited into the study.

Selection of 'Controls'

The choice of an appropriate 'control' group is the issue which will usually cause the greatest discussion amongst investigators planning a 'case-control' study. While the issues involved in selecting 'controls' are complex, and often particular to the circumstances of the study, it is important to keep in mind the central purpose of the 'control' group. This is to provide an indication of the level of exposure to the risk factor in a 'healthy' population to which the exposure experienced by the people who have developed the disease can then be compared. Put in the simplest terms, suppose that a 'case-control' study was carried out to test the hypothesis that regular consumption of a particular kind of herbal tea led to the occurrence of pancreatic cancer. Say that 40% of 'cases' were found to be drinkers of the herbal tea, such a finding would be of much less interest if 40% of the general population were regular herbal tea drinkers than if only 2% were. In this example, the 'controls' are there to represent the same types of people as the 'cases' and allow an estimate to be made of the 'normal' pattern of herbal tea drinking.

In practice, to find 'controls' which are representative of a general population from which the 'cases' are presumed to have arisen, can be extremely difficult. For example, some 'case-control' studies using hospital 'cases' take as their 'control' group, patients who attended the hospital for the treatment of diseases other than the one which is the subject of the study. This approach has advantages in that access to controls is usually relatively easy and information can be gathered in a similar fashion to the 'cases'. It is also open to a number of potential sources of bias. For example, the hospital may have different catchment populations for the disease which is the subject of the study (the 'cases') and for the disease from which the 'control' group patients were suffering. In such circumstances, the 'controls' may not be representative of the general population from which the 'cases' were drawn, so the degree of their exposure to the risk factor may be an unreliable basis for comparison with the 'cases'.

'Controls' which are drawn from the general population do not suffer from this drawback but are less easy to identify and to gain cooperation from. The way in which they provide information may also be different to the 'cases' in ways which may introduce bias.

The relative advantages and disadvantages of different types of controls has led to many investigators using two sets of 'controls' in 'case-control' studies, one drawn from hospital and the other from the community.

Matching Cases and Controls

A great deal of emphasis is often placed on the question of 'matching' in 'case-control' studies. This is the process whereby 'controls' are matched to 'cases' on the basis of certain characteristics which are also known to be present in the 'cases'. The purpose of 'matching' is to eliminate the effect of so-called 'confounding' variables. Confounding can occur in other types of epidemiological investigation and is a term used to describe circumstances where there are factors, in addition to the risk factor under study, which may influence whether the disease occurs. If such confounding factors are unevenly distributed between study groups then they can distort the comparisons which are being made (and hence the conclusions which are drawn). One of the commonest confounding variables is age. The occurrence of many diseases is strongly associated with age. If, in a case-control study, there are major differences in the age structure of 'cases' and 'controls', this may distort other more important comparisons between the two groups. In descriptive epidemiological studies, standardisation (described in Chapter 1) is the method through which the confounding effect of age is reduced.

The technique of matching should be used very sparingly because there are serious problems which can result from over-matching. With modern statistical analytical techniques the matching of characteristics of cases and controls can also be undertaken during the analysis stage. The tendency in 'case-control' studies now is to take account of confounding variables (except age and sex) in the analysis of results rather than eliminate them at the study design stage of matching.

Assembling Data on the Exposure

Data on the exposure to the hypothesised risk factor(s) amongst 'cases' and 'controls' is usually obtained retrospectively by one, or both, of two main methods. Firstly, it is obtained by abstracting information from medical or other records pertaining to the 'cases' and the 'controls' and secondly, from the 'cases' and 'controls' (or where there have been deaths, their relatives) by interview.

Inherent in these approaches are further potential sources of bias. Records may not provide either comprehensive or detailed information to fully satisfy the requirements of the investigation. This is hardly surprising because such records seldom will have been created in the knowledge that they would be needed for a study. For example, retrospectively obtaining data on exposure from medical records of lung cancer patients, and hospital patients with other diseases (used as controls), it would be more likely that a smoking history would be recorded in the lung cancer patients because of the known association between that disease and cigarette smoking than in those with other diseases.

A further potential source of bias arises when exposure data are obtained retrospectively by interview. A person with the disease may be more likely to remember or report an exposure (perhaps because he is trying to rationalise the presence of the disease) than a person serving as a control who is disease-free. For example, a surgeon notices that many female patients presenting at his outpatient clinic with breast lumps give a past history of localised trauma. To investigate this further, he takes two groups of women: one group comprises those who have presented to the outpatient clinic with a breast lump, the other comprises a sample of healthy women of similar ages. Each group of women is asked if they can recall having any bang, knock or bruise of the breast during the previous 12 months. A much higher occurrence of such trauma is found in the group with breast lumps than amongst the control group of healthy women. Should it then be concluded that localised trauma predisposes to the formation of breast lumps? This is possible but unlikely. Women who have developed a breast lump are often in a very anxious state and their principal fear is that the lump is malignant. They will often cling to any alternative explanation of the origin of the lump. Hence, when such women are questioned about a history of trauma they are far more likely to remember and volunteer some trivial occurrence, than will those women without breast lumps.

Since data are obtained retrospectively on the exposure, whether by abstraction of case notes or by interview survey, the serious problems arise when there are differences in the completeness of information or selectivity between the two groups ('cases' and 'controls'). The investigator may not be aware of it and may draw misleading conclusions – such as in the examples given above. It is not possible fully to guard against this but, an additional measure which may help, is to ensure that the person gathering the data (whether abstracting it from records or questioning patients) relies on a structured format and is 'blind' to whether the individuals are 'cases' or 'controls'.

There is evidence to show that recall bias can be influenced by the seriousness of the condition being studied (cancer vs. an infection); the perceived importance of the event in the life of the individual (childbirth vs. drug exposure); the respondent (patient vs. proxy); the length of time since the event, and the phraseology used either in the questionnaire or by the interviewer.

Analysis of Data from Cohort and Case-control Studies: Measures of Risk

A common measure of association derived from epidemiological studies of causation is the *relative risk*. This measure expresses how many more times the disease occurred in the group which were exposed to the risk factor than the group which was not.

Relative Risk

In a cohort study, the relative risk is calculated from the ratio of incidence rates in the exposed group and the non-exposed group:

Incidence of the disease in the exposed group = I_e
Incidence of the disease in the non-exposed group = I_n

Relative risk = $\dfrac{I_e}{I_n}$

If no association, relative risk = 1

Odds Ratio

In a case-control study, incidence rates cannot be calculated because the subjects do not necessarily represent the population as a whole. However, an estimate of the *relative risk* is produced by the *odds ratio*.

Table 2.8   The findings of a case-control study

Exposed to risk factor	With the disease 'cases'	Without the disease 'controls'
Yes	a	b
No	c	d
Total	a + c	b + d

The odds ratio is a measure of the association between the risk factor and the disease and is calculated:

Step 1: Odds of a person in the case group having been exposed to the risk factor
$$= a/c$$

Step 2: Odds of a person in the control group having been exposed to the risk factor
$$= b/d$$

Step 3: Ratio of odds $= \dfrac{a/c}{b/d} = \dfrac{ad}{bc}$

This ratio is constructed by dividing the odds of the case group having been exposed to the risk factor by the odds of the control group having been exposed (Table 2.8). The calculation of these indices and the statistical theory underlying them is beyond the scope of this book but they have been introduced in outline to give an insight into the way in which the results of these more specialised epidemiological studies may be presented and interpreted

Aside from the relative risk, it is possible to calculate other measures of risk when examining associations between possible risk factors and diseases.

Attributable Risk

An alternative approach is to examine the difference in disease occurrence between the exposed and unexposed groups rather than the ratio. Such an approach is used to construct the *attributable risk*.

Data from a cohort study could thus be analysed:

Incidence of the disease in the exposed group $= I_e$
Incidence of the disease in the non-exposed group $= I_n$
Attributable risk $= I_e - I_n$
If no association, attributable risk $= 0$

The attributable risk is useful in examining the absolute additional risk which individuals experience as a result of their exposure.

Population Attributable Risk

Another measure, the *population attributable risk* is a measure of the extent to which the amount of the disease which occurs in the population is due to the risk factor. The population attributable risk is useful in terms of assessing the public health impact of a risk factor and hence the benefits which could be obtained by preventive action.

It is calculated by multiplying the attributable risk by the prevalence P of the risk factor in the population:

$$(I_e - I_n) \times P$$

A relatively small excess (i.e., attributable) risk of developing a disease where a large number of people are exposed to the risk factor would yield many additional cases.

The benefits of preventive action could be great. Alternatively, an attributable risk which was large but where relatively few people were exposed to the risk would not produce a large burden of disease in the population and the scope for major preventive action would be limited.

Analysis of Case-control Study Data

Table 2.9 shows data from one of the earliest case-control studies ever carried out; an investigation in the 1950s into the possible causes of childhood cancer. One of the factors investigated was whether irradiation of the foetus by abdominal X-ray examinations of the mother during pregnancy was associated with childhood cancer.

Table 2.9 Analysis of data from a case-control study

	Cases	*Controls*
Abdominal X-ray of pregnant mother (exposed)	141	81
No abdominal X-ray of pregnant mother (unexposed)	1,125	1,204
Total	1,266	1,285
Odds ratio 1.86; 95% confidence interval 1.40–2.47		

Source: Adapted from Stewart AM, Webb J, Hewitt DA. A survey of childhood malignancies. BMJ, 1958; 1:1495–1508.

The data are shown to illustrate the way in which such an analysis can be presented (not to describe the study in detail). As Table 2.9 shows, there was a significantly elevated odds ratio of childhood cancer in children who were irradiated *in utero*. The authors concluded that foetal irradiation by diagnostic X-raying of the pregnant mother was a risk factor for childhood cancer.

Analysis of Cohort Study Data

Table 2.10 is an example of a different way in which data from a cohort study can be analysed. This is because it is only a comparison of incidence and there is no calculation of risk. However, the risk calculation is added to the table. The data are from a large study in which married women using different forms of contraception were followed-up and information was gathered on a range of health outcomes. The aspect of the study shown in Table 2.10 examines the relationship between use of oral contraceptives and the subsequent development of two inflammatory bowel diseases (ulcerative colitis and Crohn's disease).

Table 2.10 Analysis of data from a cohort study investigating the association between oral contraceptive usage and the occurrence of chronic inflammatory bowel disease

Use of oral contraceptives	Woman-years of observation	Ulcerative colitis		Crohn's disease	
		Number of cases	*Incidence/1000 women-years*	*Number of cases*	*Incidence/1000 woman-years*
Never used	75,950	8	0.11	6	0.08
Ex-user	67,319	7	0.10	4	0.06
Current user	61,116	16	0.26	8	0.13
Total	204,385	31	0.15	18	0.09

Source: Vessey M, Jewell D, Smith A, Yeates D, McPherson K. Chronic inflammatory bowel disease, cigarette smoking, and use of oral contraceptives: findings in a large cohort study of women of child-bearing age. BMJ, 1986; 292:1101–3.

There was a higher incidence of both ulcerative colitis and Crohn's disease in current oral contraceptive users than in women who had never used the pill or had given up using it (Table 2.10). While the difference did not achieve statistical significance for Crohn's disease, it did for ulcerative colitis. Incidences in those who had stopped using oral contraceptives were similar to those who had never used them.

The authors concluded that while the associations between oral contraceptive use and chronic inflammatory bowel disease could not be regarded as established, they provided important clues to its causation.

Establishing a Causal Relationship

As has been made clear, both cohort and case-control studies are observational in nature. To investigate hypotheses of cause and effect they rely on observing real life events: people who are exposed (or expose themselves) to risk factors and those people who develop disease. If an association is found it is probable that the relationship between exposure and disease is not, in fact, one of cause and effect.

It is important, therefore, to consider the possible explanations for any association between a risk factor and a disease, whether the association has arisen as a result of a descriptive epidemiological study or from carrying out a cohort or a case-control study.

Three possible alternatives for such an association should be reviewed before detailed consideration is given to establishing whether it could be causal. The three are either that the association has arisen by chance, or that it may be spurious, or that it may be a secondary association. A brief description of each follows.

Association is a Chance Occurrence

The association between the factor and the disease may be a chance occurrence which would generally not be found on another occasion. Statistical tests exist, however, to allow a statement to be made of the probability with which the observed association would have arisen by chance on the hypothesis that there is, in fact, no association between the factor and the disease.

Association is Spurious

The apparent association between causal factor and disease may not be real, but a product of the way in which the investigation was carried out. For example, suppose that it was intended to investigate the association between place of delivery (cause) and perinatal mortality (effect). A comparison of two groups of women might show that the perinatal mortality for those delivered in consultant obstetric units was higher than for women delivered in general practitioner maternity units. It might be concluded that general practitioner units were safer places in which to have a baby. Such a conclusion is almost certainly fallacious, however. In general, consultant obstetric units, because of their special expertise and equipment, deliberately select women at high risk for delivery in their units. Thus, the consultant unit might have a higher perinatal mortality rate than the general practitioner unit because of this fact alone, and not because the quality of care was inferior. This source of bias (selection bias) where like is not being compared with like is very important. Other sources of bias (such as those described in the section on case-control studies) can also yield spurious associations between risk factors and diseases.

Association is Secondary

A factor and a disease may appear to be associated in a causal fashion when in reality the reason for their association is that both are related to a third factor. Thus, an association is found between countries with a high proportion of television owners and the frequency of coronary heart disease. The fact that these two factors are strongly associated does not mean that they are causally related and that television causes coronary heart disease. A more reasonable explanation is that television ownership is an indicator of societies with lifestyles which themselves are causally related to coronary heart disease.

Criteria Which Infer a Causal Association

If an association between a factor and a disease is found which probably did not occur by chance, is not spurious and not due to a secondary association, then this does not prove that the association is causal. However, six criteria, if present, help to infer that the association is causal:

(1) **Plausibility**. Greater weight is given to a possible causal factor if it seems to fit in with what is known about the pathology of the disease.

(2) **Consistency**. The association would, if causal, be expected to persist when studies were carried out by different investigators working in different populations at different times.

(3) **Temporal relationship**. Clearly, to assess causality it is necessary to show that the factor preceded in time the development of the disease.

(4) **Strength**. A causal relationship is more likely to be present when there is a marked difference in frequency of the disease in people who have been exposed to the factor than amongst those who have not. An additional piece of evidence which is strongly indicative of causality is the presence of a dose-response relationship: with increasingly greater exposure to the risk factor the incidence of the disease rises.

(5) **Specificity**. An ideal finding would be that the postulated causal factor was related to the disease in question and no other. This is, however, not always the case since a factor may be causally related to more than one disease.

(6) **Change in risk factor**. If the factor is removed or reduced and the incidence of the disease falls, this strongly indicates that the factor is causal.

Randomised Controlled Trials

Another type of study design which is not observational in nature, as are cross-sectional studies, cohort and case-control methods, is the so-called 'intervention' design. This usually takes the form of *a randomised controlled trial* (RCT).

In it, two or more groups are assembled. They receive defined interventions (for example, treatments, health education messages, dietary modification) which are controlled by the investigator and they are then monitored to detect events which are hypothesised to result from these actions (for example, relief of pain, improvement in health, loss of weight). The best established context of the RCT is the clinical trial in which new therapies are assessed in comparison with old methods of treatment or of placebos ('dummy' treatments).

Outline of Methodology

The main feature of the *interventional* method, which sets it apart from observational studies, is the aim of producing groups of patients comparable in respect of features known to affect the outcome, except for the different interventions which it is planned that they will receive. Other unknown differences between such groups may, of course, still be present but the usual means of negating their effects and enabling valid inferences to be made is through introducing *randomisation*. This process involves dividing the group of subjects (or any subgroup or subgroups with particular characteristics) into two parts: one part becoming the 'experimental' or 'intervention' group and the other the 'control' group. The outcome or end-point of the study is then assessed as the two groups are followed-up in an identical way.

Clinical trials of therapies are much more commonplace than RCTs evaluating preventive measures. This is, in part, because of the difficulty involved with large numbers of subjects being required for the latter and a long time span to await the appearance of outcome measures. Perhaps the most frequently occurring type of preventive trial is the trials of vaccines that have been carried out. However, a number of RCTs of coronary heart disease preventive measures have been conducted, as well as a small number in the field of screening (for example, breast cancer). The importance of undertaking a statistical calculation of the numbers of patients necessary to detect a difference between treated and untreated groups must be emphasised.

Choice of a Study Population

The planning of a randomised controlled trial necessitates an early decision, in principle, on the number of people who will comprise the study population. This in turn will depend on the number of interventions to be tested and the expected differences in outcome between the interventions as these parameters will determine the statistical power of the study to prove or otherwise the hypothesis to be tested. In the simplest form of randomised controlled trial there will be two groups: one which receives the intervention and the other which does not.

Having made this decision, the first stage in assembling the study population will be to identify a base population from which the study groups can be drawn.

The choice of this base population will influence the extent to which the findings of the investigation can be generalised to other populations.

This is a factor which is sometimes overlooked in the eagerness of investigators to eliminate other (albeit equally important) sources of bias in designing the randomised controlled trial. However, it can be extremely important in determining the value of the findings of the investigation. In the evaluation of a therapy, it is commonplace to draw the study group from amongst the admissions to a hospital. If, for example, the hospital is a centre of excellence and admits only the most complex cases within a particular diagnostic category (say patients with hypertension) then the findings on the effectiveness of the therapy under study would not be generalisable to all patients with the disease (in this example hypertension) but only to those with the same degree of complexity.

Eligibility

The next step in the process of assembling the study population is to decide upon criteria for eligibility. These will include a precise operational definition of the disease status of the patients (for the disease under study); age, sex and possibly other characteristics; and, the presence or absence of other clinical features (such as complications of the disease or associated conditions).

Randomisation

Once patients have been found to be eligible for the trial on the basis of diagnostic and other criteria previously laid down, then, and only then, does randomisation take place. It is an essential requirement that after eligibility for the trial has been confirmed, no further influences can be brought to bear on whether patients are allocated to particular groups. Anything other than random choice (for example, the deliberate placing of very ill patients in a non-treatment group) will introduce bias.

There are various techniques through which randomisation can be accomplished: for example, the use of random number tables, the opening of sealed envelopes containing the treatment category, or computer randomisation methods.

The process of randomisation thus involves placing individuals from amongst the eligible population into either 'intervention' or 'control' groups in such a way that they have an equal chance of ending up in either of the groups. Its purpose is to eliminate the effect of confounding factors which can influence the outcome of the study independently of the intervention. Randomisation probably never truly eliminates the effects of confounding but it does minimise its potential effect and is a more effective technique than those used in observational studies (for example, matching in case-control studies) to eliminate confounding.

Specification of the Intervention

A very precise specification of the nature of the treatment or other measures to be used, is also necessary, together with rules for the method of administration or the conditions under which the treatment should be administered. For example, in the evaluation of a preventive measure, criteria might be laid down as to who is to administer, say, a health education message, whereas with the treatment the route of administration of a drug must be specified.

Placebo Effect

A further element of the investigation is to specify the conditions of the 'non intervention' group and it is here, in trials of clinical therapies, that the 'placebo' is brought into play. The so-called 'placebo effect' is the change in a patient's outcome or health status which can be achieved simply by being given an inactive therapy or through being a participant in a study. The psychological processes involved in this phenomenon are not fully understood.

It is easier to correct for this influence in trials of therapies. In such cases, both groups of patients (the 'intervention' and the 'non-intervention' groups) are given tablets, one set containing the active treatment under investigation, the other pharmaceutically prepared to look, smell, and feel like the active treatment but which is, in fact, inert as far as the disease under investigation is concerned.

Patients are therefore 'blind' as to whether they are receiving the real treatment or the placebo. It is also better to keep the investigators in ignorance so that they do not use their knowledge of the patients' treatment category consciously or unconsciously to influence their assessment of the patient's status following intervention (a 'double-blind' study).

It is much more difficult to use a placebo process in randomised controlled trials other than those evaluating drug therapies. For example, in a trial to test the effectiveness of an intra-abdominal surgical technique, it would almost certainly be unethical (as well as inappropriate) to anaesthetise patients in the control group, then open and close their abdomens as a placebo operation.

Assessment of the Outcome or End-point

Very clear study rules need to be laid down to ensure that outcomes for the patients in the two groups of the trial are clearly defined, assessed, and recorded in a standard way. The outcomes (or end-points) which are the subject of the investigation, will vary according to its aims but might include: (in a trial of a new therapy) improvement or worsening in a patient's condition, death, length of survival; or (in a preventive trial), the onset of disease, death, change in physical or physiological characteristics such as weight, serum cholesterol, fitness.

There is a danger of bias when either the patient, the clinician or investigator (who is responsible for assessing outcome) is aware of which groups have received the intervention as opposed to the non-intervention (control) measures. This source of bias can be minimised (as described above) by ensuring that neither the patient nor the investigator is aware of which experimental group is the intervention group. This is called a 'double-blind' study. The code identifying the two groups is only broken at the end of the study.

It is important to ensure that if patients drop out of the study, or fail to complete their treatment (non-compliance) that they are included in the analysis according to the randomised group to which they were originally allocated (on the basis that there was an intention to treat). To do otherwise would be to introduce potential bias.

Ethical Issues

In the conduct of a study involving human populations a strict ethical code must be obeyed. A number of organisations have laid down codes of practice or guidelines for the conduct of research investigations involving people. Of particular importance are those which have been produced by the World Medical Association, the World Health Organisation and the Royal College of Physicians of London. Health Authorities are required to have Research Ethics Committees (LRECs) to which application must be made for approval of research to be undertaken on NHS patients, their records or using NHS premises in their area. Since 1997, where the research will take place within the bounds of five or more LRECs' geographical boundaries, approval from a Multi-Centre Research Ethics Committee must also be obtained. The Committees will wish to satisfy themselves that due regard has been taken for the safety of the participants in a study, that proper arrangements for consent are in place, appropriate information on the trial and its aims is available for participants and that the trial is scientifically valid – capable of coming to conclusions and likely to yield important information that could not be obtained by other means.

Investigating Health Service Problems in Practice

The previous section dealt with the use of two major epidemiological methodologies (cohort and case-control studies) to investigate disease causation. It began by pointing out that these methodologies were infrequently used in day-to-day practice (aside from the use of the case-control method in the investigation of communicable disease outbreaks). It was also emphasised that it is essential to have a good understanding of the methodologies. Their strengths and weaknesses must be fully appreciated, not just for the occasions when they are used, but to enable the published work of others to be properly evaluated. This is especially important if decisions about health care priorities and programmes are to be based upon such studies.

This section of the chapter contains a description of the kinds of investigation which might be carried out by those playing a part on a day-to-day basis in identifying the health problems within a population and ensuring an appropriate range and quality of health services is available to address them.

There is a great deal of misunderstanding about this area of public health practice and this seems to be for a number of reasons. Firstly, this field of investigation is seldom debated and certainly is not the subject of texts, such as those written about case-control or cohort studies, which deal with the possible approaches and methodologies systematically and in-depth. Secondly, and perhaps as a consequence of the first reason, health service problem investigation is often denigrated as flawed or unscientific, particularly by those investigators used to undertaking studies using the more formal epidemiological methods. Thirdly, the investigation of a health service problem usually leads to a report which is presented to a health service policy-making board or as an aid to decision-making at an operational level within the management structure of the service. All energies are usually deployed to this end and it is less common for the investigator to set aside the time to write up his study separately for submission to a journal.

The approach of investigators based in academic institutions is very different. A report will always be produced (or internally published) for the funding body and wider circulation but major emphasis will also be placed on identifying those aspects of the study which can be written up for submission to journals. This will often result in one or more publications in major peer review journals, all of which adds to the standing of this type of investigative work.

This debate is epitomised by the phrase which is sometimes used to describe the type of investigative work undertaken within the health service: 'quick and dirty'. As with any catchphrase, it is easy to see why it has gained widespread usage but the juxtaposition of these two terms 'quick' and 'dirty' when applied to any form of bona fide public health investigation is both inappropriate and unfortunate. The term 'dirty' is intended to convey the impression of crudeness or unreliability in either the study methods used or the findings. It is only necessary to think of a cohort study of disease causation, taking many years to carry out, with consequent consumption of resources, having had a seriously flawed design at the outset, to realise that 'dirtiness' can equally apply to large-scale investigation using methods traditionally associated with scientific purity.

The importance of this issue cannot be over-emphasised because it draws attention to fundamental principles which should apply equally to the investigation of a circumscribed and urgent problem in a health service as to the study of possible risk factors for the genesis of a disease which poses a large-scale public health problem.

Whether using routinely available data on *ad hoc* and limited data-gathering exercise, conducting a population survey, a case-control or a cohort study, the investigator

Peer review?

should have a clear view of the aims of the investigation and the questions which need to be answered by it. He or she should choose the appropriate method to carry out the investigation (bearing in mind the prevailing constraints including time and money). He or she should be aware of the strengths and weaknesses of the approach chosen and, most importantly, should present the findings of the study in a way which makes clear the extent of the conclusions which can be drawn from them.

Thus, some studies are more limited in scope than others because of time constraints, the availability of resources or the quality of available data. Even in such circumstances, however, good investigations can still be carried out, provided that it is made clear precisely what conclusions can be drawn from them (bearing in mind the limitations of the data). This does not make them 'dirty'.

It is also worth bearing in mind that decisions about health service priorities and the allocation of resources are being made on a daily basis and, sadly, too often on purely subjective grounds. Even a limited investigation, if carefully carried out, potentially can improve the quality of decision-making. Some practical pointers to the use of public health investigations are shown in Table 2.11.

Table 2.11   Pointers to use of investigations in public health practice

- Be clear about objectives
- Do not be drawn into impossible tasks
- Follow the general principles of purer methods (e.g., sampling, defining criteria for inclusion of cases, maintaining high response rates, avoiding bias)
- Do not try to do too much
- Be aware of the limitations of your data
- Pay particular attention to the presentation of results
- Decide how to disseminate conclusions and recommendations
- Make every effort to make full use of the data

Source: Donaldson LJ, Kirkup W. Hospital Medicine, 1998; 59:1–54.

Examples of Investigations of Health Service Problems

This section of the chapter describes a small number of examples of investigations of health service problems which have been carried out as part of the practice of departments of public health. Each was the subject of a comprehensive report with presentation of data and while they are too extensive to be described in full here, the main features of each, together with some illustrative data, are included.

It is important to bear in mind that any investigation, no matter how small-scale, must be carefully planned; the first stage of which is to clearly set out the aims or questions the investigators are seeking to address or answer. It is always surprising in reading reports of investigations in public health, even those submitted to editors of journals for publication, to see that the aims of the investigation were not identified at the outset.

The main purpose of the examples, however, is not to describe investigations from start to finish in exhaustive detail (space alone would prohibit this). Rather, it is to give the reader an understanding of some of the practicalities of designing and executing such investigations and, particularly, to show how they can be used to provide insights into, and solutions to, health problems and the working of health services.

A Survey of the Health and Social Status of Elderly People in an Ethnic Minority Group

This investigation set out to describe certain aspects of the health and social status of people aged 65 years and over belonging to the Asian population of a City in the East Midlands area of England. An Asian person was defined as a person not of United Kingdom descent originating from India or Pakistan or, of Indian or Pakistani descent, originating from East Africa.

Context and Problem Definition

The population in which the study was carried out was Leicester, a city in the East Midlands area of England, which at the time had a population in which approximately 1 in 4 people belonged to ethnic minority groups. The largest group of old people in the population of Leicester who belonged to an ethnic minority group were those born in India (mainly in Gujerat or the Punjab) although the majority had come to Britain via East Africa.

At the time of the investigation, a great deal of service provision work was being undertaken within the Asian community of Leicester by health, social services and voluntary organisations but there was little objective information on the pattern of health and social need.

Carrying out the Investigation

The first step in this study of elderly Asians was to gain the cooperation of the local community to the investigation.

The Asian community has strong networks and relatively well-defined leadership so that it was possible to gain agreement and support for a large exercise, of the sort which was being contemplated, by discussing it with a small number of people who then took on the responsibility to inform the local community so that they would be prepared for the approach by the investigators.

It is important at this stage in planning an investigation to strike a balance between keeping the population to be surveyed properly informed and conveying only so much information about the detail of the survey that their responses to particular questions will not become prejudiced by prior thinking about what responses are needed. Thus, in the Leicester survey, the community leaders offered to publicise the forthcoming field work by a series of radio programmes. This offer was declined in favour of a more low-key dissemination of information to the community.

The next stage in the planning of the survey was to select a suitable sampling frame. A number of alternatives were considered. It was felt that the electoral roll could not provide satisfactory coverage of the elderly Asian population. The possibility of identifying elderly Asians by door knocking in known Asian areas was seriously considered but informal discussions within the Asian community indicated that this approach might run into serious difficulty. Asian people are often initially wary of enquiries which seem to be of an official nature and it was feared that the response of relatives, on the doorstep, might be to seek to protect the elderly by denying the interviewer access. A further factor was that there had been recent reports in the local newspaper of people posing as survey workers in order to try to rob Asian people. On balance, it was felt that the greatest degree of cooperation could be achieved if the individuals to be approached were identified in advance so that they could receive a personal letter which explained the aims of the survey before an interviewer called to see them.

The sampling frame eventually chosen was the central register of the Family Practitioner Committee (now a function of health authorities) and agreement was reached on this by seeking the permission of the Committee and its advisors.

The next major stumbling block was that the sampling frame did not categorise patients records by ethnic status (nor is this even now a routine variable recorded in health information systems). However, experience had been gained in using the Asian naming system to identify and classify Asian people into broad cultural and religious groupings. In this way, all the names of Asian appearance occurring amongst people of age 65 years and over (the elderly for the purposes of this investigation) were extracted from the sampling frame by trained staff and used as the basis for drawing the sample.

It is well documented that general practitioner registers are inflated above their true value by people whose names appear on them but who are no longer strictly members of them, having died or moved away. The Asian population was also a relatively highly mobile group which added to sampling frame inflation and made it particularly important to eliminate errors (which was done by checking against individual general practitioners' records when individuals could not be traced).

Those identified as members of the sample were written to in the Asian languages in order to seek their cooperation, and to indicate that an interviewer would be calling. Data were collected using a questionnaire which was administered by Asian-language-speaking field workers in the homes of the elderly people.

The areas of enquiry included demographic details (sex, date of birth, country of origin, religion, current and past employment status); family life and social contact; aspects of lifestyle; level of physical capacity; language and communication; knowledge and use of health and social services.

Findings and Implications

Three illustrative examples from amongst the range of information yielded by this investigation are shown in Tables 2.12 to 2.14.

Table 2.12 shows that while 5% of elderly Asians lived alone and 13% with someone of their own generation, the most frequent household configuration for these old people was multigenerational. Overall, as Table 2.12 shows, 82% lived in a household with two or more generations and the most common type of household was that in which there were three generations (usually the elderly person, their children and their grandchildren). There was little variation in household composition between religious groups.

Table 2.12 Composition of households in which elderly Asians lived, by religion (percentages)

Household composition	Hindu	Sikh	Muslim	All religions
Lived alone	5	4	4	5
One generation	13	19	9	13
Two generations	23	17	31	24
Three generations	56	56	49	55
Four generations	3	4	7	3
With non-relatives	>1	>1	>1	>1
All households N (100%) =	100 (510)	100 (73)	100 (138)	100 (721)

Source: Donaldson LJ. Health and social status of elderly Asians: a community survey. BMJ, 1986; 293:1079–82.

Further analysis (not shown in Table 2.12) revealed that of those old people who lived in multigenerational households, about one-fifth, whether they were married or widowed, shared a bedroom with someone else, most commonly grandchildren.

This pattern of household structure of the elderly Asians was in marked contrast to that of the indigenous elderly where, for example, 46% of old people lived alone.

These data had major policy implications. Participation and acceptance within the family remained a key feature of old age in the Asian Community of Leicester (this was confirmed by other findings of the investigation, not just those relating to household structure). While elderly Asians were at an advantage in having the immediate help and support of other household members, the implication for services was that the situation would be very sensitive to changes in kinship patterns. Furthermore, within existing households, the opportunities for privacy were diminished and there was no way of knowing how harmonious life was within these large multigenerational households. Organisations in Leicester providing sheltered accommodation at the time were seeing instances of family conflict leading to rejection of elderly members, and it was possible that this would become a larger problem.

Another very important aspect of the investigation related to the language skills of the old people. It was common for respondents to report that they could speak more than one language. Overall, half of the sample could speak a second language and almost a third could speak a third language. Almost all Hindus spoke Gujerati and a substantial minority Hindi, Swahili or English. Sikhs nearly all spoke Punjabi with English and Hindi being the languages next most commonly spoken. Muslims were the most diverse linguistically: after Gujerati, they were likely to speak Urdu, Kutchi and English.

Table 2.13 The percentage of elderly Asian men and women who said that they could speak, read or write English

English ability	Males (n = 389)	Females (n = 337)	Both sexes (n = 726)
Spoke English	37	2	21
Read English	24	< 1	13
Wrote English	21	< 1	11

Source: Donaldson LJ. Health and social status of elderly Asians: a community survey. BMJ, 1986; 293:1079–82.

It was in relation to English-speaking ability that particularly important findings were made. As Table 2.13 shows, a fifth of the sample could speak English but the proportion speaking it was very low amongst elderly women (only 2%). Moreover, it was also found (not shown in Table 2.13) that 63% of women could not read in any language.

Even for the old people who said that they could speak English, in three of six common social situations, more than half considered that they would have had difficulty making themselves understood without an interpreter (Table 2.14).

The investigation's findings in relation to language indicated the extent to which the old people were dependent on others for contact outside their community – particularly in health settings.

The finding that nearly two-thirds of Asian women were illiterate, in all languages, was of immediate importance in that it implied that simply translating leaflets on health education or welfare benefits would not be adequate.

Table 2.14 Elderly Asian's assessment of their own ability to use English in a range of everyday situations expressed as a percentage

| Situation | Ability to make themselves understood | | | |
	Easily	With difficulty	Only with interpreter	Total (n = 145)
Asking for cost of fare on a bus	68	22	10	100
Asking for goods in an English shop	64	27	9	100
Returning faulty goods to an English shop	47	31	22	100
Telephoning to rearrange an outpatient appointment	43	23	34	100
Giving directions to an English person	52	31	17	100
Explaining a problem to a doctor	41	21	38	100

Source: Donaldson LJ. Health and social status of elderly Asians: a community survey. BMJ, 1986; 293:1079–82.

A useful alternative to the conventional approach to posters and leaflets was considered to be the Asian language radio programmes (which were listened to a by a high proportion of the old people interviewed) and home videos (ownership of rental video recorders was also relatively high in the Asian community of Leicester).

The language findings of the investigation also emphasised the need for interpreters as an integral part of health and social service provision.

Comment and Overview

The investigation yielded valuable information for policy makers and planners in the health, social services and voluntary sectors. As a type of investigation in public health, the study was of the cross-sectional type and the techniques adopted were generally those described in the section of this chapter dealing with such studies. However, as with any other such investigation carried out in practice, its design and conduct had a number of special features which were variations on the textbook account of the study methodology concerned. This was particularly so because there had been relatively few surveys which had set out to gather data directly from people belonging to this ethnic minority group. It was important to seek the cooperation of community leaders to ensure success in the field-work and to ensure that there were people skilled in interviewing in the Asian languages if valid information was to be obtained.

An Investigation into the Population's Access to Specialist Services Provided in a Limited Number of Centres

The Northern Region was one of 14 health regions into which the NHS in England was divided for administration and planning purposes at the time. It had a population of approximately three million and stretches from the border with Scotland in the north down to Yorkshire in the south, over to Cumbria in the west and Cleveland in the east. The region was made up of health districts with resident populations of varying sizes.

Many services were present in every district general hospital but some, because of their high cost or highly-specialised nature, were provided in one, or a small number of hospital centres within the region. At the time that the investigation (described in this section) was carried out, heart surgery was provided in only one centre in the Northern region. Patients who were thought to require coronary artery surgery (and other open-heart procedures) were referred to the specialist centre by general practitioners or consultants in other parts of the region. Ophthalmology and some other specialist surgical services were provided at a number of hospitals (but not all) so that a patient requiring cataract surgery, for example, would be treated by one of these services.

The investigation aimed to describe the extent to which patients in different parts of the region, particularly those outside the district in which the regional or sub-regional centres were located, received treatment.

Context and Problem Definition

The Regional Health Authority – the statutory body accountable at the time for services in the region (Regional Health Authorities were abolished in 1996) – had been concerned to examine the extent to which the population in different places received access to services which, though located in only some centres, were funded on the basis that they would be available to the whole population.

Carrying out the Investigation

Data were assembled from routinely available hospital inpatient data. Patients treated by services provided on a regional (for example, cardiothoracic surgery) and a sub-regional (for example, ophthalmology) basis were classified according to health district of residence and to the smaller local government districts of residence.

The extent to which residents of these different populations were treated as inpatients or day cases by each of these regional or sub-regional services was then calculated.

A small number of local government districts were omitted from the analysis because they were served by hospitals in a neighbouring health region and therefore all possible hospital admissions from within the population could not be captured in the analysis.

Data were analysed in two main ways. Firstly, simple hospitalisation rates were produced for different operations in relation to the populations living in health or local government districts. This enabled the number of operations per thousand (or ten thousand) population to be examined and compared.

Secondly, standardised hospitalisation ratios (SHRs) were produced. The concept is similar to the standardised mortality ratio (SMR) which is described in Chapter 1. It allows for differences in the age and sex composition of the resident populations and hence enables a more valid comparison to be made. For example, a district with a young age composition could be expected to record low rates for cataract operations (cataracts being more common in the elderly). SHRs enable a comparison of this district's operation rates with other districts' rates to be made allowing for the different age compositions. In the investigation described here, the regional SHR for each specialty was, by definition, 100 and SHRs for individual resident populations were compared to this regional average value. A figure above 100 denoted more hospital discharges, and a figure below 100 denoted fewer hospital discharges, amongst residents of a particular area, than might have been expected given the experience of the region as a whole.

Findings and Implications

Two examples are given here to illustrate the findings and show the kinds of issues which were raised by the investigation. The first relates to cataract operations, the second to coronary artery by-pass operations.

Table 2.15 shows the SHRs for cataract surgery in relation to local government district of residence, together with information on the location of the sub-regional ophthalmology services which were undertaking the surgery. It can be seen that there was a two-fold variation in the likelihood of a person being admitted for cataract surgery according to where they lived. To some extent, the likelihood of being admitted was higher in resident populations with greater geographical proximity to the service but some local government districts with a service within their boundaries appear to have substantially lower admission rates than others. These lower rates often apply to adjacent local government districts predominantly served by this same service.

Table 2.15   Extent to which residents of local government districts in the northern region received cataract surgery operations

Place of residence	Standardised hospitalisation ratio (inpatients and day cases)
Castle Morpeth	128
Durham	127
Darlington	123*
Newcastle	122*
Gateshead	112
Derwentside	109
Stockton	107
North Tyneside	106
Blyth	103
Wansbeck	103
Sunderland	98*
Carlisle	96*
Copeland	95
Middlesbrough	93*
Tynedale	92
Sedgefield	88
Wear Valley	88
Berwick	85
Allerdale	81*
Alnwick	81
Easington	78
South Tyneside	76
Langbaurgh	75
Eden	71
Hartlepool	61
Chester-le-Street	60
Region	100

*Local government districts which had, within their boundaries, an ophthalmology unit.

Table 2.16 displays the data for coronary artery by-pass operations and clearly shows that the highest admission rate was for residents of the host district, with the lowest for a district (South Tyneside) some eight miles away. Other districts further from the host district (for example, North Tees, 36 miles away) had higher resident access rates.

Table 2.16 Extent to which residents of district health authorities in the northern region received coronary artery by-pass surgery (1984–85)

Place of residence	Inpatient discharges per 1000 resident population
Newcastle	0.27*
North Tyneside	0.22
Northumberland	0.20
North Tees	0.17
East Cumbria	0.16
Durham	0.16
Darlington	0.15
Gateshead	0.12
North West Durham	0.12
South Tees	0.12
Hartlepool	0.11
West Cumbria	0.11
South West Durham	0.11
South Cumbria	0.10
Sunderland	0.09
South Tyneside	0.07
Region	0.15

*District health authority with cardiothoracic unit.

The interpretation of data on the use of health services is made difficult by the absence of any general understanding of what constitutes need. Thus, when comparing admission rates to a particular hospital service from two or more populations, there is no way of knowing, in any of the communities concerned, the size of the pool of patients requiring treatment. Therefore, it is not possible to say what level of hospital admission would have been appropriate in the investigation described.

Demographic differences can account for some variation in admission rates when diseases are more common at certain ages. For example, coronary heart disease is more common in older males; if one district contains more older males than another with the same total population, then it is to be expected that they will record higher admission due to this disease. This was tested as a possible source of variation in Table 2.16 where unstandardised rates are used but it was found to be a very minor source of variation. It cannot be responsible for any of the variation documented in Table 2.15 however, because there the data are presented as SHRs which allow for any demographic differences between the districts.

It may be wondered why SHRs were not also the method of presentation of the data for the coronary artery by-pass surgery analysis. They could equally well have been. The reason SHRs were not used was due to the potential impact of the presentation of the findings of the investigation on a health authority which included lay members.

SHRs (or SMRs for that matter) are usually quite well understood by people without a background in public health if the concept is simply explained as part of the presentation of data. Their power of impact is as a comparative measure, showing the extent of variation between populations. Used alone, however, they can sometimes have reduced impact with the lay person because of the abstract nature of a relative measure.

Therefore it is sometimes important to give the target audience a feel for absolute values. There is additional impact in being able to picture the number of people being admitted for every thousand or ten thousand in the population.

While such data must be interpreted cautiously, it is unlikely that differences of the size in the examples described could have resulted from limitations in the data (considerable validity checks were in any case carried out).

As was indicated earlier, broad knowledge of the population and its pattern of disease and mortality does not suggest that the variation could have arisen from differences in morbidity and demography. The cataract data were in any case standardised to eliminate the effect of differences in age-structure, the strongest correlate with incidence. Mortality rates from coronary heart disease in the Northern Region were amongst the worst in the country and districts such as South Tyneside (with low access to coronary artery by-pass surgery) were amongst the worst within the region. There was no evidence either that Newcastle's population was being over-treated (another theoretical explanation for the differences).

Thus, the investigators felt it a fair assumption that the variations represented the differing extent to which need was being recognized and acted upon by patients and doctors.

The underlying factors which determine the extent to which a given level of need is translated into inpatient care include: patient consultation rates (with general practitioners); general practitioner referral rates (to hospital consultants); availability and accessibility of hospital facilities; thresholds for admission and treatment (by individual consultants); secondary referral rates (from one hospital consultant to another).

Tentative ideas about the main sources of the variation in the investigation described here, were that the differential coronary artery by-pass admission rates may have partly been explained by the availability, in district services, of physicians with expertise in cardiology who were able to recognize and refer appropriate cases. This certainly seemed to fit with existing knowledge of the pattern of district service. For example, in Newcastle, a specialist cardiology team was in place and many general practitioners would refer cases to them as a first choice. The North Tees physicians also had expertise in the specialty which may explain higher access rates in a more geographically-remote population.

The data for rates of cataract extraction seemed to be more closely related to geographical proximity to a service-providing centre. Beyond this, descriptive data like these can only be used for discussion and exploration of issues and not to draw conclusions.

Comment and Overview

This investigation used routinely available data and hence was relatively rapidly carried out and limited in its scope. Nevertheless, it stimulated a debate at the time, at the highest policy-making level within the region and one which ranged across issues such as: the siting of specialist services; the level and distribution of consultant posts in particular specialties; resource-allocation policy; general practitioner referral patterns and the prioritisation of patients on waiting lists. It led to the establishment of a second cardiothoracic centre in Middlesbrough – in the southern part of the region. In the late 1990s this second centre was well established and dealing with a large work-load. The strong clinical impression of the cardiologists and cardiothoracic surgeons appointed to the new service was that it was dealing (in its first few years of operation) with very severe coronary heart disease in much younger people than they had seen in other centres where they had worked.

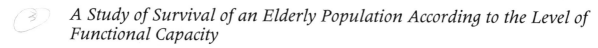

A Study of Survival of an Elderly Population According to the Level of Functional Capacity

Context and Problem Definition

The entire population of people aged 65 years and over who were in any type of insti-tutional care (hospitals or residential homes) in Leicestershire was enumerated on a single day. Amongst other information gathered on each elderly person at the time was an assessment of their functional capacity in relation to basic activities of daily living. This institutional elderly population was then followed-up over a three-year period to determine survival. The aim of the study described was to examine survival in relation to different levels of incapacity and independence in each type of care.

Carrying out the Investigation

A total of 4490 people aged 65 years and over had been enumerated in a one-day cen-sus in the full range of institutional care provided by the public (NHS and Social Services) and the independent sector (private and voluntary) in the health district. Hospital beds, nursing home and residential care places were all covered. A range of data were gathered on each patient or resident but included in the original survey was an assessment of their functional capacity in relation to mobility, urinary inconti-nence, faecal incontinence, washing/dressing and feeding. The scale used had been validated as a survey instrument. Copies of death returns were then gathered over a three-year period and details of deaths occurring amongst any of the original popula-tion were recorded. A life-table analysis of mortality was then carried out to produce survival times from the time of the initial assessment. The basis of this standard life-table approach was that exposure to the risk of death was grouped into a number of person-years of observation. For each patient or resident, it was known whether or not they died and the time from initial enumeration. The exposure time then ran from the starting date to the date of death or if they did not die to the end of the correspond-ing follow-up period. Confidence intervals were calculated for the proportion surviving. A regression analysis of the life-table allowed differences in survival in dif-ferent groups to be compared, taking account of other factors that appreciably affected survival. The statistical methods are referred to here in general terms in order to allow an understanding of the principles of the analysis (for a more detailed account the reader is referred to the original paper).

Findings and Implications

The rate of survival at all time-periods after assessment up to the end of the three-year observation period fell with increasing incapacity. For example, two years after hav-ing been assessed as 'bedfast', 36% of old people were still alive compared to 73% in the group who had been 'fully ambulant'. A similar pattern was observed for people falling into different categories with respect to urinary incontinence. Data for this are shown in Table 2.17 to illustrate the pattern which was similar for each 'activity of daily living'. In all these activities, the differences in the rate of survival between incapacity groups remained highly statistically significant even after adjustment for differences in age, sex and duration of stay using regression analysis.

Table 2.17 Percentage survival (with 95% confidence limits in brackets) from time of assessment by degree of urinary incontinence

Time from assessment	Not incontinent	Needed raising or sending	Incontinent once	Often incontinent	All degrees
6 months	90.7 (89.4–91.9)	85.1 (80.8–88.6)	82.3 (78.0–86.0)	73.5 (70.4–76.4)	85.4 (84.2–86.5)
1 year	84.1 (82.5–85.7)	74.1 (69.1–78.7)	70.1 (65.2–75.0)	61.1 (57.7–64.4)	76.5 (75.1–77.9)
2 years	69.6 (67.6–71.6)	56.5 (51.0–61.9)	48.2 (43.0–53.3)	41.1 (37.8–44.5)	59.6 (58.0–61.2)
3 years	57.3 (55.1–59.5)	43.3 (38.0–48.8)	35.9 (31.1–41.0)	28.9 (25.9–32.1)	47.3 (45.6–48.9)

Source: Donaldson LJ, Jagger C. J Epidemiol Community Health, 1983; 37:176–9.

The analysis for the different types of care (Table 2.18) showed a pattern which would have been expected given the much higher levels of dependency that occur in some settings compared to others. What was more surprising was that when differences in levels of functional capacity (and also age and sex) between the different types of care were allowed for in the statistical analysis, most of the differential survival disappeared. This was true of the three types of NHS care and the homes for the elderly.

Table 2.18 Estimated percentage survival (95% confidence limits not shown here) to various times after admission to different types of care

Time from admission	NHS geriatric beds	NHS psychiatric beds	NHS acute beds	Homes for the elderly	Private nursing homes	All types of care
6 months	61.9	77.2	75.0	81.0	80.4	72.3
1 year	49.5	64.4	67.4	68.8	64.4	60.9
2 years	37.2	49.2	59.9	53.9	53.4	48.4
3 years	27.4	38.7	53.2	43.3	40.0	38.5
5 years	10.6	21.8	49.8	27.0	23.5	22.5

Source: Donaldson LJ, Jagger C. J Epidemiol Community Health, 1983; 37:176–9.

The findings demonstrated the power of this relatively simple measure of incapacity in an elderly population to predict survival. Moreover, it seemed to be an important core characteristic of health status almost irrespective of where an elderly person was being cared for.

Comment and Overview

This investigation established that gathering data on functional capacity of an elderly population can provide an important basis for summarising its health status. The approach does not require complex procedures and has a range of other potential uses including planning services and rehabilitation policies, evaluation of the components of care and assessing the impact of individual institutional regimes. The whole question of the importance of such measures to the concept of healthy life-expectancy is discussed further in Chapter 8.

An Investigation into the Reasons for the Delayed Discharge of Patients Hospitalised with Fractured Neck of Femur

Fractured neck of femur is a common injury in the elderly and one which is responsible for a high proportion of admissions to acute orthopaedic hospital inpatient services. In the past, many patients were treated conservatively through traction, with the consequent high mortality and morbidity associated with prolonged bed rest in elderly people. Today, the approach to clinical management is based upon early surgical intervention to allow rapid mobilisation and to give the greatest chance of returning the elderly patient to her pre-fracture level of independence. Nevertheless, the high volume of cases, the underlying frailty and associated medical problems which many elderly people have, together with the fact that the fracture often brings to light unsatisfactory home and social circumstances, means that hospital stays can easily become prolonged.

The investigation described here set out to examine the factors which were leading to extended hospital stay in patients admitted to the major hospital dealing with trauma cases in a large health district in the East Midlands part of England.

Context and Problem Definition

An acute orthopaedic ward may not be the best environment in which to meet the continuing care needs of the elderly person who is not able to return home, nor may it be the most appropriate use of scarce acute-sector resources. The issue is encapsulated in the emotive and even hostile term, 'blocked bed', which is sometimes used to describe the occupation of a bed in an acute hospital specialty by an elderly person who is judged not to be acutely ill or deemed to have stayed there longer than what is perceived as being within the normal confines of an acute illness.

The investigators decided that, to tackle this problem, it would be valuable to understand what specific stages of care account for the hospital stay (for example, pre-operative stabilisation, postoperative complications, placement problems). Unfortunately, routinely available hospital data provided details of the total length of stay but not its components.

The Leicestershire Health District is a large urban and rural population, with approximately 850,000 residents at the time of the investigation, of whom about 15% were aged 65 years and over. The organisation of trauma and orthopaedic services was such that a high proportion of injuries (including fractured neck of femur) occurring in the population of Leicestershire were treated at one large centrally placed hospital.

Carrying out the Investigation

The investigators began by formulating an operational definition of fractured neck of femur so that decisions would be taken about which cases to include and which to exclude. The study entry criterion decided upon was: 'the presence of an intracapsular or extracapsular fracture of the femur down to 1 cm below the lesser trochanter'. There were no exclusions.

The study population was a consecutive series of admissions to hospital over a 20-week period from October to February. The choice of this time period was dictated by the resources available to undertake the study and the need to produce a result reasonably quickly.

A system was established whereby a member of the investigative team visited the wards of the hospital daily to identify the patients who had been admitted and who met the entry criterion. While time-consuming, such an arrangement was preferable to ensure completeness of capture of the study population rather than relying on busy nursing or medical staff to notify cases.

Each of the patients had a stage of care identified for each day of the hospital stay using a methodology adapted from one developed by North American investigators. This was based on the application to each day of care of the question: 'Why is this patient in hospital now?'.

After discussion with the clinical team, each day of each patient's stay was assigned to one of the following categories:

(a)   Preoperative, no perceived problems, awaiting surgery.
(b)   Preoperative, awaiting medical assessment or therapy before surgery.
(c)   Postoperative, condition improving, no complications.
(d)   Postoperative, complications of surgery have developed and are prolonging the stay.
(e)   Postoperative, medical difficulties have developed which would have required hospital admission regardless of surgery.
(f)   Medically and surgically fit for discharge, but hospital stay continues for other reasons (e.g., awaiting geriatric assessment or bed, arrangements being made for domiciliary services, arrival of caring relatives awaited).
(g)   Receiving conservative therapy, no operation.

As Table 2.19 shows, almost all the bed-days were spent by the patients awaiting a theatre session (10%); recovering from surgery without complications (51%) or waiting to leave the orthopaedic ward despite being medically and surgically fit to do so (28%). Other analyses (not presented here) were performed on the number of days spent in each stage.

Table 2.19   Number of patient-days spent in each stage of acute hospital care by people with fractured neck of femur

Stage of care*	Number of patient-days	Percentage of total stay
A	492	10
B	141	3
C	2690	51
D	59	1
E	56	1
F	1437	28
G	292	6
Total	5167	–

*See text for definition of stages. *Source:* Robbins JA, Donaldson LJ. Analysing stages of care in hospital stay for fractured neck of femur. Lancet, 1984; 1:1028–9.

It was calculated that, if all patients who were fit for surgery had been taken to theatre without delay, 492 hospital-days could have been saved. Moreover, if it had been possible to discharge or transfer patients when they no longer needed to remain in hospital for medical and surgical reasons, 1437 hospital-days could have been saved.

It was further estimated that by combining both of these strategies, the average duration of stay could have been reduced by eight days.

Comment and Overview

The methodology adopted contained elements of the cohort study approach, the study population being a consecutive group of patients admitted to hospital and then followed-up during their hospital stay. While the period of the year chosen to recruit the cohort could have been unrepresentative of all patients' experience (for example, if there had been strong seasonal differences), there was no evidence that overall length of stay varied markedly at different times of the year. The use of caring staff to contribute to the classification of the days of care, is open to the criticism that through the knowledge of being studied they could have modified their assessment of each patient. However, one of the senior investigators was in active clinical practice and had made his own baseline assessment of the patients and review of the medical records. Thus, a more independent judgement was also available.

The investigation provided a focus for policy discussion. It pinpointed and addressed the problem of extended hospital stay in this group of elderly patients and provided the focus for in-depth review of the whole issue, including the timing of surgery (with implications for out-of-hours staffing of operating theatres, the availability of on-call radiographers) and arrangements for assessment, rehabilitation and future placement (with implications for greater involvement of geriatricians and social workers earlier in the acute hospital stay).

An Investigation to Describe Rapidly an Emerging Problem for Which Little Information was Available

From time-to-time, a health (or health service) problem will suddenly come to the attention of the public through critical comment in the local or national media in such a way that there may be a high level of disquiet or a loss of confidence in services.

Just such a major crisis was caused when a sudden increase in the number of children suspected of having been sexually abused were taken into local authority care in Cleveland, a county in the north east of England, over a three-month period in the summer of 1987.

As is sometimes the case in such circumstances, little information was available to be able to define the size or nature of the problem so that it could be discussed rationally and objectively.

This example describes an investigation which was carried out very rapidly to provide such information.

Context and Problem Definition

The Cleveland crisis came about because of a number of factors. Firstly, there was a sharp rise in admissions of children with a diagnosis of suspected sexual abuse to one of the main hospitals in the county (Middlesbrough General Hospital). Many of these children were then made the subject of court orders (under the then child protection legislation) which led to them being retained in the hospital as a 'Place of Safety' for further assessment and investigation.

The presence of these additional children who were physically active, boisterous and, in some cases behaviourally disturbed, placed enormous pressure on the physical facilities available and on the nursing staff who were also trying to care for acutely ill children. The Social Services department (as the lead agency in child protection services) did not have the resources, in terms of skilled social work staff, to respond to this rapid increase in cases referred to it.

The presence of large numbers of parents whose children were being kept largely in one place, focused parental anger and led to involvement of Members of Parliament who publicly and effectively articulated the collective sense of indignation and concern. Finally, the open airing of professional differences of opinion on the validity of the diagnoses led further to the impression of confusion. In the first few weeks of the crisis, the services underwent a period of major instability and perceived loss of public confidence.

Much of the prevailing media comment led the public to believe that the number of cases being diagnosed was large and unprecedented (amounting to 1 in 10 of the population). This added to the sense of incredulity and the impression that a wholesale mistake had been made by the professional staff involved.

At this stage, however, no firm data were available on the numbers of children involved. Therefore, numbers could not be related to the population of origin or valid comparisons made with elsewhere in the country or with other countries. In addition, many professionals expressed public disquiet at the frequency of anal abuse diagnosed – particularly in very young children and in girls. Thus, part of the initial controversy resulted from a failure to be able to quantify and describe the problem in population terms. Coupled with this, the perception that parents were being denied their rights; that social workers and paediatricians had acted over-zealously (apparently seeking out abuse where it did not exist); that undue reliance had been placed on an unproven diagnostic technique (the reflex anal dilatation test) added to the sense of public concern and turmoil.

A Judicial Inquiry was established by the Minister for Health, for which evidence was prepared on a wide range of aspects on the background to the problems in Cleveland. As part of this evidence, information was gathered to describe the population of children who were the subject of the diagnosis of suspected sexual abuse.

Carrying out the Investigation

The investigation began by assembling all cases of sexual abuse or suspected sexual abuse in children coming to the attention of paediatric services or of the social services department over the three-month period. These cases were identified by searching hospital records of all paediatric admissions (sexual abuse was not a diagnosis recorded in routinely available hospital inpatient data) and the cases referred to the social services department over the same period.

A precoded structured pro-forma was designed to record data extracted from the children's records. The main areas of data recording were: demographic and administrative; mode of presentation; main clinical findings; subsequent management; details of referral for other medical opinion (where this occurred).

High standards of confidentiality were observed when extracting the data. Medical staff undertook the work personally. Analyses were carried out on an aggregated and anonymised basis only so that no children or families could ever be identified.

Cases were classified into three categories according to the way in which they came to light:

(a)   *Index cases* – the child in a family (or group of children) who, on presentation, first gave rise to the suspicion that sexual abuse may have occurred.
(b)   *Sibling of index case* – brother or sister of index case, who was examined because of the suspicion of child sexual abuse in the index case.
(c)   *Contact of index case* – a child connected with the index case (but not a brother or sister), who was examined because of the suspicion of child sexual abuse in the index case.

Findings and Implications

Figure 2.20 shows the time at which children were diagnosed over the three-month period. The crisis broke publicly following the peak of diagnoses in the week commencing 15 June 1987.

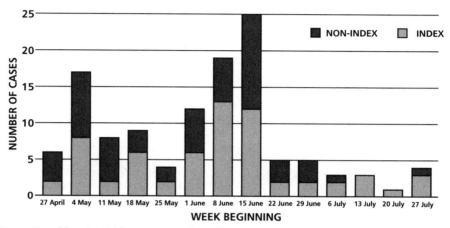

Figure 2.20 Time at which cases of suspected child sexual abuse were first diagnosed in Cleveland.

Source: Donaldson LJ. Evidence given to the Judicial Enquiry into Child Abuse in Cleveland, 1987.

Table 2.20 shows the overall rate for the three-month period was 9.8 per 10,000 population, which is equivalent to approximately 1 case in 1000 children (aged 0–14 years). The rate for girls of all ages was approximately twice that for boys and the highest rate was in girls up to the age of 4 years.

Table 2.20 Age- and sex-specific rates of occurrence for cases of suspected child sexual abuse per 10,000 population during the three-month period from May to July 1987 in Cleveland

Age-group (years)	Male	Female	Both sexes
0–4	5.4	19.2	12.2
5–9	8.9	17.7	13.2
10–14	4.4	4.2	4.3
0–14	6.2	13.7	9.8

Source: Donaldson LJ. Evidence given to the Judicial Enquiry into Child Abuse in Cleveland, 1987.

Table 2.21 shows an analysis of anal or vaginal physical signs recorded by the doctors following their examinations of the children.

The figure and the two tables show only a small selection of the analyses. Nevertheless, they illustrate the role in which simple descriptive data can play in throwing light on a problem. In this investigation, they illustrated that the problem was far less common than some of the exaggerated early impressions had suggested. Furthermore, they emphasised that part of the numerical problem arose from children who had been examined because they were siblings or contacts of children suspected of being sexually abused. On the other hand, the doctors' findings of signs of anal abuse even in very young children emphasised the centrality of these physical signs to the debate and demonstrated the need to address issues of 'normality' and 'abnormality'.

Many of these issues were the subject of extensive scrutiny by the Judicial Inquiry.

Table 2.21   Presence of anal and vaginal signs in all cases of suspected child sexual abuse diagnosed in Cleveland May/June 1987 (percentages)

Physical signs	Male	Female	Both sexes
Anal only	100	28	51
Vaginal only	N/A	9	6
Both	N/A	60	41
Neither	0	2	2
Not stated	–	1	1
Total	100 (*n* = 38)	100 (*n* = 82)	100 (*n* = 120)

N/A = Not applicable. *Source:* Donaldson LJ. Evidence given to the Judicial Enquiry into Child Abuse in Cleveland, 1987.

Comment and Overview

The study could not, and did not purport to, provide a definitive estimate of the size of the problem of sexual abuse in the population concerned. Neither did it set out to examine the validity of the diagnoses made. It also used a retrospective method of enquiry whose primary source of data – medical and social services records – was not created specifically for investigative purposes. Nevertheless, a prospective study would probably have proved impossible in the light of the attention which had been focused on the issue, circumstances would have certainly influenced the way in which information was recorded.

However, given that its limitations were made clear (which they were at the time) the investigation fulfilled a useful purpose in helping to correct a misleading anecdotal impression. This can be an important and useful role for investigations in public health medicine in a situation where absolutely no data are available, and when decisions are being made and conclusions drawn on purely subjective grounds. The investigation also proved invaluable in designing a conceptual framework for categorising the cases (index, non-index) so that the size of the problem which arose from children being diagnosed at presentation could be distinguished from the extent to which children contributed who were only included by virtue of their association with other cases. This approach was subsequently adopted by the Judicial Inquiry in its own case analysis.

The investigation also highlighted the need for further study: in particular for population-based studies of the size and distribution of sexual abuse using agreed criteria for their case definition and to improve the quality of routinely collected statistics held on child protection registers.

An Investigation to Examine the Implications of the Phasing out of Large Mental Hospitals

It has been long-established policy of British Governments in the field of services for people with mental illness to shift the balance of care from hospital to community. An important element of this policy has been to provide care for mentally ill people in need of hospital care in facilities which are integrated within district general hospitals.

The most visible manifestation of these policies has been the closure (or re-designation), in many parts of the country, of the past cornerstone of care for the mentally ill:

the large mental hospitals, many of which are buildings which housed Victorian asylums.

The investigation described here set out to identify some of the practical problems of implementing these policies by assessing the levels of physical, mental and social functioning of mentally ill people in institutional care within a large health district in the East Midlands part of England.

Context and Problem Definition

One of the key determinants of the success of the policies described above, was the ability of local psychiatric services to satisfactorily reduce the number of patients requiring nursing care on a longer-term basis. In practice, this was, and still is, an issue about suitability for discharge of patients who have already spent much of their lives in a psychiatric hospital setting. It is also about preventing the accumulation of a 'new' long-stay group arising from younger patients who are admitted for what are intended as short spells of hospital inpatient care.

Further key factors for policy success were, and also still are: the adequacy of community-based psychiatric services to care for mentally ill people who would previously have ended up in hospitals and to have adequate ways of helping elderly, severely mentally ill people, whose physical and mental frailty make it extremely difficult for them to be returned from hospital to the community.

The investigation set out to evaluate each patient within psychiatric inpatient hospital care facilities in the health district of approximately 850,000 population and to assess their level of physical, social and mental capacity relevant to care requirements.

Carrying out the Investigation

The method chosen for the investigation was a one-day census in which each patient was identified and the assessment carried out. With over one thousand beds or hospital places in psychiatric facilities in the district, the investigation was a very major exercise and required careful planning and detailed preparatory work in advance of the date which was agreed for the census.

Nursing and medical staff completed a 47-item assessment schedule on each patient in their care, the assessment covering eight main areas: demographic and administrative; current diagnoses; ward behaviour and nursing problems; current treatment; employment status and occupational therapy; contact with the outside world; rehabilitation prospects; and, family dependants.

In many of these areas of assessment, standard scales or measures were used which had been validated in earlier studies (these will not be described in detail here).

Findings and Implications

At census point, there were 1087 inpatients of whom 1052 (96%) were resident in two large mental hospitals. Table 2.22 shows that the largest group of psychiatric inpatients was the very elderly. Thirty seven per cent of patients were 75 years or older, a much greater proportion than the very elderly population of the health district as a whole (5% were aged 75 years and over). The table also indicates that while the proportion of very elderly people was lower amongst those who had been resident for the shortest and longest times, even in these length-of-stay groups it was still very substantial.

Table 2.22 Cumulative percentages of psychiatric patients in different length-of-stay groups who were a given age or older

Age (years)	Length of current stay (years)					
	< 1	1–2	2–5	5–10	10 and over	All lengths of stay
85 and over	8	17	19	15	7	11
75 and over	29	56	51	39	31	37
65 and over	45	70	70	57	59	56
55 and over	58	82	80	78	82	72
45 and over	67	88	88	88	92	81
35 and over	78	92	96	94	98	89
25 and over	88	97	100	100	100	95
15 and over	100	100	100	100	100	100
(n =)	(413)	(174)	(92)	(121)	(286)	(1086)

Source: Levene LS, Donaldson LJ, Brandon S. How likely is it that a district health authority can close its large mental hospitals? Br J Psych, 1985; 147:150–5.

Comparing the bottom row of figures in Table 2.22 gives an impression of the relative sizes of the different length-of-stay groups. While the largest proportion (413 out of 1086, or 38%) of patients had been in hospital for less than one year, 26% were inpatients of more than ten years standing, and more than half this latter group were elderly (65 years of age or older). The remaining group of patients, whose stay had extended beyond a year but was less than ten years, made up 36% of all inpatients; a third of these were under 65 years of age.

Table 2.23 Percentage of psychiatric inpatients aged under 65 years with different social withdrawal (SW) scores, by length of stay

SW score*	Length of current stay (years)					
	< 1	1–2	2–5	5–10	10 and over	All lengths of stay
0–4	81	46	61	86	65	72
5–9	12	28	28	10	28	19
10–14	4	20	11	4	6	7
15–16	3	6	0	0	1	2
All scores	100	100	100	100	100	100
(n =)	(220)	(50)	(28)	(51)	(117)	(466)

*Higher scores denote more severely incapacitated patients. *Source:* Levene LS, Donaldson LJ, Brandon S. How likely is it that a district health authority can close its large mental hospitals? Br J Psych, 1985; 147:150–5.

Dementia was the most common diagnosis in patients of all lengths of stay, except the very long-stay group, amongst which schizophrenia predominated.

The social withdrawal rating scale used in the investigation provided an indication of patients' level of social functioning within the hospital, and gave an indication of their chances of discharge. The possible score derived from this rating scale ranged from a minimum of zero to a maximum of 16 points. A score in the 0–4 range had been shown from previous studies to indicate that psychiatric inpatients have the potential for discharge.

Overall, more than half of all patients had scores above the 0–4 range. However, the patterns were so different for elderly, compared to younger patients, that data are presented for the two groups separately (Tables 2.23 and 2.24).

Table 2.24 Percentage of psychiatric inpatients aged 65 years and over with different social withdrawal (SW) scores, by length of stay

SW score*	Length of current stay (years)					All lengths of stay
	< 1	1–2	2–5	5–10	10 and over	
0–4	28	14	19	15	41	26
5–9	37	30	31	29	37	34
10–14	28	44	34	30	20	30
15–16	7	12	16	26	2	10
All scores	100	100	100	100	100	100
(*n* =)	(185)	(122)	(64)	(69)	(168)	(608)

*Higher scores denote more severely incapacitated patients. *Source:* Levene LS, Donaldson LJ, Brandon S. How likely is it that a district health authority can close its large mental hospitals? Br J Psych, 1985; 147:150–5.

Of patients under the age of 65 (Table 2.23), almost three-quarters, regardless of length of stay, had low social withdrawal scores, but less than half of those with a duration of stay of 1–2 years had such scores. Furthermore, another finding of the study (not tabulated here) showed that one-quarter of patients aged under 65 years old with a 1–2 year length-of-stay were not fully continent of urine. These findings strongly suggest that disability in this group was intrinsic to the disorder, rather than a consequence of institutionalisation and that major efforts at treatment, rehabilitation or training would need to be directed at these patients.

The patients under 65 years of age with a length of stay of ten years or more (comprising a quarter of all patients aged under 65 years) were people in the main with low social withdrawal scores, but it is this group who are most used to institutional life and therefore potentially the most difficult to return to the community.

Three-quarters of all residents in the over-65 years age-group (Table 2.24) had substantial social withdrawal and two-thirds were not fully continent of urine.

The group of patients aged over 65 years who had been in hospital for less than one year had lower social withdrawal scores overall and therefore seemed to have greater potential for discharge.

Overall, the investigation clearly showed that the presence of large numbers of elderly patients was the most important feature of the short-, intermediate-, and long-stay groups of patients in psychiatric hospitals. Those elderly patients who had been in hospital for longer than ten years were less incapacitated, both socially and physically, than their shorter-stay counterparts, though they clearly exhibited much higher levels of incapacity than younger patients. Nevertheless, it seemed possible that for a proportion of this group of very long-stay elderly patients some alternative less dependent form of care could have been provided. However, prolonged exposure to an institutional way of life, coupled with advancing years, made it likely that this care would need to continue to be provided in a very protected environment.

It was noted that while the elderly group amongst the long-stay patients would dwindle (because of deaths), this could be a slow process and optimism about reduction of numbers in this category needed to be tempered by the observation that there were substantial numbers of elderly mentally ill people in the intermediate-stay groups. Moreover, the continuing demand for hospital places from patients in the community and the possible development of a younger long-stay group would create further pressure on the same facilities.

Comment and Overview

The findings of an investigation such as the one described here could not provide a blueprint for future services, but they did identify several key issues.

Firstly, the large existing number of elderly disabled patients, together with the expectation of a further increase in their numbers, presented the most serious obstacle to hospital closure. It was noted that alternative facilities would take time to develop and were likely to consume even more resources than currently being expended. If admission and treatment facilities were to be transferred to general hospital units, while the existing mental hospitals remained open, they were in danger of becoming repositories for the disabled elderly, with consequent major problems in maintaining staff morale and high standards.

[handwritten: places where things are stored]

A second issue identified by the investigation was the high disability scores amongst patients with a duration of stay exceeding one but less than two years. This suggested that services were focused upon the acute episode or on the rehabilitation of long-stay patients and that the needs of medium-stay patients were being comparatively overlooked. The transition from acute admission to long-term resident is often insidious, and concentration on treatment issues may delay efforts at social rehabilitation.

The findings on aspects of physical disability (although not discussed in detail here) were also of major policy importance. Incontinence, for example, is a significant impediment when alternative accommodation is being sought. The substantial number of patients, even in the younger age-groups, who were incontinent of urine suggested this as a target symptom demanding special attention. It also pointed the way for studies to examine the role of medication in causing and reducing incontinence, the development of behavioural programmes in incontinence management, and the criteria for more vigorous intervention with this problem.

The investigation as a whole exposed a wide range of policy issues relevant to the organisation of psychiatric services in the health district concerned.

Conclusions

This chapter has described an important facet of public health, namely, the study methodologies and investigative approaches which must be mastered if the full range of health and health service problems are to be addressed. The practice of clinical medicine is often compared to a series of detective stories in which the clues to the diagnosis of a patient's clinical problem are investigated. In population medicine, the mysteries of health and disease in entire populations, some extremely complex, are also very challenging. The benefits of solving these problems in terms of delaying death, preventing disease and improving the quality of health care are enormous. To develop the analogy, while the clinical detective is pursuing the ordinary criminal, the public health investigator is on the trail of the Godfathers of syndicated crime.

Chapter 3

The Promotion of Health

Introduction

As the twenty first century begins, concern amongst the population living in Britain and other industrialised nations, about health and its relationship to individual lifestyle, and to the environment, has never been greater.

This is evident not just in the behaviour of individuals but also through shifts in societal attitudes as reflected, for example, in the response of major manufacturers to consumers' wishes and expectations as well as in the increasing preoccupation of mass media with health issues.

Examples which illustrate this greater health consciousness are numerous. They include the widespread adoption of jogging and other forms of regular aerobic exercise amongst the adult population; the removal of artificial substances from foodstuffs and the resultant marketing success of manufacturers promoting products which are additive-free. There has been a growth in the number of public places where cigarette smoking is not permitted and a major increase in sales of low-alcohol drinks. In the workplace, more and more companies have adopted stress-reduction and other health programmes for their employees.

All these are welcome signs that individuals and societies are now more receptive than at any other time to initiatives which will promote health and prevent disease. Yet, the challenges remain formidable. The leading causes of death and disability in Britain remain as they did for most of the twentieth century: heart disease, stroke, cancer, chronic bronchitis and accidents. Knowledge about the causation of these problems helps to provide the potential for a major impact to be made on them through health promotion programmes. Despite this, consistent success in reducing the burden of illness and premature death from these causes has remained elusive. Inequalities in disease experience between different social strata are greater than ever and addressing their wider determinants – education, employment, reduction of poverty, physical and social environment – remains fundamental to successful action.

Health services should have as their major aims to reduce the amount of illness, disease, disability and premature death in the population and also to increase the numbers of people who spend a high proportion of their lives in a state of health rather than ill-health. Health services do not have direct control over all the factors which can influence these aspects of the health of the population so it is necessary to emphasise multisectoral approaches at local level and pan-governmental coordination at national level.

This chapter describes the main strategies available to promote health and prevent disease, beginning with an historical account of the development of thinking about the causation of disease.

Origins of Disease and its Causation

Early Concepts

The writings and teachings of Hippocrates had an impact far beyond his lifetime, which began on the island of Cos near the Ionian coast of Asia Minor, about 460 BC and ended (legend has it) when bees swarmed on his grave producing a special honey: the cure for stomatitis in infants. Hippocrates is regarded by many as the father of medicine, although medicine was practised before this time. Indeed, writings on such matters date back to the earliest civilizations. In Hippocrates' time, however, there were no boundaries between medicine, art, religion or philosophy.

Hippocrates. Engraving, 1665.

Source: The Wellcome Institute Library, London.

One of the main contributions of the Hippocratic School lay in focusing intellectual attention on medicine in its own right, a science, founded on the observation of facts and the recording of clinical experiences. One of the major teachings was that the body contained four humours: blood, black bile, yellow bile and phlegm. In health, the humours mingled together and were in harmony or balance; in disease there was a derangement of this mixture.

Hippocrates was the first to seek to explain the origins of disease and in so doing he put forward many observations which do not seem out of place even today. He distinguished between diseases which were endemic (always present in a given area) and those which at times become excessively common (epidemic). In suggesting a role for exercise, diet, climate, water and the seasons, he foreshadowed modern views of the importance of the interrelationship between man and his environment in the causation of disease.

Many of his aphorisms resonate with modern causal thinking, for example:

'Those naturally very fat are more liable to sudden death than the thin.'

During the time of the Roman Empire which eclipsed its Greek predecessor, it is the name of another Greek, Galen, who lived in the second century AD, which stands out in the history of medicine. He is said to have cured the emperor Marcus Aurelius of abdominal pain. Whilst his observations on the nature and cause of disease added little to the Hippocratic writings, he did much to advance knowledge in relation to anatomy and physiology. It was also the Roman Empire which introduced sanitation and domestic water supplies, thereby making a significant contribution to public health.

Throughout the Dark and Middle Ages, Europe was ravaged by disease and pestilence: the plague, smallpox, diphtheria, tuberculosis and leprosy. Millions of lives were lost to these scourges of mankind. It is clearly apparent from reading about the measures which were adopted at the time to combat these diseases that they were understood to be contagious. For example, sufferers from leprosy were isolated and required to carry bells to warn of their approach. However, there was no suggestion at this time of a contagious agent; rather, such diseases were held to be caused by changes in the composition of the atmosphere ('bad air') arising from stagnant or decaying organic matter.

Fracastorius (1478–1553), a Veronese poet and physician, is best remembered for writing a long poem about syphilis or the 'French disease'. His views on the general nature and cause of infectious diseases were, however, remarkable and were expressed some 200 years before such ideas were embraced as new and revolutionary. Fracastorius compared contagion in disease to the putrefaction that passes from one fruit to another when it rots. Moreover, when he referred to the essential nature of infection he suggested that minute particles or seeds were conveyed from person to person and propagated themselves. This first mention of the possibility that diseases are caused by specific germs attracted little attention at the time it was published.

The Miasma

Thomas Sydenham (1624–1689) was essentially a practical physician who regarded experimental physiology, so much in vogue at the time, with contempt. His philosophy was to set aside all theory and begin by observing and recording symptoms and signs and their progression (march of events) in the sufferer from the particular ailment. He is greatly revered for his classical descriptions of diseases such as gout, measles, scarlet fever and pneumonia. He is often called the English Hippocrates because his observational method had many similarities with his distant Greek predecessor. Yet, despite his genius in this respect, Sydenham added little to the understanding of why people became ill. But because of his stature, his Miasmic theory of the causation of disease – little more than a re-expression of earlier ideas – was much more influential than it deserved to be. The Miasma was an unidentified vapour believed to result from mysterious changes in the air. It is easy now to scoff at such an apparently preposterous suggestion. Nonetheless, as recently as the second half of the last century, many medical officers of health in their annual reports still related epidemics of infectious diseases to bad odours arising in a locality.

However, the fact that the true nature of infectious disease had not been revealed, did not impede progress.

Bills of Mortality

An important, though less spectacular contribution to this progress, was the start of mortality data gathering. Before causes of disease can be investigated or preventive measures initiated, it is essential to have an indication of the size of the problem. Statistics which would allow the various outbreaks of infectious diseases to be traced, originated from the work of a man who died in impoverished circumstances towards the end of the seventeenth century. This man, John Graunt (1620–1674), analysed the statistics which he gleaned from the Bills of Mortality. These Bills were broadsheets issued weekly and listed, for the London parishes, the numbers and (in a crude fashion) causes of death. They were purchased by well-to-do people who could forewarn themselves of an outbreak of the plague and forsake the city for less hazardous surroundings.

Graunt laid the foundation for the work of his illustrious successor William Farr (1807–1883), whose statistical writings from the office of the Registrar General served as the basis for the great sanitary reforms.

London's dreadful visitation: or a collection of all the Bills of Mortality. London: E. Cotes, 1665.

Source: The Wellcome Institute Library, London.

The Broad Street Pump

There is one episode on the road to the discovery of the true nature of infectious disease which has assumed almost romantic proportions to students and practitioners of public health medicine: that of the investigation of the London cholera outbreak of 1854. John Snow (1813–1858), apprenticed as a doctor in Newcastle upon Tyne could justifiably have settled for one claim to immortality when he later became the first man to introduce anaesthesia in childbirth. He used chloroform in the delivery of two of Queen Victoria's children. Yet, it was his interest in cholera and his painstaking investigation of an outbreak of this disease which earned him a further place in medicine's Hall of Fame.

Cholera is a major infectious disease which spreads rapidly and causes death by the gross fluid depletion that results from the intense diarrhoea produced by the infection. It is rare today in the Western world, but is still a serious cause of mortality in some developing countries. During the early nineteenth century, however, epidemics of cholera swept through London killing thousands of people.

Snow's own words best describe the outbreak in 1854:

> ' The most terrible outbreak of cholera which ever occurred in this kingdom is probably that which took place in Broad Street, Golden Square and adjoining streets, a few weeks ago. Within two hundred and fifty yards of the spot where Cambridge Street joins Broad Street, there were upwards of five hundred fatal attacks of cholera in ten days. The mortality in this limited area probably equals any that was ever caused in this country, even by the plague; and it was much more sudden as the greater number of cases terminated in a few hours. The mortality would undoubtedly have been much greater had it not been for the flight of the population.'

By plotting the geographical location of each case Snow deduced that the deaths had occurred amongst people living in close proximity to the Broad Street pump (many families at this time had no water supply in their own homes but used such a communal supply). There were one or two pieces of evidence, however, which did not at first seem to fit Snow's theory of the complicity of the pump. Firstly, a workhouse with 535 inmates in the street very close to the Broad Street pump experienced only five deaths from cholera amongst its population. Secondly, a brewery in Broad Street itself, had no fatalities amongst its workforce. Snow investigated these differences and found that the workhouse had its own pump on the premises whilst the workers in the brewery never frequented the Broad Street pump. Finally, Snow turned his attention to a woman and her niece living at a considerable distance from Broad Street who, nevertheless, died of cholera during the epidemic. As a result of his interview with neighbours and next of kin, Snow ascertained that the woman had a particular liking for the flavour of the water of the Broad Street pump and sent her son to it every day for a bottle to drink.

On completing his enquiries Snow sought an interview with the Board of Guardians of St James' parish (who were in charge of the pump) and as a result of his representations the pump handle was removed and the epidemic which was already declining came to an end.

The importance of the removal of the pump handle was symbolic of a new understanding of the nature of the disease, for Snow had demonstrated that disease can be conveyed by water and specifically that cholera is a waterborne disease.

In a less dramatic but similarly painstaking series of other investigations, Snow further clarified the mode of transmission of cholera. In London, at that time, a number of private companies supplied water to its residents and Londoners paid for their supply. Snow turned his attention to the water supplies of two of these companies: the Lambeth company and the Southwark and Vauxhall company which both supplied similar areas of London. The pipes of both companies in some cases went down the same street, so that it was possible to identify individual households supplied by one or other company. The death rate from cholera in the areas of London supplied by these two water companies was much higher than it was in places supplied by other companies. Both obtained their supply from the lower part of the Thames which was, then, the part most greatly contaminated by sewage.

A chance occurrence in 1852 provided Snow with a marvellous opportunity for a natural experiment. In that year the Lambeth water company changed its intake to another source which was free from sewage. Snow obtained the addresses of all people dying of cholera and sought information on the source of the water supply to each household. During the epidemic in the year 1853 Snow found that there were 71 fatal attacks of cholera per 10,000 households supplied by the Southwark and Vauxhall company, compared with only five per 10,000 in those supplied by the Lambeth company. In other words, people getting their water from the polluted part of the Thames had 14 times more fatal attacks of cholera than those getting their supply from the purer source.

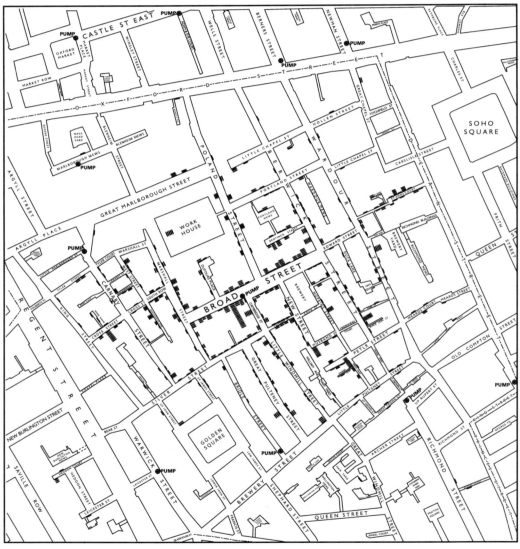

Snow's map of Soho with black units indicating deaths
from Cholera from 19 August to 30 September 1854.
Source: The Wellcome Institute Library, London.

Snow's theory of the mode of transmission of cholera then appeared to be vindicated. He considered that cholera was spread from person-to-person, the sick to the healthy, rather than by contact with any Miasma or similar substance. Moreover, he deduced that this spread took place via morbid material from the alimentary canal of the sufferer which was then swallowed by other people and had the power of multiplication in the body of the person it attacked.

Even so clear an explanation, backed by Snow's careful scientific observations, failed to convince the many doubters who still categorically rejected the idea of a specific contagion in the cause of disease.

The Germ Theory

The invention of the microscope around 1670 had allowed living organisms to be seen for the first time. Leeuwenhoek (1632–1725), a Dutchman, examined a range of materials such as saliva, blood, water and faeces and made drawings of microorganisms including what are now clearly recognizable as bacteria. No attempt was made, however, to associate these living organisms with disease in man. For example, there is no evidence that Snow saw them as the morbid material he suggested as a cause of cholera. Indeed, a separate controversy existed as to the origins of these micro-organisms themselves. Some scientists believed that they arose *de novo* (by spontaneous generation) from the fluids in which they were discovered.

Two names stand out as those who transformed causal thinking and finally gave birth to the germ theory of disease which had been so slow in its gestation: Louis Pasteur (1822–1895) and Robert Koch (1843–1910).

Lister carbolic spray in use. Engraving from W W Cheyne, Antiseptic Surgery, 1882.

Source: The Wellcome Institute Library, London.

Pasteur firmly rejected the idea of spontaneous generation, a long-standing theory which held that tiny particles were present in the air which formed into living material. He believed that microorganisms came from the air and settled on the culture media in which they were found. To prove his theory, he conducted an experiment in which he filled two flasks with suitable culture medium. These flasks were then heated to kill any organisms that were likely to be present in the medium; one was covered and the other left open. Bacteria quickly appeared in the uncovered flask but not in the covered one, thus firmly refuting the idea of spontaneous generation.

Development of preparation and staining techniques allowed Robert Koch, a doctor working in the town of Wollstein, Germany, to isolate the tubercle bacillus (1882) and the cholera vibrio (1883). In a very short period of time a wide range of organisms were identified and linked to disease in man: *Bacillus anthracis* (anthrax), *Corynebacterium diphtheriae* (diphtheria), *Mycobacterium leprae* (leprosy) and *Salmonella typhi* (typhoid fever). The practical applications of the work were not slow to be realised. Joseph (later Lord) Lister took up Pasteur's ideas and using carbolic acid during surgery founded the modern methods of antisepsis that transformed the nature of the hospital wards from places where virtually every postoperative case became septic and developed fever.

There are many other examples of the growing understanding of the ways of combatting sepsis. Ignaz Philipp Semmelweis (1818–1865) was born in Hungary, trained as a doctor in Vienna and became an obstetrician. In his early career he took an intense interest in the high rates of sepsis in the lying-in hospitals. Many women in these times died from puerperal fever.

Semmelweis conducted careful epidemiological research in which he observed the incidence of puerperal fever in different settings. He noted that medical students came from the dissecting room and, with only a cursory washing of hands, examined the women in labour.

Semmelweis made his students scrub up carefully and as a result mortality in the labour wards fell dramatically.

Such was the enthusiasm with which the medical establishment now embraced the germ theory of disease that attempts were made to link virtually every known disease to a specific causal contagious agent. Claim and counterclaim abounded. It was left to the Nobel laureate, Robert Koch, who had begun his career as a general practitioner in Germany, to impose a scientific discipline to check this bandwagon effect in which the hunt for microorganisms in diseases led to causal inferences being made on very flimsy grounds.

Koch's postulates, sometimes also referred to as the Henle–Koch postulates (Koch was Henle's pupil), may be summarised as follows:

(1)   The organism should be isolated in pure culture from each case of the disease.
(2)   It should not occur in any other disease as fortuitous and non-pathogenic occurrent.
(3)   Once isolated it should be grown in a series of cultures.
(4)   This culture should reproduce the disease on inoculation into an experimental animal.

It is clear today that Koch's postulates, if interpreted literally, are too rigid and would exclude most viral diseases and also many bacterial diseases from having a proven causative agent. Nevertheless, they served as an important landmark at the time.

The Search for Other Causative Agents

Almost at once, the germ theory of the causation of disease dispelled myths, superstitions and ill-conceived quasi-scientific theories which had stood for centuries. It should be remembered that, at that time, the infectious diseases were the major killing diseases, so the excitement produced by the revelation of the causative role of microorganisms was quite understandable. Nevertheless, there were other landmarks in causal thinking in which specific agents other than microorganisms were linked with diseases.

The possibility that factors in Man's occupation could be a cause of illness and disease was largely ignored in ancient writings, despite the grim and inhuman working conditions which often prevailed; for instance, in the quest for valuable metals in the mines of ancient Egypt, Greece or Rome. After the Renaissance, there emerged a man who is generally regarded as the father of occupational medicine: Bernardino Ramazzini (1633–1714). His *De Morbis Artificium*, published in about 1700, was a systematic study of diseases arising from occupational factors. When in his writings he recommended that, in addition to other questions and examinations, the doctor should ask the question 'What is your occupation?', he could scarcely have realised the enormous importance of his words.

Subsequently, occupational medicine has had a long and distinguished history. Discoveries such as Percival Pott's observation in 1775 of the occurrence of scrotal cancer in chimney sweeps as a result of persistent contact with soot or the cerebral effects of mercury poisoning in the hat-making trade (the basis of Lewis Carroll's *Mad Hatter*) opened new vistas when considering possible causes of disease.

Another field of study in disease causation is to be found in those conditions which arise because of lack or excess of some specific substance in the diet. A classic account is to be found in the work of James Lind, a surgeon in the Royal Navy at a time when long voyages were commonplace and provisions taken on board were those that could withstand such voyages without perishing. Sailors were afflicted after a time at sea by a strange malady: lethargy, and weakness, pains in the joints and limbs and swelling of the gums. This was scurvy and it cost many thousands of lives on the great sailing ships of the time. In 1747 Lind performed an experiment in which he added different substances to the diet of 12 sailors on such a voyage. He divided his patients into pairs and supplemented the diets of each pair with: cider, elixir vitriol, vinegar, sea water, a mixture of nutmeg, garlic, mustard and tamarind in barley water, and two oranges and one lemon daily. Only the sailors given oranges and lemons recovered. Thus, long before vitamin C was isolated, Lind had determined the cause and instituted preventive measures to redress the dietary deficiency. Sailors on long voyages took supplies of fruit juice and the tendency to use limes led to the nickname 'limeys' for British sailors.

The Importance of the Host

In parallel with the development of the concept of a contagion in the cause of infectious diseases, attention was also being directed to the capacity of the person to resist infection. It had been known since ancient times that people who had suffered from certain diseases and survived, rarely contracted the same disease a second time.

This observation led to the practice in smallpox of deliberate inoculation with material from a diseased person, in the belief that a milder infection would ensue than from a natural infection. The risks were great since the people being inoculated were acquiring a real attack of smallpox. Smallpox was one of the major scourges of the past, often called the 'minister of death'. It is estimated that during the eighteenth century 60 million people died from the disease in Europe alone.

Towards the end of the eighteenth century Edward Jenner (1749–1823), a country physician in Gloucestershire, decided to investigate a piece of local folklore relating to the disease. It was well-known by country people that milkmaids often acquired, from infected cows, a disease called cowpox which gave rise to a pustule on the finger or crop of pustules on the body. It was believed that girls who contracted this mild disease would not contract smallpox when they were exposed to it. This observation is probably the origin of the rhyme:

> 'Where are you going my pretty maid?'
> 'I'm going a-milking, Sir', she said.
> 'What is your fortune my pretty maid?'
> 'My face is my fortune, Sir', she said.

In 1779, Jenner took material from the sore of a milkmaid called Sarah Nelmes who had cowpox and scratched it on to the arm of a boy, James Phipps. In an experiment which would be considered quite unethical today, the boy was later inoculated with smallpox. He did not develop the disease and Jenner's experiment was repeated on others with similarly successful results. Thus, the practice of vaccination became widespread, although it was a very different procedure from that practised today. Material was scratched from arm-to-arm amongst vaccinees without any antiseptic precautions and complications were thus common.

Hand of Sarah Nelmes. Coxpox pustule. From Jenner's Inquiry, 1798.

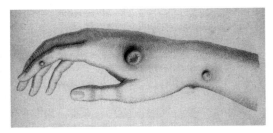

Source: The Wellcome Institute Library, London.

Despite its obvious historical importance and success in retrospect, it is surprising that Jenner's discovery was not universally accepted at the time. In many quarters of the medical establishment he was bitterly denounced as a charlatan. Jenner had earlier been elected to the Royal Society as a Fellow following the publication of a treatise on the Natural History of the Cuckoo. Yet, The Royal Society showed little interest in his cowpox discovery and it was many years before Jenner received his just professional and public acclaim for a discovery which effectively began one large element of preventive medicine – immunisation.

Almost a century later, a further great advance was made in knowledge of how to protect the host against disease. On this occasion, Louis Pasteur – who had developed techniques of immunisation of animals against anthrax – turned his attention to rabies in humans. Rabies, a disease of the dog, was one of the most feared diseases because of its universal fatality. At different periods in history it had been attributed to the sun, the weather or the dog star. Although existing technology meant that he could not see or produce a free culture of the rabies virus, Pasteur reasoned that it existed in the saliva and nervous system of infected animals and was the mode of transmission of the disease. He injected material from infected animals attenuated by desiccation into other animals and protected them against the disease.

In July 1885, a nine-year-old boy from Alsace, Joseph Meister, was brought to Pasteur's laboratory by his mother. The child, whilst walking to school on his own, had been pounced on and bitten 14 times by a mad dog before it was beaten off by a labourer. Pasteur was a chemist, not a physician, and consulted with his medical colleagues as to whether his success in the immunisation of animals against rabies justified using it on a human being. It was decided that the child faced almost certain death and thus a course of immunisation was begun which lasted ten days. The child survived and Pasteur allowed himself the following excess of emotion when he wrote to his family:[1]

> '...perhaps one of the great medical facts of the century is going to take place; you would regret not having seen it!'

Pasteur had further success with another celebrated case. A shepherd boy, Jean-Baptiste Jupille, had fought off a rabid dog which had been terrorising a group of children. He had been badly mauled. Six days after the attack Pasteur treated him with his new vaccine. The fourteen-year-old shepherd boy survived.

Jean-Baptiste Jupille (b. 1871) being attacked by a rabid dog. Statue in the Institut Pasteur, Paris.

Source: The Wellcome Institute Library, London.

Pasteur was the subject of criticism from many sections of the scientific and medical establishment who did not accept his claims. But as with Jenner, Pasteur's contribution to public health would turn out to be lasting and immense. A new era in preventive medicine had dawned.

Despite the attention which was directed towards producing specific immunity in the host to allow a person to resist disease, concern with other more general factors was singularly absent.

Apart from the investigation of specific dietary problems like scurvy, the relevance of nutrition to health was largely ignored. This was despite the fact that the majority of the population at most periods of history was seriously undernourished. Such a state limits the individual's ability to resist infection, and compounds the sequelae of the disease. Even so, this was not recognized and measures against under-nutrition were not taken until well into the present century.

The Multifactorial Concept of Cause

The concept of cause embodied in the germ theory is of a one-to-one relationship between causal agent and disease. It was soon realised however, that a more complicated relationship existed for most diseases. For example, it is only possible to develop pulmonary tuberculosis by being infected with the tubercle bacillus. Yet, not everyone who is exposed to it becomes infected and only a minority of cases will proceed to pulmonary tuberculosis. Thus, the realisation that some people developed the disease because of their nutritional status or their genetic make-up led for a time to a 'seed and ground' model of causation, in which there was seen to be an interplay between causal agent and host. This was quickly superseded by the modern view of cause, which is the multifactorial one. It is now recognized that a disease is rarely caused by a single agent alone, but rather depends on a number of factors which combine to produce the disease. These factors may be grouped together under three main headings:

(a)   *Agent* – a specific agent may be recognized or presumed depending on the level of current knowledge. It may be a microorganism, a chemical or physical agent, or the presence or absence of a particular dietary substance.

(b)   *Host* – the involvement of the host in the causation of disease is today a much wider concept than it was in the past. Constitutional factors such as genetic make-up and general nutritional status are still important. More recently, however, the behaviour or lifestyle of an individual, whereby he sets out on a road which will end in disease or ill-health, is seen to be of growing importance. A true understanding of the cause of many diseases means appreciating the complexity of factors (such as education, family and social background, occupation, economic status) which lead people to behave in a particular way.

(c)   *Environment* – similarly, the concept of environment does not merely encompass physical, chemical and biological elements which have a bearing on health, but also the socio-cultural milieu in which the person lives. In this way, many factors can be seen as implicated in the causal pathway of many of the common diseases. On the larger scale, the political and economic climate can have a distinct bearing on health. Moreover, the general attitudes and expectations of society through stress and many other manifestations, can become part of the web of causation.

This classification considerably simplifies what, for many diseases, is a highly complex interrelationship. For example, even though the causation of lung cancer is amongst the most straightforward, with about 90% of cases attributable to the effects of smoking, it still remains unclear why some people can smoke heavily for most of their lives and not develop the condition, leading to the challenging thought that if the whole population smoked we would probably regard lung cancer as caused by a genetic predisposition.

Health Promotion Strategies

Extensive debates have taken place and a great deal has been written about the concept of health and how it should be defined. One early formal definition was produced by the World Health Organization in 1946:

> 'Health is a state of complete physical, psychological and social well being and not simply the absence of disease or infirmity.'

Over the years which followed the promulgation of this concept of health, the definition was considered too idealistic, and just too difficult to convert into operational goals upon which action could be based. However, the World Health Organization's post-war definition was seen to be in harmony with a modern concept of health. Programmes to improve health have become much more wide-ranging. They have placed greater emphasis on individuals' perceptions of their own health status and have stressed the importance of psychological, social and environmental measures in achieving true health improvement in populations.

This more profound view of health, whilst acknowledging the importance of improving lifestyles, health services and environment, sees even more fundamental conditions as needing to be met if high levels of health in populations are to be achieved (Table 3.1).

Table 3.1 Prerequisites for health

- Peace
- Shelter
- Education
- Food
- Income
- A stable ecosystem
- Sustainable resources
- Social justice
- Equity

Source: Ottawa Charter for Health Promotion, 1986.

A modern public health movement began to take shape in the early 1970s based upon ideals of improving health and tackling some of the seemingly intractable problems of chronic disease and its consequences.

Probably the main turning point in focusing attention on prevention, after many years of relative neglect, and introducing the concept of health promotion, was the publication in 1974 of a report by the Canadian Government. This report, written by the Canadian Minister of Health (Marc Lalonde), 'A New Perspective on the Health of Canadians',[2] can be viewed in retrospect as a major international breakthrough, which placed health promotion high on the agenda of governments across the world. In Lalonde's 'health field concept', health was recognized as being a function of lifestyles and the environment, as well as being influenced by human biology and health care provision.

Of particular significance to health world-wide, was the resolution of the thirtieth World Health Assembly at Alma Ata in 1977 that:

'The main social target of governments and of the World Health Organization (WHO) in the coming decades should be the attainment by all citizens
of the world by the year 2000 of a level of health that will permit them to
lead a socially and economically productive life.'

The adoption of the 'Health for all by the year 2000' theme led to many initiatives
around the world and has been specifically developed by the WHO European Region
of which Britain is a member State. This has resulted in the formulation of targets
across a broad range of health promotion and disease prevention fronts addressing
two main issues: firstly, to reduce health inequalities between and within countries
and, secondly, to strengthen health as much as to reduce disease. Four principal areas
of action were identified as part of the Health for All in Europe[3] process:

(1)   Ensure equity in health by reducing the present gap in health status between
      countries and groups within countries.
(2)   Adding life to years by ensuring the full development and use of people's
      integral or residual physical and mental capacity to derive full benefit from
      and to cope with life in a healthy way.
(3)   Add health to life by reducing disease and disability.
(4)   Add years to life by reducing premature deaths and thereby increasing life
      expectancy.

The publication by the British Government in the early 1990s of a White paper
called 'The Health of the Nation'[4] further raised the profile of health improvement as a
national priority.

The Labour Government which came to power in the spring of 1997, set out a new
policy direction in 'Our Healthier Nation',[5] restricting the number of targets to manageable numbers, emphasising the wider determinants of ill-health (e.g., poverty,
employment, education, the environment), acknowledging the importance of reducing inequalities in health, and emphasising the importance of partnership in
achieving goals (Table 3.2). Accountability of different individual groups and bodies
for achieving results is captured in the notion of a three-way partnership between
individuals, communities and government (Table 3.3).

Table 3.2   Goals of our 'Our Healthier Nation'

- To improve the health of the population as a whole by increasing the length of
  people's lives and the number of years people spend free from illness.
- To improve the health of the worst-off in society and to narrow the health gap.

Source: Saving Lives: Our Healthier Nation. London: The Stationery Office, 1999 (Cm 4386).

It is a popular misconception that efforts directed at promoting health and preventing disease have a limited overall impact on health care. Some people argue that they
merely create a larger number of elderly people who then require expensive forms of
care. This overlooks the fact that many diseases caused by preventable factors do not
lead to sudden death, but they do produce a chronic lingering state of ill-health during
which time the person involved will be a major consumer of health and social services. An important aim should be to secure a maximum period free of ill-health. This
could enable individuals' levels of health and functional status to be improved considerably in their later years, so that the elderly do not become dependent until much
nearer the ends of their lives. This approach of aiming for healthy life expectancy (or
more negatively the 'compression of morbidity') is fundamental to modern public

health policy (Figure 3.1). It is also discussed in Chapter 8 in relation to older aged populations.

Table 3.3 Ways of beating accidental injury: examples of how everyone can play their part

Individuals can:	*Local partnerships can:*	*National government will:*
• Install and maintain smoke alarms • Improve driver behaviour • Maintain a physically active lifestyle • Use safety devices in the home and at work • Avoid drinking and driving • Learn resuscitation skills	• Conduct a 'safer community' audit • Introduce area-wide road safety measures • Develop local safe routes to school • Help people at higher risk to modify their homes • Increase smoke alarm ownership • Provide prompt emergency treatment to accident victims	• Coordinate government strategy • Revise road safety targets • Promote safer travel to school • Educate the public and professionals on falls prevention • Review housing fitness standards • Promote fire safety

Source: Saving Lives: Our Healthier Nation, London: The Stationery Office, 1999 (Cm 4386).

The approaches used in the promotion of health are somewhat different from those used in the diagnostic and therapeutic branches of medicine. Firstly, whilst some research evidence is available to inform decisions about which interventions are likely to be effective; for example, in changing the population's behaviour in the direction of healthier lifestyles, evidence of effectiveness is not as widely available as it is in clinical fields of medicine. Therefore, in the past, formulating local policies and designing public health programmes has been based on consensus as to what seems the right approach to take. Secondly, there is seldom any single measure which will be effective alone. It is usually necessary to consider a range of approaches as part of a coordinated programme if there is to be any genuine impact on the health status of the population. Moreover, many of the actions which can bring about improvement in health are not those over which health services have direct control. Increasingly, it is being recognized that to be effective, health promotion programmes must be multisectoral in nature and involve the active participation of the public.

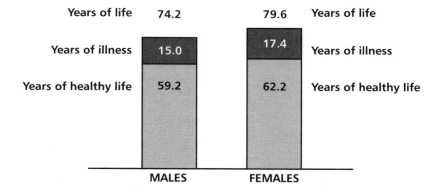

Figure 3.1 Life expectancy and healthy-life expectancy at birth.

Source: Our Healthier Nation: London: The Stationery Office, 1998.

In practice, the term health promotion used alone or in combination with disease prevention, embraces a wide variety of perspectives from preventing premature death; to legislative and fiscal measures to improve health; the promotion of individual responsibility for the maintenance of healthy ways of living; to mobilising the support of communities to health advocacy; to education and information as part of health improvement programmes (Table 3.4).

Table 3.4   Broad components of a health promotion strategy

- Building healthy public policy
- Creating supportive environments
- Strengthening community action
- Developing personal skills
- Reorientating health services

Source: Derived from the World Health Organization European Region Health Cities Project.

The activities within the field of health promotion can be grouped into three overlapping spheres: prevention, health education and health protection (Figure 3.2).

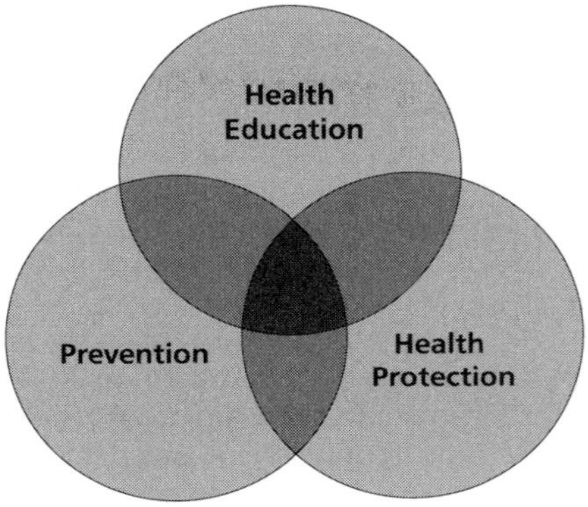

Figure 3.2   A model of health promotion.

Source: Tannahill A. What is health promotion? Health Education Journal, 1985; 44:167–8.

This model recognizes that there are distinct aspects to the health promotion process and at the same time, acknowledges their mutual interdependence. Thus, for example, the successful implementation of a motor vehicle seat belt programme is aimed at reducing death and injury in road accidents (prevention). It resulted from the passage of legislation (health protection) but, for its success, the programme relies upon the public understanding the benefits of the protective measure and adopting health-orientated behaviour (health education). This particular example would fall in the area where the three circles in Figure 3.2 overlap. The following sections deal with health promotion under these three broad headings but it must be remembered that a combination of approaches is invariably required and that the underlying philosophy must be broad-based as set out in Table 3.4.

Prevention

Reducing the risk of disease, premature death, illness or disability or any other undesirable health event is the orientation of preventive activity within the health promotion process. Traditionally, prevention has been classified into three types (Table 3.5).

(a) **Primary prevention**. This approach seeks to actually prevent the onset of a disease. The ultimate goal of preventive medicine is to alter some factor in the environment, to bring about a change in the status of the host, or to change behaviour so that disease is prevented from developing. Many of the triumphs of public health in the past, relating to the infectious diseases, were brought about by primary prevention.

(b) **Secondary prevention**. This level of prevention aims to halt the progression of a disease once it is established. The crux, here, is early detection or early diagnosis followed by prompt, effective treatment. Special consideration of secondary prevention aimed at asymptomatic individuals is necessary. This subject is covered later in the chapter in the section on screening. Whilst it may seem to be merely a logical extension of good clinical practice, careful evaluation is necessary before early disease detection is carried out on a population scale.

(c) **Tertiary prevention**. This level is concerned with rehabilitation of people with an established disease to minimise residual disabilities and complications. Action taken at this stage aims at improving the quality of life, even if the disease itself cannot be cured.

Table 3.5   Spectrum of health and disease with the main strategies for prevention at each level

	Stages			Outcomes		
	Health	*Asymptomatic*	*Symptomatic*	*Disability*	*Recovery*	*Death*
Intervention strategies	Health education*, immunization, environmental measures and social policy	Presympto-matic screening	Early diagnosis and prompt effective treatment	Rehabilitation		
Levels of prevention:	Primary	◄——— Secondary ———►			Tertiary	

* Some of these strategies, particularly health education, can also operate at other levels.

A preventive component of a population-based health promotion programme can involve specific interventions or procedures to reduce the risk of disease occurrence. Immunisation and vaccination programmes are an example of a primary preventive approach to reduce or eliminate the infectious diseases of childhood (such as whooping cough, measles, rubella, poliomyelitis, mumps) which can still have serious consequences. In practice, specific preventive techniques will often be used in combination with another element of health promotion. In this example, health education would be an essential element in order to raise parents' awareness of the benefits of immunisation, to give a balanced account of any risks and encourage them to bring their children into the programme.

The field of secondary prevention is an important one for health services and public health practice and is therefore dealt with at greater length in the remainder of this section on prevention.

Screening: the Detection of Disease in its Presymptomatic Phase

In its widest sense the term 'screening' implies the scrutiny of people in order to detect the presence of disease, disability or some other attribute which is under study. There are a number of kinds of screening, each of which is carried out for a particular purpose. These can be summarised as follows.

Protection of the Public Health

This type of screening has its origins in long-established methods to control infectious diseases. For example, people entering a country are often subjected to tests or examinations designed to detect the presence of infectious diseases or a carrier state. An immigrant in this category would be judged as a potential risk to the indigenous population and might be refused admission altogether or only admitted after appropriate treatment. Mass chest radiography was originally introduced in Britain to identify cases of tuberculosis which could then be isolated from the rest of the population.

Prior to Entering an Organisation

It is a universal requirement that all potential recruits to the armed forces should undergo screening by medical examination. This practice dates from the time of the Boer War when a similar screening exercise revealed the high levels of ill-health which so shocked the government and resulted in a wide range of measures aimed at improving the health of the nation. In addition to the armed forces, industry may use the medical examination as a screening tool in the pre-employment context. In some cases, this may also serve to protect the public (for example, in the case of airline pilots or train drivers), but its essential purpose is to benefit the organisation so that it recruits a healthy workforce.

Protection of Workforce

In addition to the pre-employment medical which is compulsory in certain occupations, many industries have a statutory obligation to screen their workforce. This is usually for the protection of workers in industries which have a high risk of disease due to hazards in the working environment (for example, ionising radiation).

For Life Insurance Purposes

Most life insurance companies screen prospective policy holders, either by a questionnaire about their health or by direct medical examination. Their aim in so doing is to allow them to load the policy against high-risk clients.

The Early Diagnosis of Disease

This form of screening is concerned with the detection of disease in its early stages so that early treatment for that disease may be started. It can be defined as:

> '...the systematic application of a test or inquiry to identify individuals at sufficient risk of a specific disorder to warrant further investigation or direct preventive action, amongst persons who have not sought medical attention on account of the symptoms of that disorder.'[6]

With chronic degenerative disorders like late onset diabetes mellitus, often first seen in their later stages, this may seem to be a logical extension of clinical practice.

This argument, coupled with the fact that many population surveys showed a high frequency of previously unrecognized abnormalities, led in the early 1960s to the advocacy of presymptomatic screening for disease on a large scale.

It is important to draw the distinction between proactive screening of the kind described so far in which members of a geographically-defined population are called by invitation to be offered screening (for example, a cervical cancer test) and opportunistic screening in which people attending a health facility – such as a general practitioner's surgery or a clinic – for one purpose may be offered a screening test (e.g., a blood pressure measurement).

It does not follow that population screening should be carried out whenever technology allows a disease to be detected in its presymptomatic phase. A number of criteria first drawn up by Wilson and Jungner for the World Health Organization[7] have been extensively used in the past to judge whether to screen. They are described below.

- *Is the disease an important health problem?* Before channelling resources on a large scale the problem must be deemed to be a serious one. Nevertheless, importance is, of course, a relative concept. Some health problems may be important because they are very common. Others, although rare, may have serious consequences for the individual or society as a whole.
- *Is there a recognisable latent or early symptomatic stage?* In order to detect a disease in its early stages there must be a reasonable time period during its natural history when symptoms are not manifesting themselves.
- *Are facilities for diagnosis and treatment available?* If a screening programme were to reveal large numbers of patients with a particular disease, facilities to provide the necessary follow-up investigation and treatment would have to be available.
- *Has the cost of the programme been considered in the context of other demands for resources?* At no time in the foreseeable future are there likely to be unlimited resources that would permit every proposal to be followed through. Proposed expenditure on any one health option must, therefore, be weighed against other proposals.
- *Is there an agreed policy on whom to treat as patients?* This brings in the question of borderline cases. In any population, disease exists in a spectrum of severity. At the less severe end of the spectrum, there is a problem of differentiating people with the disease from normal people. Strict criteria must be laid down, therefore, about what constitutes the particular disease, before screening is carried out.
- *Does treatment confer benefit?* This is perhaps the most important consideration of all and it raises fundamental ethical principles. The presymptomatic screening of people for the presence of disease differs from normal medical practice. In the usual situation the patient makes contact with a doctor because he has recognized that he is ill and in need of medical care. The doctor attempts to formulate a diagnosis and give the best treatment available to the patient, based on his experience and current medical knowledge. In the screening situation the 'patient' has not recognized that he is ill. In fact he probably believes himself to be healthy. The doctor (or screener), in offering him the opportunity to be screened, implies that a health benefit will result, i.e., the early treatment of the disease (if present) and favourable outcome. The reality is that only in a few diseases is there any convincing evidence that striving for early diagnosis on a total population basis, and hence early treatment, affects the outcome for the patient. Thus, it is essential, before

embarking on a screening programme for a particular disease, to review all the evidence and decide whether early diagnosis and treatment will truly benefit the person being screened. Or whether, on the other hand, the outcome is no different for a person detected through screening than for someone who is treated at such time as the condition manifests itself clinically. The phenomenon by which a screening test simply makes evident at an earlier stage a disease without actually affecting its course (but apparently leads to longer survival because of the earlier detection) is known as *lead-time bias*.

The Wilson and Jungner criteria have subsequently been developed further and a new list of criteria is shown in Table 3.7.

Choosing the Screening Test

Having decided to embark on a programme to screen for the presence of a particular disease in a population, the next issue centres on which test to choose for the purpose. Usually those proposing to carry out the screening will have a particular method in mind for detecting the disease, whether it is a blood test, a urine test, an examination or a questionnaire. When making the choice, however, a number of general criteria should be borne in mind. The test should be *cheap* and one that can be carried out *rapidly* by trained non-medical personnel. It should be *acceptable* to the majority of people and this usually rules out very painful or time-consuming procedures. The test should be *reliable*. In other words, the same result would be expected if it was repeated by a different observer altogether or by the same observer on a number of occasions.

Finally, and most importantly, the *validity* of the test must be known. By validity is meant the test's ability to measure or discover what the investigator wants to know. How good is the test at discriminating between people who have the disease and people who are healthy? Validity is usually expressed in terms of *sensitivity* and *specificity*.

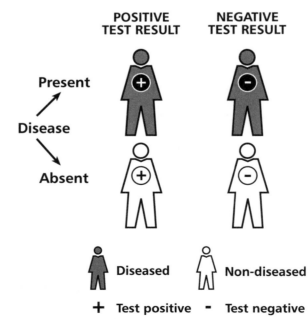

Figure 3.3 Possible outcomes of a screening test.

Applying a screening test to a population may divide people into four possible types (Figure 3.3). Firstly, there may be people who have the disease and give a positive result on screening *(true positives)*; secondly, people who are healthy, or non-diseased, and give a negative result on screening *(true negatives)*. If a screening test was ideal, these are the only categories of people who would exist. No test is perfect. So, two further categories are possible: people who, despite having the disease, are classified as healthy by the screening test *(false negatives)* and healthy people who are classified by the screening test as diseased *(false positives)*.

The concepts of sensitivity and specificity take account of these problems (Figure 3.4). The sensitivity of the test is a measure of its ability to detect the disease when present. A very highly-sensitive test would have no (or very few) missed cases (false negatives).

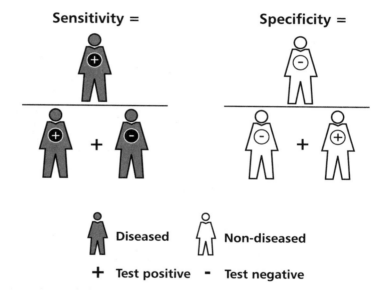

Figure 3.4 Results of a screening test showing sensitivity and specificity.

The specificity of the test is a measure of its ability to identify healthy people as non-diseased. A test of high specificity would have no (or few) people wrongly labelled as diseased (false positives). It is seldom possible to have a test which is 100% sensitive and 100% specific. Usually a compromise level must be agreed. Figure 3.5 shows (diagrammatically) different levels of sensitivity and specificity. Clearly, a level of 60% would be unlikely to be acceptable. A level of 90% might possibly be, depending on the diseases in question, but a higher level than this would usually be sought. In making a decision on what levels of sensitivity and specificity will be accepted, the practical implications of the choice must be realised. A sensitivity below 100% means that some people with the disease will be missed and the consequences of this depend on the particular disease concerned. A specificity below 100% means that some healthy people will be told that they might have the disease, with the ensuing anxiety that might result from this. It is important to stress that screening tests cannot be regarded as diagnostic and those people with positive results must undergo further examination and investigation to establish a definitive diagnosis.

Two measures of effectiveness of a screening test previously described, sensitivity and specificity, are estimates of the probability of particular test results in individuals who either have, or do not have, the condition in question. Thus, sensitivity is the probability of a positive result given that the individual has the condition, and specificity the probability of a negative result given that they do not. This is the complete reverse of the situation in reality, where a clinician will know for an individual patient whether the test result is positive or negative, but not whether they actually have the condition being tested for – because of the occurrence of false positive and false negative results. The positive predictive value estimates the probability, given a positive test result, that the individual in question will turn out to have the condition. In practice what clinician and patient want to know is: given that we have a positive test result how likely is it that the disease is really present? Positive predictive value is therefore a useful summary of the effectiveness of a screening test. It depends on both the sensitivity and specificity of the test, as well as the prevalence of the underlying condition, as an example will demonstrate.

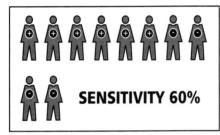

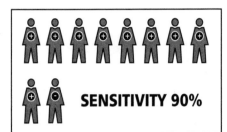

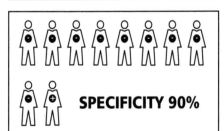

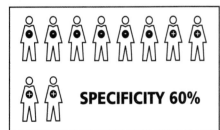

Figure 3.5 Differing levels of sensitivity and specificity tests.

Suppose that a screening test has a sensitivity of 90% and a specificity of 98%; suppose that the prevalence of the condition being screened for is 2% in the population to be tested. Now consider a typical group of 1000 of that population. From the prevalence, 20 of them will have the condition, and 980 will not. Of the 20 with the condition, the sensitivity tells us that on average 18 will yield a positive test result, and 2 will be false negatives. Of the other 980, the specificity tells us that on average about 960 will generate a negative test result, whilst about 20 will be false positives. In total, then, there will be 38 (18 plus 20) positive results, of which 18 are true positives. Hence the probability that an individual testing positive actually has the condition is 18 out of 38, or 47%. This is the positive predictive value of the test, and a little reflection should confirm that the higher the sensitivity, specificity and prevalence, the higher will be the positive predictive value. However, the numbers quoted are not untypical of real examples, showing how the diagnostic value of screening tests may be very limited even where sensitivity and specificity are quite high. This is because of the effect of a typical prevalence value, where those without the condition greatly outnumber those with it.

The question of the validity of a screening test, as expressed in sensitivity, specificity, and positive predictive value is thus an extremely important issue. A knowledge of these principles is, however, of value far beyond the arena of screening. Great benefit would result to the patient, to the standard of medical practice and to the health service, if such a scientific approach were taken to many of the diagnostic tests and examinations in common use today. For example, if we are told that colonic cancer is diagnosed by barium studies we might not accept that at face value without asking 'How good are barium studies at diagnosing colonic cancer?... How does it compare with other diagnostic techniques?... How many cases of colonic cancer do I fail to identify if I only investigate them by doing a barium study?'.

Evaluating Screening Programmes

Many screening programmes in health services around the world have been introduced in the past before there was a proper understanding of the basis upon which they should be evaluated. Policy on population screening is not just concerned with whether to introduce new programmes, but with the attitude that should be taken to existing programmes (Table 3.6). This is a difficult area because stopping a programme would be portrayed by sections of the media as withdrawal of a service and may produce adverse public reaction. Moreover, in countries which do not have national health systems, it is less easy to regulate the offering of screening tests to healthy populations by private sector providers.

Table 3.6   Broad public health policy options when taking an evidence-based decision about a population screening programme

---

- The proposed programme should not be introduced
- The proposed programme should be introduced, provided that the skills and resources are available to ensure adequate quality standards
- The programme that is currently being offered to the population should be stopped
- The policy for a programme currently being offered to the population should continue (with modification as appropriate)

Source: First Report of the National Screening Committee. London: Department of Health, 1998.

Calls for the introduction of new screening programmes have become increasingly common as technological advances have produced relatively cheap, non-invasive diagnostic tests which provide early markers of the presence of disease. Within the United Kingdom, this issue was addressed by the establishment in 1996 of a National Screening Committee to advise on the case for implementing new screening programmes and modifying or withdrawing existing ones.

Many of the criteria to be taken into account when evaluating the case for a population screening programme have been described in the foregoing sections of this chapter but the main areas which must be addressed are set out in Table 3.7.

Table 3.7 Evaluation of a proposed screening programme: summary of aspects to consider (do not rely on this table in isolation – see text for fuller description)

Aspect	In particular
• Research evidence	Of benefits and risks
• Priorities and other strategies	Importance of the health problem, whether other control strategies (e.g., primary prevention, treatment) are more appropriate
• Properties of the test	Validity (false positives, false negatives), positive predictive value, convenience, safety, acceptability
• Clinical consequences	Effectiveness, acceptability, cost, side-effects of diagnosis and treatment following screening positive
• Resources	Costs of testing, organisation of the programme, diagnosis and treatment of the cases of disease detected
• Quality assurance	System needed to monitor, assure and improve quality if programme established
• Ethical and moral	Confidentiality of data

Example of a Population Screening Programme in Current Use: Presymptomatic Breast Cancer Screening

Breast cancer is one of the leading causes of premature death amongst women in many Western countries. In the absence of individual risk factors on which to base a strategy of primary prevention, the main issue in this disease relates to presymptomatic screening. An early important study on the impact of screening apparently healthy women for breast cancer was a randomised controlled trial of women enrolled in the Health Insurance Plan of New York.[8] Two groups of 31,000 women were assigned either to annual screening (in the form of breast palpation and X-ray mammography) or to routine medical care with no such annual screening. Follow-up over a number of years showed a lower mortality from breast cancer in the screened group, but only amongst older women. There was no apparent benefit from screening women aged under 50 years of age.

Introduction of a National Breast Cancer Screening Programme in Britain

In 1987 the British Government launched a national programme to detect breast cancer in its early stages. The decision to adopt a population screening approach to reduce the impact of this disease was taken after consideration of the report of an expert committee on breast cancer screening[9] under the chairmanship of Sir Patrick Forrest, then Regius Professor of Clinical Surgery at the University of Edinburgh. The committee, having evaluated the evidence for and against screening, recommended that a national programme should be established and laid down an organisational model.

Organisation of Screening

Breast cancer screening involves the use of low dose X-ray of the breast (mammography) to detect small cancers in previously asymptomatic women.

The programme of breast cancer screening operating in Britain contains the following elements.

- ***The offer of screening***. Eligible women in the target age-group (50–64 years) are identified through a computerised population listing. Automated systems then enable a computerised call and recall system to operate so that women can be mailed with invitations to attend initial screening or follow-up visits at three-yearly intervals. Each woman receives a personalised letter of invitation mentioning that her general practitioner endorses the screening programme and is being kept informed.

- *The initial screen*. Women who are called for screening attend a conveniently situated centre (often in a local hospital) or a mobile facility (used in parts of the country with rural or widely-dispersed populations). Women who attend the screening programme for the first time have an initial screening procedure which involves a two-view, low-dose X-ray (mammogram) being taken of the breast. On subsequent screening rounds the initial screen consists of a single-view X-ray. This technique is capable of detecting abnormalities as small as 1–2 mm in diameter. The method needs careful technique by the radiographers who take the mammogram and skilled interpretation by radiologists. Following the initial screen, approximately 10% of women will be recalled for further assessment though many will be cleared following this second assessment.

- *Further assessment*. Women who undergo further assessment following the initial screen will typically have further mammographic views taken of the suspicious area of the breast as well as a clinical examination and may also have ultrasound examination. After this, or directly following the initial screen (depending on the nature of the abnormality), some women will be assessed by a specialist team usually comprising a surgeon, a radiologist and a pathologist, all of whom are skilled in the diagnosis of breast abnormalities. Triple assessment covers imaging, clinical assessment and associated pathology procedures. The nature of the examination at this stage of the screening programme will vary according to the clinical circumstances but may involve a fine-needle aspiration cytology or wide-bore needle histology in which the needle is guided to the abnormality using either X-rays or ultrasound. Some women may require further investigation and would be referred for an open diagnostic surgical biopsy, whilst other women with a confirmed diagnosis will then have primary surgery.

  Approximately 2% of women who have attended the initial mammographic screening will eventually require a surgical biopsy. Specialist assessment teams of the type described are not provided in all local hospitals. There are a limited number in each part of Britain serving larger populations. This may be inconvenient for some of the small number of women who need the service and have to travel further afield but it is essential if quality control is to be maintained. Specialist skills can only be kept at a high standard if staff see sufficient diseased people to remain experienced.

- *Treatment*. Definitive treatment of a breast malignancy may involve simple removal of the breast lump ('lumpectomy') or more extensive surgery by removal of the breast with or without radiotherapy. Although radical treatments were clinically fashionable in the past, there is little scientific evidence to show that they improve survival or reduce the rate of recurrence of the cancer. Early detection of very small cancers allows the use of techniques which conserve the breast and is more likely to remove the abnormality at a pre-invasive stage. It is thus less mutilating to the patient and more likely to be successful.

- *Counselling*. It is important that all women who attend screening should understand the basic screening process and why they are being offered screening. They are also informed that most women who have to undergo a second assessment do not have cancer. This considerably reduces the anxiety of women who have screening. Women who go on to assessment may be seen by a specialist nurse in the breast unit. Finally, it is important that adequate counselling is available for women who do have cancer both pre- and post-surgery.

- *Health education*. Education of the public about the availability of presymptomatic screening and its purpose is an essential and integral part of the programme. This helps to gain the maximum uptake of the invitation to be screened and ensures that women who need to be followed-up comply with the necessary arrangements.
- *Screening frequency*. Present national policy is that the interval between mammographic screening should be three years.
- *Screening of women outside the target age-groups*. There is no scientific evidence, as yet, that screening of women in the population who are under the age of 50 years reduces mortality from the disease. This is an issue which has caused controversy in some localities because the public and media have presumed that younger women are being discriminated against or that insufficient resources have been made available to offer them the service. It is important that the public understands the reasons for this policy decision which is in line with one of the key principles for embarking on a presymptomatic programme (*Does the treatment confer benefit?*). Current national policy is to provide screening only if it is specifically requested by women aged 65 years and over but this may change as studies of screening in older women report their evaluations. Women under 50 years do not have access to screening on demand, but may be referred by a general practitioner if there is a particular personal or family history of the disease.

Evaluation and Quality Control

Whilst presymptomatic screening for breast cancer has been successful in reducing mortality amongst study populations, the ultimate test of its efficacy is in the impact it makes on the disease in a general population. It is too early to assess the effect of the national breast cancer screening programme in the population of Britain.

These benefits are most likely to be achieved if the programme is strongly rooted in quality. This means adopting quality assurance principles. For example, achieving the highest possible uptake of invitations to be screened and ensuring that staff involved at all levels in the screening process are highly skilled. It also requires the establishment of systems and standards for continuous improvement in call and recall arrangements, radiology and radiography, pathology, surgical treatment, health education, and communication with the women being screened.

Following a number of serious failures – mainly in local screening programmes in England in the 1990s – in which cases had been missed and large numbers of women were recalled for re-screening, the management of quality assurance for both breast and cervical screening was strengthened through regional arrangements.

Health Education

Expressed most simply, health education seeks to improve health and to prevent ill-health by enabling people to follow and sustain particular actions and choices. Such a broad definition, however, has little utility since it conceals an enormous variety of aims from the general to the very specific. Health education may, for example, seek to: promote regular exercise in a population; ensure that hypertensive patients adhere to their prescribed treatment schedule; get more pregnant women to attend antenatal care at an earlier stage of their pregnancy than hitherto; and to achieve high uptake of immunisation programmes.

Health Education Concepts

One way of defining health education is by its purpose. Table 3.8 summarises four different ways of conceptualising health education activity. The first is to inform people so that they understand the basis of health risks and the nature of disease causation and are in a position to make informed choices (*the educational model*). The second way of viewing health education (the so-called *health improvement model*) is concerned not just to inform people but to equip them with practical skills to exercise choice and resist pressures to conform to particular social pressures. The *preventive medical model* sees health education as a process through which people are persuaded to pursue medically approved behaviours, whilst the fourth approach is a *radical-political model* of health education. It seeks to achieve fundamental change in social and economic policy through education about the social, environmental and political influences on health.

Table 3.8   Health education defined by its possible purposes

Model	Purpose
• Educational	To provide information and create well-informed people
• Self-empowerment	To empower choice and foster personal growth
• Preventive medical	To prevent disease by persuading people to adopt medically-approved behaviours
• Radical-political	To raise awareness of the need for health policy, to stimulate people to tackle the social, environmental and political influences on health

Source: Adapted from: Whitehead M, Tones K. Avoiding the Pitfalls. London: Health Education Authority, 1991.

Process of Health Education

The process of health education is complex, but it is often viewed in three phases:

(1)   Imparting knowledge
(2)   Changing attitudes
(3)   Altering behaviour

This used to be seen as a sequence in which people are first provided with information which emphasises the benefits and risks of following particular courses of action. As a result of this, a change in attitude results in a change of behaviour in the direction required to achieve the particular health education goal.

However, this simple sequential process is now largely discounted as a basis for action. For example, behavioural change can occur without alteration of attitude. A motorist may wear a seat belt to conform with the law, even though he maintains a negative attitude towards its use. This should not detract from the importance of imparting knowledge about health, whether it is with the intention of changing behaviour, or for other reasons.

Each of the phases of health education is very complex and much is still unknown. The supplying of information to increase an individual's knowledge about a particular health risk is not a straightforward proposition to be embarked upon without careful research. The source of the information is important. It has been said in the past that more credence is usually given if a message comes from a member of the health professions than a lay person or government spokesman.

It is by no means certain, however, that messages emanating from purely professional sources are always the correct approach, particularly, for example, when addressing the process of health education in young people. It is important that young people receive both formal and informal education about health issues. One fundamental approach which provides a long-term strategy for health education is to incorporate health-related messages into a person's value system during primary socialisation. Children are born with certain basic patterns of behaviour which are genetically determined. However, during early life they learn skills, attitudes and values which determine how they will function and interact with other members of society. This process of socialisation is not influenced solely by parents, although the family is clearly central to it. A number of other influences directly affect the process such as, school, peer groups, youth organisations and the mass media. The potential for health education to inculcate its messages as part of this process of socialisation is clearly enormous since, by this means, attitudes to health and health-related behaviour are established from a very early age.

The inclusion of health education themes within the National Core Curriculum in schools is an important development. Nonetheless it is also important that, whether in the school setting or in other contexts, health education in childhood does not just involve the imparting of knowledge. It must also seek to equip children with the ability and skills to understand and cope with influences such as peer pressure, the media, product promotion and advertising.

Approaches to Achieve Change

At a broader population level, health education is not simply a way of conveying information about health and risks. It must seek to influence young people's values towards healthy options in ways which have as much appeal and attraction as the allure of the risk taking alternatives. For example, in considering health promotion programmes to cut down the incidence of unprotected casual sex in young people, traditional approaches which centre on urging general sexual restraint are unlikely to be successful. Such approaches fail to address the reality and motivation of risk-taking behaviour in young people. Researchers who have worked extensively in the field of health education and health promotion of young people have identified ten points which should be borne in mind when directing health messages at young people (Table 3.9). Although the example is taken from the field of HIV infection and AIDS, these pointers have a more general applicability.

The process through which attitudes are changed is one which has stimulated a great deal of research, particularly by social psychologists. It has been suggested, for instance, that a change in attitude (resulting in consequent health behaviour) will occur if the individual's perception of the benefits of the action (the seriousness of the disease and his susceptibility to it) outweigh his perception of the barriers to his taking this action. Any individual's belief system is likely to result from a vast complexity of factors, which may be cultural, social, familial, formally educational or experiential. Health education must attempt to come to grips with these issues if the process of behaviour change is to be successful.

Table 3.9   Designing health promotion programmes for young people: 10 key points

- Clear, realistic and measurable objectives
- Start with what young people already know and think
- Convey clear and accurate information
- Challenge and correct misinformation and prejudice
- Avoidance of over-reliance on mass media methods
- Use the language and imagery of youth
- Education sensitive to individual background and culture
- Personalise the risks
- Use fear appeals with caution
- Encourage appropriate use of legislation and political measures

Resources allocated must be used wisely. This means that every health education programme should seek to evaluate itself. In other words, it should seek to determine how successful it has been in achieving its declared objectives. Steps forward will only be made by designing programmes based on evidence of what has been shown to be effective.

One important aspect of health education in the process of helping people to adopt and sustain healthy lifestyles is direct contact with a person skilled in risk assessment and counselling. Here, too, it is important to use evidence of effectiveness of the approaches which should be adopted.

Health Protection

The question of using legislative means to secure health goals is an issue which often provokes bitter controversy. The counter argument usually hangs on the immorality of removing the individual's freedom to choose. The relationship between the State and the individual as expressed in law is a major theme in political philosophy.

Measures which prevent the spread of disease are accepted without question; for example, legislation to ensure adequate standards of hygiene by food producers and handlers, or to maintain a pure water supply. Other proposals which affect individual freedom such as the wearing of seat belts, or restriction on smoking in public places, cause controversy.

Influencing Individuals' Choices

In addition to measures which seek to prohibit or enforce a particular action, another approach which may or may not involve legislation, is to attempt to channel an individual into a particular action. The consumer's choice may be influenced by economic means, for example, increasing taxation on cigarettes and alcohol or by subsidising products known to be beneficial. Other approaches seek to limit choice other than by economic pressures. An example of this is the restriction of smoking in public places.

The introduction of such measures can result in complex reactions, so they need to be carefully monitored to see if they produce the desired effects. There is evidence to support the approach of increasing the price of alcohol in order to achieve reduction in consumption. On the other hand, if the price is too high it could encourage people to make alcoholic drinks at home.

Modifying the Environment

Another way in which policy changes can influence the health of individuals and the community is by action taken to adjust the environment. For example, measures which control atmospheric pollution and noise levels, or those which limit the effect of radiation and other environmental hazards are contained within a legal framework which acts to modify the environment in such a way as to meet health aims. These issues are discussed fully in Chapter 10 but it must be remembered that this is not just an issue of ecology in the sense that it is usually understood. The home, the workplace and places where the public gather are linked to health in a complex range of ways. Designs for safety, policies on matters such as smoking and drinking, and the prevalence of product advertising can affect people's outlook and influence the choices which they make.

The health service alone is relatively limited in influencing these matters within the general population, but in its own premises and workforces it has considerable influence. The scope for the health service working in a concerted way with business and commerce, and other public bodies, is enormous and, as yet, largely unexploited.

An emphasis on multisectoral collaboration is likely to be a common feature of successful health promotion programmes in the future. For example, in the area of health risk-taking amongst young people, which is discussed in other sections of this chapter, there could be important roles for the drinks and leisure industries in creating and promoting attractive and acceptable, alcohol- and drug-free environments and in extending the range of recreational and leisure opportunities available to young people.

Modifying Individuals' Risks and Resistance

It is likely that, as scientific advances in human genetics progress, the scope for prevention through changing an individual's risk status will greatly widen. These developments in genetics already have a wide range of applications. In future, there is likely to be greater opportunities to avoid or modify environmental mutagens, thus reducing the incidence of many diseases. Prevention or better treatment of communicable diseases will occur as further effective vaccines are developed and antiviral agents come into wider use. Many more conditions will be detectable antenatally and whilst this may lead to an increase in the number of pregnancies being terminated, it is also likely that gene therapy applications will widen.

Protective Technologies

In some fields of health protection, goals are achieved through the development and application of technology. Some examples in the field of accident prevention are discussed later in the chapter. The use of cycle helmets by children to reduce the impact of head injuries; the use of speed ramps around schools to slow traffic, and the design of motor vehicles are all measures with the potential to contribute to the reduction in mortality and morbidity from accidents. Technological solutions are also widely used in the food industry to prevent the transmission of communicable diseases caused by microorganisms and their toxins.

Emphasis of Health Promotion Strategies

The modern approach to health promotion seeks actively to involve and empower the communities whose health it is aimed at improving. Many different approaches are combined to produce successful strategies to improve the health of populations. Specific content will vary according to the community whose needs are being addressed and the nature of the problems which are encountered. In considering health promotion as three components – health education, prevention and health protection – it must be remembered that the underlying philosophy of health promotion strategies must be broad-based. The approaches derived from the World Health Organization's Healthy Cities programme, described at the beginning of this section on health promotion, captures the main component of such strategies very well (Table 3.4). The approach of community development has become increasingly important and is achieved with an emphasis on community participation. Such participation is a process through which people in the community concerned can have a say or play a part in determining policies and programmes aimed at improving the population's health. Community participation is an active process which allows the people living in it to have ownership (Figure 3.6).

Degree	Participants	Illustrative mode
High	*Has control*	Organisation asks community to identify the problem and make key decisions on goals and means. Willing to help community at each step to accomplish goals.
	Has delegated	Organisation identifies and presents a problem to the community, defines the limits and asks community to make a series of decisions which can be embodied in a plan which it will accept.
	Plans jointly	Organisation presents tentative plan subject to change and open to change from those affected. Expect to change plan at least slightly and perhaps more questions. Prepared to modify plan only if absolutely necessary.
	Is consulted	Organisation tries to promote a plan. Seeks to develop support to facilitate acceptance or give sufficient sanction to plan so that administrative compliance can be expected.
	Receives information	Organisation makes a plan and announces it. Community is convened for informational purposes. Compliance is expected.
Low	*None*	Community told nothing.

Figure 3.6 Degrees of community participation in development programmes.

Source: Brager, Specht. Community organising. Columbia University Press, 1973.

Inequalities in Health

Why some individuals are more or less prone to ill-health than others is a recurring theme of epidemiology, and has obvious practical implications for public health. One aspect that has attracted a great deal of attention and debate is the relationship between deprivation and poor health.

The observation that those less well-off in a society experience much higher levels of premature death has a long history, and has been found consistently across a range of measures of deprivation. More recently, the findings have been extended to include various causes of acute and chronic illness as well as mortality. A relatively early example of a systematic analysis is due to Stevenson, a Registrar-General who, in 1911, grouped occupations into 'social classes' to demonstrate a gradient in standardised mortality ratios, rising steadily from lowest in social class I to highest in social class V (see also Chapter 2). This observation has been confirmed on numerous occasions since, in a wide variety of settings. Stevenson's methodology would not pass muster today: not least because he moved some occupations between his social class groups in order to improve the degree of fit with mortality statistics. In addition, his over-reliance on social class as a variable to analyse has been criticised, partly on the above grounds and partly as reflecting an obsession with social status. However, the persistence of three- or four-fold variations in health and mortality has remained a consistent one, despite improvements in the overall health of the population evident through the twentieth century.

The subject of inequalities in health related to deprivation came to national prominence in the 1980s through the report of a government-appointed working group generally known after the chairman of the group, Sir Douglas Black, as the Black Report.[10] The group had been established in 1977 when Sir Douglas was Chief Scientist at the Department of Health and Social Security. By the time the report was complete, in 1980, there was a new government which did not endorse the group's recommendations. However, the report, originally made available in limited numbers for discussion and subsequently published independently as a paperback, stimulated wide-ranging debate and considerable further research into the topic.

The Black Report confirmed again the gradient of mortality from social class I to V, both for total deaths across age and gender groups, and for a very wide range of specific causes of death. Although data were less complete, the same findings were evident for morbidity, and the report also looked at time trends and international comparisons. As a whole, and despite subsequent criticism of its reliance on social class as a measure of deprivation, the report stands as a striking testimony to the degree and consistency of inequalities in health. Finally, the report suggested explanations of the observed differences. They might be artefactual (social class V consist of fewer and fewer individuals as time goes by, who may be unrepresentative of any real group in society); due to natural and social selection (healthier individuals will prosper while unhealthier people will 'drift' by reason of their actual or latent incapacity to lower social classes); materialist or structuralist (due to the direct effects of poverty and material deprivation) and cultural or behavioural (adoption and maintenance of unhealthy lifestyles including smoking, poor diet, physical inactivity and alcohol).

Subsequent reaction focused largely on often heated debates about the relative contributions of these mechanisms to the observed health differentials. Concern that the true role of material deprivation was being obscured by the focus on alternative explanations led Townsend, a member of the Black Group with coworkers Phillimore and Beattie, to adopt a different approach to the investigation of health differentials.[11] They looked at the populations of 678 local authority wards in the Northern health region of England, a region which included some highly disadvantaged areas. Rather than relying on social class, they constructed a 'social index', (see also Chapter 1) deliberately intended to reflect material deprivation, from four census variables: unemployment, non-car ownership, non-owner housing occupation and overcrowding. When they ranked the wards according to this index (based on the 1981 census), there were remarkable correlations with premature death rates, chronic ill-health, low birthweight and a composite health indicator made up of all three (see for example Figure 1.3). If the health experience of the 136 wards with the best health record had applied to the 788,000 people in the worst 136 wards, there would have been significant benefits: fewer premature deaths, less sickness and disability and fewer low-birthweight babies at high risk of complications.

In the mid-1990s, the same investigators repeated the investigation using 1991 census data. They found that the health gap had widened between the most deprived and least deprived ward populations, principally due to a decline in the relative health of the most deprived wards. Overall, there was a four-fold difference in health index between the lowest fifth of wards and the highest.

Townsend's work showed the strength of the association between material deprivation and poor health, and led to behavioural and lifestyle explanations being challenged. In North America, and more recently in Britain, one focus has been on low income as a predictor of morbidity and mortality. The same gradients of ill-health and premature mortality have been evident, but recently a new twist has been added to the story. This is the suggestion, largely associated with Wilkinson,[12] that the degree of variation in income levels in a society may be as important, or more important, than an individual's absolute income. This depends on the repeated observation, that measures of the spread of income within populations are better correlated with poor health than are the average levels of income. Those favouring the hypothesis point out in support that a large spread in income levels would be expected to reduce the cohesiveness of a society (and there is evidence that this is so from locality-based studies), that less cohesive societies lead to more social isolation and that social isolation may lead to poor health.

This view that the degree of dispersion of income levels may be more important than the absolute level has been challenged, by some observers. It is argued that if the effect of income on health is most pronounced at low income levels and becomes less so at higher levels, so that a 'law of diminishing returns' applies and the relationship is curvilinear rather than straight-line, then this alone could explain the observed effects at population level. This is because the most 'efficient' way to distribute income in a population would be evenly, since the effect of adding additional income is greatest at low levels; a move towards a more uneven distribution would, in effect, remove income from those at low levels where it is doing most to improve health and redistribute it to those at higher levels where it would have a smaller effect. Whichever view may turn out to be correct, the overall implication remains the same: the greater the discrepancy between those least well-off and those best-off in a society, the higher the overall levels of ill-health and premature death.

Other important factors are relevant to the relationship between social inequalities and health. Education has repeatedly been found to be a significant predictor of health status, whether this is at an individual level (progress to higher education, academic qualifications) or at a population level (proportion in higher education, spending per capita on education). It is not known whether the effect operates because individuals are better informed and equipped to make positive lifestyle choices, or because educational achievement leads in general to higher income, less likelihood of unemployment, and better living conditions.

There has been a change in the way that stress is seen as a cause of ill-health. In the past, attention focused on occupations which were considered to generate high stress levels, and on personality types that were thought to be prone to stress (or to an 'unhealthy' response to stress). More recently, it has been recognized that a range of social, economic and workplace circumstances operate in concert to generate a long-term psychological state which ultimately predisposes to poor health and mortality. In particular, a wide range of forms of social disadvantage creates the circumstances in which people's health experience has been found to be very affected (Table 3.10).

Table 3.10   Some forms of social disadvantage which adversely affect health

- Having few family assets
- Social exclusion
- Insecure employment or unemployment
- Lack of control over one's work
- Poor housing
- Poorer education during adolescence
- Weak social support
- Bringing up a family in difficult circumstances
- Slow growth and development *in utero* and early childhood.

Source: The Solid Facts: social determinants of health. Copenhagen: WHO Regional Office for Europe, 1998.

This issue of which programmes can be effective to reduce inequalities in health has been widely debated and at the end of the 1990s, possible approaches were summarised by expert groups (Table 3.11).

Table 3.11   Recommendations for policies to tackle inequalities in health

- Income maintenance policies that provide adequate financial support for people who fall into poverty
- Education and training policies that help prevent poverty in the long-term
- More equitable taxation and income-distribution policies
- Targeted investment in new and improved housing
- Investment in community development
- Expansion of childcare and pre-school education, particularly for children living in disadvantaged circumstances

Source: Benzeval M, Judge K, Whitehead M (Eds). Tackling inequalities in health: an agenda for action. London: King's Fund, 1995.

The health inequalities debate was given fresh impetus in 1998 when the report was published of an Independent Inquiry into Inequalities in Health,[13] led by Sir Donald Acheson, formerly the government's Chief Medical Officer. The Report made many wide-ranging recommendations for reducing health inequalities which had implications for government generally and a broad range of local agencies. Sir Donald identified as priorities:

- the importance of evaluating government policies for their impact on health inequalities;
- policies affecting the health of families with children; and
- steps to reduce income inequalities and improve the living standards of poor households.

Some Health Problems

To illustrate the public health challenges faced by those concerned with promoting health, some examples of health problems relevant to the population of Britain are discussed in the sections which follow.

Coronary Heart Disease and Stroke

Coronary heart disease results from total or partial occlusion of the coronary arteries. This is brought about by deposits of a fibrofatty substance, called atheroma, in the inner part of the coronary arteries which, as a result, become thickened so that the space through which the blood flows is narrowed. This process of narrowing of the coronary arteries can be added to by deposits of blood clot.

These changes in the coronary vessels produce a number of main clinical manifestations: sudden death, heart attack (acute myocardial infarction), angina pectoris, heart failure and abnormal heart rhythms.

The impact on the population is major in deaths, years of life lost prematurely, hospital bed-days used, major surgical procedures performed and working days lost to the economy. Coronary heart disease is commoner in males than females until late middle age when the male excess gets smaller (Figure 3.7).

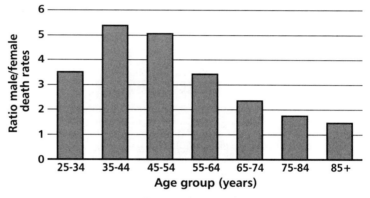

Figure 3.7 Ratio of male to female mortality rates from coronary heart disease in England, 1995.

Source: Office for National Statistics.

Stroke or cerebrovascular disease results from reduction in the supply of arterial blood to the brain. The pathological basis of stroke is more diverse than that of coronary heart disease. Atheroma of the cerebral arteries with thrombus formation is one of the common underlying processes. Haemorrhage from a cerebral vessel either associated with atheroma or a ruptured aneurysm is a second mechanism. A third is through an embolism lodging in a cerebral artery and obstructing it.

The clinical manifestations of a stroke are often devastating: loss of consciousness (from which the person may not recover); weakness or paralysis (usually) of one side of the body (arm, leg, face); loss or impairment of speech, emotional lability, loss of other functions (such as continence of urine or faeces). Cerebrovascular disease can also result in loss of function without the acute occurrence of a stroke. Of particular importance is its role in the causation of one of the forms of dementia. Dementia varies in the way in which it affects mental, physical and social functioning but (as is discussed in Chapter 8) it can affect all three.

As with coronary heart disease, stroke has a major impact on the person concerned and on the family. If the person survives, he or she will often be seriously impaired and unable to function independently. A spouse, or a middle-aged son or daughter (with children of their own) may then have to assume the burden of care.

The impact in population terms is also considerable. The large number of deaths; the demand for hospital care during the acute episode; the need for rehabilitation, and longer-term residentially-based care; and the pool of chronic disability created, make stroke a major public health problem.

Despite a decline in mortality since the peak of the 1970s (Figure 3.8), coronary hearth disease remains very important as a cause of premature death, chronic ill-health and disability. When compared to other European countries mortality from coronary heart disease is worse in the United Kingdom than most parts of Western Europe (Figure 3.9).

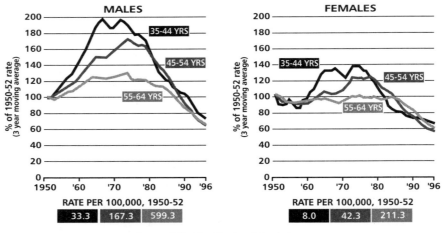

Figure 3.8 Change in mortality rates from coronary heart disease in England and Wales, 1950–96.

Source: Office for National Statistics.

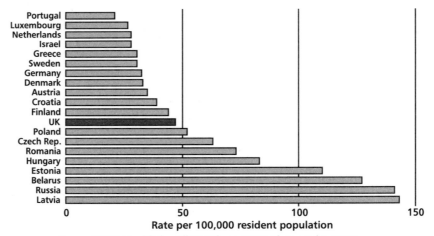

Figure 3.9 Standardised death rate from coronary heart disease in those under 65 years.

Source: WHO 'Health for All' Database, 1998 (data are for 1995).

Rate of death from stroke has declined in Britain and some other countries, particularly during the 1970s and 1980s, whilst it remains an important cause of death from middle-age onwards. Internationally, the United Kingdom fares better in comparison with other parts of Europe than for coronary heart disease mortality (Figure 3.10).

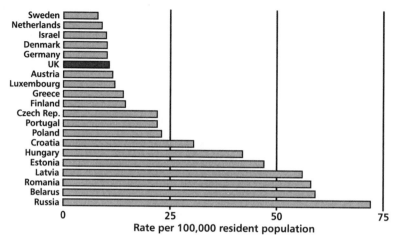

Figure 3.10 Standardised death rate from stroke in those under 65 years.

Source: WHO 'Health for All' Database 1998, (data are for 1995).

Risk Markers for Coronary Heart Disease

The causation of coronary heart disease has been the subject of extensive epidemiological investigation over many years and the evidence relating to markers of risk is well established.

Whilst it is clear that the causation of the disease is multifactorial, it is possible to identify and quantify individual risk markers. There are three major independent risk factors:

(1) *Cigarette smoking*

The main data regarding smoking and coronary heart disease may be summarised as follows:

(i) Autopsy studies have shown that cigarette smoking increases the extent of atheroma formation in the coronary arteries.

(ii) Cigarette smoking is a major risk factor in the genesis of acute myocardial infarction (AMI) in both sexes and the risk is dose-related (i.e., increases with the amount smoked). The greatest risk of AMI in smokers compared to non-smokers is in the youngest age-groups, the differences decrease in the older age-groups. This age-related effect could be due to the elimination (by death) of susceptible individuals at younger ages or probably, more importantly, the greater influence of risk factors other than smoking in the older age-groups.

(iii) Although cigarette smoking is an independent risk factor in AMI, it may also act in a synergistic fashion with the other major risk factors.

(iv) The occurrence of sudden death is strongly related to cigarette smoking and though the risk for smokers compared to non-smokers decreases with age, it persists even into the older age-groups.

(v) Studies point to a number of ways in which smoking damages the cardiovascular system. Smoking causes reduced transport of oxygen, increased blood clotting, increased LDL (bad) cholesterol, reduced HDL (good) cholesterol and vascular dysfunction.

Thus, smoking is a major risk marker for coronary heart disease in both men and women. Coronary heart disease mortality is lower in ex-smokers than in those who continue to smoke.

(2) ***Raised blood pressure (hypertension)***

Increased levels of the systolic and the diastolic components of blood pressure are both strong independent predictors of coronary heart disease risk. Those who have high levels of blood pressure have three to four times the chance of developing coronary heart disease when compared to those with normal blood pressures.

(3) ***Raised blood cholesterol***

There is little doubt about the importance of raised serum cholesterol as a risk marker at population level. Higher average blood cholesterol levels lead to higher mortality from coronary heart disease in comparisons of populations. Conversely, populations with very low cholesterol levels, such those in the rural areas of Japan, have very low rates of coronary heart disease. It appears that there is a continuous curvilinear relationship between blood cholesterol and coronary risk throughout the range. This has important implications. Firstly, as there is no cutoff level above which risk begins to rise, there is no such concept as the 'normal' level which confers only a baseline risk – 'lower is better' whatever the level. Secondly, because blood cholesterol follows a roughly normal distribution in the population, there are many more people in the central part of the distribution than in the upper tail, and although their risk is more modest than those with very high levels, they contribute the great majority of the incident cases. This is sometimes known as the 'Rose paradox', after the epidemiologist who pointed out the phenomenon in relation to coronary heart disease. Thirdly, the implication of the Rose paradox is that much more improvement in population health will result if the whole curve is shifted to the left (everyone reduces their cholesterol level little) than if the relatively few in the upper tail reduce their cholesterol to the mean. Strategies to reduce the mean and those which address high risk individuals are complementary, and need not be mutually exclusive.

The level of cholesterol in a group of people is clearly related to risk of developing coronary heart disease, but because many other factors are also involved, it alone is not a good predictor of subsequent mortality from the disease for individuals. In addition, the relation is complicated by the different classes of lipids in blood. Cholesterol is carried in the plasma attached proteins. Two main classes of these protein-lipid complexes (lipoproteins) are Low Density Lipoprotein (LDL) and High Density Lipoprotein (HDL). The level of LDL cholesterol is the major component of total plasma cholesterol and is directly related to coronary heart disease risk. HDL cholesterol, on the other hand, is inversely related. Recent research suggests that LDL cholesterol may only become harmful when it is oxidised, so that low dietary intake of antioxidants (e.g., substances in fruits and vegetables, and vitamin E) may contribute to coronary heart disease risk. There is as yet insufficient evidence to identify any particular nutrient, but increasing consumption of fruit and vegetables is prudent advice. In addition, the effect of blood lipids on coronary artery disease is only one part of the pattern. It appears that this factor interacts with others such as smoking, hypertension and physical inactivity, and its overall contribution in any individual is hard to distinguish.

There is a strong international correlation between high levels of intake of saturated (mainly animal) fat and high rates of coronary heart disease. Similarly, high average saturated fat intakes are strongly correlated with national average serum cholesterol levels. This relation is more difficult to identify within populations because of the large intra- and inter-individual variation both in plasma cholesterol and in dietary intake. In addition dietary assessments are notoriously imprecise. However, clinical studies show clearly that, on average, higher intakes of saturated fat (of carbon chain lengths C12–C16) reliably increase plasma cholesterol, while polyunsaturated fat reduces it, though to a lesser extent. There is considerable inter-individual variation this response, but the mechanics for this are not clear. A number of intervention studies using diet or drugs has now clearly demonstrated that reduction of plasma cholesterol reduces risk of coronary heart disease not only in people who have had a previous coronary heart disease event, but also in those at risk. Other nutritional factors which may influence coronary heart disease risk include total dietary fat (high intakes of which predispose to obesity, and increase the tendency of the blood clot); fruit and vegetable consumption (probably due to their content of antioxidants); dietary sodium (which increases the likelihood of high blood pressure); folic acid (inadequate intakes of which increase blood levels of homocysteine, which is an independent risk marker for coronary heart disease), and obesity which increases blood pressure and plasma cholesterol. There are two other major strands to aetiological research on diet and coronary heart disease. The first puts forward evidence of influences in early life being a determinant of coronary heart disease in adulthood and the second postulates a role for an insulin resistance syndrome (syndrome X). Diet and metabolism will remain an important area for research into coronary heart disease causation.

Beyond these three major risk markers for coronary heart disease, a number of others have been implicated in its causation:

(4) *Physical inactivity*
Regular vigorous physical activity confers protection against coronary heart disease. Physical inactivity strongly increases the likelihood that a person will develop coronary heart disease. If other adverse factors are present then the beneficial effect of exercise may be lost.

(5) *Obesity*
Risk of coronary heart disease is higher amongst individuals who are above the average weight for their height. Whilst obesity is a marker for coronary heart disease, it is often present with other risk markers such as hypertension and raised serum cholesterol. When these and other factors are controlled for during analysis of survey data, obesity is not identified as an independent marker of risk. Nevertheless, it is a marker which is amenable to preventive action even though its effect on risk is indirect.

(6) *Genetic predisposition*
The increased occurrence of coronary heart disease in close relatives, particularly of a person who has developed the disease at a young age, is well recognized. Much of the association is explained by inheritance of two risk factors: hypercholesterolaemia and hypertension.

(7) *Stress*
In the minds of the public and in media coverage, stress often seems to be a major risk marker for coronary heart disease. There is little evidence of such a simple relationship between risk factor and disease operates. Stress is difficult to define and measure and thus studies to elucidate its role have been

inconclusive. There is some evidence that particular personality types have an excess risk. When explaining risk to the public it is important that discussion of stress does not obscure the importance of the major risk markers (such as cigarette smoking). However, the role of stress resulting from long-term social disadvantage and the workplace is increasingly being seen as important (see previous section on inequalities in health). However, an important new role for stress has been defined through studies of social, economic and work-related influences on coronary heart disease mortality. Thus, factors such as high-demand jobs coupled with low control appear to put people at high risk. Low levels of social cohesion in a community are also associated with high levels of coronary heart disease mortality. These psychosocial and social determinants appear to be mediated through a form of 'social stress', the biological processes of which are not yet elucidated.

(8) *Diabetes mellitus*
The presence of diabetes mellitus increases a person's risk of developing coronary heart disease.

Risk Markers for Stroke

The predominant risk marker for the development of stroke is raised blood pressure. Linear increases in the frequency of stroke occur with rises in both systolic and diastolic blood pressure. Numerous controlled trials of hypertension have shown that a reduction in the occurrence of stroke can be achieved in treated, compared to control, groups. As a consequence, factors (such as obesity) which contribute to hypertension are also risk markers in stroke. Risk is also increased with pre-existing heart disease, diabetes mellitus and previous stroke or transient cerebral ischaemic attacks. Alcohol intake above recommended safe levels increases the risk of stroke. Serum cholesterol and cigarette smoking are associated with increased risk of stroke though the relationship is not as strong as for coronary heart disease. People with sickle cell anaemia are also at increased risk of stroke.

Prevention and Control

Strategies to reduce the impact of coronary heart disease as a public health problem must be based largely on primary preventive measures aimed at the principal risk factors. It remains to be seen what the impact will be, in population terms, of the therapeutic approaches such as thrombolytic therapy administered immediately after an acute myocardial infarction or the revascularisation techniques (coronary artery by-pass graft and angioplasty).

Past experience has shown that, certainly as far as acute myocardial infarction is concerned, people do not interpret the symptoms and summon medical help immediately, so that a substantial proportion of fatalities occur before patients are in a position to receive therapy. Some element of public health education should be devoted to raising people's awareness of the early symptoms of heart attacks so that they present more quickly and in providing people with the skills for cardiopulmonary resuscitation.

Health promotion strategies directed at the principal risk markers for coronary heart disease are discussed in other parts of this chapter. An example is shown in Table 3.12. It is important to emphasise the multifaceted nature of such programmes, the need for coordination, and the key role for multisectoral collaboration. The approach of programmes like the Bradford Heartsmart (Table 3.12) initiative is essentially developmental but this is to do with the emphasis of action and the philosophy underlying it. Specific interventions can take place within the overall framework of such a broad-based strategy; for example, interventions directed at encouraging the uptake of exercise, detecting high blood pressure in primary care, smoking cessation, and improving diet.

Table 3.12 Principles underlying a coronary heart disease prevention strategy: Bradford Heartsmart, an example

---

- To tackle inequalities in health by targeting resources to areas and communities of disadvantage
- To work with communities to develop heart-health and stroke initiatives, maximising opportunities of community empowerment and participation
- To tackle issues of heart-health and stroke using an holistic approach
- To develop a sustainable approach to heart-health and stroke
- To work in health alliances to promote partnership between the public, private, voluntary sector and communities

---

Source: Director of Public Health for Bradford. Change of heart: tackling variations in heart-health in Bradford. Bradford Health Authority, 1997.

Scope for the prevention of stroke lies with reducing risk factors which are important in the production of hypertension (including the reduction of obesity), smoking cessation policies, and strategies to increase safer levels of drinking in the population.

Aside from these primary preventive measures the other major control measure in stroke is to recognize and effectively treat established hypertension. Rapid advances have taken place since the 1960s in the development of anti-hypertensive drugs which are effective without having the severity of side-effects of earlier drugs. The step from clinical trials, demonstrating control of hypertension and hence reduction of stroke, to advocating population detection on a wide scale is not a straightforward one. Many complex issues are raised. First is the question of screening an apparently healthy population to detect abnormality (and the principles here are discussed fully later in this chapter). In the case of hypertension, the benefits of reducing or delaying death and disability from its sequelae must be balanced against the physical, social and psychological impact of putting a sizeable proportion of the population on therapy for life. This is in addition to the direct financial consequences. Secondly, there are other important practical issues raised by the population approach. Even if cases of hypertension are detected, to bring their blood pressure under control would not be easy to achieve across a whole population. Non-compliance with therapy by patients, particularly those with mild hypertension, is an important cause of failure of anti-hypertensive therapy. It may be difficult to persuade people who do not experience symptoms to remain diligently on therapy over a period of many years. Similarly, some individuals may experience side-effects which may lead to them discontinuing therapy.

For these reasons, identification and treatment of hypertension on a case-finding rather than a population basis is the preferred strategy. Such an approach can be carried out effectively in general practice with the backup of hospital specialist departments in the management of the patients detected.

Accidental Injury

The word 'accident' implies an event which happens purely by chance but accidents do not occur at random. Some groups of the population – for example, children, the elderly or those in particular occupational groups – are at much greater risk than others. The perceived inappropriateness of the term 'accidents' has led some to call for the adoption of the term 'injury'. However, here the term accident is adopted because of its widespread everyday use.

Age is a powerful influence in determining the risk of accidents in a number of ways. Firstly, it influences the degree and nature of exposure to particular hazards. Secondly, it is related to skills, competence and attitudes in particular activities. The young child and the elderly person, although for very different reasons, are at greater risks as pedestrians and fall more often than do others in the population. Young children are still developing physically, mentally and socially and are unaware of dangers such as speeds or distance; in addition, their attention easily wanders. The elderly person may have limited mobility and failing vision or eyesight. Thirdly, age may influence the ability of a person to withstand injuries sustained in an accident.

Accidents account for approximately 13% of years of life lost under the age of 65 years and they are a particularly important cause of preventable death and incapacity in the younger age-groups (Figure 3.11).

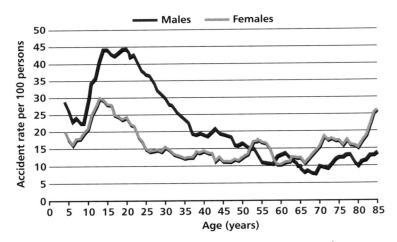

Figure 3.11 Annual rate of major accidents by age.

Source: Health Survey for England 1996. London: Department of Health, 1998.

They also result in substantial numbers of non-fatal injuries each year and considerable health service expenditure. Accidents occur as a result of road traffic accidents, falls, poisoning, drowning and fires. They occur in the home, on the roads, in a variety of outdoor locations and in the workplace. Particular categories of road users (for example, pedestrians, motorcyclists, pedal cyclists, car drivers) have differing risks of dying or being injured in an accident.

Accidents as a cause of death in Britain declined during the 1980s, motor vehicle traffic accidents are at lower levels than many other countries (Figure 3.12) but still represent an unacceptably large public health problem.

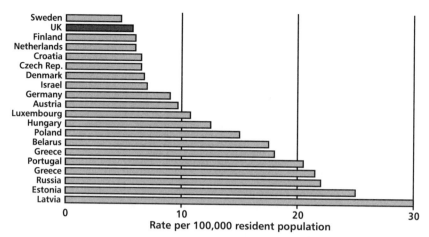

Figure 3.12 Standardised death rate from motor vehicle traffic accidents in those aged under 65 years.

Source: WHO 'Health for All' Database, 1998 (data are for 1995).

For many young people, car driving and motorcycle riding represent two ways in which they can experience the thrills of risk-taking. Most studies of young motorcyclists have found that excitement and adventure are the prime motivating forces behind their behaviour on the road and this is often reinforced by motorcycle manufacturers' advertising. The risk of serious injury or death from motorcycling is estimated to be 100 times greater than the safest form of travel by road (bus) and 25 times greater than driving a car.

At the same time, car advertising reflects an increasing concern about safety features. Rigid passenger compartments as well as front and rear crumple zones are almost standard, whilst seat belts fitted both in the front and back of new cars are now a legal requirement in Britain. Furthermore, even more sophisticated safety features are appearing such as anti-lock brakes, collapsible steering columns and inflatable driver crash airbags. However, despite improvements to car design, travelling in motor vehicles still accounts for a substantial number of deaths each year. The largest proportion of these deaths occur to those between 15 and 24 years of age and are probably connected to young people's relative lack of driving experience and also to the element of risk-taking. An additional and extremely worrying aspect of this behaviour by young people on the roads is the rising incidence of joyriding in stolen cars – sometimes with fatal consequences.

An important aetiological factor in road accidents is alcohol. It is present in about a quarter of fatal accidents involving car users and pedestrians. Misuse of alcohol is also implicated in other types of accidents such as falls, fires and drowning. Smoking is an additional important factor in fires which start in the home.

The importance of road traffic accidents as a cause of death and serious injury in childhood is emphasised by the fact that they account for about a quarter of all deaths of children under the age of 15 years. Whilst, the rate of deaths and serious injuries in road accidents is lower in Britain than most other European countries, the rate of pedestrian deaths amongst children are at relatively high levels in Britain. Indeed, pedestrian road accidents are the single commonest cause of accidental death in children, accounting for 40% of all accidental deaths in the 5–14 year-old age-group, and over 20% of accidental deaths in the younger and less mobile children from 1 to 4 years of age.

The impact of children's use of pedal cycles in the older age-group when they start to go on to the open roads is also evident in the rate of occurrence of death and severe injury.

Data on the true occurrence of home accidents which do not result in death cannot be routinely obtained. Many such accidents are self-treated or are treated by a general practitioner. However, a surveillance system which examines a sample of accidents in the home and which are then treated in hospital, shows that the commonest mechanism was fall, accounting for half the accidents in children and nearly three quarters of those in elderly women.

Accidental deaths occurring in occupational settings have declined substantially since the 1960s.

Prevention and Control

As a public health problem, accidents have been the subject of detailed study internationally, particularly in North America, where a great deal of work has been undertaken to develop ways of classifying them in a form which helps consideration of how they can be prevented. Fundamental to this is the view that the agent which produces an accident is energy in one of its five forms, that is, mechanical, chemical, thermal, electrical or various forms of radiation (for example, ultraviolet rays, X-rays). It is the sudden and harmful transfer of these types of energy to human beings which causes the injury (Figure 3.13). For instance, a teenager might get on a friend's motorcycle without any lessons or instruction and crash into a parked car breaking his leg (mechanical energy); a toddler might open and drink from a bottle of turpentine which his mother is using for decorating and be poisoned (chemical energy); an elderly woman might drop a smouldering cigarette into her lap after she has fallen asleep in her chair and sustain a deep burn on her thigh (thermal energy); a middle-aged man might cut through a cable on his lawn mower and receive an electric shock (electrical energy); the pale-skinned holidaymaker from Britain, with little previous exposure to the sun, might sunbathe on a Greek Island beach and be seriously sunburned (solar radiation). The size of the transfer of energy, its duration, its distribution and the body's ability to resist it are all factors which determine the type and severity of the resulting injury.

All these are examples of incidents which would be readily acknowledged by most people as accidents. In each case, the energy source has caused the injury to the person concerned through a transmitting agent or vector. In the examples given here, the agents were the motorcycle, the turpentine, the smouldering cigarette, the electrical cable and the sun's rays.

The individual's susceptibility to being injured by the transmission of the energy is always an important aspect of an accident. Everyone, every day, is in contact with or is using many forms of energy. If the energy source is under control then it is not usually harmful. However, when it exceeds the ability of its user to control it, then an accident can occur. The balance between an energy source and the human being controlling it is therefore a crucial one. The balance can be tipped in favour of the energy source when it suddenly becomes stronger or more difficult to control. For example, a car skidding on an icy road surface risks causing the driver or the passengers injury as mechanical energy source becomes more powerful and gets out of control. The balance can also be altered if the person controlling the energy source lacks sufficient skill, the necessary physical attributes or relevant experience to exert full control over it. An elderly woman with arthritic hands who picks up a frying pan full of hot oil risks a scald injury due to her reduced capacity to exert full control over a source of thermal energy. A young, physically-able person would not find such difficulty.

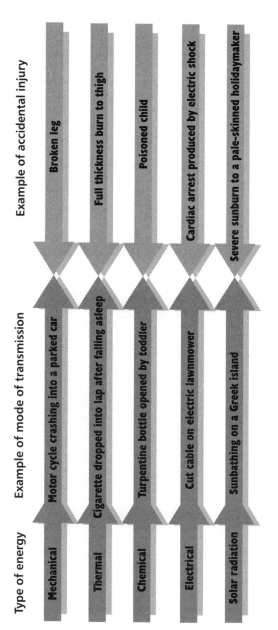

Figure 3.13 A concept of accidental injury based upon the exchange of one of five forms of energy with the human body.

Source: Adapted from Haddon W. American Journal of Public Health, 1968; 58:1431–8.

This description of accidents as interchanges of energy between their source and a man, woman or child is not just an interesting theoretical idea. It has proved to be an excellent basis for planning comprehensive action to minimise the unfortunate consequences of such impacts.

Many of the approaches used in the past to prevent accidents, and which are often still used today, are based upon the concept of accidents arising from acts of carelessness or stupidity. Successful solutions are therefore seen as those which ensure that people take a much greater degree of personal responsibility for their actions and adopt behaviour which appears less likely to result in accidental injury. Education, particularly of young children, regarding individual behaviour and road safety still remains an important component of accident prevention strategies. Yet, additionally, today's thinking places greater emphasis on safer product and environmental construction, drawing upon methods of research, innovation and design from within fields such as science, engineering and psychology.

This stems from a recognition that if a major proportion of crashes cannot be prevented, then structural modifications to reduce and distribute impact forces might at least minimise injuries and enhance the chances of survival.

This approach has been developed to identify three critical stages to an accident: pre-event, event and post-event. The factors which determine whether an accident will occur and what its impact will be are influenced by the interplay between a diversity of elements at each of these stages. This concept has been developed into a matrix which can help in understanding the causes of injuries arising from accidents and, even more importantly, can assist in designing prevention and control measures.

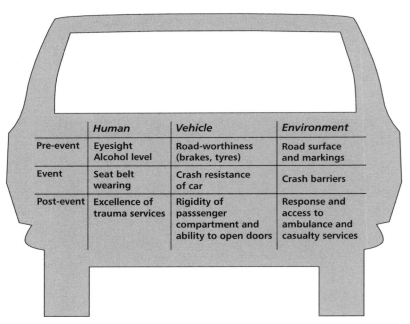

Figure 3.14 The accident prevention matrix applied to road accidents.

	Human	*Vehicle*	*Environment*
Pre-event	Eyesight Alcohol level	Road-worthiness (brakes, tyres)	Road surface and markings
Event	Seat belt wearing	Crash resistance of car	Crash barriers
Post-event	Excellence of trauma services	Rigidity of passsenger compartment and ability to open doors	Response and access to ambulance and casualty services

Source: Adapted from Haddon W. Public Health Reports, 1980; 95:411–21.

These ideas can be illustrated by considering such a matrix when it is applied to a car crash (Figure 3.14). The pre-event stage (in this example 'pre-crash') involves all the influences which determine whether the accident will occur in the first place, including the human factors; for example, how good the driver's eyesight is, how experienced and skilled a driver he or she is, and whether he or she has been drinking alcohol. Other important pre-crash factors will include the functioning state of the vehicle as well as aspects of the physical and socio-cultural environment (for example, tyre pressure and tread, effectiveness of brakes, provision of zebra crossings and adequacy of road surface). Once the accident has taken place, its seriousness and the severity of injuries sustained by those people involved through the transfer of mechanical injury to their bodies will also be determined by the same groups of influences: human (for example, whether a seat belt was worn); vehicular (for example, how crash-resistant the car body shell was); physical environment (for example, whether crash barriers were present alongside the road), and socio-cultural environment (for example, attitudes to seat-belt wearing). Post-crash, a range of factors will determine whether those injured survive the crash and, if they do, how well they recover or are free of long-term disability. It is here that vital issues such as rapid response by the trauma services come into play.

It will be clear from this illustration that a comprehensive strategy to reduce the toll of injury, disability and premature death arising from car crashes should not just involve measures directed at drivers themselves. It should also include targets for improved vehicle construction and design so that, as far as possible, drivers and passengers are 'packaged' to withstand the mechanical energy released if the car should crash. Similarly, roads which permit clear visibility, which have well-constructed surfaces, good signposts, clear lane markings and adequate crash barriers are also factors which, if targeted in an accident prevention programme, would contribute to the saving of lives and serious injuries.

Health education of children and parents in restricting the areas of mobility of young children, teaching them road safety procedures and imparting knowledge about the dangers are also important components of strategies to reduce accidents to children in traffic. Legislative measures in Britain in the second half of the twentieth century included the mandatory wearing of crash helmets by motorcyclists, and compulsory wearing of front and rear seat-belts by drivers and passengers in cars. A major problem in road accident prevention is alcohol. The Road Safety Act 1967 made it an offence to drive with more than the prescribed limit of alcohol in the blood. During the 1980s, the number of deaths on the roads associated with drinking and driving fell substantially. The introduction of the roadside breathalyser test and its use by the police initially received widespread media attention and has done so periodically since then. The original legal limit was 80 mg of alcohol per 100 ml and it has remained at this level but a number of countries subsequently introduced lower legal limits than this. The problem of alcohol in pedestrian accidents is often overlooked, though it is undoubtedly important. It is difficult to envisage any acceptable legislative measure similar to the breathalyser being used in pedestrians, though existing legal provision for dealing with drunk and disorderliness has little impact on this problem.

A similar multifaceted approach is required to prevent non-transport accidents. For example, in home accidents, improvements in the design of buildings and products can reduce the chance of accidents. In some areas, this may be backed-up by legislation or by voluntary codes of practice agreed with manufacturers. Public awareness of these hazards has helped to encourage action to prevent the sale of such things as dangerous toys and to introduce the childproof medicine container. Health education also has an important part to play in preventing home accidents by making people aware of the dangers.

Strategies to reduce deaths and injuries in the workplace rely on a strong legislative framework. Appropriate training is an important element in workplace safety. Unlike health education aimed at the general public to prevent accidents in the home or on the roads, education of the person at work can be a mandatory component of training programmes in which knowledge and skills are formally assessed. As such, it has the potential to be more effective than population health education programmes. Factory design operating procedures, adequate maintenance of machinery are also important measures in preventing accidents in the workplace. Special measures are required for occupations or processes where there are particular hazards. The most successful programmes are undoubtedly those where an organisation's management demonstrates a strong commitment to occupational health and safety.

Sometimes a major accident and its subsequent investigation can lead to accident prevention measures being introduced. This has occurred following airline and other transport disasters and also following other forms of accidents where there was major loss of life.

The transfer of energy idea has been used to provide a comprehensive accident prevention framework. In it (Table 3.13), there are ten types of strategy for intervening to control the release or impact of energy. This approach is extremely valuable, not necessarily in applying all measures to every accident prevention programme but in allowing all options to be carefully thought through prior to designing the particular programme.

Table 3.13   Accidents as energy forces: countermeasures to prevent injury

Countermeasure	Accident type	Example
1 Prevent the creation of a form of energy in the first place	Poisoning caused by a chemical agent	Stop production of the agent
2 Reduce the amount of energy marshalled	Hot water scald	Limit temperatures in hot water systems
3 Prevent the release of the energy	Mauling by wild animals	Caging tigers
4 Modify the rate of release of energy from its source	Fire started by electric kettle boiling dry	Shut-off valve on the kettle
5 Separate in space and time the energy source from the individual who might be harmed	Burn from hot fat in frying pan	Keep toddlers out of the kitchen when cooking
6 Interpose a barrier between the energy source and the susceptible individual	Child poisoned by tablets	Child-proof medicine container
7 Modify the basic structure of the hazard	Strangulation of baby in cot sides	Narrow space between bars in cots
8 Strengthen the resistance of the susceptible individual	Head injury in child cyclist	Widespread use of cycle helmet
9 Counter the damage done by the energy source	Lacerating wound due to broken glass	Apply first aid to stop further loss of blood
10 Stabilise and rehabilitate the person damaged by the energy	Multiple injuries in car crash	Rapid transfer to major accident and emergency department and provision of care

Source: Adapted from Haddon W. American Journal of Public Health, 1970; 60:2229–34.

The Misuse of Substances

One of the most important influences on health is behaviour associated with the use and misuse of substances such as alcohol, drugs and tobacco.

Whilst the use of these substances occurs at all stages of life, their adoption in childhood and adolescence poses a particular problem to the health of young people. Moreover, such patterns of behaviour established early in life can carry forward into adult life with long-term consequences in terms of dependency, illness and premature death.

Alcohol

There are three main spheres of behaviour associated with alcohol misuse: intoxication, excessive use and dependence (Figure 3.15). A spectrum of health and social consequences is associated with each.

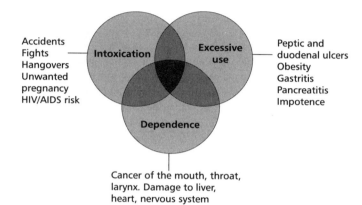

Figure 3.15 Drinking alcohol and its effects

Drinking patterns vary greatly internationally (Table 3.14). In Britain, drinking levels also vary between regions with the most damaging patterns of alcohol use being seen in the Northern parts of England and Scotland. Alcohol is related to deaths from accidents and violence and disease, more so in men than women (Figure 3.16).

Table 3.14 The 25 Countries with the highest alcohol consumption (litres of alcohol per capita)

Country	Litres per capita	Country	Litres per capita
Portugal	11.3	Belgium	8.9
Luxembourg	11.2	Greece	8.8
France	10.9	Slovak Republic	8.6
Hungary	10.1	Netherlands	8.2
Spain	10.1	Italy	7.9
Czech Republic	10.0	Cyprus	7.9
Denmark	9.9	United Kingdom	7.7
Germany	9.5	Australia	7.6
Austria	9.5	Bulgaria	7.5
Switzerland	9.2	Russia	7.3
Romania	9.2	New Zealand	7.3
Republic of Ireland	9.0	Finland	7.0
		Latvia	6.9

Source: Tables for World alcohol consumption in 1997. Extracted from World Drink Trends, 1998 edition.

However, for middle-aged men and post-menopausal women low levels of alcohol consumption have a protective effect against coronary heart disease.

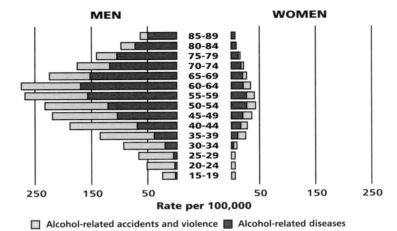

Figure 3.16 Alcohol related mortality per 100,000 person-years.

Source: Makela P. European Journal of Public Health, 1998; 8:43–51 by permission of Oxford University Press.

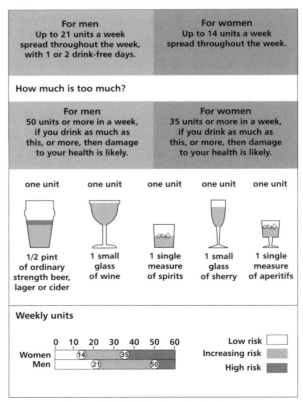

Figure 3.17 Sensible drinking levels.

Source: Health Education Authority.

The central thrust of Western European strategies to reduce the impact of alcohol as a public health problem is in encouraging more people in the population to adopt sensible patterns of drinking. Such strategies are built on the concept of safe and sensible alcohol intake expressed in terms of units of alcohol consumed (Figure 3.17). Until the mid-1990s, advice from expert committees, endorsed by the British Government was that sensible and safe drinking levels should be expressed in weekly units of alcohol. In 1995 the government redefined the limit on a daily basis in the light of a review of the scientific evidence. Weekly limits take no account of the risks of consuming large amounts on one or two drinking sessions in a week. Current guidance provides indicative daily safe levels as well as advice on avoiding 'binge' drinking and abstaining altogether in some contexts (e.g., operating machinery). However, many health programmes still work to the weekly limits because these are easier to assess.

More men in Britain than women drink above safe and sensible levels (Figure 3.18). The highest proportion drinking above the former guidance on 21 units per week was in younger adult age-groups.

For some people, alcohol use occurs early. Although true dependence on alcohol is rare amongst young people, problems with intoxication are not. Intoxication, raises short-term risks such as: accidents, antisocial behaviour, casual sexual relationships, vandalism, joy riding, theft and damage to property.

Figure 3.18 Alcohol consumption: percentage of men and women drinking over safe and sensible limits.

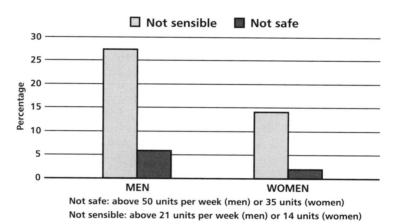

Not safe: above 50 units per week (men) or 35 units (women)
Not sensible: above 21 units per week (men) or 14 units (women)

Source: General Household Survey for 1996. London: The Stationery Office, 1998.

Surveys of young people who have tried alcohol or who drink it often have shown that whilst they know about the risks of dependence on alcohol, they are not aware of the risks associated with intoxication and excessive consumption in the short-term.

Table 3.15 shows findings from a survey of young people's drinking habits and presents a disturbing picture of the central part which alcohol plays in some young people's lives and the reasons why it is important to them.

This poses an enormous challenge for those addressing the health needs of the population. Particularly so when considering the problems of communities where drinking patterns are set at levels determined by social and cultural norms and expectations. Issues such as unemployment and social disadvantage can also turn a reliance on alcohol into a necessity of life providing a purpose and continuity which is otherwise lacking.

Table 3.15 Some findings from surveys of drinking amongst young people in the Northern region of England

- 70% of children under age for legal drinking were developing a regular pattern of consumption
- 26% of 16 to 20 year olds were heavy drinkers
- 37% of young people drank alcohol because it made them feel good
- 29% of young people drank alcohol to get drunk
- 45% of young people who drank excessive amounts of alcohol said they did so because they had nothing else to do

Thus, strategies can rely only in part on educating the public on safe and sensible drinking levels. They must create environments which provide alternatives to alcohol and demand for it. They must also provide practical help and support to people who need it. They must provide opportunities for local communities to develop programmes which will produce change in attitudes and behaviour. The fundamental aim is to shift the overall population patterns of alcohol misuse to safer and less damaging levels. There are many other important ways and contexts in which initiatives can be taken (for example, programmes centred on the workplace, in the prisons or associated with probation services, within ethnic minority communities and with homeless people).

There is also an important role for health services and other organisations. The identification of serious alcohol problems and intervention to resolve them is an important role for primary care services. The provision of help for people who have become dependent on alcohol or are suffering serious effects because of excessive use can include the creation of day centres in which skills training, counselling and befriending services can be provided. They also include treatment services (inpatient, residential, outpatient, day care) which can provide detoxification programmes, family therapy and other specific treatment and support services. Few local services are based upon health service initiatives alone. The most successful are those in which the emphasis is on close collaboration between health, local authority and voluntary organisations skilled in these areas of service. Self-help groups can also be very effective and some benefit from support and encouragement from statutory agencies.

Action at national policy and governmental level can play a part in the reduction of alcohol misuse. There is a close, observable relationship between the price of alcohol relative to personal disposable incomes, alcohol consumption and alcohol-related harm indicated by deaths from chronic liver disease. Put simply, if people have more disposable income and there is a fall in the price of alcohol in real terms, then it is likely that consumption of alcohol will rise and there will be a corresponding increase in the harm produced by it. The price of alcohol is largely affected by the amount of tax the government decides to put on it.

Drug Misuse

The predisposition to drug misuse lies in a wide range of influences. Deprivation, unemployment, social exclusion, poor educational status are all important factors in creating conditions where children and young people are more likely to misuse drugs. But all social groups are at some risk, including well-educated young people. In addition, particularly high-risk groups are young people who are in care, homeless or involved in truancy from school. Generally, also family and peer group influences are important. It is noteworthy that drug misuse can also be the cause of deprivation and unemployment, not just the result.

The proper initial focus for consideration of the problem of the misuse of drugs in the population is on young people. For them, there are many paths leading to experimentation. A first offer of drugs most commonly comes from a friend or member of their peer group and not, as is popularly imagined, from the stereotypical drug pusher skulking by the school gates or in a darkened alley.

The 1990s saw a major rise in so-called 'recreational drug use' – in young people this is often in the context of attending a nightclub. This issue captured wide public attention in the mid-1990s with media coverage of the deaths of a number of teenagers who had been supplied tablets of Ecstasy at 'raves'.

Routinely available information is very limited on the frequency of occurrence of various forms of drug-taking in the population. The nature of the activity, the fact that relatively few people are in contact with statutory services and the fear of detection or prosecution means that data are very difficult to obtain. Surveys properly designed and carried out to establish patterns of behaviour in local populations can be very valuable. They are likely to yield up-to-date information which has an immediate relevance to decisions on policy, service provision or preventive programmes.

In England, the Department of Health's Regional Drug Misuse Database (RDMD) system provides data on trends in drug misuse and use of treatment services to service providers, health authorities and central government, so that they can monitor existing service provision and plan how best to provide services to meet the needs of drug misusers. It is the only national system for collecting information about people receiving treatment for drug misuse problems.

A range of agencies in the statutory and voluntary sectors, from Primary Care Groups to residential rehabilitation services, submit data on people presenting for treatment for problem drug misuse for the first time, or for the first time after a break of six months or more.

Locally, Drug Actions Teams (DATs) collect information from the main agencies involved in drug misuse work – health, local authorities, probation, police and education – about their activity and expenditure levels.

Many young people have tried drugs and approximately one in ten may use drugs every year (Figure 3.19). During the 1990s there was an increase in drug use amongst schoolchildren and at younger ages. Males misuse drugs more than females. In Britain, peak incidence of drug misuse is in the teens and twenties age-group, becoming relatively uncommon amongst people in their thirties but this may change over time as generations which have taken drugs in childhood grow older.

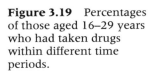

Figure 3.19 Percentages of those aged 16–29 years who had taken drugs within different time periods.

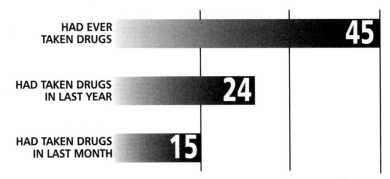

Source: Tackling drugs to build a better Britain. London: The Stationery Office, 1998.

Use of 'recreational' drugs (such as Ecstasy, amphetamines or LSD) are often used alone or in combination with other drugs or alcohol. Hard drug use (heroin, cocaine) was relatively uncommon in Britain in the late 1990s compared to some other countries but there was considerable variation between different parts of the country (Figure 3.20). The categories of drugs which most people associate with drug misuse or addiction comprise a wide range of substances, some of which have a bona fide therapeutic role and others which do not.

• **Cannabis** ('marijuana', 'pot', 'grass', 'hashish') whose active ingredient is an extract of the flowers and leaves of a plant known as *Cannabis Sativa* is not a new discovery. Known for 2000 years, it was brought into Europe during the Napoleonic Wars becoming, at the time, fashionable with influential authors. Many young people today experiment with it whilst adults use it in a more controlled way socially for pleasure, much in the same way as alcohol is used. Cannabis is a mood-altering drug which tends not to cause dependence or aggressive antisocial behaviour. Most commonly, it gives rise to feelings of relaxation, talkativeness, hilarity and heightened appreciation of sensory experience. It has been suggested that use of this soft drug can lead to harder-drug use but there is no firm evidence to support this. Nor is there evidence which proves that long-term cannabis use causes lasting physical or mental damage, although it is likely that frequent inhalation of cannabis smoke over a period of years will contribute to bronchitis, respiratory disorders and possibly lung cancer.

Figure 3.20 Percentages of those aged 16–29 years who had ever taken different drugs.

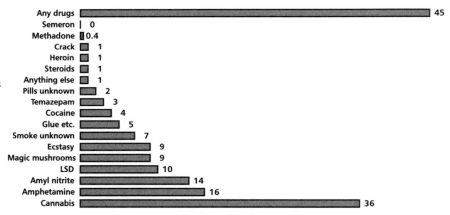

Source: Tackling drugs to build a better Britain. London: The Stationery Office, 1998.

• **Hallucinogenic drugs** were a major source of interest during the 'flower power' era of the 1960s when their ability to induce altered states of perception led to them becoming an integral part of the youth culture. Many will remember their principal exponent, Timothy Leary's celebrated phase: 'turn on, tune in, drop out'. The best known example is the synthetic drug LSD (lysergic acid diethylamide) although psilocybin and psilocin occur naturally in Liberty Cap, and are known as 'magic mushrooms'. Hallucinogenic drugs cause an altered state of mind which may involve perceptual disorders, hallucinations, delusions, paranoia and panic. There is no physical dependence as tolerance develops rapidly. Adverse psychological effects are possible

– especially among regular users – and some prolonged serious psychological reactions have been reported. These usually occur in individuals with existing or latent mental illness.

- *Ecstasy* (MDMA) containing a mixture of hallucinogen and stimulant was a small-scale part of the recreational drug scene in the United States during the 1960s. In the 1980s it emerged as a drug used by young people in Britain when a new form of dance music became popular. The risks of Ecstasy have been mentioned earlier and whilst the number of actual deaths have been relatively few, the drug produces a rise in body temperature and this combined with dehydration and strenuous exercise associated with dance clubs can be a potentially lethal combination. On top of this many suppliers of Ecstasy in the club scene provide 'E' tablets which contain very little of the drug itself and many contain combinations of other drugs, other harmful ingredients or have no active content at all. Knowledge of the nervous system effects of Ecstasy is not yet clear although emerging evidence would suggest there is damage.

- *Heroin* is one of a group of opiate drugs which also includes codeine, morphine, pethidine and methadone. The drugs are mainly used therapeutically to produce pain relief. As well as being analgesics, they have psychological effects such as reduced sensitivity to and emotional reaction to pain. Dependency withdrawal symptoms may be severe. Misuse of opiates is a major health, social and legal problem world-wide. A major risk to people injecting drugs, particularly those using shared needles or equipment, is becoming infected with the Human Immune Deficiency Virus (HIV) which causes the Acquired Immune Deficiency Syndrome (AIDS). Similarly, intravenous drug misuse can lead to Hepatitis B and Hepatitis C infection.

- *Cocaine* is another drug whose misuse is on a world-wide scale. It acts as a nervous system stimulant and increases alertness, delays sleep and diminishes fatigue. Tolerance and physical withdrawal symptoms do not occur although users may develop strong psychological dependence on the heightened feelings of physical and mental well-being induced by the drug. A common route of administration is by inhalation or sniffing which makes it more convenient to take and increases the pyscho-active effects. Although sometimes associated with the lifestyle of the rich and famous, it is a strong feature of drug taking in poor inner city areas, particularly in North America, where in its freebase form (cocaine freed from the acid hydrochloride) it is called 'crack'.

- *Drug misuse fashions and designer drugs* are a feature of the drug, club and dance scene at street level amongst the young. It is a rapidly-changing and quickly-evolving world. The drugs which are sold and used vary from month-to-month and year-to-year in what they contain, what they are called, how they are packaged and in the way in which they are taken. The extent to which such drugs can insidiously become a dangerous component of an otherwise harmless craze was shown in the north-east of England in the early 1990s through the creation and sale of 'tabs'. These were small pieces of blotting paper impregnated with LSD bearing pictures of Teenage Mutant Hero Turtles and Viz comic characters. So-called designer drugs also come and go. Similarly, the types of drugs which are injected can rapidly change depending on availability, price and prevailing fashions. Cocktail drug use and combinations of alcohol and drugs are also common.

- ***Benzodiazepines*** (tranquillisers) may only be supplied through a doctor's prescription but prescribed or stolen benzodiazepines are available on the illicit market. They are commonly prescribed drugs in Britain and are primarily used in cases of anxiety, other kinds of psychological disturbance or for sleeping problems. They are manufactured in different potencies to be effective over different time spans: long-, medium- or short-acting.

    All benzodiazepines produce feelings of tranquillity at low to moderate doses because they depress mental activity and alertness. If continued for longer, however, the therapeutic effect fades and the individual becomes tolerant to the drug. There is a risk of drug dependency if the drug dosage is increased by either the doctor or the patient without the doctor's knowledge.

    Dependence is mainly psychological, as the drug is relied on to help the individual cope with situational pressures or psychological problems, although there are a range of physical symptoms associated with withdrawal. These include headache, dizziness and blurred vision through to incontinence, vomiting and severe stomach cramps. Although not life-threatening, the symptoms can be extremely distressing and tend to be more noticeable with the short-acting drugs. The withdrawal syndrome can closely resemble the original complaint, tempting both the doctor and patient to continue the treatment or even increase the dose.

    As benzodiazepines do not tend to produce positive feelings of pleasure, euphoria or well-being, they are not especially popular as recreational drugs. They may be used, however, when the main drug of choice is not available or to enhance the effects of other depressant-type drugs such as alcohol or opiates. They can also be used to offset the effects of amphetamine sulphate (speed) and there is increasing evidence of them being used illicitly in injectable form.

- ***Volatile substances*** are inhaled as vapours from a wide variety of substances including glue, paint thinners, nail varnish remover, typewriter eraser fluid and cigarette lighter fuel. Volatile substance abuse (VSA or 'sniffing') remains a serious problem amongst children and adolescents. Sniffing can be a solitary or a group activity. The product is sometimes placed in a small plastic bag, for example a crisp packet, which is held over the nose and mouth. Although this has caused few deaths directly in the United Kingdom, more deaths have been associated with aerosol or butane gas inhalation or plastic bags placed over the head. Fortunately, these practices are much less common. The effect of volatile substance abuse is one of dizziness, unreality and euphoria, although some experimenters feel nauseous or drowsy. Pseudo-hallucinations, commonly occur and the effects can last from 15 minutes to three-quarters of an hour after inhalation stops.

    The behavioural signs in young people are similar to those produced by use of other drugs: aggression and irritation, lowering of inhibitions, secretive behaviour and poor performance at school. These can, however, also be part of normal adolescent behaviour. Physical signs such as anorexia, vomiting, skin rash, irritation of the eyes or nasal passages may occur in children who sniff frequently. Solvent abuse is a classic example of experimentation and risk-taking behaviour amongst children and young people. Often responding to curiosity or the pressure of peers they form a habit. Very rarely does the behaviour carry on into adult life. Tragically, some young people die every year because of Volatile Substance Abuse through behaviour which leads to an accident, from the toxic effect of the substance, or from inhalation of vomit due to suffocation.

- **Steroids** are a class of drugs used for a wide range of therapeutic purposes but can be misused. They are particularly prevalent in the body-building world where injected use brings the added risk of Hepatitis B and HIV infection due to shared needles and syringes.

Prevention and Control

A national strategy for tackling drug misuse was published in the late 1990s following the appointment of the first United Kingdom Anti-Drugs Coordinator (Drug Czar). This comprehensively addresses all aspects of the problem (Table 3.16).

At local level district Drug Action Teams draw together key senior staff for a wide range of agencies to deliver a coordinated approach.

Table 3.16 Key elements of a comprehensive strategy to tackle drug misuse

- Help young people to resist drug misuse
    - culturally attuned drug information credible to target audience
    - early broad life-skills development, appropriate skill reinforcement later
    - target high-risk groups
    - peer and community support programmes
- Protect communities from drug-related crime and antisocial behaviour
    - sustained treatment for offenders
    - target police resources on detection of drug-related crime, dealer and supplier networks
    - mobilise and involve local communities
    - detect drug use in particular settings (e.g., clubs, workplaces, driving)
- Enable people with drug problems to overcome them and live healthy crime-free lives
    - good access to services
    - accurate information, advice, help for drug misusers
    - integrated programmes for groups with special needs (e.g., mentally ill, prisoners)
    - effective coordination through Drug Action Teams
- Stifle availability of illegal drugs on the streets
    - international action to reduce drug crops and illicit manufacturing
    - reduce the amount of drugs coming across the UK borders
    - break up dealer networks within Britain
    - reduce street dealing and availability of drugs in communities
    - ensure full cooperation and collaboration between all agencies

Source: Mainly derived from: Tackling drugs to build a better Britain. London: The Stationery Office, 1998.

Confidential counselling, advice and information services should be available and easily accessed by drug users, relatives and friends. Detoxification programmes, maintenance schedules and other prescribing regimes to reduce the effects of dependency can be provided in the community with close cooperation from general practitioners. Heavily dependent individuals and those with polydrug problems need access to specialist services and may require inpatient admission and extended support through rehabilitation and aftercare.

In many parts of Britain a key role is played by voluntary organisations with expertise in the drug misuse field and it must be acknowledged that many people who have problems are more comfortable in using these informal, non-statutory services. Most residential rehabilitation services are provided by this sector. Moreover, voluntary organisations and their staff may also have more credibility with young people in relation to relevant health promotion and disease prevention programmes.

It is very important that regional and local services develop in an integrated and coordinated way, making use of the expertise of health, local authority, other statutory services and these voluntary organisations.

Tobacco

Cigarette smoking is the commonest preventable cause of death in Britain. It is estimated that smoking was responsible for 120,000 premature deaths in Britain each year by the end of the 1990s. Smoking is implicated in the causation of cancer of the lung, coronary heart disease, stroke, peripheral vascular disease, diseases of the lung (such as bronchitis and emphysema), cancer of the larynx, oesophagus, pharynx, oral cavity, pancreas and bladder. Women who are smokers have more low birthweight babies and more thrombo-embolic disease (particularly if they are taking the oral contraceptive pill).

There are potential risks to non-smokers through passive smoking (inhalation of the components of cigarette smoke in the environment). Apart from the smoking-related diseases described above there is an increased risk of upper respiratory disease in children living in a household where the adults smoke.

Figure 3.21 Cigarette consumption in the United Kingdom.

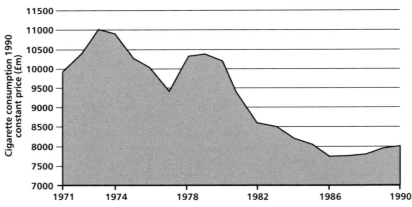

Source: Health Update Revised Edition. Health Education Authority, 1995.

The total number of cigarettes sold each year in the United Kingdom (Figure 3.21) increased steadily during the twentieth century reaching a peak at the end of World War II and then increasing again during the late 1950s through into the mid-1970s. From the late 1970s through the 1980s and 1990s consumption began to decline. The economic implications of smoking remain major (Table 3.17).

In 1996, approximately 28% of adults smoked, a proportion which represents a substantial decline since the 1970s but the decline may now have levelled out. There is a marked social class gradient (Figure 3.22). Many more men used to smoke than women but the gap has narrowed considerably.

Most people start smoking when they are in their teens and then continue the habit into adult life. Substantial proportions of children have tried cigarettes or have actually started smoking on a regular basis (in 1996, 13% of children aged 11–15 years smoked regularly).

Table 3.17   The economics of smoking in Britain: some facts

- £10 billion (approximately) was the value of the cigarette market in the United Kingdom in the 1990s
- 50 million working days lost to industry because of smoking-related illness
- £1.2 billion spent by the National Health Service (and on benefits) each year in dealing with diseases caused by smoking
- £6.5 billion earned by the Treasury per annum from tobacco duty and value added tax
- £600 a year spent by a 20-per-day smoker
- £90 million a year spent on cigarettes by children aged 11 to 16 years

Source: Data from various sources apply to mid-1990s.

To acknowledge that a huge pool of premature death, disease and disability could be eradicated if cigarette smoking became uncommon is not to underestimate the difficulties of effecting change in behaviour.

There is no single solution to the problem. Policies to reduce cigarette smoking in the population must not only recognize the addictive nature of tobacco but also the general availability of tobacco and tobacco products; the social acceptability of smoking; the pressures on people to start smoking and to continue doing so, and the commercial promotion and advertising of cigarettes. They must also find ways of providing help and support to smokers who wish to give up.

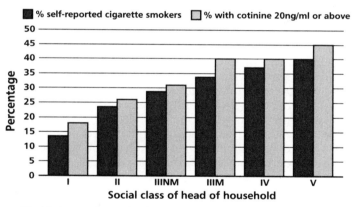

Figure 3.22 Smoking prevalence and cotinine levels for males by social class.

Source: Health Survey for England 1996. London: Department of Health, 1998.

It is illegal to sell cigarettes and other tobacco products to children under the age of 16 years. Unfortunately, it is all too evident that this law has not been well enforced. Children in Britain have been able to buy cigarettes quite easily with relatively few prosecutions each year of shopkeepers for illegal sales.

The breadth of the approach which is necessary is illustrated by the measures and programmes listed in Table 3.18.

One of the most powerful channels for cigarette manufacturers to influence people and therefore to increase their sales and income as companies is through the medium of promotion and advertising. Other influences can be equally strong although not necessarily calculated to produce a specific effect. For example, the use of cigarettes by models or actors as props can glamorise smoking and reinforce its apparent desirability as a lifestyle.

Of particular concern during the 1980s and early 1990s was the extent to which cig-arettes were promoted through the sponsorship of sport and sporting events, cigarette advertising on television already having been banned in Britain. At that time the Brit-ish Government also had a voluntary agreement with the tobacco industry which restricted televised coverage of tobacco-sponsored events. In 1998, the government published a White Paper 'Smoking Kills' which set out how it will phase out advertis-ing sponsorship in conjunction with other European Union countries. A wide range of other tobacco control measures were also included in the White Paper.

Table 3.18 Measures to reduce cigarette smoking in the population

- Eliminate advertising and promotion
- Regular, innovative programmes to keep no-smoking issues constantly in the public eye
- Regular increases in duty on cigarettes
- Varied and carefully chosen warnings on cigarette packets
- Reduction of smoking in public places and workplaces
- Support services to help smokers quit (including nicotine replacement)
- Health education for school children
- Enforcement of laws prohibiting the sale of cigarettes to young people
- Action to target smuggling

Nutrition

Any consideration of the relationship between nutrition and health in an industrial-ised country like Britain must begin by setting the problem in an international context. In many developing countries of the World, large sections of the population are in a state of chronic malnutrition caused by the lack of adequate amounts of food. At times of war and natural disaster, as is all too evident from the widespread media coverage such events receive, situations rapidly turn to famine and large numbers of people die.

In many developing countries, protein-energy malnutrition, particularly amongst children, is present to some degree in the population all the time. In famine, or other circumstances of acute food shortage, the severe forms of protein-energy malnutri-tion, marasmus and kwashiorkor, become common. Often, there is also failure of sanitation, poor hygiene and the lowered resistance to infection (which accompanies malnutrition). This leads almost inexorably to outbreaks of communicable diseases, which then contribute to the high loss of life.

Whilst public health practitioners in the Western World grapple with a set of nutri-tional problems, mainly associated with dietary excess and imbalance, their counterparts in Third World countries, for example, are confronted with public health problems related to nutrition which are of an awesome magnitude.

This section is concerned with nutrition in industrialised countries, like Britain, where the dietary issues concern the balance of nutrients in the diet and whether they are present in sufficient quantities. In such countries, therefore, the issues in nutri-tional policy concern the measures necessary to avoid dietary deficiency diseases as well as those necessary to promote health and proper growth and development in childhood.

The importance of diet in the causation of chronic disease has been considered ear-lier in this chapter as part of the discussion of risk markers for coronary heart disease and stroke. Diet may also be related to the causation of a number of other major chronic diseases. for example, some forms of cancer and hypertension. Advice is obtained from the Committee on Medical Aspects of Food and Nutrition Policy (COMA). This suggests that the risk of cancer would be reduced by:

(1) Avoiding obesity and weight gain in adult life (endometrial and post-meno-pausal breast cancer).

(2) Increasing intake of a wide variety of fruits and vegetables (colorectal and gastric cancer).

(3) Increasing non-starch polysaccharides dietary fibre (colorectal and possibly pancreatic cancer).

(4) Avoiding very high intakes of red and processed meat (colorectal cancer).

Studies of diet as a risk factor in chronic diseases are notoriously difficult to carry out and thus conclusions about causation must be drawn with great caution. In relation to cancer, there are a number of possible causal associations. Dietary fibre may reduce the risk of occurrence of cancer of the large bowel. Alcohol above safe levels is a well established risk factor for cancer of the mouth and larynx and has also been linked to the causation of breast cancer. Despite claims which have been made for the protective effect of β-carotene in some cancers, the evidence from intervention trials has not only failed to show any beneficial effect, but in fact demonstrated worse outcome in those receiving β-carotene supplements. The relevance of this study in a high-risk group to the general population is not clear, but COMA advises against the use of purified high-dose nutrient supplements to avoid cancer. COMA also concluded that there was moderately strong evidence that dietary fat was not specifically related to cancer risk (except indirectly via an association with obesity). Evidence is not properly established relating to the often mooted risks of different types of dietary fat on the development of cancer at various sites. Although a controversial subject for many years, the association between high sodium intake and dietary hypertension, has led expert committees in a number of countries to recommend reductions in the amount of salt in the diet.

Part of public health policy involves gaining expert advice on the nature of the link between diet and health. In the United Kingdom such advice from COMA is generally published as Reports to Government. One such COMA Report on Dietary Reference Values (DRV)[14] sets out authoritative estimates of the range of requirements for micro-nutrients in the United Kingdom population, and of the desirable balance of macro-nutrients (fat, carbohydrate, protein) providing energy. These DRVs provide benchmarks against which surveys of people's diets can be assessed for risk of nutrient deficiency, or of the development of chronic disease. Government also commissions surveys of the British diet and of the nutritional status of the population. The National Food Survey has measured household food purchases in Great Britain continuously since 1940, and is the major tool for monitoring dietary trends. In addition, the National Diet and Nutrition Survey (NDNS) Programme measures the weighed food intake of around 2000 individuals, together with physiological data e.g., height, weight, blood pressure, and measures of nutrition status (e.g., plasma levels). Each such survey covers different age-groups of the population and the cycle is repeated approximately every 12 years. These surveys provide data on trends in diet and nutrition, as well as allowing comparison with recommended intakes, and with biochemical or other health-related reference ranges. For example, the government and public health services of most industrialised countries have issued guidelines for healthy eating which are the basis of many health promotion programmes. An example is shown in Table 3.19. Such diets aim to reduce the proportion of energy derived from fat (particularly saturated fat), to increase the amount of starchy foodstuffs and to increase the amount of fish, fruit and vegetables eaten daily.

Obesity is a major nutritional disorder in the industrialised world. It is an important cause of premature death and is associated with the development of a number of chronic diseases, including coronary heart disease, diabetes mellitus and hypertension. Measures of obesity vary for purposes of assessing its prevalence in the population. One commonly used measure is the Body Mass Index (BMI) which is calculated by dividing the person's weight in kilograms by the square of their height expressed in metres.

Table 3.19 Example of healthy eating guidelines

Dietary guideline

1   Enjoy your food
2   Eat a variety of different foods
3   Eat the right amount to be a healthy weight
4   Eat plenty of foods rich in starch and fibre
5   Eat plenty of fruit and vegetables
6   Don't eat too many foods that contain a lot of fat
7   Don't have sugary foods and drinks too often
8   If you drink alcohol, drink sensibly

Source: Eight guidelines for a healthy diet, Health Education Authority. London: 1997.

This measure can be used to construct a definition of 'obesity' and 'overweight' and then assess the status of the population in relation to their weight against these defined concepts (Figure 3.23).

Figure 3.23 Prevalence of overweight or obese adults.

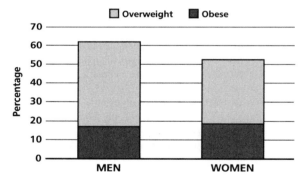

Source: Health Survey for England 1996. London: Department of Health, 1998.

A major element in strategies to achieve goals in nutrition and health, is to ensure that the public is well informed about the issues, the risks, and of ways of reducing them through dietary modification. There is an important role for parents in introducing their children to healthy eating alternatives and helping them to realise the importance of patterns of eating to their future health and well-being.

The achievement of fundamental population change will, however, require much broader and concerted action. People's patterns of eating and their choice of food is governed by a wide range of factors, for example: family income, access to different types of food, the behaviour of other members of their social network and the powerful forces of product marketing and advertising. For children in particular, what their parents can afford and choose to give them to eat is an important part of their early dietary experience.

To create a culture within Britain where healthy food choices are widely available and are adopted by a large proportion of the population poses a formidable challenge. Health services can play an important part by setting targets and gathering appropriate information about current dietary patterns. They can also take the lead in those areas where health care professionals are in a position to assess and advise people about their present food intake and provide information and assistance which will help them to make beneficial modifications. This is particularly important in the primary care setting where a relatively high proportion of the population is in regular contact with the health service. There are particular responsibilities for doctors and nurses assessing the growth and development of children to ensure that their daily nutritional requirements are being met, and to ensure that undernutrition is recognized early and corrected.

Health care professionals also have an important part to play in counselling the smaller number of people who come into contact with the hospital service as patients. It is important that the health service ensures that adequate skills and expertise in this field exist amongst their professional staff, notably that sufficient skilled dieticians are available.

Schools have a particular responsibility to introduce nutrition and health issues in the health education curriculum. They can also create catering policies which help children to develop positive attitudes towards eating for health and which will enable them to become used to healthier food.

Similarly, catering facilities in the workplace offer major opportunities to help adults to adopt and sustain nutritional behaviour conducive to health.

The food industry in all its diversity is another key element in population-based nutrition and health strategies. Industry is influenced by government which can enjoin it at national level. It is also influenced by consumer demands and expectations. Increased labelling of food with nutritional information has been an important step forward in educating consumers about nutrition and health. A greater availability of healthier options (for example, containing less saturated fat) in processed food is still required. Similarly, such options are still in the minority amongst the choices offered by restaurants and fast-food catering outlets.

The growth of vegetarianism in young people has also been important in opening up the issue of food and health to public debate (though the prime motivation behind the movement is concern for animal welfare and not health consciousness per se).

As with many other lifestyle-related issues, the greatest challenges are with social groups within the population in which behaviour has proved intractable to change. The issue of poverty, the extent to which a limited household budget is spent on food, (particularly for its younger members) and the presence of 'food deserts' in many disadvantaged communities are a major concern when considering the public health problems of some parts of the population in Britain.

Infection With the Human Immune Deficiency Virus (HIV)

The World Health Organization (WHO) has estimated that, by the end of the 1990s, there will be approaching 40 million people living with HIV and Acquired Immune Deficiency Syndrome (AIDS) worldwide. More than 14 million deaths have occurred due to AIDS since the beginning of the epidemic. Very many more people are already infected with HIV than the number who have developed AIDS. It is estimated that the number of HIV-positive people will also increase greatly, if no vaccine or cure is available.

The emergence of AIDS as a global threat has been spectacular. The disease was first recognized in 1981, although testing of serum taken at the time led to the realisation that it was spreading rapidly amongst some populations in the middle and late 1970s.

The Nature of HIV Infection

HIV belongs to the retrovirus group and, by infecting a subset of the T-lymphocyte population (so-called CD4 cells), gradually destroys the normal immune response mechanism. During 1981, in the United States of America, increasing numbers of cases of opportunistic infection (particularly *Pneumocystis carinii pneumonia*) and unusual tumours (e.g., Kaposi's sarcoma) were reported in previously healthy homosexual or bisexual men. The presenting clinical features are often general: weight loss, fever, malaise, lymphadenopathy. The fully developed AIDS syndrome often involves opportunistic infections or patterns of malignancy infrequently seen in people with normal immune systems, although any one of a wide range of infections or malignancies can occur.

People can be HIV positive and remain asymptomatic for long periods of time. However, the precise proportion of such people who will eventually develop AIDS is not fully established. The first therapy to have had an impact on HIV infection and AIDS was the anti-viral drug zidovudine (AZT). This drug is now used in combination with other anti-retroviral drugs. They increase survival for patients with AIDS and delay the onset of symptoms and progression to AIDS in people who have HIV infection. Drug treatments are strategies of containment not of cure but until research yields a more effective alternative, they remain the mainstay in the treatment of infected people.

Modes of Transmission and Risk Groups

In Western Europe, North America and Australasia, the majority of new cases of HIV infection and AIDS up to now has been amongst homosexual or bisexual men, people who inject drugs and (in the earlier phase of the epidemic) haemophiliacs who were given infected blood products. In African countries, the majority of cases of the disease has occurred amongst heterosexual people. In these populations, considerable numbers of babies have become infected through transmission of the virus from their infected mothers during late pregnancy, childbirth or via breast feeding. By the late 1990s nearly 70% of the world's infected people lived in sub-Saharan Africa yet only a tenth of the world's population lives in the area. By this time rapid expansion of the epidemic had occurred in the Far East (China, Thailand, Vietnam), in India and in Central and Eastern Europe. Migrant workers, people in the sex trade and intravenous drug users were the major sources of the spread of infection.

Table 3.20 Modes of transmission of Human Immune Deficiency Virus (HIV) infection

- Penetrative heterosexual or homosexual intercourse with an infected person
- Intravenous drug abuse (usually involving sharing of infected needles or equipment)
- Infected mother-to-child during pregnancy or labour or through breast feeding
- Inoculation of infected blood through a variety of potential means (including medical and dental procedures); risks to health care workers and cross-infection of patients
- Transfusion of unscreened blood or blood products

Over 70% of adult cases world-wide are associated with unprotected heterosexual intercourse. Mother-to-child transmission accounts for most childhood cases world-wide whilst around 10% of adult infections occur through intravenous drug users sharing equipment. Transfusion of infected blood or blood products accounts for 5 to 10%. The main modes of transmission of the infection are shown in Table 3.20.

The Challenge of Prevention

In Britain, whilst the number of cases of HIV infection arising from heterosexual transmission is mainly associated with time spent in sub-Saharan African countries, it is still much less common than those arising from homosexual or bisexual exposure; however, it is rising and is likely to become much more common. It is important to remember that changes in attitudes to sex and sexuality in Britain from the late 1960s onwards led to a situation prior to the AIDS epidemic, where changes in individual behaviour increased the chances of acquiring the virus. For example, the growth of non-barrier methods of contraception came about because they were seen as a surer way of preventing pregnancy, of demonstrating sexual liberation and of enhancing sexual pleasure. Changing attitudes to relationship-building, particularly amongst young people, meant that multiple sexual experiences before a stable relationship was established were increasingly seen in a positive light. The 'coming out' movement amongst gay men was also characterised by freer sexual behaviour.

Such powerful societal trends and the individual behaviour which stems from them are difficult to modify or reverse. Yet, this is precisely what is required to halt the AIDS epidemic in Western countries such as Britain. For example, the transformation of the image of the condom from an unfashionable and less effective form of contraception (than the contraceptive pill) to one which is perceived as an essential and potentially life-saving component of a casual sexual encounter, is a major challenge for public health educators. Persuading people, particularly the young, to return to more stable long-lasting relationships and to cut down one-night stands is equally challenging.

The importance of changing behaviour, especially in young people and in high-risk groups is a major element of the global war against AIDS.

The British Government ran a major public education campaign between 1986 and 1987 (relatively early in the occurrence of the epidemic). The campaign made heavy use of the mass media: television, radio, cinema and posters. A leaflet was delivered to every household in Britain giving information about HIV infection and AIDS. A tele-phone information system, the National AIDS Helpline, was also established.

Britain was widely praised internationally for its willingness to take an early, high-profile involvement in combatting the threat of AIDS through public health educa-tion. Undoubtedly as a result of this early action, Britain has remained a low prevalence country compared to many other parts of Europe.

The campaign was evaluated and found to have been extremely effective in increas-ing awareness about HIV infection, AIDS and the risks of transmission. Sexual behaviour amongst the population of gay men shifted with a reduction in the average number of sexual partners, and other changes in sexual behaviour (e.g., safer sex practices).

There is good evidence that young people understand the risks. There is less evi-dence of any major shift in behaviour on their part. Young people continue to take risks with casual or unprotected sex. A particularly telling example of the dangers for young people in these health risk-taking years is provided by an example of the results of a survey carried out in the North East of England. It shows (Table 3.21) the extent to which students would protect themselves by wearing a condom for casual sex accord-ing to their level of alcohol intake. Those who drank more were more likely to get involved in casual sex without wearing a condom. This example illustrates the way in which two behaviours in young people can produce a level of risk which could result in personal disaster and, ultimately, even death.

Table 3.21   Extent to which students risked casual sex without a condom

	Percentage of students risking casual sex without a condom	
Alcohol intake	*Male*	*Female*
Non-drinker	4	4
Light drinker	9	6
Medium drinker	19	12
Heavy drinker	33	23

Source: Based on the result of a survey of 1874 students in three establishments (University, Polytechnic and Technical College) in the Tyne/Tees National Union of Students area.

When addressing the problem of changing behaviour in young people, it is vital that national campaigns are accompanied by strong regional and local campaigns and activities. As is discussed earlier in this chapter, it is also important that initiatives taken with young people are attractive to them and are designed to be consistent with the way in which they think and view the world.

One of the problems for public education programmes for HIV infection in a country like Britain is that a number of target groups are being addressed simultaneously (Table 3.22). Thus, the health education initiative must continue to target the sexual behaviour of gay men without leading the rest of the population to believe that HIV infection is a disease of homosexuals. Similarly, whilst heterosexual transmission is still at a low baseline in this country and mainly confined to people from high prevalence parts of the world, it is more difficult to persuade people that the threat to them is indeed real. Campaigns and programmes must also be appropriately targeted for example, gay/bisexual men, intravenous drug abusers, prostitutes, travellers to high-risk areas of the world.

Table 3.22   Particularly high-risk groups for HIV prevention in Britain

- Gay men, in particular young gay men
- Bisexual men and other men who have sex with men
- Injecting drug users
- Men and women who travel to, or have links with, high-prevalence areas where heterosexual transmission is common (e.g., sub-Saharan Africa)
- People who already have HIV infection or AIDS
- Female sexual partners of men in these groups
- Babies of HIV infected mothers

Source: Adapted from HIV and AIDS Health Promotion: an evolving strategy. London: DoH, 1995.

Public education, whilst a vital element of programmes to prevent and control HIV infection in the population, is only one part of a comprehensive range of measures which have been adopted. For example, well-organised needle exchange schemes are particularly important in reducing risk amongst intravenous drug abusers. Free, open-access genitourinary medicine clinics provide the main entry point for most HIV/AIDS patients. Other key elements of the overall programme include training of staff in the care of infected people as well as in the risks of transmission during the process of patient care.

Counselling, Treatment and Care

Other measures include ensuring that patients with symptoms or the full-blown disease have access to the best specialist services and that people in risk groups, or the worried, will have access to locally-based confidential counselling and blood testing services. The counselling service has two distinct functions. For those requesting an HIV test for insurance purposes, or as part of antenatal care, pre-test discussion will be less extensive than for those who believe they have put themselves recently at risk. Post-test counselling places the emphasis on helping the individual to cope with their HIV infection, for instance, advising them of the availability of specialist treatment and care, counselling and support for partners and family.

Most children with HIV in the United Kingdom are infected as a result of transmission of HIV infection from their mothers either before or during birth or afterwards through breastfeeding. There is clear evidence that the risk of transmission can be greatly reduced by interventions such as antiretroviral therapy, elective caesarian section and the avoidance of breastfeeding.

It is important that services for HIV infection and AIDS are flexible and diverse. For example, availability of counselling services in different health care settings. Health authorities and local authorities work closely with voluntary organisations to provide non-statutory alternatives for some components of care.

Surveillance and Legislation

Information on the prevalence of HIV infection and AIDS in Britain is reported on a voluntary and confidential basis by clinicians to the national Communicable Disease Surveillance Centre in England and its counterpart in Scotland. Other information on the prevalence of HIV infection includes data from unlinked anonymous surveys which use blood left over after completion of diagnostic testing. These surveys provide essential public health information about the prevalence of HIV in high-risk groups e.g., genitourinary medicine clinic attenders and injecting drug users, and in the general population (e.g., pregnant women).

The *AIDS (Control) Act* 1987 required health authorities to provide details on the number of people with AIDS reported in the previous year and since records began in 1982. The Act was amended in 1988 to include the number of people with HIV infection reported. The Act also placed additional responsibilities on health authorities to report annually to the Department of Health on various aspects of the prevention, control and treatment of AIDS and to provide local statistics.

The Act was introduced to provide the Secretary of State for Health with a picture of activity underway and planned in each part of the country. The publication of local reports also gives health professionals and the public in each locality an opportunity to assess the progression of the epidemic, the services which are provided and action being taken to combat the infection.

Conclusions

This chapter has described the background and the approaches used, in one of the main aspects of public health practice – the promotion of health.

Many of the health problems in a population are capable of major reduction, if not elimination, through these measures. Similarly, the promotion of health as a positive state to be attained by as many people in a population as possible is another important goal for this aspect of public health practice.

The potential for change is enormous if ways can be found to modify risk factors on a population scale and to help people adopt and sustain lifestyles which are supportive to health rather than harmful and injurious. However, the underlying influences on health – for example poverty, lack of educational opportunity, social exclusion – are powerful and reducing their impact is an enormous challenge.

One of the keys to success lies in shaping the behaviour and values of children and young people. It lies in enabling them to lay the foundations for a life which will achieve the maximum of the biological span and in which most of those years will be characterised by health rather than illness, chronic disease or disability.

If these challenges can be met, as the world has entered a new Millennium, then the scale of public health achievement will be as great as the historical discoveries whose descriptions began this chapter and which transformed the health landscape of the past.

Chapter 4

The National Health Service

Introduction

The last decade of the twentieth century was a time in which governments throughout the world have examined critically their health care systems and asked fundamental questions about how best they can continue to serve their citizens in the new Millennium. The driving force for health care reform has been the dilemma of how to meet ever increasing demand for health services, whilst containing costs to ensure that scarce resources go further. In many countries this has led to the design of new ways to organise and allocate funds to health services.

Change has created a new environment: health care organisations have increasingly become managed rather than being led by professional staff as in the past; health service workforces have had to adapt rapidly to ever-changing roles and responsibilities; and, traditional notions of clinical freedom have been reassessed as responsibilities at the bedside and to the boardroom have become intertwined. This process of change has inevitably been accompanied by tensions as well as perceived benefits as traditional attitudes and practices have been challenged.

This chapter describes the factors which influence the demand for health services, the historical development of the National Health Service, its present structure, and the way in which it functions.

Historical Perspective

The Poor Law

The development of services for the sick, aged and infirm in Britain is inextricably linked to the attitudes of society towards the poor at various points in history for it is often the case that sickness and old age are states which coexist with poverty.

Much of the responsibility for the poor, aged and sick in medieval Britain fell on the church and on parishes, which often levied local taxes to assist them in providing relief. With the dissolution of the monasteries and religious fraternities by Henry VIII, considerable hardship was created, leaving large numbers of elderly and sick people with no means of support. Many individual items of legislation passed during the reign of Elizabeth I were rationalised in 1601 with the passage of the Elizabethan Poor Law (most commonly referred to as the 'Old Poor Law'). Under this law the 'impotent poor' (for example, the old or sick) were to be cared for in poorhouses or almshouses, whilst the able-bodied paupers were provided with work in houses of correction. Much of the responsibility for the administration of the Old Poor Law rested with individual local parishes in the form of parish overseers. Whilst tyranny undoubtedly existed, there were also many examples of caring parishes. Dissatisfaction with the Old Poor Law mounted for several reasons.

Firstly, and at the simplest level, the law was proving an increasingly costly exercise. The system of 'outdoor relief' was becoming widespread in many parishes. It proved simpler to administer payments in cash or kind to the poor, but because of the economic problems of the time, the size of the pool of such needy individuals and their families had grown. Secondly, some critics considered that the regimes in houses of correction were too comfortable for their inmates. This climate of opinion led ultimately to the establishment of a Royal Commission of Inquiry into the Poor Law and the subsequent Poor Law Amendment Act 1834 (the 'New Poor Law'). Many commentators regard this resulting legislation as being strongly aligned to the Utilitarian philosophy of Jeremy Bentham (1748–1832), and his follower Edwin Chadwick (1800–1890), the latter being intimately involved in the framing and implementation of the legislation.

It was believed that the old system of poor relief and the condition of the houses of correction might actually encourage idleness and pauperism. The New Poor Law was intended to abolish pauperism by measures based on deterrence. The system of outdoor relief for the poor was abolished. Those in need of support had to apply for it and were offered the workhouse. The workhouse regime was harsh and austere, deliberately designed to pose a very unattractive prospect for those applying for poor relief. By this central tenet of 'less eligibility' (the person receiving poor relief could not be better off than the worst-paid independent worker) it was reasoned that only those who were truly needy would accept poor relief in the form of the workhouse.

Under the New Poor Law, responsibility was taken out of the hands of individual parishes, which were grouped together as Poor Law Unions (administered by Boards of Guardians), and placed under the control of a central body headed by three Poor Law Commissioners, the aim being to introduce a uniform process of administration. Although separate provision was laid down for the sick and aged, in practice few Unions allowed themselves the expensive luxury of separate workhouses and in many mixed workhouses the able-bodied pauper rubbed shoulders with the sick, the old and infirm, children and the mentally handicapped.

Gradually, many workhouses set aside annexes or 'wards' for the care of the sick pauper. In a few, individual workhouse infirmaries were to be found and the rudiments of a domiciliary service for the sick poor were also present. Standards within such premises were, however, pitifully inadequate, with overcrowding and insanitary conditions prevailing. 'Nursing' was carried out by other inmates. Moreover, the crux of the problem was still that the law implied that poverty was a result of idleness or waywardness on the part of the individual. Florence Nightingale commented that these civilian hospitals were just as bad as, or worse than, the squalid military hospitals which she so strongly condemned in the Crimean War. Towards the end of the century, conditions had become so appalling that Parliament authorised the building of separate infirmaries with trained medical and nursing staff.

The Local Authority Hospitals

In addition to the Poor Law medical service, the major local authorities (County and County Borough Councils) provided a separate publicly owned system of hospitals which had its origins in the isolation hospitals for infectious diseases and asylums for the mentally ill and handicapped. However, in many regions of the country in the early part of the present century, local authority hospitals were also treating other, more general illnesses. Following the transfer of the powers and responsibilities of the Poor Law to local government by a further Act of Parliament in 1929, the local authorities also took control of and administered the Poor Law infirmaries, thus creating some degree of unity. The local authority hospitals fell mainly under the jurisdiction of the Medical Officer of Health who delegated his responsibility in each hospital to a Medical Superintendent.

Voluntary Hospitals

A small number of hospitals had been provided from earliest times by ecclesiastical bodies and some have survived to this day (e.g., St Thomas's Hospital in London). However, the main alternative to the publicly owned hospital system was the voluntary hospital movement, which sprang up in the middle of the eighteenth century and was run by independent organisations obtaining their finance from donations, charitable funds and subscriptions. Mostly they were established to cater for the deserving poor, the undeserving poor continuing to look to their local poor house for care. Over time, great variation occurred in the size and function of the voluntary hospitals as they become the main focus for medical practice. In general they provided a standard of care which was far above that provided by the State and indeed served as a model which the latter strove to attain. Each voluntary hospital had its own committee of governors and medical care was provided by visiting physicians and surgeons who were almost always in private practice and provided their services to the voluntary hospitals free of charge but the prestige of a hospital affiliation enabled them to build up their practices.

Although the system was variable, patients who could afford to pay were often asked to do so whilst others provided themselves with some security for illness by making weekly payments to one of the hospital contributory schemes. As the involvement of the medical profession in the voluntary hospitals grew with the flourishing of teaching and research, so their function began to alter. Admission policies were selective, with an emphasis on patients with illnesses which were of a short-term or acute nature, thus ensuring a rapid turnover, or those with diseases which were of particular interest. There was little place for the elderly or chronically sick. It was this emphasis on acute medicine which was partly responsible for the extension in the last century of the State-owned hospital service to fill the gap.

The Emergency Medical Service

As part of the preparation for the anticipated receipt of military and civilian casualties during World War II, a hospital service was created in 1938 to be administered directly by the Ministry of Health. The number of beds in some hospitals was increased, temporary buildings were erected or premises extended, and some of the former poor law institutions were renovated or upgraded. Some centres were created with specialist facilities; for example, rehabilitation, plastic surgery and neurosurgery, and the Ministry laid down what the functions of the existing hospitals should be on a regional basis.

The Emergency Medical Service is of considerable importance in the development of the health service. Although its influence was short, in the context of the long period of evolution of the service it represented a watershed for the hospital service. It resulted in the review and classification of all hospitals provided by the wide variety of agencies and brought their administration for the first time under a central authority in the shape of the Ministry of Health. This laid the foundation for the unified hospital service when the National Health Service came into being shortly after the war had ended.

Primary Care

Medical services for those who did not receive care in hospital was slower to evolve. Under the Poor Law, domiciliary care or treatment by the Poor Law Medical Officer existed in some parts of the country, but the standard was very variable and care was generally very basic. Other forms of care were provided by a variety of other agencies, such as free dispensaries run on charitable lines or outpatient departments within voluntary hospitals. Other developments during the nineteenth century provided private panel systems or clubs where, by paying a retention fee, the patient could claim the services of a doctor in time of need. Friendly societies and a few industries operated similar schemes.

The National Health Insurance Act 1911 (the Lloyd George Act) was the most influential development in primary care. The scheme was directed at relieving hardship amongst working men during periods of illness. When it was introduced in 1912, it was confined to workers earning less than £160 per year and was based on contributions from the employee, the employer and the State. It entitled the insured man to choose his own general practitioner from a local panel of doctors (hence the term 'panel system') and to secure treatment (including prescribed drugs) and other consultations free of charge on demand. The exclusion of dependants' wives and children from the scheme, together with the denial of the right of insured people to receive free hospital inpatient care, meant that considerable hardship was left untouched. Moreover, a sizeable proportion of the population still paid a fee to their general practitioner for advice or treatment.

This system continued (although the eligibility was subsequently increased) until the National Health Service was established in 1948. Until then, general practitioner services were administered throughout the country by a network of insurance committees responsible for making available these services for all insured people in their locality, and representing almost half of the population.

Other Local Authority Services

The new industrial towns, which were the products of the industrial revolution, forced the consideration of health problems on a population or community-wide basis. As a growing proportion of the population came to live in towns and work in factories so, in turn, their circumstances were characterised by scarce and over-crowded housing of a very poor standard, pollution, inadequate sanitation, a contaminated water supply and limited diet. Such conditions were ripe for the infectious diseases to flourish, ravaging the population and taking a high toll in mortality – particularly amongst the young.

Once again the impetus for change was the doctrine of the utilitarian philosopher Jeremy Bentham (1748–1832). The great milestones along the path to reform were the public health reports and legislation in the middle of the nineteenth century, which bore the mark of Edwin Chadwick, this time in the guise of public health reformer, and his champion Thomas Southwood-Smith (1788–1861) who like Chadwick had been Bentham's secretary.

Chadwick promoted 'the sanitary idea' and his efforts led to a Sanitary Commission in 1839 which reported in 1842. The report was a landmark in public health in pointing to the importance of increasing the provision of a pure water supply, effective sanitation, drainage and disposal of sewage and improved standards of housing. A Public Health Act in 1848 followed. It established a new national body, the General Board of Health and led to the establishment of local sanitary authorities. The first Medical Officer of Health was appointed in Liverpool in 1847 and other local authorities soon followed suit.

These were all developments which contributed to the reduction in mortality in the last quarter of the nineteenth century and the early twentieth century. When the National Health Service was established in 1948 public health responsibilities, including the control of the spread of infectious diseases and the environmental hazards, remained a function of local authorities.

Local authorities then turned their attention to personal health services for people in the community, a major feature of their work during the present century. The Poor Law had provided, towards the end of the last century, a form of community service (for example, for expectant mothers and children) but this was patchy and inadequate. During the first 20 years of this century, the health visitor system was developed and maternity and child-welfare clinics were opened. Thus by 1948, the local authorities not only had responsibility for a large part of the hospital service but for a whole range of community services. When the National Health Service was established they continued to be responsible for community services but lost responsibility for hospitals.

The personal social services, which were provided by the local authorities for groups like the elderly, children, the physically and mentally handicapped, also had diverse origins. In a few cases, services arose from voluntary or charitable organisations, in most others from the structure of the Poor Law with its strong orientation towards institutional care. Although local authorities subsequently assumed responsibility for certain services, it was not until the implementation of the National Assistance Act 1948 that they became responsible for providing comprehensive welfare services.

The Welfare State and The National Health Service

In the summer of 1941 the government appointed Sir William (later Lord) Beveridge (1879–1963) to chair a committee of senior civil servants charged with undertaking a survey of existing national schemes of social insurance and allied services and making recommendations. The Beveridge report, published a relatively short time later in December 1942, contained a series of sweeping proposals and recommendations which laid the foundation for the modern welfare state.

Beveridge based his proposals for a compulsory social security scheme on three assumptions: that there would be a policy for the maintenance of employment, a system of children's allowances, and a comprehensive health service.

The basis of the report was enacted by the post-war Labour Government and the subsequent legislation was contained in five main acts:

(1) The Family Allowances Act (1945) provided for cash allowances to the second and subsequent child.

(2) The National Insurance Act (1946) established a comprehensive contributory national insurance scheme.

(3) The National Insurance (Industrial Injuries) Act (1946) made provision for insurance against accidents, injuries and prescribed diseases due to a person's employment.

(4) The National Assistance Act (1948) finally replaced the Poor Law, placing on local authorities the responsibility for the elderly, the handicapped and the homeless, and setting up a scheme for financial assistance on a national basis to those in need.

(5) The National Health Service Act (1946) created a comprehensive health service available to all citizens.

With the commencement of the National Health Service on 5 July 1948, the Minister of Health became statutorily responsible for providing a comprehensive health service for the population of England and Wales. All hospital property, whether it had been in the voluntary or municipal sector, came under the control of the Minister, including all but a small number of privately owned hospitals. Thus, the Minister inherited a wide array of buildings and accommodation with varying origins, traditions, functions and differing levels of upkeep and which were spread unevenly throughout the country. However, the administrative merging of these made it possible to plan a hospital service for a locality, and to rationalise the distribution of, and to make arrangements for, the training of medical, nursing and technical staff.

England was originally divided into 13 regions (four in London and the home counties and nine in the rest of the country) with regional hospital boards whose chairmen and members were appointed by the Minister. A further region, Wessex, was created later to make a total of 14. These regional boards appointed hospital management committees to be responsible for the day-to-day running of individual hospitals or groups of hospitals. Teaching hospitals had separate arrangements, being administered by Boards of Governors appointed by the Minister and responsible directly to him rather than the regional hospital boards.

The National Health Service also provided general medical, general dental, ophthalmic and pharmaceutical services on a contractual basis with local Executive Councils. Thus, with the advent of the National Health Service, primary medical care was also provided free and as a right for all who wished to request it.

Aside from therapeutic services which were based in hospitals or general practice, the National Health Service laid down a range of other services concerned with the health of the population which were delivered mainly by major local authorities (Counties and County Boroughs). This was the only part of the new service which had specific responsibility for the prevention of disease. However, little detail was specified giving considerable scope for innovation by individual local authorities. The authorities discharged their functions through Health Committees whose chief officer was the Medical Officer of Health. In addition to the general responsibility for developing a preventive function, local authorities were charged with providing a range of supportive services. These included a wide variety of 'community' services (such as health visitors, home nurses, domiciliary midwives and home helps) to provide care, support and advice to people in their own homes; a responsibility for the control of infectious diseases including immunisation and vaccination; the care of expectant mothers, infants and young children; the provision of an ambulance service and the provision of health centres.

The last of these, health centres, were seen as a major role for the local authorities at the time but were very slow to get off the ground. As early as 1920 the Dawson Report had recommended that local authorities provide, equip and maintain health centres where groups of doctors and other health care staff could work together. By 1966 only 28 purpose-built group practice premises, housing about 200 general practitioners, had been established.

The first experiments with local authority nursing staff attached to practices occurred in the late 1950s and early 1960s. General practice at this time was experiencing problems. The perception that general practitioners were failed hospital doctors was commonly held. The general practitioner's income was wholly dependent on the number of patients registered with them, and they received no assistance from the government towards the provision of adequate premises or supporting staff. In consequence morale amongst general practitioners was low. Many United Kingdom graduates emigrated to North America.

In 1966, as a result of The Charter for the Family Doctor Service, a new contract for general practitioners introduced major change. A three-part payment system of basic practice allowances, capitation fees and item-of-service payments was supplemented by group practice allowances and incentives for doctors to work in under-doctored areas. Partial reimbursement of the salary costs of practice clerical and nursing staff was instituted, and funds were made available for the building or upgrading of premises.

These steps encouraged a trend towards group practices, the employment of ancillary staff, the imaginative development of premises and an expansion in the range of services offered to patients. Attached district nurses and health visitors developed steadily and practices progressively sought to accommodate these staff in their premises. These positive developments were accompanied by the expansion of vocational training for general practitioners, which became mandatory in 1982, and the establishment of academic departments of general practice in the medical schools.

After a period of 25 years of relative stability, a new General Practitioner contract introduced in 1990 brought about a major shift in emphasis in the following areas: health promotion; systematic chronic disease management; consumer responsiveness; preventive care targets; population surveillance.

To meet the challenges posed by the new contract most practices employed more staff, particularly practice nurses and practice managers, and a large majority became computerised. Practice income, on average, increased. The 1990 contract demonstrated that, with the appropriate financial incentives, practices could respond and develop their services rapidly.

Reorganising The National Health Service: 1974 and After

Between 1948 and 1973 the health service was organised in a so-called 'tripartite' fashion whose three components were:

(a) the hospital service (administered by Regional Hospital Boards and a network of hospital management committees at a local level) and teaching hospitals (administered by Boards of Governors);
(b) the family practitioner services (with contracts held by Executive Councils);
(c) the local authority health services (which operated within the sphere of local government administration to provide public health services in the form of infectious diseases and environmental hazard control, preventive services and community-based services).

A Unified Health Service: 1974

In 1974, the first major administrative reorganisation of the National Health Service took place. Its aim was to provide a better, more sensitive and coordinated public service. Before 1974, it had never been the responsibility, nor had it been within the jurisdiction of any single named authority, to provide a comprehensive health service for the population of a given area. As a result it had not been easy to balance needs and priorities rationally and to plan and provide an integrated service within the resources available. From 1974, local authority health services were brought within the National Health Service along with hospital services. The service was organised geographically around 14 Regional Health Authorities and below them Area Health Authorities.

The Introduction of General Management

A further restructuring took place in 1982. The 1982 restructuring attempted to solve further problems by removing one administrative tier (Area Health Authorities) and devolving from the centre the responsibility for providing the service within available resources. New district health authorities were created and were left to decide on the type of organisational structure most suited to local needs. Before the impact of this 1982 reorganisation could be fully realised, further major changes in the organisation of the service were stimulated by a National Health Service Management Inquiry in 1983. The most noticeable consequence of this, the 'Griffiths Report', was the introduction for the first time, of general managers at various levels within the health service.

Sir Roy Griffiths had criticised the consensus style of administration in the NHS at that time, which gave each member of a team of equal partners (administrator, nurse, doctor and treasurer) in effect a right of veto over decisions; he wondered who could tell a latter-day Florence Nightingale who was in charge of the wards and other services. He recommended that a single general manager should be appointed to each District Health Authority, accountable to the board, responsible for unit general managers at operational level. In this way, there was in theory, for the first time since 1948, a clear line of accountability, with a single nominated individual at each point. In practice, there were considerable tensions, particularly between the new general mangers and the professionals providing services, and the 1980s were marked by a series of clashes over financial targets and service responsiveness.

The Creation of an Internal Market: 1990

The National Health Service and Community Care Act 1990 followed the White Paper 'Working for Patients', the end product of a review of the National Health Service undertaken by the Thatcher Conservative government. This review had been prompted by unwelcome publicity in the winter of 1987 which had focused on two perceived shortcomings:

(1) Incidents of hospitals closing beds, deferring or redirecting admissions or sending doctors on extended leave to limit workload in order to stay within budget, despite continued real increases in health service funding.
(2) The existence of 'perverse incentives', whereby extra workload in the most efficient, effective and sought after hospitals was not matched by extra funding, and these hospitals were the first to have to limit their services.

The 1990 National Health Service reforms introduced a new approach to funding and regulating the delivery of hospital care. The proposals ended the conflicting roles of the then District Health Authorities (DHAs) in which operational involvement in health care provision (in local hospitals) within their geographical boundaries was coupled with serving the needs of the population. The proposals also ended the system of funding which was seen as offering no incentive to hospitals to treat more patients, improve quality, or to provide a wider range of services.

The 1990 reforms introduced a number of new features to the way in which the National Health Service functioned. The principal thrust of the 1990 reforms was to separate responsibility for purchasing health care from its provision. District Health Authorities and General Practice Fundholders became service purchasers, funded according to the health needs of their population. Hospitals and other provider organisations were free to concentrate on improving the quality, effectiveness and efficiency of health care in order to win service contracts, the means of regulating service delivery between purchasers and providers.

- *National Health Service Trusts* (whether hospitals or other providers of services) were created and had their own Trust Boards directly accountable to the Secretary of State and significant freedom in the way they could employ staff and invest in capital infrastructure. Trusts were dependent upon contracts with purchasers for most of their income, keeping services provided in line with the requirements of the populations they served.
- *Fundholding General Practices* were given their own budgets to cover some hospital and community services, prescribing and practice staff in the first part of the 1990s. Later, new organisations were developed (for example, general practitioners pooling their budgets in 'multi-funds' to work together).
- *Changed Health Authority membership* replaced large and cumbersome authorities with streamlined 'boards' based on a more business-like model capable of a sharper and quicker focus on priorities. Additionally, for the first time, chief officers were also board members.
- *New funding arrangements* clarified markedly the previously confused relationship between populations, service workload and resources. For the first time, central funding could be allocated to purchasers on the basis of population size weighted for level of need. From there, funding flowed through service contracts to hospitals and other providers of services according to the amount of work that they were contracted to do (this was often referred to as 'money following the patient'). This arrangement was intended to remove the perverse incentive whereby the hardest working hospitals were the first to use up their fixed allocation and be obliged to cap workloads.

Despite all the reassurances which were given, the public in Britain seemed to hold to the view that these reforms concealed a hidden agenda to privatise the National Health Service. In addition, where problems did occur – as they do from time-to-time in any health service – the media and the public were quick to attribute them to the organisational changes introduced in 1990. Moreover, the managerialism which swept into many public services in the late 1980s and early 1990s was also unpopular with the public. The idea of salaries which were more competitive with the private sector and employee benefits (such as 'company cars') was anathema to a public to whom the National Health Service was a cherished institution sustained by the tax payer. Money not directed towards patient care was readily seen as money squandered.

Looking back on this important period in the history of the NHS it is difficult to assess fully the benefits of the changes. It must be remembered that, at the start of the decade, many other countries were also experimenting with health care system reform. The changes in Britain to separate purchasing from provision of service were in keeping with an international philosophy towards the public sector. Undoubtedly, the discipline of being explicit about the cost and quality of health services was long overdue. However, the central concept of an internal market – bringing the perceived benefits of competition to a publicly funded system, increased bureaucracy and set up significant transaction costs which could only be justified as an indirect cost of service if the overall system led to greater efficiency and drove up quality. The incoming 1997 Labour Government judged that it had not been successful and abolished the internal market replacing the philosophy of competition with one based on partnership and collaboration.

The next section of the chapter deals with the structure and function of the present health service in more detail. The present arrangements reflect changes brought about by the policies of the Labour Government elected in 1997.

The Present Structure and Function of The National Health Service

The Labour Government which came to power in Britain in the summer of 1997 sought to end the experiment with competition within an internal market. Therefore new policies were introduced in the late 1990s with the framework for dismantling the internal market set out in a White Paper: 'The New NHS – Modern and Dependable'.[1] The separation of planning and provision of care was retained, so too was the devolution of management responsibility for running local health care organisations. However, a new emphasis was placed on collaboration and partnerships rather than competition as well as reducing the bureaucracy which had been necessary to support the mechanisms of the previous internal market.

The main elements of the structure and functioning of the NHS created by the modernisation programme, initiated in 1997 and legislated for in 1999 (Figure 4.1) are:

(1) Local planning mechanisms which, through the formulation of a three-year Health Improvement Programme, draw together all relevant parties to establish how health needs will be met and how health will be improved in the population served.

(2) Grouping together of general practitioners and other primary care workers in Primary Care Groups and Trusts to commission services for the local community and where appropriate to deliver services (e.g., primary and community health services, community hospitals).

(3) A greater emphasis on improving the health of communities through public health programmes addressing national and local targets to reduce mortality, increase healthy years of life and narrow inequalities.

(4) A duty of quality placed on all health organisations.

(5) A stronger framework of accountability for performance of local services which is monitored and managed by an executive arm of the central government, Department of Health, the NHS Executive.

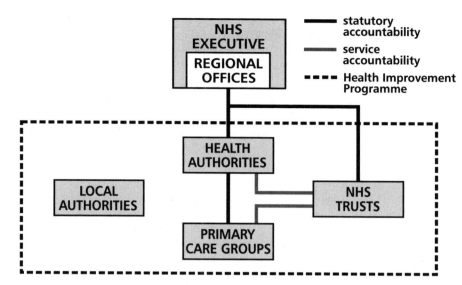

Source: The New NHS: Modern and Dependable. London: The Stationery Office, 1997.

Figure 4.1   Organisational structures.

Whilst there is considerable scope for local decision-making in the provision of health care to the people of Britain, services are delivered within a clear national framework which is underpinned by legislation. This places responsibility for securing the appropriate services in response to the population's needs in the hands of statutorily defined health authorities in England and also provides a clear chain of accountability to the Secretary of State for Health and hence to Parliament.

To raise standards and levels of cost-effectiveness without specific elements of the system of health care which create incentives has proved difficult in the National Health Service over the years. Whilst the inherently high standards of professionalism in the service, the altruism of staff, the setting of fixed budgetary limits, and a focus on management performance have all helped to push the service in this direction, the system of organisation of the health service has not in the past had the momentum to provide major consumer-orientated changes quickly and spontaneously.

The health service now in existence in Britain is probably best described as a managed system in which the perceived benefits of local autonomy and choice have been introduced, whilst aiming to ensure comprehensive coverage of the community's needs and equality of access to services.

The next two sections of the chapter set out in more detail the main structural and managerial elements through which the health service is organised and the processes through which health care is secured and provided.

The Main Elements of Structure and Management of The National Health Service

The Department of Health

The Secretary of State for Health is accountable to Parliament for the National Health Service in England, whilst the Department of Health has a number of major functions, including the management of the National Health Service and the Personal Social Services. The Department of Health is staffed by senior and junior civil servants, which includes professional staff (e.g., the Chief Medical Officer and the Chief Nursing Officer), technical and scientific staff and health service managers.

Although ultimate accountability for the National Health Service at national level rests with the Secretary of State for Health, he or she is assisted by five Ministerial colleagues: two Ministers of State and three Junior Health Ministers, also called Parliamentary Under Secretaries, one of whom is for Public Health.

Whilst the Secretary of State for Health determines policy for the National Health Service, as well as on health matters more generally, he or she receives advice from a range of sources including senior civil servants, health service managers, health professionals, external advisers and expert committees. His or her main source of day-to-day advice on the running of the National Health Service comes from staff in the NHS Executive. A Parliamentary Select Committee on Health also scrutinises and comments on the work of the NHS and addresses other contemporary themes in health and health care.

Different arrangements exist for health services in other United Kingdom countries (see later).

National Health Service Executive

The day-to-day management of the National Health Service in England is in the hands of the Chief Executive of the NHS Executive who is supported by a team of other senior managers (or 'directors' as they are usually called). The size of this group of senior managers and areas of individual responsibility will often change to reflect prevailing priorities in the National Health Service or career progression of the individuals concerned. At any one time, for example, the team is likely to include the Directors of the NHS Regions, a Director of Finance, a Director of Human Resources, a Medical Director, a Director of Nursing and a Director of Research and Development, as well as Directors covering other areas of responsibility.

This team of directors, is formed as a Management Board, the National Health Service Executive, under the leadership and chairmanship of the Chief Executive.

The broad aims of the NHS Executive could be described as:

- To ensure, through the National Health Service and within available resources, significant improvements in the health of the population through the delivery of services providing health promotion, prevention and diagnosis of illness, and high quality cure, care and rehabilitation.
- To ensure that these services are provided effectively, efficiently and economically, in response to identified needs and with regard to the wishes of the patients.
- To ensure that the National Health Service provides the structure and support for its staff satisfactorily to carry out their jobs and develop their careers.

The NHS Executive as the national tier of the service provides Health Ministers (and thus the government) with advice and help in developing policies for the National

Health Service as well as leading the implementation of such policies throughout the service. The NHS Executive also must ensure that the health service delivers its objectives. It is responsible for the strategic management of the NHS.

The role of the NHS Executive can be captured in three main elements: planning (setting direction for the local service), development (helping the local service to fulfil its functions), and control (ensuring that the local service delivers results).

It is helpful also in clarifying the overall purpose of the NHS Executive to do so in the form of a challenge: how does it add value? In any large and complex organisation the role of the headquarters relative to the work performed by the operational organisations at local level is a much discussed subject. The style of such a relationship is all important if local services are not to feel that they are being increasingly interfered with or disempowered.

The NHS Executive seeks to deliver its role by making clear what is expected of the service and how success will be judged, by facilitating the work of local health organisations, by intervening only when things go wrong ('the coach more than the cop'), and by requiring certain information to be supplied for monitoring purposes.

The main interface of the NHS Executive with the health service in England is through its regional offices. These organisations, each staffed by about 130 managerial and professional staff, lead the process of service development and improvement working closely with the local health organisations (health authorities, NHS Trusts, Primary Care Groups and Trusts) within their regions. The Regional Offices of the NHS Executive coordinate the implementation of national policies, manage and monitor performance, encourage and facilitate development, and intervene when problems cannot be resolved at local level.

In addition, the NHS Executive and Department of Health staff will often be in contact with staff at operational level (whether managers, doctors, nurses or other professional staff) through site visits to see at first hand and to learn about service developments and problems.

The management of the health service at national level is also characterised by a great deal of team work involving staff of all disciplines. On any one day, government buildings will contain a substantial number of meetings involving managers from national, regional or local level as well as doctors, nurses and other professional staff. Such meetings will vary in their purpose, format and content but will range from single *ad hoc* events to discuss a particular issue, through working parties considering service programmes, to more permanent advisory committees.

This is an important and democratic part of the management of the service and ensures that there is commitment to national policies and programmes by those working in the field and that action initiated by the NHS Executive is informed by the knowledge and expertise of those closer to the operational service level.

Health Authorities

Below the Department of Health, the next organisational and managerial level of the health service consists of health authorities.

The broad functions of a health authority could be specified as follows:

- Providing strategic leadership for health and health care in their area and ensuring commitment of all organisations to achieving agreed goals and objectives.
- Assessing health need and health status in the local population and ensuring that service response and other activities in their area effectively meet need and improve health status.

- Allocating resources in such a way that, as far as possible, they will achieve maximum health improvement and maximum health care benefit and ensuring financial stability of all health care organisations.
- Monitoring and regulating the commissioning and provision of health care in their area to ensure that local populations have access to a choice of services which are of high quality.

Health authorities are staffed by a team of managerial and professional staff, each of whom is ultimately accountable to the Authority's Chief Executive who in turn is accountable to the health authority's chairman and board of non-executive directors (or 'members' as they are often called). Individual health authorities have taken different approaches to the organisation of their core staffing structure but in most the Director of Public Health (and his or her department) will play the major role in relation to health needs assessment and in advising on aspects of the commissioning process – particularly in relation to achieving public health goals, clinical content and standards of care. Other senior managers and professional staff within the health authority will usually take the lead in other areas of work such as: developing Primary Care Groups; resource allocation and financial management, as well as in monitoring and assessing the impact of the health improvement programme.

In carrying out these functions, health authorities maintain close working relationships with local general practitioners. They seek their views on the services provided and on issues which affect the provision of care – such as likely patterns of referral of patients to hospital. They support and help to develop Primary Care Groups in their area. They must also have strong mechanisms for taking account of the views and wishes of service users and carers.

A strong partnership and joint working is also maintained with the local government authorities and this is particularly important in improving the public health and in providing services for people with long-term care needs (e.g., the elderly and mentally ill). The partnership between health authority and other agencies is particularly important in drawing up the health improvement programme – the planning document which determines what will be done for the local population and how it will be delivered (Figure 4.2).

Aside from their responsibilities to support and develop Primary Care Groups as organisations, health authorities are also responsible for contracting with general medical practitioners, general dental practitioners, ophthalmic opticians and community pharmacists. These various primary care practitioners continue to be paid mainly on a so-called *independent contractor* basis. Health authorities must maintain lists of these contractors and take responsibility for their remuneration. In some parts of the country health authorities have grouped together to establish at 'arms-length' agencies to deliver these duties on their behalf whilst retaining overall accountability for them. Other administrative functions relating to primary care are also the responsibility of health authorities; for example, appraisal of doctors' surgery premises; arranging for improvements to premises; reimbursing doctors for the employment of practice staff and the investigation of complaints.

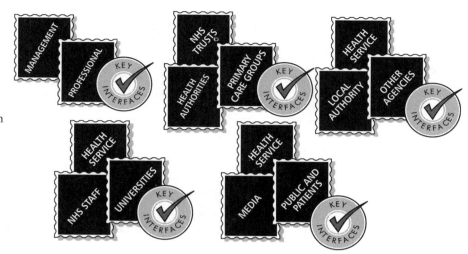

Figure 4.2 Good health care depends on partnerships.

NHS Trusts

Health Authorities and Primary Care Groups negotiate agreements for services with hospitals and other providers of service to secure the volume, range and quality of service which they require.

NHS Trusts are a service entity which had not previously existed, created by the National Health Service and Community Care Act 1990. The purpose of the Trust concept was to create considerable managerial freedom and autonomy for hospitals, community units and other providers of care or services (for example, ambulance services) whilst retaining them under the overall organisational umbrella of the National Health Service.

The managerial team of an NHS Trust is headed by a Chief Executive with a Board of Directors which comprises a non-executive chairman and non-executive directors (appointed by the Secretary of State for Health after open competition) together with executive directors (which must include a Medical Director, Finance Director, and Nurse Director).

NHS Trusts have a number of local freedoms. They are free to determine separate terms and conditions of service and levels of remuneration for their staff; and within certain restrictions, they are permitted to buy and sell land, buildings or other assets.

NHS Trust hospitals participate in local service planning and contribute to the formation of Health Improvement Programmes. They enter into service agreements with health authorities, Primary Care Groups and Trusts and other commissioners of health care, to provide defined services. Usually, the health authority and Primary Care Groups within whose boundary the NHS Trust Hospital is situated will be the largest funder of the Trust's services, but the Trust hospital will often have agreements with other health authorities or Primary Care Groups within a region especially if it provides more specialised services which are not present in every general hospital.

NHS Trusts, particularly those which are hospitals, have a responsibility to maintain a balance of services for patients and to ensure that major investment decisions such as new buildings, equipment or employing new specialist doctors are consistent with priorities in the local Health Improvement Programme.

The Secretary of State for Health retains reserve powers to intervene in a Trust's affairs in the rare circumstances where it may be necessary. Health authorities have a reserve power which they can exercise if it is considered that capital investment decisions or the establishment of senior medical staff posts by a Trust are not in accordance with strategy set out in the Health Improvement Programme.

Private and Voluntary Hospitals

The majority of hospitals and other providers of services in the British health service are within the framework of the National Health Service (usually as NHS Trusts) but a proportion of care and services is provided by hospitals managed by private or not-for-profit organisations. Health authorities and Primary Care Groups may purchase care, through agreements, from providers in the private and voluntary sector, although the principal purchasers of private health care are still the patients themselves either paying directly or through medical insurance plans.

Primary Care Groups and Trusts

The concept of Primary Care Groups was introduced by the new Labour Government in its 1997 White Paper 'The New NHS' as part of its plans to abolish the internal market. The objectives seem to have been:

- to continue – and enhance – the emphasis on general practitioners as commissioners of hospital services on behalf of their patients in their locality, whilst abolishing the contentious general practice fundholder scheme;
- to provide the flexibility to integrate the provision of primary and community care, bringing together primary care services – general practitioners, practice nurses, and other attached staff with community nurses, health visitors and others previously employed by NHS Trusts;
- to devolve decisions on local services whilst freeing Health Authorities to adopt a more strategic role focused on the health of large populations;
- to improve the health of, and address health inequalities in, their locality;
- to develop an integrated approach to both commissioning and provision of health and social services by involving Social Services officers directly on the Boards of Primary Care Groups.

By mid-1999, each Health Authority was given the task of working with general practitioners, Local Authorities and others to establish a framework of Primary Care Groups, each covering a population of around 100,000, with involvement of all general practitioners. In England, 481 Primary Care Groups became operational in April 1999 with populations ranging from 46,000 to 257,000.

Primary Care Groups (PCGs) can operate with different levels of responsibility and it will be possible for PCGs to become Primary Care Trusts (PCTs).

- *Level 1* is a PCG established as a committee of the Health Authority. It holds an actual prescribing budget for its constituent practices, but has responsibility for less than 40% of the PCG unified budget: responsibility for the majority of secondary care commissioning remains with the Health Authority.
- *Level 2* is a PCG with responsibility for at least 40% of the PCG unified budget, rising to at least 60% in the second year at Level 2.
- *Level 3* is a free-standing, legally established PCT responsible for commissioning the majority of services for its population (certain services will continue to require specialised commissioning arrangements).
- *Level 4* is a PCT which both commissions and provides primary and community services. The legislation is enabling and does not restrict the size, scale or capacity of PCTs. It is possible, for example, to use the new operational flexi-

bilities to allow closer working with Local Authorities and to provide personal medical and dental services under the Primary Care Act.

It is not expected that all Primary Care Groups will want, or be able, to take on responsibility for commissioning all hospital and community health services at once. Each Primary Care Group will be different in organisational terms – in their development, in the skills they have available or their experience of managing complicated commissioning responsibilities. The degree of responsibility for commissioning secondary care services is a matter for each Primary Care Group to determine in conjunction with its Health Authority. This will often depend upon the knowledge, experience and local circumstances within each Primary Care Group. Thus it is a matter of local judgement and agreement as to how fast, how much and with what control commissioning responsibilities shall be delegated.

Structure of The NHS in Wales, Scotland and Northern Ireland

There are differences in Wales, Scotland and Northern Ireland in the administrative structure of the NHS, although many of the principles are the same as in England; however, with devolution of government to elected assemblies the pattern is changing.

Pressures on Health Services

Modern health services face increasing calls on their limited resources. In industrialised nations of the world, the sources of this growth in demand are demographic (particularly the ageing of populations), advances in medical science and technology, greater patient expectation of what health care can do for them, and innovations in service delivery (Figure 4.3).

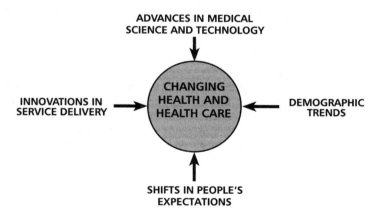

Figure 4.3 The main factors influencing change.

For any individual health care organisation, such as a hospital, the consequences of rapid growth in demand are enormous. It results in pressure to balance three conflicting imperatives: managing within a financial budget, meeting the needs of patients who present as emergencies, and maintaining high standards of care for all patients – in particular, keeping response-times short (Figure 4.4).

Figure 4.4 The *bulging triangle*: implications for a hospital of increasing demand.

If the three are not met, one element of the triad will be sacrificed (in Figure 4.4 one side of the triangle will burst open). For example, a massive surge of emergency admissions during the winter months as large numbers of people are admitted with severe respiratory illnesses can mean planned admissions being cancelled. Meeting the needs of emergency admissions and continuing to keep waiting times short for patients requiring planned surgery, means ensuring that the budget will not be over-spent through loss of financial discipline.

These issues can be viewed positively as well as negatively. To some extent the increased demand for health services is a reflection of success. Some diseases can be treated more effectively if diagnosed earlier, a new service innovation immediately generates its own demand (patients are able to be treated who could not be before), and patients expect more from the service.

Nevertheless, most health services during the 1980s and 1990s faced a series of financial crises as health service costs increased rapidly. Health service inflation has historically risen faster than general inflation, mainly because of price rises in drugs and equipment.

Key Functional Processes of Health Service Delivery

The overall purpose of health services in Britain is to improve the health of the popu-lation; to provide advice, assessment and treatment for patients, and to enhance the quality of life for those with special and long-term care needs (for example, the elderly, the mentally ill, the disabled and those with chronic diseases). There is also a responsibility to deliver services efficiently and, where appropriate, to address prob-lems of inequity (Figure 4.5).

The process begins with the formulation of strategic goals and aims at national and local level and ends with a process through which health authorities in an area come together with the Local Authority and other agencies to implement changes agreed in these strategies.

Figure 4.5 Main functions of the health service.

Setting Policy and Strategy

The direction for the improvement of health and development of health care through the activities of the health service is set at a number of levels. National policy is formulated by Ministers and the National Health Service Executive drawing widely on expert advice and information. One of the most difficult issues is how to set priorities. Although, in theory, a number of areas of policy will have particular emphasis and importance, the reality is that the health service has to cope with multiple priorities and ensure progress on almost all of them. This is in contrast to the approach taken in private sector business where good management practice would see a company concentrating on a relatively small number of clearly expressed goals.

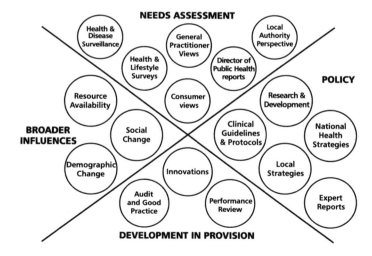

Figure 4.6 Input to the planning process.

In the health service, the flow of new ideas, information, policy guidance and new initiatives is constant and one of the major challenges is to channel this stream into manageable courses to inform and stimulate health care development.

The range of potential inputs to this planning process is very diverse and encompasses information arising from health needs assessment, developments in provision, policy and strategy as well as wider influences such as the availability of resources, demographic and social change (Figure 4.6). There is a need to evaluate information, some of which is quite technical. It is important, for example, to draw in the research and development perspective to ensure that a proper evaluation is undertaken of new technologies and interventions which are claimed to be beneficial to patients or to the population. Policy and strategy set at national level is developed and extended within Health Improvement Programmes which are formulated and implemented at local level through a process of service agreements and through the establishment of health programmes.

Business Planning

Business planning is a management process common to all organisations within the health service. It is often the process through which strategy is turned into action; it is the bridge between setting strategy and negotiating and forming service agreements. It is a continuous process rather than a discrete exercise.

The boards of Health Authorities and NHS Trusts set objectives and goals for the organisation, identify likely available resources, assess the organisation's strengths and weaknesses as well as opportunities for, and threats to, growth and development (commonly known as SWOT analysis).

Contributions to the business planning process also come from the operational level of service. These involve identifying options for change in management and operational practices and in investment requirements. They also involve evaluating current service levels, comparing the performance of other organisations ('benchmarking') and expressing the aspirations and requirements of the different functions within the organisation. In the case of hospitals, these will be the clinical services, the operational support services such as catering, and portering as well as the general management functions.

The crux of business planning is the bringing together of these two processes and producing a business plan which sets the direction for the coming year. The National Health Service is no different from any commercial business environment in that it is not possible to plan accurately for *exactly* what will happen in the year ahead. The business plan must therefore consider the implications of all likely situations which may arise during the course of the year. Financial planning is a key element of the business plan. The costs of action plans and programmes can usually be forecast with a reasonable degree of accuracy but the organisation also needs to make provision for potential financial pressures which cannot be foreseen. This is called risk assessment and contingency planning.

The business plan document is a series of objectives and goals supported by specific programmes or action plans as the means to achieve them. The programmes and plans are prioritised and matched to likely available resources. Precise timescales are set for implementation. The plan will also identify the lead person in the organisation responsible for the implementation of each action. However, producing the business plan document is not the end of the business-planning process. The document provides the benchmark against which the organisation's performance is measured and evaluated and this review must be continuous if the business-planning process is to be effective.

Service Agreements

The service agreement is the means through which the commissioner of care (health authority, or Primary Care Group or Trust) secures a particular level and quality of services from hospitals or other providers of care for its population. It replaced the former system of contracting.

Patients who present to hospital as emergencies, either through referral by their general practitioner, by presenting themselves to an Accident and Emergency department, after calling an ambulance or by telephoning NHS Direct, may require any element of the possible range of help which hospital-based specialist services are capable of providing. This may include specialist opinion, investigation, therapy with drugs or other measures including operative intervention.

The majority of the non-emergency demand will arise from clinical workload generated by general practitioners referring patients following consultations. Thus, depending on the clinical specialty concerned, a relatively large proportion of the elective work of the hospital service will involve providing specialist assessment or an opinion (usually on an outpatient basis) on patients referred by a general practitioner. Such patients may require further investigation or treatment by hospital-based specialist services but many will be referred back to their general practitioner with advice on further management of their problem.

A group of patients, in addition to baseline investigation, will require more complex or advanced forms of investigation before their problem is defined. They may require further specialist intervention to resolve or alleviate their problem (provided either on an inpatient or outpatient basis) or they may again be referred back to the care of their general practitioner with advice only on treatment.

A further group of patients at any one time will have their problem defined as a need for intervention by specialist services – either in the form of an operation, another type of procedure or some kind of non-operative treatment. Some will have the condition or treatment monitored, others will have further specialist interventions, either in response to changes in their health or at predetermined times as part of their overall clinical management plan.

It is not possible within this diversity of patient's clinical problems (and the consequent variation in care requirements and resource consumption) to accurately predict (in advance) the numbers who will require particular programmes of care.

Service agreements are therefore concerned with covering eventualities and they can be framed to do so in a number of ways ranging from a broad catch-all approach to a more specific basis for some groups of patients or some treatments. Service agreements are set following discussion and negotiation between commissioner of services and the hospital or other provider and should be seen as part of continuing contact between the two, in the context of the Health Improvement Programme.

Health Improvement Programmes

The central plank of the 1997 changes to the NHS was the requirement for all relevant participants in a locality to contribute to the production of a health improvement programme. Health Authorities are charged with drawing-up these plans, with full participation of the relevant Primary Care Groups and Primary Care Trusts, NHS Trusts and Local Authorities and other local agencies. Improvements to health are better achieved by combining the work of all agencies whose activities have a health-improving aspect. Health Improvement Programmes specify the local health priorities in the context of national policies and local requirements, and the key service changes and developments resulting. Health Improvement Programmes must be approved by each of the participants in the process, and form the framework within which the annual operational plans of the NHS bodies are prepared: specifying levels and changes of staffing, revenue and any capital investment required.

This approach may have particular benefits in the improvement of health where, for example, the aim might be to reduce mortality from coronary heart disease or stroke or to reduce levels of teenage pregnancy. Health authorities lead the process of designing health programmes to achieve the desired change, but with the full participation of primary care bodies, NHS Trusts and the Local Authority. Programmes may involve health education campaigns through local media, counselling of high-risk individuals or working with non-health service bodies to create more opportunities for healthier leisure pursuits. Approaches to the promotion of health are described in detail in Chapter 3.

Evaluation and Monitoring

The process of evaluation and monitoring of health services should be a continuous one. The basis for it is something which should be agreed before implementing service contracts or health programmes. The lessons learned from the evaluation process can be used to inform the next year's decisions about service development and investment of resources.

Health Action Zones

Another concept introduced by the Labour Government's NHS White Paper was that of Health Action Zones. By 1999 some 30 Health Authorities in England were part of a Zone and thus eligible to access significant additional resources to pursue the Zone's aims and objectives.

Health Action Zones are a way of Health Authorities, Primary Care Groups and NHS Trusts working in partnership with other government departments, local authorities, the voluntary sector and the private sector to devise innovative ways to improve the population's health. The government invited Zones to identify ways in which regulations could be loosened (and other barriers to collaborative and partnership working broken down) to enable new, innovative solutions to long-standing health problems to be tried. Zone status was granted for a seven-year period.

NHS Direct

NHS Direct was introduced in the late 1990s. It is a nurse-led telephone helpline service to respond to public enquiries on a variety of health matters and acts as a gateway into all local health services. The service provides professional advice, 24 hours a day, 365 days a year. In December 1999 it covered 32 million people in England (65% of the country) with the intention that the service will cover the whole country by the end of the year 2000. The intention is that the service should be expanded to provide a range of health information and services to help people maintain their health, to know how to deal with common ailments as well as providing advice on how to act on symptoms and signs or access services.

Healthy Living Centres

The concept of a Healthy Living Centre was launched at the end of the 1990s from National Lottery Funds. The scheme is managed by a so-called New Opportunities

Fund. The overall target of the initiative is to commit funds to establish or develop centres accessible to around 20% of the population of the United Kingdom by 2002. The aim of the initiative is to target areas containing the most deprived sections of the population in order to reduce health inequalities and improve the health of the worst-off in society. There is no blueprint for projects. The initiative will be flexible enough to allow for innovative proposals and the different needs of different communities with key players locally working in partnership. Some of the projects which may be funded include: health screening services, reproductive health groups, food cooperatives, employment, training and skills schemes, anticrime and community safety programmes, credit unions, cafes, physical activity programmes, dietary advice, arts programmes, stress management activities, parenting classes, counselling, complementary therapy, creches and childcare facilities, smoking cessation classes, drug prevention programmes, community gardening, prenatal and postnatal groups, community music, exercise classes, environmental initiatives, general practitioner referral schemes, and access and transport schemes.

Quality of Health Care

In a modern, consumer-oriented society one of the cornerstones of the process of supplying goods and services is an emphasis on quality. In turn, one of the principal stimuli in a market economy for improving quality and raising standards is competition amongst suppliers and providers to produce a better product or service as economically as possible, and which meets the expressed needs or wishes of the purchaser. The question of quality and its improvement within a publicly funded health care system cannot be viewed quite in this way.

In the early years of the NHS there was no formal and comprehensive approach to quality assessment and improvement. Much faith was placed in the fact that if standards of professional training and practice were high then they would guarantee that the practitioner delivering the service will do so at a uniformly high quality. Over time, it has become recognized that the complexity of defining and measuring quality in the health-care field is much greater than in many other sectors (for example, industry). This has been an impediment to developing a formal quality framework in health service provision. Moreover, the approach to assessing and improving quality can be potentially very threatening to professional staff, such as doctors and nurses, particularly if it is felt that health service managers may also wish to become involved in discussions about the quality of the services they provide. In the past, this was sometimes a barrier to progress.

By the late 1990s the climate had changed and there is now a widespread acceptance that quality and its improvement should be a central component of all health services. This section of the chapter describes some of the key themes underlying the approach to quality in health care and gives an account of the main mechanisms through which quality of care can be influenced.

Concepts and Definitions of Quality

The development of conceptual frameworks to define quality of health care has spawned a major literature on the subject in biomedical and health services journals – particularly since the 1970s.

Structure, Process, Outcome

One of the most important and widely-respected classifications of quality in health care is that originally propounded by the North American Avedis Donabedian[2] in which there are three aspects:

- *Structure* – one aspect of assessing the quality of health care is to examine the amount and nature of facilities and staff available. Examples of such *structural* measures would be: hospital beds per thousand population, and the number of senior doctors per thousand population. The structural aspects of quality in health care are often used in making comparisons between health services in different parts of a country or in international comparisons. Thus, variation may be found between services in the number of surgeons per head of population or in the number of ophthalmology out-patient clinics available to different populations.

  Such differences in the structural aspects of health care quality can be useful in initiating discussions about the adequacy of health care facilities available to different populations. They can also be valuable in stimulating change or improvement where, for example, levels of staff or facilities are very low compared to those which are agreed as being required to operate an effective service.

  The main problem with relying on structural measures to assess how 'good' or 'bad' a health service is, is the fact that there is seldom adequate evidence to demonstrate what levels of facilities or staff are required to produce good results for particular types of patient care. It by no means follows, for example, that one service with a higher number of surgeons per head of population than a neighbouring service will yield better results for hernia repair operations (low in-hospital complication rates and low long-term recurrence rates).

  Thus, whilst structural measures are still an important aspect of assessing the quality of health care, they are of limited value when taken alone and are best regarded as only one part of an overall concept which also embraces process and outcome measures.

- *Process* – a second attribute of quality is concerned with what is done for and to a patient, or group of patients, and how well it is done. Assessment of the quality of care based on the *process* approach can be wide-ranging. For example, the evaluation of a programme for control of high blood pressure (hypertension) might involve: establishing how adequately the population at risk of developing hypertension had been identified; how thoroughly diagnostic criteria had been determined; how valid and accurate were the blood pressure readings which were taken; how other associated medical conditions were detected and managed; whether agreed treatment protocols were being followed; whether patients were complying with treatment regimes; what proportion of patients who had been diagnosed as hypertensive had their blood pressure stabilised at agreed levels; how often patients were followed-up, and how adequate were their subsequent clinical assessments.

  All these are examples of *processes* of care which can be used as a basis for assessing aspects of the quality of clinical services given to hypertensive patients. In practice, assessing quality in this way requires establishing agreed standards of good practice in the process of care concerned against which the actual service can be compared and hence assessed. Whilst the process approach adds much greater depth to the assessment of quality than the structural approach, it cannot be viewed in isolation from it nor from the third attribute, outcome measurement.

- *Outcome* – the final attribute of quality in the Donabedian triad is the outcome of the health care episode for the patient. Does she or he get better? Are there any clinical complications? Is he or she satisfied with the care delivered? Does he or she survive the illness or disease occurrence?

Outcome is the final arbiter of the quality of care provided. There are numerous possible approaches to defining outcomes of health care or of a health service's activity.

One approach which is often quoted and easily remembered is based on the *five D's: death, disease, disability, discomfort* and *dissatisfaction*. Thus, for example, assessment of the outcome of care for a man admitted to hospital as an emergency for treatment of a ruptured aortic aneurysm might take account of whether he survived (*death*); whether the aneurysm was technically well-corrected surgically (*disease*); whether he returned to 'normal' physical, psychological and social functioning after discharge from hospital (*disability*); whether he remained free of residual pain (*discomfort*), and whether the interpersonal as well as the technical aspects of the nursing and medical care and the environment in which it was provided were pleasing to him (*dissatisfaction*).

This and similar classifications of outcomes are probably best used for illustrative purposes because most are either too simplistic or too detailed to be generally applicable. A great deal of work has been undertaken in defining appropriate outcomes for use in clinical trials or service evaluations of particular health problems or therapies.

Table 4.1 Maxwell's dimensions of quality

- Access to services
- Relevance to need (for the whole community)
- Effectiveness (for individual patient)
- Equity (fairness)
- Social acceptability
- Efficiency and economy

Source: Maxwell RJ. BMJ, 1984; 288:1471–1472.

An important issue in considering outcome as an aspect of health care quality is to remember that there is a *population* and a *patient care dimension*. A conceptualisation of health care quality in the mid-1980s by Maxwell captures this wider scope and incorporates the population dimension (Table 4.1). Like the Donabedian formulation its principal use has been in shaping debate and improving strategies rather than in routine management and evaluation of services.

The practical application of outcome assessment of the quality of health services, to day-to-day health service management, whether at the population or at individual patient care level, is still in its infancy. Partly, this is because of the virtual absence of routinely available data through which outcome can be assessed. This situation is rapidly changing as greater emphasis is being placed on the importance of the outcome dimension in assessing the quality of care and finding ways of using more widely the specific outcome measures which have been developed.

The Donabedian classification has been dealt with at length because it remains the most enduring and widely-respected conceptual approach through which the quality of health care can be defined and assessed. It is important, however, to remember that these concepts are closely interrelated as well as dynamic. Determining the way in which health facilities (*structural*) are used (*processes*) to produce the end result of care for the patient (*outcome*) is the real route to improving the quality of care.

Technical, Interpersonal, Amenities

Donabedian has also pointed out that health care has different attributes upon which judgements about quality can be made. The health professional's definition of high quality care would probably rely heavily on *technical* considerations (for example, how well the therapeutic or investigational aspects of the care were delivered). On the other hand, many patients would place a high or low value on the care they receive based on the *interpersonal* or *amenity* attributes of their care (for example, kindness, courtesy, explanation, information-giving and standards of lighting, heating, food, toilet and washing facilities).

All are important quality considerations and it cannot be assumed that high quality in one attribute automatically means high quality in the others. For example, a surgeon may be excellent in the domains of communication and empathy with his patients but obtain less satisfactory surgical results than a colleague who is a masterly technical surgeon but treats his patients in an impersonal manner.

Clinical Effectiveness, Appropriateness, Efficacy

Another way in which quality can be viewed is the extent to which the clinical interventions carried out by health professionals deliver good outcomes of care. The main concepts involved here are: efficacy, appropriateness and effectiveness (Table 4.2).

Table 4.2   Aspects of quality of a clinical intervention

Aspect	Meaning	In other words
Efficacy	The ability of an intervention to produce the desired outcome under ideal conditions (i.e., in the environment of a clinical trial)	What is the right thing to do?
Appropriateness	The application of the most effective intervention from the range of alternatives available to the particular patient's circumstances	Is the right thing being done to the right people at the right time?
Effectiveness	The performance of an intervention in producing the desired outcome in an ordinary service setting	Is the right thing being done, right?

It is important to distinguish efficacy from effectiveness because the two terms are often confused or misused. Efficacy is whether the intervention (e.g., drug or operation) delivers a particular outcome (e.g., restoration of lost function, relief of pain, five-year survival) under ideal conditions. For example, what was the efficacy of the intervention when it was first subjected to research evaluation in a randomised controlled trial? Effectiveness, on the other, hand assesses how well the intervention yields the desired outcome under everyday circumstances – such as a busy hospital service.

Appropriateness is whether the intervention which has been applied to a particular clinical situation is the right one. It is often reflected in under- or overuse of a particular treatment – patients not receiving (say) an operation when they would have benefitted from it, whilst others are receiving the operation where they will not derive improved outcome from it.

The Philosophy of Total Quality Management (TQM)

The experience of the commercial sector, both industrial and service, can inform strategies for quality improvement and quality management in health care. This wider quality debate is most clearly apparent in the recent history of North American and Japanese manufacturing industry. It is not so long since the Japanese were renowned for producing cheap, poor quality merchandise, and American industry predominated in such areas as camera production, stereo and hi-fi equipment manufacture. Today, the Japanese have gained a major share of the North American and, indeed, world markets in consumer goods. They now produce and export merchandise which competes with alternatives on quality – not simply price.

The reason for this dramatic turnaround in the competitiveness and market position of Japanese industry is widely recognized as being grounded in the adoption of relatively simple theories of quality improvement. Ironically, the theorists who have been credited with stimulating this process in Japan are American – particularly W Edwards Deming[3] and Joseph M Juran.[4]

In the industrial field and in the service industries, this approach is based on the philosophy that by continually improving the processes of production (or the delivery of service) expensive consequences such as scrapping defective products, expenditure on warranty agreements and remanufacturing will be avoided. By concentrating on quality productivity will improve. It is called Total Quality Management (TQM) or Continuously Quality Improvement (CQI).

The traditional approach to quality control in industry was initially based upon the concept of inspection to detect defects. This has a number of disadvantages. Firstly, and most importantly, it does not gain commitment of the whole workforce to improving quality. Instead, the issue is seen as the concern of a separate quality department or inspector. This instills in the workforce a feeling that they are not being trusted and, even worse, creates the situation in which they will only achieve a high standard of work when being watched or inspected. Secondly, when the process of manufacture is not properly designed, and the raw material inadequate, then no amount of inspection will remedy the problem. This approach inspects out poor quality, rather than building in good quality to the systems of management and production.

The TQM or CQI approach seeks to reduce the importance of inspection as a quality tool and instead to involve the whole workforce, using to the full, their knowledge and expertise of the process of manufacture constantly to improve it so that the defects, errors and poor products are eliminated.

The overall benefit for a company which is engaged effectively in TQM or CQI is success of its business. Reduction in errors and defects not only increases quality, it reduces costs (from remanufacture, replacement goods, inspection), improves profitability and, by satisfying customers, attracts more of the market share.

Whilst a key element of TQM or CQI is reducing unnecessary variation in the production process, another is the emphasis on the customer and his or her wishes and expectations. This customer ethos extends not just to the external customer but also to internal customers within the organisation. Indeed, in TQM or CQI terms, the very definition of quality of the product or service relies heavily on the customer's views of what constitute good or bad quality.

The potential applications of TQM or CQI to the health care field are not yet fully apparent such that large numbers of practical examples cannot be cited. However, perhaps one example at this stage will illustrate the potential benefits of quality improvement to a health service. A complication of hospital care, particularly in the elderly, is that of pressure (or 'bed') sores.

In this example, good quality care would be a hospital inpatient stay for an elderly person in which he or she was free of pressure sores. An approach in which all nurses on the ward discussed, planned and reviewed the process of nursing care so that pressure sores were eliminated would have advantages over an approach in which a matronly figure inspected patients for evidence of pressure sores for which individual nurses could then be blamed for failing in their duty.

The former, TQM-based, approach would reduce or eliminate pressure sores (improve quality of care); reduce costs (length of stay reduced, no need for skin grafts or other treatment); increase productivity (by enabling other patients to be admitted and treated), and improve market share (Primary Care Groups would be more likely to commission services from a hospital with a reputation for a low incidence of pressure sores).

Thus, there are parallels between TQM or CQI in the business sector and in health care. In this example, the health service's aim of eliminating pressure sores could be seen as analogous to a Japanese electronic company in which concentration on improving the processes of production of television sets led to products in line with customer requirements (improved quality); reduced costs (fewer defects resulting in re-work, scrapping, payment of warranty agreements); increased productivity (less workforce time devoted to remanufacture or correcting defects), and increased market share (more satisfied customers).

The introduction of TQM or CQI is not simply a matter of exposing and adopting the techniques, it requires major organisation-wide change of the culture and orientation. It places major responsibilities on senior management to create the kind of participative environment in which all members of the organisation are valued, their skills and efforts rewarded, and an environment in which there is a recognition that employees generally want to do their best and should be comprehensively and actively involved in the process of quality improvement.

One of the organisational approaches borrowed from private sector experience, business-school teaching and the many management gurus who have written inspirational texts, is that of restructuring. The concept of making an organisation 'fit for purpose' (including delivering quality strategies) has led to 're-engineering', 'downsizing', 'right-sizing' and a variety of other methods of reshaping organisations. Whilst these have often been adopted enthusiastically by the senior management of health care organisations, they have also been less popular with staff. Many health professionals are organised in fairly traditional hierarchies and practitioners enjoy considerable autonomy in the delivery of their role. Sudden and dramatic reorganisations threaten job security and require entirely new models of working. They are sometimes less successful in developing the health care organisation than more subtle and low-key ways in which health care professionals are drawn into the management process.

Many different approaches have been advocated to create a quality organisation. They have important common features which have been shown to be successful (Table 4.3) including that the organisation should be well-led, have good systems in place, listen to and be supportive to staff and create a positive culture for quality improvement.

Table 4.3   Quality management: an organisational philosophy

- Leadership from the top
- Empowerment of staff
- Teamwork
- Prevention (rather than correction) of adverse outcomes
- Analysing, simplifying and improving processes
- Strong customer focus

Quality Improvement: Approaches and Influences

A wide range of ways exist which can bring about improvements in the quality of health care provided and some of these are described in this section.

Quality Improvement Through the Health Care System

In a health care system, such as the National Health Service, in which there is a framework for different kinds of health care organisations to operate and interact with each other, there are forces which can influence quality.

Firstly, general practitioners' referral patterns of patients to particular hospitals and the NHS Trusts, with which Primary Care Groups place service agreements, will be based upon experience. Thus, for example, poor experience of patients with an obstetric service (such as lack of attentiveness of staff or a high perinatal mortality rate) should lead those funding the service to negotiate improvements in the quality of service from the hospital concerned. If this does not then take place, the ultimate sanction is that work will be placed with another hospital which is able to provide the quality of service required. Secondly, service agreements enable the opportunity to make explicit requirements for the quality of service to be provided. This, then, is a further stimulus for improving quality within in the health care system.

Evidence-based Practice

Every day, throughout each health service in the world, hundreds of thousands of decisions are taken by doctors, nurses and other health professionals during the diagnosis and treatment of illness. No systematic approach to improving quality of health care can afford to overlook the importance of clinical decision-making.

For many years it has been recognized that there is wide variation in such decision-making. Between different health services internationally, thresholds for surgical intervention in patients with broadly similar clinical problems have been observed to vary greatly. Hysterectomy is one of many examples. Such variation is also seen between different parts of the same country and even different members of the same clinical team.

It has also long been acknowledged that the science and the practice of medicine do not go hand-in-hand in the way that they should. The failure to translate the results of research into practice quickly and effectively has meant that too few patients benefit in the way that they should from medical advances. It is also one of the reasons why there is wide variation in medical practice in many fields of care. This point can be reinforced by an example from obstetrics.

In the early 1970s, research carried out in Canada[5] focused on the babies of women who went into premature labour. Such babies are prone to respiratory problems partly caused by immature lungs. Treatment after delivery with an agent called

Surfactant helps their lung function but they will often also need a period of intensive care. Some will not survive, some will spend a long time in intensive care, some will have permanent disability. The Canadian study showed that if selected women in premature labour were given an injection of corticosteroid before delivery, these problems are significantly reduced.

The benefits of this therapy were clear. It could save lives, reduce disability and produce major savings in the use of intensive care resources and drugs (corticosteroids are very cheap compared to *Surfactant*).

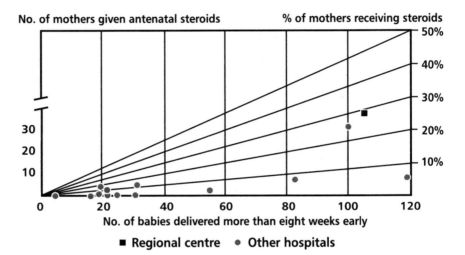

Figure 4.7 Use of steroids to prevent deaths and complications in premature babies: variations amongst maternity units.

The study appeared in a major medical journal at the time, later studies confirmed the finding. The issue would have been widely read and talked about by obstetricians and in professional circles. It did not, however, impact in a major way on practice. The pattern of corticosteroid usage in premature labour ten years later in one part of Britain is shown in Figure 4.7 and it is likely to have been similar in most parts of the country. The practice had only been adopted in a minority of eligible cases. The level of usage was higher in the regional teaching centre, but even there it was greatly suboptimal. Improvements in the region studied then took place.

This and many other examples which could be chosen from other fields of medicine have influenced health services during the 1990s to look critically at how clinical practice could be made more effective.

Particularly influential was work from McMaster University in Ontario, Canada, which formulated the concept of 'evidence-based medicine'. It rapidly became an international movement. The original proponents of evidence-based medicine saw it as a paradigm shift in medical practice rather than merely a change in emphasis. Clinical decisions in the past relied upon intuition, impression and experience. The evidence-based medicine movement saw a future in which many more clinical decisions were based on the findings of valid research relevant to the particular patient's condition (Table 4.4).

Table 4.4   Evidence-based medicine

A process of life-long, self-directed learning in which caring for one's own patients creates the need for clinically-important information about diagnosis, prognosis, therapy, and other clinical and health care issues, and in which clinicians:

- convert these information needs into answerable questions;
- track down, with maximum efficiency, the best evidence with which to answer them (whether from clinical examination, the diagnostic laboratory, the published literature, or other sources);
- critically appraise that evidence for its validity (closeness to the truth) and usefulness (clinical applicability);
- apply the results of this appraisal in their clinical practice;
- evaluate their own performance.

Source: Sackett DL, Straus SE, Richardson WS, Rosenberg WMC, Haynes RB: Evidence-Based Medicine; How to practice and teach EBM, 2nd Edition. Edinburgh: Harcourt Brace, 2000.

Evidence-based practice has not been free of controversy. Generally, health policy-makers and managers have welcomed it enthusiastically as a route to improving quality and reducing clinical variation. Within the health professions it has been embraced – but not in all quarters. Some have seen it as implying the end of clinical judgement based upon experience and the dawn of a mechanistic approach to patients. This is not the aim of evidence-based practice. It sees an important place for traditional skills (the art of medicine) but believes that clinical judgements should have a strong scientific basis as well as an experiential one.

The introduction of an evidence basis to professional practice, and health care more generally, is a complex task involving a number of important steps (Figure 4.8) which are described in the next four sections. It is part of the overall approach to clinical governance (see later).

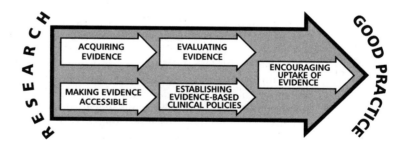

Figure 4.8   Evidence-based practice: key steps and activities.

Producing Information Through Research

There is a need to ensure that, where there is a lack of research evidence in relation to a particular disease problem, its diagnosis and its clinical management, that research is commissioned to fill in the gaps. The NHS has a research and development programme which was established in the early 1990s to address this need, identify priorities and fund research.

Evaluating Research to Produce Evidence

Using the results of research studies to aid a clinical decision is not straightforward either. Say the decision is whether to perform carotid endarterectomy in a woman of

65 years who has suffered a number of transient cerebral ischaemic attacks. How many studies are necessary before the correct use of the intervention is proved? How good are the studies on which current evidence is based? Does the evidence apply to all patients with transient ischaemic attacks or were the original studies limited to selected groups of patients? These are just some of the questions which are raised when the use of information from published research studies is considered. The importance of evaluating the quality of the research evidence is now appreciated. Thus, for example, one clinical trial on the use of therapy may not be enough if it was not big enough to yield a benefit in the treatment compared to the control group (if such a benefit was present). Five clinical trials may not be enough to constitute good evidence if they were all flawed in their methodological design.

Different levels of evidence may be available depending on the state of research in the particular field and it is important to be clear what quality of evidence is being relied upon to formulate a clinical policy (Table 4.5). Part of the task of developing evidence-based practice involves ensuring that health professionals are trained in the evaluation of research evidence. Techniques and training programmes have been devised to enable health professionals to acquire so-called critical appraisal skills.

Table 4.5 Categories of evidence

Ia	– Evidence from meta-analysis of randomised controlled trials
Ib	– Evidence from at least one randomised controlled trial
IIa	– Evidence from at least one controlled study without randomisation
IIb	– Evidence from at least one other type of quasi-experimental study
III	– Evidence from descriptive studies, such as comparative studies, correlation studies and case-control studies
IV	– Evidence from expert committee reports or opinions or clinical experience of respected authorities, or both

Source: Eccles M, Freemantle N, Mason J. BMJ, 1998; 316:1232–1235.

It has also been recognized that clinical staff cannot be expected to undertake this evaluation themselves from scratch prior to taking clinical decisions across a busy service. Increasingly, databases and information systems have been developed to provide topic-based summaries of research evidence which can be made available to health professionals. One of the best established is the Cochrane Collaboration which was started in Oxford, England, and is now an international network. The Cochrane Collaboration prepares, maintains and disseminates systematic reviews of research (usually randomised controlled trials). This process yields summaries of the effectiveness of treatments and other interventions in particular fields of care. In this way, clinicians can obtain information. A systematic review is a type of secondary research which takes the findings of the original (primary) research and carefully assesses them using a strict set of criteria. Often this will mean pooling data from the original studies and reanalysing them: a technique called meta-analysis. It is important to recognize that this form of secondary research is itself open to bias if the methods are wrongly applied or it is undertaken superficially. Just as there can be bad randomised controlled trials there can also be bad systematic reviews and bad meta-analyses.

Making Evidence Available to Clinical Staff

Systems like the Cochrane Collaboration which is well established, rigorous in its methods and well-respected scientifically are very important in the development of evidence-based practice.

Aside from specialist evidence databases, there are many initiatives which circulate in short, easy-to-assimilate form: summaries and advice in a way that is of help to clinical decision-makers. They take the form of specialist journals dealing with evidence-based health care, clinical effectiveness bulletins and newsletters.

Making this clinical information available, particularly specialist databases like the Cochrane Collaboration, but also good summaries on effective care, has been made much easier by the Internet. Nevertheless, individual practitioners must have the ability to gain access to these electronic media easily. Hospitals and other health care organisations have an important role in providing the infrastructure of information technology.

Implementation: Incorporating Evidence into Practice

Providing easy access to high-quality evidence is vital in developing clinical environments in which evidence-based practice will flourish; however, it does not guarantee systematic uptake.

Training of clinical staff is important – particularly in critical appraisal skills (mentioned above) and in the use of information technology. The promotion of teamworking is important so that individual departments regularly evaluate their work and explore ways of improving it.

An important way of doing this is through medical and clinical audit. Clinical audit is the approach through which health professionals critically examine their own and each other's practice, so that the lessons learned from such a scrutiny can be used to make improvements in professional practice, and hence the quality of care.

The term *clinical audit* is largely a British one. It is a form of peer review. It is not a new phenomenon, examples of it having been practised can be found much earlier in this century, and in even more distant medical history. However, the early 1990s saw such audit being formally introduced as part of the contracts of all senior hospital medical staff in the National Health Service and as an integral part of postgraduate continuing education programmes.

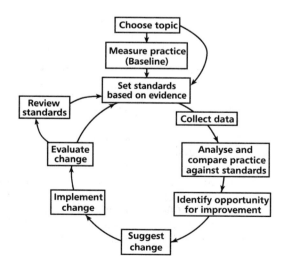

Figure 4.9 The clinical audit cycle.

Any clinical audit programme must be methodologically sound, such that appropriate conclusions can be reached and hence appropriate action planned and undertaken. If this is not the case, then the time and effort involved will have been wasted. Valid techniques must be in place to allow the audit to take place continuously as part of the day-to-day work of a clinical team, so that it is multidisciplinary in focus.

The process through which effective clinical audit is conducted is by progress around the audit cycle (see Figure 4.9). A key component of the cycle is the setting of standards based upon evidence comparing current practice against these standards. The setting of standards is something for all members of the clinical team to agree upon but should be undertaken using the best available medical evidence and knowledge drawn from specialist research databases (such as the Cochrane Collaboration) and from appraisal of the research undertaken by members of the clinical team themselves.

One of the main ways in which new clinical policies are formulated is through setting out clinical practice guidelines. As described this can be undertaken as part of the clinical audit cycle. Many clinical practice guidelines setting out the best way to manage a particular health problem are written by national or international bodies, drawing on the best evidence and expert opinion (Table 4.6). Increasingly in England, statements about what represents good practice in particular fields will be made by the National Institute for Clinical Excellence (NICE) – see later.

Table 4.6   Clinical practice guidelines – examples of evidence-based guidelines for tonsillectomy in children

Disease	
Recurrent Tonsillitis	Tonsillectomy if: episodes < 5 days, 6 attacks a year for 2 years or 8 attacks in 1 year
	or
	episodes > 5 days, 4 attacks a year for 2 years or 6 attacks in 1 year
	or
	one attack with symptoms so serious hospitalisation needed
	Lower threshold if heart disease, diabetes, 2 febrile convulsions, obstructive symptoms or otitis media
Sleep apnoea	Adenotonsillectomy if parental account of very loud breathing/snoring and referral to sleep studies unit to determine cause
Secretory otitis media	Not an indication for tonsillectomy

Source: Donaldson LJ, Hayes JH, Barton AG, Howel D, Hawthorne M. The Journal of Otalaryngology, 1999; 28:24–30.

Changing professional behaviour to conform with evidence of best practice is thus a complex process (Figure 4.8). Research into the factors which influence change in professional behaviour has shown that no single measure will be effective but that multifaceted strategies are important. The factors which have been shown to contribute to such change are shown in Table 4.7.

Table 4.7 List of measures which may achieve professional behaviour change which have been subject to evaluation by trials

Intervention	No. of studies
Educational material	12
Conference	17
Outreach visit	8
Use of local opinion leader	5
Patient-mediated intervention	10
Audit and feedback	31
Reminder system	52
Marketing	3
Multifaceted intervention	15
Local consensus process	8

Source: Oxman AD, Thomson MA, Davis DA, Haynes RB. Canadian Medical Association Journal, 1995; 153:1423–31.

Clinical Governance

As part of its policies for the NHS introduced in 1997, the Labour Government set out a new strategy for quality. These proposals acknowledged that, in the past, issues such as achieving financial balance and meeting workload targets had perhaps started to dominate the agendas of many health care organisations in the NHS.

The government's White Paper created a new style of NHS which aimed to redress this balance. For the first time, all health organisations have a statutory duty for quality improvement through clinical governance. Now, well-managed organisations are seen as those in which financial control, service performance and quality are fully integrated at every level.

The new concept (Table 4.8) resonated strongly with that of corporate governance. Corporate governance is a framework of organisational procedures and behaviours introduced to the private sector following a report called the Cadbury Report (chaired by Sir Adrian Cadbury). This was set up in response to a number of high-profile scandals in the City of London during the early 1990s. The principles of corporate governance were later extended to public sector bodies in Britain. The resonance of clinical governance with corporate governance was important because if it was to be successful then it needed to be underpinned by the same strengths as corporate governance: rigour, an organisation-wide approach, and placing a clear accountability on the leadership of the organisation.

Table 4.8 Definition of clinical governance

Clinical governance is a framework through which NHS organisations are accountable for continuously improving the quality of their services and safeguarding high standards of care by creating an environment in which excellence in clinical care will flourish.

Source: A First Class Service: quality in the new NHS. London: Department of Health, 1998.

The organisations which make up any health service will vary in their performance against quality criteria. A hypothetical quality curve is shown in Figure 4.10. Health care organisations at the left-hand tail of the curve will be those which have demonstrated failures in standards of care whether detected through complaints, audit, untoward incidents, or routine surveillance. The challenge here is to learn lessons which can be built into future service delivery. Similarly, looking at the innovative organisations at the right-hand tail of the distribution, good practice must be recognized, the scope for more general applicability identified, and methods found to transfer it both locally and nationally. This process of learning lessons – both from exemplar and the problem services – was never tackled systematically before and was an important part of the clinical governance proposals. In addition to addressing these tails of the quality curve (Figure 4.10), a major movement of any curve of this kind towards improved quality requires that health organisations in the middle range are engaged ('shifting the mean').

Thus, the thrust of clinical governance is also to improve quality across the board not simply to concentrate on the best and worst organisations. The task is largely a developmental one – of organisations and staff. Clinical and management systems, quality improvement mechanisms, the work of teams and individuals all need to be aligned to produce a new kind of health organisation.

When considering different hospitals and Primary Care Groups the feature which distinguishes the best from the others is probably their culture. An organisation which creates a working environment which is open and participative, where ideas and good practice are shared, where education and research are valued and where blame is used exceptionally is likely to be one where clinical governance is prospering.

Figure 4.10 Variation in the quality of organisations.

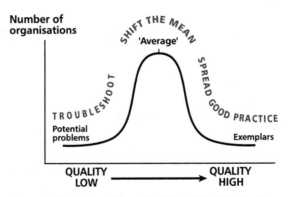

Source: Scally G, Donaldson LJ. BMJ, 1998; 317:61–65.

Clinical governance involves the integration of many aspects of quality (including those discussed in this chapter) which have previously been dealt with in a rather fragmented way (Figure 4.11).

Clinical governance places accountable officer status for clinical governance on the Chief Executive of the health care organisation, with regular reports to Board meetings (of equal importance to monthly financial reports), and day-to-day responsibility in the hands of a senior clinician. It is for each organisation to work out these accountability arrangements in detail and ensure that they are communicated throughout the organisation.

Two external bodies facilitate and reinforce the local duty for quality. The Commission for Health Improvement and the National Institute for Clinical Excellence. These are described later in this chapter.

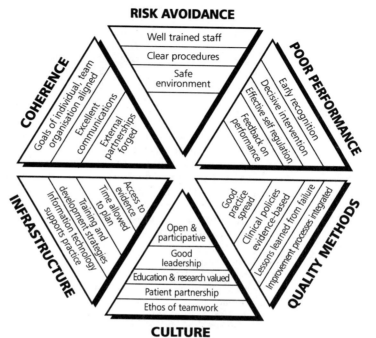

Figure 4.11 Integrating approaches of clinical governance.

Source: Scally G, Donaldson LJ. BMJ, 1998; 317:61–65.

Patient Partnership

In the past, concern with quality has largely focused on improving standards of diagnostic and treatment techniques delivered by doctors and other health care professionals. This perspective on quality improvement is still very important but increasingly attention is being given to seeking and acting upon the views and expectations of users and potential users of health services. In a message to the United States Congress in 1962, President John F Kennedy identified four basic rights of consumers (Table 4.9). These rights embody fundamental principles which, if applied to health services, would constitute a powerful commitment to users of services. In Britain, there has been a trend in health service and other public services to formulate charters and entitlements for patients as consumers of services. Such an approach is aimed at raising standards and ensuring greater accountability in the delivery of public services. This approach deliberately encourages patients to have high expectations of services and uses the criteria set out (e.g., response times) as one of the levers for improving quality.

However, genuine empowerment of patients as consumers of health care requires a cultural shift in the way in which services are traditionally delivered. It involves not only listening and talking to patients about the care which they receive, but also genuinely taking their views and opinions into account when designing services. It also means enabling them to make informed choices and becoming partners with health professionals in the care provided.

Table 4.9   Basic right of consumers

- The right to be informed
- The right to be heard
- The right to choose
- The right to safety

Source: President John F Kennedy. Message to
the United States Congress, 1962.

The true involvement of patients in health care is limited by a range of factors. Infrastructure within local services is often lacking, and health care professionals do not always have the training or skills to enable patients to participate effectively in their care. Particular groups of patients such as those who are in ethnic minority populations or who are disabled can experience even greater barriers. Strategies must be actively pursued if patient partnership is to become a central part of high-quality health care (Table 4.10). A regular national survey of user and patient experience was introduced in the late 1990s.

Table 4.10   Aims of a strategy to develop patient partnership in health care

- To promote user involvement in their own care, as active partners with professionals
- To enable patients to become informed about their treatment and care and to make informed decisions and choices about it if they wish
- To contribute to the quality of health services by making them more responsive to the needs and preferences of users
- To ensure that users have the knowledge, skills and support to enable them to influence NHS service policy and planning

Source: Patient partnership: building a collaborative strategy. Leeds: NHS Executive, 1996.

Complaints

The number of formal complaints made by patients is relatively small in relation to the total episodes of care provided by the health service. Though this undoubtedly represents a generally high level of satisfaction with the public health care system in Britain, there is some evidence that people who wish to complain do not do so either because they do not know how or because they believe that it would be pointless to do so.

Complaints made by patients about their care represent an important opportunity to learn lessons about possible service failures, which can then be translated into improvements in service quality. An important factor in judging the quality of a health service should be how quickly and effectively complaints are resolved. Patients will wish to see their concerns taken seriously; their complaint investigated, quickly, fairly and using processes which they understand; with a clear explanation given, and follow-up action taken.

People who are unhappy about the clinical care they receive in National Health Service hospitals face several options for expressing their dissatisfaction. They can raise their concerns informally with the health professional concerned to have them settled by discussion and explanation; they can make a complaint formally to health service management, where it will be dealt with using the NHS Complaints Procedure. Alternatively, they can take their complaint to law.

A new NHS Complaints Procedure came into effect in the mid-1990s following dissatisfaction about the complexity, delays, and fragmentation inherent in previous complaints procedures. It aims to address some of the concerns described above by providing a speedy, fair and thorough response to complaints.

Under the procedure, each health care organisation in the NHS must designate one of its senior officers as a Complaints Manager to oversee the operation of the complaints procedure within the organisation, and to act as a point of contact for the public. In addition, each organisation must appoint one or more conveners. One of these conveners must be a non-executive director of the health care organisation's board (but it should not usually be the chairman). Other conveners can be appointed, but they must not be employees of the health care organisation.

Attempts to Resolve Locally

A complaint can be brought by any patient or on their behalf (with their permission) by someone else. When a complaint is made, the person receiving it will often be a member of staff who is in direct contact with patients on a day-to-day basis (e.g., a doctor, a nurse, a receptionist). He or she should clarify the complaint and try to resolve it to the patient's satisfaction. If the complaint cannot be resolved by such a front-line member of staff, or it is made in writing or it is serious, it should be referred to the Complaints Manager who will investigate, organise a meeting with the complainant, if appropriate, and compile a report. At the end of this process, it is a requirement for the complainant to receive a written reply from the Chief Executive of the health care organisation concerned.

The Convener and Whether to Establish an Independent Panel

If the complainant is dissatisfied with this response – in other words, the complaint cannot be resolved locally – then they can refer it to the Convener with a request that an Independent Review Panel should be established. The complainant is asked to set out their continuing grievance and the person being complained against is advised. The Convener then takes a decision on whether to convene a panel in consultation with an independent lay chairman drawn from a list of such individuals held by the NHS Executive. The Convener and the independent lay chairman may also need to take independent clinical advice depending on the nature of the complaint. Such a panel would not usually be established where litigation by the Complainant seems imminent, where further action could still result in local resolution, or where the health care organisation could not reasonably have been expected to do any more. However, if a convener turns down the request for an Independent Panel, the Complainant is given a full explanation in writing and advised of their right to complain to the Ombudsman if they wish.

The Independent Panel

An Independent Review Panel arises from the decision of a convener (as described above) and responds to the terms of reference established by that convener. The Independent Review Panel has three members: an independent lay chairman drawn from a list held by the NHS Executive, the Convener and, for NHS Trusts, a representative of the health authority that places service agreements with the Trust. In a health authority complaint the third member is an independent person drawn from the list held by the NHS Executive. If there are clinical aspects to the complaint, then at least two independent health professionals advise the Panel.

Independent panels establish the facts relating to a complaint, listen to the views of the complainant and all relevant parties, and produce a report which describes the events and the issues, draw conclusions and make recommendations.

The Independent Panel's report is made available to the complainant, those complained against and the Board and management of the health care organisation to enable follow-up action to be taken.

Primary Care

General practitioners (and others providing family practitioner services) must have in operation a practice-based complaints procedure. If a complaint cannot be resolved locally (within the practice) then it passes to the health authority whose convener initiates the complaints procedure described above. In addition, many practices use conciliators.

Health Service Commissioner (Ombudsman)

An independent Health Service Commissioner (Ombudsman) reports to Parliament. This official has powers to investigate complaints from members of the public who consider that they have suffered injustice as a result of a failure in a service provided by a health authority or a hospital, or failure to offer a service it has a duty to provide, or other examples of maladministration – including failure to properly operate the complaints procedure described above.

A member of the public must always complain first to the responsible health service organisation before referring the matter to the Commissioner. Many complaints relate to waiting time for hospital treatment, lack of communication from health professionals to patients and relatives, failures in services, poor handling of complaints themselves, or the administration or management of health services. The Health Service Commissioner produces an annual report in which he comments on the issues which have been reported to him and which he has investigated. He also produces regular anonymised reports of selected investigations.

Courts

A patient has recourse to the courts of law where he or she may allege clinical negligence. Settlements are often made out of court and this is the main route of complaint through which he or she can obtain financial retribution. This is an increasingly common route for complainants in Britain, and is a major feature of medical practice in the United States of America where patients are much more litigation-minded and doctors are inclined to plan their clinical management in a way which is least likely to lead to litigation – even if it may not be the best approach to a particular clinical problem (so-called 'defensive medicine').

Community Health Councils

Community Health Councils (CHCs) represent the interests in the health service of the public to health authorities and act as the official watchdog for the local community, inevitably receiving adverse comments. They have no specific duty to investigate complaints but many do advise complainants about their entitlements under the NHS complaints procedure and may attend with individuals at the hearings of complaints.

Each Community Health Council employs a small team of management and administrative staff headed by a Chief Officer. The Council itself is made up of members with a particular interest in the health services. Half are appointed by the local authorities, one-third by voluntary organisations and one-sixth by the Secretary of State for Health. Although no upper or lower limit for membership is set, CHCs typically comprise 18–24 members. One of the members is appointed as chairman.

There is a CHC for the area covered by each health authority (a few have two). Councils have right of access to information from health authorities, have the right to visit hospitals and other NHS premises and have access to health authorities and NHS Trusts; in particular, to the senior officers managing services.

Health authorities have a statutory duty to consult CHCs about any substantial service developments and variations in services that might be under consideration; for example, the closure of a hospital or change of use of facilities. CHCs publish annual reports and health authorities are required to publish replies to reports, stating action taken on specific issues contained in them.

Some Important National Structures Dealing with Quality

An important part of a system to promote continuous quality improvement in health services is the role of bodies which are external to local services. These can take various forms but essentially can operate in an inspectorial or a facilitatory manner, sometimes both. The majority operate on a national basis.

This is a subject which can arouse very strong feelings. A hospital or other health care organisation which is subject to formal inspection by an external body seeking to check for problems can sometimes react very negatively to its relationship to such a body. Traditionally, whilst external scrutiny was intended to keep organisations on their toes, it had the drawback of engendering a climate of apprehension. Those being inspected were motivated to conceal rather than be open about problems. This was particularly so where the external body had the power of sanction when it found procedural errors or poor performance.

Over time, there has been a tendency for external bodies to re-orientate themselves so that their outlook is more positive and constructive in dealing with the organisations they monitor or inspect. Sanctions are still needed in any system for dealing with extremes of poor performance. However, the overall benefit to quality improvement is likely to be much greater if, when weaknesses are identified, the external agency and the individual organisation work together to identify action to improve them in a less judgemental way.

Operating this way, an external body can provide valuable developmental support to an organisation seeking to improve the quality of its services as well as acting as a safeguard for the public against very poor standards of care being allowed to prevail unchecked.

Commission for Health Improvement

The Commission for Health Improvement has a major role in reviewing both local and national arrangements for improving the quality of clinical services. Its reviews are in the form of a rolling programme of all service providers to assess local clinical governance arrangements and their capacity to assure and improve services. As part of this rolling programme, the Commission looks at local implementation of National Service Framework standards and the take-up of guidance produced by the National Institute for Clinical Excellence (see later). In addition, the Commission provides expert advice to hospitals, Primary Care Groups and other service providers and planners of health care on the development of clinical governance within their organisations and localities. The Commission has the capacity for rapid investigation of service problems – for example, where these have failed to respond to local efforts or where these are giving rise to serious concerns about the quality of care for patients. In such circumstances, the Commission investigates and develops recommendations for action to put these right – although it is the responsibility of the organisation concerned to develop an action plan for implementation of recommended changes. The Commission pays special attention to progress made by the organisation when it is next visited as part of the Commission's rolling programme. Where the Commission has identified the need for significant service development, it may arrange to revisit the organisation on a shorter timescale, bringing forward its place in the review programme.

National Institute for Clinical Excellence

A second external body is responsible for coordinating and validating the flow of information on clinical and cost-effectiveness to health care organisations and health professionals within the NHS. The National Institute for Clinical Excellence (NICE) is responsible for providing authoritative national guidance on clinical standards, effective interventions and spreading good practice. Clinical practice guidelines are produced, and evaluation of new technologies carried out, by a wide range of bodies regionally, nationally and internationally. It is important that local health services and practitioners have a clear idea about what source they should rely on. NICE has a role in appraising such material and providing validation where appropriate.

Health Advisory Service 2000

The Health Advisory Service focuses on a number of service areas, in particular: mental health problems, the elderly, the elderly mentally-ill, children and adolescents with mental health problems. It carries out its function through two joint Chief Executives and a small number of full-time staff. However, extensive use is made of senior professional and managerial staff (from within the health service) who work on a temporary or part-time basis to assist the Health Advisory Service with particular initiatives. It was set up in 1997 as an independent charity with terms of reference:

> '...to develop a pro-active advisory and consultancy service with the aim of improving the delivery of health and social care services for mentally ill and elderly people. This is to be achieved by adopting a multidisciplinary approach based on the interpretation of evidence-based clinical practice and organisation and personal development.'

National Service Frameworks

National Service Frameworks are national service plans first introduced in 1999 which aim to improve service quality and reduce variation in outcome of care by setting out national standards and defined service models for particular services or care groups.

The first two National Service Frameworks covered coronary heart disease and mental health and frameworks for elderly people and diabetes mellitus are being produced in the years 2000 and 2001 respectively.

The Audit Commission

The Audit Commission is a body which has overall responsibility for the external financial audit of all local authorities as well as the National Health Service in England and Wales.

Part of its role involves ensuring the best use of the public funds which are allocated to the authorities concerned. In addition to examining the way in which funds are used within individual authorities, the Commission also undertakes regular reviews of specific subjects and makes recommendations which particularly focus on value for money issues. For example, the Audit Commission has examined the use of acute hospital beds, day case surgery, and community care. The usual method of conducting these reviews is for the Commission's staff to study services in a number of parts of the country and draw up a report based on its findings. Health authorities are then encouraged to examine the implications for their local services in the light of the Commission's report and implement changes as necessary.

National Clinical Audits of Services

Although the majority of clinical audit activity is carried out as an integral part of clinical governance at local level, there are examples of clinical audit initiatives on a regional or a national scale.

A number of initiatives are organised as confidential enquiries. The Confidential Enquiry into Perioperative Deaths (CEPOD)[6] which was first established on a pilot basis in three Health Regions in the late 1980s, was later extended more widely.

The main focus of CEPOD is to audit hospital deaths which occur within 30 days of a surgical or gynaecological procedure. The audit seeks to identify those deaths which are attributable to 'avoidable' surgical or anaesthetic factors.

In CEPOD reports, issues which have been described include deaths which were associated with avoidable factors. These included situations where inadequate time and attention had been given to resuscitating patients or dealing with intercurrent medical conditions before they were operated upon; instances of lack of adequate supervision of junior surgeons and anaesthetists by consultants; and situations where surgeons who were generalists were operating on patients with conditions which would have been better dealt with by a surgeon with specialist skills in the field concerned.

The results of the CEPOD studies are only made available in aggregated and anonymised form. Thus no individual doctor or patient can be identified. This is an essential prerequisite of any peer review based upon voluntary notification of cases and participation if the continuing cooperation of the professionals concerned is to be achieved.

An initiative like CEPOD produces improvement in the quality of care in two main ways. Firstly, the knowledge of those involved that they are participating in a peer review process may in itself raise standards by making them more aware, and self-critical, of their practice. Secondly, the formal report of the results of a major peer review exercise of this kind, containing analyses and recommendations, is a means through which the profession can amend existing practices. Where necessary, change can take place in the organisation of clinical care. Training programmes can be established to address the issues raised.

Other nationally organised confidential enquiries include the Confidential Enquiry into Stillbirths and Deaths in Infancy (see Chapter 6); the Confidential Enquiry into Maternal Deaths (also see Chapter 6); the Confidential Enquiry into Suicide and Homicide by People with Mental Illness (see Chapter 7). These enquiries are now under the auspices of the National Institute for Clinical Excellence.

Prescribing and the use of Medicines

Prescribing of medicines is one of the main interventions used in the delivery of health care. Medicine usage accounts for a substantial proportion of the health service's budget each year (Table 4.11); and in most developed countries medicines account for an increasing proportion of health care expenditure and of the Gross Domestic Product. Governments and health care providers have therefore developed strategies to promote the cost-effective use of medicines.

Table 4.11   NHS total cost and expenditure on pharmaceutical services, United Kingdom

Year	Total NHS Cost (£m)	FHS[a] medicines bill (£m)	FHS medicines bill as a % of total NHS cost	FHS medicines bill as a % of total GDP[b]	FHS medicines per head (£)
1986	19,141	2,090	10.9	0.55	37
1987	21,037	2,291	10.9	0.55	40
1988	23,317	2,544	10.9	0.55	44
1989	25,492	2,849	11.2	0.56	50
1990	28,337	3,067	10.8	0.55	53
1991	32,124	3,352	10.4	0.58	58
1992	35,796	3,754	10.5	0.62	65
1993	38,336	4,156	10.8	0.65	71
1994	39,859	4,531	11.4	0.67	78
1995	41,627	4,850	11.7	0.68	83
1996	43,183	5,248	12.2	0.70	89
1997	45,116	5,735	12.7	0.72	97
1998	47,245	6,268	13.3	0.75	106

Source: ABPI Annual Review, 1998.
a FHS = Family Health Services
b GDP = Gross Domestic Product

A range of data are available to enable trends in general practice prescribing to be examined. They are provided by the Prescription Pricing Authority which analyses prescriptions written by general practitioners. Analysis of such data allows comparisons of medicine usage between general practices and health authorities in a number of key respects; for example, the number of prescriptions written, the net ingredient cost and the therapeutic class of drug used. The presentation and discussion of such comparative data allows the quality of prescribing, as well as the use of resources, to be explored which ultimately potentially benefits patient care. For example, the NHS in England uses such prescribing data, adjusted for age-sex weighted populations, to derive a range of 'prescribing indicators' which are issued regularly to all health authorities. Similar data are not routinely collected nationally to allow prescribing and medicine usage in hospitals to be examined. However, most hospitals now have computer-based systems for issuing drugs to wards and clinics and these enable patterns of medicine usage to be examined at a local level.

In the early 1990s new arrangements were introduced for the monitoring and management of medicine usage in primary care through the Indicative Prescribing Scheme. Under this scheme, each general practice must set an indicative prescribing amount which is a non cash-limited estimate of each practice's annual prescribing needs. The scheme enables targets to be set for more rational prescribing and enhances opportunities for greater efficiency in the use of resources.

The Control of Medicines

With the increased availability of new pharmaceutical products in recent years there has been growing concern about the safety and side-effects of medicines. The availability of medicines in the United Kingdom is controlled on the basis of their safety, quality and efficacy.

The legal basis for monitoring and control of medicines for both human and animal use is the Medicines Act 1968, and a series of European directives and regulations of the European Commission which have harmonised medicines regulation in the European Union. Since the Act originally came into force, regulations, orders and information leaflets have been issued by government departments on various aspects of the control of medicines.

Responsibility for control of medicines is vested in the 'Licensing Authority' which is, in effect, the Secretary of State for Health, acting on behalf of all United Kingdom Health Ministers. The controls have a wide variety of aspects. A licensing system governs the development, marketing, manufacture, import and wholesale distribution of 'medicinal products'. Criteria are laid down for what constitutes a medicinal product and powers exist to extend the definition. The licensing system also covers the issue of new medicinal products for the purposes of conducting clinical trials to evaluate a new therapy in human beings. Medical and dental practitioners are exempt from the licensing procedure in so far as they have freedom to prescribe an unlicensed product on their own professional responsibility, when this is judged to be in the patient's best interests. The question will hardly ever arise since the majority of practitioners will be prescribing medicinal products which ultimately derive from a manufacturer or supplier which will itself hold a licence under the regulations. However, a doctor or dentist may import a medicinal product without licence provided that it is to treat a specific patient and not to build up a stock for general usage. He or she may also manufacture (make up) an unlicensed medicine for an individual patient and maintain a small stock. The use of unlicensed products is rare in general practice, but much more frequent in hospital medicine because of clinical trials and other specialised patient needs.

European System

With the development of the Single Market within the European Union (EU), medicines regulation has become increasingly pan-European. In 1995, a new system for the authorisation (licensing) of medicinal products was established. This is designed to promote both public health and free circulation of pharmaceuticals within the EU. The system is based on cooperation between national regulatory bodies.

There is now a choice of procedures for introducing medicines to the European Market. In the centralised procedure, successful applications lead to the granting of a European Marketing Authorisation by the EU Commission. This process is compulsory for biotechnology products, and optional for other innovative medicines. Interferon Beta-1b for multiple sclerosis was the first product to be introduced throughout Europe by this new machinery and, by the late 1990s, more than 80 new medicines had been authorised in this way.

A decentralised procedure applies to the majority of conventional medicines, where application is made to EU member States, followed by mutual recognition. For products to be marketed only in one member State, a national authorisation continues to be granted by the relevant regulatory body. Because of the transnational nature of the pharmaceutical market, use of this procedure is declining.

Aside from licensing, other aspects of medicines regulation include controls on legal classification (prescription-only or non-prescription availability of medicines); promotion and advertising (both to the medical profession and the public); post-marketing safety surveillance or pharmacovigilance, and product information labelling and package leaflets. As medicines licensing moves to earlier availability of new therapies, post-authorisation regulation has an increased role in monitoring safety and ensuring that the information which reaches health professionals and patients facilitates safe, correct use and is up-to-date.

The Medicines Act makes no provision for regulating the price of medicines or their availability under the National Health Service. The licensing process is concerned solely with quality, safety, efficacy and it does not take into account factors such as the clinical need for the new medicine or relative efficacy between drugs. Indeed, consideration of these issues as part of the licensing process would be unlawful under The Medicines Act and European Union directives on medicines licensing. Instead, the Secretary of State for Health controls prices through the Pharmaceutical Price Regulation Scheme (PPRS) which is a voluntary agreement between the government and the major pharmaceutical companies operating in the United Kingdom. In addition, the availability of, and reimbursement for, medicines prescribed in the National Health Service is regulated by the National Health Service Act 1977.

The Secretary of State for Health administers The Medicines Act and regulations and relevant European directives through the Medicines Control Agency (MCA) of the Department of Health which is staffed by doctors, pharmacists and scientists as well as administrative and clerical staff.

The Medicines Control Agency's main functions include:

(a)   Direct involvement with all aspects of licensing, both of medicinal products and of manufacturing and wholesale facilities.

(b)   Providing an inspectorate to ensure compliance of manufacturing procedures with the product licence and Good Manufacturing Practice.

(c)   Monitoring adverse reactions to medicinal products (together with the Committee on the Safety of Medicines) and taking steps to optimise safe usage.

(d)   Taking enforcement action in relation to breaches of the Act and regulations.

(e)   Providing information on risk–benefit to health professionals and patients and ensuring advertising is not misleading.

(f)   International liaison, particularly through the European Community and the World Health Organization.

The Act allowed for the establishment of a Medicines Commission. Members from the relevant professions are appointed by the Secretary of State for Health and advise him or her in relation to the execution of the Act. Upon the recommendation of this Commission, the Secretary of State has established a range of expert committees to provide advisory functions on specific topics; for example, the Committee on Safety of Medicines (CSM). Many of these standing committees have themselves established expert subcommittees to deal with individual aspects of their overall responsibility; for example biological products.

A particularly important role of the Committee on Safety of Medicines and the Medicines Control Agency is to involve members of the medical profession and the pharmaceutical profession directly in the process of detecting untoward reactions from drugs. This is undertaken through the 'yellow card' system, whereby individual medical practitioners can report, in strict confidence, a suspected adverse reaction in an individual patient. The Committee on Safety of Medicines maintains a confidential register of such information that it has obtained from this and other sources. This database contains more than 360,000 adverse drug reaction reports and constitutes a major source of information on drug safety. Anonymised analyses from the register are available to health professionals on request.

In response to drug safety information received through yellow cards or from other sources, the Licensing Authority has powers to revoke a product licence or, where there is an immediate risk to public health, to suspend the licence for a period of three months. When such regulatory action has been taken, it becomes unlawful for anyone to promote the use of that medicine (although its use by a practitioner in individual patients is still legally permissible). Alternatively, the product licence may be varied and the manufacturer required to issue a new data sheet (now replaced by the Summary of Product Characteristics) with revised dosage, contraindications, precautions or warnings. An example of the value of this system of reporting is provided by the events which led (in August 1982) to the suspension of the product licence for the anti-inflammatory drug Opren (benoxaprofen). The Committee on Safety of Medicines had received more than 3500 reports of adverse reactions to the drug, including 61 deaths, mainly in the elderly, when the suspension of the product licence was made (initially for three months) under the terms of the Medicines Act, 1968. More recently, the anticholinergic drug, Terodiline, was voluntarily withdrawn from the market by its manufacturer, after the United Kingdom yellow card system had revealed an association with serious cardiac arrhythmias.

Drug Safety

Before a drug receives a marketing authorisation (product licence) the Licensing Authority must be satisfied that it is safe in relation to its intended use. This is a relative judgement, termed the risk/benefit analysis. For example, a new anticancer drug or an antiviral agent for use in AIDS would be permitted to exhibit more frequent or serious toxicities than a new addition to the penicillin group of antibiotics. Information on safety of new drugs is generated through a range of animal studies including carcinogenicity, mutagenicity and reproductive toxicity in several species. Appropriate standards of chemical and pharmaceutical quality must also be achieved. After appropriate animal testing, new drugs are introduced into clinical use through a continuous process of clinical development that is conventionally divided into four phases:

- *Phase 1 studies* constitute first use in humans, where the clinical pharmacology of the drug is investigated in small numbers of healthy volunteers or patients.
- *Phase 2 studies* comprise clinical investigation for efficacy and safety in larger numbers of patients, typically 200–300.
- *Phase 3 studies* are formal randomised clinical trials on a substantive scale, in up to more than 1000 patients.
- *Phase 4 studies*, also known as post-licensing studies or post-marketing surveillance (PMS), consist of further surveillance, particularly for safety, in large populations after the drug has been launched.

Adverse reactions to drugs can be broadly subdivided into two groups. Type A (augmented) reactions are exaggerated responses to the drug's normal pharmacological action; for example, bradycardia with beta-blocking drugs. They are common, predictable, usually dose-related, and rarely fatal. Type B (bizarre) reactions are unrelated to the drug's normal actions, usually not dose-related, and uncommon. However, they are often serious and may carry a high mortality; for example, hepato-renal syndrome caused by benoxaprofen, or oculomucocutaneous syndrome caused by practolol. Much effort in adverse-reactions monitoring and post-marketing surveillance is therefore directed at identifying and avoiding Type B reactions.

Information and Quality in Prescribing

The doctor actually carrying out the prescribing, whether based in hospital or in general practice, has a number of channels through which to learn about the efficacy of various alternative therapies, and their potential hazards and side-effects:

(a) *From pharmaceutical companies* – either directly from medical representatives of the companies concerned, via advertising in medical journals or by advertising literature mailed to him or her.

   As this is a major source by which medical practitioners acquire information about medical products and because of the large sums of money at stake in the drug industry, there has been concern about the potential for pharmaceutical companies to make unjustified or misleading claims about the efficacy or safety of their products. Control on standards in advertising to the professions is maintained through regulations issued in accordance with the Medicines Act 1968. Companies that promote unlicensed products, or make therapeutic claims beyond the terms of the product authorisation, may face criminal prosecution. It is a legal requirement that the practitioner must receive an SPC setting out objectively full details about the product with written promotional material sent to him and at any visit by a medical representative. In addition to this, a Compendium of SPCs is published by the Association of the British Pharmaceutical Industry (ABPI) and mailed free of charge to all medical practitioners and pharmacists. It contains SPCs from the majority of prescription-only products on the market from ABPI member companies, so that details of dosage, route of administration, contra-indications, markings, precautions, side-effects and other details are available in one volume. The ABPI also operates a voluntary code of practice which covers promotion of medicines to prescribers by its member companies. Breaches of the code are investigated by the ABPI's Prescription Medicines Code of Practice Committee (PMCPA), to which health professionals can refer complaints. Another publication which contains brief data on many drugs and is produced by a commercial organisation and sent regularly to doctors is the Monthly Index of Medical Specialties (MIMS). This also contains advertising material.

(b) *Drug Information Service* – most health authorities provide a hospital-based service staffed by pharmacists with special expertise to maintain and provide information on drugs and medicines from a number of different perspectives including indications, relative merits, efficacy, side-effects, safety and costs. This impartial advice or information is open to all medical practitioners, pharmacists and other relevant professionals working within hospitals and primary care in the district.

(c) *British National Formulary* **(BNF)** – this is produced by the medical and pharmaceutical professions and is brought up-to-date and sent without charge to doctors and pharmacists within the National Health Service every six months. It is orientated towards the treatment of specific disorders grouped by therapeutic category and thus provides an impartial opinion on indications for, and the relative merits of, various alternative drug therapies.

(d) ***The medical literature*** – articles in the medical journals will report clinical trials of new or existing therapies for particular conditions, as well as reporting potential side-effects. Some more specialised journals deal specifically with prescribing.

(e) ***Postgraduate education or training*** – in the course of study for postgraduate examinations or through attendances at lectures and seminars many practitioners will keep abreast of recent developments in therapeutics.

(f) ***Evidence-based prescribing guidelines*** – these are now available in many disease areas (for example, asthma, angina pectoris, depression, peptic ulcer) or for major innovations in treatment (e.g., interferon beta for multiple sclerosis, statins for primary and secondary prevention of coronary heart disease, donepezil for Alzheimer's disease). Such guidelines may be developed and issued nationally by government or professional bodies, or by local health bodies. They are increasingly viewed as an important contribution to achieving effective health care, and also to proper management of the introduction of new drugs. The National Institute for Clinical Excellence has an important role in appraising such material and providing validation as necessary.

There is increasing emphasis on seeking ways to improve the quality and cost-effectiveness of prescribing through education programmes, publications, drug information services, the development of limited formularies in general practice and in hospitals and audit of drug therapy. Audit may be performed on a 'macro' scale, through drug utilisation review (DUR) in which patterns of prescribing and outcomes of drug therapy are studied in populations. Drug utilisation review was pioneered in Scandinavia and the United States of America, and is now developing rapidly in the United Kingdom and the remainder of Europe as part of the growing discipline of pharmaco-epidemiology.

A complementary approach is the review of drug therapy for effectiveness, safety, cost-utility and patient convenience in individual patients. This is increasingly seen as an integral component of the clinical audit process at patient, practice or hospital level.

Resources for the Health Service

The health service in Britain represents a major area of government expenditure. This section of the chapter describes how the resources of the health service are determined and deployed. In addition to financial resources, there are three other major elements of the health services resources: its staff, its estate and its information.

Financial Resources

The National Health Service is mainly funded from public finances. In its first full year of operation, the National Health Service cost approximately £10 per head of population but by the late 1990s this had increased to around £800 per head in 1998. Over the same period the proportion of the Gross Domestic Product (GDP) dedicated to health care increased from 3.5% to 5.8%.

Spending on health care, and the proportion funded by public expenditure, varies greatly between different countries of the world (Figure 4.12).

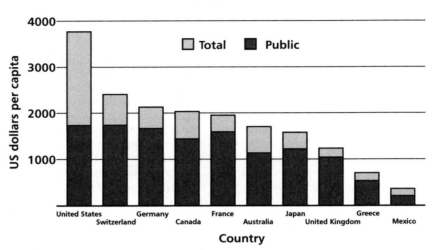

Figure 4.12 Total and public expenditure per capita on health care expressed as US dollars at purchasing power parity rates.

Source: OECD Health Data 1998: A Comparative Analysis of 29 Countries, 1998.

In the past, an annual Public Expenditure Survey (PES) was undertaken to determine the levels of funding for public expenditure programmes including for the NHS. These involved Ministers of the various Departments of State submitting bids to the Chief Secretary to the Treasury who then made proposals to the Cabinet on public expenditure levels. These were usually accompanied by an economic assessment by the Chancellor of the Exchequer. The PES process was used to determine expenditure levels up until the financial year 1998–1999.

On coming to office in 1997, the Labour Government announced a Comprehensive Spending Review of all government departments' spending. This would cover all aspects of departmental expenditure, and that no aspects would be excluded.

The Chancellor of the Exchequer announced the outcome of the Comprehensive Spending Review in the summer of 1998 which provided, at that time, for additional resources for the NHS in England totalling £18 billion over the years 1999–2000 to 2001–2. A second spending review will determine the resources available for the years 2001–2, 2002–3 and 2003–4.

The National Health Service is tasked with using its resources in the most effective way possible. Improvements in efficiency and value for money are expected year-on-year, while conditions are set which ensure that the NHS continues to drive up quality. It also receives income from other sources such as income generation, land sales, prescription and dental charges and fees paid by private patients in National Health Service hospitals.

Resources committed to the National Health Service fall into two broad categories:

- *revenue* – which is money spent on day-to-day running costs such as medical and non-medical staff, drugs and other consumables; and,
- *capital* – which describes money spent on items such as buildings or equipment.

Revenue funding is allocated to health authorities on the basis of the relative needs of their populations. A weighted capitation formula is used to determine each health authority's target share of available resources to enable it to commission similar levels of health services for populations in similar need.

For the financial year 1999–2000, funding for hospital and community health services, prescribing and discretionary general medical services was brought together into a single funding stream at Health Authority (HA) and Primary Care Group (PCG) level. Unified allocations enable HAs and PCGs to deploy resources flexibly to best meet the health needs of their population.

As discussed in an earlier section of the chapter, PCGs are established as committees of Health Authorities and receive budgets from their Health Authorities. PCG budgets are determined on the basis of its registered population (adjusted for list inflation and the unregistered population in its area) and coincide with the population bases for HA allocations. The methodology and formula used for PCG budgets is the same as that used for HA allocations; however, there is local flexibility in the pace of change for PCG budgets. Health Authorities remain statutorily responsible and accountable for the budget for health care in their geographical area, which includes monitoring the use of funds by their Primary Care Groups.

Capital allocations are made for block and discretionary capital. Block capital is issued to all NHS trusts to maintain the asset base and is available for minor developments, equipment replacement, and maintenance. Discretionary capital is available for major capital developments which trusts cannot fund from their block allocation. Public capital is supplemented by investment provided by the Private Finance Initiative (PFI). The majority of new major hospital developments are provided by PFI.

Typically, a PFI consortium will consist of a large construction company (to build the scheme), a design team (to design the facility) and one or more facilities management companies (to provide, for example, estates, security, portering and cleaning services). The hospital facility is managed by the consortium with a Trust paying regular revenue payment for the use of the hospital.

Human Resources

The most important asset of a service industry like the health service is the people it employs (Table 4.12). Either directly, or indirectly, they are the means through which the patients or consumers of health services receive the help they need.

The health service has traditionally employed a wide range of professional staff. Doctors, nurses, physiotherapists, clinical psychologists, occupational therapists are examples but there are many others. In addition, there are many groups of staff which perform specialist technical jobs; for example, medical physicists and information technologists. During the 1980s and early 1990s there was much greater emphasis on general management posts and managements posts in relation to specialist functions such as finance and personnel. Finally, a further group of staff essential to the efficient and effective running of the service is the very wide range of personnel providing an infrastructure of support to other levels of the service; for example, drivers, porters, catering staff, ward clerks, records officers, medical secretaries, engineers, laboratory technicians and public relations officers.

Table 4.12 NHS staff directly employed in hospital and community health services in England

Staff groups	Numbers
Nursing, midwifery and health visitors	332,900
Medical and dental	57,000
Scientific, therapeutic and technical	100,400
Healthcare assistants	17,900
Support staff	66,800
Administration and estates staff	167,000
Ambulance staff	15,200
Other staff	800
Total	758,100

Source: The Government's Expenditure Plans 1999–2000, Department of Health, The Stationery Office, 1999. (Data refer to 1997).

The 1990s also saw a much greater awareness on the part of the NHS on identifying the workforce implications of its policies and for developing staff who were equipped for the new health policies which were being put in place.

Major changes have taken place in the professions. For example, the traditional role of nurses has been greatly extended into areas such as prescribing, clinical assessment of patients, dealing with minor injuries, providing community care and health promotion services. These areas would in the past have been the sole province of doctors but today nurses have a much greater degree of autonomy in them. Similarly, other professions have extended their roles whilst all health care professionals, including doctors, have had to develop skills in areas such as primary care, health promotion, information technology, evidence-based practice and counselling and advising patients.

The Medical (and Dental) Workforce

Within the health service doctors usually work in hospitals or in the community (as general practitioners or in specialist areas of clinical practice such as community paediatrics). Other doctors work in the field of public health medicine.

Throughout his or her working life a doctor must now embrace lifelong learning – a commitment to continuing professional development.

On completion of the undergraduate programme of basic medical education the newly-qualified doctor must spend a year as a preregistration house officer (PRHO) gaining experience within the broad disciplines of medicine and surgery. Recently, provision to gain experience in general practice has been included. At the end of the PRHO year, if the doctor's progress is satisfactory, the General Medical Council will grant him or her full registration.

After the PRHO year, the first phase of specialist training (basic specialist training) takes place within the senior house officer grade and will ordinarily last two to three years. Such training prepares the doctor for competitive entry *either* to a five- or six-year higher specialist training programme *or* to a period of training in general practice which usually lasts no more than one year.

Under the reforms to specialist training, introduced in the early 1990s, higher specialist trainees (specialist registrars) now follow a systematic approach to their training delivered through specially designed training programmes. During this time they follow a curriculum, receive regular feedback on their performance, have opportunities to develop and refine knowledge, skills and attitudes, and will participate in an annual review of their progress informed by regular in-programme assessments. Satisfactory progress leads to the award of the Certificate of Completion of Specialist Training (CCST), entry to the Specialist Register held by the GMC and eligibility for appointment as a consultant. There are separate but parallel arrangements for general practice. Here, satisfactory completion of the period of vocational training leads to the award of a Certificate of Prescribed or Equivalent Experience either of which is required before the doctor may work as a general practitioner in any capacity other than as a trainee.

The supervision of specialist training is the responsibility of the Specialist Training Authority of the Medical Royal Colleges (STA). Royal Colleges and their Faculties, acting on behalf of the STA and with its approval, determine and publish the curricula for training programmes, monitor and assure the quality of training and attest to the standard reached by individual doctors. Each Royal College or Faculty has a network of regional advisers and tutors who advise the College nationally and the postgraduate dean locally. Parallel arrangements apply to general medical and dental practice. For example, the Joint Committee on Postgraduate Training for General Practice (JCPTGP) supervises training and is responsible for setting and monitoring the standards of training, the curriculum to be followed and for attesting that individual trainees have attained the required standard to enter general medical practice.

A local university with a medical school and the NHS, in England, jointly appoint the postgraduate dean. He or she is responsible for managing the delivery of medical and dental education to the standards set by Royal Colleges and their Faculties. Each manages a budget for postgraduate education and will commission training from trusts. A deanery includes a number of associate deans with diverse responsibilities, a dental postgraduate dean and a director of general practice education. The management of individual training programmes is conducted under the aegis of the deanery specialty training committees (STCs). A network of clinical tutors also supports postgraduate deans. They are usually based in, and with particular responsibilities, for a Trust or hospital. Most are part-time with clinical commitments as consultants within their hospital. Some are now taking on the broader role of Director of Medical Education for all doctors in their hospital Trust. Clinical tutors are responsible for organising local programmes of education and for managing study-leave budgets. They are normally responsible for the hospital postgraduate centre (including the library and information services). Associate deans and a network of tutors, course organisers and trainers also assist the director of general practice education and the dental postgraduate dean.

Royal Colleges and their Faculties together with postgraduate deans provide complementary mechanisms for assuring the quality of training. These include programmes of hospital visiting. All training-grade posts and programmes within the NHS must have both valid educational (college/faculty) and postgraduate dean's approval.

The Public Health Workforce

In addition to doctors working in hospital and in general practice, the medical workforce of the National Health Service also comprises public health doctors. The specialty of public health medicine is entered as part of a structured programme of postgraduate medical training. Training involves in-service and academic components. Trainees sit a two-part examination leading to Membership of the Faculty of Public Health Medicine of the Royal College of Physicians of the United Kingdom.

A number of consultant-level posts exist for doctors who have satisfactorily completed training in public health medicine. Directors of Public Health are the senior public health doctors at health authority and regional level in England (the titles of health authorities and of the senior public health doctors differ in Scotland and Northern Ireland). They form part of the health authority's senior management team and head a department of public health within the authority.

There are also posts of Consultants in Public Health Medicine. They, too, are based within health authority departments of public health. Some public health doctors specialise in communicable disease control and where this is the case they may be appointed to posts as Consultants in Communicable Disease Control (see also Chapter 9). Other public health doctors work within academic institutions such as Medical Schools where they major on teaching and research and usually have honorary contracts with health authorities to undertake public health duties within the National Health Service.

Within the health service, the role of departments of public health and the doctors who staff them differs from place-to-place but in the majority the work will encompass health needs assessment in the population, disease surveillance and control, the design of health promotion programmes as part of the local Health Improvement Programme, and advising the health authority and local Primary Care Groups and Trusts on a wide range of health policy and public health matters. Each Director of Public Health is required to produce an Annual Report on the Health of the Population in his or her locality. Such reports vary in format but will usually draw attention to the main health problems and issues as well as making recommendations for action.

During the 1990s, public health became more and more multidisciplinary in its orientation. People enter public-health training from a variety of professional backgrounds and will, after studying for a postgraduate qualification such as the Masters in Public Health, take part in a structured training programme. Increasingly, the public health workforce is seen from the perspective of the contribution necessary to develop capacity and capability to deliver public health goals and programmes. The post of non-medical specialist in public health was created in the White Paper 'Saving Lives: Our Healthier Nation', published in 1999. Thus, six main groups of staff can contribute to the public health through their work:

- those who have undertaken specialist training in public health (whether medically or non-medically qualified);
- those professional staff outside the health sector but whose organisations contribute to improving the health of the population (e.g., local authority staff such as environmental health officers, social workers, housing officers);
- health care professionals involved in the care of the patients (such as hospital doctors, nurses, midwives, health visitors, general practitioners);
- staff with expert or scientific skills fundamental to public health such as epidemiologists, toxicologists, nutritional scientists, health economists and environmental scientists;
- those with no traditional public health role but whose work could make a major contribution to public health (e.g., town and city planners, engineers and architects);
- Chief Executives of health and other organisations who are managerial leaders of institutions which can impact on population health.

This more holistic view of a public health workforce, which goes beyond simply those staff who are employed in traditional public health posts, will become increasingly important as a wider multisector, multi-agency philosophy of public health is adopted to address fundamental social, economic and environmental causes of ill health and health inequalities.

Workforce Planning Mechanisms

Extensive planning mechanisms exist for determining the size, skill mix and educational needs of the NHS workforce. For staff other than doctors and dentists, education and training needs are assessed by locally-based educational consortia comprising representatives of health authorities, NHS Trusts, Primary Care Groups and non-NHS providers of health services. These education consortia place contracts with institutions of higher education (mainly universities) for the delivery of education and training. The consortia are organised on a regional basis and there is a Regional Education and Development Group (REDG) which looks at overall strategy and coordinates the work of its constituent consortia. By April 2000 each NHS employer was expected to have in place an annual local workforce plan. Local education and development plans aim to have in place continuing professional development (CPD) arrangements for each member of staff. This is part of the goal of life long learning which was a growing part of the philosophy on education and training in all sectors which emerged in the late 1990s.

In relation to the medical workforce, an extensive advisory structure helps to develop national policy (including in some areas manpower controls). At local level Postgraduate Deans work closely with Local Medical Workforce Advisory Groups (LMWAGs) which are made up of a wide range of NHS interests.

The Estate

A major element of the resources of the health service is its estate: the buildings, land, plant and equipment from which services are delivered. The management of the resources which make up the estate is a complex and wide-ranging process. It involves the deployment of existing capital assets to meet service needs and strategic decisions about new investments. The planning and building of new hospitals is itself a complex process and includes the establishment of an initial business case, detailed planning and design, acquiring land, procurement, construction and commissioning (see also the preceding section on capital funding allocations).

Management of the estate also involves maintenance and renewal of building machinery and equipment. It involves ensuring that rigorous safety standards are met and, increasingly, it involves addressing environmental issues (such as energy consumption and waste management).

Information

The fourth element of the health services resources, information, is considered in Chapter 1.

Social Services

Local authorities must set up arrangements to discharge social services functions which are placed on them by law. Smaller authorities can agree to establish a joint social services committee or appoint jointly a Director of Social Services. The organisational structure of social services within a local authority varies around the country but social services authorities are accountable for the quality of services provided. The Social Services Inspectorate carries out national programmes of inspection of the services provided in all authorities. Local authorities must assess people whom they consider may need community care services such as: older people, people with disabilities, people with mental illness and people who misuse alcohol or drugs. They are required to produce Community Care Plans based on an assessment of local needs. They are also required to produce Children's Services Plans. Social Services must work closely with other local agencies (e.g., health authorities, education authorities and the criminal justice system).

Conclusions

The basic principles of the National Health Service have remained intact since it was introduced after World War II. This is despite a number of major reorganisations which have changed its structure and management. Also, when viewed internationally, it is generally acknowledged as a relatively efficient system of delivering health care to the population. Changes which will occur in the first few decades of the twentieth century and beyond are likely to include: a further growth in diagnostic and treatment technology, further ageing of the population, a greater emphasis on the promotion of health, a change in the role which the hospital will play in the health care system, and rising consumer expectations (Figure 4.13). It will be important for the National Health Service to adapt to and meet these challenges as they occur.

Figure 4.13 The changing philosophy of the National Health Service.

EARLIER DECADES	2000 AND BEYOND
■ Treatment emphasis	■ Public health emphasis
■ Service-based planning	■ Population-based planning
■ Demand-led priorities	■ Needs-driven priorities
■ Reactive	■ Proactive
■ Hospital-care centred	■ Primary-care centred
■ Provider dominated	■ Consumer informed
■ Professional opinion and therapeutic fashions	■ Evidence-based standards

Chapter 5

Physical Disability

Introduction

Many disease processes are wide-ranging in their impact. In some, the result is disability: a state in which the individual may experience loss or limitation of physical function; reduced opportunities in social functioning; economic hardship or disadvantage, negative attitudes and prejudice. Aside from disease, disability can arise through other causes, such as fetal abnormalities and accidents.

Disability is an important issue for public health for a number of reasons. Firstly, the proportion of people who develop disability could be reduced with more effective health promotion measures aimed at eliminating the underlying causes. Secondly, the effective use of treatment and rehabilitation services directed at restoring function in people who are already ill or injured can reduce residual disability. For example, an active multiprofessional approach to the clinical recognition, treatment and rehabilitation of people with stroke helps to prevent long-term major disability in some of those affected. Thirdly, disabled people have special needs. It is a responsibility of those planning and providing services to ensure that the needs of disabled people are clearly identified and that an appropriate and personalised response is made to them. To undertake this task properly poses enormous challenges. It is not simply a question of making adjustments in the delivery of health services. The needs of disabled people are very wide-ranging and addressing them requires approaches in many areas (Table 5.1).

Table 5.1 Some key areas of need for disabled people

- Medical care
- Building and environmental design
- Transport
- Employment (including equal opportunities)
- Education
- Communications
- Leisure
- Financial
- Social interaction
- Carer support
- Information

Perhaps the greatest challenge is to create an infrastructure of help, support and care which enables disabled people to be fully integrated within society as well as creating a climate in which they are recognized and respected as individuals, with commensurate rights and entitlements. Disabled people must never be regarded as passive recipients of care. This chapter deals with the nature and causes of physical disability as well as the needs of people who are so affected and the range of responses which can support them.

The Meaning of Disability

Whilst many classifications and definitions of disability have been formulated, the most widely accepted is that adopted by the World Health Organization in the early 1980s.[1]

In this a sequence is recognized:

disease or disorder → impairment → disability → handicap

Progress through the sequence is not necessary or inevitable but each of the terms has been given a particular meaning which is helpful in exploring the concepts both for individual need and for population needs assessment.

- *Impairment*: Disturbance of the normal structure or functioning of the body, which may be temporary or permanent.

  A state of impairment represents a deviation from normal bodily function or status, irrespective of whether it arose from injury, disease or congenital malformation. It is concerned with parts or systems of the body that do not work.

- *Disability*: Loss of, or restriction in, functional ability or activity as a result of impairment.

  A disability represents a limitation in tasks or activities, either physical, social or psychological, arising from the impairment. Disability is about things people cannot do.

- *Handicap*: A disadvantage for a given individual, resulting from an impairment or a disability that limits or prevents his or her fulfilment of a role that would be expected (depending on age, sex, social and cultural factors) for a group of which that individual is a member.

  Handicap is very dependent on the structure and attitudes of the society in which the individual exists; handicap therefore is a relative concept.

Practical Implications

The applicability of these concepts depends very much on the underlying cause of the disability, the characteristics of the individuals and the community or society in which they live. Even for particular causes of disability, people can vary greatly in the impact which the disease process has upon them. For example, a person with diabetes mellitus, by definition, is impaired since there is a disturbance to normal functioning of one organ of the body. For many diabetic people, careful self-regulation of their disease through urine glucose monitoring, diet, exercise and insulin injection will mean that they are not disabled: there is no loss or restriction of functional ability or activity because of their impairment. On the other hand, a diabetic person whose disease has progressed or been badly controlled may have complications of the illness (for example, blindness, poor circulation to the limbs) which will seriously interfere with his or her ability to function. Diabetic people will be handicapped if, for example, they are unable because of their disease to follow a particular occupation or career which would otherwise have been open to them.

Numerous other examples can illustrate the way in which the components of disablement are manifest. A person with red/green colour blindness has an impairment but is unlikely to have a disability if there is no restriction of activities. However, their choice of occupation could be restricted. For example, normal colour vision is required for driving trains. This would give rise to a handicap or disadvantage. A young woman who has been rendered paraplegic in a road accident and is confined to a wheelchair will be impaired, disabled and also handicapped.

Of even greater importance than a conceptual framework when considering the needs of disabled people are the ways in which disability is perceived by society and its individual members, the way in which disabled people themselves are affected by these attitudes and the extent to which they cope with them.

As a result of the way in which disabled people may be treated by other members of society, they themselves may develop feelings of frustration, resentment and serious loss of self-esteem. It is particularly important that health and social care professionals supporting disabled people (and their carers) are sensitive to their perceptions and have the training to deal with complex problems (Table 5.2).

Table 5.2   Perceptions of quality care by disabled people and their carers: some wants

- To be respected and understood by professionals providing services
- To be given an accurate diagnosis and prognosis sensitively
- To be involved in the planning and decision-making about their care and services

Source: Seminar report: be prepared for action. Ferring: Disability and rehabilitation open learning project, 1998.

The Assessment of Need

There are no comprehensive data available to describe the size of the problem of disability and its nature at local population level. This is for a number of reasons. Firstly, most information systems are derived from contact with hospital services, whilst many disabled people will be living in the community and will not necessarily be receiving care from hospital-based services. Secondly, the needs of disabled people have not, in the past, been a high priority for service providers. Therefore, building up accurate information on the numbers of those disabled people and on their needs has not been a concern. Thirdly, for information on disability to be of any value, it must encompass some of the definitional issues which were discussed in the previous section. Gathering valid data on this basis is extremely complex in practice.

Causes of Disability

The major underlying causes of disability (Figure 5.1) are consistent across a number of surveys. In examining population need locally, some insights into the size of the problem of disability can be derived by estimating the number of people with conditions such as stroke. This disease-based approach does not provide information on the full range of disability nor does it yield data on levels of incapacity amongst disabled people, the most important issue when assessing need and planning service responses. Some information is available from the national sample survey, the General Household Survey, which asks questions about long-term incapacity. Disability registers maintained by social services authorities under Section 29 of the National Assistance Act yield data of variable quality and are only of very limited use for local needs assessment.

Figure 5.1 Classes of disorder giving rise to disability in the world.

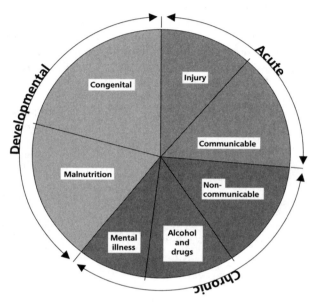

Source: Wood P, Bradley E. The epidemiology of disablement. In: Goodwill C J, Chamberlain M A (Eds), Rehabilitation of the physically disabled adult. London: Croom Helm, 1988.

Pattern in the Population

The most comprehensive information on the numbers of people with disability and the nature of their problem comes from a series of national surveys undertaken during the 1980s. Originally commissioned by the government in 1984, the Office of Population Censuses and Surveys (OPCS) carried out four separate surveys between 1985 and 1988. In 1995 the Health Survey for England repeated major parts of the 1985 disability survey series using an adapted form of the World Health Organization's questions for determining levels of disability.

The Health Survey covered private households in England and found that 18% of those aged 16 years and older had at least one type of disability out of the five covered. Overall, 4% of men and 5% of women were judged to have a serious disability. The prevalence of disability increased with age for both men and women with about three-quarters of men and women aged over 85 years having at least one disability (Figure 5.2).

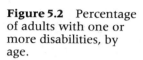

Figure 5.2 Percentage of adults with one or more disabilities, by age.

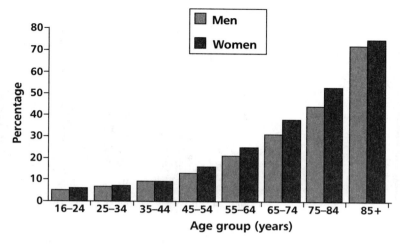

Source: Health Survey for England 1995, London: The Stationery Office, 1997.

The most commonly reported cause of disability was disease of the musculoskeletal system (in particular, arthritis) – see Table 5.3. There was a strong relationship between disability and lower social class (Figure 5.3). For men of working age who had a disability, 35% of those with any disability and 56% of those with serious disability were permanently unable to work. The comparable figures for women were slightly lower (Figure 5.4). Overall, 5% of children (boys and girls aged 10–15 years) had at least one disability and 1% had a serious disability.

Table 5.3 Reported causes of all disabilities among adults

Health complaint	Percentage[a]
Diseases of the musculoskeletal system and connective tissue:	34
• arthritis	21
• others	13
Diseases of the ear and mastoid processes	24
Diseases of the circulatory system	16
Diseases of the respiratory system	10
Eye disorders	8
Diseases of the nervous system (other than eye or ear)	5
Injury and poisoning	4
Endocrine, nutritional and metabolic diseases and immunity disorders	3
Neoplasms	2
Mental disorders	2
Others	13

a. Percentages add to more than 100 because some informants had more than one complaint.
Source: Health Survey for England 1995, London: The Stationery Office, 1997.

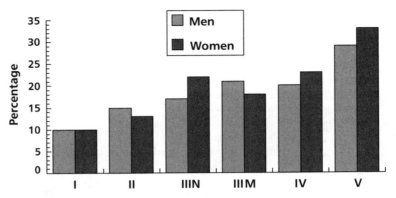

Figure 5.3 Observed percentage with one or more disabilities among adults, by social class.

Source: Health Survey for England 1995. London: The Stationery Office, 1997.

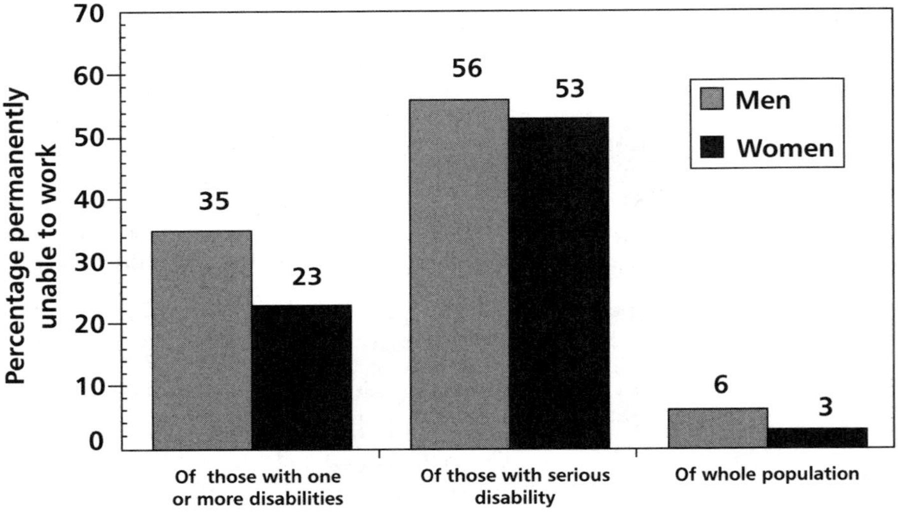

Figure 5.4 Percentage of adults of working age who are permanently unable to work.

Source: Health Survey for England 1995. London: The Stationery Office, 1997.

These major national surveys were very important in describing the size and nature of the problem of disability in the population. Increasingly, it will be necessary to gather similar data at a more local population level if the needs of disabled people are to be properly assessed and then addressed by those planning and providing services.

Visual and Hearing Disabilities

People with sensory disabilities are individuals with special needs within the disabled population. The three principal categories are people with blindness, those with deafness and those who are both deaf and blind. There are various definitions of blindness and deafness in use depending on the context.

The National Assistance Act 1948 defines blindness as 'that a person should be so blind as to be unable to perform any work for which eyesight is essential'. There is no statutory definition of partial sight. However, in practice this category refers to those who, although not blind within the meaning of the Act, are substantially and permanently handicapped by defective vision caused by congenital defect, illness or injury.

Social services authorities are required to maintain registers of people in their areas who are blind or partially sighted. Individuals are not obliged to register in order to access social services, although some concessions provided by other agencies and not related to social services are available only to people who are registered. The concessions available for blind people (e.g., the blind person's income tax allowance) are generally more significant than those available to partially sighted people, so there is a stronger incentive for blind people than for partially-sighted people to register. Even so, it is estimated that registers significantly under-record the prevalence of blindness.

Social services authorities are advised to register people as blind or partially sighted only when they have been certified as such by a medical practitioner with experience in ophthalmology (usually a consultant opthalmologist). Absolute standards are not laid down, but the advice is that most people with visual acuity below 3/60 Snellen can be certified blind, and also people with greater visual acuity but a very contracted field of vision; people with visual acuity between 3/60 and 6/60 with full field, or with greater acuity but a contracted field, may be certified partially sighted.

Social services authorities are also required to maintain registers of people who are deaf or hard of hearing. As with visual impairment, there is no requirement for individuals to register to access social services, although some unrelated concessions provided by other agencies may be available to those who do. There is no requirement for a person to be medically certified as deaf or hard of hearing before he or she is registered.

Different agencies use different terminology, but in helping users to access services it is often useful to distinguish between those who are:

- **'deaf'** (often written with a capital D): people who are born deaf or who become profoundly deaf in childhood and whose preferred language is British Sign Language (BSL);
- **'deafened'**: those who become profoundly deaf after acquiring spoken language in the usual way and who identify mainly with hearing people;
- **'hard of hearing'** or **'partially hearing'**: those who are hard of hearing but not profoundly deaf (mainly older people).

'Deafblind' is used to refer to people who have a severe degree of both visual and hearing impairment. It is not precisely defined, but does not necessarily imply that a person is completely blind or completely deaf. It has been estimated that 40 people in every 100;000 are deafblind. People aged over 65 years are thought to account for more than 50% of those who are deafblind, and the incidence of deafblindness increases sharply after the age of 75 years. Causes of deafblindness vary, as does the point in life when a person becomes deafblind:

- Until recently, the most common cause of dual sensory impairment among newborn babies was rubella contracted by the mother during pregnancy. Vaccination has reduced the incidence of rubella, but congenital deafblindness can also result from premature birth and birth trauma. Many of those who are deafblind from birth also have other disabilities, (e.g., learning disability).
- Some genetic conditions mean that people will become deafblind by the time they are young adults. For example, Usher's Syndrome results in deafness from birth and gradual loss of sight in late childhood.

- As the population ages, the number of people who are deafblind because of age-related visual and hearing impairment is growing.

Figure 5.5 Median hearing impairment for mid- and high-frequency as a function of age and noise emission (men only).

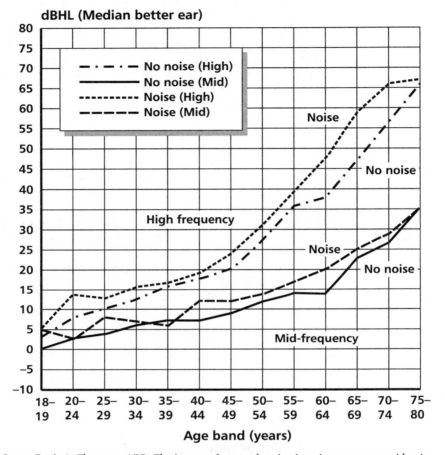

Source: Davis A, Thornton ARD. The impact of age on hearing impairment: some epidemiological evidence. Proceedings of the 14th Danavox symposium. Presbyacusis and other age-related aspects. Jensen JH (Ed), 1990.

It is important to take account of the particular needs of deafblind people in planning services: mainstream services for people who are either visually or hearing impaired may not be appropriate, as they are likely to assume, for example, that a visually-impaired person has unimpaired hearing, which a deafblind person, by definition, does not. Social services authorities may be able to provide some figures on the number of people in the area whom they know to be deafblind, but it is important to recognize that, because of their disabilities, deafblind people may be less likely to access services on their own initiative. It is therefore all the more important for service providers to take active steps to identify the level of need.

The prevalence of hearing loss in the adult population of Britain is not available from routine data sources but can be derived from well designed surveys (Figure 5.5).

Services for Disabled People

During World War I, rehabilitation regimes including physiotherapy, hydrotherapy, remedial exercises and occupational therapy were organised for orthopaedic cases. Meanwhile, the work of St Dunstan's Hospital for blinded soldiers and sailors showed how experts with a medical approach could train disabled people to acquire self-reliance and compensatory skills.

The large number of military and civilian casualties sustained during World War II brought about rapid innovations in rehabilitation methods and in special schemes for disabled people. Under the Emergency Medical Service, a large number of hospitals were taken over by the Ministry of Health for the care of war casualties and evacuated civilian patients. The improved resources together with a commitment towards war casualties stimulated a progressive attitude. The range of occupations for which disabled men were trained greatly widened to include, for example, skilled engineering work. Rehabilitation methods similar in principle to those used in orthopaedic practice, were applied to other categories of sick and injured people. Furthermore, an increasing emphasis was placed on the involvement of patients in their own treatment through techniques such as group exercise and remedial games.

The development of services for the rehabilitation of people with spinal injuries, although a specialised field, has also done much to stimulate improvements in rehabilitation services generally.

As with other groups with special needs the emphasis in providing help, support and care for people with physical disability must lie in comprehensive needs assessment by all relevant agencies working together. To meet the large range of health, social and other needs of people with a disability, requires well-coordinated and managed services and a personalised approach in organising the care and support required. The health service is only one of the agencies involved in providing such care. Social Services authorities have the lead role in community care.

Medical and Rehabilitation Services

A cornerstone of the health services' response to the problem of disability is the provision of high quality rehabilitation services. In the past, such services have grown up around wartime medicine: notably World War II and the Vietnam War. Survivors of serious injury often had considerable residual disability and their function was often considerably improved by targeted intensive rehabilitation programmes.

In Britain, although there have been some centres of excellence for rehabilitation medicine, the majority of local services have had to make do with general, rather than special, expertise. This is rapidly changing. It is now recognized that an organised, team-based approach to rehabilitation is an essential feature of local services for people with disability. Not only has there been a growth in rehabilitation as a specialty of medical practice, but there has also been increased recognition of the value of therapy services. The continuing growth of voluntary and charitable organisations and of the disabled persons movement have also been important forces for change. It was the advent of the disabled persons independent living movement in the United States of America that was a major force in the development of rehabilitation and disability services in that country.

Rehabilitation services have a number of functions. Firstly, they must undertake a full assessment of the disabled person, ideally in their home or other place of residence. This will enable functional capacity to be assessed and the scope for restoration of lost functions and acquisition of new skills to be identified. It will also identify the need for special equipment to be supplied or for adaptation to the person's day-to-day living environment. Secondly, rehabilitation services will set out to establish a clear care plan, agreed with the person concerned and their carers (if any). Thirdly, the service will set-in-hand measures and services to deliver the care plan. The circumstances vary greatly. In some cases, rehabilitation will begin following an acute hospital admission; for example, because of stroke or traumatic injury. In other cases, rehabilitation services may be offered to someone who has had a long-standing problem; for example, multiple sclerosis, but has never previously had help of this sort.

It is important to recognize that people with disability often have long-term care needs which will continue to benefit from rehabilitation services and the notion of rehabilitation as a single course of therapy is increasingly outmoded. This means that rehabilitation services will not be exclusively provided on a hospital site but will be delivered on a community-basis. Local rehabilitation teams are multiprofessional, using skills such as physiotherapy, occupational and speech therapy in addition to those of medicine and nursing.

Within the National Health Service there are increasing numbers of Consultant posts in Rehabilitation Medicine which are filled by people with specialist training. In addition to being core members of local rehabilitation teams, such consultants perform a liaison and specialist advisory role with consultants in other disciplines (for example, neurology, geriatric medicine, orthopaedics, rheumatology) where conditions giving rise to disability are commonly seen amongst their patient population.

Whilst many hospitalised patients will be able to receive help from the rehabilitation team and still remain within the service which is treating their underlying problem, some designated hospital inpatient facilities are required specifically for the treatment of disabled people. During the latter part of the 1990s, there was a clear trend to establish a three-tier system of rehabilitation services. Local general hospitals have specialist inpatient units (stroke units are common but more widely orientated disability units are also developing). Community teams then provide a link to the hospital-based service. Some of these community teams cover the full range of rehabilitation services and deal with all problems. Others are more specialised (e.g., community multiple sclerosis teams, stroke early discharge teams).

Specialist facilities are also required for the rehabilitation of people with acute traumatic injury of the spinal cord and people who have sustained head injuries. The physical, psychological, social and financial consequences of both of these types of disability are profound and justify the specific attention of services to ensure high standards of care for the groups of patients concerned.

It is also important to ensure that services specifically address the needs of young adults so that the transition from childhood to adulthood is as smooth as possible. In many areas advisory services for the disabled young school-leaver have been developed.

Many disabled people require specialist medical, surgical and nursing treatment to deal with locomotor and bladder problems. Close liaison is needed between the rehabilitation team and the hospital services concerned to ensure that the nature and timing of any intervention is the most appropriate.

Disabled Living Centres

A major focus of local services for disabled people can be the Disabled Living Centre. Such centres are still infrequent in Britain but where they exist they act as a valuable resource and information facility and provide a wide range of aids, appliances and equipment to help disabled people. Centres will undertake assessment of people to judge what sort of aids and equipment are most appropriate to their needs and will also provide advice and supervision on their use in the home environment. In some cases, this will involve home visiting by the Centre's staff. Most Disabled Living Centres provide many additional services. Typically they will give information and advice to disabled people and their families on issues such as health and social services, employment, benefits and entitlements, and sports and leisure opportunities. Their advisory function in relation to benefits may extend to an advocacy role and to representing disabled people at tribunals and hearings. They will also often serve as an educational resource to pass on expertise about caring for disabled people. Many Centres are funded from charitable sources but additional funding is usually also provided by health and local authorities. A local Disabled Living Centre can provide continuity of support, advice and help to empower and enable those with disability to have access to the complex range of services which are available.

Some Specialist Services

Whilst services such as those provided by the Disabled Living Centre are intended to be accessible to all disabled people in a particular locality, the nature of some people's disabilities will mean that they have needs which can only be met by more specialised services. The nature of such services has developed in different ways around the country either in response to a particular need, or because of local initiatives, or as a result of the enthusiasm and commitment of certain individuals or organisations. Nevertheless, there are some specialist services which are more generally available. These may be based at Disabled Living Centres or delivered from other locations.

Continence Services

Many disabled people experience a degree of urinary incontinence. This subject is discussed more fully in the chapter on elderly people but much of the core service is the same. Because the embarrassment and stigma of incontinence of urine or faeces is particularly great, an important function of continence services is to promote awareness of the problem as well as to provide practical help and support. Continence services are usually run by a continence adviser, invariably with a nursing background, who assesses the extent of the person's problem and advises on the most appropriate continence treatment, including continence and toileting aids.

Stoma Care Services

A stoma is an artificial opening to the outside of the body from one of the internal organs. The more common types of stoma are created after bowel surgery for diseases such as cancer of the bowel, ulcerative colitis and Crohn's disease. A stoma may also be created involving the urinary tract. People who have a stoma have special needs for advice, counselling and practical support. Although this may be provided by the hospital surgical service which created the stoma, increasingly, specialist services using trained stoma care nurses or therapists provide pre-operative counselling, after care and continuing support to patients.

Pressure Sore Services

Pressure sores are a particular hazard for disabled people. Their consequences can be serious and their treatment is potentially very costly. They are preventable. Many pressure sores develop amongst people who are hospitalised, particularly the elderly. The avoidance of pressure sores in this group relies upon high quality nursing care. Similarly, for people who are confined to bed in their own homes, skilled nursing care in the community will reduce the occurrence of pressure sores. For disabled people who are in wheelchairs or whose mobility is seriously restricted, it is important that they receive advice and counselling from expert staff on the measures they need to take (regular shifting of position, weight distribution cushions, special mattresses) to avoid developing a pressure sore.

Counselling Services

The psychological consequences of disability are, for most affected people, profound. Counselling and psychological intervention can provide, therefore, an important and much valued element of core services for disabled people. Therefore, it is very important that this domain of disability and handicap is not regarded as a need to which services respond as an afterthought. There are very strong arguments for a counsellor being a core member of the professional team of every local disability service.

Driving Assessment Services

The dominant feature of many disabilities is restriction of physical mobility with its potential to limit social contacts and produce difficulty in coping with aspects of independent living such as shopping, leisure, or visiting places of entertainment. For many disabled people, a car or other means of personal transport will be one of the most important features of their lives. Disability arising from a wide range of causes will affect people's ability to drive (for example, stroke, epilepsy, muscular dystrophy, amputation, rheumatoid arthritis). A person's fitness to drive must be taken into account by the Driving and Vehicle Licensing Authority (DVLA) based in Swansea whose staff (making use of medical advisers) will decide whether the disability could constitute a danger when driving. Medical reports and assessments will usually be required from the person's local doctor.

A disabled driver has three main needs. Firstly, to be fully assessed. Secondly, to be advised on the type of car most suited to his or her needs (with adaptations and modifications where appropriate). Thirdly, to receive advice on how to finance the purchase.

There are a number of assessment centres for disabled drivers around the country which provide these services including the opportunities to try out particular vehicles and adaptations. Some also offer advice on wheelchairs and pavement vehicles. It is important that local disability services have good links with them so that they can ensure disabled people have access to the centres, even though they may live some distance away.

Prosthetics and Orthotics

A prosthesis is a device which replaces a missing part. For example, the fitting of an artificial limb to a person who has lost all or part of their limb due to amputation because of trauma, vascular disease or cancer.

There are many other types of prostheses and they are becoming increasingly sophisticated as a result of advances in modern science and technology as well as higher expectations of people themselves.

The fitting of prostheses is one which *par excellence* requires a service based upon an ethos of high quality and patient-centred care. In the case of an artificial limb, the scope of the service should involve pre-operative counselling, the operation itself, the assessment and fitting of the prosthesis, gait training, after-care and support. Such an approach requires general practitioners, surgeons, physiotherapists, occupational therapists, other members of the rehabilitation team and prosthetic fitters, engineers and suppliers working closely together. Increasingly, for example, it is recognized that the quality of a surgical amputation is a vital determining feature of a successful prosthesis for the patient. The idea that amputations should be left for the most junior member of the surgical team to gain experience is no longer acceptable. It is a growing practice for amputations to be performed by senior surgeons who undertake larger numbers of such operations and who work closely with the prosthetic and rehabilitation teams.

An orthosis is an appliance or piece of equipment which is attached to the body to enhance function. Orthoses can range from splints or collars applied to support an arthritic joint to calliper-type devices used to assist movement where muscles are weak or paralysed, to devices which support or redistribute weight (for example, special footwear). The orthosis is usually arranged following a prescription by a consultant. Orthotics is a well established service for disabled people but it could be better integrated into rehabilitation services. Many orthoses are supplied by private firms whose orthotist also does the assessment. This can lead to a conflict of interest. However, the NHS Supplies organisation is well qualified to offer advice on contracting, quality and value for money. NHS Supplies has an Orthotic Strategic Supplies Group which includes representatives of users. This group works with manufacturers to make devices more cosmetically appealing and to exploit the latest developments in technology.

In some instances the Orthotic and Prosthetic services are being integrated using the same management structure and facilities of the Disablement Service Centre; which is starting to improve the overall provision of orthoses.

Wheelchair and Special Seating Services

Wheelchairs are an important aid to mobility for disabled people. The majority are prescribed and supplied at local level by a therapist. Some disabled people will require a more specialised chair and, in such cases, assessment and supply may have to be arranged at a centre dealing with special problems and serving a wider population. A wide range of wheelchairs (non-powered and powered) are available both for indoor and outdoor use. The wheelchair service is also responsible for assessing and providing special seating for disabled people with major postural problems.

Communication Aids

Difficulties with speech and communication are an important consequence of some causes of disability. For this reason, a speech therapist should also be a member of the team providing core rehabilitation services for disabled people at local level. In addition to speech therapy services, some people can greatly benefit from a mechanical aid to communication. Each person should receive careful individual assessment to determine which of the many possible aids to communication are best suited to their needs. Communication aids are normally provided through a network of Communication Aids Centres. Equipment ranges from simple voice amplifiers, to devices controlled by non-affected parts of the body (for example, eyeball, finger, chin, toe) which will link up to electronic typewriters, computers, or to the more complex communication and environmental controls systems. Until the late 1980s the main supplier was Possum which became the term used by health professionals to refer to this kind of equipment. During the 1990s the range of approved manufacturers has been added to and an increasingly varied range of environmental control equipment is supplied.

Technical Aids and Medical Physics Services

The supply of technical aids specifically tailored to an individual's needs is an essential part of disability services. The Medical Physics department of a hospital will be the usual route through which such services are delivered. A range of 'aids for daily living' is also supplied by social services departments.

Aids for Sensory Disabilities

It is important to ensure that sensorily-impaired people have had a proper clinical assessment. They must also have access to medical and surgical treatment where they can potentially benefit from it. Having said this, a proportion of sensorily-impaired people will not have a problem which is amenable to specific intervention. The approach is then to ensure that they receive aids and equipment to minimise the degree of disability and handicap caused by their condition. In the case of the deaf, this can mean the fitting of a hearing aid, or other devices to assist amplification of sound, aids to the home (such as lights on telephones and door bells), and vibration devices for the profoundly deaf.

Similarly, the range of aids and equipment for blind people is now quite large. Longer-term measures used in the rehabilitation of blind people include teaching them to read Braille and Moon and touch-typing. Some of these services are more appropriate for the younger blind rather than very elderly people. The Wireless for the Blind Fund can arrange for any registered blind person in need of a radio to have one. Free membership is available to blind people for the Braille National Library for the Blind and for the Royal National Institute for the Blind which also has a large talking book library.

Braille dials can be fitted to most gas and electric cookers. Clocks and watches are available with special markings and embossed playing cards, chess, dominoes, draughts and other games are obtainable.

Primary Care and Community Services

Many of the services for disabled people already described in this section are delivered to people living in the community. Most disabled people will be registered with a general practitioner. Through this, they will have access to the services provided by a Primary Care Group or Trust, including home nursing, dietetic and chiropody services, as well as general medical care. However, many disabled people may not be in regular contact with their general practitioner. Thus, whilst general practitioners provide a logical point of contact for disabled people, the numbers and requirements of disabled people in the practice population may not be clearly identified. Community social care services such as meals-on-wheels, home-helps and care assistants which are most often provided for older people (described in Chapter 8) can also be provided to younger disabled people.

Day Care

Day care should be an important component in the network of services for disabled people. It is mainly provided by either social services departments or by certain voluntary organisations, although specialist hospital facilities may develop a day care service alongside acute work.

Regular attendance at a day care centre can facilitate important social contact and access to other specialist services. On a more practical level, meals are usually provided in the day care setting. Such measures also provide a safe and comfortable environment. Some day care, particularly that provided by voluntary organisations, has social integration as its main aim. It focuses on providing social activities for both able-bodied and disabled people. Such organisations tend to operate on an informal, drop-in basis.

Support for Carers

Adequate support for those providing informal care to people with special needs is an increasingly important aim of statutory services. It is a key feature of the formal arrangements for community care described at various points in this book in relation to other care groups. Carers must be fully involved in the assessment process, not only as partners with statutory agencies in providing care for disabled people, but also as individuals who themselves may have special needs.

The support which carers need has two dimensions. The first is aimed at providing the carer with a break. Services such as sitting services, respite care services, emergency cover and holiday care are all examples of what is required to enable the carer to be relieved of the task of caring for a short time. It is particularly important that respite services are available when carers want them, and that there is continuity of care among respite personnel. The second type of support for carers is aimed at helping the carer directly in the caring role. Examples would be education about lifting the disabled person and preventing pressure sores or in managing incontinence. Opportunities to form and participate in carers' support groups are also useful. Here, as is the case with all disability services, it is extremely important that health and social services agencies work together so that the full spectrum of carers' needs can be addressed.

Residential Care

Different agencies are involved in providing residential accommodation: local authorities, voluntary organisations and the private sector. The NHS has responsibility for those with continuing health care needs. The type of residential accommodation needed by disabled people depends on individual requirements.

Employment and Training

Work, although a means of financing household necessities and leisure pursuits, also provides status and self-esteem for the individual and is the basis of many social contacts. Indeed, for some it represents the main focus of their lives. The work orientation of many modern societies is a source of additional pressure for disabled people. Even those who are more severely disabled will perceive work as a means of drawing closer to other members of society.

Careers guidance is important to help people, particularly young people, decide which option is best for them to fulfil their potential. The Careers Service, as part of its ongoing work, will focus its help on those who need it most including those with learning difficulties and/or disabilities.

There are in-place a number of measures to help disabled adults and young people access and remain in employment. Work-based provision for young people is important and includes Modern Apprenticeships, National Traineeships and other specific training provision.

The majority of disabled adults will be helped through the mainstream employment and training measures delivered by the Employment Service and Chambers of Commerce/Training and Enterprise. Advice is available from the local Jobcentre. This provision includes Programme Centres which modularise training to meet individual needs, Work Trials and work-based learning for adults.

In addition, there is a range of specialist disability measures. Disabled people have access to the specialist Employment Service Disability Employment Advisers in the local Disability Service Teams. As well as providing general advice to individuals and employers they will be able to give details of the specialist disability measures.

These include Access to Work which provides help in the form of equipment, aids and adaptations, fares to work and communicator/interpreter support. The Job Introduction Scheme provides a subsidy to employers for an agreed number of weeks to employers to assess an individual's suitability for a particular job. The Supported Employment Programme provides employment for people whose disabilities are more severe. This is provided by organisations such as Remploy and voluntary bodies and local authorities and can be supported placements with employers or in sheltered workshops or factories.

Work Preparation is available to help individuals to get to work by addressing their specific employment-related needs that result from their disability and prevent them from retaining, taking up work or vocational training of a type that would otherwise be suitable for them.

In addition to work-based learning for adults, mentioned earlier, there is specialist residential training provision for adults at 15 colleges throughout the country. These are accessed by disabled people in collaboration with their local Disability Employment Adviser in the first place.

Benefits and Allowances

Table 5.4 Financial benefits and entitlements according to disability and need

Need	Response
Incapable of work • previously employed • insufficient NI contributions • insufficient to live on	Statutory Sick Pay/Incapacity Benefit Severe Disablement Allowance Income Support
Unemployed	Job Seekers Allowance/Income Support
Incapable of work	Job Seekers Allowance/Income Support
Working at least 16 hours a week	Disability Working Allowance
Injured or contracted disease at work	Industrial Injuries Disablement Benefit/Reduced Earnings Allowance
Vaccine damage	Vaccine Damage Payment
Injury due to violent crime	Criminal Injuries Compensation
War disablement	War Disablement Pension/War Widows Pension
Retirement	Retirement Pension/Income Support
Help with personal care	Disability Living Allowance Care Component/Attendance Allowance/Independent Living Funds
Problems with walking	Disability Living Allowance Mobility Component/Motability Scheme/Road Tax Exemption/Orange Badge Scheme
Practical help at home	Care Services (Home-help, meals-on-wheels) from social services and/or NHS
Help with NHS glasses, hospital fares	Health Benefits
Housing problems, renovation or other housing grants	Housing Benefit, Council Tax Benefit
Caring – for at least 35 hours a week	Invalid Care Allowance
Disabled children	Child Benefit/Guardian's Allowance/One Parent Benefit/Family Credit/Disability Allowance/Family Fund/Health Benefits
Insufficient Income	Income Support/Job Seekers Allowance/Family Credit/Disability Working Allowance/Social Fund Community Care Grant/Budgeting Loan/Crisis Loan
Other	Other benefits from other government departments such as Department of Employment or local authority (e.g., leisure pass, bus pass) or private sector (e.g., rail passes)

Source: Barnes MP. Broader Issues in Rehabilitation – Handicap and Participation. In: Barnes MP, Ward AB (Eds). Textbook of Rehabilitation Medicine. Oxford University Press, Oxford, 2000.

Note: legislation in this field is rapidly changing and subject to modification. This table should be regarded as giving a general indication of the types of support available in the late 1990s.

Many disabled people have a lower earning capacity than other members of society and are over-represented in the lower socio-economic groups. By the nature of their disability as well as on the basis of their level of income, disabled people are entitled to a wide range of benefits, special payments and income support. People who care for those with a disability also have certain entitlements. The whole system of financial support is quite complex and changes rapidly but the broad categories of need which require a financial response from the State are more stable (Table 5.4). An important component of services for disabled people and their carers is a mechanism to ensure that they are receiving their full entitlements. In practice, this means the provision of leaflets and other printed information in an easily readable form coupled with access to people who are skilled in the interpretation of the regulations and who can give specific advice and help. It is not surprising that specialist advisory staff are often in great demand where they are part of a Disabled Living Centre.

Conclusions

The value attached to disabled people and the extent to which they are regarded and treated as full members of the population is an important indicator of how caring a society is. Identifying the numbers of people in the population who are disabled, describing the nature of their disability and the needs which result from it has not been accorded a high priority in the past. Assessing need at both individual and population level is a key prerequisite to the provision of appropriate services and requires attention being given to gathering and maintaining high quality information. Services for disabled people will be most effective when they are based on such needs assessment and when they are founded on teamwork – both at the organisational (health, local authority and voluntary agency) and at the individual level (doctors, nurses, therapists, social workers).

Chapter 6

Mothers and Children

Introduction

Until about 70 years ago, childbirth was an event which threatened the life of both mother and baby. Deaths of women in labour were not uncommon and children's funerals were a prominent feature of everyday life.

Throughout the ages, children have been subjected to harsh and inhuman treatment and, until this century, infanticide in England was regularly practised. Not everyone appreciates that the famous politician and Prime Minister of the last century, Benjamin Disraeli (1804–1881), was also a novelist. A quotation from *Sybil; Or The Two Nations* is an eloquent commentary on life at that time for some mothers and children:

> 'About a fortnight after his mother had introduced him into the world, she returned to her factory and put her infant out to nurse: that is to say, paid three pence a week to an old woman, who takes charge of these newborn babies for the day and gives them back at night to their mothers as they hurriedly return from the scene of their labour to the dungeon or the den, which is still by courtesy called 'home'. The expense is not great: laudanum and treacle, administered in the shape of some popular elixir, affords these innocents a brief taste of the sweets of existence and, keeping them quiet, prepares them for the silence of their impending grave. Infanticide is practised as extensively and as legally in England as it is on the banks of the Ganges: a circumstance which apparently has not yet engaged the attention of the Society for the Propagation of the Gospel in Foreign Parts.'

From the beginning of the present century up to modern times there has been a steep decline, both in maternal deaths and in mortality in the early years of life and later childhood. There is still considerable scope for improvement. In particular, many traditional inequalities between different sections of the population persist.

This chapter deals with the health of children and of mothers around the time of childbirth. The main ways of assessing health and need in these sections of the population are described. The scope for the promotion of health in the early years of life is discussed in relation to the prevention of fetal loss and of fetal abnormalities as well as the measures required to improve health amongst women of childbearing age. The range of services which are provided for mothers and children are described and where appropriate, set in their statutory framework.

Births, Deaths and Fertility

Registration of Births and Stillbirths

Registration of births, and stillbirths is a legal requirement. The information is collected by the local Registrar of Births, Marriages and Deaths and transmitted to the Office for National Statistics.

In England, Wales and Northern Ireland, every birth must be registered:

- by a parent or other informant;
- with the local Registrar;
- within 42 days of birth.

Information collected as part of birth registration covers: date and place of birth; the baby's name and surname and its sex; the name, address and place of birth of parents; the occupation of the father, and the mother's maiden name (or surname at marriage). Confidential information is also collected (but not entered in the register) which includes dates of birth of mother and father; date of parents' marriage (if appropriate whether the mother was previously married); number of previous children (with present and previous husbands), and whether live or stillborn.

As with live births, the same legal obligation exists to ensure registration of stillbirths. The legal definition of a stillbirth as amended by the Stillbirth (Definition) Act 1992 is:

'A child which has issued forth from its mother after the 24th week of pregnancy and which did not at any time after, having been completely expelled from its mother, breathe or show any other signs of life.'

Notification of Births

In addition to birth registration, a parallel process of birth notification takes place. The midwife, doctor or other attendant at the birth is required to notify within 36 hours the health authority in which the birth occurred. The information usually reported in this notification includes: birthweight, length of gestation, parity and the presence of fetal abnormality.

It is important to understand that registration and notification of births serve different purposes. Registration is essentially intended to collect information for statistical purposes. Notification is intended to alert health services to the birth of the child so that the necessary care can be provided to support the mother and her new baby. Here there is a need for urgency in passing on the information about the birth of the child. There is also an exchange of information between the health service and the Registrar of Births and Deaths. The local health authority passes brief information of the notification of births to the Registrar as they are received in order to assist in obtaining full registration. The only medical information which is transferred is birthweight. It is incorporated with the cooperation of Registrars and is not a legal requirement. When added to the other data collected at birth registration, it allows statistics of live and stillbirths to be compiled to include this important variable.

Registration of Deaths

As with births, deaths of babies must also be registered, in this case within five days of their occurrence. In the mid-1980s new certificates were introduced in England and Wales to cover stillbirth and neonatal death (death of a baby born alive but dying in the first four weeks of life). Certification accords with World Health Organization standards. The certificate includes information on both maternal and fetal causal factors (Table 6.1). Deaths occurring after the neonatal period are certified by a doctor and are also then registered with the local registrar of births, marriages and deaths.

Table 6.1   Cause of death categories in the certification of stillbirth and neonatal death

- Main diseases or conditions in the fetus or infant
- Other diseases or conditions in the fetus or infant
- Main maternal diseases or conditions affecting the fetus or infant
- Other maternal diseases or conditions affecting the fetus or infant
- Other relevant causes

Ascertainment and Validity

Ascertainment of births through the registration process in Britain is high. The vast majority of births are registered by the parent or another proper informant. Any birth where there has been contact with a health care professional will in addition be picked up through the cross-check of the notification system. There are a small number of births (for example, as a result of concealed pregnancy) where there may be further delay in registration. On the whole, in Britain the quality of information on birth certificates is very good, although there may be problems with the names used by parents on certificates.

Ascertainment of death in infancy is also virtually complete. Only those deaths which are concealed following criminal violence may fail for a considerable period to be recognized. However, there is delay in the registration of those deaths where there has been a Coroner's inquest. Information on cause of death as registered is not always reliable. It is most likely to be accurate if there has been a post-mortem examination.

Internationally, systems for birth and death registration vary and may be weak in some parts of the developing world. It is important to bear this in mind when comparing mortality rates in infancy and childhood internationally. In some parts of the developing world, particularly those where there is internal disruption due to war or famine, information on infant and perinatal mortality is available only from *ad hoc* surveys, usually conducted by international aid organisations.

Indices of Fertility

Crude Birth Rate

The number of live births, expressed as a rate per 1000 total population per annum, is the annual crude birth rate. Although often quoted, it is a poor indicator of fertility because included in the denominator are men, children and post-menopausal women, (the limitations of 'crude' rates are discussed in Chapter 1).

General Fertility Rate

A better denominator is used in the general fertility rate, which is calculated by expressing the number of live births per 1000 women in the population of child-bearing age (by convention this is usually taken as those aged 15–44 years).

Age-specific Fertility Rates

Because there are differences in levels of fertility amongst women of different ages within the child-bearing years, an even more precise measure of fertility is obtained by calculating the number of births to a specified age-group per 1000 women of that same age-group. For example, the fertility rate for women aged 20–24 years is calculated by taking the number of live births occurring to mothers aged 20–24 years and expressing them per 1000 women aged between 20 and 24 years in the population.

Total Period Fertility Rate

The total period fertility rate is a convenient summary of all the age-specific rates. This rate is the sum of the age-specific fertility rates, in this case expressed as live births per woman of a single age, rather than per 1000 women. It measures the average number of live-born children per woman which would occur if the current age-specific fertility rates applied over the entire 30 years of the reproductive span. It therefore takes account of differential fertility within the different reproductive age-groups, whilst providing a convenient summary measure in a single figure. It can be thought of as reflecting the average number of children which would be born to women who experienced the age-specific fertility rates of the year in question throughout their reproductive lives. It enables comparisons to be made between countries and within the same country over time because it is not affected by the age distribution of women in the reproductive age-groups.

Cohort Measures of Fertility

All indices of fertility so far described have referred to births at a specific period of time, most often a single year. However, births in any given year occur to a cross-section of women, married at different ages and with differing numbers of previous children. Temporary fluctuations in 'period' indices may simply reflect the timing of births within a reproductive lifespan without any important change in the number of children women will have by the time they have come to the end of their reproductive years. A cohort of women is a population of women who were born in a particular year (generation or birth cohort). Studies of fertility, following such cohorts of women, observe the occurrence and timing of births in their reproductive lifetime. The cohort fertility rate (which gives the completed family size for women born around the same time) provides a much more stable basis for commenting on trends and predicting future levels of fertility than do measures based on a specific period of time (Figure 6.1). The cohort fertility rate has the disadvantage that it cannot properly be calculated until the cohort concerned has completely passed out of the childbearing years.

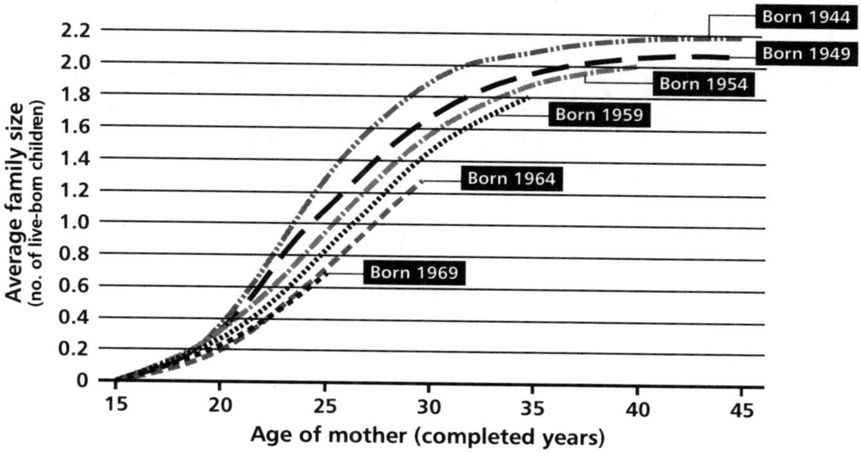

Figure 6.1 Cohort fertility rates for women born in England and Wales at various times.

Source: Armitage B, Babb P. Population Trends, 1996; 84:7–13.

Trends in Fertility

A fall in fertility in Britain during the economic depression of the 1930s stimulated considerable national concern about the long-term growth of the population. An increase in the birth rate occurred after World War II, since when fertility has been dominated by two distinct trends. During the decade between the mid-1950s and the mid-1960s, the number of births, the crude birth rate, the general fertility rate and total period fertility rate all rose reaching a peak in the mid-1960s (the so-called 'baby boom' generation). The succeeding decade showed a sharp fall in the same indices of fertility. In 1977, the crude birth-rate, the general fertility rate and the total period fertility rate, all fell below their corresponding values in 1933 – the previous lowest level of this century. Trends in these indices over the last several decades are shown in Table 6.2. By the beginning of the 1990s, fertility had increased well above its low point in 1977 but not to the high level of the 1960s. Changes in the fertility rates in the 1960s and 1970s have not been properly explained and were largely unpredicted. The 1990s saw a slight recovery from the low of the mid-1970s but has remained below the natural population replacement level of 2.1. This did not stop the population growing during the 1990s because the number of deaths remained below births and inward migration.

Table 6.2 Changes in various indices of fertility for selected years (England and Wales)

Fertility index*	Year or Period							
	1933	1940–42	1950–52	1960–62	1978	1980–82	1990	1998
Crude birth rate	14.4	15.6	15.6	17.6	12.1	12.9	13.9	12.1
General fertility rate	59.4	61.3	72.1	88.9	60.1	61.8	64.3	59.0
Total period fertility rate	1.72	1.81	2.16	2.77	1.73	1.81	1.84	1.73

Source: Office for National Statistics. *See text for definitions.

The greatest number of births occur in the 25–29 year-old age-group but fertility rates amongst younger women declined from the late 1960s onwards. For example, in England and Wales in 1966, 176 live births occurred for every 1000 women aged 20–44 years. By 1977 the figure was 76 per 1000. Fertility amongst older women rose slightly during the 1980s and 1990s so that the gap in fertility rates between older and younger women narrowed. These trends were also reflected in mean age at childbirth (Table 6.3).

Table 6.3   Mean age at live childbirth in England and Wales

Year	All births	First birth	Second birth	Third birth	Fourth birth
1964	27.2	23.9	26.8	29.3	31.0
1977	26.5	24.4	26.8	28.8	30.6
1989	27.3	25.3	27.6	29.5	30.9
1998	30.3	29.2	30.7	31.8	32.7

Source: Office for National Statistics.

There has also been an increase in childlessness over successive cohorts of women. Amongst the 1945 cohort, 34% were childless at 25 years of age compared with 61% for those born in 1969. There has also been an increase in childlessness over successive cohorts of women. There may be some catching up in the older years for this cohort but not enough to reverse what seems to be the genuine option of childlessness for more couples.

Another trend during the 1980s and 1990s in the United Kingdom was the increase in the proportion of births which occurred outside marriage (from around 7% in the mid-1960s to 32% in the mid-1990s). Generally, levels of fertility have been higher for women born outside the United Kingdom.

Factors Affecting Fertility

In few societies do women produce the maximum number of children of which they are physiologically capable.

Factors which determine sexual behaviour in society are wide-ranging and complex. They include the influence of society's norms and expectations, the family, the law, social and psychological factors, religion and lifestyle. Availability and use of contraception, levels of economic prosperity and patterns of marriage and cohabitation may also have independent effects on the number of children a woman may have.

A number of explanations have been put forward to account for the changes in fertility which have occurred during the twentieth century.

Three common interpretations of the trends are as follows:

(1)   *Contraceptive availability.* The widespread availability of modern contraceptive methods, particularly the introduction of oral contraception in Britain in the early 1960s. However, fertility fell in a similar way in the 1930s, when contraceptive technology was primitive. Trends in fertility, similar to those seen in Britain over the last 20 years, occurred in other industrial societies in Western Europe, North America and Australia and not all had well-developed Family Planning Services. It seems unlikely that the availability of the oral contraceptive pill is the entire story.

(2) *Level of affluence*. Levels of income and attitudes towards future prosperity are said to be influential. Hence, a parallel is drawn between the economic depression of the 1930s, which is considered to have been largely responsible for the reduction in fertility at that time, and the downturn in fertility in the early 1970s when an economic recession also prevailed. However, the decline in fertility had started well before the financial crisis brought about by the increase in oil prices in 1973; so, once again, this cannot be the whole explanation.

(3) *Working women*. More women of childbearing age now enter the labour force. It is believed that women restrict their family size in order to remain at work. However, the upward trend in the proportion of married women at work was just as steep during the rise in fertility in the early 1960s as it was during the decline in the 1970s.

It is probable that all three factors, as well as others, influence fertility in a complex manner that is not fully understood – which illustrates the difficulty in predicting trends in fertility, even in the relatively short-term.

Health and Need Amongst Children and Women in Pregnancy

Internationally, comparison of maternal, infant and childhood mortality is a vital epidemiological tool and these three measures are powerful indicators of the general health of the population. Traditionally they have been used as an indicator of a nation's health since they are closely related to standard of living, inequalities in social and economic measures within the country concerned and with the quality of medical care. In the developed world differences still occur across populations in maternal, perinatal and infant mortality because of these underlying influences. However, as rates have fallen during the twentieth century, the number of deaths in developed countries has been relatively small. Measures of mortality are not, therefore, as useful – particularly when looking at smaller populations. It is also important to measure disease and disability and to concentrate on underlying factors in exploring unexplained deaths or fetal abnormalities.

Maternal Mortality

Improvements in the general health of women, general medical advances (for example, the advent of antibiotics and blood transfusion), a reduction in the number of illegal abortions, together with improved standards of obstetric care and anaesthetic care, all contributed to a major decline in maternal mortality during the twentieth century (Figure 6.2). In 1847 the maternal mortality rate was around 6 per 1000 total births and fell to around 4 per 1000 births by 1937. A sharp fall in the rate occurred after 1937, probably due to the introduction of sulphonamides. The rate in 1994–96 was 12.1 per 100,000 maternities. The denominator 'maternity' for this rate refers to pregnancies which result in a live birth or stillbirth.

A maternal death is defined by the World Health Organization as:

> '…the death of a woman while pregnant or within 42 days of termination of pregnancy, from any cause related to or aggravated by the pregnancy or its management, but not from accidental or incidental causes.'

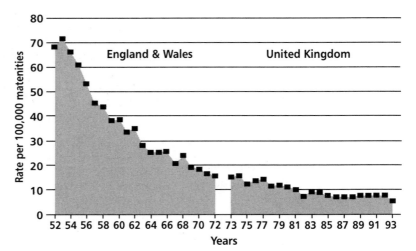

Figure 6.2 Post-war trends in maternal mortality per 100,000 maternities.

Source: Report on Confidential Enquiries into Maternal Deaths in the United Kingdom. London: HMSO, 1996.

Maternal deaths are subdivided into 'direct', 'indirect', 'fortuitous' and 'late'. Direct maternal deaths are those resulting from obstetric complications of pregnancy, labour and the puerperium. Indirect maternal deaths are those arising from an existing disease or from one which developed in pregnancy and whose effects were accelerated or altered by the pregnancy. Fortuitous maternal deaths are those resulting from causes not related to or influenced by pregnancy. Late deaths are those which occur 42 days after delivery, miscarriage or termination and these can be either *direct, indirect* or *fortuitous*.

A detailed confidential enquiry into maternal deaths is carried out in the United Kingdom and reports at three-year intervals. The enquiry into a maternal death is initiated in England by the Director of Public Health (DPH) of the district in which the woman was usually resident (or equivalent public health chief officers in other United Kingdom countries). Using a standard enquiry form, information is collected from the various health staff concerned with the care of the woman. These may include general practitioners, midwives, health visitors, consultant obstetricians and anaesthetists.

The completed form, together with the Director of Public Health's comments, is forwarded to an obstetric assessor (and, where appropriate, to an anaesthetic, pathology or midwifery assessor). Pathology assessors review details of post-mortem or other pathological investigations. The assessors add their comments and opinions regarding the cause of death. The forms are then sent to the Director of the Enquiry. Central assessors review all the recorded information and act as final arbiters in evaluating the factors which may have led to death. Strict confidentiality is observed at all stages and reports based on the analysis are published every three years. The reports draw general conclusions about causes of maternal deaths and changes over time and they make recommendations for action based upon the lessons learned. The enquiry is now under the overall auspices of the National Institute for Clinical Excellence (NICE) – see Chapter 4.

Since the 1970s, the two leading causes of direct maternal death have been pulmonary embolism and hypertension in pregnancy (Figure 6.3).

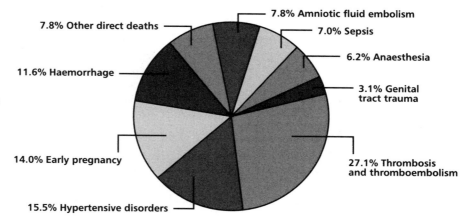

Figure 6.3 Causes of direct maternal deaths: United Kingdom, 1991–1993.

7.8% Amniotic fluid embolism

7.0% Sepsis

6.2% Anaesthesia

3.1% Genital tract trauma

27.1% Thrombosis and thromboembolism

15.5% Hypertensive disorders

14.0% Early pregnancy

11.6% Haemorrhage

7.8% Other direct deaths

Source: Report on Confidential Enquiries into Maternal Deaths in the United Kingdom. London: HMSO, 1996.

Despite the relatively low level of maternal deaths compared to the past, reports of the confidential enquiries into maternal mortality continue to make recommendations which, if implemented, would bring about further improvements. The most recent triennial report contains important public health messages concerning nutrition, smoking, alcohol, the correct use of seat belts and domestic violence. Cases in which substandard care was judged to have been present in maternal deaths are highlighted in the report. Past reports have highlighted issues such as: diagnostic errors; inappropriate treatment; the need for better communication between doctors, midwives and other professional staff involved in caring for pregnant women; greater involvement of consultants during pregnancy and labour, and a failure to recognize and act upon potential problems when they develop.

Mortality in Early Life

Death rates in infancy are constructed differently from the mortality rates of later childhood and adult life. Births occurring during the same period as the deaths, not the population of a particular age-group, is the denominator. 'Infancy' is taken as the first year of life and thus, the *infant mortality rate* in a given period of time (usually a year) is the number of deaths of children under the age of one year (numerator) per 1000 live births in the same period.

The infant mortality rate has long been regarded as an important measure of the health of a community. However, it is a rather crude indicator because deaths occurring during different periods of the first year of life usually reflect different groups of causal factors. It has become customary to consider deaths in infancy in a number of different time periods:

(a) *Perinatal deaths* – deaths from the 24th week of gestation up to six completed days of life.
(b) *Early neonatal deaths* – deaths between birth and six complete days of life.
(c) *Late neonatal deaths* – deaths from seven to 27 completed days of life.
(d) *Neonatal deaths* – deaths in the first 27 completed days of life.
(e) *Postneonatal deaths* – deaths at 28 days but under one year of life.

Table 6.4 Definitions of annual mortality rates of infancy

• Stillbirth rate	Number of stillbirths per 1000 total births per annum
• Perinatal mortality rate	Number of stillbirths together with deaths up to six completed days of life per 1000 total births per annum
• Early neonatal mortality rate	Number of deaths up to six completed days of life per 1000 live births per annum
• Late neonatal mortality rate	Number of deaths between the 7th and 27th completed days of life per 1000 live births per annum
• Neonatal mortality rate	Number of deaths in the first 27 completed days of life per 1000 live births per annum
• Postneonatal mortality rate	Number of deaths at ages 28 days and over but before the end of the first year of life per 1000 live births per annum
• Infant mortality rate	Number of deaths from the first day of life to the end of the first year of life per 1000 live births per annum

The formal definitions of these rates are shown in Table 6.4. The various mortality rates are constructed around these different periods of infancy (Figure 6.4). The numerator is all deaths occurring within the period of infancy in question (usually during a calendar year), the denominator is the number of registered live births during that same calendar year. The exceptions to this general rule are stillbirths (babies born dead after 24 weeks of gestation) and perinatal deaths (stillbirths plus babies dying in the first week after birth) where the denominator in each case is total births (i.e., both live and stillbirths). In other words, when stillbirths are included in the numerator then the denominator is total births, not live births alone. Records of infant deaths are routinely linked nationally to their birth certificates. This enables such deaths to be analysed using data collected at birth registration (which is more extensive).

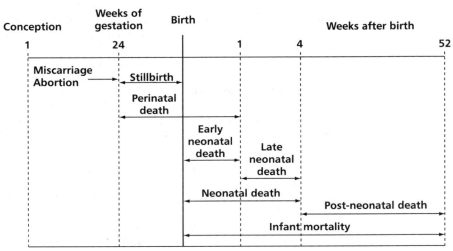

Figure 6.4 Subdivision of deaths in infancy.

Perinatal deaths

Amongst the reasons for using this index, which groups together stillbirths and deaths in the first week of life, is that the factors responsible for these two types of death are often similar, being those operating before or around the time of birth. Another practical reason is that it overcomes some of the difficulties (particularly in making international comparisons) of variation between different localities as to which conceptuses are regarded as stillborn and which as having been born alive but died shortly after birth. Information on perinatal deaths is determined from national death certification and birth registration data. In addition, each region in England, together with Wales and Northern Ireland, is required to participate in a confidential enquiry of stillbirths and infant deaths (CESDI). In this way, causes of death are established and potentially avoidable factors can be identified.

Just 50 years ago in Britain, one in every 20 babies was either born dead or died within the first week of life. By the late 1990s, these major risks of fetal life and of birth had receded to the extent that only one in 120 babies failed to survive the first week of life. Whilst the perinatal mortality rate has fallen steadily (Figure 6.5) there is still considerable regional variation (Figure 6.6). However, the perinatal mortality rate varies between localities and fluctuates from year-to-year. Conclusions based upon comparisons between places and within places over time must be very cautiously drawn because the variations observed may be arising from very small numbers. A statutory change to the definition of stillbirths (commencing from the 24th week of gestation not the 28th as previously), introduced in October 1992 has implications for the interpretation of trends over time. Figure 6.7 summarises the factors contributing to perinatal death together with ascertainment processes. This is useful to consider when making international comparisons or exploring or interpreting variation between localities.

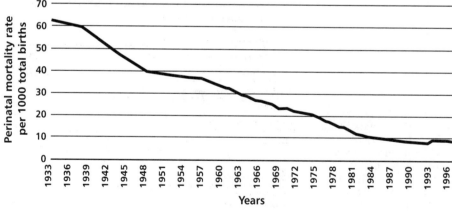

Figure 6.5 Perinatal mortality in England and Wales.

Source: Office for National Statistics.

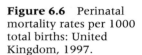

Figure 6.6 Perinatal mortality rates per 1000 total births: United Kingdom, 1997.

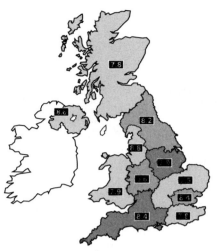

Source: Office for National Statistics.

Much of the reduction in perinatal mortality has been associated with an overall improvement in the health and nutrition of the population; also, far fewer women are having a large number of pregnancies. In addition, over the last several decades there have been major technological advances in the care of pregnant women and the newborn. Such treatments are now accepted as commonplace today but at the time of their introduction may have appeared to be as unnatural as some of the techniques used in the care of women in labour or very tiny babies today. Natural childbirth arguments have led to the acknowledgement that high-technology care is not necessarily appropriate for every mother but recent improvements in perinatal mortality would have been hard to achieve without it.

Figure 6.7 Conceptual model of the relationship between quality of antenatal and perinatal care, risk factors for perinatal mortality, and registration procedures and practices in the construction of the perinatal mortality rate.

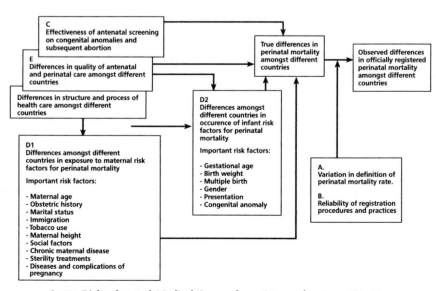

Source: Richardus *et al.* Medical Care, volume 36, number 1, pp. 54–66.

Low birthweight is the most important factor which is linked to perinatal death. Survival of babies with very low birthweight has improved over the last twenty years, although the most marked change did not occur until after 1980. This improvement is due in part to the wider availability of intensive care facilities for newborn babies together with advances in technology in this field of care.

It is important to understand the factors which contribute to, or are directly associated with, low birthweight or perinatal mortality and to identify those elements where there are clear associations and opportunities for improvement. If lethal congenital malformations are left to one side, the major factors associated with low birthweight are plural pregnancy, poor nutrition, low socio-economic status, teenage pregnancy and smoking and drinking in pregnancy. Many of the factors associated with low birthweight and perinatal mortality are interrelated. Their independent contribution is hard to assess.

The association between smoking and low birthweight was first reported in the mid-1950s and there is now no doubt that smoking during pregnancy has an adverse effect on the unborn child. The more the mother smokes, the greater the risk to the baby. The average reduction in birthweight of a baby born to a smoker is of the order of 150 to 250 grams. Smoking is also associated with impairment of the child. The increased risk of perinatal mortality due to smoking has been estimated at 28%.

Drinking alcohol is also potentially damaging to the developing fetus. Heavy alcohol consumption, particularly in early pregnancy, can lead to a baby being born with fetal alcohol syndrome. This is characterised by retarded growth, abnormalities of the face and of the nervous system, as well as abnormal behaviour of the baby in the period after birth.

Women from poorer social backgrounds are one-and-a-half times more likely to produce a low-birthweight baby or suffer a perinatal death than those in the other social classes. Similarly, the youngest and the oldest women who are pregnant have much greater risks of poor outcomes of their pregnancies. For teenage pregnancies, the opportunities to effect change include better sex education, easier access to contraception and wider availability of counselling and support services as well as enhanced antenatal care for young expectant mothers (this issue is discussed more fully later in the chapter).

Some parts of Britain have large ethnic minority populations. Some women within ethnic minority communities are at higher risk of perinatal loss than pregnant women as a whole. The factors contributing to such differences are not fully understood but include the presence of certain mother and baby illnesses, dietary practices and the availability, or otherwise, of services which are responsive to the special needs of women in ethnic minority groups – including interpreters translations of written materials and familiarity of health care professionals with cultural and religious beliefs. Innovative approaches to this problem have already been taken in some parts of Britain – such as special link workers to ensure that the needs of ethnic minority mothers are more comprehensively met. In areas where ethnic minority populations are present, the need for services to be appropriately targeted and designed to respond to these mothers and their families should be recognized and actively addressed.

The immediate causes of perinatal death are identifiable and provide another means of assessing the scope for their prevention. This can be seen by examining the component parts of perinatal mortality in one health region (Figure 6.8), as an example.

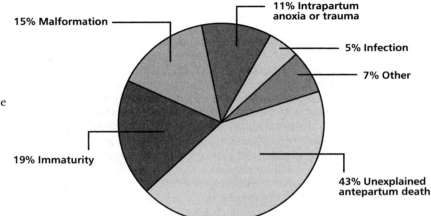

Figure 6.8 Immediate causes of perinatal death, 1996.

Source: Northern Perinatal Mortality Survey Annual Report.
Newcastle upon Tyne: HMSO, 1997.

A number of major causes account for the majority of all perinatal deaths. These are congenital malformations, asphyxia or injury to the baby during labour or birth, immaturity, respiratory disease, or infection. In addition over 40% are classified as unexplained antepartum deaths. Many such losses could be avoided if it were possible to eliminate all the deaths due to raised blood pressure in the mother; poor fetal growth; problems developing for the first time during labour; and if antenatally recognisable, but untreatable, malformations had been identified through screening and the parents opted to terminate the pregnancy. Techniques for supporting the breathing of small babies immediately after birth have improved so much that the risk of delivering a baby ten weeks early is now often less than the risk of allowing some pregnancies to continue. Good antenatal care at this time makes it possible to monitor the baby's health as well as the mother's.

Other causes of pregnancy loss present a greater challenge. The deaths which occur before the onset of labour in the absence of any serious malformation account for an even higher proportion (around 50%) of all perinatal loss amongst babies weighing 1kg or more at birth. High blood pressure in the mother accounts for some such deaths. Raised blood pressure can develop rapidly and without warning between the 28th and 32nd week of pregnancy – especially in a mother's first pregnancy. This can easily go unrecognized (especially if there is any ambiguity as to how care is being shared between the hospital and general practice services). Signs of poor fetal growth at this time, even in the absence of any problem with the mother's blood pressure, can point to a situation where the risks of early delivery are less than the risk of leaving the pregnancy to run its normal course.

Neonatal, Postneonatal and Infant Deaths

At the end of the last century, about 150 children in every 1000 live births died during the first year of life. The decline in this rate since then has been both consistent and dramatic. By 1936 it had fallen to 58.7; by the beginning of the 1960s it had halved again and by the late 1990s it was around six deaths per 1000 live births. The decline is unlikely to have been due to a single event. Better nutritional standards, better education and improved environmental conditions of the large working-class population of late Victorian England, together with the emergence of the middle class, have all contributed. Improvements in medical care and the advent of comprehensive vaccination programmes have also played a part.

Deaths occurring in the first year of life are a fair reflection of the health of a population generally. For descriptive epidemiological purposes, infant deaths are usually divided into neonatal and postneonatal deaths (definitions given earlier). The factors affecting neonatal deaths have many similarities with those which influence perinatal mortality.

Postneonatal deaths are more strongly related to social and economic factors as reflected by place of residence, father's occupation and social class. Even since the mid-1970s, there have been further sharp declines in neonatal and postneonatal mortality and in infant mortality as a whole (Table 6.5). The data are presented in tabular, rather than graphical form to show the extent of fluctuation in these rates. Whilst neonatal mortality fell for each successive year of the observation period, the postneonatal mortality rate has declined over the whole period but less steadily. Indeed, in the mid-1980s, there was much concern that infant mortality had apparently risen due to an increase in postneonatal deaths.

Table 6.5   Trends in components of infant mortality, England and Wales

Mortality rate*	Year								
	1980	1982	1984	1986	1988	1990	1992	1994	1997
Stillbirth	7.2	6.3	5.7	5.3	4.9	4.6	4.3	5.7	5.3
Neonatal	7.7	6.3	5.5	5.3	4.9	4.6	4.3	4.1	3.9
Postneonatal	4.4	4.6	3.9	4.3	4.1	3.3	2.3	2.1	2.0
Infant	12.0	10.8	9.4	9.6	9.0	7.9	6.6	6.2	5.9

Source: Office for National Statistics. *See text for definitions.

Undertaking analyses using routinely available national data shows that infant mortality varies according to birthweight, multiple pregnancy, marital status and social class as defined by occupation. The assessment of marital status has been made more complex by the fact that more children are born outside marriage but statistics can distinguish registrations of birth which are made by both parents (even if unmarried) or by the mother alone.

As a result of rules for certification of stillbirth and neonatal death (introduced in 1986), causes of neonatal deaths are analysed by the main maternal and fetal conditions but not by a single underlying cause. The conditions cited most often for neonatal deaths are congenital malformations, prematurity and respiratory distress syndrome.

For postneonatal deaths, where certification rules are different, a single underlying cause can be analysed. The leading causes of death in this period are: 'sudden infant death syndrome' (SIDS), diseases of the respiratory system, other infections and congenital malformations (Figure 6.9). Since the early 1970s, death certified with terms such as 'cot death', 'sudden unexpected death in infancy' or 'sudden infant death syndrome' (SIDS) have been separately identified and analysed for epidemiological purposes. The category is defined as 'sudden death of an infant or young child, which is unexpected by history, and in which a thorough post-mortem examination fails to demonstrate an adequate cause of death'.

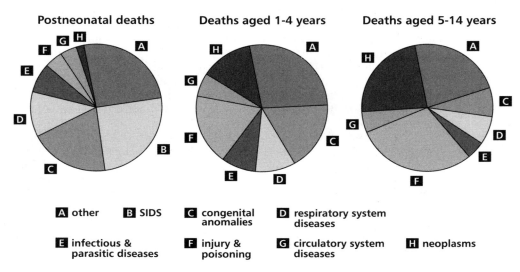

Postneonatal deaths   **Deaths aged 1-4 years**   **Deaths aged 5-14 years**

A other   **B** SIDS   **C** congenital anomalies   **D** respiratory system diseases

E infectious & parasitic diseases   **F** injury & poisoning   **G** circulatory system diseases   **H** neoplasms

Figure 6.9   Main causes of childhood mortality in England and Wales, 1997.
Source: Office for National Statistics.

The whole issue of sudden unexpected deaths in apparently healthy babies is one which has caused a great deal of public concern. At the same time as interest in this syndrome rose, its frequency as a certified cause of death increased in the mid-1980s, whilst respiratory causes declined. This suggested a change in certification practice. The postneonatal mortality rate as a whole is strongly influenced by changes in the occurrence of the sudden infant death syndrome. A major fall in mortality attributed to SIDS occurred during the first half of the 1990s when the Department of Health issued advice which was widely publicised about babies' 'sleeping position'.

Figure 6.10 Infant mortality per 1000 live births, selected countries.

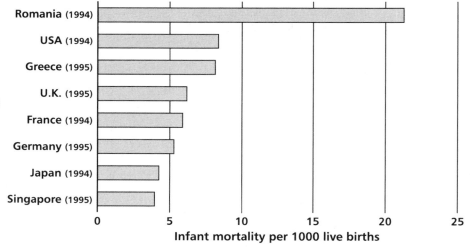

Source: World Health Organization.

Research had shown that the 'prone' position increased risk so parents were told to place babies on their backs. Advice also contained warnings about overheating of babies through placing too many covers on them and about keeping them in an environment free of cigarette smoke. The 'Back to Sleep' campaign is thought to be a major contributor to the fall in mortality due to sudden infant deaths but would not explain all of it.

Dramatic improvements in the infant mortality rate has occurred in most of the countries in the European Union. The scope for further improvement is evident from the lower rates of some other countries (Figure 6.10). Developing countries and Eastern European countries have much less favourable rates whilst Japan at the end of the 1990s had the lowest infant mortality rate in the world.

Fetal Abnormalities

An important cause of fetal death as well as impairment, disability and handicap are the disorders which develop during intra-uterine life. The decline in other causes of death over the last several decades has meant that congenital abnormalities have accounted for an increasing proportion of infant deaths – estimated as a quarter of all such deaths towards the end of the 1990s. Such abnormalities also cause some of the deaths which occur in later childhood.

Some information on the frequency of congenital malformations and other fetal abnormalities in the population is derived from a national monitoring system which was introduced in the mid-1960s following the thalidomide tragedy. The system is voluntary and takes account of abnormalities detected at or within 10 days of birth. It relies upon health authorities extracting information on congenital malformations contained within birth notifications made to them with additional information being supplied by doctors, nurses and midwives. Minor abnormalities are excluded from the reporting system. The national monitoring system is run by the Office for National Statistics. Returns are analysed monthly and subjected to statistical analysis and any significant increases are reported to the health authority concerned. The system is primarily a method of surveillance to compare trends over time. It is of less value exploring variations in incidence between different localities, testing aetiological hypotheses and detecting overall prevalence. Problems with under-reporting, with accuracy of notification, and the fact that late detections cannot be included are serious drawbacks. Despite these limitations, congenital malformation statistics from the national monitoring scheme yield much valuable information. Table 6.6 shows rates of congenital malformations for some selected causes.

Table 6.6 Babies born with selected congenital malformations (England and Wales, 1996)

Condition	Number	Rate (per 10,000 total births)
Talipes	596	9.1
Hypospadias and epispadias	513	7.9
Cardiovascular abnormalities	481	7.4
Cleft lip (with or without cleft palate)	405	6.2
Down's Syndrome	319	4.9
Central nervous system abnormalities	239	3.7
Cleft palate	151	2.3
All babies notified	5,465	83.7

Source: Office for National Statistics.

Surveys at regional or local level, where a higher degree of ascertainment can be achieved, can provide better data for exploring differences in prevalence and risk factors. An important cause of fetal abnormalities is a group of conditions called neural tube defects which occur in differing forms, including that of spina bifida. Neural Tube Defects (NTD) arise from a failure of normal development of the central nervous system during the first few weeks of embryonic life; specifically, the failure of proper closure of the neural tube. A spectrum of disorders may result depending on the site and severity of the defect:

- *Anencephaly* – failure of development of the forebrain, its coverings and the skull. This defect is incompatible with life; most affected infants are stillborn, whilst the remainder usually die within hours of birth.
- *Spina bifida occulta* – failure of fusion of the vertebral arches with no protrusion of tissue and seldom any neurological impairment.

Spina bifida cystica in two forms:

(1) *Meningocoele* – This less serious and less common form consists of a protrusion of meninges, but not the spinal cord, through a defect in the vertebral column. The sac consists of spinal membranes and is covered by skin ('closed' NTD). After surgical closure, prognosis is usually good, with minor residual impairment.

(2) *Myelomenigocoele* – This type is more serious and more common (accounting for 80–90% of all spina bifida cystica births). In this 'open' NTD the protruding sac contains spinal cord which is partly uncovered. This defect often results in severe handicap of the nervous, urinary and locomotor systems, even if surgical treatment is undertaken (although this depends on the spinal level at which the defect occurs). Hydrocephalus and learning disability may also be accompanying features.

NTD is a world-wide phenomenon. Its aetiology is not fully elucidated. It has declined sharply in England and Wales (Figure 6.11) and a number of other countries. There is a strong social class gradient for the prevalence of NTDs: they occur more frequently in social class IV and V than in I and II. In part, the fall has been due to a reduction in the natural incidence of the condition for reasons which are so far unexplained but which may be due to dietary and environmental factors. Support for this theory came from an important seven-year Medical Research Council study which showed that the risk of conception of a second child with such a defect is greatly reduced if the mother took folic acid supplements prior to conception of the next child. The Department of Health subsequently issued guidance that all women planning a pregnancy should consume additional folic acid prior to conception and in the first 12 weeks of pregnancy in the form of folate-rich foods supplemented by an extra daily dietary supplement of folic acid.

Another factor which has contributed to the decline in NTD-affected babies is the advent of techniques for detecting open neural tube defects during pregnancy. Prenatal diagnosis enables parents to be offered the option of terminating the pregnancy and so avoid giving birth to a severely handicapped baby or one who may die in the perinatal period. About one-third of the reduction in the number of babies born with open neural tube defects in the last ten years is estimated to be due to screening and termination.

Another important fetal abnormality is Down's syndrome which is discussed more fully in Chapter 7. Screening for Down's syndrome and NTD is discussed again later in this chapter.

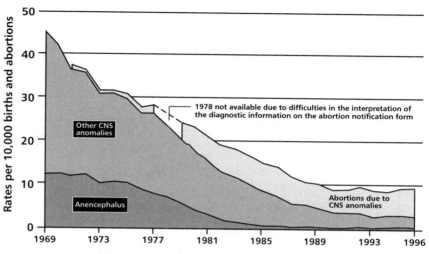

Figure 6.11 Notification rates of anencephalus, other central nervous system (CNS) anomalies, and legal abortions due to central nervous system anomalies in fetus (England and Wales).

Source: Congenital Anomaly Statistics 1995 and 1996. Series MB3 no. 11.
London: The Stationery Office, 1998.

Health and Disease in Childhood

Beyond the first year of life, mortality rates for the remainder of childhood (until the age of 15 years) are expressed in relation to the numbers in the population at risk. Deaths in childhood in England and Wales, like mortality in infancy, have fallen during the twentieth century (Figure 6.12). The main reason for this improvement has been a substantial reduction in the importance of infectious diseases as a cause of death in this age-group. In the 1930s, one in every two childhood deaths were attributed to one of five diseases: pneumonia, tuberculosis, diphtheria, measles and whooping cough. By the late 1990s, these diseases accounted for a very small proportion of deaths. The change has been brought about by a combination of socio-environmental changes (such as improvements in standards of nutrition, housing and sanitation); preventive measures (immunisation), and therapeutic medical advances (antibiotics in particular). The decreased impact of infectious diseases means that the mortality rates, within the different phases of childhood and after the first year of life, are lower than at any other period of life.

Whilst this overall improvement in childhood mortality has occurred other conditions have assumed greater importance (Figure 6.9). Injuries and poisoning are now responsible for quarter of childhood deaths (half of these are road accidents) between the ages of one and 14 years. Cancers account for a substantial minority of the remainder (particularly in older children) with leukaemia prominent amongst them.

In childhood mortality, inequality amongst different social groups persists. There is a marked upward gradient in mortality for both boys and girls from Social Class I to Social Class V. For boys, the ratio of mortality in Social Class V as compared to Social Class I is about 2:1 and somewhat less for girls. The gradient is less marked as children become older. The steepest gradients are for accidents and respiratory disease.

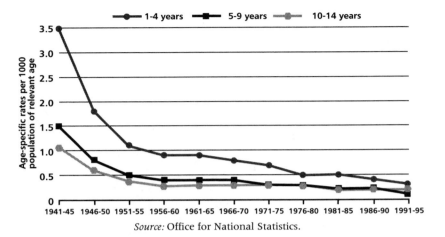

Figure 6.12 Child-hood mortality rates in England and Wales.

Source: Office for National Statistics.

There are various measures of morbidity available. None of these are as robust as the measures of mortality. The three main national sources are parents perception of their childrens' health as reported by the General Household Survey, morbidity statistics from general practice relating to children, and information from hospital episode statistics. The national study of morbidity statistics from general practice 1991–92 gave information from a sample of practices about consultation patterns for children. Across childhood a third of consultations are for diseases of the respiratory system. In contrast, injury and poisoning which is the major cause of childhood death accounted for only 13% and 19% of consultations of children aged 0–4 years and 5–15 years respectively.

Hospital episode statistics (HES) are collated nationally on inpatient and day care surgery episodes. For the majority of serious diseases of childhood (e.g., asthma, epilepsy and diabetes), HES are of only limited value in describing overall morbidity.

There are specific data-collection systems for some conditions. The British Paediatric Surveillance Unit receives notification from paediatricians on certain rare disorders (e.g., AIDS, galactosaemia, drowning and Reye's syndrome) and produces information on incidence and prevalence. Cancer registries hold information on childhood cancers, often supplemented by detailed regional treatment and follow-up registers – for leukaemia in particular. Detailed national surveys of children's dental health were carried out in the mid-1970s, 1980s and 1990s.

Local information on specific conditions may exist as registers; for example, for paediatric renal disease, diabetes and specified tumours. These often start as treatment registers or for research and may not necessarily have a population base to which the incidence of disease can be related.

Preventing Unwanted Pregnancy

Contraceptive Methods

Since the 1960s contraceptive methods have been dominated by the so-called 'high technology' measures – the oral contraceptive pill, new hormonal delivery systems and, to a lesser extent, the intrauterine device (IUD).

Data indicating the usage of these different methods are available from routine statistics collected on people receiving family planning services. This is a selected group not representative of the whole population. An impression of contraceptive practices of the general population is obtained from special surveys.

The pattern of contraceptive use by women is shown in Figure 6.13. Since the mid-1980s, however, the use of condoms has increased substantially. This trend is almost certainly accounted for by the advent of HIV, the virus that causes the Acquired Immune Deficiency Syndrome (AIDS).

Figure 6.13 Estimated current use of contraception for all women aged 16–49 years.

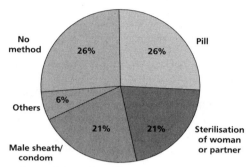

Source: Contraception and Sexual Health. London: The Stationery Office, 1997.

The effectiveness of various methods of contraception is illustrated in Table 6.7. The estimates are based on the percentage of women who became pregnant using the method for one year. A major feature is the variation between failure rates of careful and consistent users and those who are less attentive. For example, use of the diaphragm/cap is up to 95% effective and is less effective with less careful and consistent use.

Table 6.7 Efficacy of contraceptive methods (% per 100 women per year) with correct and consistent use

Methods that have no 'user' failure	
Injectable contraception	over 99% effective
Implants	over 99% effective in first year (over 98% per year over 5 years)
Intrauterine system (IUS)	over 99% effective
Intrauterine device (IUD)	98-over 99% effective (depending on IUD type)
Female sterilisation	over 99% effective 1 in 200 lifetime failure rate
Male sterilisation (vasectomy)	over 99% effective 1 in 2000 lifetime failure rate
Methods that have 'user' failure	
Combined oral contraceptive	over 99% effective
Progestogen-only oral contraceptive	up to 99% effective
Male condom	up to 98% effective
Female condom	up to 95% effective
Diaphragm or cap + spermicide	up to 96% effective
Natural family planning:	
- combining two or more fertility indicators	up to 98% effective
- new technologies (Persona)	up to 94% effective

Source: T Belfield. *Contraceptive Handbook,* 3rd edition, Family Planning Association, 1999.

Safety of Methods

Most published data about mortality from the use of contraceptives concentrate on the risk from the method itself. Some investigators, however, deal with the wider aspect and calculate cumulative mortality. Thus, not only is there inherent risk of death from the method included but also risk from pregnancy as a result of method failure. Additionally, in the case of the oral contraceptive, the potential beneficial effects of reducing the risk of ovarian and endometrial cancer are taken into account.

Precise risks are difficult to determine and detailed information is limited to hormonal contraceptives, intrauterine devices, sterilisation and other hormonal delivery systems. Risk related to the oral contraceptives has been most studied in this and other countries. The diseases which are more common among women while they are taking the combined pill include various disorders of the circulation – especially thrombosis, stroke and certain cancers such as breast cancer. However, the benefits of the pill include a reduction in the risk of endometrial and ovarian cancer.

IUDs can be used by all women providing they are not at risk of acquiring an infection.

Sterilisation involves a one-time risk associated with surgery, unlike the sort of continuous exposure of the other two methods. It has been estimated as one death per 12,000 laparascopic sterilisations and 0.1 per 100,000 procedures for vasectomy.

Provision of Services

Family planning services in Britain are provided in three main ways: by general practitioners, in community family planning clinics, sexual health clinics and in departments of obstetrics and gynaecology of local hospitals. Despite the move, during the 1990s, towards more family planning services being delivered by general practitioners, it has been national policy to maintain a choice of service and hence the community family planning clinics have been preserved (albeit in smaller numbers than in the past). Women and men may prefer to visit such a clinic rather than their general practitioner for a number of reasons. They may prefer anonymity, it may be easier to see a woman doctor, there may be a fuller range of contraceptive methods and they will often regard the staff of the family planning clinic as 'specialists' who have more detailed knowledge.

A number of principles underlie the provision of good family planning services (Table 6.8). These include ensuring that certain quality criteria are fulfilled, providing good access and enabling groups with traditionally low uptake (but who may be in particular need) to receive services. Of particular importance are the problems of sexual health amongst teenagers where the risks of unwanted pregnancy are particularly high. In addition, effective family planning services must also give advice about reducing the risks of sexually transmitted diseases. Attendance for family planning advice also provides an opportunity for opportunistic health promotion including offering cervical screening to women whose test is due or overdue. Many general practitioners now offer family planning in the context of a 'well women' service.

Table 6.8   Factors to be considered when organising family planning services

- Ensure the number, times and locations of clinics meet the needs of users
- Provide choice of male and female professional staff
- Make available a wide choice of contraceptive methods
- Provide accessible, objective consistent information that is evidence guided
- Ensure the service is staffed by those with skill and knowledge of contraceptive methods and sexual health
- Provide opportunities to discuss related subjects (for example, premenstrual tension, HIV)
- Offer an appointments system with flexibility to allow walk-in attendances (especially for emergencies)
- Provide facilities for children

Teenage Pregnancy

Teenage pregnancy is of major concern. In the late 1990s the United Kingdom had the highest teenage conception rate in Western Europe (Figure 6.14). Whilst the actual number of pregnancies in the 13–15 year-old group is small compared with the number in 16–19 year-olds, there is some evidence that pregnancy in very young girls (under 14 years) is sometimes a result of intrafamilial sexual abuse and the need for child protection investigations should be considered in all cases of very young girls who become pregnant.

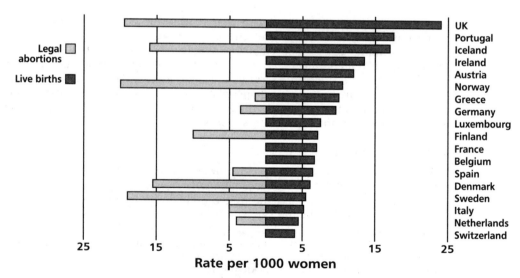

Figure 6.14   Live births to women aged 15–19 and abortions.
Source: Eurostat & UN Demographic Yearbook, 1996.
(Legal abortion figures not available for all countries).

Young women who become pregnant as teenagers are more likely to have: low educational achievement (before the pregnancy); come from families on income support and have mothers who were themselves teenage mothers. They are likely to have low self-esteem and lower aspirations than other girls of the same age. Those who choose to continue the pregnancy may well not complete their formal education and have reduced employment opportunities. The range of risk factors is in fact very diverse (Table 6.9). Very young mothers (under 16) are at higher risk of many of the complications of pregnancy, and their babies are at higher risk of stillbirth and neonatal death than mothers in the 20–29 age-group.

Table 6.9   Factors associated with early sexual initiation, contraceptive use, and teenage pregnancy

Individual	Family	Educational	Community	Socio-economic	Contraceptive
• Knowledge • Self-esteem • Skills base • Cognitive maturity • 'Experimental' behaviour • Age of first intercourse • Emotional maturity	• Parent/child communication • Mother or sister teenage pregnancy history • Family structure (including single-headed families)	• Academic attainment/ educational goals • Truancy • Sex education	• Social norms (sexual activity/ pregnancy) • Peer influences • Cultural and religious influences • Media influences • Child abuse	• Poverty • Employment prospects • Housing and social conditions	• Contraceptive services • Awareness • Availability • Accessibility

Source: Effective Health Care Bulletin, volume 3, number 1. University of York, NHS Centre for Reviews and Dissemination, 1997.

Although many pregnancies in the 16–19 age-group are unplanned and can cause disruption to education and work, it is important to note that a significant number occur to married women who have chosen to be pregnant. This is particularly the case in some ethnic groups where early marriage is the norm.

Traditional family planning services are unlikely to meet the needs of teenagers and the rising rates of teenage pregnancy in the 1990s led to reconsideration of how to deliver contraceptive advice and services alongside 'safer sex' messages to young people. Many areas now provide young people's clinics, often in town centre shopping areas rather than traditional health service premises. These clinics may also offer drug education and advice and counselling services.

Table 6.10   Tackling teenage pregnancy

- *A national campaign*, involving government, media, voluntary sector and others to improve understanding and change behaviour

- *Joined-up action* with new mechanisms to coordinate action at both national and local levels and ensure that the strategy is on track

- *Better prevention* of the causes of teenage pregnancy, including better education in and out of school, access to contraception, and targeting of at-risk groups, with a new focus on reaching young men, who are half of the solution, yet who have often been overlooked in past attempts to tackle this issue

- *Better support* for pregnant teenagers and teenage parents, with a new focus on returning to education with child care to help, working to a position where no under 18 lone parent is put in a lone tenancy, and pilots around the country providing intensive support for parents and child

Source: Social Exclusion Unit. Teenage Pregnancy. London. The Stationery Office, 1999 (Cm4342).

A major initiative was taken in 1999 by the British Government through its Social Exclusion Unit (SEU), which set out a comprehensive action plan to tackle the problem (Table 6.10). New health service standards for effective and responsible contraceptive advice and treatment for young people, new models of sex education in schools using 'peer educators' (usually specially trained year 12s) are important elements. It is vital that sex education contributes both to developing self-esteem and the ability to make choices and also involves both sexes. The SEU report announced new guidance for schools on sex and relationships education. It also described a local implementation fund for integrated and innovative programmes (including, for instance, peer mentoring) in high-rate areas.

Abortion

Abortion is defined as 'the emptying of a pregnant uterus up to the 24th week of pregnancy'. Spontaneous abortion (often referred to a 'miscarriage') occurs in an estimated 9–15% of recognized pregnancies – usually for unknown reasons. A criminal abortion is one procured deliberately and unlawfully. A termination of pregnancy is the legal ending of a pregnancy.

The Abortion Act 1967 became law in April 1968. It enabled the legal termination of pregnancy (by a registered medical practitioner) to take place in a National Health Service hospital, or premises approved by the Secretary of State for Health. Amendments were made, by the Human Fertilisation and Embryology Act, 1990. The current requirements are that two registered medical practitioners should certify that certain defined indications for abortion have been met (Table 6.11); that the abortion should be performed by a registered medical practitioner, and that the procedure should be undertaken in a National Health Service hospital or other approved premises. The Abortion Regulations 1991, requires any terminations to be notified within seven days to the Chief Medical Officer of the Department of Health or to the Chief Medical Officers of Wales and Scotland according to where the termination takes place.

Table 6.11 Statutory grounds for abortion under The Abortion Act 1967 and amended by The Human Fertilisation and Embryology Act 1990

A	The continuance of the pregnancy would involve risk to the life of the pregnant woman greater than if the pregnancy were terminated.
B	The termination is necessary to prevent grave permanent injury to the physical or mental health of the pregnant woman.
C	The pregnancy has NOT exceeded its 24th week and that the continuance of the pregnancy would involve risk, greater than if the pregnancy were terminated, of injury to the physical or mental health of the pregnant woman.
D	The pregnancy has NOT exceeded its 24th week and that the continuance of the pregnancy would involve risk, greater than if the pregnancy were terminated, of injury to the physical or mental health of any existing child(ren) of the family of the pregnant woman.
E	There is a substantial risk that if the child were born it would suffer from such physical or mental abnormalities as to be seriously handicapped.

The factors which can influence the abortion rate in a population are diverse (Table 6.12). The proportion of terminations undertaken (Figure 6.15) on non-residents of England and Wales reached a peak of 34% in the mid-1970s.

Table 6.12 Some factors which can influence the
rate of abortion in a population

- Prevailing legislation
- Social attitudes
- Contraceptive efficacy and usage
- Scope for diagnosis of fetal abnormalities
- Fertility patterns
- Age structure of female population

The proportion has fluctuated however, being partly influenced by the liberalisation of abortion laws in countries from which a high proportion of non-resident abortions were drawn. The impact of these factors is well illustrated by the position of women from the Republic of Ireland (which prohibits abortion). Between the beginning of the 1970s and the start of the 1990s, there was a sixteen-fold increase in the number of women from that country having abortions in England and Wales. The highest rates of abortion are among the 16–19 year-old and the 20–24 year-old age-groups.

The proportion of conceptions overall which end in termination of pregnancy is around 20%. However, the figure is much higher for very young and older women: 52% (for the under 16s) and 34% (for the over-40s) respectively. The figure for the latter group reflects terminations undertaken as a result of screening for congenital abnormalities – Down's syndrome in particular.

Critics of the abortion law have considered that liberal interpretation of the grounds for abortion has led to termination of pregnancy on demand. There is ample evidence from surveys of women who have had abortions that they do not regard it as a substitute for contraception but rather as a last resort in the case of failure or mistake.

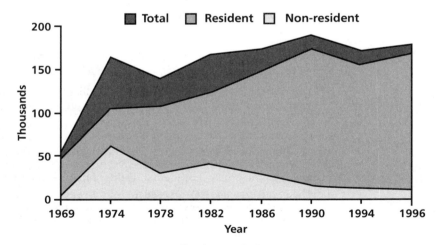

Figure 6.15 Trends in number of legal abortions in England and Wales.

Source: Office for National Statistics.

Infertility Services

There are various formal definitions of 'infertility', most of which embody concepts of exposure to the risk of pregnancy over a certain period of time: for example, 'a failure to become pregnant over a period of two years whilst engaging in sexual intercourse without contraceptive use'.

There are a number of important influences on fertility. Factors both inherited and acquired, and of a short- or long-term nature, affect the physiological reproductive capacity of both males and females. Examples of acquired factors amongst women are infections, such as gonorrhoea, chlamydia or other pelvic inflammatory conditions which may prevent conception by causing scarring and blockage of the fallopian tubes. Acquired infertility in men is less well understood and less easy to treat.

Failure to conceive may produce as much distress as an unwanted pregnancy. Formerly, adoption was the sole resort of couples who were childless. The widespread availability and use of effective contraceptive methods, and changes in the law relating to termination of pregnancy, have had the effect of reducing the number of babies offered for adoption. This has, to some extent, been countered by the development of methods of assisted reproduction in couples of low fertility, and by the acceptance of the use of donor sperm for men who are infertile.

With treatment, about a third of infertile couples can achieve a successful pregnancy (though success rates vary according to a woman's age, other clinical factors and the performance of the service). The investigation of sub-fertility and infertility should involve both partners. Approximately 30% of problems relate to the male partner, 30% to the female and in the remainder there is no apparent cause.

In general terms, infertility and subfertility are usually due to failure to produce sperm or to ovulate, or to a mechanical blockage in the vas deferens or the fallopian tubes. Treatment of female subfertility and infertility may include drug-induced ovulation. This may result in multiple pregnancy.

More recent developments have included *in vitro* fertilisation (test tube babies), where ovulation is artificially induced; the eggs are harvested, fertilised under artificial conditions and placed in the uterus. A further development of this technique is gamete intrafallopian transfer (GIFT) where ovulation is also artificially induced; the eggs are harvested and are then mixed with semen and returned directly to the fallopian tube. A further technique for male infertility is Intra Cytoplasmic Sperm Injection (ICSI) in which sperm are taken from the testis and injected directly into the egg *in vitro*, which after fertilisation is placed in the uterus. Because more than one ovum may be used in order to give an increased chance of pregnancy, these methods may also give rise to multiple pregnancy. It is now recommended that, in general, no more than two eggs should be replaced. The whole question of artificial fertilisation has been addressed by the passing of the Human Fertilisation and Embryology Act 1990, and the resulting regulatory authority.

Childless couples may go to very considerable lengths to acquire a child. Recent years have seen the appearance of surrogacy where a fertile woman is willing to bear a child for one who is infertile. There are a number of ethical questions surrounding this issue which have still to be addressed. Concerns arise particularly over the level of payments to surrogate mothers.

Maternity Services

During most of the second half of the twentieth century, the focus of maternity services was to reduce risk to mother and baby. The services became hospital-based, medically orientated and made extensive use of high-technology. The focus was on reducing maternal and perinatal mortality. In the early 1990s, the Parliamentary Health Select Committee made a report which for the first time focused on women's needs and preferences. This led to an Expert Group report called *Changing Childbirth* which set out a set of principles for a 'woman-centred' maternity service (Table 6.13). Issues addressed included how to create a service which was woman-centred care with sharing of information on risk, whilst providing continuity of care and the appropriate lead professional (not always a doctor) for the woman's needs.

Table 6.13   Principles of good maternity care

- The woman must be the focus of maternity care. She should be able to feel that she is in control of what is happening to her and able to make decisions about her care, based on her needs, having discussed matters fully with the professionals involved.
- Maternity services must be readily and easily accessible to all. They should be sensitive to the needs of the local population and based primarily in the community.
- Women should be involved in the monitoring and planning of maternity services to ensure that they are responsive to the needs of a changing society. In addition care should be effective and resources used efficiently.

Source: Changing Childbirth. London: HMSO, 1993.

Antenatal Care

The whole process of antenatal care is geared to a healthy outcome of pregnancy both for mother and baby. Increasingly, the traditional antenatal period is being extended to include the concept of preconception care. Women in the childbearing years are now encouraged to think about the prospect and implications of pregnancy before it happens. Well-women clinics provide a focus for discussion about lifestyle, contraception, and the timing of conception. The role of folate in preventing neural tube defect has been described earlier and women planning a pregnancy are recommended to take an additional daily supplement.

It is important that the woman is enrolled into a programme of antenatal care as early as possible after pregnancy is confirmed. The most common model of antenatal care is a shared approach between the midwife, the general practitioner and the local hospital department of obstetrics and gynaecology.

Antenatal care encompasses a wide range of activities including: advice on lifestyle (for example, smoking, alcohol, drugs, diet); screening for maternal illness (for example, hypertensive disease, diabetes, infection); the recognition and treatment of abnormalities in pregnancy; the detection of fetal abnormality; assessment of fetal size, development and well-being; psychological preparation for delivery (including antenatal classes), and education about the importance of breast feeding and parenting. The content of antenatal care has evolved over time as a development of medical and midwifery practice rather than on the basis of evaluating the efficacy of specific interventions on the outcome of pregnancy. Increasingly it is being recognized that a modern service must develop not on the basis of tradition but on evidence of what is proven to be effective as well as a parent's views and preferences.

The Prevention and Recognition of Fetal Abnormalities

There are certain groups of women who are at higher risk of fetal abnormality. Parents with a family history of certain genetically determined diseases or who have had a previously affected child, for example with cystic fibrosis, should be offered genetic counselling. They may decide to avoid pregnancy. In some cases it is now possible to determine whether a fetus is affected by the genetic/chromosomal abnormality by early chorion villous sampling or amniocentesis. An increasing proportion of fetal abnormalities can now be recognized by ultrasound screening in the antenatal period. Parents can be counselled and offered termination. Although such decisions are difficult, an even more ethically-challenging area is that of population screening of pregnant women for fetal abnormality – e.g., for neural tube defect and Down's syndrome (see below). The aim here is to offer the women a choice about screening which if accepted may lead to a diagnosis. Women can then be offered the opportunity to discuss all the options available to them, which could include termination of the pregnancy. Major questions arise about informed consent to testing; health care professionals' ability to offer non-directive counselling, and guilt and distress caused by mid-trimester termination.

Some women are at higher risk of fetal abnormality due to their own health status. For example, women with diabetes require preconceptual care, planning and monitoring of the pregnancy and delivery. Prescribed drugs in pregnancy can cause abnormalities and women on long-term medication (e.g., sodium valproate for epilepsy), require preconceptual advice and possible changes to their drug regime.

The effects of smoking and alcohol on fetal growth and development have been described earlier. An increasing problem is that of opiate abuse in pregnancy and, to an extent related, HIV infection in pregnancy.

Rhesus Haemolytic Disease in the Newborn

This disorder arises from a genetic difference between a mother and her baby, whereby they have different blood groups. Each member of the population belongs to one of four main blood groups: A, B, AB and O but also falls into two other broad groups, rhesus-positive and rhesus-negative. In Britain, 85% of the population is rhesus-positive carrying the rhesus antigen (commonly the 'D' antigen) on their red blood cells. A rhesus-negative woman can conceive a rhesus-positive baby if the father is rhesus-positive.

If at some time during pregnancy, or at delivery, fetal (i.e., rhesus-positive) red blood cells pass into the maternal circulation, then the (rhesus-negative) mother may respond by producing antibodies against the rhesus antigen. The risk is that these antibodies (anti-D antibodies) can then cross back through the placenta and haemolise the red cells of the fetus. The result is anaemia, jaundice, brain damage and even death in subsequent pregnancies where the baby is rhesus-positive. This kind of bleeding occurs most commonly at delivery. However, it is also associated with invasive prenatal diagnosis – amniocentesis, chorionic villus sampling, fetal blood sampling, antepartum haemorrhage, abdominal injury, intrauterine death and abortion.

In the 1950s, haemolytic disease of the newborn accounted for over 1000 stillbirths and neonatal deaths each year. The development of postpartum exchange transfusion, intrauterine transfusion, and early induction of labour, reduced the number of deaths to 708 by 1969. However, it was the introduction of postnatal anti-D (antibody to rhesus-D antigen) prophylaxis in 1969 which led to the major reduction in infant deaths attributable to rhesus haemolytic disease from 46 per 100,000 then, to 1.6 per 100,000 by 1990.

All rhesus-negative women, currently receive intramuscular anti-D within 72 hours of delivery. This destroys any rhesus-positive fetal red cells circulating in the mother's blood before they can stimulate continuing maternal antibody formation. In addition pregnant rhesus-negative women who have risk factors or invasive prenatal interventions or abdominal trauma during pregnancy also receive anti-D.

However, a small number of rhesus-negative women continue to develop anti-D antibodies during pregnancy. The most important cause in 1% of all rhesus-negative women without obvious risk factors, is occult transplacental bleeding. There is good evidence from large studies that this could be reduced to 0.2% or less by giving two additional injections of anti-D routinely at 28 and 32 weeks of pregnancy. Therefore guidelines on treatment with anti-D might in future include routine antenatal prophylaxis.

Detection of Neural Tube Defect

The possibility of early detection of open neural tube defect (NTD) came in the 1970s when it was noted that a substance called alpha-fetoprotein (AFP) was present in increased amounts in the amniotic fluid of women carrying babies with anencephaly or spina bifida. A later discovery, that raised AFP levels could be detected in the serum of mothers carrying NTD fetuses, meant there was a potential for a screening test.

Serum AFP screening followed by amniocentesis for those with high levels has now largely been superseded by ultrasound scanning. The fetal anomaly scan at around 18 weeks gestation is a safer method of detecting NTD. If NTD is confirmed parents are offered (with appropriate counselling) the choice of terminating the pregnancy.

The Detection of Down's Syndrome

Screening for Down's syndrome using amniocentesis at 15 weeks pregnancy (or chorion villous sampling before 15 weeks) has been offered to older mothers (over 35 years) or those who had a previously affected child or one partner with known chromosomal abnormalities since the 1980s. These techniques look for abnormal cells. However, because most babies affected by Down's syndrome are born to women aged below 35 years, the screening of older women makes a limited impact on the overall number of affected babies born. More recently, maternal serum screening for Down's syndrome has been developed using a variety of serum markers. This involves a second trimester maternal blood test to assess a number of markers. Results, taking account of the woman's age and the gestation of the fetus, are interpreted as low or high risk and those with high-risk results are offered diagnostic amniocentesis. Again, women are then offered termination of pregnancy if the diagnosis is confirmed, with the principle of informed choice being key.

Intrapartum Care

During the second half of the twentieth century in Britain, there was progressive closure of smaller local maternity units, often on the basis that they could not fulfil professionally-set standards for care during labour. This trend took place with medical professional support and accorded with Department of Health policy.

There will always be some mothers for whom underlying medical problems or complications of pregnancy mean that delivery away from immediate obstetric and paediatric assistance entails risk. There will similarly be many mothers whose delivery will be so straightforward as to entail virtually no risk at all. In between these two are a group of mothers who may face a higher risk of complications in labour because of, for example, their age or that it is their first baby; it is these women, who, were they to be given a free choice, would truly have to weigh up the risks and the advantages of either having their baby at home or in hospital.

Those in favour of home delivery argue that labour should take place in the more intimate atmosphere of their own home with those members of their family or friends that they might wish around them. They would also argue that the technology of a modern labour ward dehumanises what is an intense, emotional and essentially normal experience. There are others who would argue that the risk of something going wrong at very short notice is such that they are willing to trade the familiar and comforting environment for safety. Evidence can be produced on both sides to support the arguments advanced for both points of view. Unplanned home births occur either in very young mothers (concealed pregnancy) or by too rapid events in mothers who planned a hospital birth and have the expected very high perinatal mortality.

It seems unlikely that there will be any major shift away from the specialised obstetric unit as the main focus of care into the early years of the twenty-first century. However, there is greater flexibility and choice in provision than in the past. When women do choose to have their baby in a specialist unit, it is essential that they receive the highest standards of care available. This includes, for example, access when needed to the equipment necessary to detect fetal distress and the availability of epidural anaesthesia. In turn, this means ensuring that units are well equipped and staffed with highly trained personnel. Some large units now contain dedicated midwifery-led units where women can opt for low-technology midwife-led care with the safeguard of adjacent high-technology services.

In rural areas there are still some small general practitioner and midwife led maternity units. A safety-net, in the form of an obstetric flying squad, has been provided for those mothers delivering at home or in the smaller more remote rural maternity units. Traditionally this has consisted of an obstetric team comprising, usually a midwife, an obstetrician and an anaesthetist who could be available almost immediately to go out by ambulance to an obstetric emergency. However, obstetric flying squads are decreasing in number; partly because of less frequent calls due to fewer home deliveries; partly because, in many cases, it is a paediatrician who is required, (rather than an obstetrician), and partly because of an increase in the use of paramedics in the ambulance service.

Quality Measures for Maternity Services

The report produced in the early 1990s, 'Changing Childbirth', described several indicators of success in developing women-centred services. In addition, the professional bodies have developed standards against which clinical practice should be audited. For example, the Royal College of Obstetricians and Gynaecologists recommends that the ventouse (vacuum extraction) should be the first choice as the method for instrumental delivery. In England in the early 1990s ventouse accounted for only 17% of instrumental deliveries; by the mid-1990s the proportion had risen to 45%. Similarly, there is ongoing debate about what is the most appropriate rate for caesarian section in populations of women. In the mid-1990s in England 15.5% of deliveries were by caesarian section compared with 10.4% a decade earlier.

Paediatric Services at Birth

The majority of babies require no resuscitation at birth. Some will require temporary assistance with airway clearing. Others will require full resuscitation and transfer to special care. This includes premature babies, babies with congenital anomalies and congenital infections, and those who are found for whatever reason, to be asphyxiated at birth.

There are four categories of babies requiring care:

(a) *Level 1 Intensive Care (Maximal Intensive Care)*
     Care given in an intensive care nursery which provides continuous skilled supervision by qualified and specially trained nursing and medical staff. Such care includes support of the infant's parents.

(b) *Level 2 Intensive Care (High Dependency Intensive Care)*
     Care given in an intensive or special care nursery which provides continuous skilled supervision by qualified and specially trained nursing staff who may care for more babies than in Level 1 Intensive Care. Medical supervision is not so immediate as in Level 1 Intensive Care. Care includes support of the infant's parents.

(c) *Special Care*
     Care given in a special care nursery, transitional care ward or postnatal ward which provides care and treatment exceeding normal routine care. Some aspects of special care can be undertaken by a mother supervised by qualified nursing staff. Special nursing care includes support and education of the infant's parents.

(d) *Normal Care*
     Care given by the mother, or mother substitute, with medical or neonatal nursing advice if needed.

The majority of general hospitals in Britain which have an obstetrics service are equipped to deal with babies in categories (c) and (d) in special care baby units. In addition, they are almost all capable of dealing with babies in categories (a) and (b) in the short-term. However, for very tiny and very pre-term babies there is no doubt that the outcome is better if they are treated in units where long-term ventilation is a standard procedure. The development of such regional or subregional units has also led to the establishment of neonatal flying squads: these consist of an experienced junior paediatrician or consultant, accompanied by an experienced neonatal nurse who go out with a fully equipped incubator to peripheral hospitals and stabilise and then supervise the transfer of the baby requiring high-dependency care back to the subregional centres.

Whilst in the short-term, facilities need to be available to ventilate babies with respiratory distress in all hospitals offering an obstetric service, current evidence suggests that given the medical and nursing expertise required to deal with babies who need long-term ventilation, high-dependency neonatal care should be provided in a smaller number of centres in each health region.

The increased workload produced by low-birthweight survivors means that many hospitals providing this type of care have experienced great pressure on their facilities. An example of this trend in one health region is shown in Figure 6.16.

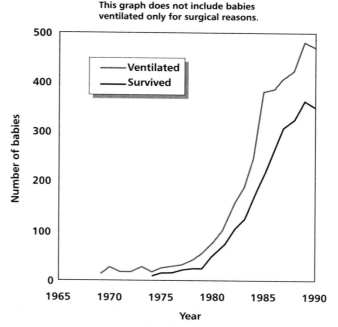

This graph does not include babies ventilated only for surgical reasons.

Figure 6.16 Trend in the number of babies who received help with breathing after birth in an English health region.

Source: Northern Regional Health Authority, Collaborative Study of Perinatal Mortality.

Services for Children

Historical perspective

Services exclusively dedicated to the welfare of children developed slowly and sporadically in Britain during the eighteenth century. A dispensary for children of the poor was established in London in 1769 and, as part of its service, children were visited at home. A hundred years later this feature was developed when a home visiting service by 'respectable working women', to help and advise on child welfare matters, was established in Manchester and Salford. At the beginning of this century, a comprehensive Health Visiting Service was established in Huddersfield to combat the high infant mortality rate. A local Act made notification of birth to the Medical Officer of Health compulsory so that a home visit could be made shortly after the birth. This pioneering service was followed by national legislation which was, at first, permissive but later, through the Notification of Birth Act 1915, made compulsory. A few years later, local authorities were empowered to make arrangements for safeguarding the health of mothers and children, including the provision of free antenatal and postnatal clinics. Child Welfare Clinics provided by local authorities became more numerous and a national scheme for training health visitors was inaugurated. Universal compulsory education introduced in 1870 and 1880, revealed the extent of poor hygiene, malnutrition and handicapping conditions prevalent amongst school children. Further legislation was soon passed to give powers to local authorities to make provision for blind, deaf, mentally handicapped and epileptic children. The first full-time School Medical Officer was appointed in London in 1890 and other places followed suit. However, it was the disquiet about the nation's health, following the discovery of the poor physical condition of recruits for the Boer War, which finally persuaded the government to introduce a school health service. Medical inspection of school children was made compulsory in 1907 and as there was no National Health Service, provision was also made for the treatment of school children. This arrangement continued until the National Health Service was established in 1948.

In the eighteenth and nineteenth centuries, young children were often admitted to women's hospital wards, usually accompanied by their mothers who helped to care for them in hospital. In 1852, the Hospital for Sick Children in Great Ormond Street, London, was opened and shortly afterwards many other children's hospitals were built. A register for Sick Children's Nurses was established in 1919 and the emerging new specialty of paediatrics assumed increasing importance during the late 1920s and early 1930s.

Woodcut: a mother and ten children in a damp and dilapidated room; anon., c. 1864.

Source: George Godwin, Another blow for life. London, 1864.

Over the past one hundred and fifty years social attitudes to children have changed. In early Victorian times, children were on the whole viewed as amoral beings who needed instruction and discipline in order to become 'civilised' human beings. There was widespread and systematised abuse of children both in working conditions in the developing industries and also child prostitution – particularly in the big cities. Understanding of the psychological and emotional needs of children developed over the first half of the twentieth century.

The Rights of Children

It was only in the late 1980s that there was an international statement regarding the rights of children: the United Nation Convention on the Rights of the Child. In England and Wales the Children Act 1989 for the first time described the duties and responsibilities of parents rather than parental rights in relation to their children. The Children Act defined children in need as those children who would not be able to achieve maximum physical, psychological and emotional development without the provision of services. Children in need include those children who have physical disability, inadequate family support or may indeed be in need of protection from abuse. Each local authority must identify children in need and publish information about services available. Such services include advice, provision of family centres and day care services and child protection investigations.

The Education Act 1993 defined children with special educational needs who would require additional educational services in order to achieve their full education potential. Added to the statutory definitions is the wider concept of vulnerable children, a term which is usually used to describe those children who live in poverty and who may have significant social, emotional and physical needs.

Health Services for Children

It has been recognized for many years that children differ in many ways from adults. Increasingly there is now awareness both of the wider needs of children as individuals who are developing both physically and emotionally, and of their changing physiological stages at various ages. Greater recognition exists of the importance to children of the quality of care they receive from their parents and families. In response to these needs a range of specialist services for children has developed; for example, paediatric oncology, and paediatric renal services. Children and young people have rarely been asked how they feel about the health services provided for them and what they would prefer. Parents are usually used as proxies, but studies demonstrate that children's concepts of illness and health care differ greatly from those of adults. Children account for up to one-quarter of general practitioners' consultations and just over a quarter of accident and emergency workload. The health needs of children should be met by staff specifically qualified in child health and with appropriate communication skills.

Child health services are provided in a variety of settings: from community services to secondary care in local hospitals, with professionals increasingly working in both settings at local level, to tertiary specialised care which may be provided in only a few major hospital centres which aim to deliver care through the local networks. Child health services cover the range of: promotion of healthy behaviours; disease prevention (for example immunisation against communicable diseases of childhood); recognition, diagnosis and treatment of disease, and the management and care of children with chronic disease, disability and handicap. Most children are healthy and have few contacts with the health service over the whole of their childhood other than routine surveillance, contact with the local general practitioner and the occasional visit to the Accident and Emergency Department. However, 1 in 4 will have been admitted to hospital once or more by the age of two years. The challenge for those with an interest in the health of children is to identify those the children who are in need of services to support them in reaching their full potential and to ensure that they receive them.

Integrated Child Health Services

Organisational arrangements within the health services and between agencies may create barriers to providing high quality care for children. A large number of professionals may be involved in the care of one child and, without overall coordination and proper communication, there can be real frustration for families. For example, consider the hypothetical care of a child with severe epilepsy and learning disability. She has recently been referred for a further clinical opinion from a paediatric neurologist in a specialist centre but is admitted after a prolonged seizure to the local general hospital under a consultant paediatrician whom the family do not know well. Meanwhile, there is an ongoing assessment being led by the Education Department of the local authority for which the child has seen an educational psychologist and a speech therapist both of whom the family have not met before. On top of this, the child has regular reviews with the consultant community paediatrician. A health visitor has been involved in trying to obtain additional safety equipment and home adaptation liaising with social services and the housing department, whilst the child also sees the local general practitioner for recurrent ear infections. The family has real concerns about the child's school placement. To whom do they turn? It is vital for children with complex needs (such as the girl in this example) that their care is coordinated and that parents feel that professionals are working together to ensure that the child receives the services which are needed.

The current model preferred by professional bodies in the United Kingdom is an integrated or combined child health service where community child health services are offered locally including, for example, secondary-level care in outpatient and day care investigation, with close relationships with the local hospital and tertiary centres where inpatient care is offered. The local focus is essential because it is at this level that proper relationships can be established between health services and local authority education and social services departments.

The perceived fragmentation of wider services for children in need led to the development of children's service planning which requires that local authorities work with local health services to produce integrated children's service plans which cover the range of children in need and services necessary to met those needs. In many areas this has allowed a widening of focus from child protection and disability issues to the whole area of vulnerable children, and children living in poverty.

Child Health Surveillance

For the past thirty years or more, the regular surveillance of children's growth and development has been an integral part of the child health service. The scope of such surveillance has varied over the years – particularly when the value of some kinds of screening of apparently healthy children to detect abnormalities has been challenged. Effective child health surveillance requires high quality communication and information systems at a number of levels. Firstly, there is a need to maintain databases to identify children at birth: to ensure that they are called-up for their regular assessments, for immunisation, vaccination and to enable the findings of examinations as well as immunisation status to be recorded. Secondly, there is a need for exchange of information between all health care professionals involved in child health; for example, the general practitioner, the health visitor, the paediatrician and the community health doctor. Increasingly, parent-held child health records are being developed as a way of overcoming some of the traditional logistic difficulties of maintaining continuity and accuracy of records.

The service is delivered by general practitioners, consultant community paediatricians, child health doctors, health visitors, school medical officers and school nurses. The organisation of the service varies around the country but services mainly differ in the extent to which they are based with general practice or whether there is greater emphasis on community health services. In recent years the value of routine non-targeted health visiting and school health services has been questioned. In many areas, health visitors and school nurses have developed expertise in specialised areas such as child protection and health promotion.

Health Promotion in Childhood

The subject of health promotion and the importance of developing healthy lifestyles and behaviours early in life is described fully in Chapter 3. It is important to recognize the opportunities available for health promotion as a result of the regular contacts with children and their parents which occur throughout childhood. This applies whether the child is presenting with a problem to the general practitioner or to the hospital service or for routine child health surveillance. Opportunities for health education on issues such as immunisation and vaccination, accident prevention, safety, nutrition, passive and active smoking, and drug and alcohol misuse should be taken by health professionals whenever possible. In addition, health professionals need to work with colleagues in education to maximise the opportunities for health promotion in schools.

The Protection of Abused and Neglected Children

Although injury to children by their parents is not a new phenomenon, it only became widely recognized in the early 1970s. In 1962, the term 'battered child syndrome' was first used by an American paediatrician, Dr. Kempe, and was taken up by the media.

In Britain, widespread attention was first focused on child physical abuse in 1974, following an inquiry into the death of seven year old Maria Colwell. This inquiry uncovered serious deficiencies in professional practice and in the response of services. Its main historical importance is that it acted as a stimulus to the establishment of a procedure for dealing with the problem. A series of major public inquiries have since discovered a consistent pattern of failure of professional practice, lack of communication and poor coordination of services.

Recognition of the widespread nature of child sexual abuse was much slower in coming. Although it was recognized amongst professionals who were dealing with the issue, the public were largely unaware of it, at least as a major problem. All this changed in the late 1980s when the sexual abuse of children became a prominent issue for the public, the media and for politicians. Esther Rantzen, the broadcaster, launched 'ChildLine', a free telephone counselling service for child victims of sexual abuse.

In Cleveland in 1986, the admission to hospital of large numbers of children suspected of being sexually abused led to an enquiry chaired by Lord Justice Butler Sloss. The subsequent report stated that there was not only lack of communication but also a lack of understanding by the agencies involved, of each others' functions in relation to child sexual abuse, as well as fundamental differences in approach amongst professionals of the same discipline.

The crisis in Cleveland raised new issues. Firstly, it brought into the open the fact that child sexual abuse might be a much greater problem than had previously been realised. Secondly, it drew attention to the need for a balance between the rights of parents and the power of professionals to take action to protect children. Although the Cleveland Inquiry report was far-reaching and was a force for the introduction of much new guidance on the detection and management of child sexual abuse, the lessons were not fully learned.

The Children Act 1989 was framed against the background of enquiries into physical abuse occurring in the 1970s and 1980s and the ongoing issues in Cleveland. Although the Act clearly established what is often referred to as 'the paramouncy principle' (i.e., that the welfare of the child is paramount), there are also strong messages about the need to care for children whenever possible within their families and to seek to avoid court orders when possible. Even in the Act, which was on the whole welcomed by all those involved in child care, there was expression of the intrinsic conflict between the need to protect children and recognition of the important to the child of its family.

Size of the Problem

The spectrum of child abuse is now recognized as extensive. It covers physical injury to the child, sexual activities involving a child, emotional ill-treatment, and severe neglect. There are no reliable data to describe the size of the problem of child abuse in the population. By its nature it is a problem that may not be recognized or which may be concealed. Children recorded on child protection registers provide an estimate of the problem, although undoubtedly it is an underestimate.

Recognition and Referral of Cases

Health visitors are the group of NHS staff most likely come into contact with and recognize cases of child abuse. Children may also be brought to the general practitioner or accident and emergency departments. Consultant paediatricians and community child health doctors will be involved in the diagnosis of physical abuse and neglect. However, the most common source of child protection referrals is through education and those providing other local authority services to children and families. There has been criticism of health care professionals' role in child protection. Sometimes these problems reflect a lack of training in recognition of the physical signs of abuse. On other occasions criticism has been made of health care professionals' reluctance to refer to social services departments. Varied explanations are given for this but there do appear to be genuine concerns about preserving the integrity of the doctor–patient relationship with the family (particularly for general practitioners) and concerns about breaching the confidentiality of the parent or carer. Another group of health care professionals for whom these conflicts are particularly difficult are those who deliver adult mental health care services; for example, psychiatrists, psychotherapists and community psychiatric nurses. These professionals may receive disclosures of abuse by adult abusers.

It is vital that child protection training is multi-agency and that different groups of professionals understand the roles and responsibilities of others.

Investigation and Assessment

An early decision needs to be taken as to whether the child is in need of urgent protection. If so, an application can be made to the court for an Emergency Protection Order. Such action will not usually be warranted and the first step will be a strategy discussion between representatives of the various agencies to plan the investigation of the suspected abuse. There is always the possibility that legal action may be taken by either the social services department (to protect the child) or by the police (to prosecute an alleged perpetrator of abuse) or by both agencies.

Staff undertaking this type of work from whatever agency must be appropriately skilled and trained. Detailed national and local guidance covers how the various types of investigation should be carried out, especially in relation to interviewing and examining the child. It is essential that this is done with great sensitivity otherwise the investigation process could further damage an already vulnerable child. High standards are also required in recording findings and evidence which may be required subsequently for the child protection conference and by the court.

The Child Protection Conference and Registration of Cases

The child protection conference (sometimes called simply the case conference) is a vital part of the child protection procedures. It is the forum in which representatives of all agencies concerned come together to review information related to the child and to plan the action required. The conference will also seek advice on assessment from relevant experts (for example, a child psychiatrist, an educational psychologist).

There are two main types of conference: the initial child protection conference and the child protection review. An initial child protection conference takes place after the investigation and initial assessment. Its timing varies. In some cases, it needs to take place extremely quickly but in any case it would not normally be later than a week after the initial referral. The child protection conference has only one major decision to make – which is whether to register the child. The process of registration leads to the designation of a key worker who is a social worker from the social services department or the NSPCC (National Society for the Prevention of Cruelty to Children). He or she is responsible for the development of a plan for the protection of the child, coordinating all other agencies as well as coordinating further assessment and, if necessary, preparation of the application to court for a Care Order. It is important to realise that it is not the purpose of the child protection conference to establish whether abuse has taken place.

Children, parents and other family members should usually be involved in some part of the conference though this can be problematic and not all care professionals agree with such an approach.

The Chair of the child protection conference is held by a senior representative of the lead agency (either social services department or NSPCC). The skills and knowledge of the chairperson are very important. Poor chairing can make the difference between a child being adequately protected and being left vulnerable to further abuse. Representatives from each agency and each care professional should be invited to attend the child protection conference.

The review conference serves a different purpose. It assesses the current status of the child, reviews the current child protection plan, the level of risk and decides whether registration should continue.

A key feature of the approach to the problem of child abuse at a local level is the establishment and maintenance of child protection registers to record all cases of abuse and those in which a child is at risk of abuse. It is a requirement that such a register is maintained in each social services area. There are three broad objectives of such a register:

(1) To provide a record of all children in the area who are currently the subject of an interagency protection plan and to ensure that the plans are formally reviewed at least every six months.
(2) To provide a central point of speedy enquiry for professional staff who are worried about a child and want to know whether the child is the subject of an interagency protection plan.
(3) To provide statistical information about current trends in the area.

A child's name can only be entered onto the register after a child protection conference if there is significant risk of harm leading to the need for a child protection plan or a likelihood of such harm.

The categories of abuse for registration are:

(a) Neglect
(b) Physical injury
(c) Sexual abuse
(d) Emotional abuse

The removal of a child from the register is considered at every review child protection conference but all those present at the conference must agree that the abuse (or risk of it) is no longer present for deregistration to occur. Other aspects of register maintenance include: ensuring confidentiality, communication of changes of registered details, updating with additional reports, and notification of details to another area if the family moves house.

Area Child Protection Committees

The Area Child Protection Committee is the body in which all the agencies come together to formulate, review and monitor child protection policies. The main functions of the Area Child Protection Committee are set out in Table 6.14.

Table 6.14 Main functions of Area Child Protection Committees

- To establish, maintain and review local inter-agency guidelines on procedures to be followed in individual cases
- To monitor the implementation of legal procedures
- To identify significant issues arising from the handling of cases and reports from inquiries
- To scrutinise arrangements to provide treatment, expert advice and inter-agency liaison and make recommendations to the responsible agencies
- To scrutinise progress on work to prevent child abuse and make recommendations to the responsible agencies
- To scrutinise work related to inter-agency training and make recommendations to the responsible agencies
- To conduct reviews required in cases where there are adverse incidents
- To publish an annual report about local child protection matters

Source: Working Together Under the Children Act 1989. HMSO, 1991.

Prevention of Child Abuse

As in so many fields involving human behaviour, successful preventive measures are very difficult to establish. If better methods could be devised to identify families where violence or neglect is likely to occur, then the necessary corrective measures could be taken. More frequent visiting to give support to isolated families may reduce the risk. As more attention is focused on the problem of child abuse, various schemes are being established, such as 'self help' groups and the 'crying baby' 24 hour service, where health visitors respond to crises.

A longer-term measure is to develop the teaching of parenthood in schools, with emphasis on child development and the emotional needs of babies and children.

Where sexual abuse is concerned, there is general agreement that it should be openly discussed with young children and their families, both before it occurs, in sensitive prevention programmes and afterwards, and in the form of therapy. It is also necessary to educate preschool and day care managers and teachers about the recognition of symptoms and the kinds of threat that children might receive to prevent them from revealing the abuse.

Children 'Looked After' by Local Authorities

At any one time, some 55,000 children in England will be looked after (in the care of) local authorities. Care in this context encompasses a wide variety of settings ranging from fostering through various types of residential care to secure institutions (Table 6.15). Children need care of these kinds for a variety of reasons. For example, they may have been abused or neglected, their parents may not be able to cope with their upbringing, they may have severe behavioural or emotional disturbance, or their family may have broken down and fragmented.

Table 6.15 Children looked after by local authorities in England, 1999

Placement	Percentage
Foster placements	65
Children's homes	12
Schools (and homes, hostels)	2
Placed with parents	11
Placed for adoption	5
Other	5
Total	100
(Number =)	(55,300)

Source: Department of Health.

A child being considered for care by the local authority should have a full assessment so that the choice of placement can be made in a way which reflects his or her individual needs. In the mid-1990s concern was expressed about the delivery of health, social care and education services to 'looked after' children. A report commissioned by the government highlighted failures of care – in particular, for highly vulnerable children and those with challenging behaviour. Children with frequent changes of foster placement were not receiving continuous education and were not receiving basic health services such as routine immunisation. A number of children suffered further abuse in foster care or residential care. A number of children leaving local authority care are known to become homeless others are at risk of prostitution, drug addiction and criminal behaviour. Children looked after by local authorities are, by definition, a most vulnerable and needy group. Meeting their needs presents a real challenge to providers of services. In 1999, a Quality Protects initiative was launched. It aims to improve the management and delivery of children's services in local authorities. The challenge is to promote independence through enhancing the life chances of children who need social services and to ensure that those who need safeguarding are properly protected. Life chances for looked after children are not good and therefore a significant amount of attention is given in the initiative to improving outcomes for this group of children and young people.

Conclusions

The health of a population's children is an important indicator of its overall health status. Over this century, the industrialised world has witnessed a major reduction in the number of babies lost around the time of childbirth. Despite the fact that a high proportion of pregnancies now have a successful outcome for mothers and babies, a minority of babies still die or survive in a damaged or impaired state. A small number of mothers also die because of pregnancy or childbirth. An important role for public health is to identify the scope for further reductions in this pool of potentially avoidable death, morbidity and disability. Health services working alone or with other agencies have a responsibility to improve the health and well-being of children. This can be through the promotion of health; the application of preventive interventions (such as immunisation); the maintenance of good surveillance; the provision of high quality diagnostic, treatment and rehabilitation services; or making available alternative forms of care, protection and support for children in need.

More than at any other time of life, health and disease in childhood encompasses emotional, psychological, environmental and social influences as well as specific risk factors. Responding to the health challenges of the future will involve a vigorous and imaginative public health approach to the needs of mothers, infants, children and adolescents. For, it is amongst these groups that the foundations of a Nation's health are laid.

Chapter 7

Mental Health and Learning Disability

Introduction

Mental health is not just the absence of mental disorder. It is a state in which a person is able to fulfil an active functioning role in society, interacting with others and overcoming difficulties without suffering major distress, abnormal or disturbed behaviour.

Whilst attitudes in society are changing, both mental illness and learning disability continue to carry a stigma for those who suffer from them, and, to a lesser extent, those who care for people who suffer from them. Many health professionals still find the pursuit of a career in this field of care unattractive compared with alternatives involving the care of acutely physically ill patients in high-technology surroundings. Yet, this group of the population has special needs which can pose formidable challenges for those seeking to provide the most appropriate care. The field of work can offer scope for innovation just as great as in the other therapeutic fields of medicine and surgery.

This chapter deals with the extent and range of mental illness and learning disabilities found in the population, the needs of people who suffer from them, and the spectrum of services available to meet those needs.

The Needs of People with a Mental Illness

The spectrum of psychological disorders which can incapacitate people and interfere with their ability to function normally is very large. Whilst distinctions are often made between major and minor mental illnesses, disorders of the mind can be very distressing and disruptive to individuals and their families, even when they do not amount to a full-blown psychiatric illness. For example, a thirty-year-old woman with three small children who develops uncontrollable panic attacks when she enters a shop can be so incapacitated by this problem that she is unable to go outdoors unaccompanied. Moreover, she may be so distressed that she needs to ask her husband to stay away from work to be with her, thus putting his employment position in jeopardy. Similarly, the teenage girl who develops an eating disorder at the time of school leaving examinations can perform so badly that she may lose important career opportunities, yet her condition may not amount to full-blown anorexia nervosa.

Many so called 'minor' mental illnesses are treated in primary care settings or do not necessarily come to the attention of specialist services, so that routine data are not available to enable them to be quantified within the population.

A smaller number of people suffer from very serious psychiatric disorders which can have a major social impact. Psychotic diseases such as schizophrenia are examples of this kind of condition. These are usually long-term illnesses for which people require medication, support and periodic episodes of hospital care during the course of many years. Whilst most people who have developed the disease over the last twenty years have been able to maintain a home outside hospital, there is a group of people with chronic psychotic disease who were diagnosed at a time when modern drugs were not available. Many such people are long-term residents within large psychiatric hospitals which have, in effect, become their homes. Their inability to lead an independent life is in part a feature of the long-term nature of their illness but in part also caused by a dependence on the routines and habits of institutional life developed over many years. With the advent of programmes of care which have largely replaced the large long-stay psychiatric hospitals with more modern forms of care, this group of chronically mentally ill people must be considered as having special needs. This group is being replaced by a group of younger people with severe mental illness who tend to be in and out of hospital and may need continuing NHS care.

Also amongst the more severe mental illness problems within the population is the group of people whose disorder of the mind leads them to commit crimes such as assault, rape, murder, theft and arson. Although the numbers of mentally disordered offenders is very small (probably no more than a few thousand across the United Kingdom), they pose problems which are complex to solve and have needs which require highly specialised forms of care.

Prevalence of Mental Illness in Populations

Describing the size and nature of the problem of mental illness in the population, and the range of needs experienced by people with mental illness, is very difficult. Not least are the problems of diagnosis and disease classification. Whilst variation between psychiatrists in the use of disease labels is not of major importance when addressing the needs of individual patients, it causes difficulty when it is necessary to aggregate diagnostic information to produce estimates of the size of particular pools of psychiatric morbidity at population level. There is also a lack of routinely available population-based information. Traditionally, information on psychiatric morbidity has been based on contacts with services, usually hospital services.

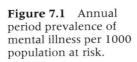 **Figure 7.1** Annual period prevalence of mental illness per 1000 population at risk.

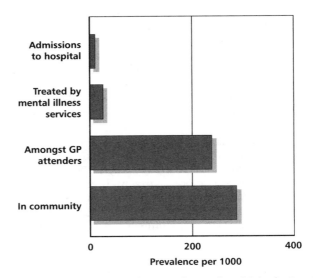

Source: Adapted from Goldberg D. Indicators of Mental Health in the Population. Department of Health Workshop, 1990.

Establishing the frequency of psychiatric morbidity in the general population has been a major area of epidemiological research since the 1960s and the subject of important studies even before that. Early studies concentrated on people already in contact with mental health services but it was quickly realised that this represented only a small proportion of total psychiatric morbidity (Figure 7.1). Findings of early community-based surveys suffered from the difficulties of producing the types of psychiatric diagnoses so that survey instruments could be applied to large populations, by non-medical (but trained) interviewers and then yield valid assessments of morbidity in the population.

One of the most influential early studies of mental illness in a population was carried out in New York in the mid-1950s. The Mid-Town Manhattan Study was based on a single home interview of a randomly selected sample of 1.7% of households to identify adults aged 20–59 years, together with information from searching records of hospitals and other agencies (to identify people who could have been missed in the household survey). The survey questions covered 120 manifestations of mental illness, mainly drawn from symptom-based psychiatric screening tools of the day. Psychiatrists then classified the responses gathered by the field interviewers. The results were presented as a continuum of mental health (Table 7.1) not as a series of diagnostic categories. As a result, the prevalence of mental 'illness' appears quite high. For this reason, the study is often criticised by those who seek to establish the prevalence of mental illness in precise diagnostic groups. Yet, it would have been impractical at the time to carry out a full psychiatric assessment on each member of the sample. Moreover, the variation in diagnostic approach between psychiatrists would have limited the extent to which the findings could be generalised.

Table 7.1   Classification of people's mental status in an early community study: Mid-Town Manhattan

Mental health	Percentage of sample
Well	18.5
Mild symptom formation	36.3
Moderate symptoms	21.8
Marked symptoms	13.2
Severe symptoms	7.5
Incapacitated	2.7
N(100%) = (1660)	100

Source: Srole L *et al*. Mental Health in the Metropolis. New York: McGraw-Hill, 1962.

In more recent years, views have differed as to the approach which should be used to establish the prevalence of mental illness in the population. Broadly, when the aim is to explore causation, disease categories are more useful. When the aim is to examine need for services, functionally-based measures are usually preferable.

This is particularly so when attempting to quantify the problem of severe mental illness in a population. Using diagnostic criteria to identify cases of schizophrenia would be of value in a study of the aetiology of the disease. Establishing criteria for defining, and then subsequently identifying, people with 'severe enduring mental illness' would be much more helpful in reviewing the configuration of services for this group of the population. Moreover, many reported studies of severe mental illness have differed in the age-groups studied, in whether patients in institutions were included and in the clarity and rigour of the definitional criteria used. A broad estimate of the frequency of some of the major mental illnesses in the population of England is shown in Table 7.2.

Table 7.2 Estimated frequency of mental disorders in the adult
population over 16 years of age

Mental disorder	Point prevalence %	Lifetime risk %
Schizophrenia	0.2–0.5%	0.7–0.9%
Affective psychosis	0.1–0.5%	1%
Depressive disorder	3–6%	>20%
Anxiety states	2–7%	N/A
Dementia (over 65)	5%	N/A
Dementia (over 80)	20%	N/A

N/A = not available or not applicable. *Source:* The Health of the Nation.
London: HMSO, 1992.

The development of standardised diagnostic and assessment scales has greatly
improved the value and comparability of population-based studies of mental illness.
Good population data on the prevalence of mental illness in Great Britain were provided by a series of population surveys carried out in the mid-1990s. The presence of
neurotic-type illnesses was assessed using a standardised scale, the Clinical Interview
Schedule (CIS-R), which comprises 14 sections, each covering a particular area of
neurotic symptoms (e.g., anxiety, phobias, panic disorders). Assessment was also
undertaken for the presence of psychotic illnesses but in this case, after an initial
screen by the lay interviewer, a follow-up clinical interview was conducted by a psychiatrist before the problem was said to be present. About 1 in 6 adults aged 16–64
years old living in private households had experienced a neurotic disorder in the week
before interview (Figure 7.2). The most common neurotic disorder was mixed anxiety and depression (77 per 1000) with generalised anxiety affecting 31 per 1000. A
range of other neurotic disorders (e.g., phobias, panic attacks) affected between 8 and
21 people per 1000 population.

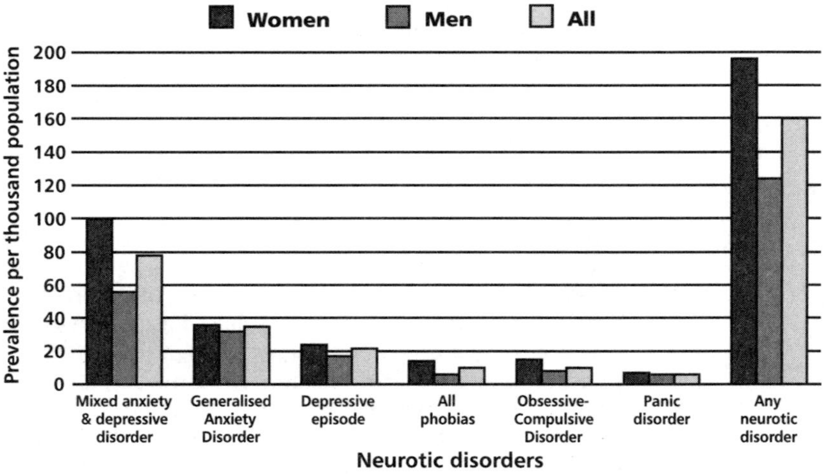

Figure 7.2 Weekly
prevalence of neurotic
disorders.

Source: OPCS Surveys of Psychiatric Morbidity: Great Britain. Report 1. London: HMSO, 1995.

For all neurotic disorders the prevalence was: (a) higher in women than in men; (b)
higher in divorced and separated men and women but lowest for those who were
married or cohabiting; (c) highest for people who were unemployed and lowest in

those working full time; (d) highest for women in Social Classes IV and V and lowest for women in Social Classes I and II (a similar but less marked pattern was found for men); (e) highest for lone parents and lowest for couples with no children and adults living with their parents; (f) higher for those in rented accommodation than those who were owner occupiers.

The data gathered in studies on the prevalence of psychotic and more severe forms of mental illness were based on separate samples of people living in private households and in mental health institutions, so that it is difficult to cite exact population-based estimates of prevalence. Disease-based prevalence studies have estimated the prevalence of schizophrenia in the range shown in Table 7.2 (higher in deprived or high-risk populations). An approach which is of practical value gives a range of prevalence estimates for severe mental illness in relation to different community settings (Figure 7.3).

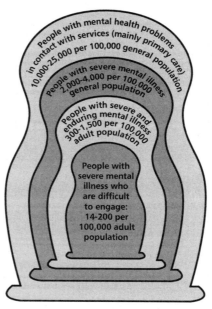

Figure 7.3 Estimated number of people with different degrees of mental health problem in the population.

Source: Keys to engagement. London: Sainsbury Centre for Medical Health, 1998.

In this diagram the largest 'Russian Doll' represents the people who present mainly in primary care with mental health problems of this group is estimated as between 10% to 25% of the population each year. Within this group are those other 'Russian Dolls' representing the frequency of people in the population with severe mental illness, severe enduring mental illness and the group with severe mental illness who are difficult to engage with services (e.g., homeless, violent, drug abusers, complex social problems).

As with other groups of hospital patients, Hospital Episode Statistics is the method by which statistics on psychiatric inpatients are collected from National Health Service psychiatric hospitals and psychiatric units in England and Wales. Detailed information is collected about each admission and discharge and a notional census of all psychiatric inpatients is carried out once a year (see Chapter 1 for a fuller description).

In addition to these routinely collected statistics, many surveys have investigated psychiatric illnesses using populations of psychiatric inpatients and outpatients. The danger in such studies arises when the assumption is made that admission rates to hospital for particular conditions are synonymous with their incidence in the population.

The fact that fewer people in one area are admitted to hospital than in another may not necessarily be an indication of a lower occurrence of mental illness. It may be reflecting the availability of facilities, the policy for admission, the social stigma attached to mental illness in general or to a particular institution for its treatment, or the tolerance of the community towards abnormal behaviour. Other factors determining whether or not people with a particular psychiatric illness come to the attention of hospital-based services may be the extent to which they or their relatives perceive an abnormality and consider it necessary to make contact with services. This, in turn, may depend upon whether the abnormality interferes with social functioning either in the person's job or in the discharge of other social responsibilities.

Some Primary Health Care Teams routinely collect data on contacts of patients with general practitioners or other primary health care workers. Such data are not yet gathered comprehensively throughout the country and can be of variable quality. However, a number of studies have looked at various aspects of psychiatric morbidity in general practice. Studies of the general practice population give an indication of the distribution of less severe psychiatric conditions and highlight the importance of the psychological components of illness to the work of the general practitioner. In addition, this population gives a fuller indication of the natural history of mental illness. There are, however, special difficulties which limit the conclusions which may be drawn from the results. Rates of psychiatric illness reported by general practitioners vary widely. The report of a single general practitioner is of little value when extrapolated to the whole population. The patients in the practice may not be typical, and the diagnostic criteria and classification adopted by the general practitioner may not be satisfactory.

Psychiatric case registers record and collect information concerning contacts made by individuals residing in a defined geographical area with a specified set of psychiatric services. Having identified an individual making contact with services, a register monitors any future contacts so that the patient's record is cumulative. Amongst the best known psychiatric registers developed in the United Kingdom were those in Camberwell, Salford and Aberdeen. They have been used to trace the natural history of disease, to identify groups at high risk and to determine the pattern of use of services as well as the extent to which needs are being met. The maintenance of registers is labour-intensive if accuracy is to be achieved. Thus, there are few such registers in Britain as a whole. A fuller description of the concept of disease registers is to be found in Chapter 1.

The Mental Illness Needs Index (MINI) is a social index specifically designed to predict likely levels of need for mental health services for a geographic sector definable in terms of electoral wards in Britain. It was developed primarily to assist local managers, commissioners and national-policy-makers in allocating resources.

Risk Factors for Schizophrenia

Schizophrenia is one of the psychiatric illnesses which has been most extensively studied using epidemiological approaches. Studies of risk factors have yielded a fascinating range of influences on the frequency of the disease (Table 7.3). Familial risk is now well established and a great deal of subsequent work has been to elucidate whether this is due to genetic or environmental causes. Socio-demographic risk factors for schizophrenia have been classified into mutable (for example, marital status) and immutable (for example, ethnic origin). It must be remembered however that mutable risk factors may occur because of the disease and not vice versa. A good example of this kind of problem is the relationship between schizophrenia and social class.

Table 7.3 Potential risk factors for schizophrenia

Risk factor	Approximate relative risk
Familial factors	
• Schizophrenic parent	12
• Two schizophrenic parents	37
• Schizophrenic sib	
- Monozygotic twin	55
- Dizygotic twin – same sex	18
- Other sib	8
• Schizophrenic second-degree relative	3
Mutable sociodemographic factors	
• Low socio-economic status	3
• Single status	4
Immutable sociodemographic factors	
• Ethnic group status	2
• Modern industrialised nation	2
Other risk factors	
• Rheumatic disease	0.2
• Winter birth	1.1
• Stressful life events	2.7

Source: Eaton WW. Epidemiology of Schizophrenia Epidemiologic Reviews, 1985; 7:105–125.

One of the earliest and best known examples of the use of hospital admissions to study mental illness was the investigation of the relationship between schizophrenia and social class carried out in the 1930s in Chicago.[1] First-admission rates to hospital for schizophrenia were used to pinpoint differences in its frequency between parts of Chicago. The question of selection bias (discussed above) is not further raised here, except to say that first-admission rates for schizophrenia at that time are probably a fair approximation of incidence, since most people were hospitalised at some stage during their first episode of the illness. It was observed that the mental hospital admission rates for schizophrenia were highest in the central slum districts, with much lower rates in the outer residential areas of the city. One interpretation of these observations was that since the poor areas contained many people of lower socio-economic status, it was therefore the environment, lifestyle and living conditions of people in the lowest stratum of society that predisposed them to the disease. This hypothesis seemed to be substantiated by a later study which looked at first-admission rates to all psychiatric services, including outpatients in a defined geographical area, New Haven, Connecticut.[2] The results appeared to show that people in lower social classes had a higher incidence of schizophrenia. This phenomenon became known as 'the breeder hypothesis'; adverse social circumstances being seen as generating mental illness. Some doubt was shed on this reasoning by the observation that poor areas and social isolation do not necessarily go together, at least in European cities, and that schizophrenic patients quite often moved into isolated areas before admission to hospital.

Table 7.4 Social class distribution of schizophrenic patients and their fathers (males, first admissions aged 25–34 years, England and Wales, 1956)

Social Class	Patients at admission		Fathers at patient's birth	
	Observed	*Expected*	*Observed*	*Expected*
I	12	12	14	8
II	21	44	42	42
III	178	203	192	192
IV	52	55	66	68
V	90	39	55	59
Total	353	353	369	369
Not Stated	18		2	

Source: Goldberg EM and Morrison SL, Schizophrenia and Social Class. Br. J. Psychiat., 1963; 109:785–802.

British researchers then provided important new evidence. Their findings are presented in Table 7.4. They compared the social-class distribution of young male patients diagnosed with schizophrenia on first admission to mental hospitals with that of their fathers at the time of the patient's birth. It was found that although the patients had a marked excess of jobs in the lower social class categories, they had been born into families with a similar social-class distribution to that of the general population. The implication was that there had been a 'drift' downwards in the social classes of schizophrenic patients as a result of their illness. This contradicts the 'breeder hypothesis' which suggested that socio-economic deprivation is of major aetiological importance. It is now more generally believed that the preponderance of lower social class patients with schizophrenia is due to the disabling effect of the illness (the drift hypothesis) rather than through poor environmental circumstances (the breeder hypothesis), although the debate is one which has continued within the field of psychiatric epidemiology and some consider the question unresolved.

Suicide and Severe Self-harm, Homicide

Suicide

The classic work of the famous French Sociologist Durkheim (1858–1917) on suicides during a period of over 30 years, is a landmark in his own discipline and in social psychiatry.

Durkheim, by studying statistics from various European countries as well as by analysis of case records, concluded that suicide was a relatively stable characteristic with a fixed rate for a given society which reflected its culture. He considered that factors in society, such as the degree of social cohesion, exercised a powerful effect on the individual which might predispose him to suicide. Durkheim's studies were spread over many years and one of his conclusions was that suicide rates were higher amongst Protestants and the well-to-do and lower amongst Catholics and poor people. He also found suicide more frequent in males than females with an increased rate in elderly people.

Although published statistics rely solely on officially confirmed suicides, misclassification is a problem. The potential sources of error should not affect the large, observed variations of suicide rates over time.

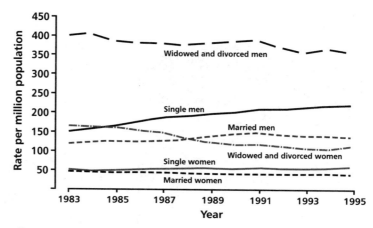

Figure 7.4 Suicide rates* by marital status and sex for people aged 15–44, England and Wales, 1982–96.

*3-year moving averages plotted on central year.

Source: Kelly S, Bunting J. Population Trends. London: Office for National Statistics, 1998.

In the immediate post-war period, suicides in England and Wales increased to a peak in the mid-1960s and then fell until the mid-1970s. Thereafter suicides increased to a peak in the early 1980s amongst women and the late 1980s amongst men. From then until the late 1990s, suicide rates in both sexes fell (more so in women than men). These overall trends conceal contrasts between the age and sex groups. Suicides amongst males aged 25–34 years increased during the 1980s whilst those amongst older males fell. Suicide rates amongst women aged 15–24 years increased slightly during the 1990s but are relatively low compared to males. Amongst different marital-status groups, there has been decline in suicide rates except amongst single people (Figure 7.4). Certain groups of the population in Britain have higher rates than others (Table 7.5).

Table 7.5 High-risk groups for suicide in Britain

- Young men
- Young women from the Indian subcontinent
- Men from the Republic of Ireland
- Unemployed people
- People who have been in local authority care during childhood and adolescence
- People who have suffered bereavement or loss
- People detained in prison, particularly young men
- Vets, farmers, pharmacists, doctors, nurses and others who have ready access to means of killing themselves
- People with a previous episode of deliberate self-harm
- People with severe mental illness

Hanging was the commonest suicide method amongst men and poisoning by solid or liquid substances in women (Figure 7.5). Suicide rates appear to be influenced by accessibility to the means to commit suicide. For example, the reduction, during the early 1990s, in poisoning by gases may reflect the difficulty in using car exhaust fumes since the advent of catalytic convertors.

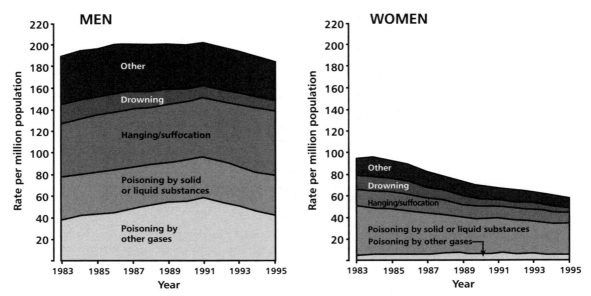

Figure 7.5   Standardised suicide rates* by sex and method, England and Wales, 1982–96.
*3-year moving averages plotted on central year.
Source: Kelly S, Bunting J. Population Trends. London: Office for National Statistics, 1998.

Homicide

When things go wrong in mental health services, they tend to attract considerable media attention. This is particularly so in the case of homicides committed by people with mental illness. Currently health authorities are required to set up independent inquiries into homicides committed by people who have been in recent contact with specialist mental health services, and the Department of Health expects the main findings and recommendations at least to be made public.

A sample of such homicides in England when considered by a National Confidential Inquiry revealed that 89% were male, 53% were single and 52% were unemployed. The most common method of homicide was the use of a sharp instrument (44%) and the victims were most commonly family members (35%) or acquaintances (31%). In all, 17% of those convicted of homicide had symptoms of mental illness at the time of the offence whilst 5% of these had symptoms of psychosis.

Severe Self-harm

Severe self-harm can be defined as a non-fatal incident in which a person causes self-injury or self-poisoning. The term 'attempted suicide' used to be applied to acts in which people tried to kill themselves but were not successful. It was then realised that of the people who were labelled attempted suicides, a certain proportion were not intending to kill themselves but had other, more complex, motivations such as making a statement about their own worthlessness or expressing the depth of their distress. Distinguishing those people who seriously wished to kill themselves, but had failed, from those who had other intents is obviously extremely problematic.

Because of these issues of motivation and intent, the frequency of severe self-harm in the population is difficult to define accurately. Estimates are based on cases of poisoning or self-injury admitted to hospital. However, from hospital data it is difficult to distinguish between accidents and admissions which result from a deliberate attempt at self-harm. Furthermore, it has been suggested that estimates based on hospital inpatient statistics may miss between one-fifth and one-third of cases. Those who sought help from their general practitioner or a hospital accident and emergency department will not be included nor will those who did not make contact with any medical authority. Thus, figures based on hospital cases for poisoning must be an underestimate of the true number of self-harm in a population. However, from any hospital statistics it is estimated that there are about 100,000 cases of adverse effects of medicinal agents (mainly overdose) each year in Britain.

Risk Factors and Risk Assessment

A number of risk factors predispose people to suicide or self-harm (Table 7.6). The approach to the assessment of risk and hence the prevention of suicide and self-harm involves: checking for the presence of risk factors; undertaking a careful clinical examination in which the person's past history of previous incidents of self-harm together with their ideas about suicide are explored; whether they have a plan to harm themselves, and an intent to do so are also strong predictors.

Table 7.6   Risk factors for self-harm

Variables	*Higher risk*	*Lower risk*
Age	Older	Younger
Sex	Male	Female
Marital Status	Separated, divorced, widowed	Married
Living arrangements	Living alone	Others at home
Employment status	Unemployed, retired	Employed
Physical Health	Poor, especially terminal, painful, debilitating illness	Good
Mental Health	Mental illness, especially depression, schizophrenia, chronic sleep disorders	Good
Substance Abuse	Alcoholism, illegal drug misuse	None

Source: Learning materials on mental health: risk assessment. Manchester: University of Manchester, 1996.

The majority of suicides by people with mental illness occur when the risk is perceived to be low, which raises questions about the adequacy of risk assessment but may equally be a reflection of the limits of current knowledge about suicidal risk factors and the difficulty faced by clinicians in predicting patients' behaviour.

Risks can be managed – much depends on the individual case but the key to good risk management involve a multidisciplinary, multi-agency approach, well trained staff and a great deal of direct contact with the patient.

The Department of Health in England funds the Royal College of Psychiatrists to conduct a national confidential enquiry into cases of suicide and homicide by people with mental illness. Systematic study of such cases has highlighted a range of problems which are commonly found when such deaths occur (Table 7.7). Lack of effective communication, poor teamwork and inadequate care planning and supervision are features which seem particularly important.

Table 7.7 Common problems in services where there were suicides or homicides involving mentally ill people

- Failure of communication between professionals
- Lack of clarity about care plans
- Lack of time for face-to-face contact with patients
- Inadequate staff training
- Poor compliance with treatment
- Insufficient use of legal powers to supervise patients

Source: Report of the confidential enquiry into homicides and suicides by mentally ill people. London: Royal College of Psychiatrists, 1996.

Supervision Registers

Following a number of high-profile tragedies involving mentally ill people in the early 1990s in England, all NHS Trusts were required to introduce supervision registers. These registers should identify those people with a severe mental illness who may pose a significant risk to themselves or to others and to ensure that local services are targeted on them.

Trends in the Care of Mentally Ill People

Early Practices

In the Dark and Middle Ages the treatment of mental illness was governed by ignorance and superstition. If the mentally ill had delusions of a religious nature, they were often revered; if their utterances were blasphemous they were held to be possessed by demons and treated, in the first instance, by exorcism by a priest. If this was unsuccessful, then they would be subjected to physical restraint, pain and degradation. This quasi-religious view of mental illness later gave way to the notion that insane people were practitioners of the Black Arts. In Britain alone, thousands of women and children were subjected to the ducking stool or burned at the stake as witches of whom many must have had mental illnesses. The last woman to meet her death in this way did so in Scotland in 1722.

Britain in the Eighteenth and Nineteenth Centuries

In the early years of the eighteenth century, a number of singularly unpleasant fates could befall the person who was mentally ill, depending on the circumstances in which he found himself. There was then no organised service to provide care for the mentally ill.

The Pauper Lunatic

If the manifestations of his illness led him into the trap of poverty, the pauper lunatic became subject to the conditions of the Poor Law. Under the old Poor Law, which dated from Elizabethan times, the responsibility for paupers rested with individual parishes, each of which had an overseer who raised money by taxation to provide for them. The standard of poorhouses varied greatly from one part of the country to another but in many of the larger cities the workhouse began to emerge as the principal type of provision. A report by the Poor Law Commissioners which gave rise to the Poor Law Amendment Act 1834, saw the workhouse as the fulcrum of the State's policy on the poor. There was almost an obsession on the part of the authorities to prevent exploitation by malingerers. The workhouse with its frugal, and in many cases, inhuman surroundings, was seen as the way to deter the lazy and workshy and to extract the maximum productivity from the able-bodied pauper. The policy on the pauper lunatic was expressly to exclude him from the workhouse. Nevertheless, the majority found their way into it, although they were not recognized or treated as a separate category. The law dealt with the vagrant very strictly and thus the mentally ill who left their own homes to wander abroad as beggars would often find themselves in prison. Similarly, criminal insanity was not recognized. Hence, if a person's mental condition led him to commit a crime, he would be judged by penal law and usually find himself in one of the already crowded prisons.

Because of the deep shame attached to mental illness many families of poor and well-to-do alike sought to conceal its presence amongst their relatives. This led to the practice of keeping 'single lunatics' in remote places. It was not uncommon for a family member to be secured in a cellar like an animal for years at a time.

The Private Madhouse

For the wealthy, though escaping the indignity of the workhouse or the prison cell, insanity brought confinement in one of the private madhouses which proliferated in England at the time. These were run for profit and the fate of their inmates was scarcely better and, in many cases, worse than that of the pauper lunatic in the workhouse; shackling and deliberate ill-treatment were often the order of the day.

Bedlam

Originally founded in 1247, as a priory by the Order of St Mary of Bethlehem, Bethlehem Royal Hospital in London was the largest, and for some time, the only public hospital in England devoted to the care of the insane. It existed largely on public subscriptions. The treatment meted out to inmates was as harsh as that in the private madhouses. The mentally ill were chained in confined surroundings and often subjected to bizarre and whimsical therapies, such as bleeding, purging or the induction of vomiting. Towards the end of the eighteenth century the general public could be admitted to the hospital and for the fee of one penny amuse themselves by watching the antics of the inmates. The name of the hospital, corrupted in common parlance to 'Bedlam', gave the English language a new word which was synonymous with mindless disorder and chaos. Discharged patients were given badges to allow them legitimately to exist as beggars without falling foul of the harsh vagrancy laws of the time. These 'Toms O'Bedlam' soon found their ranks swelled by imposters who had forged their badges.

A ward in Bethlem about 1745. From Chapters in the history of the insane. London: Kegan Paul, 1882.

Source: The Wellcome Institute Library, London.

The Humanitarian Movement

At the beginning of the nineteenth century, concern began to grow amongst a few enlightened reformers and to a lesser extent by public opinion about the appalling way in which the mentally ill were treated. In part, this came about through the existence of islands of compassion in the approach to mental illness. Outstanding in this respect was William Tuke, a Quaker, who founded the Retreat at York where the mentally ill were not manacled and restrained but were treated humanely. The success of this venture made a deep impression on attitudes to mental illness and its treatment.

Equally important were the revelations made by various select Parliamentary Committees of the circumstances of those housed in public asylums and private madhouses. One of the most well known examples is the visit made by Edward Wakefield, MP and his colleagues to Bethlehem Hospital. During their visit they discovered one of the inmates, William Norris, who was half naked and chained to the wall in such a way that he could stand up or lie down but not sit. This wretched man had been kept in this way for nine years and by the time he became a *cause celebre* was in the terminal phase of tuberculosis. Similar discoveries of conditions in private madhouses led to legislation bringing them under licence, although it must be admitted that conditions changed little at first. Another important advance was the County Asylums Act, 1808, which recommended that Local Authorities should build asylums to provide treatment for the mentally ill. The programme was not compulsory and consequently, implementation was very slow in most parts of the country but it was designed to cater mainly for the pauper lunatic, who would otherwise have found himself in the workhouse.

Under the Madhouse Act 1828 (with subsequent amendments), the Metropolitan Commissioners in Lunacy, consisting of medical practitioners, barristers and lay people appointed by the Lord Chancellor, became the guardians of insane patients and made reports.

The culmination of the reform movement was the passing by Parliament of the Lunatics Act 1845. In it, the power of the Lunacy Commissioners was greatly extended so that they were responsible for inspection, licensing and reporting on all places in which the mentally ill were housed or cared for. They were able to investigate and report the circumstances of the mentally ill in prisons and workhouses (which had previously been outside their jurisdiction), as well as in public hospitals, asylums, private madhouses and other licensed premises. Further measures introduced in the Act were the tightening up of procedures for certification of the mentally ill and the compulsory keeping of records by institutions treating them.

Into the Twentieth Century: the Open Door Policy

During the early years of the twentieth century, the mental hospital, closed and often situated in a remote locality, served a predominantly custodial role with little attempt to treat mental illness or to forge links with the community. One of the first rays of light on this depressing scene was the widespread establishment of psychiatric outpatient clinics, which together with the move towards voluntary admission, were by-products of the enlightened Mental Treatment Act 1930.

In 1948, mental hospitals, along with other types of hospital, became part of the National Health Service and were no longer the responsibility of the Local Authorities. The local authorities were given statutory responsibilities for providing community care, which comprised care and aftercare, as well as prevention.

Most of the hospital facilities for the mentally ill, inherited by the National Health Service, were in buildings erected during the last century and even earlier. These large mental hospitals had been designed to provide an isolated, self-sufficient community, often enclosed by high walls with the objectives of protecting society from the patient and of protecting the patient from the outside world. Few new mental hospitals have been built since the start of World War II so that serious overcrowding of existing hospitals reached crisis point by the mid-1950s. For instance, a typical large hospital designed to accommodate 1800 patients might contain 2700, be serving a catchment population of about one million covering four or five different local authorities and be staffed by three consultant psychiatrists. Thus, serious thought was being given to the idea of building new hospitals. The discovery of the psychotropic drugs, which helped to accelerate a trend in the reduction of psychiatric hospital inpatients (Open Door Policy), arrested this development. A similar picture was seen in the United States of America and other countries. This more optimistic outlook in treatment led to changing attitudes to mental illness amongst professionals and the public. Locked doors were opened and many more patients left hospital to live in the community, where local authorities began to provide an increasing quantity of supportive services.

In a way, the Mental Health Act 1959 served as the legislature's imprimatur on a wagon that was already rolling. In a relatively short space of time, the mantle of isolationism fell away from mental hospitals and a real working partnership sprang up between hospital and community services. It was as if a latter-day Joshua had blown his trumpet and the high walls around the mental hospitals had fallen down.

The population of mental hospital inpatients reached a peak in England and Wales in 1954, at just over 152,000. By 1975, this figure had been reduced to 98,000 and by the beginning of the 1990s, there were 59,000 mental illness beds.

From before the beginning of this century until the end of World War II, there was a slow increase in the number of admissions to mental illness hospitals and units in England. From the late 1940s until the early 1970s, there was an increase in annual admissions from around 25,000 to 160,000. During the course of the 1970s, admission rates remained stable, varying only slightly in an upwards or downwards direction but from then onwards episodes of inpatient care have increased and lengths of stay have decreased. In other words, modern psychiatric inpatient facilities are now used much more intensively than they used to be with a focus on treatment rather than a custodial approach to care.

Care in the Community: Ideals and Concerns

Current national policy on care of those with serious mental illness in Britain can be traced back to the famous speech by Enoch Powell in 1960s when, as Minister for Health he declared that the 'watertower' hospitals for those with mental illness had had their day and should be replaced with modern forms of care.

This policy was further developed in the White Paper, 'Better Services for the Mentally Ill' which was issued in the mid-1970s. It proposed a reduced role for the large mental hospitals, many of which were the former asylums of Victorian times. In turn, there was to be greater development of locally-based services so that inpatient facilities for the mentally ill would be provided in the district general hospital alongside those for people with other illnesses. Greater emphasis on community care was seen as the best way to enable some patients who would formerly have been treated in hospital to be supported in their homes or in settings closer to their families and friends.

Progress on policy implementation viewed in the round was slow during the 1970s and 1980s. Whilst the ratio of beds in larger psychiatric hospitals to those for the treatment of mental illness in district general hospitals fell from 8:1 in the mid-1970s to about 2:1 at the beginning of the 1990s, there was still substantial reliance on the old psychiatric hospitals as a major provider of service. By the early 1990s, 80 such hospitals were still open in the country as a whole. The economic consequences of such closures were formidable with substantial capital expenditure as well as additional revenue required to develop replacement services in general hospitals and in the community.

In some parts of Britain (especially the inner cities), a failure to re-provide a sufficient range of community services in tandem with psychiatric hospital closure programmes led to ex-hospital patients wandering the streets in a state of neglect. By the early 1990s, services for the mentally ill were still in the transitional phase. After 20 years of a programme based upon closure of large, old psychiatric hospitals, the alternative of acute hospital care in a general hospital setting, with associated day and outpatient facilities, together with smaller more local residential care and with packages of community care tailored to individual needs was still a goal to be striven for rather than a reality everywhere in the country.

Moreover, a series of high-profile incidents in which members of the public were attacked or killed by patients with severe mental illness who had been discharged from psychiatric services led to a loss of public confidence in the policy of closing down the larger mental hospitals.

Despite these concerns the late 1990s saw a much wider range of more flexible locally-based services developing. Much hospital treatment of people with mental illness became provided on an outpatient, rather than an inpatient basis, and many people with mental health problems received care in their own homes or in residentially based settings within local communities.

Local Mental Health Services: the Modern Approach

The cornerstone of the care for people with a mental illness or other mental health problem is a well structured and coordinated system of care at local level. The precise pattern of care varies throughout Britain because different models of service have developed according to local circumstances.

A number of principles should govern high quality care for people with mental health problems (Table 7.8). Increasingly it is recognized that the structure of local services must be flexible enough to cope with the wide range of needs of patients with the various forms of mental ill-health as opposed to providing a homogenised service. For both ethical and practical reasons (e.g., patient compliance) it has also been understood that care must rely more heavily on user and carer views on how services should be delivered. Furthermore, successful locally-based services are those which are well-coordinated, integrated, organised on a multi-agency basis and delivered by multidisciplinary teams as opposed to older models of care which stressed the primacy of the psychiatrist.

Table 7.8   Key principles governing high quality mental health services

- Care built around the individual's needs and views of users and carers
- A range of services that function as a system should be available
- Services should be sensitive to local needs, resources and culture

Source: Laying the foundations. London: Sainsbury Centre for Mental Health, 1998.

The ideal of rapid access to coordinated care which responds to an immediate problem experienced by a mentally ill person but also provides a full assessment of need and longer-term treatment and support as required has not been achieved everywhere. An indication of the diverse range of services required to provide a comprehensive service for a population is shown in Table 7.9.

Table 7.9   Range of services for people with severe and enduring mental illness

Community support:	• Primary care
	• Crisis intervention
	• Community-based alternatives to acute care
	• Assertive outreach
	• Support with daily living
	• Generic community mental health services
24 hour care, residential provision, and housing:	• Ordinary housing with intensive support
	• Sheltered accommodation
	• Group homes/shared housing
	• Medium support hostels
	• Residential homes
	• High support accommodation
	• 24-hour nursed accommodation
	• Acute inpatient care
	• Low secure units
	• Medium secure units
	• Special Hospitals

continued ▸

Table 7.9   Range of services for people with severe and enduring mental illness (cont'd)

Daycare and daytime activities:	• Ordinary employment • Supported employment • Adult education • Employment rehabilitation places • Clubhouse • Day centre • Day hospital • Drop-in centre
Financial support:	• Welfare advice centre

Source: Keys to engagement: London: Sainsbury Centre for Mental Health, 1998.

Primary Care

Most minor mental health problems and less severe mental illness (e.g., some forms of anxiety and depression) are managed throughout their natural history in primary care settings. The balance in the work undertaken by the general practitioner, the community psychiatric nurse or other health professional will depend on the nature of the patient's problems, the clinical skills of the various practitioners in the Primary health care team and the philosophy of care adopted. Many patients with longer-term enduring mental illness will also receive their continuing support (including monitoring of their medication and their social functioning) from members of the primary care team. The close integration of primary care services with more specialist mental health services as well as with other agencies (both statutory and voluntary) providing care, help and support for people with a mental health problem is a particularly important component of good local services.

Community Mental Health Teams and Centres

In most parts of Britain, Community Mental Health Teams have been developed to serve the needs of local communities. They deal predominantly with people who have more severe mental health problems. The precise model of service varies but the best are made up of staff from all relevant local agencies who deliver multidisciplinary care in a way which is 'seamless' as far at the client is concerned. Some teams operate from special Mental Health Resource Centres. Such a base can enable a multidisciplinary team of staff with skills in the assessment, treatment, continuing care and rehabilitation of people with mental health problems to cross services easily. Teams can comprise, for example, psychiatrists, community psychiatric nurses, psychologists, specialist social workers, psychotherapists, counsellors, occupational therapists as well as welfare rights and benefits advisers. Their strength is to enable users of services to be dealt with through a single point of delivery, avoiding some of the fragmentation and lack of coordination of the past.

Community Mental Health Teams and Centres can also provide a variety of specialised forms of care. Examples would include day care, respite care and responding to the emergencies and crises which can occur in the lives of enduringly mentally-ill patients. 'Assertive Outreach' schemes can also be delivered from these settings –

these are services which aim to prevent patients with the most complex problems in the community from being lost to the caring services, becoming non-compliant with their medication and then requiring an inpatient admission.

Residential Care

Many types of residential care exist for people who would in the past have been in old long-stay hospitals. Services and projects vary. Some provide specialist staff (e.g., nurses) living with residents, others providing a measure of independent living with back-up support. The range needs to include capacity for intensive support for it to be provided over the longer-term as well as round the clock if necessary.

There has been increasing evidence in recent years of a lack of 24-hour staffed accommodation for people with severe and enduring mental illness. These people are sometimes described as the 'New Long Stay' and although a relatively small group (about 5000 in England) they can end up occupying acute inpatient beds inappropriately. They need access to 24-hour care and support and recognition of the fact that they are chronically ill. The concept of 24-hour staffed accommodation is not new and is seen as a key component of effective comprehensive mental health services.

Continuing care facilities will always be needed for those people whose illnesses are too severe in impact, and chronic in nature, to live on their own. Rather than being provided in traditional hospital wards, these services should be available in more intimate and community-based care settings such as hostels, group homes and supported lodgings. Services provided in this way not only reduce the dislocation of the individual from society but also, when provided in a comprehensive network, allow easier progression to more independent forms of accommodation as the person's condition permits. The spectrum of care for people with mental illness living in the community is quite wide. It ranges from independent living accommodation (for example, single flats in shared accommodation) to shared group accommodation (with or without support), to living as part of a family (including fostering), to hostels and staffed housing schemes.

Acute Hospital Care

A proportion of people with acute or relapsing mental illness will still require admission to a facility with 24-hour medical and nursing care. Stays in such facilities are much shorter than they would have been in the past. Many admissions are to mental health units in District General Hospitals developed during the 1970s and 1980s to reduce the stigma of mental illness and to facilitate access to other health services. However, some professionals believe that the inclusion of psychiatric wards with District General Hospitals is not conducive to either optimal care for mentally ill patients or those with physical illnesses in adjacent wards. Such professionals favour smaller free-standing units rather than wards within general hospitals for treating patients with acute illness.

Length of stay for patients with mental illness has fallen substantially over recent years. However, because people with such illnesses often require long-term support, it is important that they are not lost track of and that aftercare arrangements are in place which enable them to be followed-up within the community.

Care Programme Approach

The Care Programme Approach (CPA) was introduced in England in the early 1990s to provide a framework for the care of mentally ill people. The requirements of CPA are relatively simple in that all people receiving specialist mental health services will have a named key worker and a care plan agreed with them which will be subject to regular review.

Secure Accommodation and Offenders With Mental Illness

A small group of people with mental health problems need secure accommodation because they are a danger to themselves or others.

Such services exist within a range of levels of security dependent upon the degree of risk posed by the patient. At the lower end of the spectrum are locked wards within mental health units while as more security is required to cope with the patient's problems (often associated with offending behaviour), medium secure care (within what were previously called Regional Secure Units) are available. The small number of patients deemed extremely dangerous can be cared for within conditions of high security within the Special Hospitals. In England in the late 1990s these were at Ashworth, Rampton and Broadmoor. It is accepted that all patients should be cared for in the condition of the lowest security which can prevent danger to themselves or others.

Figure 7.6 Examples of the diversity in pathways of care for people with mental illness.

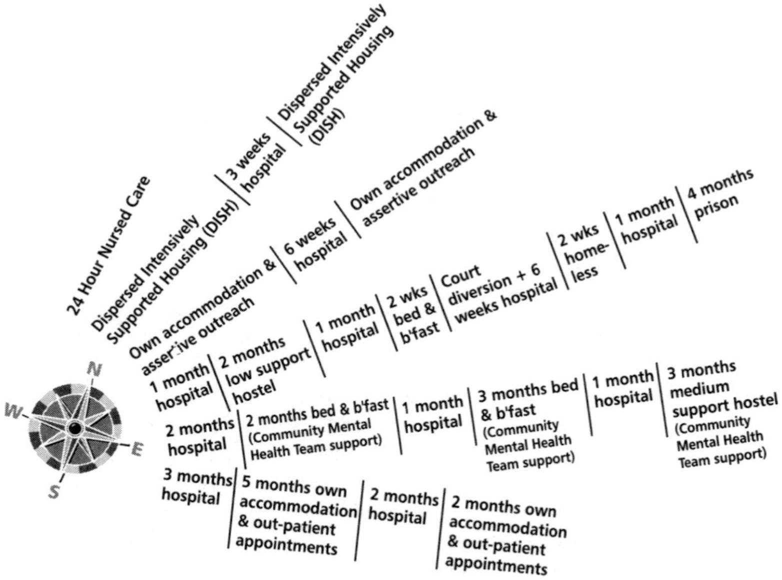

Source: Keys to engagement. London: Sainsbury Centre for Mental Health, 1998.

Many patients need help when they become embroiled in the criminal justice system as a result of their mental illnesses. It has for some years been recognized that those who commit crimes as a result of mental ill-health should receive care rather than custody. Although many mentally disordered offenders still end up with the prison system due to the still patchy nature of services for this difficult group of people, the early 1990s saw a considerable growth in services to divert them away from the criminal justice system. Such initiatives include education and training for police officers, lawyers and those involved in administering criminal justice within the courts. This enables the recognition of mental illnesses in those who come before them and so referral to teams of mental health specialists who can formally diagnose whether mental illness is present and arrange for an admission into hospital. It is likely that the future will see still further growth in such initiatives as well as still greater liaison and cooperation between agencies such as the police, probation, social services and mental health services.

It is important to recognize that individual's with mental illness have quite complex pathways of care over their lifetime (Figure 7.6).

Groups with Special Needs

The onset of mental illness is often accompanied by the inability of the individual concerned to participate fully in society. In severe mental illness, the resulting dislocation can be near total with the loss of friends and employment and, in some cases, estrangement from family. Care will usually be directed towards integrating the individual into society using services such as sheltered employment, day care, accommodation in the community and creating opportunities for social contact. Ideally, a key worker will ensure that the mentally ill person is receiving and benefiting from the various elements of the care package. The importance of a range of other components in a comprehensive network of services for people with mental health problems cannot be over-stated. Such services will include community psychiatric nursing, social work services, day resource centres and supported employment projects to help mentally ill people regain the ability to earn a living. In time, the development of such a comprehensive range of services will reduce the need for acute admissions as people's conditions will be monitored and stabilised in the community.

The needs of certain groups requires particular attention if services are to be truly comprehensive. Homelessness is both a precipitating factor in poor mental health (especially for diseases such as anxiety and depression) and can also be a result of the social dislocation which often accompanies major mental illness (as described above) which can easily lead to loss of accommodation. Services have traditionally struggled to engage with mentally ill people who have no fixed abode who often only come into contact with them following a major crisis such as a suicide attempt or via the criminal justice system. In certain of the inner city areas of Britain which tend to have a larger than average proportion of homeless people, specialist multidisciplinary teams have been established to maintain contact and thus to attempt to prevent a crisis. More generally, the provision of adequate housing for previously homeless patients discharged from acute psychiatric care is a key issue in maintaining future mental health. Projects which bring together local authority housing departments, housing associations, social services and the NHS are particularly important.

Making services appropriate for, and acceptable to, minority ethnic communities is also a challenge. Issues such as varying cultural norms of what constitutes acceptable behaviour may have contributed to the over-representation of people from certain minority ethnic groups within those diagnosed as suffering from mental illnesses as well as to those groups having a greater than average proportion of their admissions to hospital being subject to the compulsion of law as opposed to voluntary. Focused effort on behalf of the statutory mental health services working in conjunction with local minority communities is essential if services are to be fully effective.

Children and adolescents who have mental illnesses require specialist services. Apart from the fact that children's mental ill-health can manifest itself in ways different from that of adult illnesses, there is a need for a different range of agencies to be involved in child and adolescent mental health. Of these the most notable is the education services in whose settings disruptive or disturbed behaviour is often first noticed and which have a statutory duty to provide education to the child throughout their illness. Such services include child psychiatry, child psychology, education welfare services, special educational services (including special schooling for children with 'severe emotional and behavioural difficulties' who cannot be managed within the mainstream) as well as (where appropriate) the input of the probation service and the voluntary sector.

People who misuse substances (whether legal or illegal) to the extent that it adversely affects their social functioning may have a recognized mental illness. However, most do not and cannot be defined as mentally ill. For those without concurrent mental illnesses, services include inpatient or community-based detoxification, specialist counselling from drugs teams as well as such services as needle exchanges. Those patients with concurrent mental illnesses (those with the so-called 'dual diagnosis') require not only these services but also the input of mainstream psychiatric services if their care is to be optimised. The quality of this liaison between specialist drug and alcohol and mainstream mental health services is of key importance for this numerically quite small but challenging group of patients.

Users' Views, Advocacy and Carers' Needs

All services for people with mental illness must share the aim of allowing maximum autonomy. It is increasingly recognized that people should have influence over the care that they receive and that when this is encouraged by services, a positive outcome from treatment is more likely. Mechanisms like patients' councils have been established to facilitate this process. Advocacy and other schemes to involve users can help people with mental illness express their views on services. User-led services are an increasingly common development.

Mental illness, particularly when it first develops in an acute form, can be extraordinarily stressful and difficult for families and friends of the affected person. As with other groups with special needs, the role of informal providers of care is of fundamental importance in the planning and delivery of services. Needs assessments of mentally ill people must also include an appraisal of their carers' needs. Statutory services must seek to involve carers in planning their response to the individuals' problems and also provide support to the carer. The absence of such support can lead to the collapse of the informal caring arrangement and the consequent admission of the mentally ill person to the statutory services.

Legislation and the Mentally Ill

At the beginning of the present century, the basis of legislation for the mentally ill was the Lunacy Act 1890. In this Act, no distinction was made between mental illness and so-called mental deficiency. The main failing of the 1890 Act was, however, that it was deeply entrenched in a legal framework. Asylums could only admit patients who had been certified and this was often performed only as a last resort. As a consequence, sufferers from mental illness were admitted only when the condition was severe and this served to enhance the stigma attached to mental illness in the mind of the public.

Gradually, after World War I, a greater proportion of patients were admitted to mental hospitals without compulsory procedures being involved. This situation received legislative recognition in the Mental Treatment Act 1930, which had been preceded by a Royal Commission on Lunacy and Mental Disorder. Subsequently, the proportion of voluntary admissions to mental hospitals continued to increase. Compulsory admissions remained essentially a judicial procedure, with the final decision being taken by a magistrate. This situation continued until the Mental Health Act 1959 cleared the way for a more liberal approach. This Act was based on the report of a Royal Commission and embodied the basic principles of its recommendations, which were that the mentally disordered should be treated in the same way as those suffering from physical illness and that compulsory admission and detention should be used as infrequently as possible. The procedures became a mainly medical rather than a judicial affair.

Subsequent legislation removed much of the general provisions for the care and treatment of the mentally ill and handicapped. This has been incorporated in other Acts. The Mental Health Act 1983, consolidated the Mental Health Act 1959, as amended by the Mental Health (Amendment) Act 1982. It is principally concerned with the grounds for detaining patients in hospital or placing them under guardianship and aims to improve patients' rights and to protect staff, in a variety of ways. A code of practice under Section 118 of the Mental Health Act 1983 is prepared from time-to-time for the guidance of professional staff in the implementation of the Act.

In the late 1990s, the government decided to review the Mental Health Act 1983 to ensure that the current legislation was updated to support the effective delivery of modern patterns of care for people with mental disorder. This review will also ensure that there is an appropriate balance of safety in relation to the rights of individual patients and the wider community.

The intention is to develop an appropriate legislative framework to provide a prompt and effective legal basis to ensure that patients receive treatment and supervised care including a legal basis for requiring treatment in an appropriate setting.

The trend in legislation for the last 40 years has been to recognize the legitimate rights of those with mental disorder and to ensure that their liberty to refuse treatment is not taken away unless there is no safe alternative.

Compulsory Admissions

The majority of patients with mental illness are admitted to hospital in much the same way as someone entering hospital for medical or surgical treatment. They are required to consent to treatment and are generally able to leave the hospital if they choose to do so. Compulsory detention and treatment of people with a mental disorder is governed by the Mental Health Act. Compulsory detention and treatment of an individual will only take place when the person represents a serious risk to themselves or other people.

Mental Health Review Tribunal

The basic function of the Mental Health Review Tribunal is to consider applications for discharge of those patients, compulsorily detained in hospital or under guardianship orders, and to ensure that no patient is detained compulsorily without good reasons. The appointment of the Mental Health Review Tribunal is the responsibility of the Department of Health and three categories of members (legal, medical and lay) are recognized. A panel of members exists in each of the NHS regions from which tribunals are formed to consider cases as necessary. Each tribunal comprises at least three members, one from each category, with the legal representative acting as chairman. An application for discharge may be made by the patient himself, his next of kin, the Secretary of State for Health or the Home Secretary, depending on the section of the Mental Health Act under which the patient is detained.

Property of Mentally Ill Patients

The Court of Protection is responsible for the protection and management of the affairs and property of patients who are incapable, because of mental disorder, of managing and administering their own affairs, irrespective of where the patient may be living.

Mental Health Act Commission

This is a special health authority, which has about 80 part-time members – Commissioners – who are appointed by the Secretary of State for Health from the professions of medicine, nursing, social work and psychology, as well as lay members. The Commission has a wide brief. It can investigate complaints and keep under review all aspects of the care and welfare of detained patients. Second independent opinions can be given by medical members of the Commission or by doctors appointed by the Commission. Furthermore, it can submit proposals for the content of a Code of Practice to the Secretary of State for Health.

The Needs of People with Learning Disability

Accurate and respectful descriptions of this subgroup of the population have proved difficult to establish. Early legislation used and defined terms, such as mental defective, idiot, imbecile and feeble-minded which, although they were felt to be scientifically valid descriptions at the time, have subsequently become terms of abuse. The Mental Health Act 1959 introduced the term 'subnormal' and the definition encompassed subnormality of intelligence as well as the concept of social incapacity. The term was traditionally confined to those individuals who were handicapped in childhood. It excluded those who acquired their learning disability in later life; for example, people with permanent and severe impairment of the central nervous system caused by road accidents.

There was much debate about whether to include people with learning disability in the 1983 Mental Health Act at all. Thus, it was something of a compromise that the concept of 'abnormally aggressive and seriously irresponsible conduct' deliberately limited their inclusion to the minority of people with learning disability who needed some sort of legally supervised care because of their behaviour.

The Education Act 1981 introduced the term 'learning difficulties' but this was a definition of educational progress and thus did not recognize the social aspect of mental handicap. At the beginning of the 1990s, the Department of Health in England formally adopted, for use within the health and social services, the term 'people with learning disabilities' instead of 'mental handicap'. In some other countries, the term 'mental retardation' is used despite its negative connotations.

Internationally, both scientific study and health service practice have yielded a bewildering diversity in terminology, conceptual frameworks and classification of this group of conditions. Different approaches are based on, for example, causes, disorder or injury to the brain, low intelligence on formal testing, socially maladaptative and personality dependency. It is important to establish what taxonomy is being used. Without this, it is impossible to establish which people are being counted in epidemiological studies or in needs assessment of populations.

Table 7.10 Taxonomy: different approaches

- Intellectual impairment
  - Criteria   *Intellectual:* intelligence or development tests.
  - Main categories   *Severe:* IQ <50 (or 'severe and moderate').
                       Mild: IQ 50–69
- Learning disability
  - Criteria   *Usually educational:* e.g., reading or numeracy tests but should reflect learning dysfunction, not merely achievements
  - Main categories   *Various,* according to legal, administrative and professional contracts
- Mental handicap/retardation
  - Criteria   *Social:* e.g., dependency or maladaptation scales
  - Main categories   *Severe:* co-extensive with severe intellectual impairment, if IQ <50 is used as a necessary criterion. *Mild:* many factors in selection, varying in different communities

Source: Adapted from: Fryers T. Paediatric and Perinatal Epidemiology, 1992; 6:181–192.

Three approaches have been used for classification in this context (Table 7.10). The intellectual impairment approach, widely used in the past, is based upon the idea of low intelligence. Intelligence is measured by intelligence tests and usually expressed as the intelligence quotient (IQ). The IQ measure is distributed within the population in a way which has some similarities with other characteristics of people (such as height). Although much criticised, this approach to classification has remained popular precisely because it is so readily measurable and can be expressed in terms of severity (based upon IQ scores). Thus, 'severe intellectual impairment' is the term used to describe people with an IQ less than 50 whilst the term 'mild intellectual impairment' is used for people with an IQ between 50 and 69 (Table 7.11).

The second approach to classification is to view the problem in terms of the resulting disability, principally in learning. Thus, the concept of 'learning disability' has emerged. Although valid ways of measuring learning disability are not well developed, it is important to recognize that it is not simply a case of assessing IQ (as for intellectual impairment). Not all sources of disabled learning in children and adults are associated with impaired intellect, although they are clearly closely related.

Recently, a third approach has gained currency which attempts to assess the effects of the individual's disability on daily living skills and on their social functioning. In this approach the quantified intellectual level of a person is held to be less relevant than its results as expressed in these terms. A wide range of tools are now available to assess individuals on this basis. Typically this model can offer benefits when planning services to meet an individual's personal needs.

Table 7.11　Differences between severe and mild learning disability*

	Severe (IQ below 50)	*Mild (IQ 50–70)*
Social class distribution	Evenly distributed	Strongly aggregated in Social Class V
Prevalence	4 per 1000; almost all are in contact with services	10 per 1000; only one-third are in contact with services
Education	School for severe learning difficulties	School for mild learning difficulties but many in ordinary schools
Employment	Most attend training/education centres; but work has become an option for more people	Many in open employment, although usually in poorly paid jobs
Physical handicap	High proportion have additional physical and/or sensory handicaps	Most do not have a additional physical handicap

* traditional 'mild'/'severe' categorisation on IQ not always used.

For the remainder of this chapter the term 'learning disability' is used except where describing epidemiological studies by other authors (who have used the terms 'mental handicap', 'severe intellectual impairment' and 'mental retardation').

Frequency in the Population

As will be evident from the discussion of the taxonomy and aetiology of learning disability, assessing the size of the problem in a population and making comparisons between different places or over time is particularly difficult because of the complexity of issues surrounding definition and classification.

Despite the limitations of measuring IQ and of relating intellectual impairment to handicap, the most comprehensive epidemiological data relate to the frequency of people in populations with an IQ of less than 50 (severe intellectual impairment, but often also referred to in studies as severe mental handicap or severe mental retardation). Reasonably reliable estimates are also available for the more clear-cut syndromes which are associated with learning disability (for example, Down's syndrome).

The two most often used measures to express the frequency of learning disability in the population are the birth prevalence (number of affected infants per 1000 births) and age-specific prevalence (number of affected people in particular age-groups expressed per 1000 people of that same age living in the population concerned).

Most data on the frequency of learning disability in the population are derived from epidemiological surveys. Routinely available health service data are not generally useful sources although the establishment of population-based registers is becoming more common (see Chapter 1 for a fuller description of case registers). Notifications of congenital abnormalities (see Chapter 6) can provide estimates of the population frequency of some conditions which cause learning disability.

When considering the frequency of severe intellectual impairment it is important to examine rates of occurrence in birth cohorts (children born in the same year) as well as within different age-groups of the population. The prevalence of severe intellectual impairment varies between similar birth cohorts in different populations, both nationally and internationally. Similarly, birth prevalence shows changes over time. For example, it was relatively low in many developed countries of the world for birth cohorts of the early 1950s (1.8–4.0 per 1000) and higher for birth cohorts in the early 1960s (3.5–5.5 per 1000). Factors likely to affect birth prevalence at different times include: survival of impaired infants due to better neonatal intensive care, detection of fetal abnormalities through screening and termination of affected pregnancies, and changes in maternal age. Differences in birth prevalence then work through to be reflected in age-specific prevalence ratios as the cohort concerned grows older. Changes in survival of affected children and the prevalence of disabilities caused in later life to otherwise unimpaired people (e.g., head injuries) are the other main factors which affects such age-specific prevalence figures.

These main epidemiological features of severe intellectual impairment are shown in Table 7.12.

Table 7.12   Key epidemiological features of severe intellectual impairment* in developed countries

- Geographical variation within similar birth cohorts
- Variation over time in successive birth cohorts in the same population
- Many countries experienced low prevalence in early 1950s' births and high prevalence in early 1960s' births
- Variations in age-specific prevalence due to cohort variations in incidence and mortality
- Improved survival at all ages
- More males than females
- Social class gradient for incidence and mortality

* Equates broadly to severe learning disability. *Source:* Fryers T. Mental retardation in the developing world. Tantam D, Duncan A (Eds). Psychiatry for the Developing World. London: Gaskell Press, 1993.

Aetiology of Learning Disability

Causes of learning disability are mostly multifactorial processes. When considering the impairment of individuals, it is important to recognize that the precise mechanisms of causation of many forms of learning disability are not yet fully established, even though the principal causal agent can often be identified. For example, it is recognized that alcohol intake during pregnancy causes the fetal alcohol syndrome (which can include learning disability). However, the amount of alcohol which will induce such damage is not well established nor is it clear which maternal or fetal characteristics predispose to the syndrome. When considering causes of learning disability at population level they must be viewed more broadly. The influences on the population frequency of learning disability in different places or over time can be diverse. For example, the frequency of learning disability resulting from the fetal alcohol syndrome will vary according to the availability of alcohol in the society concerned, attitudes to pregnancy and childbearing, as well as the price of alcohol.

There is a wide range of factors and conditions associated with increased frequency of learning disability. These include: causes of neurological impairment; factors concerned with general genetic endowment; deprivation, and educational underfunctioning. Causes of neurological impairment (i.e., organic causes of learning disability) can be classified as pure primary disorders, primary disorders with secondary neurological damage and pure secondary disorders.

Pure Primary Disorders

A number of disorders which result in learning disability are present at the time of conception and result from an abnormal chromosome formation. The nuclei of normal human cells contain 23 pairs of chromosomes: one of each pair is derived from either parent. There are two types of chromosome: one pair which determines sex (sex chromosomes) and the other 22 pairs which are called autosomes. Males have 44 autosomes, one X and one Y sex chromosomes; females have 44 autosomes and two X sex chromosomes. Chromosome abnormalities may involve either the sex chromosomes or the autosomes and may be due to abnormalities in chromosome number (more or less than the usual complement) or in their structure. Specific chromosomal abnormalities are associated with particular diseases.

- *Down's syndrome*. The physical characteristics of Down's syndrome (although each is not present in all cases) include narrow slanting eyes with prominent epicanthic folds; short stature; small ears; short broad neck; furrowing of the tongue and a tendency for the mouth to hang open; a single transverse palmar crease; prominent and characteristic skin ridges on the palms of the hand, fingers and soles of the feet. Congenital abnormalities of the heart and intestinal tract occur more frequently in these children than in other infants.

  Within the spectrum of Down's syndrome there is a range of cognitive ability but the IQ usually lies somewhere between 20 and 55 with a small proportion of affected people having an IQ greater than 50. People with Down's syndrome are usually described as humorous, cheerful and affectionate. Whilst it would be wrong to accept this as a stereotype, many people involved in the care of children with Down's syndrome would agree with this description of their personalities.

  People with Down's syndrome always possess extra chromosomal material in the cells of their bodies. The presence of an extra discrete autosomal (i.e., non-sex) chromosome is called 'trisomy'. In 94% of cases of Down's syndrome, all or part of an extra chromosome resembling the normal number 21 pair of chromosomes is present in the cell; this most common variant of Down's syndrome is called 'trisomy 21'. It arises because of a failure of separation of chromosomes (non-disjunction) during cell division in the formation of the ovum. The fetus developing from this ovum, when it is fertilized, has 47 chromosomes rather than the usual 46. In a less common form of Down's syndrome (3–5% of cases) the extra chromosomal material becomes joined to another chromosome: the so-called 'translocation type'. These are familial with a high risk of recurrence in families, so there are opportunities for prevention through genetic counselling. In a third rare form (1–3% of cases), non-disjunction occurs after fertilization so that only some of the cells of the body are abnormal (mosaicism) and people show some signs of Down's syndrome but not all. They may be of normal intelligence.

  The birth prevalence of Down's syndrome in the absence of screening is of the order of 1.3–1.8 per 1000 live births. The precise aetiology of Down's syndrome is unknown but the most striking feature is the strongly increased risk of trisomy 21 with increased maternal age. Antenatal screening for Down's syndrome is discussed in Chapter 6.

- *Fragile X syndrome*. This is a sex chromosome disorder which can result in severe intellectual impairment although only in a minority of males and almost never in females. About 80% of boys will have an IQ less than 70, a smaller proportion of girls have impairment, mostly in the mild category. Females may carry and pass on the abnormality but be unaffected themselves.

Primary Disorder with Secondary Neurological Damage

A second group of disorders do not affect the constitution of the individual per se but a genetic abnormality leads to abnormal or arrested development.

- *Phenylketonuria*. This is a rare recessively inherited condition (birth prevalence 0.05–0.2 per 1000 births) in which the absence of a specific enzyme leads to a failure in the ability of the body to convert the amino acid phenylalanine to tyrosine. Normal diet thus becomes a direct hazard to the child. Phenylalanine accumulates in the blood and tissues and has a toxic effect on the brain, leading to convulsions and, if untreated, severe damage. The deficiency of tyrosine leads to paucity of melanin formation and thus lack of pigmentation giving rise to the other characteristics of the syndrome: blonde hair, blue eyes, pale skin and a tendency to infantile eczema. The treatment is to eliminate phenylalanine from the diet until the central nervous system is mature.

    Since it is an essential amino acid, this cannot be done completely but if a special diet is instituted as early as possible, there is a chance of limiting the degree of damage resulting from the condition. This has led to the practice of screening all new born babies by taking a few drops of blood and testing for excess phenylalanine (the Guthrie test).

- *Sporadic congenital hypothyroidism*. Congenital hypothyroidism occurs sporadically within the population (birth prevalence 0.1–2.0 per 1000). It is important to realise that this results from a mutation and not from iodine deficiency (see below). Thyroid failure ensues and if the condition is not recognized early and treated with thyroid replacement therapy, severe intellectual impairment can result.

Pure Secondary Disorders

A third group of disorders arises because of an environmental factor interacting with a normal fetus after conception. The mechanisms are not understood fully in all cases but the range of factors which can lead to learning disability is wide.

- *Infections*. Maternal exposure to rubella (German measles) virus, particularly during the first trimester of pregnancy, puts the developing fetus at risk of the congenital rubella syndrome. The manifestations include congenital heart disease, deafness, blindness and learning disability. Many other infections of the mother during pregnancy, in particular cytomegalovirus and toxoplasmosis, can cause learning disability in the offspring. Congenital syphilis, acquired by the mother and passed to the fetus, was in the past an important cause of learning disability as part of a general multisystem disorder. Infections acquired postnatally can also lead to learning disability: for example, meningitis, encephalitis, malaria.
- *Alcohol Intake in Pregnancy*. Learning disability can arise from consumption of alcohol during pregnancy usually as part of the fetal alcohol syndrome (see also Chapter 6).
- *Rhesus incompatibility*. The problem of rhesus incompatibility and its prevention is discussed in Chapter 6. The cerebral damage caused by jaundice

(kernicterus) may result in cerebral palsy and learning disability; though this condition is now largely preventable.

- **Exposure to radiation**. Excessive use of diagnostic X-rays in pregnancy has, in the past, led to radiation being identified as a risk factor for learning disability. This is not an important cause today and the use of ultrasound has in any case superseded X-rays as a diagnostic technique in pregnancy.

- **Perinatal factors**. Two factors are of particular importance during the process of birth which may lead to injury of the brain and some degree of neurological impairment: hypoxia and birth injury. Hypoxia in the fetus may occur for a variety of reasons such as pre-eclamptic toxaemia, antepartum haemorrhage, anaesthetic complications, excessive sedation during labour, respiratory distress in the infant, pressure on the umbilical cord or prolonged labour. Trauma during delivery is particularly likely to occur with abnormal presentation of the fetus or with instrumental delivery. Fortunately, with modern obstetric care and the tendency towards early caesarian section in difficult cases, birth trauma, is probably less common today. Prematurity with low birthweight is strongly associated with the later development of learning disability. It is unlikely, however, that the relationship is one of direct cause and effect but is probably explained by the fact that babies in this category are much more susceptible to adverse factors during delivery and afterwards. Indeed, intellectual impairment, epilepsy and cerebral palsy are sequelae of the same processes and problems.

- **Iodine deficiency**. When considering learning disability world-wide, iodine deficiency disease is an important cause of severe intellectual impairment. Other features may be associated, including the full syndrome of cretinism. In parts of the world where iodine is not present in sufficient quantities in water or in the diet, the solution is population-based prevention strategies including dietary supplementation or injection (this lasts several years).

- **Neural tube defect**. Learning disability can be a feature of the group of disorders called neural tube defect which are described fully in Chapter 6.

- **After birth**. A wide variety of elements of the postnatal environment may lead to neurological impairment and learning disability. In the early postnatal period hypoglycaemia is a serious problem which, if uncorrected, can cause convulsions and cerebral injury. Infectious diseases have already been discussed. Head injury, either accidental or deliberate (as part of child abuse), may have similar repercussions. One of the effects of excessive exposure to inorganic lead, either as a result of pica (ingestion) or environmental pollution, is varying degrees of intellectual impairment. There is no evidence of lead causing damage to a degree resulting in identified learning disability but it probably does cause slight reduction in children's IQs at all levels of exposure.

General Factors

Causes which are not associated with an underlying organic process can be considered in terms of the complex interrelationships between genetic endowment, deprivation and educational underfunctioning. In general these factors are relevant to mild degrees of learning disability.

The number of people with IQ scores in the range 50–69 is a reflection of the statistical distribution of IQ within the population. Whether they are then labelled as intellectually impaired or suffering from a learning disability (in effect 'abnormal') is a socially-determined phenomenon.

Today, mild forms of learning disability are seen much more through the processes which influence whether people with mild degrees of intellectual impairment or other characteristics are identified and labelled as having a learning disability. This varies between localities, countries and societies. Factors which influence this are the structure and orientation of services, professional attitudes and training, employment and training practices, social and cultural expectations, family and kinship structures, as well as legislation in relation to health, welfare, education and employment.

Prevention of Learning Disability

As described in the section on aetiology, some forms are potentially preventable. Preventive strategies can be grouped into three categories directed at processes before conception, processes during fetal life and birth, processes after birth.

Processes Before Conception

If social attitudes lead to reduced births in older women or lowering of maternal age overall this would reduce the frequency of Down's syndrome. The birth prevalence of a range of disorders could be reduced by minimising inherited disease in identified families by use of genetic counselling, screening and offering parents the choice of termination of pregnancy. Examples of causes of learning disability which can be addressed by these kinds of strategies include: genetic counselling after one child (for example, translocation Down's syndrome); screening for carriers and pre-conceptual counselling (for example, Tay Sachs disease), and population screening. This is a rapidly moving field and as technologies advance new opportunities for prevention will open up. Other preventive measures directed at processes before conception include reduction of hazardous factors in the environment (such as drugs, chemical exposures and industrial radiation).

Processes During Fetal Life and Birth

Preventive approaches at this stage include targeting the nutritional status of pregnant women; folate supplementation to avoid neural tube defects; minimising harm to the fetus (reducing alcohol intake and smoking during pregnancy; measures to prevent rhesus haemolytic disease); screening to detect fetal abnormalities and offering parents termination of the affected pregnancies, as well as generally good obstetric and neonatal care.

Processes After Birth

Preventive measures after birth include protection (as far as possible) against communicable diseases which can cause intellectual impairment, early recognition of problems such as hypothyroidism and phenylketonuria and strategies to reduce accidents and their impact.

Services for People with Learning Disability

The philosophy of service provision for children and adults with learning disability must be based on a clear set of values which seeks to place individuals at the centre of a care process which regards their particular needs as paramount.

At its heart is a responsibility placed on all statutory and other agencies, under the lead of the social services authority, to identify individuals (such as those who have a learning disability) with special needs and to design an appropriate service response to meet those needs whether it be a placement in the community, or in a residentially-based setting. All agencies must work together and all professionals must collaborate to provide appropriate care.

It is also important that services identify the needs of carers of those with a learning disability and provide help and support to them. Running through the modern approach to care is the concept of normalisation in which, as far as possible, the person with learning disability is given the same rights and entitlements as other members of society. Some values and principles underlying service provision are shown in Table 7.13.

Table 7.13   Key features of good quality health services for people with learning disabilities

- Shared values of person-centred services; equality of access; support to use services; and social inclusion
- Partnership and cooperation by all stakeholders working together effectively and with service users and carers
- Shared responsibility to promote healthy lifestyles and to avoid adverse experiences
- Availability of information about needs
- Using guidance documents and reports
- Training, development and workforce planning

Source: Derived from: Signposts for success in commissioning and providing services for people with learning disabilities. Leeds: NHS Executive, 1998.

Living at Home or in the Community

Children and adults with a learning disability can successfully live at home, only being admitted to residential or hospital care when serious problems develop with their health or with their behaviour.

Parents of a child with a learning disability will need a great deal of counselling as well as practical support to help them come to terms with the birth of an affected baby. Thereafter, as the child grows older, many will continue to require emotional support, advice and practical help including welfare benefits. The presence of a person with a learning disability can give rise to special problems in a family. Both day services and respite care provide some relief for parents. There are some schemes for placing carers in the family home to give parents an opportunity to get away. Aside from short-term care, support for a family can be given by a health visitor, a community learning disability nurse, social worker or voluntary worker. Usually this takes the form of advice and information about service availability. Families are often helped by being put in contact with other parents with similar problems. Practical assistance with transport for visiting or workload (for example, nappy service) is usually very valuable.

The provision of adequate and suitable housing can often ease the problems of helping with a person who has a learning disability. A frequently voiced concern amongst parents is the future for the son or daughter when they die. Some voluntary sector initiatives attempt to meet part of the problem with trustee schemes. Support for families to consider the future and options for continuing support needs is vital.

Most health localities in England have at least one multidisciplinary community team for people with learning disabilities. Such teams are made up of people from a variety of professional backgrounds but most have a social worker, a community learning disability nurse, a psychiatrist or a psychologist and usually a therapist (physiotherapist, occupational therapist, or speech therapist).

Teams provide a domiciliary service to people with learning disability and their families. Core team members make routine visits to clients' homes. They provide advice and assistance with current day-to-day problems, they advise on welfare benefits, arrange respite care and advise or assist with any problem behaviours. They have an important role in coordinating domiciliary services and can also be helpful in breaking down organisational barriers which sometimes exist between agencies. On the other hand, they have to deal with issues relating to the blurring of professional boundaries whilst maintaining their own professional identities and, at the same time, sharing their skills.

The range of services available to people with learning disabilities who are no longer able to (or who do not) live in their family home is very wide and varies in type around the country. People with minor degrees of incapacity can often live in flats or houses with a small number of their peers. Such facilities may have local assistance but in any case will usually be supported by a community team.

Education of Children

A key issue for families with a child with learning disability is education. Schools and local education authorities are under a duty to identify and make suitable provision for all children with special education needs. Around 20% of children will be identified as having special needs at some time in their school careers, with around 3% having sufficiently severe and complex needs to require a 'statement' of special needs for their local education authorities.

A child with learning disability may attend an ordinary preschool playgroup or one for children with special needs similar to theirs. A playgroup gives the child an opportunity of benefiting from contact with other children, to learn through play as well as providing a period of relief to the parents. A child with learning disability may be admitted to a nursery class in an ordinary school. This is usually at the discretion of the headteacher and often for a trial period. Problems can arise because of lack of staff to cope with the extra requirement needed for a child for special needs.

Children with a 'statement' of special educational needs can be exempted from some or all of the demands of the national curriculum, as laid down by the Education Reform Act 1988. The exemption from, or modification of, the national curriculum is detailed in the child's statement of special educational needs. This is a legal document which sets out the child's individual needs and the ways in which the local education authority will meet them.

Specialised provision is made at schools for children with moderate, severe or profound and multiple learning difficulties. These children often also have severe physical and sensory disabilities.

A small number of children are educated in residential schools, some run by local education authorities but most run by the voluntary or the private sectors. The vast majority of children live at home and go to school on a daily basis. Transport is often provided for them.

Many young people with severe learning disabilities remain at school until they are 19 years of age. Others attend local colleges of further education where specialised courses are made available. A small number of young people attend special residential colleges, run either by the voluntary or the private sectors. Whichever type of college is chosen, the aim of the course is the same: a successful transition to adult life and the maximising of social functioning. There is a range of government employment and training measures which help people with learning disabilities to access employment.

It is recognized that many children with learning disabilities benefit from early educational intervention. In some parts of the country peripatetic teachers visit the home and work with parents. Parents are encouraged to stimulate their children and teach them skills. A number of different schemes for use by parents in teaching their children are in operation in Britain.

Education and Training Centres for Adults

Centres, formerly called adult training centres, are run by local authority social services departments to provide a place for adults with learning disabilities to go during the daytime. Their main activity was originally light assembly work which was subcontracted by local firms. The centres are now called social educational centres or resource centres, which more accurately reflects their modern purpose. Over the years the emphasis has switched to the development of social and personal skills, further education and work experience with an emphasis on individualised learning programmes and clients going outside the centre into community resources for much of the week.

Whilst training centres remain part of the network of provision, there has also been a trend to encourage and support people with learning disability to take paid employment within the general workforce where appropriate.

Residential Care

Local authorities now provide directly only about one-third of non-health-service care. The type of residential care which can be provided by the local authority social services departments varies with the degree of social competence of the individual. Social services authorities arrange residential and nursing home care much of which is organised by other providers (both voluntary and private sectors). In 1998, there were 8000 residential and nursing care homes for adults with learning disabilities in England, containing 53,000 places.

The person with a learning disability may be placed with foster parents, in lodgings, in a home or a hostel specifically for people with learning disabilities or an unstaffed home or hostel supervised by supporting social work staff.

The typical local authority hostel of early community care developments had about 25 beds with attached staff accommodation. Such hostels are now often divided into smaller units and few new hostels of that type are being built. An increasingly common form of community accommodation is that provided by independent trusts. These are organisations consisting of several participating agencies; for example, a housing association, a health authority, a social services authority and a voluntary organisation.

Voluntary organisations dedicated to the interests of people with learning disabilities also operate community housing. Many of these houses are ordinary dwellings in ordinary streets. Most of them are staffed during the daytime and some will have a member of staff awake during the night. Others may have a member of staff sleeping in the house at night.

Whilst the average home in the average street is where most people with learning disability live and always have lived, there are those who disagree that this should be the only model. An alternative view is provided by the supporters of special villages and residential communities. It is suggested that residential villages have the advantage of containing various-sized residences, all with a domestic home-like atmosphere and at the same time ready access to a wide range of services. There is a view that people with severe forms of learning disability feel less isolated and more protected in a village setting than in the general community.

A pragmatic case has been made in some parts of the country for the re-use of hospital sites for large settlements but with modern style accommodation. However, the geographic remoteness and the perceived stigma attached to those sites could militate against this and this model of care remains controversial amongst professionals in the field.

The private sector has emerged as a major provider for community services for people with learning disability. Many of these homes cater for rather large numbers of people and there is concern because they do not necessarily fit the ordinary life model with its emphasis upon family-sized groups living together.

Family placement schemes, where the person with learning disability lives with a family in a private household, gained popularity during the 1990s. These can provide either a permanent home or be used for respite care on a regular basis.

Hospital Provision

At the end of the 1960s there were 7400 children and 52,000 adults aged 16 years or older in hospitals for the mentally handicapped. The White Paper published in 1971 called 'Better Services for the Mentally Handicapped' envisaged that by the beginning of the 1990s hospital beds for mentally handicapped people would be reduced to 33,000. At the end of the 1990s there were some 6000 people with learning disabilities living in old long-stay hospitals.

For some years, first admissions fell whilst readmissions increased disproportionately, suggesting that while fewer people were admitted more of them were undertaken for special purposes, such as respite care. However, the provision of respite care in hospital has decreased during the 1990s and is now more commonly provided by the social services authority or through family placement.

Different health authorities have adopted different approaches to the issue of closure. The issues associated with planning, organising and financing the resettlement of people into the community are only one part of planning for community services. There are many people with learning disability who live with elderly parents and for whom provision will also eventually have to be made. Comprehensive community services must respond to where, how and with whom the person will live, how they wish to spend their time (work- and leisure-related activities) and providing specialised services as necessary.

People with learning disabilities have greater health needs. They are more likely to have mental health problems, physical disabilities and other chronic conditions e.g., epilepsy. Clinical assessment, diagnosis and treatment, usually have historically been undertaken in a hospital setting. With the reduction in size of these hospitals and the desire of policy-makers to develop services close to home, free-standing community mental health centres, providing assessment and treatment units, are becoming increasingly common.

Challenging Behaviour

Some people with learning disability exhibit very disturbed behaviour. If the behaviour is such as to place the physical safety of the person or others in serious jeopardy or make impractical the use of community facilities, the term 'challenging behaviour' is applied. The disruptive behaviours are usually aggression and self-injury.

It has been estimated that 10–15 people with learning disability per 100,000 of the total population demonstrate behaviours which present a serious challenge to current services. There is a view that people demonstrating seriously aggressive or self-injurious behaviours should be cared for wherever possible by specialists visiting them in their own homes as that is the environment in which the behaviour has been manifest. Another view is that 'challenging behaviour units' should be planned for a health district or on a shared basis between several health districts. Such units can operate as part of an assessment and treatment unit.

Secure (Forensic) Units

People with a moderate or severe learning disability who have committed crimes (such as arson, assault, rape) may be admitted to one of the special hospitals in England or they may be admitted to a regionally-based secure unit for treatment. It is a general view that this group should be treated in specialised units and not as part of the general forensic psychiatric services.

Voluntary Organisations

There is a range of voluntary organisations solely or partly orientated towards the needs of people with a learning disability. Many have a long tradition of providing care and support for this group. This can include the provision of residential accommodation day nurseries and playgroups, social clubs and recreational centres, holiday homes and outings and toy-lending libraries.

Advocacy

The desire to involve people with learning disability in decisions about their own lives has resulted in a need for advocacy services. A system of citizen advocacy is one way of ensuring personal representation A citizen advocate is often a volunteer who has had some training for the role and who works on a one to one basis with the individual. Self-advocacy is being promoted amongst disabled people themselves and aims to equip them with the skills and self-confidence to make their voices heard in relation to service providers.

Conclusions

The mental health status of a population is an important component of its overall health, though difficult to conceptualise and measure. By careful study design, including giving particular attention to defining terms and ascertaining cases, important information can be yielded on the pattern of mental illness and learning disability in the population. This in turn can enable: ideas about disease causation to be generated, trends over time to be monitored and health needs assessments to be carried out.

Methods for the promotion of mental health and the prevention of mental illness in the population are not well developed. This is partly because of the complexity of describing mental health and partly because the aetiology of many mental illnesses has not yet been elucidated. In the field of learning disability, the scope for prevention is greater and is likely to grow as techniques advance in antenatal detection and treatment of fetal abnormalities, as well as in genetic-risk identification.

Services for people with mental illness and learning disability must be wide-ranging in nature. Although they are very different in kind, these two groups must be characterised by teamwork at the level of the professionals providing the care, and by strong partnership and coordination at the level of the agencies organising the care. Increasingly, high quality care is seen as that provided in non-institutional surroundings, within, or close to, the community. Its hallmark is that the type of service should be based upon, and matched to, an assessment of the individual's needs. At the same time, protection of the public from the small number of mentally ill people who pose a risk to society is a vital part of modern services.

Chapter 8

Health in Later Life

Introduction

At one time, descriptions of the problems of old age would have dwelt little on what group constituted the elderly of a population. The definition would have been based solely on age and would have chosen a cut-off point of 65 years (sometimes 60 years for women). In Britain, these ages would have also coincided with the normal times of retirement from work.

Today, the concept of old age is much more fluid with considerable diversity in the perspectives taken to describe it. On the one hand, it is well recognized that chronological age is only a rough guide to the biological age of an individual. Examples can be cited of alert and active octogenarians as well as people who have appeared to age prematurely. It has been suggested that we should think only about biological age, as measured by the abilities and performance of the individual. On the other hand, for most record keeping and administrative purposes, the convenient label of chronological age is still necessary.

Improvements in the general health of the population have meant that higher levels of dependency are now found at later years of age. Many health and welfare services view the age of 70 years or even 75 years as the start of the elderly age-groups for planning purposes, rather than the traditional 65-years-old watershed.

The concept of a fixed age of retirement fundamentally changed in Britain and many industrialised countries, particularly during the 1980s and 1990s. The transition to old age, if viewed through retirement, may be entered for some people today as late as 70 years (for example, the radio broadcaster who has continued to work and may even have fathered a second family). For others, the transition may be quite early, in their 50s (for example, the primary school headmistress who married young, has grown-up children and who decided to opt for early retirement as part of a restructuring of the teaching profession).

In the new millennium, health and social policy discussions about the elderly in the population are likely to adopt a more flexible and functional way of defining the later years of life. Such an approach has emerged in the use of a social life cycle comprising four stages (Table 8.1). For characterising the later years of life, it is the Third and Fourth Ages which are important. Some definitions regard the Third Age as beginning after full-time work has ended. However, this fails fully to take into account the position of women. Some women may not have worked during the period of their life when they were responsible for bringing up children but chose to work when their children left home. The definition of the Third Age shown in Table 8.1 encompasses these issues in a more subtle notion of a period of life free from the formal structures and constraints of full-time work and career-building, as well as a time in which family responsibilities do not include dependent children. The Fourth Age is then the final period of life in which dependency and disability occur. However, this kind of conceptualisation does not capture certain aspects of social exclusion, including unemployment. It must not be seen as a classification which conveys wider significance about the circumstances of later life.

In this chapter, the demographic origins of the present older population are described. So are the adverse physical, mental, social and financial factors which are frequent accompaniments of advancing years. The spectrum of services available to attempt to meet the problems of people in later life is also examined. Some special health problems are dealt with in a separate section of the chapter.

Table 8.1   The social life cycle and ageing

•	*First Age:*	The period of childhood and socialisation
•	*Second Age:*	The period of work and family raising
•	*Third Age:*	The period free of the formal structures of full-time work and dependant children
•	*Fourth Age:*	The period of eventual dependency and disability

Source: Derived from The Carnegie Inquiry into the Third Age, Final Report, *Life, Work and Livelihood in the Third Age*. The Carnegie United Kingdom Trust, Fife, 1993.

Health and Need in Later Life

The onset of mental and physical frailty, the advent of chronic diseases (most of which occur more commonly in old age) lead many older people to have multiple, rather than single, reasons for needing help, support or care.

These considerations make it particularly important that a clear picture is built up of the health and social needs of the older population if the best kinds of services are to be developed to meet its needs. As with many other fields of care, no single measure or source of data can be relied upon to provide a comprehensive picture of the health and social status of an older population and the extent to which these translate into needs.

To describe the characteristics of such a population in the depth required to plan effectively to meet its needs, it is necessary to draw upon a wide range of sources of information. Even then, in many places, relevant information will not be routinely available. In such circumstances it may be necessary to consider conducting local surveys.

Demographic Implications of an Ageing Population

In the United Kingdom in 1901 there were 1.8 million people over the age of 65 years out of a population of 38.2 million – representing 4.7% of the total, and only half a million people 75 years and older, or 1.3% of the total population. By the late 1990s, the situation had changed dramatically: an estimated 15.7% of the population were aged 65 years and over, and 7.2% were aged 75 years and over.

It is a popular misconception that these population changes were due to advances in medical science, new drugs and high-technology allowing older people to live longer. The real explanation lies before the turn of the nineteenth century. At that time, most deaths occurred in infancy and childhood. When mortality started to fall, more children survived into adult life and younger age-groups were predominant in the population. As mortality rates fell further and birth rates also started to decline during the twentieth century, the older age-groups began to make up a much greater part of the population than they had done earlier.

The age structure of any population is often represented graphically by so-called 'population pyramids'. The age structure of the population of Britain at the beginning of the nineteenth century, when plotted graphically, did indeed resemble a pyramid. There were large numbers of young people at its base and very few elderly people at its peak. In this respect it resembled some present day developing countries. By near the end of the nineteenth century age structure of Britain's population causes the graph to look more like a box than a pyramid, with a relative shrinking in the numbers of young people and a larger proportion of elderly people (Figure 8.1).

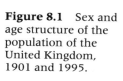

Figure 8.1 Sex and age structure of the population of the United Kingdom, 1901 and 1995.

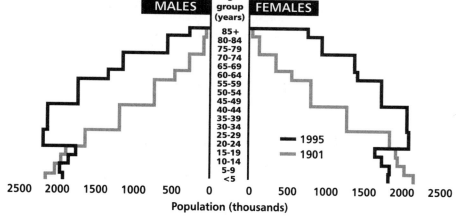

Source: Data from Office for National Statistics.

Changes in population age structure are part of what is call the *demographic transition*. The pattern can be seen not just in historical comparisons but in different countries of the world today. Broadly, populations start in a position where mortality and fertility are high and move to a point where both are low. The demographic transition (Table 8.2) started to gather pace in Britain and other industrialised countries during the late nineteenth and first half of the twentieth centuries and in many developing countries not until the last third of the twentieth century.

Table 8.2 Stages of demographic transition

Fertility	Mortality	Population
High birth rate	High mortality in early life	Predominantly young
High birth rate	Mortality falls in early life	Still predominantly young
Birth rate falls	Mortality falls further	Proportion of adults increases
Birth rate low	Mortality falls across all ages	Proportion of elderly sharply increases
Birth rate low	Mortality falls further especially in later adult life	Proportion of very elderly rises

In exploring the reasons for the demographic transition in Britain's population, it is necessary to identify the time at which improvements in mortality started to occur and why. Relatively little improvement in mortality occurred from the sixteenth century through to the latter part of the nineteenth century (Figure 8.2). For most of this period of several hundred years, a person could expect to live only on average until their mid-30s. Such fluctuations as there were coincided with periods of famine and epidemics of communicable diseases. Better agricultural methods and food distribution during the eighteenth century enabled higher levels of nutrition to be achieved by more people. The major impact on mortality was made by the measures taken by the public health and social reformers during the late nineteenth century. Proper disposal of sewage, purer water supplies as well as less crowded, higher-quality housing all helped to reduce the incidence, spread and consequences of the major communicable diseases of the day. As has been previously mentioned, the big improvement was for mortality in infancy and childhood.

Figure 8.2 Life expectancy at birth: England 1541–1994.

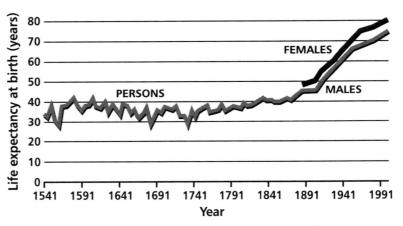

Source: Health Inequalities. Drever F, Whitehead M (Eds). London: Office for National Statistics, 1997.

By the time the beginning of the twentieth century was reached, a male child could expect, on average, to live a further 48 years, whereas a male child born towards the end of the twentieth century could expect on average to live well into his 70s (Figure 8.3). Even greater improvements in survival have taken place in women. This is a result of a complex relationship between behavioural, social, environmental, economic and genetically-linked factors. The excess male over female mortality can be largely accounted for by higher mortality from coronary heart disease, lung cancer, cirrhosis of the liver and fatal accidents.

Life expectancy for people who have already lived to the middle and later years of their lives has also increased during the twentieth century. A man aged 60 years in 1901 lived an average of 13 further years. Towards the end of the 1990s, the comparable figure was 18 years (Figure 8.3). Thus, whilst the major changes in the age structure of the population of Britain in the twentieth century have been due to changes in birth rates and improvements in expectation of life, more recently, additional ageing of the population has been produced by falling mortality rates in old age. When a population is already ageing but has relatively low fertility and low mortality rates, changes in death rates in the older age-groups are the major determinant of further population ageing.

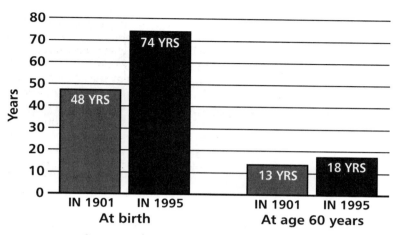

Figure 8.3 Expectation of life for males in the United Kingdom: 1901 vs. 1995.

Source: Data from Office for National Statistics.

Expectation of life at birth varies greatly between countries. At the end of the twentieth century, Japanese women are predicted to have the greatest life expectancy at birth. However, the gap between industrialised countries and some developing countries is still marked (Figure 8.4). The demographic transition which occurred in many developing countries in the late twentieth century (and is still occurring) has had slightly different origins. Social, public health and economic improvements have been important. However, these populations have also benefited from immunisation programmes in childhood, modern birth control methods, and more advanced medical care. None of these technological influences was available to assist the speed of the demographic transition in Victorian and Edwardian Britain or the other industrialised countries of the Northern Hemisphere. The relative speed of these demographic transitions is illustrated by examining the time it has taken for populations to age (Figure 8.5).

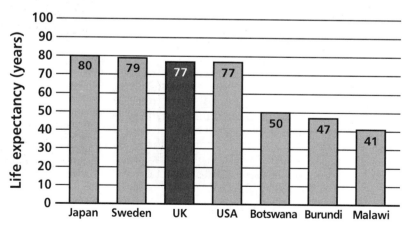

Figure 8.4 Life expectancy at birth for selected countries.

Source: Derived from The World Health Report, 1997. Geneva: WHO.

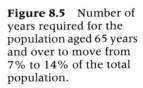

Figure 8.5 Number of years required for the population aged 65 years and over to move from 7% to 14% of the total population.

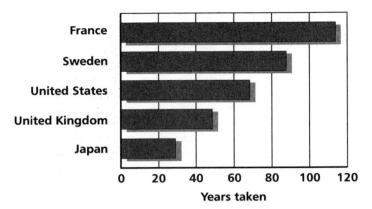

Source: MacFayden D. International demographic trends. In: Improving the health of older people: a world view. (Eds: Kane RL, Evans JG, MacFayden D). Oxford: Oxford University Press, 1990.

Whilst in many developing countries, the numbers of elderly people occupy a relatively small proportion of the total population, the annual growth in numbers of older people in these countries is exceeding that of their developed counterparts. Population ageing is thus becoming an issue for the world population as well as for developed countries like Britain, other parts of Western Europe, the United States and Japan. These changes are illustrated in comparisons of the distribution of deaths and population by age-group in the world's population (Figure 8.6).

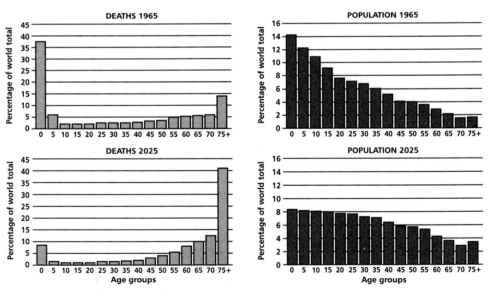

Figure 8.6 Deaths and population in the world by age: 1965 and 2025.
Source: The World Health Report, 1997. Geneva: WHO.

Demographic and Social Factors Affecting
Informal Support for the Elderly

Much of the care and support given to elderly people in the population is still provided informally by their children or other relatives. In considering the needs of the elderly population it is important, therefore, to take account of the size of the pool of potential informal carers as well as the numbers of economically active people necessary to sustain a more dependent older population. A broad indication is provided by comparing the extent to which the numbers of elderly people within a society are balanced by those in adult age-groups prior to conventional retirement age. Table 8.3 shows that, for a number of industrialised areas of the world, the so-called aged dependency ratio (those aged 65 years and over versus those aged 15–64 years) increased over the twentieth century and will continue to increase rapidly into the first few decades of the twenty-first century. In Europe, for example, this will mean that whilst at the beginning of the 1990s there were about 19 people aged 65 years for every 100 people aged between 15 and 64 years, by the year 2030, 34 people aged over 65 year olds will be present in the population for every 100 younger adults.

Table 8.3 Aged dependency ratios* in countries of the Organisation for Economic Cooperation and Development

	1990	*2000*	*2010*	*2020*	*2030*
United Kingdom	4.1	4.2	4.0	3.3	2.7
France	4.7	4.0	3.9	3.0	2.5
Germany	4.6	4.3	3.6	3.3	2.5
Italy	4.8	3.9	3.3	2.8	2.1
USA	5.3	5.3	5.2	3.9	3.0
Canada	6.1	5.4	4.9	3.6	2.6
Japan	5.8	4.1	3.1	2.4	2.3

Source: United Nations' 'World Population Prospects 1950–2050 (The 1996 revision)'.
*The 'aged dependency ratio' is defined as the population aged 15–64 years divided by the population aged 65 years and over.

The aged dependency ratio is an index which can only give a general indication of the potential support available to older people in a population. To obtain a fuller impression it is necessary to explore information on family size and structure, patterns of geographical mobility and cultural attitudes to family life.

Family size fell during the twentieth century. The change away from the Victorian tendency to have large families has meant that there are fewer children available to give support to parents as they become old and frail. However, in more recent times, the proportion of women who never married, and therefore would not have children potentially available to give support as they grow older, has declined and is projected to fall still further thus counteracting some of the earlier trends. The extent to which very elderly women are likely to have no surviving children (and hence less potential source of support) is also projected to fall. These higher marriage-rates mean that more women will have the potential support of a spouse and one or more children.

Such demographic considerations do not, of course, give any indication as to what level and type of support from children actually materialises when the elderly parent needs it. Other factors relating to marriage and family-building have potential implications for the informal support available to people as they grow old. If, for example, there were more marriages in which both partners agree not to have children (perhaps to enable the woman to pursue a full career) there would be implications for future generations of older people. Moreover, the increased divorce rate which has been such a feature of the later decades of the twentieth century in Britain, will also have an impact. Firstly, divorced elderly people who have not remarried will not have the support of a spouse when they begin to develop the problems associated with old age. Secondly, younger people who become divorced (whether or not they remarry) will have more complex family relationships which may weaken their capacity or commitment to provide tangible support to their elderly parents when it is needed.

Increased geographical mobility also affects the pool of potential supporters of older people. The direct effect of this on the availability of informal care for elderly people is difficult to judge as improved transport now makes travel more straightforward. However, making the not unreasonable assumption that mobility is likely to be greater for those under 75 years of age than for those above it, it is quite possible that the effect of this change will be to reduce the level of informal care available when compared with the past.

It is difficult fully to discern the implications of all these factors on the actual support given to people in later life. However, of equal importance to the numerical assessment of potential supporters in the light of socio-demographic changes of the kind described above, is the actual response made by grown-up children and other relatives of old people when they do need help. Many men and women who are in their middle years of life, with dependent children of their own, will at some time be faced with the problem of how to respond when one or more of their surviving elderly parents or parents-in-law becomes too frail, too ill, or simply too lonely to maintain an independent way of life. Sometimes, this will be precipitated by the sudden death of the spouse of one of the elderly people concerned but more often it will be a situation which builds up gradually.

Depending on the extent of need of the old person, the type of support provided by families varies enormously, ranging from a regular telephone call from a son or daughter, to periodic or regular visits, to the elderly person actually taking up residence with their children and grandchildren.

The way in which such situations are resolved depends upon a complex interaction of factors including: geographical proximity of the families; the nature of the housing of the elderly person and of the family; the quality of family relationships; the attitude of the elderly person towards independent living, and financial considerations. Informal care is extensively provided to older people.

Future Population Changes and Implications

The immediacy of the problems encountered by the older population is highlighted by a simple demographic fact. They are not a homogeneous group. Disproportionate increases in the very elderly (Figure 8.7) produce higher levels of dependency and greater needs and demands for health and social services.

Table 8.4 Numbers of centenarians in England and Wales: actual and future projections.

Year	Number aged 100 years or more
1961	554
1981	2,228
1996	5,523
2036	39,000

Source: Office for National Statistics.

The very elderly also tend to be proportionally highly represented in the most intensive forms of non-home based care such as hospital inpatient care. In addition to their having the highest rate of hospital admission, this group also have a much longer average duration of stay in such care when compared to other sectors of the older population.

Thus, overshadowing the more subtle factors which determine the need for care within the elderly population are some stark and simple facts. Well into the twenty-first century, there will be an inexorable increase in the numbers of people who are in the oldest age-groups. These are the people who are the frailest, sickest, poorest and most likely to be living on their own. The most dramatic manifestation in the growth of the very old in the population is the increase in the number of centenarians (Table 8.4).

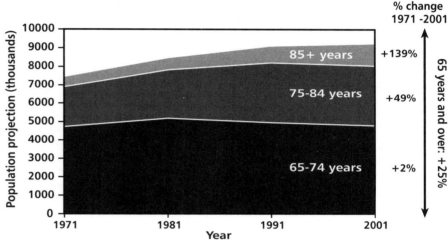

Figure 8.7 Projected elderly population of the United Kingdom.

Source: Data from Office for National Statistics.

Ill Health, Loss of Function and Need

One of the characteristics of any ageing organism is that the older it becomes the greater is the risk of impairment, disease or death. In most organisms, including man, the risk of death fluctuates during the early years of life before beginning to rise progressively with time.

Ageing is related to disease in three main ways:

(1) **Altered response to disease** – some diseases are overcome less easily when they occur in elderly people than in younger people; for example, pneumonia and fractures.

(2) **Diseases associated with ageing** – some diseases are so closely associated with ageing that they occur to some extent in all individuals as they age. The best example of this is arteriosclerosis.

(3) **Increased risk with ageing** – many diseases, although not exclusive to ageing individuals, occur much more commonly when old age is reached. Examples of this are many of the common cancers.

The hallmark of the occurrence of disease in older people is the presence of multiple pathology. Very old people rarely suffer from a single disease, but several chronic degenerative processes. Some surface for the first time in old age, others are carried over from middle age. In addition to multiple pathology, there are other properties of ill health in later life which are important when designing medical care responses (Table 8.5). Very old people often display impaired adaptability to disease so that their health problems manifest themselves in different ways, making them difficult to diagnose. Rapid deterioration and a relatively high incidence of complications are also features of disease in very old age. The importance of rehabilitation services in recovery is much more important than it is in younger age-groups. So is the environment in which care is provided.

Table 8.5 Some features of illness in later life

- Multiple pathology
- Risk of dependency
- Presentation of problems often not typical
- Side effects and complications frequent
- Limited resilience
- Care environment important
- Multidisciplinary care essential

The assessment of the types of diseases experienced by an elderly population has a place in assessing its health status but this approach is not appropriate on its own. It is particularly relevant to consider the way in which pathological processes manifest themselves by interfering with the old person's level of functioning (in relation, for example, to particular aspects of self-care) or producing disability.

The activities which have been considered in the context of limitation of function in later life are broad and include: those activities concerned with self-care (for example, washing, dressing, eating and using the toilet); walking and other movements; mobility in the wider sense (for example, the ability to move from house to shops), and the performance of socially-allocated roles and self-determination. Some data on activities of daily living amongst older people are available through national surveys and some from study of local populations. Such data can be invaluable in assessing the needs of older people in a locality and planning the response of services. All information on functional capacity shows a strong relationship between increasing age and loss of independence in such functions (Figure 8.8).

The use of a functional capacity perspective of elderly people's needs has led to the formulation of the concept of active life expectancy. It separates the years of relatively healthy life from those characterised by disability, major illness or dependency. As has been discussed in Chapter 3, one of the aims of public health is not just to enable more people to live into late old age but to 'compress morbidity' so that active life expectancy is as close as possible to the number of years lived *per se* (Figure 8.9).

It is likely that information on functional capacity will become a predominant feature in assessing the needs of older populations. This approach has many attractions (Figure 8.10). Defining, for example, the help an elderly woman requires against an assessment of her ability to wash, dress, cook and go out to the shops is of relevance to most caring professionals. It gives a focus for a multidisciplinary approach to care. In addition, assessments of functional capacity provide a common currency which enables the aggregation of data to population level; so that it is possible, for example, to describe the proportion of a local elderly population with incontinence of urine and organise an appropriate service response.

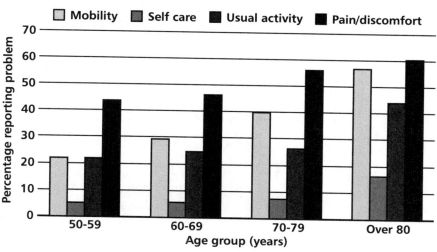

Figure 8.8 Self-reported limitation of function and pain: United Kingdom.

Source: Derived from: Kind P *et al.* BMJ, 1998; 316:736–41.

There is a growing problem of isolation amongst elderly people, particularly in the inner-city areas from which the young have migrated. Loneliness can be a major factor in many of the problems of the elderly. It can cause apathy and lack of interest. It can lead to problems such as malnutrition, hypothermia, and general self-neglect.

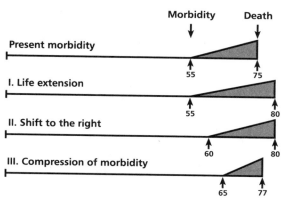

Figure 8.9 Scenarios for future morbidity and longevity.

Source: Fries JF. J. R. Soc. Med., 1996; 89:64–8.

Elderly people's social networks are a vital aspect of the assessment of their need for care as they grow older. It does not, of course, automatically follow that an elderly person living alone is socially isolated. It does raise, however, the importance of the nature of social contacts (as opposed to their number) in the lives of elderly people. For most elderly people, their main social contacts are either with those with whom they live or with relatives outside their home. The potential impact of social and demographic changes related to these issues was discussed in the previous section. Much less is known about the extent to which other societal changes have influenced elderly people's own perceptions of the importance of social networks. For example, an old person living alone in an inner-city area who enjoys regular social contact with relatives and friends may be so fearful of personal attack that she would much rather be resident in a sheltered housing scheme than remain in her own home any longer.

Consistent with public health emphasis on healthy life expectancy
Easily matches need to health service response
Well suited to multidisciplinary needs assessment and care
Not an abstract concept, has meaning for care workers
Allows data aggregation to describe older populations at different levels: locality, district, region

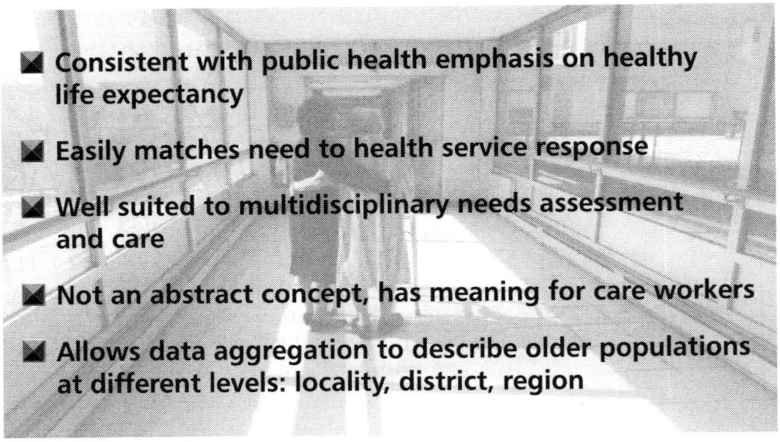

Figure 8.10 Advantages of using functional capacity measures to describe the health of older populations.

Whilst the social networks of older people will be based heavily on relatives, friends and neighbours are also important. The number of social contacts which people maintain in later life is very variable and depends upon their social and educational background, their ethnic groups, the type of community they live in as well as personal attitudes and outlook. There is some research evidence suggesting that health and mortality in later life are both affected by the strength of older people's social networks.

700
600
500
400
300
200
100
0
Income (£)
547
152
345
Non-retired
Retired on state pension
Other retired

Figure 8.11 Gross weekly income for one-man, one-woman households.

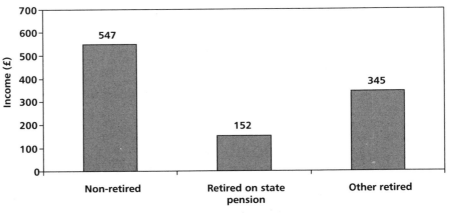

Source: Family Expenditure Survey, 1997–98.

Changes in the position of elderly people in society are also closely related to the economic effects of growing old. Retired people, mainly dependent on state pension, as might be expected have lower income than other groups (Figure 8.11). State pensions and other welfare benefits provide the main source of income for elderly people. Older people spend a higher proportion of their income on basics – housing, fuel, food – than do younger people.

A key issue may well be the distribution of income among the older age-groups. There is evidence that this distribution widened considerably during the latter part of the twentieth century with major differences in standard of living between those dependent upon state benefit for their income and the smaller number with other income such as investments and occupational pensions.

Ethnic Minority Elders

In the last few years of the twentieth century, ethnic minority communities made up about 6% of Britain's population. The proportion was much higher in certain conurbations. Their relatively young age-structure reflects a high birth-rate (in some groups), and the waves of immigration which occurred in the 1960s and early 1970s and (for those who came from Afro-Caribbean countries) in earlier years still.

Whilst the numbers of older people belonging to ethnic minority groups are as yet small compared to the indigenous elderly, their numbers will increase as the structure of the minority populations begins to resemble that of the majority (Table 8.6).

Table 8.6 Proportion in older age-groups amongst selected ethnic minority populations in Great Britain, 1995–97

Ethnic group:	Proportion (%) aged (years):		
	45–59	60–74	75+
White	18.6	13.9	7.0
Indian	15.5	6.5	1.2
Pakistani	9.0	4.3	0.6
Bangladeshi	8.6	4.9	0.2
Black–Caribbean	13.4	11.3	1.4

Source: Office for National Statistics.

Relatively little information is available on the health of older people in the ethnic minority populations and it is important not to fall into stereotypic assumptions about the needs of ethnic minority elders. For example, it is widely believed that old age is a greatly revered state in some ethnic minority communities within Britain. Hence it is assumed that an elderly person will enjoy the warmth, support and care of an extended family, so that little attention should be given by statutory services to meeting the needs of this group of elderly people.

Whilst this may be the ideal shared by people in some ethnic minority communities themselves, patterns of geographical mobility and other factors will mean that it is unlikely always to be realised. Contrasts between this cultural ideal and the social reality may give rise to problems for elderly people belonging to ethnic minority groups as well as leading to false assumptions amongst those responsible for providing services.

Nevertheless, a population survey of the health and social status of elderly people of 'Asian' descent in Leicestershire (described as an example of a public health investigation in Chapter 2) is one of the few to provide objective data on need amongst the ethnic minority elderly in Britain.

It showed similar levels of incapacity to the indigenous population, but a greater direct involvement with the extended family. Wider social contact was seriously limited, however, by lack of literacy and language skills which may also limit contact with the helping agencies in the health and social care arena.

In responding to the needs of older people from ethnic minority communities it will be especially important for health services to ensure that they are aware of and work with varying cultural norms. Knowledge of, and sensitivity to, issues such as diet, religious practice and observance and the role of the older person in his or her own community will be of particular significance.

Some Special Health Problems of Later Life

A number of specific health problems of later life which are amenable to prevention or which have major medical care implications are considered briefly in this section. Cardiovascular disease and cancer which are particularly important causes of illness and disability in older people are discussed in Chapter 3. Respiratory infections which are a common cause of emergency admission to hospital amongst older people are considered in Chapter 10. Sensory impairment (loss of vision and hearing) are discussed in Chapter 5.

Hypothermia and Excess Winter Deaths

Accidental hypothermia is said to be present if a deep body (core) temperature falls to below 35 °C. The term 'accidental' is used to distinguish this type of hypothermia from that which might be induced deliberately for therapeutic purposes. The diagnosis of hypothermia must be confirmed with a special low-reading thermometer inserted rectally. Such instruments are becoming an increasingly common part of the equipment of doctors and nurses working in the community.

It is estimated that 3–4% of people aged 65 years and over who are admitted to hospital have a core body temperature below 35°C. Over 90% of cases of accidental hypothermia occur indoors.

The elderly person with hypothermia does not usually shiver or complain of being cold because of an impaired perception of temperature change. However, the skin is pale and cold to the touch and consciousness is clouded leading to drowsiness, disordered thought and speech. Coma is more likely the lower the body temperature becomes. Movement and reflexes are sluggish. Speech may be slurred and the hearing and respiratory rates are slow and characteristic changes in an electrocardiograph may be present. The blood pressure may also fall. Some patients with hypothermia may become agitated and restless, and if tranquillisers are prescribed this can complicate their serious condition.

Fatality amongst patients with hypothermia is high. Treatment, usually in hospital, consists of gradual rewarming (if conducted too rapidly this may be fatal) and other supportive measures, such as administration of oxygen, intravenous fluids, and broad-spectrum antibiotics.

The main causes of accidental hypothermia are defective thermo-regulatory mechanisms (a consequence of ageing) and exposure to cold through low environmental temperature. Other factors such as immobility due to general infirmity, mental impairment, strokes, falls, effects of medicines, certain illness (for example, infections, endocrine disorders) may be superimposed.

Reducing the occurrence of accidental hypothermia in later life can be addressed through community programmes directed particularly at the homes of older people living alone. Living accommodation can be reviewed to ensure that there is a high enough indoor temperature. This can be maintained by a combination of heating, draught reduction and insulation measures. In addition, health education advice to older people should emphasise moving around (if possible) to increase body heat by metabolic activity and to ensure adequate nutrition and clothing, especially in advanced age. Financial support through the benefits system for heating, insulation and cold weather payments are particularly important. In addition, all health and social care professionals and informal carers should be made aware of, and be vigilant for, the danger signs of hypothermia, especially in cold weather. It is also valuable to ensure a basic knowledge of those issues amongst members of the general public coming into regular contact with older people (for example, milkmen, postmen).

Hypothermia has been discussed in detail because deaths from this cause in later life are a tragedy which effective public health action can help to avoid. However, the issue of death due to cold weather is a much more complex question which has been subjected to extensive epidemiological study.

Measuring mortality in the winter months (usually December–March) as a proportion of mortality at other times of year yields an index called excess winter deaths. Whilst this index has fluctuated during the twentieth century, it has persistently showed an excess of winter deaths in older age-groups. The excess mortality is due to circulatory illness (ischaemic heart disease and stroke), respiratory disease (particularly influenza) accidents and violence (including hypothermia), as well as a range of other causes.

The excess winter mortality rises sharply with age in the older age-groups (Table 8.7) and is worse in the years with influenza epidemics.

Table 8.7 Mean excess winter death index* by selected cause of death in women

	Age-group (years)		
Cause:	45–64	65–74	75+
Coronary heart disease	18	20	25
Respiratory disease	54	57	58
Accidents and violence	12	20	38
All causes:	11	18	27

Source: Curwen M. In *The Health of Adult Britain 1841–1994*. Office for National Statistics, London: The Stationery Office. 1997 (data relate to 1976–1983). * Excess winter mortality as a percentage of non-winter mortality.

Falls

Accidents are a common cause of death, disability and hospital admission in later life. Falls are the single most important cause of accidental death in older people, the remainder resulting from road traffic accidents, burns and a variety of other reasons.

The propensity of older people to fall over has long been recognized. Many falls in the elderly will produce no injuries. However, partly because of the increased fragility of bones in old age, a fracture is a common outcome of a fall. Fracture of the neck of the femur is a particularly serious example which can result from seemingly quite trivial falls or no apparent trauma (e.g., rising out of a chair). Even with a modern approach of immediate operation (to pin the fracture or replace the hip joint) and early mobilisation, fatality can still be as high as 25%. A less serious fracture, such as Colles' fracture of the wrist, may still be a considerable handicap for an elderly woman attempting to cook her meals and do her housework with an arm immobilised in plaster.

The types of falls have been classified into:

(a) ***Trips or accidental falls*** – which account for more than one-third of all falls in the elderly. There is a decline in the proportion of falls due to this cause in the very elderly, possibly because of their decreased mobility, combined with the growing importance of other causes.

(b) ***Drop attacks*** – which are sudden falls (without warning), not the result of a trip, in which consciousness is retained throughout. The precise mechanism is not clear although it may be due to a momentary reduction in the flow of the blood through the vertebral artery.

(c) ***Giddiness*** – this is a less common precipitant of a fall, possibly because the slow development of an attack allows the elderly person to grab hold of something or to sit down. Giddiness is, however, a more important factor in falls amongst the very old. There are very many reasons why giddiness can occur such as hypertension, cardiac insufficiency, transient attacks or side-effects of therapy.

(d) ***Loss of balance*** – may also be caused by a variety of factors, perhaps disorder of the labyrinthine apparatus.

A large number of underlying risk factors have been reported in studies of falls in older people but it is difficult to identify their relative contribution with certainty. The main groups of such risk factors are identified in Table 8.8. All cases of falls amongst older people should be investigated to determine whether there is any underlying correctable problem.

Table 8.8 Potential risk factors for falls and injury in older people

Risk factor	Example
• Nutritional status	Vitamin D and calcium deficiency
• Environmental hazards	Loose carpets, poor lighting
• Medication	Antidepressants, hypnotics
• Lack of exercise	Poor muscle strength, bone loss
• Medical problems of old age	Poor vision, dementia

Source: Adapted from: Preventing falls and subsequent injury in older people, Effective Health Care, volume 2, number 4, 1996.

Approaches to prevention of falls are largely directed against the underlying risk factors. In the home, simple measures such as: minimising the use of stairs and steps; attending to loose stair-rods, uneven carpets and dangling flexes; improving lighting; and providing non-slip bath mats can be effective. Ready availability of simple aids to daily living in retail outlets is also important. There would seem to be little doubt that such improvements to the design of the environment of older people's homes would have an impact. However, there is little evidence from research studies to show how best to effect such an improvement to this aspect of health on a population-wide basis. Local schemes exist in which health visitors or other workers undertake programmes of visits with the aim of bringing about environmental improvements but few have been rigorously evaluated to see whether they are cost effective.

The role of dietary supplements (in particular vitamin D and calcium) and hormone replacement therapy in reducing bone loss (and hence the risk of fracture) has been established in study populations. However, the cost effectiveness of population-based preventive strategies is not yet established.

Urinary Incontinence

Urinary incontinence is a common problem in the elderly. It is perhaps the most embarrassing, distressing and ultimately humiliating sequel to old age. Moreover, its onset is often the reason why the elderly person is judged as no longer fit to remain in his or her home, rejected in a family or friend's home or considered an unsuitable candidate for certain forms of residential care.

Urinary incontinence has been defined by the International Continence Society as:

> '...the involuntary loss of urine which is objectively demonstrable and is a social or hygienic problem.'

The causes of urinary incontinence are many and may arise from local factors, for example, bladder neck obstruction (most often due to prostatic enlargement), stress incontinence (usually due to weakening of pelvic floor musculature following childbirth), urinary tract infections or general factors. General factors in the elderly which may lead to incontinence are often multiple and not clear-cut. A common reason for urinary incontinence is loss of inhibition of need to void when the bladder is partly full. This mainly occurs at night and may be associated with early brain failure. Emotional upsets resulting from bereavement, accidents or illnesses can give rise to incontinence of either a transient or permanent nature. Confusion arising from organic cerebral disease (including stroke) or side-effects of sedatives or psychotropic drugs can also lead to incontinence. Other drugs such as rapidly-acting diuretics may also contribute. Incontinence may be a feature of limitation of mobility so that the elderly person is unable to reach the toilet in time to avoid an accident. Estimates of the occurrence of urinary incontinence suggest that the overall prevalence is around 10% in older adults.

In order for continence of urine to be maintained five conditions need to be fulfilled (Table 8.9). Approaches to management need to identify which of these factors is contributing to the loss of continence in the individual concerned and to address the problem.

Table 8.9 Factors necessary to maintain urinary continence

- Adequate function of the lower urinary tract to store and empty urine
- Adequate cognitive function to recognize the need to urinate and to find the appropriate place
- Adequate physical mobility and dexterity to get a toilet and use it
- Motivation to be continent
- Absence of environmental barriers to continence

Source: Ouslander JG. The efficiency of continence treatment. In: Improving the health of older people: a world view. (Eds, Kane RL, Evans J G, MacFayden D). Oxford: Oxford University Press, 1990.

The cornerstone of management of urinary incontinence in the elderly is making a correct diagnosis of the cause together with a sympathetic and understanding attitude on the part of the professionals. This means good assessment; for example by a continence adviser with expertise and experience in this field. It cannot be over-emphasised that the presence of incontinence is a deeply emotional issue both for the elderly people who have it and relatives, friends and neighbours who are in contact with them. Incontinence is seldom the result of a single underlying cause.

In some cases operative treatment of an enlarged prostate or gynaecological disorder, treatment of an underlying urinary tract infection, or review of a long-standing drug regime may solve the problem. Aside from these measures, probably the most important step in treating urinary incontinence is bladder training. For incontinent patients already in an institutional setting, episodes of incontinence are recorded on a fluid chart, and nursing staff ensure regular toileting of the patient to re-educate the bladder. Such bladder training may be supplemented by physiotherapy in the form of exercise for the pelvic floor muscles. Despite such measures some will continue to experience episodes of incontinence.

A wide variety of support is possible for elderly people with incontinence who are living in the community. In many parts of the country, specialised continence advisers (often with a nursing background) visit old people and make assessments as well as providing help to those whose problem has been diagnosed. The use of specialised underclothes and pads are a particularly important part of a support strategy once specific interventions have been tried or as an accompaniment to other therapies. The range of available products is quite wide and make use of disposable pads with highly absorbent materials.

Mental Illness in Elderly People

Mental illness in the elderly can take many different forms. Some degree of depression is the commonest disorder and affects approximately 15% of the population aged 65 years and over. In addition to the causes of the disease amongst younger people, depression amongst elderly people can be precipitated by any of the major life-events which are common in this age-group: for example, the loss of a spouse, retirement, or the onset of physical illness associated with pain. The manifestations of depression can be quite wide-ranging and include: apathy, social withdrawal, neglect of personal appearance, tearfulness, sleep disorders, loss of appetite and suicide. Although, for many old people, the episode of depression may resolve with professional help, in others the condition becomes chronic.

Another serious mental illness of later old-age is dementia, a disorder of brain functioning which leads to deterioration in the capacity of the mind affecting areas such as memory, decision-making, understanding and the use of language to communicate with others. Old people with dementia can also have disturbances of normal behaviour which lead them to wander, sleep irregularly and fitfully, and to exhibit disruptive and antisocial behaviour. Another practical aspect of the effect of dementia on elderly people is the extent to which they are able to care for themselves. Progressive loss of function in this respect is an important feature of the disease. Dementia varies in the way in which it affects the mental, physical and social functioning of any individual elderly person but it is capable of affecting all such areas of functioning (Table 8.10).

Minor degrees of memory impairment and temporary confusion may not necessarily threaten an old person's capacity to maintain an independent existence in the community. However, more severe and sustained problems of this kind, especially when coupled with disturbed or erratic behaviour and an inability to perform basic activities of daily living, will lead rapidly to a state of dependency.

Table 8.10   Practical features of dementia

Progressive impairment of intellectual functioning
- Memory problems
- Loss of sense or time
- Loss of sense of where or who they are
- Speech difficulties

Personality and behavioural changes
- Neglect of personal care and hygiene
- Incontinence
- Emotional stability
- Loss of social inhibitions

Dementia affects around 5% of people aged 65 years and over whilst closer to 20% of over-85s will exhibit some signs of it. Dementia is of two main types. The first and most common is Alzheimer's disease, in which there are permanent changes in the brain characterised by loss and severe abnormalities of nerve cells and their processes. In particular, nerve cells which produce important chemical substances for brain activities are lost. Alzheimer's disease accounts for about half of all cases of dementia amongst the over-65s. Dementia is much less common in middle-age and early old-age but, when it does occur here, Alzheimer's disease is commonly found. The second type of dementia is associated with disease of the arteries of the brain causing death of small or large areas of brain tissue, so-called multi-infarct dementia.

Aside from these two main types of dementia, there are other less common forms, including Huntingdon's chorea, Parkinson's disease and Creutzfeldt–Jakob disease. In addition, the symptoms and signs of dementia can be produced by vitamin B-12 deficiency, brain tumours, thyroid disease and chronic alcoholism.

Some of these less common forms of dementia are treatable but where Alzheimer's disease or multi-infarct dementia are the underlying pathologies, treatment is not effective and clinical management is aimed at containing and ameliorating the effects of the disease. New generations of drugs are entering the field but it is too early to assess their clinical and cost effectiveness on a widespread basis.

As the population ages still further, the estimated number of people with dementia will increase sharply. This has major implications for service provision.

Other groups of elderly people with mental illness are important and need services. Many of those with psychotic illnesses such as schizophrenia have grown old within large, old-style psychiatric hospitals. With the policy of phasing out such long-stay institutional-type facilities these patients have particular needs which must be matched by appropriate community services if they are to leave what has effectively become their home over many years. Amongst elderly people admitted to hospital for treatment of acute medical, surgical or orthopaedic conditions, so-called 'confusion' (more properly 'delirium') is not uncommon. Many cases can be managed clinically if identified at an early stage and underlying factors treated.

Services for People in Later Life

It often surprises people to learn that the majority of elderly people are able to lead an independent existence in their own home. However, with advancing age and the impact of the negative forces of old age, this independence is less easily maintained. The main categories of need were discussed in the previous section and are summarised in Table 8.11. When elderly people are no longer able to manage on their own, a wide range of services may be available to provide help, support and advice.

Table 8.11   Key features that determine health need in later life

- Social networks and support
- Income level
- Presence of disease or illness
- Mobility and capacity for self-care
- Housing quality and neighbourhood environment
- Sensory impairment
- Personal security
- Access to services

National Service Framework

Chapter 4 has described the concept of a National Service Framework a new planning mechanism introduced for 1999 which sets out standards for particular fields of care and models of service organisation which represent good practice. A National Service Framework for older people will be produced in 2000.

The Promotion of Health in Old Age

Some specific health problems which affect people in later life have been described in earlier sections as has the concept of healthy life expectancy. The main conditions which contribute to incapacity and dependency in old age are: cardiovascular disease, joint disease and fractured neck of femur, cancer (particularly of the breast, lung, prostate, colon and rectum), dementia and depression, and eye disease (cataract and glaucoma). Measures to promote health and prevent disease earlier in life can help to improve health in later life by delaying the onset of some of these chronic diseases. However, action in old age itself can also have an impact. Health promotion strategies addressing factors such as good diet, exercise, smoking cessation as well as the control of high blood pressure and high blood cholesterol can be effective.

A wider perspective on the promotion of health would also include programmes which prepare older people psychologically for retirement and which address their social welfare in ways which prevent problems and crises occurring.

Primary and Community Care

The majority of elderly people will continue to live in the community either with their spouse, with their children or other members of their family or, increasingly as they grow older, alone. For some considerable time, the central objective of policy for care in old age in the United Kingdom has been to enable elderly people to remain in the community for as long as possible. For most people in later life, their ability to reside in their own home is a potent symbol of autonomy, independence and self-determination.

The nature of services provided in the community is critical in determining successful outcomes of care for old people who do have needs. For example, occupational therapists, district nurses, home helps and health visitors are vital professionals whose input to the care of housebound old people can help to convert their tenuous hold on independent living into a well-supported daily routine enhanced by social contacts. Similarly, the availability of day and respite care backed up by good transport to provide widespread access can be another key ingredient of support for the vulnerable elderly. Services which are available on a 24-hour, seven-day-a-week basis to provide, for example, night nursing, toileting, bathing or sitting services will often make the difference between a hospital or residential care admission and sustaining an old person with a reasonable quality of life at home.

Whether organised around the Primary Care Group or Trust directly, or based within a community health service unit, or located within a hospital's management structure (as an outreach function), health professionals other than doctors are an essential element of the network of health care delivered to elderly people in the community.

Although the health visitor is mainly concerned with the youngest age-groups, a proportion of her caseload may be meeting the needs of older people. Her training equips her to detect early signs of disease and disability and to take the necessary action to ameliorate these conditions. A knowledge of the complex network of services available can enable her to play a part in obtaining the assistance which an older person may require.

Community nurses also have a major role in caring for the elderly. Of all the patients treated at home by nurses in Britain, almost half are elderly. Increasingly, in many parts of the country, although overall responsibility remains in the hands of a qualified nurse, nursing auxiliaries assist with some duties such as bathing, washing hair, cutting toe-nails and generally performing home nursing tasks. The role of the fully trained nurse is in assessment of older people and the delegation of the personal care to nursing auxiliaries and care assistants whom she supervises. Recently, community nurses have been instrumental in developing and delivering new models of care to elderly people – such as community rapid-response teams which, following referral by the general practitioner, social worker or hospital professional, allow up to 24-hour a day nursing support to be put into a person's home for a short period (typically 2 weeks). The aim of such services is to help an at-risk elderly person overcome a crisis in their functioning (e.g., following a fall) and prevent the need for a hospital admission. Such approaches can also facilitate safe early discharge following an acute hospital admission. Other health professionals working in the community, such as chiropodists and dieticians, are also part of the care team supporting old people.

Specialist nursing services such as community psychiatric nurses, (for example, for older people with severe depression or dementia) or palliative care nurses (for example, for elderly people with end stage cancer) are a valuable adjunct to these general community services.

There is a statutory requirement for social services departments to respond to all request for the assessment of need in older people. This is led by the social services authorities, but all agencies and professional disciplines should collaborate. On the basis of such assessments, a care manager may be appointed (normally from the social services department but possibly from the health service if the individual requires mainly health care). He or she will take the lead in ensuring the services identified by the assessment are arranged and delivered. This role will include the commissioning of the social care components of the individual's care package.

Some older people in need can move into this process of assessment and care planning after referral from primary care services whilst, in others, the process of acute hospital admission triggers multidisciplinary assessment – see Figure 8.12. The planning of discharge from hospital is discussed again later in this chapter.

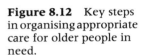

Figure 8.12 Key steps in organising appropriate care for older people in need.

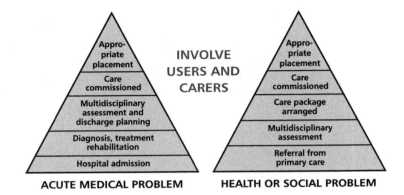

Professionals delivering services to elderly people in their own homes can include social workers and home helps. The latter group, if their traditional role is extended, can be particularly valuable in maintaining a frail or incapacitated elderly person at home. Many social services departments have developed their home help services into home care services based around a much wider range of tasks (a large proportion is provided by the private sector) in response to individual need than was previously the case. In some parts of the country, the potential for a joint health and social care approach to domiciliary care for older people is being examined via the provision of domiciliary workers who undertake both the functions of district nurse auxiliaries and local authority home care workers. This model has particular merit in meeting individual need across the health–social care divide. Other services delivered to the home and which are also an important component in the network of support, include meals-on-wheels and home laundry facilities.

Day Centres and Recreational Clubs

Many older people will attend a day centre or be a member of a club (often organised by a voluntary organisation or in some places by a church). Such facilities are places they can interact with their peers and with staff. This can help to counteract loneliness and social isolation. A hot meal is often provided midday and helps to meet the overall nutritional needs of the older people concerned. Day centres like these can also help to relieve some of the burden of care for informal carers and allow them time and space to unwind, to go shopping or to get on with household tasks.

Respite Care

Respite care can be of major importance in allowing dependent older people to remain in their own homes. Whilst the term respite care implies a single form of care service, this is increasingly incorrect. Currently, there are a variety of models of respite care which are designed to meet a range of individual needs of older people and of carers. There is still a clear role for the health service in providing hospital inpatient respite care. Other forms of respite care are provided by local authority or the independent sector. Respite care does not have to cause individuals to leave their homes. Given the importance of familiar surroundings to many older people (and especially those with mental illnesses of old age such as dementia) models of respite care involving care workers looking after the person in their own home are increasingly seen as important.

Voluntary Organisations

In Britain, voluntary organisations have traditionally played a vital role in the care of older people in the community. Whilst their role will vary according to the philosophy and infrastructure of the organisation concerned, it will invariably include raising public awareness of the issues involved as well as providing information to older people and their carers. Many voluntary organisations will additionally have a service-provision role which can encompass the delivery of specialist advice on state financial benefit entitlements, the running of day care centres, counselling, advice, and home visiting.

Caring for Carers

Understanding the full spectrum of care needs (Figure 8.13) requires an understanding of the needs of those who look after others, many of whom are themselves in middle-age (Table 8.12).

Figure 8.13 Continuing care needs in later life: key components.

ASSESSMENT OF NEED

HOME OR SPECIAL HOUSING | SUPPORT AT HOME | RESIDENTIAL PLACEMENT | NURSING HOME CARE | LONGER TERM HOSPITAL CARE | TERMINAL CARE

PLANNING OF CARE

Carers must be given practical support as partners with professionals in giving care. This should also be based on an assessment of their individual needs separate from their dependants. Above all, they should have access to high quality, up-to-date information about the availability of facilities, services, rights and entitlements. They must also be recognized as having needs of their own – requiring support and care. There might be a need for counselling and emotional support, for training in particular aspects of disease management, or health care needs of their own. Support to enable them to take regular breaks or continue in employment (if they want to) is a particularly important part of supporting carers. Much of this work is anticipatory, to prevent a breakdown of the caring relationship. A national strategy for carers launched in 1999 addressed these and many other needs of carers in a comprehensive way. (Table 8.13).

Table 8.12   Characteristics of carers in Britain

- 5.7 million people are carers
- 17% of households contain a carer
- Largest age-group of carers is 45–64 years
- 2 out of 10 carers care for partner or spouse
- 4 out of 10 carers care for a parent
- Half of all carers look after someone 75 years or older
- 18% of carers look after one person

Source: Caring about carers: a national strategy for carers. London: The Stationery Office, 1999.

Table 8.13   Strategy for carers: key elements

- Information for carers, including:
  - a charter
  - a helpline
  - information on internet
- Support for carers including:
  - involvement in planning services
  - regularly consulted
- Care for carers including:
  - help to take a break
  - special grants
  - health needs met

Source: Caring about carers: a national strategy for carers. London: The Stationery Office, 1999.

Elderly People with Long-term Care Needs Who Cannot Manage at Home

Sometimes, even with a high level of support from services it is just not feasible or humane to allow an older person to remain at home. Through multi-agency assessment, the social services authority is the lead agency which commissions care for them, unless they meet health authority eligibility criteria or if they have sufficient funds to buy private care. The choice of care will be from within the range of facilities in a locality which is best suited to their needs (Figure 8.12). Sometimes, for example, this would be a private nursing home or residential care home, provided by the local authority or by a voluntary organisation or private sector. If public funding of care is being sought, entry to residential homes will often mean the older person's financial means being assessed and if they are leaving their home permanently and have assets over a nationally-defined amount that they will pay for all (or a contribution towards) their care (see also the section below on funding of long-term care).

For a small group of highly-dependent people, the health service is expected to continue to provide consultant-led hospital inpatient care or nursing home placement.

For elderly people whose conditions are too severe for them to continue in their own homes, even with support services, there has been a growing realisation of the importance of the nature of the institutional environment and regime of long-stay accommodation. The term 'institution' itself is increasingly unfavourably regarded because it has become synonymous with the negative features of long-stay facilities which it is sought to eliminate. Places where the interior fabric is drab and decaying, furnishing is uniform, where there is a permanent smell of urine and privacy is limited, coupled with regimes which are organised and regimented to facilitate the tasks of the staff rather than the needs of the individual resident or patient, can be destructive. This lack of self-determination encourages an apathy and indifference amongst people with special or long-term care needs which may lead not only to poor quality of life but to poor outcome of care. Such long-stay institutions are also often characterised by poor staff morale, high staff turnover and problems with recruitment.

There is a broad range of facilities available for elderly people who require long-term care and support who cannot manage within their own homes. The health service continues to provide what are often called 'long-stay geriatric beds', which usually cater for heavily dependent elderly people who require very intensive nursing and/or medical care which cannot be delivered in other settings. The local social services authority secures places in homes for the elderly, aimed particularly at those frail elderly people who are not heavily physically or mentally incapacitated. The private sector provides places in private nursing homes as well as in rest or residential homes; the not-for-profit and voluntary sectors also provide some residential and nursing home care.

During the last two decades of the twentieth century, there was a major shift in the provision of such care away from the public sector towards independent providers as government policy stressed the need for the state to commission high quality care rather than directly provide it.

There are two major groups of older people who require these forms of long-term care: those who need care for considerable parts of a 24-hour period from staff with nursing training and those who need staff to give help or assistance in carrying out some of the activities of daily living such as washing, dressing, getting to the toilet and feeding themselves.

In the past, these types of care have been regarded as discrete entities, developed to a level within the population determined by the agencies which control them and with admission and care policies which were similarly individual-agency orientated. The advent of the changes to the organisation and funding of community care, at the beginning of the 1990s, helped to achieve a greater degree of integration. Under these arrangements community care plans, produced jointly between health authorities and social services authorities, must ensure that the decisions of each agency are coordinated in order that the population's needs determine the quantity of the various forms of continuing care commissioned. As already described, at the level of the individual elderly person, the system of multidisciplinary assessment aims to ensure that he or she receives the form of continuing care most suited to their needs.

The aim of all facilities which care for elderly people should be to allow the old person to have maximum dignity and self-determination. Whilst in practice the daily routine for elderly patients or residents can often seem dull and monotonous, there is much that can be done to ensure that the regime does not develop the adverse features of an institution. Older people in continuing care facilities should not spend extended periods of the day bedridden or chairfast unless their condition dictates that this must be so. Older people should receive personalised care and should not be subjected to set regimes in relation to toileting, bathing or feeding. Each continuing care facility should pursue a personalised clothing scheme to encourage the maintenance of self-respect and individuality. Elderly people should be encouraged to bring as many of their personal possessions with them as is feasible.

The older person's environment should provide a sense of security and cheerfulness. Therefore, floors should be safe to walk on and appropriate furniture, including a wide variety of chairs, provided. The layout and furnishing of the hospital or home should be designed to avoid confusion, particularly important for the elderly with dementia. Decoration should be in a non-institutional manner with soft furnishings and colour schemes of homely appearance. The communal rooms should be arranged to allow each resident to pursue their own hobbies and interests. With positive attention to building design, environment, regimes, individual care plans and staff training, adverse factors of institutional life can be reversed.

The Funding of Long-term Care

By the mid-1990s, in Britain an estimated £11.1 billion was being spent annually on long-term care of which £8.3 billion went on residential and nursing home care whilst £2.7 billion was spent on home care (Table 8.14). Of the total amount, £7.1 billion was paid for by the State directly (via NHS and Social Services) whilst other people paid £4 billion themselves. Long-term care services are usually a mixture of health and social care, and increasingly the result of a multidisciplinary assessment involving health and social care staff. The elements of the care package provided by the NHS are free to the older person, and met from NHS budgets (ultimately direct from taxation). Those elements commissioned by local social service authorities can be subject to a charge on the older person based on a test of their means. For residentially-based care commissioned by the local authority, above a certain level of capital the older person has to pay the fees in full. Below such a level they have to contribute to such fees.

Table 8.14   Expenditure on long-term care services

Type of expenditure	£million (at 1995–6 prices)
Personal social services net[1]	4,510
National Health Service	2,565
Private charges[2]	1,725
Private fees[3]	2,265
Total	11,065

Source: 'With Respect to Old Age', a report by the Royal Commission on long-term care. The Stationery Office, March 1999.

Notes:

1. PSS = expenditure on personal social services for elderly people by local authorities, net of charges.
2. Charges are paid by individuals for social services provided by local authorities usually at subsidised rates.
3. Fees are paid by individuals directly to private service providers.

This system was perceived as having serious inequity and anomalies.

A Royal Commission on long-term care reported in 1999 having reviewed the options for a new system of funding long-term care for older people and produced many detailed recommendations, but two main ones in particular were that:

- The costs of long-term care should be split between living costs, housing costs and personal care. Personal care should be available after assessment, according to need and paid for from general taxation: the rest should be subject to a co-payment according to means.
- The government should establish a National Care Commission to monitor trends, including demography and spending, ensure transparency and accountability in the system, represent the interests of consumers, and set national benchmarks, now and in the future.

Funding issues are being considered by the Government whilst it has broadly accepted the recommendation to establish a National Care Standards Commission.

Hospital-based Services

A central part of a comprehensive system of care for older people is the capacity to provide specialist assessment and treatment for older people with acute medical problems.

Older people with acute illnesses present a particular challenge for the service seeking to provide the most effective clinical management of their condition and to maximise their level of independence. Older people will often have several problems coexisting which require skilful assessment and treatment, but, as already mentioned, their functional capacity (in terms of factors such as mobility and continence) will be equally as influential in determining both recovery and future living status. Moreover, the acute presentation will often bring to light issues of family and social support which have previously not been addressed but which require resolution as part of the care plan.

Inpatient Care

The appropriate organisation of acute medical care to provide prompt and accurate assessment, treatment and rehabilitation, and ultimately a return to the community or other care facility, is a constant source of discussion amongst health policy-makers and clinicians providing services. Attention has also centred on what kind of hospital bed the older person with an acute illness should be admitted to and what the relationship should be between geriatric medicine and general medicine as specialties of clinical practice. It is now widely acknowledged that care of the acutely ill elderly person is best provided within a bed in a general hospital setting where there is access to the full range of diagnostic and therapeutic facilities.

A number of models of hospital care for acutely ill older people have evolved and these tend to take one of three main forms.

Age-defined Approach

In some localities, all patients above a certain age (usually 75 years and over) are admitted to a specialist care of the elderly service. This model of care has attractions in that it is easily understood by general practitioners and it provides a ward environment and care team especially geared to the needs of the elderly. It has the disadvantage inherent in the differences between chronological and biological ageing. With a cut-off point which is chronologically-based, say at 70 or 75 years, the 66-year-old with problems of biological old-age (such as stroke) will miss out on the assessment and rehabilitation skills of the geriatric team.

Integrated Approach

An alternative model of service is one in which all acutely ill older people are admitted to an acute medical ward which deals with other age-groups and are cared for by a group of physicians. Although one or more of these physicians will have special expertise in the care of the elderly, he or she will also participate in the care of the young age-groups.

This has the advantage that all medical staff are in touch with medical care across all age-groups and it enables more scope in the use of beds. However, there can be difficulties. Patients may be spread around the hospital, be subject to different ward routines and there can be problems in getting nursing staff to take a common approach with a split across different wards. Moreover, there is a danger that the 'urgent' will always take priority over the 'important' (for example, the younger person with a myocardial infarction rather than the elderly person with a stroke).

Needs-based Approach

The traditional model of acute care has separate departments of geriatric and general medicine but the decision about which team takes care of the patient is governed by his or her care needs. In practice, this is determined by the general practitioner or by clinical staff in the accident and emergency department.

This has the advantage that patients are selected at the time of admission according to whether they will benefit from the assessment and rehabilitation skills of the geriatric team. Patients with more straightforward medical problems (even though they are elderly) will be admitted under the care of the general medical team. The success of this model of care depends upon very close collaboration between the two departments, and a good assessment procedure in the accident and emergency department. Where this does not exist, the approach can lose much of its attraction and effectiveness.

It is the success in achieving recovery rather than the response to illness *per se* which is the real test of the quality of hospital services. This is only partly dependent on the medical input. It also crucially depends on access to non-medical advice and support from groups such as occupational therapists or physiotherapists. The role, too, of social services in ensuring discharge is coordinated with support services is vital. The assessment of older people in acute hospital beds and planning their discharge is a crucial test of the success of multidisciplinary multi-agency working in the care of older people (Figure 8.12). If it is done badly then discharge is delayed, older people occupy acute beds unnecessarily have reduced social functioning due to learnt dependence and may well therefore end up in more intensive forms of care than would otherwise have been the case.

The nature of services for the treatment of non-emergency problems of the elderly within the acute care sector is also of great importance. Many elderly people's lives are impaired by the presence of conditions which are potentially correctable. For example, many elderly women with chronic pain and severe limitation of movement caused by osteoarthrosis of the hip could have their level of independence and quality of life immediately improved by a hip joint replacement. Similarly, the lives of old people with very poor eyesight due to cataracts can be transformed by a simple operation.

Specialist hospital facilities for older people with mental illness are increasingly being provided by a Consultant in the Psychiatry of Old Age supported by a specialist multidisciplinary team working from a district general hospital with outreach facilities.

Day Hospital and Outpatient Facilities

Much of the initial assessment of older people with physical or mental illness is undertaken on an outpatient basis or by the consultant or other members of the hospital team visiting the old person's home at the request of the general practitioner. The inappropriate use of hospital beds can also be avoided by the provision of adequate day hospital care. The day hospital now has a firmly established place in most hospital services for the elderly. Day hospitals usually operate five days per week with patients generally arriving early morning and departing mid-to-late afternoon, having had their midday meal at the hospital. The day hospital is often situated close to or within a hospital which has inpatient facilities for the elderly. The emphasis in day hospitals is on active treatment and rehabilitation with multidisciplinary teamwork involving professionals such as nurses, physiotherapists, occupational therapists and speech therapists.

The day hospital also permits earlier discharge from a hospital bed so that rehabilitation takes place alongside reintegration into the community, and thus the risks of relapse and readmission are reduced. As with day centres, the day hospital can be an invaluable aid to carers in providing a respite from care (this is especially so for the most dependent elderly people).

Rehabilitation

Over recent years increasing emphasis within services for elderly people has been given to the concept of rehabilitation. This derived from a recognition that many services tended to simply accept that following an acute crisis an elderly person would become more dependent and thus might require long-term care services. Rehabilitation attempts to ensure that an older person's social and health functioning is maximised in order that they can pursue as normal a life as feasible.

Rehabilitation can take place in either a hospital or community setting and views amongst professionals are still divided over whether these are substitutes or compliments within a comprehensive network of services for elderly people.

In whatever the setting that rehabilitation is provided, it is essential that it delivered on a multidisciplinary basis rather than being seen as the preserve of any one profession. The key professionals will include physiotherapists, occupational therapists, social workers and nurses, as well as medical staff.

The evidence from successful projects at the local level is that a focused model of rehabilitation can reduce the need for admission to the more intensive care models such as nursing and residential care homes and can thus enable a greater proportion of older people to safely return to their own homes than could more traditional services.

Housing

There is little doubt that adequate and properly designed housing is the foundation upon which medical and social services for older people should be built. Over half of older people in Britain are owner-occupiers. If they are to continue to remain in the community, then their dwelling places must be adapted to meet their special needs. This can be achieved by the renovation or adaptation of existing houses or by providing specialised dwellings of the kind which are often described as sheltered housing.

Sheltered housing is provided by local authorities, by private organisations and by housing associations. Some specialised housing for older people is warden-controlled. Essentially, the warden acts as a friendly neighbour and keeps regular contact by personal visits, encouraging the elderly resident to contact him or her by means of some communication apparatus; for example, buzzer, bell or two-way speaking system. The warden does not provide a personal service such as cooking, cleaning or shopping, but can obtain help when necessary by providing a point of contact through which health and social services can be delivered. Sheltered housing is an important form of provision which allows frail, elderly people to continue to live in the community. Without such a protected environment, in which they can maintain supervised independence, they would probably be unable to cope, and the only recourse would be towards hospital or residential care.

The size of the specialised dwelling sectors is of key importance and there is no doubt that during the last few decades of the twentieth century it did not keep pace with the growth of need in the frail elderly population.

Conclusions

An ageing population brings with it increasing need for help and support from society – medical, social, emotional and financial. The ultimate aim of public health is to increase the period of later life which is free of poor health, incapacity and dependency. This will mainly be achieved by measures taken to promote health and prevent disease earlier in life but action taken in old age itself can also play an important contribution.

Greater health expectancy will make old age be a time of continuing participation in the life of the community and of personal fulfilment for many more older people. However, with ever-advancing years, the need for support for old people who become frail, ill, incapacitated or socially isolated becomes increasingly important. The key to this process is identifying and assessing individual need on a multidisciplinary, multiagency basis and then organising an appropriate response. Whilst the planning and commissioning of support and care is undertaken by social services and health services, increasingly in the actual provision of care, the independent sector will have a major part to play. Much, if not the majority, of the care provided to old people is given by informal carers (families and friends) and this must be recognized by all care agencies through the implementation of the National Strategy for Carers. Practical and emotional support for such carers is a vital part of the infrastructure of support for elderly people themselves and it is important that old people and their carers are fully involved as part of the care process.

If these services work well, many old people with problems will be able to remain in the community, well supported, close to family and friends. Throughout, however, emphasis must be placed on setting and maintaining high standards of care, whether this is to be provided in the community, in a hospital or in a residential care facility.

In these ways, quality of life and dignity for people in the final years of their lives will be sustained.

Chapter 9

Communicable Diseases and Parasites

Introduction

Once thought to be conquered, communicable diseases nevertheless continue to be an important feature of the health profile of many countries and in the developing world, they are still major killers. Throughout the 1980s and 1990s a series of food hygiene issues received media coverage in Britain for weeks at a time, from salmonella in eggs to Bovine Spongiform Encephalopathy in cattle and its relationship to variant Creutzfeldt–Jakob Disease (vCJD) in humans. In addition to food-related problems, new diseases such as Legionnaires' Disease, cryptosporidiosis and the Acquired Immune Deficiency Syndrome (AIDS) emerged as important public health problems and other diseases, thought to have been vanquished, such as tuberculosis, re-emerged together with multi-drug resistant forms.

Although deaths from communicable diseases in Britain are relatively rare now compared with the last century, they still occur. Reflecting on the fact that some children die each year from meningococcal infection is to realise that microorganisms continue to contribute to the toll of human misery. In developing countries, communicable diseases are still an important cause of premature death. Combating communicable diseases depends upon surveillance, preventive measures, and, where appropriate, outbreak investigation and the institution of control measures. This chapter outlines the services to deal with infectious conditions including the legislative framework, describes the principles of surveillance and control of communicable diseases, and provides a detailed description of the infections more commonly encountered by pubic health professionals in Britain. Some of the common communicable disease terminology is included as an annex to the chapter.

Organisation of Services

Communicable diseases do not respect geographical or administrative boundaries and efforts to prevent, control, and treat them depend upon input from a variety of local, national and international bodies. Key amongst them are Local Authorities, the National Health Service, the Public Health Laboratory Service, the Scottish Centre for Infection and Environmental Health and the Central Government Department of Health. Other national agencies (e.g., the Health and Safety Executive, the Water Undertakers and the Veterinary Laboratories Agency) also play an important role, as do international agencies such as the World Health Organization.

Local Government

Local authorities are empowered to take action in relation to the control of notifiable diseases within their boundaries. They are required to appoint a proper officer for this function who is usually a public health physician nominated from within the health authority to provide medical advice relating to communicable disease control. The person concerned is usually the district health authority's Consultant in Communicable Disease Control (CCDC), sometimes it is the authority's Director of Public Health or another consultant in Public Health Medicine who also has other duties within the health authority's department of public health medicine. The Local Authority can appoint more than one proper officer and can define the limits of their responsibilities, so it does not follow that all 'proper officers' of this function have the same powers. In Scotland the Designated Medical Officer to the local authority may be the Health Board's Consultant in Public Health Medicine (Communicable Diseases and Environmental Health) (CPHM(CD&EH)) or the Chief Administrative Medical Officer (CAMO) who is usually the Director of Public Health. The role of public health doctors in the National Health Service is described more fully in Chapter 4.

The structure of local government varies but the department concerned with communicable disease control is that containing environmental health services. Its function is usually led by a Chief Environmental Health Officer. Local authorities have a wide range of duties covering most aspects of environmental protection. The duties include the registration, inspection and investigation of food premises; involvement in the investigation of outbreaks of certain communicable diseases (mainly those which are food-borne); monitoring and dealing with other environmental hazards, and responding to concerns and enquiries from the public about environmental food quality matters. Legal powers of enforcement and prosecution with respect to the control of communicable diseases rest mainly with local authorities and their 'proper officer'.

Health Services

In addition to the formal communicable disease control responsibilities, health authorities and health boards have an important role in promoting health, preventing disease, and securing care to meet the population's needs. Thus, surveillance of communicable diseases, the identification of particular problems and the planning of preventive measures are key roles for health authorities and boards.

The health service also has responsibilities for the treatment and care of people with illnesses caused by communicable diseases and parasites. The general practitioner, with the support of the primary care team, is the person who treats the majority of cases of communicable diseases in the community. Only serious cases or those with complications are admitted to hospital. The fall in the incidence of infectious diseases over the years has led to fewer hospital beds being required for treatment. Many general hospitals are able to provide only limited isolation facilities but specialist advice and care is provided by specialist infectious disease physicians or physicians with a special interest in infectious diseases, as necessary.

Each major hospital or group of hospitals has a Hospital Infection Control Committee consisting of senior professional staff. The committee meets at regular intervals and keeps problems in relation to infection in the hospital under review. The day-to-day work is carried out by an Infection Control Doctor, usually a microbiologist on the hospital staff, and an Infection Control Nurse. They carry out regular checks on the level of infection (for example, in operating theatres) and deal with outbreaks when they occur. Reports are made at regular intervals to the committee.

The Public Health Laboratory Service

The Public Health Laboratory Service (PHLS) was originally formed as an emergency service to deal with problems anticipated in World War II, since when, it has proved to be so useful that it was established permanently. It is administered by the Secretary of State for Health through an appointed board whose headquarters, along with several of the service's specialist reference laboratories, are at Colindale in London. There are Public Health Laboratories (PHLs) serving different parts of England and Wales. Most are in hospitals and some take part in the hospital diagnostic microbiology service. They also work closely with the health authorities and local authority environmental health departments to provide microbiological investigation of communicable disease outbreaks, food and drink products, drinking water quality and routine samples of other material. Local laboratories can refer particular cases to the reference laboratories.

The Public Health Laboratory Service also has a Communicable Disease Surveillance Centre (CDSC) responsible for national surveillance of communicable disease and for providing advice and assistance to Public Health Physicians and others involved in the investigation and control of communicable disease. The CDSC is based in London at the headquarters of the Public Health Laboratory Service and has offices in each NHS Region, including centres for Wales and Northern Ireland to support both National and local surveillance and response functions. The members of staff of the centres also play an important part in educational programmes concerned with the control of infectious diseases.

The Scottish Centre for Infection and Environmental Health

The PHLS does not extend to Scotland which has its own independent network of reference laboratories, managed by the National Services Division of the Common Services Agency (CSA), reporting to the Scottish Centre for Infection and Environmental Health (SCIEH) which is also part of the CSA. A national surveillance centre has existed in Scotland since 1969 and was established following a public enquiry into a large outbreak of typhoid in Aberdeen. The SCIEH has responsibility for the surveillance and control of non-communicable environmental hazards, thus its remit is broader than that of the CDSC.

Department of Health

The Department of Health has overall responsibility in England for national policy matters in relation to communicable diseases, for example:

- ensuring that adequate and suitable hospital accommodation is available for communicable disease cases;
- ensuring adequate immunisation levels, not just at the time of outbreaks;
- maintaining international communication networks on communicable diseases matters.

The Chief Medical Officer for England is the UK government's principal adviser on communicable disease matters. The Chief Medical Officers for the other United Kingdom countries advise their Ministers directly (although in practice efforts are made to ensure that advice is consistent between the Chief Medical Officers). This is particularly important with devolved parliament and assemblies in three of the United Kingdom countries. In turn, the Chief Medical Officer will seek advice from a wide range of sources including experts within and outside the Department of Health and from the Director of the Public Health Laboratory Service (and specialists on the staff).

It is important to remember that the Chief Medical Officer advises government as a whole and not just the Department of Health. Hence, other relevant departments, for example, the Ministry of Agriculture, Fisheries and Foods, the Department for Education and Employment or the Department of Environment, Transport and the Regions may seek or receive advice from the Chief Medical Officer.

Legislation

A considerable amount of legislation exists which relates to the control of the spread of communicable diseases. For half a century, this legislation has been added to and amended as knowledge has advanced and new hazards have been identified. Most of it is enforceable by local authorities although in practice the courts are kept as a last resort and persuasion and education are mainly used. It should be noted that some public health legislation north of the Scottish border differs from that in England and Wales.

General Principles of Communicable Disease Control

When describing the spread of an infection and its control, three aspects should be considered. These are source, mode of transmission and susceptible recipient (Figure 9.1).

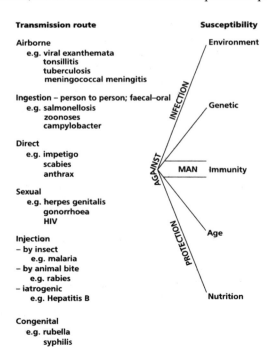

Figure 9.1 Major methods of transmission of infection.

The Source

This is the person, animal, object or substance from which an infectious agent is transmitted to a host.

Most communicable diseases in Britain are caused by either bacteria or viruses, and some of these pathogens have Man as their sole host. There are numerous exceptions. The Salmonella group of organisms have reservoirs in many domestic and wild animals. Other examples are brucellosis in cattle and leptospirosis in rats and other species. Viruses multiply only in living cells and never in inanimate substances. Certain fungi may cause infection but most, such as candida (thrush), are mild and not life-threatening except in circumstances where immunity is impaired. Medical parasitology includes the study of pathogenic protozoa, worms and insects. The first two groups often have reservoirs in wild or domestic animals, sometimes with insect vectors and complex life cycles involving several hosts.

Mode of Transmission

There are three main mechanisms through which infection can enter the body:

(1) **Direct transmission** involves the direct transfer of microorganisms to the skin or mucous membranes by touching, biting, kissing or sexual intercourse. Diseases which spread in this way include scabies (touching), rabies (biting), glandular fever (kissing) and syphilis or HIV infection (sexual intercourse). Some infections spread from pregnant mothers to their babies, for example, rubella and HIV infection.

(2) **Indirect transmission** involves an intermediate stage between the source of infection and the individual. The infection may be vehicle-borne for example, by infected food, water or vector-borne by animals or insects. Vehicle-borne infections include food poisoning, whilst malaria is vector-borne.

(3) **Airborne transmission** involves inhaling aerosols containing micro-organisms. Smaller droplets can penetrate right down to the alveoli of the lungs and be retained there. The microorganisms in the aerosols can remain suspended in the air for a long time. Legionnaires Disease is a good example of an infection due to airborne transmission, so is tuberculosis.

Measures directed at the route of transmission are key control measures for many communicable diseases. For example, typhoid and cholera may be controlled by the efficient disposal of sewage and the supply of uncontaminated drinking water.

Susceptible Recipient

Whether a person develops an infectious disease after contact with any given causal agent is governed by a number of factors such as the virulence and dose of the organism; previous exposure to the organism or an antigenic component as in vaccination conferring immunity; the age of the individual (babies up to six months have natural immunity to some infections from their mothers); the nutritional state of the person; the presence of other diseases and whether the individual is receiving immunosuppressive therapy.

Surveillance of Communicable Diseases

A prerequisite for detecting outbreaks of communicable disease is to have a mechanism in place to monitor their presence and changes in their incidence.

Surveillance is the systematic collection, collation, and analysis of data with dissemination of the results to those who need to know so that appropriate control measures can be taken. In short, surveillance is information for action. By monitoring communicable disease trends the information is used to identify epidemics or outbreaks, evaluate prevention and control programmes, set priorities for resource allocation and provide aetiological clues. A number of systems, both formal and informal, exists to enable information about communicable disease occurrences in the population to be gathered and analysed (Figure 9.2).

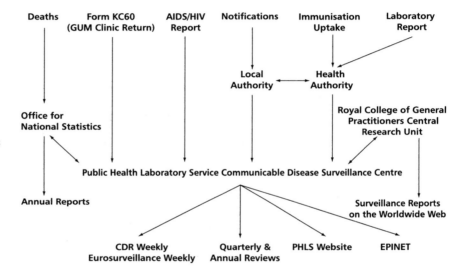

Figure 9.2 Flow of information about communicable diseases in England and Wales.

Notification of Infectious Disease

A legal duty rests on all registered medical practitioners, who are attending people suspected of having certain specified infectious diseases (Table 9.1), to notify the names and addresses of these patients. It should be noted that the list of notifiable diseases in Scotland differs slightly from that in the rest of the United Kingdom. It is important to note that notification is supposed to take place on the basis of clinical suspicion. According to the legislation a diagnosis does not have to be laboratory confirmed for notification to take place. This makes sense when considered in the context in which the legislation was drawn up. The purpose of notification is to allow public health action to be taken within the incubation period of the disease in question, thus the system needs a sensitive trigger. Waiting a couple of days for a diagnosis to be laboratory confirmed might mean that secondary spread has already taken place. The notification system should, therefore, be a sensitive, although not a specific, indicator of communicable disease in a community.

Table 9.1 Notifiable diseases in England and Wales

Anthrax	Paratyphoid fever
Cholera	Plague
Diphtheria	Acute poliomyelitis
Dysentery (amoebic or	Acute encephalitis
bacillary)	Relapsing fever
Rabies	Rubella
Food poisoning	Scarlet fever
Leprosy	Smallpox
Leptospirosis	Tetanus
Malaria	Tuberculosis (all forms)
Measles	Typhoid fever
Mumps	Typhus
Meningitis	Viral haemorrhagic fevers (including
Meningococcal septicaemia	Dengue fever, Ebola virus and Lassa
(without meningitis)	fever)
Ophthalmia neonatorum	Viral hepatitis
	Whooping cough
	Yellow fever

Notifications in England and Wales are made to the Proper Officers of the local authorities. The Proper Officers submit this information (not names and addresses only anonymised aggregated data) to the Communicable Disease Surveillance Centre which collates the information on behalf of the Office for National Statistics (ONS). In addition to the weekly returns, the Proper Officers submit returns at quarterly intervals which enable corrections to be made to the data gathered weekly. The Communicable Disease Surveillance Centre publishes weekly, quarterly and annual reports of notifications of infectious diseases in England and Wales.

In Scotland and Northern Ireland notifications are sent to the Chief Administrative Medical Officer (CAMO) of the appropriate Health Board. Notification data in Scotland are collated by the Information and Statistics Division (ISD) of the Common Services Agency and published in a weekly report produced by the Scottish Centre for Infection and Environmental Health (SCIEH).

Unfortunately, the effectiveness of the notification system is variable because there is a serious degree of under-notification of these statutorily notifiable diseases by medical practitioners. Part of the reason for this may be the fact that many doctors perceive notification simply as a means of gathering statistics and not as a tool for public health action. This is compounded by the fact that the list of notifiable diseases contains conditions which rarely occur in Britain but which appear by international agreement. Nevertheless notifications remain a key source of information about the incidence of certain communicable diseases in the population.

Laboratory Reports

The other major source of epidemiological information is reports of positive laboratory isolates. In England and Wales laboratories report certain microbiological results to the CDSC. Laboratories include those of the Public Health Laboratory Service, hospital departments of microbiology and virology, and a small number of private laboratories. In addition, there are specialist reference laboratories which undertake detailed typing work in relation to particular organisms or sources of infection. Information from them is also collated by the CDSC. A similar network in Scotland feeds into the SCIEH and, in Northern Ireland, the responsible body has been the Department of Health and Social Security.

Laboratory reporting is not yet a statutory requirement but rather a voluntary system. It complements the notification system by providing specific data about the occurrence of infectious organisms in a community.

Sentinel Surveillance in Primary Care

In England and Wales a sentinel scheme for reporting disease in general practice, under the auspices of the Royal College of General Practitioners (RCGP), includes some communicable diseases. Returns from a number of selected spotter practices are made on a weekly basis to the RCGP Research Unit. The sentinel practice scheme involves some sixty general practices covering a population of approximately 425,000 people. In Scotland there is a much larger system involving 124 general practices collecting information about almost 700,000 patients. As Primary Care Groups are introduced the opportunity to secure good quality information at a more local level should be maximised. In addition there are various 'tailor-made' enhanced surveillance schemes at both local and national level that aim to link clinical and laboratory data to provide answers to risk groups, trends and outcomes.

Other Sources of Surveillance Data

Other sources of surveillance data include the special confidential reporting system for HIV infection and AIDS which has been mentioned in Chapter 3. In addition, Genito Urinary Medicine clinics make returns to the CDSC on a quarterly and annual basis about the incidence of sexually transmitted infections.

Data on vaccination coverage are collected by a local Immunisation Coordinator who is usually either the CCDC (or CPHM(CD&EH)) or a Community Paediatrician. In England and Wales these data are collated centrally and published by the CDSC. In Scotland the data are collated by ISD and published by SCIEH. The system is referred to as COVER (Coverage of Vaccination Evaluated Rapidly).

The Royal College of Paediatrics and Child Health houses the British Paediatric Surveillance Unit which carries out a small number of time-limited surveillance projects at a time, some of which might include communicable disease topics e.g., the United Kingdom and Republic of Ireland survey of haemolytic uraemic syndrome (HUS) in children.

In addition to these usual routes, information can be gleaned about previously unsuspected cases of communicable diseases from death notifications, from reports of sickness absence (e.g., during an influenza outbreak) or from hospital inpatient statistics.

Informal communications between the CCDC or CPHM (CD&EH) and colleagues are of paramount importance. A telephone call from a general practitioner, practice nurse, microbiologist, Environmental Health Officer, a colleague in one of the water companies, or school nurse yields rapid information and these links should be nurtured.

In an attempt to speed up the passage of information many health authorities are linked directly with their reporting laboratories by means of an electronic network. CDSC is also linked electronically to many reporting laboratories.

European Surveillance Schemes

A number of European networks for the surveillance of communicable disease have been funded by the European Commission. The CDSC coordinates some of these, including Enter-net (surveillance of salmonellosis and *E. coli* O157) and the European

Working Group on Legionella Infections (EWGLI). Problems detected abroad can provide an alert in Britain.

In the late 1990s there were plans to establish a European network for the surveillance and control of communicable diseases to coordinate surveillance across the European Union. The World Health Organization also maintains global surveillance systems.

Feeding Back Surveillance Data

At local level regular bulletins are distributed to local general practitioners, laboratories and environmental health departments. Regular surveillance bulletins are also produced at regional and national level. Information is fed back by means of a published weekly report containing, amongst other things, the notification data and details of isolates derived from hospital laboratories and the Public Health Laboratory Service. In addition to the weekly report, quarterly and annual reviews are also produced for various infections. Surveillance data are also posted on the PHLS Web site. In Scotland a weekly report is produced by Scottish Centre for Infection and Environmental Health.

Investigation of Communicable Disease Occurrences

The accounts of individual communicable diseases given later in this chapter illustrate the importance of thoroughly investigating people with symptoms suggestive of an infectious cause. In this way, the organism responsible can be identified (wherever possible), the most effective treatment instituted and other potential cases or contacts can be traced (if appropriate for disease control). The rapid identification of organisms which cause illness is also essential for good surveillance of communicable diseases in the population to enable control measures to be instituted.

It cannot be over-emphasised that the key to successful communicable disease control in the population is prevention. However, when cases occur, either singly, in small or in large numbers everything possible should be learned from such occurrences. In this way, control measures can sometimes be strengthened so that new incidents or outbreaks can often be ended rapidly thus minimising the numbers of people affected.

Whilst the circumstances of communicable disease occurrences will differ in practice, a number of general principles apply when approaching an investigation. The most common reason for starting an investigation is because of an outbreak. Whatever the circumstances, the aims must be to act quickly, to establish clear operational principles and to perform a sound investigation.

How Problems Come to Light

The way in which occurrences of communicable diseases prompt investigation varies. With good surveillance systems, a sudden upsurge in the incidence of a particular disease, clustering of several cases in a certain geographical area or the occurrence of one or two cases of a very rare disease, or unusual strain type, will be rapidly detected and could be the starting point for an investigation. Some incidents will come to light in other ways. For example, a call for help may be received from an hotel after a large number of guests have developed vomiting and diarrhoea. Similarly, enquiries from the media may be made to a health authority's press office after people in a locality have reported being ill. Outbreaks reported from abroad might have implications for United Kingdom citizens. A publication by a research team may draw attention to the unusually high incidence of a particular disease or a previously unrecognized causation.

Steps in an Investigation

Broadly, investigation of an outbreak involves three tasks. These are to describe the incident, analyse the data and give public health advice. The objectives of an investigation include:

- to identify the source and mode of transmission;
- to put in place control measures which will interrupt the chain of transmission;
- to prevent secondary spread;
- to provide advice which will prevent a further outbreak occurring under similar circumstances.

It should be borne in mind that the outcome of any outbreak investigation might result in the perpetrator being prosecuted. Whilst this is rarely a primary objective of an outbreak investigation it might be a consequence of it. This means that notes need to be kept assiduously; meetings including decisions need to be formally recorded and evidence needs to be gathered correctly. The decision to prosecute rests with the enforcing authority – usually the local authority Environmental Health Department (or equivalent) – and not with health officials.

Information needs to be collected which *describes the outbreak,* (i.e., the nature and timing of the illness, where people acquired the disease, and the characteristics of the affected people). This descriptive information often yields clues to the source of an infection and its means of spread, thereby allowing early intervention. When the source is not readily apparent a more detailed analytical approach needs to be undertaken. This will often involve comparing the exposures of people who became ill with those who did not. A variety of statistical techniques are used in such analyses. The results help to draw out inferences concerning transmission and exposure to disease.

The logical sequence of action in investigating an outbreak or epidemic is outlined in Figure 9.3.

The first requirement is to *confirm the existence of an epidemic or outbreak* and to *verify the diagnosis.* This involves the collection of as much information as possible about the disease and its characteristics. Information also needs to be assembled about the expected level of such an infection under normal circumstances, and about the population which is primarily affected. This preliminary exercise will help to determine the extent of any subsequent investigation and the urgency with which it is carried out.

It is important to involve microbiological experts at a very early stage. A microbiologist can ensure that the most appropriate arrangements are made for the collection and rapid processing of clinical and environmental specimens.

Environmental Health Officers of local authorities play a key part in the investigation process, particularly of food-borne outbreaks. Their areas of expertise include inspection of premises, knowledge about food hygiene and food preparation, collection of environmental and food samples for microbiological testing, and education of, for example, food handlers. The Environmental Health Officer will also be able to judge the relevance and quality of any risk assessment systems (e.g., Hazard Analysis Critical Control Point (HACCP)) and the adequacy of record-keeping as well as examining policies on, for example, pest control. Environmental Health Officers are also empowered to interview people under caution, i.e., to collect evidence which might be used later in court if a prosecution ensues.

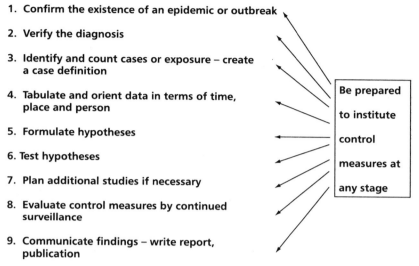

Figure 9.3 Steps in a communicable disease investigation.

1. **Confirm the existence of an epidemic or outbreak**

2. **Verify the diagnosis**

3. **Identify and count cases or exposure – create a case definition**

4. **Tabulate and orient data in terms of time, place and person**

5. **Formulate hypotheses**

6. **Test hypotheses**

7. **Plan additional studies if necessary**

8. **Evaluate control measures by continued surveillance**

9. **Communicate findings – write report, publication**

Be prepared to institute control measures at any stage

Source: Adapted from: Goodman RA, Buehler JW, Koplan JP. The Epidemiologic Field Investigation: Science and Judgement in Public Health Practice. American Journal of Epidemiology, 1990; 132:9–16.

The next step requires the *identification of the number of people affected and what they have been exposed to*. In order to do this, a working *case definition* must be created. A case definition will usually contain personal (clinical and/or demographic), temporal and geographical characteristics. When an outbreak presents the investigators might have a shrewd idea about the causative organism from a combination of the event which took place and the average incubation period. When constructing the case definition the incubation period range should be used in order to take account of what might appear to be unusually swift or late presentations.

It is surprising how often constructing a case definition is overlooked, but without it, highly misleading conclusions can be drawn from an investigation. For example, in an outbreak of food-borne illness in which people have presented with symptoms of vomiting, are people who report feelings of nausea to be counted as cases or not? In outbreaks of illnesses with ill-defined symptoms several case definitions may be used to test an association between illness and exposure, but great care must be taken to ensure that whichever case definition is used it is rigorously adhered to.

Case-finding methods will vary according to the severity or importance of the suspected disease and the setting in which the outbreak or epidemic has occurred. In a hospital outbreak, there is likely to be a clearly identifiable risk group. However, in a community outbreak this is likely to be far more complex, because people are widely dispersed. Cases are usually found either by locating other people who were exposed to the probable risk factor (for example, people on an affected aeroplane flight) or by contacting local doctors or hospitals. For diseases which do not have a clear presentation (for example, atypical pneumonia) extensive checking of possible cases, which may be recorded under a different diagnosis, on a local surveillance system or in clinical notes will need to be undertaken. This ensures that case ascertainment is as comprehensive as possible.

Once data have been collected they are arranged by time, place, and person, in the same *descriptive* epidemiological terms which are described in Chapter 2. When graphs of the occurrence of cases over time (an *epidemic curve*) are plotted it is frequently possible to distinguish different types of epidemic such as a *common or point source* (Figure 9.4), and a *propogated source* or person-to-person transmission (Figure 9.5). In the former there is a rapid upsurge to a peak and then a rapid fall-off. With the latter, the curve is much less steep and the period over which people develop symptoms is much longer either because people continue to be exposed to the infected source or because secondary cases occur.

Figure 9.4 Point source outbreak.

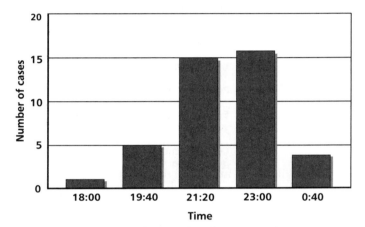

Note: A large number of cases appearing over the space of a few hours

Plotting data geographically can often provide a clue to the source of an infectious agent or the nature of exposure. This has proved particularly useful in determining the source of *Legionella pneumophila* in outbreaks of Legionnaires' Disease.

Arranging data by patient characteristics, such as age, sex or occupation may point to a particular risk group or mode of spread.

By this time, the investigators may have a very good idea about the organism responsible, and its source and mode of spread. It is still necessary, however, to determine the most likely exposure which caused disease. It is at this stage that hypotheses are formulated and those concerning causation are then tested by using appropriate *analytical epidemiological techniques*.

Care is required in choosing appropriate controls if either a *case-control* or a *cohort study* is undertaken. This reduces the risk of inadvertent biases. A discussion of the use of controls in studies of chronic diseases is contained in Chapter 2.

The precise method of gathering information from cases and controls will again depend upon the incident being investigated. With a group of tourists who are leaving shortly for their next travel destination the chosen method may be a simple listing of case details along one side of a grid and exposures down the other side. On the other hand, where there is less urgency the chosen method may be administration of a detailed, carefully constructed questionnaire. Whichever method is chosen, it is important that the interviewers ask questions in the same way so that one group of people is not prompted to remember more details than others, thus introducing an element of bias.

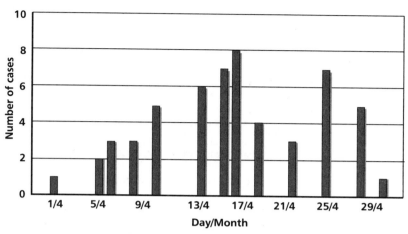

Figure 9.5 Propagated source outbreak where person-to-person transmission occurs.

Note that cases keep occurring over a long period of time; in this case over a month.

When investigating outbreaks of food-borne illness it is usual to compare exposure to different foodstuffs in those who developed illness and in those who did not. This is illustrated in the following example of an outbreak of food-borne illness amongst hotels guests in Brighton. The results of the investigation are shown in Table 9.2.

An outbreak of gastrointestinal symptoms occurred amongst a party of 136 elderly people who stayed in an hotel over the six day Christmas period. Sixty-eight people were ill. The authorities were notified about the outbreak after the guests had left.

A guest list was obtained. The guests were contacted and a standard questionnaire administered to them asking them about foods eaten and about symptoms. Stool samples were obtained from the 68 guests who had symptoms and from the nine food handlers on duty over the Christmas period. The hotel kitchen was inspected and information obtained about food handling practices, food supplies and cooking methods. Samples of food were taken but little remained from batches used over the period concerned.

Analysis of the food items revealed three which showed an independent, statistically significant association with the illness: chocolate mousse, lemon mousse and creme caramel (Table 9.2). All had been made with fresh eggs. The preparation of the mousse involved the heating of raw egg yolks over a low heat for two minutes. The creme caramel was baked in the oven for half an hour. *Salmonella enteritidis* was isolated from the stools of 29 of the 68 cases. A high proportion of these were submitted to phage typing and found to be *phage type 4*. Stool samples from food handlers were negative. No organisms were grown from the food samples which were taken. Kitchen practices were found to be good.

The investigators concluded that it was probable that the organism responsible for the outbreak was introduced into the kitchen via the eggs in the dishes containing raw eggs.

Table 9.2 An investigation of an outbreak of *Salmonella enteritidis* associated with the consumption of egg dishes

Food	Cases		Controls	
	Ate	Did not eat	Ate	Did not eat
Chocolate mousse	66	2	21	14
Lemon mousse	60	4	25	12
Creme caramel	55	9	24	13

Source: Franks CR, Harding BH, Jeffrey PA, Iverson AM, Thom BT. Communicable Disease Report 1990; (47):3 (internal publication of the Public Health Laboratory Service). Note: People who were unsure of what they ate are excluded from this analysis.

The report described is a good example of a practical investigation of a communicable disease outbreak. It should be noted that controls were members of the same hotel party. Some investigations would require controls to be chosen from other sources. Investigators also conclude the probability of the cause being eggs. Investigations establish associations; deciding whether the association is causal or otherwise is a separate process. The same rules of attributing causality apply in communicable disease investigation as in chronic disease investigation (See Chapter 2).

In outbreak investigation generally, having identified the probable source, it is important to revisit the facts and ask the following question: Does the hypothesis fit with the natural history of the disease in question? The clinical, laboratory, and epidemiological results together with those of any environmental investigations should provide a logical, biologically plausible explanation of the events which have taken place.

At this stage the investigation may be complete or the decision may be taken to conduct additional systematic studies. In any event, communicating the findings of an outbreak investigation is extremely important and the final report should contain details of the investigation, the findings and any recommendations.

Once control measures have been implemented, continuing surveillance must be put in place to monitor their effects. If the surveillance data suggest that the outbreak is continuing, despite the control measures implemented, the facts must be revisited and some, or all, of the steps described above repeated.

Instigating Control Measures

The question of when to instigate control measures during a communicable disease investigation can be very difficult. However, it is important both to investigate quickly using sound methodologies and have the best possible information available when taking such decisions. When in doubt, the balance should always lie with protection of the public.

Organisation and Management of an Investigation

All investigations involve teamwork so that coordinating the various team members is an integral part of the investigation. The exact composition of a team will depend upon the disease under investigation although core members are likely to include the CCDC (who usually leads) (or CPHM (CD&EH)) (who is also likely to lead the team), a microbiologist and an Environmental Health Officer. All Health Authorities and Health Boards have plans for dealing with outbreaks of communicable disease in the community. Similar plans exist in NHS Trusts for coping with an outbreak of hospital-acquired infection. These plans include:

- a description of the roles and responsibilities of the organisations and individuals concerned;
- arrangements for liaising with others outside the health authority including the Department of Health, reference laboratories, the CDSC, SCIEH or equivalent, the NHS Executive and neighbouring local and/or health authorities;
- the circumstances under which the outbreak control team (OCT) will be convened;
- the facilities required for an incident room;
- the arrangements in place for convening a group out of hours.

The plan will contain details of suggested membership out of an OCT, although this will need to be tailored according to individual situations, and will describe the terms of reference of the OCT. Many plans also contain a model agenda.

Good communication, both within the outbreak control team, and between the team and others is vitally important. Investigations flounder where communication is poor and this may have a detrimental impact on public confidence. An important point to bear in mind, particularly when dealing with a larger outbreak, is the relationship with the media. Possibly because of a fear of sensationalism by the local press, radio and television, many health professionals are apprehensive about having contact with the media. A single spokesperson should be appointed who is acceptable to both health and local authorities and should be available to the media at appointed times only. If either authority has a press officer he or she might be the right person to act as a spokesperson although members of the press often prefer to discuss such matters with a person who is medically qualified. In any case, it is essential that factual information is reported in an unbiased way. Reporters are quick to realise when relevant information is being withheld. They will not expect personal details about patients to be divulged but, otherwise, experience shows that a more accurate report is much more likely to result where the fullest possible information is released to the media. It is wrong to regard the media as a nuisance. Indeed, if good relations are established, particularly with local press, radio and television, this contact can be a great asset, helping, for example, to trace contacts or give health education advice.

Time is of the essence when investigating an outbreak or epidemic. The longer it takes to mount an investigation, the slimmer the chances of success. People's memories fade. The greater the time between the incident and the investigation, the lower the chances of confirming a diagnosis microbiologically. Depending on the infecting agent and the existence, or not, of a serological test vital environmental evidence might have been lost or destroyed.

Finally, outbreak investigations always provide the opportunity to learn for all concerned.

Classification of Communicable Diseases

Any classification of communicable diseases is necessarily arbitrary. No matter what system is used, some diseases will fit into more than one category. In this next section of the chapter, infections which could be placed in more than one category are described in detail once only, but cross-referenced where necessary. Not all the infections described are notifiable, but in order to keep up-to-date with this rapidly changing field, the important, emerging non-notifiable diseases are also discussed. The main features of some of the important infectious conditions encountered in Britain are described in sections which follow.

Emerging Infections

Certain communicable diseases are designated as emerging infections by the World Health Organization and warrant detailed investigation in order to determine their current and future impact.

Human Immunodeficiency Virus (HIV) and Acquired Immune Deficiency Syndrome (AIDS)

AIDS and HIV have been described in detail in Chapter 3. It is worth reiterating at this point, however, the fact that up to the end of 1998 nearly 37,500 people in the United Kingdom had been infected with HIV. Of those nearly 19,900 were reported as having an HIV diagnosis but had not progressed to AIDS; over 4600 had been reported as having an AIDS diagnosis but were still alive, and nearly 11,400 had died after developing AIDS. A small proportion of people had died without a report of an AIDS diagnosis. The success of anti-retroviral therapy has also improved survival with HIV infection, significantly increasing the interval between infection and the development of AIDS.

Transmissible Spongiform Encephalopathies (TSEs)

Creutzfeldt–Jakob disease (CJD) was first described in the 1920s. It is one of a group of diseases called transmissible spongiform encephalopathies (TSEs) which can occur in people or animals. The diseases are characterised by fatal degeneration of the nervous system.

CJD in its classical form is so far the commonest of the human TSEs but it is still rare with an annual incidence across the World of 0.5 to 1.0 cases per million population. In Britain, there have been about 35 cases per year. The average age of onset of classical CJD is between 55 and 75 years. Classical CJD has no known cause in the majority of cases. However, a minority of cases run in families (about 14%) and appear to result from mutations of genes. About 1% in the past have been transmitted as a result of medical treatments such as brain surgery, human derived growth hormone injections and corneal transplants.

The most highly publicised of the TSEs in recent years has been Bovine Spongiform Encephalopathy (BSE) because of its links to variant Creutzfeldt–Jakob Disease (vCJD), in humans. BSE is a progressive, lethal central nervous system disease of cattle, which exhibit changes in behaviour, loss of weight, loss of coordination and ataxia. There is no effective treatment. The first case in cows in the United Kingdom was recognized in 1985 and BSE was first identified as a new disease in November 1986. By the end of 1998, more than 173,000 cases of BSE had been confirmed in British cattle and more than 34,000 herds were affected. At the height of the epidemic in British cattle in 1993 the incidence of BSE was almost 1000 cases per week.

The precise nature of the agent which causes BSE is not known, but the main theory implicates an abnormal protein particle which has become called a 'prion'. Prion proteins are distributed throughout nature in normal circumstances. For example, they are found in the tissues of healthy people, animals and even in the yeast plant. It is believed that prions can cause disease when they become altered in shape, folding in an abnormal way. The abnormally shaped prion protein influences normal tissue to replicate its shape and leads to destruction of nervous tissue, particularly in the brain, giving it a 'spongy' appearance under the microscope. The pathogenic form of the prion protein is heat stable, less soluble than the normal form and is more resistant to enzyme action. A sheep TSE, Scrapie, has been an endemic disease in the UK for more than 200 years. There is still uncertainty about sheep TSEs and whether BSE may have transmitted to sheep.

It is generally agreed that the BSE epidemic in cattle was exacerbated by feeding rendered meat- and bone-meal (MBM) of bovine origin to cattle. The probability that vertical transmission of BSE could occur emerged in 1991 when, following a ban on MBM feed for ruminants (see below), a case of BSE occurred in a calf.

In 1990 the CJD Surveillance Unit was established in Edinburgh and in 1995 a new form of CJD was first suspected. Variant CJD (vCJD) in the United Kingdom is distinguishable from the classic form in a number of ways. It tends to affect younger people with a median age of onset of around 29 years. The predominant initial clinical presentation is of psychiatric or sensory problems, the onset of neurological abnormalities such as ataxia, dementia and myoclonus occurring later. The illness lasts between six months and two years before death. The definitive diagnosis of vCJD can only be confirmed by neuro-histopathological examination (usually post-mortem) and requires the exclusion of familial or iatrogenic causes of CJD. Since it was first described in 1995 to the end of October 1999 there were 48 deaths from definite or probable cases of vCJD in the United Kingdom (Table 9.3).

Table 9.3 Deaths from definite and probable cases of Creutzfeldt–Jakob disease (CJD) in the United Kingdom, 1990–1999, including variant CJD (vCJD)

Year	Sporadic	Iatrogenic	Familial	GSS	vCJD	Total
1990	28	5	0	0	–	33
1991	32	1	3	0	–	36
1992	43	2	5	1	–	51
1993	38	4	2	2	–	46
1994	51	1	4	3	–	59
1995	35	4	2	3	3	47
1996	40	4	2	4	10	60
1997	59	6	4	1	10	80
1998	60	3	3	1	17	84
1999*	39	4	0	0	8	51

Source: Department of Health press release, monthly CJD figures. Note: GSS = Gerstmann-Straussler-Scheinker Syndrome. * To 31 October 1999.

The government's Spongiform Encephalopathy Advisory Committee (SEAC) concluded that the most likely explanation for the emergence of vCJD was that it had been transmitted to people who had eaten cattle meat, organs or tissue infected with Bovine Spongiform Encephalopathy (BSE).

There is strong epidemiological and laboratory evidence for a causal link between vCJD and BSE including:

- no confirmed cases of vCJD in areas free of BSE;
- the interval between first human population exposure to potentially BSE contaminated food and discovery of vCJD is consistent with the incubation periods for some other types of TSE in humans;
- animal models: macaque monkeys inoculated with infected bovine brain

tissue developed neuropathological and clinical features similar to vCJD;
- laboratory analysis of prions causing infection in 10 cases of vCJD found to have similar molecular characteristics to those from animals affected by BSE. These characteristics were different from prions obtained from patients with other forms of CJD.

In the late 1990s new research provided further evidence that the agent which causes BSE is the same as that which causes vCJD. Measures to control the BSE epidemic in cattle were first introduced during 1988 when a ban on MBM feeds for ruminants and a policy to slaughter infected cattle were introduced. During the summer of 1989 the European Union banned the export of cattle from the UK. A wide range of measures to reduce the risk of cattle products infected with BSE from entering the human food chain were subsequently introduced.

Classic sporadic CJD has been transmitted iatrogenically by neuro-surgical instruments. Abnormal prion protein has been found in the lymphatic tissue (including tonsils) of patients who have developed vCJD. The possibility that the abnormal prion protein of vCJD might be transmitted by medical procedures led to control measures being introduced in the late 1990s to reduce the hypothetical risk of human-to-human transmission. These included the leukodepletion of blood for transfusion and the sourcing of blood products from countries outside the United Kingdom. Action was also taken to explore the possibility of using disposable instruments more widely in routine surgical conditions. Guidance is in place to ensure that precautions are taken when dealing with known and suspected cases of CJD and the disposal of instruments used in their care. A detailed account of all relevant guidance and action is beyond the scope of this book but such guidance is very extensive.

By the end of the 1990s there were a number of imponderables about vCJD including the timing and scale of a possible human epidemic but there is no doubt that BSE and vCJD are likely to occupy public health professionals well into the new century.

Helicobacter Pylori

Helicobacter pylori is one of a growing number of communicable diseases being linked with chronic disease causation, in this case peptic ulcer disease and gastric cancer. *H. pylori* is a spiral-shaped bacterium, related to *Campylobacter* (see below), and is found either adherent to the gastric epithelium or in the gastric mucus layer. It is estimated that about two-thirds of the world's population is infected with *H. pylori*. Although most people who are infected are unlikely ever to suffer symptoms, infection can be associated with chronic active, chronic persistent and atrophic gastritis in both children and adults. The organism is said to be responsible for approximately 80% of gastric ulcers and 90% of duodenal ulcers. It has been demonstrated that people infected with *H. pylori* are between two and six times more likely than uninfected people to develop gastric cancer and mucosal-associated-lyphoid-type (MALT) lymphoma. Gastric cancer is the second most common cancer globally.

Diagnosis of *H. pylori* infection is either by serology or by a urease breath test or by upper gastro-intestinal endoscopy with biopsy. In the latter case the organism can be cultured from biopsy specimens.

Treatment of *H. pylori* infection is by means of antibiotics in combination with acid-suppressing medication and eradication is successful in between 70% and 90% of patients, depending upon the drug regimen used. The two major reasons for treatment failure are antibiotic resistance or patient non-compliance.

The source of *H. pylori* and its routes of transmission are not yet known. It has been suggested that faecal–oral or oral–oral spread might be implicated and that contaminated water sources may serve as an environmental reservoir. Iatrogenic spread has been documented, occurring via contaminated endoscopes. This can be prevented by cleaning equipment properly. Until the source and routes of transmission of *H. pylori* are better understood it is difficult to give advice to the public about how to prevent infection. In the absence of specific control measures, however, it would seem prudent to reinforce the general principles about good personal and food hygiene.

Campylobacter

It might be argued that, with an annual incidence of around 70,000 cases in Britain, *Campylobacter* has emerged. It is, however, still recognized as an emerging infection. The importance of *Campylobacter* as a cause of gastroenteritis has been recognized relatively recently with the development of improved laboratory techniques for diagnosis. *Campylobacter jejuni* is a Gram-negative vibrio-like organism. *Campylobacter coli* is a similar organism which also causes illness in humans. Since it was first described in the late 1970s the incidence of *Campylobacter* infection in Britain has risen so much that it is now the most commonly recognized bacterial cause of gastroenteritis.

The incubation period for *Campylobacter* ranges between one and ten days (usually two to five days) and infection results in a range of symptoms but characteristically profuse diarrhoea (occasionally blood stained) occurs and is associated with very painful colicky abdominal pain. This can be alarming for those concerned (and often results in hospital admission) but usually it subsides and the person affected makes a full recovery. Guillain Barre Syndrome has been linked with *Campylobacter* infection, occurring rarely as a late complication of infection.

The source of the organism is probably the gastro-intestinal tract of poultry, cattle and pets. The mode of transmission is probably by food (for example, undercooked poultry), milk or contaminated water. In addition because the infectious dose is low, cross-contamination of ready-to-eat foods may also be a significant mode of transmission. Cases have occurred after drinking milk which has been pecked on the doorstep by wild birds (such as Jackdaws). One of the tantalising epidemiological conundrums relating to *Campylobacter* is, however, the fact that outbreaks of infection are seldom recognized. In part, this might be due to the absence, until recently, of a discriminatory laboratory typing scheme. Unlike *Salmonella* (see later), *Campylobacter* does not grow on food but, like *Salmonella*, it is heat-sensitive so adequate cooking should destroy it. Animal-to-person transmission (by direct contact) is generally regarded as an established route of transmison, whilst person-to-person transmission appears to be uncommon.

Verocytotoxin-producing E. coli O157 (VTEC O157)

Verocytotoxin-producing *E. coli* (VTEC) are a group of *E. coli* organisms (see later) which produce a toxin similar to *Shigella* (see later). This results in a spectrum of illness ranging from mild diarrhoea to profuse diarrhoea to bloody diarrhoea. Some cases are complicated by the development of the haemolytic uraemic syndrome (HUS). This usually affects children and may necessitate them undergoing renal dialysis. A proportion of these children will develop long-term renal damage. A particular serogroup of VTEC, *E. coli* O157 has been responsible for a number of reports of this type of illness in Britain.

Since it was first described in the early 1980s, the incidence of VTEC O157 infection in Britain has risen sharply to just over 1100 in 1998. The reservoir is predominantly cattle, in which the organism does not behave as a pathogen, although other farm animals have been discovered to be excreting the organism during outbreak investigations. There is also evidence that the organism might survive in the environment for a period of several weeks; for example, on pasture land. Outbreak investigations in Britain have shown that, whilst food-borne transmission is an important route of infection (undercooked ground beef, cold sliced meats, raw milk, untreated water) person-to-person and animal-to-person transmission are also important. The increasing vogue for children visiting open farms and city farms has brought outbreaks in its wake.

Whilst the incidence of VTEC O157 is still low compared with other gastro-intestinal pathogens there is no room for complacency given the very severe consequences of infection. There have been large, serious outbreaks of VTEC O157 infection in many parts of the world including, notably, an outbreak in Central Scotland in November and December 1996 which affected around 500 people and claimed 20 lives.

Antimicrobial Resistance

The issue of antimicrobial resistance is of global concern. Not only is antimicrobial resistance accumulating world-wide in many bacteria, but it is also emerging amongst viruses (*Herpes simplex* virus and HIV) and fungi (*Candida sp.*) as well. Of major concern in Britain are:

- **Methicillin-resistant *Staphylococcus aureus* (MRSA)**: *Staphylococcus aureus* is classically a cause of superficial or deep-seated wound infections. In 1944, when penicillin was introduced, over 95% of isolates were susceptible but this proportion has subsequently diminished to about 10%. During the 1950s resistance to penicillins and tetracyclines became a huge problem in hospitals. In order to overcome this beta-lactamase-stable penicillins were introduced in the 1960s (including methicillin and flucloxacillin) and, shortly thereafter, the first MRSA was recognized. Having sought therapeutic refuge with the aminoglycosides (e.g. gentamicin), gentamicin-resistant strains developed by the 1970s. Strains then emerged which had a peculiar ability to spread very easily in the hospital environment, so-called epidemic MRSA (EMRSA) some of which are highly invasive. A very worrying recent development has been the emergence of strains showing intermediate resistance to glycopeptides (e.g. vancomycin) in Japan, the USA and France. These strains show some resistance to all the available antimicrobial agents; unlike most other pan-resistant organisms, they pose a threat to patients who are immunocompetent, not only those who are immunocompromised.

- *Streptococcus pneumoniae*: *Streptococcus pneumoniae* is a leading cause of community-acquired pneumonia, septicaemia and bacterial meningitis. When penicillin was first introduced these organisms were highly susceptible. Low-level resistance to penicillin was first reported in the 1960s, with high-level resistance emerging in the late 1970s. High-level resistance has important therapeutic consequences, especially for the treatment of meningitis, where alternative antibiotics do not necessarily penetrate into the cerebro-spinal fluid as efficiently as penicillin. Resistance to macrolides (erythromycin) is also increasing.

- *Enterococci*: Part of normal gut flora, enterococci, which are usually harmless, pose a threat to immunosuppressed patients in hospital settings such a transplant units. The clinical spectrum of illness caused is broad, but in serious infections like septicaemia and endocarditis, enterococci prove very difficult to treat because of their high degree of antimicrobial resistance. They are intrinsically resistant to some antibiotics and readily acquire resistance to others. Penicillin and aminoglycosides (e.g., gentamicin) were used successfully in combination to treat infections due to enterococci until the mid-1980s when aminoglycoside resistance emerged. This left only the glycopeptides (e.g., vancomycin). In 1987 glycopeptide-resistant enterococci (GRE) first appeared in the UK and have rapidly spread in the hospital setting. Many GRE, especially *Enterococcus faecium*, are resistant to all currently available antibiotics so that the only recourse in serious infections is to use untested agents or untested combinations of agents.
- *Hospital-acquired Gram-negative rods*: The significance of Gram-negative rods is usually as opportunistic pathogens in immunocompromised patients in hospital and they cause considerable problems on intensive care units. Degrees of resistance vary according to the organism involved with *Escherichia coli* (a common cause of urinary tract infections in hospital and the community) and *Proteus mirabilis* being amongst the least resistant whilst *Enterobacter*, *Pseudomonas* and *Klebsiella* show much greater levels of resistance.
- *Salmonella* Salmonella typhimurium DT104: Concern about antibiotic resistance in *Salmonella typhimurium* dates back to the 1960s when a series of epidemics occurred in both cattle and man, a feature of which was increasing antimicrobial resistance. Following these epidemics an expert committee recommended that certain agents should only be available on prescription for veterinary use and that they should not be used added to animal feed as growth promoters. For a while after this the level of antibiotic resistance in *S. typhimurium* from both animals and humans subsided. However, a substantial increase in multi-resistant *Salmonella typhimurium* from food animals, particularly cattle, was again witnessed over a decade from the mid-1970s and coincided with an increase in multi-resistant isolates from humans. It followed the introduction of therapeutic antibiotics into veterinary practice which were very similar to those used in man. In the early 1990s a further upsurge in resistance occurred, due in large part to the epidemic spread of *S. typhimurium* DT104 which, at its peak, was widely distributed amongst food producing animals, not just cattle. This was quickly reflected in the human population such that, in 1996, 80% of isolates of *S. typhimurium* from humans were multi-resistant and the majority were DT104. Fortunately, the most common *Salmonella* found in man, *S. enteritidis*, remains generally sensitive to antibiotics. The use of antibiotics as growth promoters in the farming industry is a source of great concern and in the late 1990s efforts were being made in Britain and Europe to phase out their use.
- *Campylobacter*: Not much more than 10 years after their introduction, *Campylobacter* is demonstrating worrying levels of resistance to quinolones (e.g., ciprofloxacin).
- *Gonococci*: By 1944 the use of sulphonamides for the treatment of gonorrhoea was all but defeated by the development of resistance (sulphonamides had only been introduced in 1937). Penicillin resistance has developed much more slowly but there are now strains with the ability to produce penicillinase (designated PPNG) and these account for roughly 50% of *Neisseria gon-*

orrhoeae in the developing world. Although still uncommon in the UK at the moment, the emergence of strains resistant to tetracyclines and quinolones is being witnessed elsewhere.

- **Tuberculosis**: Tuberculosis is unusual amongst the bacterial infections in as much as it normally requires treatment with a combination of three or four antimicrobial agents in order to prevent the development of resistance. In order to be successful treatment needs to take place over a period of several months. Treatment with only one drug inevitably leads to resistance by selecting-out organisms which have spontaneously developed the ability to resist the drug, but even where combination therapy is used resistance may emerge due to factors such as incorrect prescribing patient non-adherence or malabsorption. Multi-drug resistant tuberculosis (MDR-TB) is defined by resistance to rifampicin and isoniazid alone or in conjunction with resistance to other drugs. Mortality from MDR-TB can be higher than 40% in HIV-negative patients and twice as much (80–90%) in HIV-infected patients. Multi-drug resistance in tuberculosis has been rare in the United Kingdom but there were two outbreaks of MDR-TB during the 1990s in hospitals in England, mainly affecting HIV-infected individuals. Outbreaks of MDR-TB in the United States have led to deaths amongst health care workers.

Combating antimicrobial resistance has become a major priority for government and the National Health Service alike. Several high-level committees have published reports detailing concerns about antimicrobial resistance including a House of Lords Select Committee and the Standing Medical Advisory Committee in 1998. Measures to tackle this important public health problem include stopping the use of antibiotics as growth promoters in animal husbandry, responsible prescribing by both the medical and veterinary professions, and educating the public not to expect antibiotic treatment for viral conditions such as the common cold and simple sore throats. An illustration of the range of measures which need to be addressed in combatting antimicrobial resistance is set out in Table 9.4.

Table 9.4   Key measures to reduce antibiotic resistance

- Keep antibiotics as prescription-only medicines
- Adhere to infection-control policies in hospitals and other health care facilities
- Raise professional, public and farming awareness
- Promote high-quality prescribing of antibiotics (and reduce their unnecessary use)
- Reduce use of antibiotics in farm animals
- Establish good surveillance of antimicrobial resistance

Gastrointestinal Infections

Food-borne Illnesses

Examples of diseases which can be transmitted by food are discussed throughout this chapter. This particular section deals with the specific causes of food-borne illness (sometimes called food poisoning) which result in the acute onset of symptoms, predominantly vomiting and/or diarrhoea.

The causal agents which are responsible for food-borne illness are bacterial (these will be considered in detail in this section), viral, parasitic and, relatively infrequently, other substances (for example, heavy metal, mushroom and shellfish toxins).

In Britain, reported food-borne illness caused by infectious agents continues to rise (Figure 9.6). Towards the end of the 1990s clinical notifications of food poisoning have risen to over 90,000 cases per year although this is likely to be a considerable underestimate of the true population burden of food poisoning. Estimates of under-reporting vary between 10- and 100-fold.

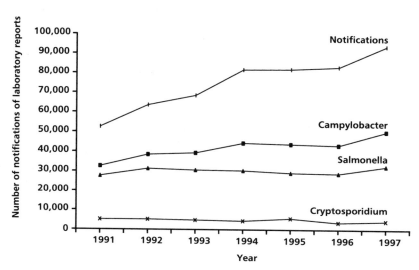

Figure 9.6 Notifications of food poisoning and laboratory reports of common food-borne (including waterborne) pathogens in England and Wales.

The increase in notifications may reflect an increased tendency on the part of the public to seek help when they have symptoms related to food poisoning, or an increased tendency of medical practitioners to investigate and report cases which presented to them. In addition, major changes have occurred in people's eating habits. With more women working outside the home, and the development of a more leisure-orientated society, there is a greater tendency for people not to cook at home. Despite these possible changes in reporting, the underlying trend in food poisoning is of a marked increase in cases and this is supported by an increased number of laboratory results of the major bacterial pathogens associated with food poisoning.

Salmonella Infections

There are some 2200 *Salmonella* serotypes which can cause illness in Man. In Britain, the reported occurrence of *Salmonella* food-borne infections increased sharply in the 1980s and has remained high ever since (Figure 9.6). Whilst part of the increase may be due to increased awareness, and hence greater reporting, it is nevertheless a matter of great public health concern.

One of the principal *Salmonella* organisms associated with illness in Britain is *Salmonella enteritidis*. Illnesses due to this one organism showed a very large increase in Britain in the mid-1980s. Illnesses caused by *Salmonella* organisms in food vary in severity. Common symptoms include fever, headache, abdominal pain, diarrhoea and vomiting. Illness usually lasts between one and seven days. However, infections can be fatal, particularly in the elderly or the very young.

Foodstuffs commonly implicated in outbreaks of *Salmonella* infection include undercooked poultry, pre-cooked meats, eggs (particularly dishes prepared with raw eggs), milk and milk products.

Clostridium Botulinum **Infections**

Toxin produced by the organism *Clostridium botulinum*, (a Gram-positive, anaerobic bacillus which produces spores that are very resistant to destruction by heat) is the cause of an uncommon but potentially fatal illness called botulism. The toxin affects the nervous system and can cause double vision, respiratory (and more generalised) paralysis in addition to vomiting and diarrhoea.

Classically, the illness is associated with the toxin accumulating in anaerobic conditions (for example, during home bottling or canning of vegetables) but it also occurs with smoked or preserved meats and fish. In the United States, outbreaks of botulism in infants have been associated with contamination of honey by spores of *Clostridium botulinum*, subsequent multiplication of the organism within the intestine and toxin formation (this is an unusual mechanism of acquiring botulism compared with primary ingestion of the toxin). In Britain, cases of botulism have been associated with foodstuffs as diverse as duck pâté and hazelnut yoghurt. The time between ingestion of toxin and the onset of symptoms is typically between five and 36 hours but can occur as early as three hours or as late as eight days.

Treatment involves the administration of antitoxin and intensive care, including respiratory support. If such care is instituted promptly and effectively then the case fatality rate can be reduced. Some people will still die from what is a very serious food-borne illness.

Bacillus Cereus **Infections**

Bacillus cereus is an aerobic Gram-positive bacillus which produces spores and is widely found in nature (for example, in soil and dust).

It produces two main types of illness both of which are self-limiting, almost always leading to a full recovery within a day or so. The first, called the *diarrhoeal type* usually takes longer for symptoms to appear (between eight and 16 hours) and gives rise to severe abdominal pain and profuse diarrhoea (often there is no vomiting). It arises from an enterotoxin which the organism releases into the bowel following infection. The second main presentation of *Bacillus cereus* infection, called the *emetic type* presents with sudden onset of vomiting relatively early (one to six hours) after ingestion of the suspected foodstuff. It is caused by a toxin produced by the organism and accumulated in the contaminated foodstuff prior to ingestion. Diarrhoea is much less common with this presentation.

The diarrhoeal type infection is associated with foods such as corn flour, sauces, soups and meat dishes which have been insufficiently heated. The emetic type infection is classically associated with rice which has been cooked, stored and reheated later.

Staphylococcus Aureus **Infections**

Staphylococcus aureus is a very commonly occurring Gram-positive coccus which causes a range of infections including superficial skin infections (for example, boils) and wound infections following surgical operations. It is a cause of food-borne illness by virtue of the production of a toxin (for example, after it has accumulated in a foodstuff following contamination by a food handler with an infected finger).

Ingestion of the contaminated foodstuff results in sudden onset (usually within one to six hours) of abdominal pain, vomiting and diarrhoea.

Foods commonly incriminated include those left at room temperature for the organism to multiply; for example, cakes, trifles, sandwiches and cold meats. Outbreaks are frequent in the summer when salad lunches and cold buffets are served out of doors, in marquees or pavilions at fetes, weddings or sporting events.

Clostridium Perfringens Infections

An illness with sudden onset of abdominal pain, nausea and diarrhoea (but not usually vomiting or fever) anything between eight to 24 hours after ingestion of a suspected foodstuff is characteristic of infection with *Clostridium perfringens* (an anaerobic, Gram-positive bacillus) which produces spores and is widely distributed in nature (soil and the gut of animals).

It typically occurs when poultry or meat dishes are inadequately cooked in the first place or reheated. The spores change into the vegetative form which multiplies during slow cooling, storage at ambient temperature or inadequate rewarming. The organism then produces a toxin when in the intestine. The illness usually lasts about 24 hours and is very seldom fatal (except occasionally in the elderly).

Yersinia Infections

Yersinia enterocolitica is a small Gram-negative bacillus which is found amongst wild and farm animals (particularly pigs), in water and sewage. It produces an illness with abdominal pain, diarrhoea and fever which is seen most commonly in children. The clinical picture can closely mimic acute appendicitis or mesenteric adenitis. Erythema nodosum can occur as a complication in up to one-third of adults who acquire infection.

The most common routes of transmission are contaminated milk or water or various foodstuffs. Another species of *Yersinia*, *Yersinia pestis*, whose reservoir is rodents, causes plague. Although a scourge of the past, it no longer occurs in Britain though it is still found in some parts of the world.

Cryptosporidiosis

Cryptosporidium is a protozoan organism with a parasitic life cycle which causes illness after the ingestion of the oocystic stage. It is a relatively commonly-reported cause of diarrhoeal illness (between 3000 and 5000 cases in England and Wales per year) and usually produces watery diarrhoea which does not usually last more than a month in immunocompetent individuals but can last much longer in immunocompromised patients. Waterborne transmission occurs and outbreaks have happened when treatment of the public mains water supply has failed. A large outbreak in the home counties in England occurred after drinking water from a borehole supply became contaminated. Expert committees have, amongst other things, reviewed the risks from domestic water supplies and have made recommendations for the control of cryptosporidiosis which may be transmitted either by direct animal-to-human spread or via contamination of water. The organism can also be spread from an infected person to others. Contact with farm animals associated with poor personal hygiene is a cause. For example, one outbreak which occurred in Britain resulted from a party of schoolchildren visiting a farm and eating food without first washing their hands.

Escherichia Coli Infections

Escherichia coli (E. coli) is a Gram-negative bacillus which is frequently found in the intestine of humans and animals. *E. coli* organisms are usually classified into broad groups in each of which there are many serotypes. *Enteropathic E. coli* (EPEC) cause outbreaks of diarrhoea in infants and are a particular problem when they occur in hospital neonatal or paediatric wards.

Enteroinvasive E. coli (EIEC) are very similar in their modes of infection to *Shigella* bacteria and occur in sporadic cases and outbreaks in similar circumstances to the latter.

Enterotoxigenic E. coli (ETEC) produce toxins and watery diarrhoea rather like that which occurs in cholera. They are a common cause of diarrhoeal illness amongst infants in tropical countries and in adults visiting tropical countries. They are one of the causes of traveller's diarrhoea and are acquired by contaminated food and water.

Verocytotoxin-producing *E. coli* (VTEC) were described in detail in an earlier section of this chapter.

Listeriosis

Listeria (more correctly 'Listeriosis') made headline news in Britain during the late 1980s when it was one of a number of food hygiene issues which aroused public concern and which led to urgent government action. The causative organism is a Gram-positive bacillus, *Listeria monocytogenes*, which is widely distributed in nature. The organism can grow at temperatures as low as those maintained in refrigerators, which is unusual for a microorganism. It is usually transmitted to Man via foodstuffs such as soft cheese, milk, pâté, cold meats, and cook-chill recipe dishes. It is mainly a danger to people whose immune system is impaired or to the very young, very old, and pregnant women. It is an important cause of neonatal septicaemia and meningitis and can spread from mother to foetus either *in utero* or through direct contact with mother's infected genital tract. *Listeria* infection in pregnant women may also cause abortion.

Non-bacterial Toxins

In addition to the many food-borne illnesses caused by toxins produced by bacteria, some toxins of non-bacterial origin can be ingested in foods (Table 9.5).

Table 9.5   Some causes of non-bacterial food poisoning

Toxin	Source	Comments
Muscarine	*Amanita pantherina, Amanita muscaria*	Toxin found in two of the more common poisonous fungi which can easily be eaten in error. Incubation period < 6 hours. Symptoms include diarrhoea, vomiting, abdominal pain, sweating, twitching, diplopia and convulsions
Amanitine	*Amanita phalloides* ('death cap')	Incubation period 6–24 hours. Symptoms include diarrhoea and vomiting, abdominal pain, jaundice and acute renal failure. Mortality 50–90%
Solanine	*Solanum tuberosum* (potatoes)	Incubation period is a few hours. Leads to headache, fever, abdominal pain, diarrhoea and vomiting. The alkaloid toxin is water soluble so peeling and soaking potatoes before cooking alleviates the problem
Scombrotoxin	Scombroid fish – tuna and mackerel. Also pilchards, herring	An increased histamine level in the fish leads to facial flushing, urticarial rash, nausea, diarrhoea and vomiting. Incubation period usually within 1–2 hours
Ciguatera fish poisoning	Toxin produced by dinoflagellates and accumulates within flesh of fish which feed on them	Incubation period usually within 1–2 hours. Causes nausea, diarrhoea, paraesthesia of mouth and feet, weakness of legs. Seen increasingly because of tendency to holiday in exotic locations. Barracuda is one of the fish implicated

continued ▶

Table 9.5 Some causes of non-bacterial food poisoning (continued)

Toxin	Source	Comments
Paralytic shellfish poisoning	Toxin produced by dinoflagellates which are eaten by shellfish. Toxin does not harm the shellfish but accumulates in the flesh	Incubation period 30 minutes to 12 hours. Symptoms include circumoral paraesthesiae, numbness of limbs, incoordination, dizziness, drowsiness. In extreme cases may cause respiratory muscle paralysis. Has been a problem in the last few years off the north-eastern coast of Britain
Tetramine*	Red whelks	Incubation period often less than 1 hour. Causes headache, dizziness, diplopia, incoordination and drowsiness
Nicotinic acid	Along with ascorbic acid added to minced beef to keep it pink	Dose-related incubation period. Causes rash and tingling of face and extremeties

Source: Christie AB (1987). *Infectious Diseases.* Churchill Livingstone: London (except * which is additional material).

The Prevention and Control of Food-borne Illness

A major reduction in the occurrence of food-borne illness could be achieved if well-established control measures were rigorously applied.

In practice this means enforcing safeguards and taking preventive action at all points in the food chain from the rearing of animals which are to be consumed by humans, to the process of food production, storage and distribution, its points of sale and preparation for eating. Concerted, coordinated action is, therefore, needed from 'farm to fork' and requires the cooperation of producers, the food and catering industries; several government departments and non-governmental bodies; the National Health Service, and local government. The need to tackle the prevention of food-borne disease across the whole food chain from producer to consumer was a major reason for the proposal to establish an independent Food Standards Agency. Legislation to establish this is planned for 2000.

There are control measures which are particular to individual organisms described in this section but the majority of measures are common to all.

Good animal husbandry, careful attention to the content of animal foodstuffs, the raising of *Salmonella*-free flocks of poultry, high standards of slaughterhouse hygiene and a range of other measures are essential steps in ensuring that, when food and drinks are consumed, they are free of harmful microorganisms and their toxins.

It is also important to ensure that strict control measures operate during the manufacture of food. Increasingly, food in Britain is bought in processed form. Whether this is as joints of meat or poultry, canned or frozen products or more elaborate heat and serve recipe dishes, measures to prevent food-borne illness must be built-in at all stages of the production process.

This has implications for the design of, and building materials used in, food processing plants; the type of equipment used and how it is maintained; heat and other treatments given to various types of food; the type and content of packaging materials; operating practices for, and training of, staff; and inspection and quality control procedures. Many of the same considerations apply to storage and distribution chains which should maintain the food in a hygienic condition in the interval between it leaving the production plant and reaching the shop, supermarket or catering outlet.

Enormous expenditure and extensive research and development takes place in these aspects of food technology, particularly by the major producers and suppliers.

Food hygiene and safety are an integral part of the food industry but the fact that there is such a large number of producers and suppliers, and the fact that even a small lapse can lead to a serious outbreak of food-borne illness, means that the task is one of constant vigilance and improvement of standards.

The storage, handling and preparation of food in the home, in institutions (such as hospitals, schools), in restaurants, cafes and other catering outlets is a vital issue for the prevention and control of food-borne illness. This will be evident from the accounts of individual causes of food poisoning earlier in this section of the chapter.

The following are the main principles and practices which are important:

- Maintenance of high standards of personal hygiene by those handling food (for example, washing hands before and after handling food, between stages of preparation and after going to the toilet).
- Separation of raw meat (which should always be regarded as potentially contaminated) from cooked meat and other foodstuffs. Avoidance of cross-contamination by using separate cutting tools and other utensils.
- Adoption of recommended standards in the design and layout of food preparation areas and kitchens.
- Keeping kitchen utensils, chopping boards and worktops clean. Cleaning again between stages of preparation and not using the same utensils and surfaces for preparation of raw and cooked food.
- Avoidance of transference of infection from the nose and throat by the fingers to food. Where cuts and sores occur, ensuring that they are covered.
- Exclusion of people with symptoms of food poisoning from food handling. Department of Health guidance on 'Fitness to Work' provides a framework for Local Authorities about periods of exclusion for foodhandlers who have been found to be suffering from infectious intestinal disease themselves.
- Attention to the temperature of storage. Fridges and freezers should be kept at the correct temperatures: below 4°C and below −18°C respectively. Thermometers should always be in place to check temperatures. Foods should not be maintained at room temperature for any length of time. High-risk foods should be held in the temperature danger zone (5°C to 63°C) for the shortest possible time. Cold foods (for example, salads, cream cakes) should be kept refrigerated and hot foods (for example, casseroles, meat dishes) should be kept hot (not warm). Frozen food, especially poultry, must be completely defrosted before cooking and, if possible, eaten immediately after cooking.
- Special care should be taken when cooking food for later use and when re-heating it. Cooling should be undertaken quickly using small quantities. Re-heating should not be undertaken more than once and should take place quickly and thoroughly. Raw foods, ideally in covered containers, should be stored at the bottom of the fridge to avoid dripping on to ready-to-eat foods.
- Shoppers should take chilled or frozen food home quickly and store it in the fridge or freezer rather than letting it stand in the car or office. It is good practice to use cool boxes, especially in the summer.
- Food should be allowed to stand for the recommended periods of time before serving after microwave cooking.
- Pets should be kept out of, and pests and insects should be eliminated from, food storage, display and preparation areas.

Ensuring proper adherence to these measures in all situations in which food is stored, prepared and served is clearly a major and difficult task. In the commercial context it requires that senior management is fully committed to food hygiene and safety and that all relevant staff are effectively trained and qualified. With the kind of transient workforces which exist in the catering and hotel industries this requires special effort. In addition, environmental health officers play a key role in education and in protecting the public.

Careful preparation of food in the home is just as important as it is for large-scale catering concerns. Even if foodstuffs are contaminated when they are bought, the measures listed above can be taken in the home to ensure that microorganisms do not cause illness either directly or through being spread to other foods.

It is essential that the public also receives information on specific issues; for example, about the risks of home bottling of vegetables and botulism (described earlier). The public needs also to be given specific advice on food-borne illness from time-to-time. For example, because of the risks of *Salmonella* transmission, current Department of Health advice to the general public is that it would be prudent not to eat raw eggs or uncooked foods made with them. To pregnant women, to the very young, to the elderly and to the sick the advice is that eggs should be cooked until the white and the yolk are hard before they are eaten.

The Law Relating to Food-borne Illness

In addition to general legislation relating to communicable diseases there is a large body of legislation relating to food hygiene and safety which is an important element in the range of control measures for food-borne illness.

The Food Safety Act 1990, and the many sets of legislation made under the Act, form the basis of this legislation. Most of this legislation is EU-based applying to all EU Members States, and also to non-EU countries who wish to trade with the EU in certain categories of foodstuff. In the UK the legislation applies to over 600,000 food businesses from slaughterhouses at one end of the food chain through to retail and catering businesses at the other end.

Under the Act, and its associated Regulations, it is a requirement that almost all food premises should be registered, licensed or approved depending on the nature of their trade. This provides local authorities, and other food enforcement bodies, with information to carry out inspections and enforce the law. With the exception of some limited categories of premises it is an offence to trade without being registered, licensed, or approved.

With its focus on consumer protection the Act, and its Regulations, place obligations on food producers and handlers to ensure the safety of food. It is an offence, punishable by fine or imprisonment, to place on the market food which could be injurious to health. The Act also provides a range of powers for enforcement action to ensure businesses meet these obligations.

In the case of a large-scale food poisoning outbreak, or evidence of widespread food contamination, where it is necessary, the Department of Health operates its national Food Hazard Warning Scheme. This is used to provide local enforcement bodies with information or advice necessary for action under the Act to investigate problems and ensure contaminated food is not sold to the public. Where appropriate, such action is undertaken in parallel with public warnings issued at local or national level to alert consumers.

Other Infective Causes of Vomiting and Diarrhoea

Illnesses characterised by vomiting, diarrhoea and associated symptoms are common in the population but not all are food-borne. Many are transmitted from person-to-person by the faecal–oral route or by droplets. Some of the organisms which can be transmitted in this way can also be food-borne.

This section of the chapter describes organisms which cause illness mainly through person to person spread, though the fact that they are not described in the previous section does not mean that some of them cannot also be spread by ingestion of food contaminated with the organism.

Viruses

A variety of viruses regularly cause diarrhoea and vomiting. A spectrum of gastro-intestinal symptoms in which viruses have been implicated has been recognized for many years and was often referred to as winter vomiting disease. Characteristics of viral gastroenteritis are that symptoms are sometimes severe but short-lived, lasting 24 to 48 hours and the incubation period is usually fairly short. Fatalities are rare but can occur in the elderly and the very young. Viruses are much more difficult to identify from specimens like faeces than are bacteria and are only present at the beginning of the acute stage of the illness so that reported cases undoubtedly grossly under-represent the true size of the problem.

The fact that people do not always present to medical care for these self-limiting illnesses, the fact that general practitioners treat symptomatically and do not collect samples, and the fact that viruses are difficult to isolate from human and food specimens means that their frequency in the population and other aspects of their epidemiology are not well understood.

Rotaviruses are RNA viruses which cause vomiting, diarrhoea and fever, mainly amongst children under five years of age. Rotavirus infection is a major cause of diarrhoea in children. The incubation period ranges from 24 to 72 hours and symptoms typically last for 4 to 6 days. The profuse watery diarrhoea in infants can lead to severe dehydration and death and rotavirus infection is a major cause of admissions to paediatric units during the winter months. Adults are less frequently affected. There are around 16,000 cases reported in England and Wales each year. Efforts to produce a vaccine against rotavirus are underway in order to combat this important cause of childhood morbidity and consequent hospital usage. Adenoviruses cause similar symptoms.

Another group of viruses which cause symptoms of diarrhoea and vomiting are the so-called 'small round structured viruses (SRSVs)', of which the most well-known is, perhaps, the Norwalk virus. The incubation period is usually 24 to 48 hours and symptoms typically last for about 48 hours. It is characterised by the sudden onset of explosive vomiting as well as diarrhoea. Whilst symptomatic, patients shed millions of virus particles into the environment which contaminate surfaces and appear to remain viable for some time, allowing them to infect others who pick them up on their hands etc. Small round viruses are an important cause of outbreaks in institutional settings like hospitals and nursing homes; they are also becoming an increasing problem for the leisure industry. Outbreaks in hotels or on cruise liners can be very difficult to control especially where susceptible people in the shape of new guests continue to be introduced at regular intervals, setting up the chain of transmission over and over again. The mainstay of control in all these settings relies on prompt and thorough cleaning of body fluid spillages and isolation of affected individuals. Even with rigorous regimens in place the chain of transmission can be very difficult to interrupt. Sewage pollution of shellfish is an important means of food-borne spread. The classic scenario is an outbreak following a romantic dinner on St Valentine's Day because of the consumption of raw contaminated oysters.

Dysentery: Bacillary

Shigella is a group of Gram-negative bacilli of which there are four species: *Shigella sonnei* which accounts for the great majority of cases of dysentery occurring in Britain; *Shigella flexneri* only an occasional cause of infection in Britain but found most frequently historically in hospitals for the mentally ill or those with learning disabilities; *Shigella boydii* and *Shigella dysenteriae* very seldom the cause of dysentery in Britain.

The disease has a world-wide distribution. In Britain, epidemics of *Shigella sonnei* occur amongst young and school-age children every seven years or so. During the last major epidemic over 17,000 cases were notified in England and Wales in one year (1992). In inter-epidemic years the number of notifications can drop approximately ten-fold. Outbreaks of sonnei dysentery are often associated with day and residential nurseries, nursery and infant schools.

There are many mild cases of this disease whilst others have few or no symptoms. When the full clinical picture occurs it is typified by diarrhoea of acute onset (with mucus, blood and pus in more severe cases), abdominal pain and fever.

The laboratory diagnosis of *Shigella* infection is made by isolation of the organisms from the faeces.

The incubation period ranges between 12 to 96 hours (usually one to three days) but can be up to seven days for *S. dysenteriae*. Patients are highly infectious during the acute stage of the illness and continue to excrete the organism for about four weeks after recovery. In a minority of cases, a chronic carrier state may develop.

The reservoir for infection is Man and transmission is by the faecal–oral route either directly or indirectly. The direct method is probably quite common. Young children carry the infection on their hands and pass it to other children or members of the family. Indirect transmission by ingestion of contaminated food or drink is also quite common.

In an established case, control measures include instituting standard precautions, including care in the handling of excreta from the patient. Bacteriological screening of well contacts is usually not necessary unless the contacts are food handlers or work in the health care field. Bacteriological screening of well contacts is not routinely recommended for *Shigella sonnei* but only for the other species.

General preventive measures include hand washing after using the toilet, the use of disposable paper towels, regular cleaning of lavatory door handles and seats and extra precautions in the preparation of food. Food handlers with bacillary dysentery should be excluded from work until three negative specimens have been obtained. In the event of an outbreak in a day nursery, all new admissions should cease and all infected children should be excluded. Three negative specimens are required before affected children may be readmitted. Once an outbreak is established in an infants school or nursery it is difficult to control the spread of sonnei dysentery even with the measures recommended. General environmental measures are less important in Britain but include adequate disposal of sewage and the control of fly populations.

Dysentery: Amoebic

Amoebic dysentery is caused by *Entamoeba histolytica,* a protozoan which can become a cyst with a tough, resistant membrane. In the human intestine it can emerge from the cyst in its active form and cause symptoms.

It is most commonly found in the tropics and subtropics. Most of the cases occurring in Britain each year are people who have contracted the disease in an endemic area overseas. A small proportion, possibly 2% of the population, are carriers.

The clinical presentation varies with many people remaining asymptomatic whilst others proceed to ulceration of the bowel and hepatic involvement. The classical clinical picture of amoebic dysentery is abdominal pain and recurrent attacks of diarrhoea containing blood or mucus. There are periods of remission and the cycle may continue for years. From this primary colonic site, in a small proportion of cases, the infection can spread to involve other organs (most often the liver). It is important to exclude amoebic dysentery when making the diagnosis of ulcerative colitis. The diagnosis is made by observing large amoebae-containing red blood cells on microscopic examination of specimens of faeces. Tests on sera are available but are positive in only a proportion of cases and, most importantly, do not identify the carrier state.

The incubation period is variable, most often two to four weeks, but can extend to months. Cysts may continue to be passed in the faeces for many years. Man is the sole reservoir either as symptomless excreter or with the chronic disease. The infection is transmitted by the cysts by faecal–oral spread. The usual vehicle is contaminated water or food – especially salads and raw fruit.

Provided proper precautions are taken in nursing the patient, no isolation is necessary nor is there any need for surveillance of contacts except to ensure that fellow travellers have not contracted the disease. The maintenance of good standards of personal hygiene and the exclusion of cases from food handling are important in preventing this disease, as is the provision of a pure water supply and an adequate sewage disposal system.

Enteric Fever

Enteric fever is cause by either *Salmonella typhi* (typhoid fever) or *Salmonella paratyphi* types A, B and C (paratyphoid fever). These are Gram-negative rods identical in appearance and only distinguished by different reactions in laboratory tests. An enteric fever-like illness can also be caused by other members of the salmonella family which usually cause gastro-enteritis.

The diseases occur in all parts of the world but endemic typhoid and paratyphoid has been virtually eliminated from North Western Europe, North America and Australasia. Imported disease, however, still occurs. The majority (approximately 90%) of the 100 to 200 or so cases of typhoid in Britain each year are contracted abroad, although cases of typhoid and occasional outbreaks have occurred indigenously. Similarly, most of the 100 or so notified cases of paratyphoid fever in Britain are contracted abroad.

The clinical picture of typhoid fever varies. Symptoms can include: pyrexia, headache, anorexia and constipation more often than diarrhoea. A classical rose-spot rash may appear on the trunk and enlargement of the spleen may also occur. Rarely, intestinal ulceration and perforation may occur. Paratyphoid fever has similar but milder symptomatology with a lower fatality rate. Clinical symptoms depend on the dose of the organism and a much larger dose is required to cause paratyphoid fever than typhoid fever. Sub-clinical cases of paratyphoid fever also occur. The laboratory diagnosis of the enteric fevers is made by isolating the organisms from blood culture (which is usually positive in the first week of illness) or from culture of faeces or urine (usually in the second and third weeks of the illness). Antibodies can be detected from the second week (Widal test) and a sharply rising titre in serial samples of sera confirms the diagnosis.

The incubation period for typhoid fever this is usually one to three weeks but can vary from three days to three months depending on the dose of organism. Paratyphoid infections have a shorter incubation period (one to ten days). Cases remain infectious for as long as the person excretes the organism, usually from the early stages of the illness until some weeks or even months after recovery. Up to 5% of typhoid fever cases become permanent carriers.

The reservoir of infection is Man. Usually the organism is found in the faeces but also can occur in the urine. A permanent residue of infection is the gall bladder and in extremely persistent carrier states where antibiotic therapy has failed surgical intervention to remove it may be considered. The mode of transmission of infection *par excellence* is by food and drink which have been contaminated by faeces of the case or carrier. Particularly implicated are those substances on which the organism can multiply: pastries, meat, milk, milk products, ice cream, raw fruit and vegetables. Contaminated water supplies have also been responsible for typhoid outbreaks.

Cases should be isolated and particular care should be taken when handling the patient's urine and faeces. Contact tracing is generally limited to identification and screening of contacts in risk groups – particularly food handlers. If the contacts are food handlers or work with vulnerable groups of people (for example, health care workers) they should be excluded from work during this period.

If the infection is traced to a food source, then a search should be made amongst the food handlers to identify the carrier. Special care must be taken to ensure that the recovered case does not return to food handling until clear of infection and many experts recommend that food handlers who have had typhoid should be found alternative employment if possible. Education of ex-patients about the risks of contaminating food is important.

Monovalent typhoid vaccine gives around 70% protection and is recommended for travellers to areas where typhoid is endemic, but it is important that travellers are aware of the risks, take precautions with their choice of food and do not drink local tap water. Other environmental control measures include adequate sewage disposal, the provision of a pure water supply and the control of flies and rodents. The public should be educated to high standards in food.

Cholera

The causative organism is *Vibrio cholerae*, a slightly curved and twisted (comma-shaped), motile, aerobic Gram-negative rod. The O1 serogroup includes two biotypes of *V. cholerae*: classical and El Tor. Both produce illnesses which are indistinguishable but they differ in laboratory haemolysis tests. The O139 serogroup has recently been recognized as a cause of outbreaks of cholera.

During the last several hundred years, classical cholera has been endemic in the basins of the rivers Ganges and Brahmaputra, from which it has spread repeatedly as pandemics to many countries of the world. Fatality rates have been high especially amongst the poor. A pandemic of the El Tor variant started in Indonesia in the 1960s and reached Western Europe. Britain has been virtually free of cholera during the present century except for the occasional imported case.

Evidence of the devastating effects which epidemics of the disease can still have in many parts of the world are seen from time-to-time on the television screens of the West when there are natural disasters (floods, earthquakes) or war. In such circumstances, sanitation can break down as people are displaced from their houses into makeshift and overcrowded camps. Cholera outbreaks then occur, often associated with huge loss of life, especially in the very young.

The characteristic clinical features of cholera are very severe diarrhoea with copious watery stools ('rice water') accompanied by vomiting and rapid dehydration. The latter causes death in a high proportion of untreated cases. The organism may be identified in cultures from specimens of vomit, faeces or in rectal swabs. A rise in antibody titre in paired samples of sera is helpful in confirming the diagnosis.

The incubation period is usually two to three days, although it may be as short as a few hours and as long as five days. The organism is excreted during the illness and for a few days after recovery. The carrier state is uncommon and usually lasts only a few months – in contrast to typhoid fever.

Man is the only known mammalian host, although recent observations from America, Bangladesh and Australia demonstrate that environmental reservoirs exist. Transmission is mainly by faeces contaminated water but also by food – particularly shellfish. Flies are not generally regarded as a significant vector although fly control is regarded as important in the epidemic setting, or in cholera wards. Direct spread from cases, carriers or contaminated objects is much less important. Gastric acid acts as a protector against infection.

Acutely-ill patients require hospital treatment with careful management to replace lost fluids and electrolytes but strict isolation is unnecessary. Surveillance of contacts is important and their stools should be examined for *Vibrio cholerae* for five days following the last exposure. Contact surveillance is of limited value, unless they have been exposed to the same source of infection. Screening of stools is not routine practice in the UK. Vaccination gives low protection and short-lived immunity and is therefore of limited value. No vaccine is currently available in the UK. People travelling to areas where cholera is known to be present should take precautions with drinking water, salads and other uncooked foods. The main environmental control measures are the protection of water supplies and supervision of disposal of sewage. Health education of food handlers and measures to protect food against flies are also important. In a country with modern water supply and sewage disposal systems, cholera is of almost no public health importance (aside from recognising occasional imported cases).

Respiratory Infections

A number of organisms described in this chapter cause respiratory infections. Acute upper respiratory infections are still the commonest manifestation of illness caused by communicable disease in the population of Britain. They range from colds, coughs, ear infections and bronchitis, to pneumonia. A wide range of organisms are responsible, most of them viruses. Although such illnesses occur throughout the year, most display a marked seasonal variation. Some common examples are: viruses causing the common cold (for example, rhinoviruses, myxoviruses, picornaviruses, coronaviruses); viruses causing sore throats (for example, ECHO virus, Coxsackie virus, adenoviruses); the Epstein-Barr virus which causes infectious mononucleosis (also called glandular fever); the respiratory syncytial virus which causes coughs, ear and chest infections; parainfluenza viruses which cause croup in children and other respiratory infections, and influenza.

There are no satisfactory control measures for this group of infections and action is directed at minimising the complications of the clinical syndrome by prompt diagnosis, symptomatic treatment and treatment of complications. Vaccine for influenza is the exception where there is scope for preventing infections.

Streptococcal Infections

Streptococci are Gram-positive, spherical bacteria which tend to form chains when they grow. An important feature which determines their classification is whether or not they produce haemolysis when grown on a medium containing red blood cells: complete (beta-haemolytic streptococci); or partial haemolysis (alpha-haemolytic streptococci) or no haemolysis at all. A further classification is made on the basis of antigenic differences in the components of the cell wall. On this basis beta-haemolytic streptococci are divided into a number of serological ('Lancefield') groups (A to G).

Group A beta-haemolytic streptococci are the most important human pathogen and often cause sore throats and tonsillitis. *Scarlet Fever* is now, fortunately, infrequent. More rarely the organism can result in a number of other infections: erysipelas, impetigo, puerperal fever, necrotising fasciitis or bacterial endocarditis. After a delay of several weeks, infection with the beta-haemolytic Group A streptococcus may result in acute nephritis, or rheumatic fever. These delayed manifestations are probably hyper-sensitivity reactions and not infections. They were much more common in the past but it is possible that they will again become problematic if virulence of the causative organism changes.

Haemolytic streptococci also cause other infections. Groups A, B and G cause several thousand cases of bacteraemia each year in Britain. The infection occurs in all age-groups but is particularly serious when it occurs in babies – especially premature babies. Much less commonly, the same groups of organism cause bacterial meningitis. Again, all age-groups are affected but the disease is a particular problem in neonates.

Streptococcal infection occurs in most parts of the world but is more common in temperate zones. Streptococcal throats are characterised by sudden onset of sore throat, fever and inflamed tonsils, with exudate and enlarged lymph glands. The tongue may have a strawberry-like appearance in the early stages of the disease. The main differential diagnosis is with viral infections of the upper-respiratory tract which are often clinically indistinguishable. If, in addition, an erythematous rash appears several days later scarlet fever is likely. At the beginning of the century this disease was a major cause of death of children but is now a milder, treatable illness. The more serious complications: bacteraemia, nephritis, meningitis, endocarditis, rheumatic fever are identified by the clinical manifestations characteristic of these conditions. The organism can usually be cultured from throat swabs, where the beta-haemolytic streptococcus will be seen surrounded by its characteristic zone of haemolysis. Blood cultures are taken where bacteraemia is suspected. Rising serum antibody titres may be helpful in aiding diagnosis.

The incubation period is usually one to three days. Most patients cease to be infective twenty-four hours after starting treatment with antibiotics, although in some, a persistent carrier state may develop.

The reservoir of infection is Man and transmission is by direct contact, droplet spread and via articles freshly contaminated with nasopharyngeal secretions. In the past, outbreaks have occurred through infected milk.

Isolation of the case is unnecessary because the patient becomes non-infective shortly after treatment is started but it is usual to keep close contacts under surveillance for a few days. In closed communities of children, prophylactic antibiotics should be considered.

Pneumonia

Pneumonia is a common cause of illness and death amongst the very young, elderly people and those with suppressed immune systems. A wide range of organisms can be responsible, the most important being *Streptococcus pneumoniae* (the *pneumococcus*).

Pneumonia is much less common in younger, previously healthy people. When it does occur in such circumstances, the common organisms are *Streptococcus pneumoniae* which may cause classical lobar pneumonia; *Mycoplasma pneumoniae,* which can cause pneumonia but is also much more commonly responsible for milder respiratory illnesses and Legionnaires' disease. In Britain, pneumonia tends to occur in small winter epidemics every four years or so. Conjugate pneumococcal vaccines are already under evaluation and first results suggest very high efficacy against invasive pneumococcal infection. A pneumococcal polysaccharide vaccine has been shown to prevent invasive pneumococcal infection but is not effective in children under 2 years of age. It is recommended for those at high risk of pneumococcal infection by virtue of underlying disease or immunosuppressive treatment, including those with an absent or dysfunctional spleen.

Legionnaires' Disease

This illness derived its name from 183 cases of pneumonia which occurred amongst nearly 4000 delegates attending an American Legion convention in Philadelphia in July 1976. The episode attracted wide publicity, particularly in view of the 15% fatality rate and it was intensely investigated. Many agents were suggested as being responsible for the outbreak, some of them fanciful, but it was eventually established that the disease was caused by a small Gram-negative bacillus (named *Legionella pneumophila*), previously unrecognized, which was isolated from the water in the air-conditioning system in the hotel. In all some 35 species of *Legionella* and about 45 serogroups have been identified. The predominant pathogen in Mankind is *Legionella pneumophila* serogroup 1.

Between one and two hundred cases are reported in England and Wales each year, mostly sporadic or in small groups. About half of the known affected people have acquired the infection abroad. A number of outbreaks have occurred.

An outbreak in which 101 people developed Legionnaires' disease (28 died from it) was associated with a hospital cooling tower in Stafford in 1985. The subsequent Committee of Enquiry made recommendations which form part of present policy to control the disease. Another outbreak affecting over 90 people in central London in 1988 was associated with a British Broadcasting Corporation (BBC) building.

The disease is most common in adults and whilst anyone can acquire the infection, those who smoke heavily, or who have a chronic disease appear to be at higher risk. Clinically, the condition is rarely distinguishable from other causes of pneumonia. Early symptoms are non-specific with fever, malaise, myalgia, headache and often diarrhoea. As the illness progresses the patient develops a high fever and non-productive cough which becomes productive. Chest signs are often unimpressive and not in-keeping with the marked changes observed on chest X-ray. The overall case fatality rate in patients admitted to hospital is about 10–15%. In addition to history and clinical features, diagnosis is made by culture of the organism from secretions, serological testing or by detection of urinary antigen (for *Legionella pneumophila* serogroup 1). Culture of the organism is difficult. Detection of urinary antigen is therefore a very useful diagnostic test since the antigen can be detected early in the illness (during the first 10 to 14 days) long before serology becomes positive. This speeds-up considerably the ability to mount a public health investigation.

The incubation period is usually between two and ten days (usually five to six days) but has been reported to be as long as 18 days. Person-to-person spread has not been demonstrated.

The bacterium is widely distributed in nature and often found in soil and water. Although not usually found in mains water supplies, it may become established in complex water systems in large buildings such as hotels, hospitals and office blocks. Surveys have shown that the organism is commonly present in systems of such buildings. The likelihood of this is increased by stagnation and water temperatures between 20°C and 45°C. Water-cooled air conditioning systems and the towers associated with them are another common source of the organism.

The presence of *Legionella pneumophila* in a system does not necessarily lead to an outbreak of Legionnaires' disease. Nevertheless, the main route of infection when it does occur, seems to be via inhalation of contaminated aerosols from, for example, cooling towers or from spa baths.

Since Legionnaires' disease was first recognized, and since the larger outbreaks occurred in Britain, a wide range of regulatory and standard-setting guidance has been put in place. This will continue to be updated as research into the organism and the disease continues. The key to control lies in preventive measures taken by those involved in the design, operation, supervision and maintenance of water systems and cooling systems – particularly in large buildings. Detailed codes of practice are available. Important aspects include regular inspection, cleaning and disinfection as well as careful temperature regulation. A cooling-tower registration scheme is now in operation to assist monitoring compliance and outbreak investigation.

A non-pneumonic infection with *Legionella pneumophila* also occurs: so called 'Pontiac Fever'. It has a much shorter incubation period (five to 66 hours) and, although the attack rate is much higher (approximately 95% in outbreaks compared with 0.1% to 5% for Legionnaires' disease), it is a much less severe illness from which patients recover spontaneously in about two to five days. Pontiac fever appears to arise as an allergic reaction to inhaled antigen, possibly from dead bacteria, rather than as a result of bacterial invasion.

Influenza

Influenza viruses are responsible for causing influenza. Three types have been identified. Epidemics are caused by types A and B. Type C is less common and associated with sporadic cases. The continual genetic evolution of influenza viruses with periodic major genetic changes (antigenic shift) enables their constant circulation.

The occurrence of influenza is world-wide. The very high fatality rate of the pandemic of 1918–19 (as many as 20 million people are estimated to have died worldwide) is thought to have been due to poor nutrition following World War I but it may have resulted from a virus of enhanced virulence. Later pandemics caused by different strains of the Type A influenza virus – the 'Asian' influenza pandemic of 1957–58 and the 'Hong Kong' influenza pandemic of 1968–69 – produced milder illnesses, but large numbers of fatalities occurred particularly in susceptible groups such as the elderly. Although sporadic cases are reported, large or small epidemics are the usual mode of occurrence. Some influenza occurs every year with larger outbreaks about every three to four years and peak occurrences in the winter months. Mortality is mainly confined to elderly people but the excess deaths from all causes which occur in the population at the time of an influenza epidemic can be very substantial.

The clinical picture is of sudden onset of headache, fever, muscle pains and respiratory symptoms which may be followed by secondary bacterial infection. Respiratory infections are often labelled as 'flu' when they are not in fact truly caused by the influenza virus. Indeed, the kind of upper-respiratory symptoms which occur with the common cold are not a feature of influenza. In the early stages of the illness, the virus may be grown in culture from throat or nasal swabs. An increasing level of antibody in paired sera at 10- to 14-day intervals may assist in making the diagnosis. A rare but important complication in children (given salicylates (aspirin) to reduce their temperature) is the development of Reye's Syndrome which affects the liver and the central nervous system. The use of aspirin is therefore contraindicated in children, particularly those under 12 years of age, with high fever.

The incubation period of influenza is short, usually one to three days and it is highly infectious – particularly during the early period of the illness. Adults are infectious for the first three to five days after clinical onset, and children a little longer, until about seven days.

The reservoir is Man, although Type A viruses have been isolated from horses, birds and swine. It has been suggested that changes in the genetic structure may arise from animal reservoirs or are mixtures of human and animal strains. Types B and C have been isolated only from Man.

Influenza is transmitted by droplet and airborne spread and directly by objects contaminated with fresh secretions from the nasopharynx. There is little value in isolating cases because of the large number of cases which occur in epidemics. Active immunisation with influenza vaccine is recommended for people at special risk of serious illness from influenza such as those with cardio-respiratory problems. UK influenza immunisation policy was extended in 1998 to include in the risk groups all those over the age of 75 years, regardless of whether they are suffering from chronic disease or not. The Chief Medical Officer issues guidance each year so that vaccination may be completed before the start of the influenza season. Immunisation is around 70–80% effective in giving protection to healthy young adults. It is less effective in the elderly, but although it does not necessarily prevent infection, immunisation modifies the severity of the illness. Regular changes in the antigenic profile of the virus mean that the vaccine components have to be reviewed each year. This is undertaken by the World Health Organization which monitors influenza activity globally in order to determine which strains are circulating and to advise on the antigenic components required for producing the vaccine each year.

Tuberculosis

Tuberculosis is caused by bacteria of the Mycobacterium tuberculosis complex: *Mycobacterium tuberculosis* (human type), *Mycobacterium bovis* (bovine type), or *Mycobacterium africanum*. Most tuberculosis in the United Kingdom is now due to *M. tuberculosis*.

Tuberculosis is endemic in most countries of the world and remains the most common bacterial cause of death in adults world-wide. The estimated incidence world-wide is 8 million cases with 3 million deaths annually, mainly in the developing world. In Britain, there had been a dramatic decline in the number of notifications and deaths from tuberculosis during the present century, but this trend began to plateau in the mid-to-late 1980s. This picture was observed in other developed countries as well. There are several reasons why this has happened including:

- increased immigration from high-prevalence countries. In immigrants to Britain, especially those of Asian origin, it has a much higher reported incidence than in the indigenous population (notifications of respiratory tuberculosis approximately 30 times higher; non-respiratory tuberculosis approximately 80 times higher);

- the emergence of HIV and consequent co-infection;
- the increase in homeless people and refugees living in overcrowded conditions;
- impaired immunity due to increasing age and chronic disease (e.g., diabetes mellitus, renal impairment).

The primary infection, if it occurs in childhood, usually occurs without noticeable symptoms. It is overcome with the body's natural defence mechanisms. The lesion becomes inactive, the person recovers and acquires tuberculin sensitivity and a degree of resistance to development of further disease. In a small proportion of children, progressive primary pulmonary tuberculosis may ensue. Rarely, a miliary form occurs in which the infection is widely disseminated through the body in the bloodstream, producing a serious illness in which there may be meningeal involvement. In the adult, pulmonary tuberculosis is the most important form of the disease and is the major source of infection for other members of the population. There is a clinical spectrum of severity but many cases may present only with a persistent, productive cough. Other symptoms include lassitude, fever, night sweats, loss of weight and haemoptysis. It is a chronic condition in which there is gradual erosion of the lung tissue with exacerbations and remissions. Diagnosis is confirmed by a chest X-ray and bacteriological examination of sputum. The adult disease is considered by many authorities to result from reactivation of lesions which have lain dormant since primary infection. A proportion of infections will also occur through first infection taking place in adult life, but the relative frequencies of such cases is not known.

Non-respiratory tuberculosis is also of importance, particularly in the Asian population, and may affect most systems of the body. Particularly common sites are lymph nodes (typically the cervical glands), the bones and joints and the genitourinary tract.

The time from exposure to development of a primary lesion can be one to three months, as demonstrated by a strongly positive tuberculin reaction. The development of secondary lesions may take years but the risk is highest within the first two years of infection.

A case is infectious as long as viable tubercle bacilli are produced in sputum. However, the degree of infectivity depends on the virulence of the organism, the closeness of contacts, the personal behaviour of the sputum-positive individual and the degree of immunity of the exposed person.

Man is the reservoir for the human type and cattle for the bovine type. Transmission is by droplets spread from an infected person; indirect spread is not thought to be important. Bovine tuberculosis is usually spread from drinking unpasteurised milk from infected cows. Pasteurisation of milk has largely eliminated this form of spread.

Strict isolation in hospital of all patients with tuberculosis is no longer necessary because appropriate chemotherapy quickly renders the organisms which are coughed up non-viable. They may, however, be demonstrated in the sputum on straining for several weeks after the commencement of antimicrobial therapy. Although outpatient treatment is the normal approach, inpatient hospital treatment may be indicated for certain clinical or social reasons and in the event of suspected or proven multi-drug resistance. In these circumstances appropriate isolation taking into account the likely infectiousness of the patient and the susceptibility of other patients, is essential. Detailed guidance has been produced by the Department of Health. Close contacts of all patients with tuberculosis should be traced and screened using tuberculin testing and/or chest X-ray if necessary. They may be the source of, or have acquired infection from, the index case. The need for further contact-tracing will depend on the individual circumstances of the case and the outcome of this first round of contact-tracing.

People who have or have had tuberculosis show a skin reaction to protein from the tubercle bacillus (tuberculin). This is administered either as a single measured dose injected intradermally (the Mantoux test) or in the form of small multiple punctures of the skin (the Heaf test). In each case, the skin reaction is assessed after a specified period of time. The degree of reaction to the test is the basis for a decision on further action. Strong reactors should be referred to a chest clinic for further investigation.

BCG vaccination, as a primary preventive measure, should be offered to negative reactors as follows: the infants of tuberculous parents; contacts of 'open' (sputum smear positive) cases; ethnic minority populations from high-incidence centres and their babies; health care staff and other occupational groups who may be at risk of exposure to infection; laboratory workers likely to deal with sputum or other infected body fluids; schoolchildren aged between 10 and 14 years; and long-stay travellers to tuberculosis high-endemic countries.

Pre-employment tuberculosis screening is recommended for special groups for their own protection and for those with whom they may associate, such as the nurses, doctors and special occupational groups already mentioned. Repeated routine X-ray examinations are no longer recommended. There have been examples of outbreaks of tuberculosis arising in children where the source of infection has been a teacher with tuberculosis. Mass radiography, which played a large part in reducing tuberculosis in the past, is no longer regarded as economic for use with the public at large.

Screening of new higher-risk immigrants to Britain should also be carried out.

Infections for Which Comprehensive Vaccination Programmes are Available

The childhood vaccination programme has, without doubt, been one of the most successful public health interventions in modern public, health bringing about huge reductions in morbidity and mortality from a range of communicable diseases in childhood, many of which were still major killers in Britain as late as the 1950s. This section describes those infections for which large-scale immunisation is available (Table 9.6). It should not be used as a practical guide for immunisation. Details of individual vaccines and their indications and contraindications can be found in a Department of Health publication on Immunisation against Infectious Disease which is regularly updated.[1] Tuberculosis is covered in the respiratory diseases section.

Table 9.6   Childhood immunisation schedule

Age	Vaccine	Comment
Birth	BCG Hepatitis B	High-risk neonates only High-risk neonates
2 months	Diphtheria, Tetanus, Pertussis (DTP) Oral Polio Vaccine (OPV) Haemophilus influenzae b (Hib)	Inactivated toxoids, killed organisms Live-attenuated viruses Chemical extract
3 months	DTP OPV Hib	

continued ▶

Table 9.6 Childhood immunisation schedule (continued)

Age	Vaccine	Comment
4 months	DTP OPV Hib	
12–15 months	Measles/Mumps/Rubella (MMR) (+ Hib if not previously given)*	Live-attenuated viruses
4–5 years (school entry)	DT OPV + MMR	
14 years	BCG (Bacille Calmette-Guerain)	Live-attenuated bacteria Given to tuberculin negative children.
15–19 years (school leaving)	OPV Td	

* If Hib has not been given before 12 months, then one dose should be given between 12 and 48 months of age.

Measles

The measles virus is a paramyxovirus. Measles occurs in all parts of the world. In developed countries it is usually a mild disease with a low mortality rate although a complication rate of 10% can be expected. In developing countries, with poorly nourished inhabitants, childhood mortality can be 10% or more. Until the introduction of mass measles vaccination, few people in Britain reached adult life without having had the disease. The use of the vaccine has altered the previous classical two-yearly epidemic and the number of notifications has fallen substantially (from 13,302 in 1990 to 3962 in 1997). Moreover the specificity of a measles notification is now very poor, i.e., most of those children notified as having measles in fact have another viral infection.

Infection with the virus produces a prodromal illness with upper-respiratory symptoms, pyrexia and spots (Koplik spots) on the buccal mucosa. Classically, the maculopapular rash appears on the fourth day of the illness but this is variable. The blotchy rash starts on the face and spreads over the body. Secondary bacterial infection of the respiratory tract and otitis media are common complications, encephalitis is rare. A very rare complication is sub-acute sclerosing panencephalitis which develops late (approximately seven years after infection) and results in death within a few months. The frequency of cases proceeding to complications has remained unchanged since the introduction of the vaccination programme. The diagnosis is usually made purely on clinical grounds. A proportion of notifications also have salivary antibody testing – approximately 2% are confirmed measles.

The incubation period is 7 to 18 days, usually 10 days. It is a very infectious illness particularly in the prodromal phase and the patient is infectious for four to five days after the appearance of the rash. The reservoir is Man.

Transmission is via droplet spread and directly by objects freshly contaminated by secretions from the nasopharynx.

Pertussis (Whooping Cough)

Pertussis is caused by _Bordetella pertussis,_ a small ovoid, Gram-negative coccobacillus which is difficult to culture and grows only on special media. It occurs throughout the world and epidemics of whooping cough tended to occur every four years; but since the early 1950s, when pertussis vaccine was introduced, their size has progressively lessened although the periodicity of epidemics remains. There were three major epidemics in late 1970s and early 1980s which were a consequence of the reduction in the uptake of pertussis vaccination. Loss of public confidence in the vaccine occurred when it was suggested that vaccination caused brain damage, claims which were subsequently shown to be invalid. Although the occurrence of the disease was at a generally lower level in the 1980s, periodic up-swings have occurred, including one at the beginning of the 1990s, leading to strengthened measures to achieve fuller immunisation uptake.

Pertussis begins with a slow onset of an irritating cough which progresses to paroxysmal attacks over a period of a few weeks and lasts for up to two months. The coughing attacks are accompanied by 'whooping' and vomiting. Pulmonary atelectasis and bronchopneumonia are common complications during the paroxysmal phase. Persisting low-grade infection encourages the development of chronic lung damage, bronchiectasis, but fortunately this has become a rare occurrence. Convulsions may occur in infants. Fatality rates are highest in children under six months. It can be difficult to diagnose and depends on the history given by the mother. Similar clinical syndromes can be produced by viral respiratory infections. Organisms can be cultured from carefully taken pernasal swabs if there is no delay in getting them to a laboratory, although the organism is isolated in less than half the swabs taken.

The incubation period is usually between six and 20 days. The patient is highly infectious during the catarrhal stages of the illness and for about three weeks after the onset of paroxysmal coughing. If treated with antibiotics, however, the infectivity period only lasts for about five days after the onset of therapy.

The reservoir is Man and transmission is mainly by droplet spread but also indirectly from objects contaminated by fresh discharges from the upper-respiratory tract.

The main control measure is prevention through the use of pertussis vaccine which is a key element of the childhood vaccination programme in Britain (the course of three doses is given at two, three and four months of age in combination with diphtheria and tetanus vaccines and Hib). Pertussis control requires vaccine uptake in excess of 90%. Although rates in Britain remained well below this level for many years, in part reflecting parental concern about the safety of earlier vaccines and litigation brought on the basis of allegations of neurological damage caused by them, vaccination uptake in the late 1990s was well above 90%. Although modern vaccines are regarded as extremely safe, research is continuing to create even safer ones.

The major concern is the protection of unimmunised and therefore susceptible infants, although the introduction of an immunisation schedule starting at two months of age should help to alleviate this problem. Although it is often advised that babies should be excluded from infected children such a measure is rarely, if ever, successful. There is an argument for protecting a vulnerable baby with a two-week course of antibiotics to stop them developing the infection. The child with the disease should be treated at the same time since erythromycin rapidly eliminates the organism, although it has little effect on the clinical course unless given in the catarrhal phase of the disease. There is increasing awareness of pertussis as a disease of adults, often responsible for infecting young unimmunised children.

Poliomyelitis

Poliomyelitis is caused by poliovirus (three serological types) which belongs to the enteroviruses. Type 1 is the most virulent, most commonly causes epidemics and is most often isolated from paralytic cases.

There has been a concerted world-wide effort to eliminate poliomyelitis by means of vaccination and world-wide eradication is now within reach. The only United Kingdom cases which occurred during the 1990s were vaccine-associated or imported when the individuals acquired polio outside the United Kingdom.

Most people who are infected with the virus remain asymptomatic whilst some develop an acute pyrexial illness in which the person affected may have a fever accompanied by headache, stiffness of the neck and gastro-intestinal upset. A minority of patients develop paralysis through involvement of the motor neurones. The diagnosis may be suspected on clinical grounds but every effort is made to confirm on laboratory evidence (e.g., viral cultures, antibodies). As we approach eradication of poliomyelitis the occurrence of a case of acute flaccid paralysis warrants detailed investigation in order to exclude wild poliomyelitis as the cause.

The incubation period is commonly 7 to 14 days, although it has been as short as 3 days and as long as 35 days. Poliovirus can appear in throat secretions as quickly as 36 hours after infection and in faeces about three days after infection. The virus is excreted in the faeces for three to six weeks or more although it can be isolated from the throat for only about a week after onset. The reservoir is Man.

The faecal–oral route is the major mode of transmission, especially in areas of poor sanitation. In areas of good sanitation spread by direct contact with pharyngeal secretions becomes much more significant. Vaccine-associated poliomyelitis has sometimes occurred when unimmunised parents have been changing the nappies of their immunised infants who are excreting the virus. This reinforces the fact that parents' immunisation status should be checked and they should be offered immunisation at the same time as their babies if necessary. They should also pay scrupulous attention to hygiene when changing nappies.

Isolation of the case is essential and contacts should be given booster doses of vaccine immediately. This is one of the few diseases where mass vaccination of all possible contacts in the neighbourhood is recommended as a control procedure in outbreak situations. In areas with modern sewage disposal systems environmental measures should not be needed.

Britain's immunisation programme is based upon a live-attenuated virus vaccine administered orally and very rarely the vaccine can cause the disease (see above). For this reason, the live-attenuated vaccine should not be used in people who are immunocompromised.

Rubella

The rubella virus is a member of the Togaviridae family of viruses. Rubella has a world-wide distribution. By the late 1990s rubella was no longer endemic and affected young men, not children.

The virus produces a mild febrile illness with upper respiratory symptoms, a fine macular rash, enlargement of the posterior cervical and occipital glands. The disease is easily confused with other viral infections and in many cases is sub-clinical. Its public health importance lies in the risk of the congenital rubella syndrome which affects infants whose mothers had the disease during the first trimester of pregnancy. Defects are rare in women infected after the twentieth week of pregnancy. At birth the infant can have a variety of defects which include cataracts, deafness, learning disability and cardiac abnormalities. In some cases these are mild and not detected for some years after birth at which stage it is too late to make a definitive diagnosis. Rising antibody titre can be demonstrated in paired sera with 10–14 day intervals during the 2–4 weeks following infection and specific Immunoglobin detected for a month or so.

The incubation period is usually 16–18 days with a range of 14–23 days. It is a highly infectious disease: the patient is infectious a week before and a week after the appearance of the rash. Babies affected by congenital rubella may shed the virus for months or years. The reservoir is Man and transmission is mainly by direct contact with droplets and respiratory secretions.

Prevention includes the fact that pregnant women should avoid contact with cases of rubella, but any pregnant woman who is in contact should undergo serological screening. The main control measure used to be a vigorous vaccination programme of schoolgirls between 11 and 13 years of age and women of reproductive age having no antibodies (sero-negative). It is important to remember that there is a risk in giving the vaccine in the early stages of pregnancy, hence its use is not recommended when there is a possibility of the woman being pregnant, although no cases of congenital rubella have so far arisen by this means.

The main thrust to eliminate the disease in the population of United Kingdom changed in 1988 with the introduction of a new immunisation policy to add to the existing policy. The live-attenuated rubella vaccine is now combined with mumps and measles as part of MMR (measles, mumps, rubella) vaccine given to all children at around 12–15 months of age or at school entry if not previously given. Staff working with pregnant women should also be vaccinated (for example, nursing staff, medical students, ambulance personnel).

Diphtheria

Diphtheria is caused by *Corynebacterium diphtheriae* which is a slender, Gram-positive rod. The organism produces a powerful exotoxin. The disease has a world-wide distribution but is more common in temperate climates. Largely due to the success of the immunisation policy in childhood, the disease is seen in Britain only as imported cases from time-to-time.

The disease is an acute upper respiratory tract infection which may affect the tonsils, pharynx, larynx or nostrils and also the skin. The characteristic feature is the presence of a greyish membrane in the throat firmly attached and surrounded by inflammation with enlarged cervical lymph glands. The main hazards (which may cause death particularly in the untreated case) are local obstruction of the respiratory passages (by the membrane) and the effects of the exotoxin on the myocardium and on the peripheral nervous system (most seriously leading to paralysis of the respiratory muscles). Throat or nose swabs are taken from the suspected case, carrier or contact and the organism is identified after culture on a suitable medium. Once isolated, the Corynebacterium should be tested for toxigenicity by injection into guinea pigs or by *in vitro* diffusion techniques. Serum antitoxin levels may further assist in diagnosis. Treatment and control measures should be taken without waiting for laboratory confirmation.

The incubation period is two to five days, although it is occasionally a little longer. Cases are seldom infectious beyond four weeks, especially with effective treatment but, rarely, a chronic carrier can shed organisms for six months or more. The reservoir is Man.

Transmission is by direct contact with another human case or carrier, usually by the airborne route, may be spread by discharges, or by fomites (inanimate objects).

In order to control the spread of diphtheria the person infected is isolated and treated with antitoxin and suitable antibiotic therapy. Close contacts should have nose and throat swabs taken and be kept under surveillance for seven days. The non-immune are immunised with the toxoid and prophylactic antibiotics may also be of value. Nose and throat swabs may identify carriers who are then also isolated and treated with antibiotics until the carrier state no longer exists. Articles that have been in close contact with the patient should be disinfected especially those which may have been contaminated with nasal or oral secretions.

Vaccination is an important control measure so non-vaccinated children should be given a full course at once and others a booster dose. If immunisation levels fall, there would be a risk that diphtheria might once again occur in epidemic form, particularly as a result of the infection being imported from parts of the world where it is still common. The key control measure is the maintenance of a high level of immunity in the child population by means of an effective immunisation programme. All children are offered vaccination at two, three and four months of age as well as boosters.

Tetanus

This serious illness is now relatively rare in England and Wales, largely due to active immunisation of children. The causative organism, *Clostridium tetani*; a Gram-positive, anaerobic spore-forming bacillus, is widely distributed in nature and is commonly found in soil. The organism is introduced into the human body by a penetrating injury; for example, during gardening. In anaerobic conditions, the spores germinate producing a powerful exotoxin which is neurotoxic. This process takes three to 21 days depending upon the severity of the wound. The average incubation period is about ten days. The patient develops painful muscular contractions initially affecting the facial and neck muscles, but going on to involve the muscles of the trunk. Involvement of the respiratory muscles leads to compromised breathing. In untreated cases mortality is high (approximately 60%). Treatment of a patient with tetanus involves surgical debridement of the wound, the administration of antitoxin, antibiotics and sedative, and intensive care nursing. People who have injured themselves, in circumstances when they may have been exposed to tetanus, should have the wound cleaned and be offered vaccine (depending upon their immunisation history) and immunoglobulin. Long-term prevention of tetanus depends upon the childhood immunisation regime.

Mumps

The mumps virus, a paramyxovirus, is spread by droplets or by direct contact with the saliva of an infected individual. The incubation period is usually about 18 days but may be as short as 12 days or as long as 25 days. The child becomes unwell with a headache, sore throat and a fever, after which the salivary glands, particularly the parotids, become inflamed. The virus persists in the saliva for several days after the onset of parotitis. Sub-clinical infection occurs in some children, and is important in perpetuating the spread of the virus.

Mumps infection may be complicated by orchitis in post-pubertal males, oophritis in post-pubertal females, meningitis or encephalitis, and rarely, pancreatitis. Permanent deafness is a rare consequence of mumps meningoencephalitis. Routine vaccination of children is the means of controlling mumps.

Haemophilus Influenzae

Haemophilus influenzae is a fastidious, Gram-negative bacillus. Non-capsulated strains of the organism are not invasive and tend to cause secondary infections of the respiratory tract. They are the commonest cause of otitis media in children. Of greater significance, however, are the six capsulated strains, which produce invasive disease.

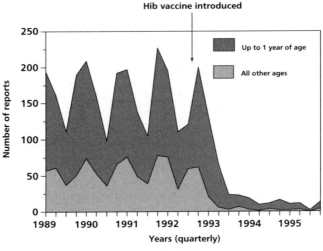

Figure 9.7 Reports of *Haemophilus influenzae* Type b (Hib) in England and Wales.

Source: PHLS, CDSC.

Haemophilus influenzae b infection (also known as Hib) used to be the most common bacterial cause of meningitis in children under the age of five years, with a peak incidence at ten to eleven months of age. A major breakthrough in protecting children against infection by *Haemophilus influenzae* b occurred with the successful development of a conjugated vaccine which confers high levels of immunity even in very young children. The vaccine was incorporated into the United Kingdom's childhood immunisation programme in October 1992 and is administered at two, three and four months of age. The incidence of Hib has plummeted since vaccination was introduced (Figure 9.7).

The disease often had an insidious onset with malaise and a high temperature before the characteristic features of meningitis appear: vomiting, headache, neck stiffness and, in infants, a bulging fontanelle. The incubation period is thought to be short (two to four days). The infection is spread by secretions from the respiratory tract which remain infectious for as long as the organisms are present, but are rendered non-infectious 24 to 48 hours after the commencement of antibiotics. Person-to-person spread, giving rise to secondary cases, does occur. The attack rate was estimated at around 5% prior to introduction of vaccine, in children under four years of age, being those most at risk. For this reason antibiotic chemoprophylaxis is recommended for all household contacts (including adults) of the index case where there are other unimmunised under-fours in the family. It should also be considered where two cases occur in children in the same nursery class, but advice on the use of prophylaxis in this specific situation should be sought from the local CCDC or CPHM (CD&EH).

In addition to meningitis, Hib was also responsible for producing other invasive diseases such as epiglottitis, pneumonia, cellulitis, septic arthritis and osteomyelitis.

Childhood Infections for Which Vaccination is not Currently Available

Chickenpox

Chickenpox is caused by the varicella-zoster virus which is a member of the herpes virus family. It is a very common infection world-wide, usually causing a mild illness in children. Chickenpox is one of the most highly infectious diseases occurring in humans and spreads rapidly and readily. It is characterised by the development of fever and a rash which first appears on the trunk. The rash is flat to start with (macular) but swiftly becomes vesicular. The vesicle fluid contains virus particles, although the skin lesions are not as infectious as secretions from the respiratory tract. Transmitted mainly by this means, it is most infectious a couple of days before the onset of the rash up to about five days after the first crop of vesicles appear. The incubation period is usually two to three weeks but can be seven to 26 days.

Usually a mild illness, chickenpox may have a profound effect in immunocompromised individuals who may suffer a fatal attack. Occasional deaths in otherwise healthy adults occur because of varicella pneumonia. Neonates are at risk of a severe generalised infection as are pregnant women. Varicella zoster immune globulin (VZIG) is indicated in certain circumstances for non-immune pregnant women and for neonates who have been exposed to chickenpox, but it is in short supply, and its use is strictly limited – specialist advice must be sought.

Herpes zoster, commonly known as shingles, tends to occur in older adults and is a local manifestation of reactivation of the chickenpox virus. The commonest distribution of the zoster rash is along the skin supplied by the intercostal nerves or over the face in the innervation of the ophthalmic branch of the trigeminal nerve. Severe ophthalmic zoster can permanently damage the cornea. Zoster infection can be treated with antiviral agents (e.g., acyclovir) which can abort an attack or shorten both the duration of symptoms and the pain associated with herpes zoster infection.

Herpes Simplex Infection

Although primary infection with herpes virus can occur at any age, it is most common in young children. Most primary infections are subclinical and it is only when the latent virus is reactivated forming the typical 'cold sores' that it is apparent that the individual is infected. In young children, however, primary infection can be manifest as a very painful acute ulcerative gingivostomatitis. Whether as a result of primary or recurrent infection, the lesions are highly infectious. The virus is usually spread by direct personal contact such as kissing. Health care workers such as dentists may develop lesions on their hands if a patient is excreting virus, the so-called herpetic whitlow.

The incubation period for herpes virus infection is two to 12 days. Halting the spread of infection depends upon avoiding contact with people who have lesions.

In recent years it has been recognized that two forms of herpes virus hominis exist. Type 1 infection leads to the problems described above, whilst Type 2 tends to be sexually transmitted and causes genital herpes, although either virus can cause genital herpes.

Cytomegalovirus Infection

The importance of this infection, caused by another of the herpes virus group, is in the severe manifestations which can result from congenital infection. As many as 5 to 10% of congenitally infected neonates are estimated to develop significant learning disability and permanent blindness.

Infants are frequently found to have microcephaly, cerebral calcification and chorioretinitis. In addition, the spleen and liver are affected and sometimes also the kidneys. The virus may be excreted in the child's urine for several months after birth.

Cytomegalovirus also causes profound problems in immunocompromised patients such as transplant recipients and in individuals infected with Human Immunodeficiency Virus. The incubation period for herpes virus infection is two to 12 days. Halting the spread of infection depends upon avoiding contact with people who have lesions.

Parvovirus Infection (Erythema Infectiosum; Fifth Disease; Slapped Cheek Syndrome)

Infection with human parvovirus B19 is now probably one of the commonest childhood causes of viral exanthem and is probably mistakenly notified as measles or rubella, more often than not. It causes a characteristic erythema on the cheeks (hence slapped cheek syndrome) and a lacy-looking rash on the trunk. The reservoir is Man and transmission is predominantly through contact with infected respiratory secretions. The incubation period varies between four and 20 days. The infection is usually self-limiting; although rare, severe complications include transient aplastic crisis. In around 10% of cases of intrauterine infection in the first half of pregnancy fetal anaemia, hydrops foetalis and fetal death can occur.

Infections Leading to Hepatitis

Hepatitis A

Hepatitis A virus is a human picornavirus. Infection is very common in the early years of life in the developing countries of Africa, Asia and Latin America, and in some around 95% of children will have been infected by the age of five years. The seroprevalence rates in Western Europe are considerably lower having fallen during the last few decades of the twentieth century; thus an increasing number of adolescents and adults in such countries remain susceptible to hepatitis A infection. Travellers are at greater risk of acquiring infection as they move to areas of higher endemicity.

Many infections with the hepatitis A virus produce no marked symptoms or cause a very mild illness. Other cases have anorexia, abdominal discomfort and pyrexia but no jaundice. Others develop jaundice which may result in a mild illness lasting about a week or a severe illness lasting several months. Recovery is slow in the latter instance but most cases make a complete recovery. Rarely, the disease can involve serious clinical manifestations, including hepatic failure. Hepatitis A is more common in children, but also affects adults who usually have a more severe illness. The clinical diagnosis of hepatitis A may be suggested by the history and clinical features but confirmation depends upon the finding of IgM antibody to hepatitis A virus during the acute phase of the illness.

The incubation period is 15–50 days (usually 28–30 days). The person is most infectious during the latter half of the incubation period and the early stages of the illness. Most people are not infectious after the first week of jaundice. The reservoir is Man and some other primates. Transmission is by person-to-person mainly by the faecal–oral route. Generally the disease occurs when hygiene is poor; for example, in those schools or nurseries where handwashing is not observed and lavatories are kept in a poor state of cleanliness. Transmission has been recorded between male homosexuals. Contaminated water and food act as vehicles and a variety of foods have caused outbreaks – notably shellfish such as mussels, oysters and clams, although these outbreaks are becoming increasingly rare.

Strict isolation of the patient is unnecessary because the stools are virus-free shortly after the jaundice appears. However, it is usual to adopt the standard precautions in handling urine, faeces and blood from the patient. Surveillance of close contacts, new cases and undiagnosed cases should be carried out. It is often difficult to trace the source of an outbreak. The long incubation period and the frequency of mild or asymptomatic illness are reasons for this. There is little to be gained from excluding contacts from school but it is wise to remove young people (who are the most susceptible) from food handling for six weeks. A high standard of personal hygiene is especially important when infectious hepatitis is prevalent.

Although human immunoglobin may give protection for about three months in special circumstances (such as before travelling to endemic areas or as a prophylactic measure after exposure), the protection afforded by immunoglobulin is falling as a consequence of the low incidence of disease (people are not being exposed). Travellers to endemic areas are therefore offered vaccination. The general environmental measures of providing uncontaminated water supply and adequate sewage disposal are important in preventing the spread of infection.

Hepatitis B

Hepatitis B virus is a hepadnavirus. The disease occurs throughout the world. In some individuals hepatitis B virus persists resulting in chronic infection, the risks being inversely proportional to the age of acquisition, i.e., around 80–90% in neonates but only around 5% in immunocompetent adults. Chronic carriers of hepatitis B, defined as the presence of hepatitis B surface antigen (HBsAg) in the serum for six months or longer, are at increased risk of developing progressive liver disease, including cirrhosis and hepatocellular carcinoma. In Britain, seroprevalence of HBsAg is low but varies geographically. For example, the prevalence among antenatal women varies between 0.05% in areas such as East Anglia and 1% in some parts of London. In Southern Europe the carrier rate is up to 5% and in the tropics 10%. In parts of the Far East, some 10–15% of people may have serum which is positive for HBsAg. Although notifications of acute hepatitis B are small in Britain (730 new cases in 1997) seroprevalence varies within population subgroups (up to 4% in homosexual men) and might expected to be higher in inner cities. Most of the carriers in Britain have no previous history of jaundice.

Patients typically present with gradual onset of 'flu-like' symptoms such as malaise, anorexia, nausea, vomiting, abdominal discomfort and aching of muscles and joints. A rash may occur in this early phase of the illness but fever is not usually a prominent feature. Clinical jaundice may then ensue or the patient may remain anicteric, the diagnosis being made by liver function and other tests. The fatality rate and likelihood of permanent liver damage in hepatitis B is higher than with hepatitis A infection. In the latter, almost all patients make a full recovery.

Three antigenic components of hepatitis B virus have been identified each with associated antibodies:

(1)   The surface or capsule antigen (HBsAg) also referred to as the Australia antigen can be detected by various techniques including radioimmunoassay and electron microscopy; it appears in the late incubation period before the onset of symptoms and remains present in both acute and chronic infection. The appearance of its antibody, anti-HBs, is generally associated with loss of infectious virus in those recovering from infection and also occurs in response to hepatitis B immunisation.

(2)   The core antigen (HBcAg) is not directly detectable in the serum; however, its antibody (anti-HBc) is present during active infection and also persists after recovery and is thus a marker of previous exposure to hepatitis B; the IgM component of anti-HBc predominates during the acute phase and anti-HBc-IgM can be used to detect recent hepatitis B infection.

(3)   The e-antigen (HBeAg) occurs when there is ongoing active viral replication and is associated with higher infectivity. Chronic carriers with low levels of viral replication are seronegative for HBeAg and seropositive for its associated antibody (anti-HBe) and are less likely to transmit infection.

The incubation period is 45–180 days, with an average of 60–90 days. The individual is infectious as long as hepatitis B surface antigen (HBsAg) is present in the blood. Chronic cases of hepatitis B should not donate blood. The reservoir is Man and possibly other primates. Hepatitis B can be transmitted from another case or more often a carrier either parenterally or sexually. Transmission may occur through heterosexual and male homosexual intercourse, intravenous drug abuse, tattooing, acupuncture, ear-piercing and medical and dental instrumentation. It is an occupational risk for health care workers and those involved in handling blood products and dialysis equipment. Hepatitis B can be transmitted from infected mothers to their babies at or around the time of birth (perinatal transmission). Blood transfusion is an unlikely method in Britain as strict screening of donor blood is now carried out.

Isolation of cases is not necessary but strict precautions are required in the handling and disposal of blood and excreta. Close household and sexual contacts of a case of acute hepatitis B or a chronic carrier of the virus should be screened for hepatitis B markers and immunisation offered to any who are neither immune nor infected. Follow-up of individuals who may have been exposed to hepatitis B infection from a point source, such as a tattooist or to a breakdown in infection control, to detect any who may have been infected, is indicated. It may be too late for post-exposure prophylaxis to be effective in many cases, but those exposed could become possible sources of infection for their own close contacts. General preventive measures include adequate precautions as part of the normal routine in all places handling human blood and its products. This includes the correct disposal of used syringes in all settings in which they are used. Specimens must be labelled 'High Risk' and sent in special containers. Special risks apply to patients and staff of renal units where vigilance should be especially high. Many renal units manage HBsAg-positive patients, most often in isolation from other patients and using dedicated machines. Whilst some might feel that infected patients would be better managed at home, patients will need to be admitted to be trained in the use of dialysis; in any case not all patients would be suitable for home treatment. The screening of potential blood donors for the carrier state has already been mentioned. Health education is important amongst special and high-risk groups such as drug takers and male homosexuals. Adequate sterilisation of instruments should be undertaken and, wherever possible, disposable needles and instruments should be employed and used once only for each patient. There is a clear need also for close supervision of tattooing, body-piercing and acupuncture. Sometimes screening procedures are also carried out on drug addicts and male homosexuals. Patients who are HBsAg-positive should be educated about the mode of spread of the disease and counselled as to behaviour to reduce the risk of transmission.

Perinatal transmission of hepatitis B infection can largely be prevented by the appropriate immunisation, commencing at birth, of infants born to infected mothers. Individuals in groups at increased risk of acquiring infection (for example, injecting drug misusers, homosexual and bisexual men, close family contacts of a case or carrier, and health care personnel) should be immunised. Specific hepatitis B immunoglobulin is available for passive protection and is normally used in combination with hepatitis B vaccine to confer active/passive immunity after exposure (for example, after being pricked by a needle from an infected person) or when immediate protection is required.

Hepatitis C

Hepatitis C virus (HCV) is a leading cause of chronic liver disease world-wide and is the principal cause of parenterally transmitted non-A non-B hepatitis. The infection is spread by injection of blood, blood products or serum (thus it can be contracted by intravenous drug abusers). Diagnostic tests were developed following discovery of part of the genome in 1989 and all blood donations are now screened. Seroprevalence amongst current or past intravenous drug users can be high in some countries and they are likely to be the main group of infected people in the UK. The incubation period is two weeks to six months (usually 6 to 9 weeks). The initial symptoms are usually mild. The majority of patients are unlikely to have jaundice. Hepatitis C leads to chronic infection in about 80–85% of people infected, of whom approximately 70% may develop chronic liver disease with persistently raised liver enzymes. Chronic HCV is a risk factor for cirrhosis and primary hepatocellular carcinoma. There is, as yet, no vaccine against hepatitis C so that prevention rests upon education and avoidance of exposure to the virus.

Hepatitis D (Delta Hepatitis)

Since hepatitis D virus (HDV) requires the presence of hepatitis B for replication, it is always associated with coexisting hepatitis B infection. HDV infection is therefore either acquired simultaneously with HBV (co-infection) by those susceptible to HBV, or subsequently (superinfection) by those who are carriers of HBV. Both natural and vaccine-induced immunity to HBV protect against infection with HDV. Like hepatitis B, the infection is spread by exposure to infected blood or body fluids. The incubation period is between two and eight weeks.

Hepatitis E

Hepatitis E is endemic throughout much of Asia and in some parts of Africa, the Middle East and Central America; cases in the United Kingdom have been most often associated with a history of recent travel to the Indian subcontinent. Hepatitis E shares characteristics with hepatitis A and is spread by the faecal–oral route and large outbreaks have occurred in some endemic areas in association with faecally-contaminated drinking water. The incubation period is 15–64 days and the clinical picture is very similar to hepatitis A. There is no evidence that infection with hepatitis E leads to chronic disease. Hepatitis E is a diagnosis of exclusion and diagnostic tests are still being refined.

Infections Leading to Meningitis

Meningococcal Infections

Meningococcal disease is caused by *Neisseria meningitidis* (Meningococcus) is a Gram-negative diplococcus. Five main serogroups exist A, B, C, W and Y. Most infections in Britain are caused by either Group B or Group C meningococci.

Meningococcal disease has a world-wide distribution. In Britain, *N. meningitidis* is responsible for causing meningitis and septicaemia which occur both as sporadic cases and in localised outbreaks, particularly in children and young adults. Overcrowded living conditions facilitate its spread. For example, outbreaks occur in boarding schools and military camps where young people are living and sleeping in close proximity.

During the 1980s, a persistent pocket of high incidence of meningococcal infection with fatalities occurred in Stroud, Gloucestershire. The reason for the higher frequency in this area was not elucidated. It gave rise to great public concern, extensive media coverage and the formation of pressure groups which called for more action and research to combat the disease. Almost 3000 cases of meningococcal disease are notified each year in England and Wales (as meningitis or meningococcal septicaemia). Notifications of meningococcal septicaemia in England and Wales rose sharply during the 1990s from 273 in 1991 to 1440 in 1997 although this was partly thought to be due to better ascertainment and a lower clinical threshold for notification. Also during the 1990s there was a shift in frequency of infection from Group B to Group C so that in 1998, 60% of infections were due to Group B and 40% due to Group C. There was also a shift to more cases and deaths in the 15–19 year age-group.

Nasopharyngeal carriage of the organism in asymptomatic individuals can be surprisingly high with up to 15–20% of individuals being carriers in some age-groups. The overall prevalence lies somewhere between 2–4% of the population.

The incubation period ranges from two to ten days, usually three to four days. The patient is infective for as long as the organism is present in the nasopharynx. Penicillin (the antibiotic of choice in the treatment of meningococcal disease) suppresses the organism but does not eradicate it. This is important since it means that people who have recovered from meningitis should receive a second antibiotic (usually rifampicin) to eliminate nasopharyngeal carriage of the pathogen.

The reservoir is Man. Transmission is by droplet spread following close contact with a carrier of *N. meningitidis*. Only capsulated strains have the capacity to cause invasive disease. Carriage of non-capsulated strains and other commensal *Neisseria species* can help to boost natural immunity. Long-term carriers of pathogenic strains rarely become cases themselves. Their natural defences have learned to cope with the organism.

In cases where meningitis does develop, symptoms are fever, headache, neck stiffness and photophobia. Acute septicaemia, which is rapidly fatal if untreated, is often accompanied by a haemorrhagic rash which does not blanch under pressure (e.g. if a glass is rolled over it). This may range from petechial, purpuric, to ecchymotic. Other symptoms may occur, such as backache and muscle pains and other organs (for example, joints, heart) may be involved. However, septicaemia can occur without typical signs of meningitis and flu-like symptoms general malaise can rapidly lead to deterioration and death. The laboratory diagnosis is made by observing the organism on direct microscopy of cerebrospinal fluid; by isolating the organism from culture of cerebrospinal fluid (CSF) or blood, or by detecting fragments of the organism's genome in blood or CSF by non-culture techniques – e.g., polymerase chain reaction (PCR).

The administration of antibiotics, even before admission to hospital, is vital to reduce mortality from this disease. The organism can be identified by non-culture techniques so administration of antibiotics should not be delayed in order that it can be grown in culture. Regular health information campaigns are necessary to make the public and parents aware of the symptoms of both meningitis and septicaemia.

Action rests largely with the general practitioner or Accident and Emergency unit in early treatment. Household contacts and other intimate contacts (for example, kissing contacts) should be traced and offered antibiotic prophylaxis as soon as possible after the diagnosis has been made; preferably within twenty-four hours. The use of antibiotic chemoprophylaxis is usually limited to people who came into close contact with the infected person in the five days prior to the onset of the illness.

The purpose of antibiotic prophylaxis is to eliminate carriage of meningococcus in the nasopharynx of the close contacts of the case. The fact that a case has occurred usually means that someone in their immediate circle is a carrier of the organism. Antibiotic prophylaxis thus reduces the chance of this carrier causing another case of disease. It is thus a population measure designed to reduce carriage. The indiscriminate use of antibiotics can do more harm than good. They may eliminate harmless, commensal *Neisseria* from the nasopharynx which, whilst present, not only boost natural immunity but also prevent pathogenic strains from gaining a foothold. This is especially the case in small children who tend to be carriers of *Neisseria lactamica*. Clearing carriage of these strains can, paradoxically, leave children open to becoming infected with pathogenic strains. The decision to widen antibiotic prophylaxis beyond close contacts, the only group in which there is compelling evidence of benefit, therefore needs to be taken with care.

Vaccines are available against Group A and C (and the less common Y and W135 Groups) and for most of the 1990s was used on a selective rather than a population basis. The purpose of vaccination was to protect against an individual's increased risk of developing invasive disease with one of these strains when involved in an outbreak. These polysaccharide vaccines are less suitable for use on a population basis for a number of reasons including:

- protection is short-lived;
- the age-group at highest risk of developing disease is not protected. The polysaccharide vaccine has been used in outbreak settings but the management of such outbreaks require specialist help and advice.

At the end of the 1990s conjugated Group C vaccines became available for the first time and their incorporation into the routine childhood immunisation schedule was commenced. The absence of an effective Group B vaccine (research is continuing) is a serious gap in the public health weaponry to combat meningococcal disease. General environmental measures include the avoidance of overcrowding and the maintenance of good ventilation, particularly in sleeping quarters in closed communities containing children and young adults. Here carriage rates may be high. Passive smoking is also a significant risk factor.

Haemophilus Influenzae B

Haemophilus influenzae b meningitis was discussed in the earlier section on infections for which comprehensive vaccination programmes are available.

Streptococcus Pneumoniae (Pneumococcus)

Although a less common cause of meningitis than *N. meningitidis* and *H. influenzae* B, pneumococcal meningitis is important because of its high associated mortality (20–40%). It occurs at all ages, but is the commonest bacterial meningitis occurring in the over 50-year-old age-group. The source of the infection may be an existing respiratory tract infection. Meningitis can occur rarely as a result of direct extension from chronic otitis media. The current pneumococcal polysaccharide vaccine is unsuitable for children under two years of age as it is not immunogenic at this age. New vaccines where the pneumococcal polysaccharides are conjugated to a protein are showing very encouraging results in clinical trials in young children.

Listeriosis

This rare but important cause of neonatal meningitis has been covered in the section on food-borne illnesses.

Other Organisms

In addition to bacterial meningitis, a variety of other organisms cause the disease. These include viruses (for example, mumps, enteroviruses, herpes simplex); mycobacteria (*M. tuberculosis* and *M. bovis*) and, much more rarely, leptospires and fungi (cryptococcal meningitis usually occurs in immunocompromised people including those with Human Immunodeficiency Virus).

Hospital-acquired (Nosocomial) Infection

Since the end of World War II there has been considerable concern about the frequency of infections acquired by patients whilst they are in hospital (nosocomial infections). This is despite improved methods of sterilisation of equipment and wider adoption of aseptic techniques. The factors involved in this are numerous and include:

- the emergence of resistant strains of organisms (partly due to the increased use of antibiotics) – this is described in an earlier section of this chapter;
- the greater survival of patients with life-threatening illness (for example premature infants) who are more susceptible to infection;
- the wider use and complexity of surgical techniques;
- the advent of modern therapies (such as immuno-suppressive drugs) which lower host-resistance;
- changing use of health services.

Surveys of infection in hospital inpatients in Britain have found huge variation in infection rates, of which almost half had been acquired in hospital. Urinary and wound infections, which are especially likely to develop whilst the patient is in hospital, tend to be endogenous (i.e., a break in the patient's natural body defences causes the patient's own normal bacterial flora to induce infection). Nosocomial infections often lengthen the patient's stay in hospital with attendant economic implications both for the individual and the service as a whole. Many organisms, some of which are usually commensals, can cause problems for debilitated patients in hospital settings and a number of these were discussed briefly in the section on emerging infections. There are two infections which deserve a special mention here.

Methicillin-resistant Staphylococcus Aureus (MRSA)

The evolution of multiple-antibiotic resistance in *Staphylococcus aureus* has been described earlier in this chapter. The main problem with MRSA in the hospital setting is the fact that staff or patients colonised represent a hazard to other patients. *Staphylococcus aureus* is a skin commensal which is carried by about 30% of the population. All staphylococci, including MRSA, are easily spread by direct contact and persist in the environment. Where patients are constantly being moved from ward-to-ward, or in and out of nursing homes and back into hospital MRSA can spread very rapidly. The primary problem in hospital is, therefore, one of cross-infection. Infection is not trivial and MRSA can cause deep-seated wound infections which prove very difficult to treat. It can wreak havoc on orthopaedic units and, if a joint prosthesis becomes infected, there is usually little choice but to remove it. Certain MRSA strains also produce powerful toxins like enterotoxins or toxic shock syndrome toxin. Invasive infection with these strains carries a very high mortality.

Nosocomial outbreaks of MRSA can be very difficult to control. Effective control measures include:

- identifying and treating carriers;
- isolating those with infection;
- strict adherence to stringent hygiene policies in hospitals including rigorous environmental cleaning.

Clostridium Difficile

Clostridium difficile is part of normal gut flora and causes problems when the use of antibiotics promotes bacterial overgrowth and toxin production. Laboratory reports of the identification of *Cl. difficile* toxin in faecal specimens in England and Wales have risen dramatically between 1986 and 1997 (594 to 12,150 respectively) although there is undoubtedly an element of increased ascertainment playing apart in this dramatically increasing trend. Like other clostridia, *Cl. difficile* produces spores which can persist in the environment and environmental contamination has been implicated in generating or perpetuating outbreaks in hospitals and nursing homes which can prove very difficult to control.

Although much nosocomial infection is human in origin, coming from other patients, staff or visitors, the source may be either human or the hospital environment (for example, dust, air-conditioning systems or instruments).

Endogenous infection is by far the commonest infection which develops in hospital patients, particularly as a result of surgical procedures or other instrumentation (for example, catheterisation). Cross-infection is classically thought of when hospital-acquired infections are mentioned and this may arise either by contamination of instruments or by transmission of pathogenic organisms on the hands and uniforms of doctors and nurses. Similarly, doctors and nurses who carry organisms in their nasopharynx can induce infection in patients. Environmental infection, occurring when organisms can survive and multiply within the hospital environment, is a potential source of problems. Obvious hazards are places like the ward sluice, but more subtle are antiseptic solutions and disinfectants, or even sometimes medication like eye-drops or parenteral feeds.

It should not be forgotten that some people who develop an infection in hospital might have acquired it at home in the community and have been admitted during the incubation period of illness.

In general terms the control of hospital-acquired infection usually involves isolation of cases (and carriers). There is no single effective control measure but continuously high standards of hygiene are essential and education of staff is necessary to achieve this. Designers of hospitals should be mindful of the risk of infection at all times. A high standard of building maintenance should be observed. Strict adherence to a routine of cleaning premises is needed. When an outbreak involving a highly infectious agent occurs, it may be necessary to close the ward to interrupt transmission and allow for cleaning and disinfection.

Occupational and Environmental Hazards

Leptospirosis (Weil's Disease)

Leptospira is a spirochaetal organism which has two species: *Leptospira biflexa* and *Leptospira interrogans* with many different serotypes. Two main serotypes cause most cases of disease in Britain – *Leptospira icterohaemorrhagiae*, and *Leptospira hardjo*.

The disease is a zoonosis which occurs in all parts of the world. In Britain it was traditionally associated with sewage workers and is now seen in farm or abattoir workers or, less commonly, amongst butchers, pest-control workers and veterinary workers. Contact with water contaminated by animal urine causes the disease. Canoeing and other water sports account for a substantial minority of the cases which occur each year. Imported infections also occur.

The clinical manifestations are sudden onset of pyrexia, headache, severe muscular pain and sometimes vomiting. Occasionally a petechial rash occurs. More severe cases develop jaundice and haemorrhagic complications. This is classical Weil's disease and up to a fifth of cases can die from it. Spirochaetes can be cultured from patients' blood and sometimes the urine. Antibodies can usually be demonstrated in the serum (a range of tests are available) but not until the end of the first week of illness at the earliest. This means that tests are unhelpful in recognising the disease and initiating treatment in an acutely ill patient. The initial diagnosis should be made on history-taking and physical examination. Early treatment is the most effective especially in reducing fatalities in severe cases.

The incubation period is usually around 10 days but may extend from four to 19 days and person-to-person transmission is rare. Many animals carry the different serotypes, including rats and other rodents, dogs, cattle, foxes and squirrels. In Britain the main risks are from rats (*Leptospira icterohaemorrhagiae*); dogs and pigs (*Leptospira canicola*), and cattle (largely *Leptospira hardjo*). Cattle become infected through grazing on fields contaminated by the urine of small rodents. In some surveys over 60% of cattle sera show antibodies to leptospira strains – particularly *L. hardjo*.

Transmission is by direct contact with water, damp soil or vegetation which has been contaminated by the urine of infected animals or, less commonly, directly from the infected urine of animals. The spirochaete enters via broken skin, via mucous membrane or may be swallowed.

Health care professionals must exercise care in handling body excretions, particularly the blood and urine of infected patients. Other people exposed to the primary source must undergo medical surveillance. Protective clothing should be worn by workers in hazardous occupations and wounds and cuts covered. Health education is important. This must be directed both at workers in high-risk occupations and at the general public. The latter should be warned about the dangers of infection through swimming in contaminated water such as that in disused canals and through other water sports such as canoeing. The control of the urban rat population is also important. General environmental control measures include extermination of rodents.

Toxoplasma Gondii

Toxoplasma gondii is a coccidial protozoan parasite found in the tissues of many animals, as well as Man. Only in the cat is there a stage of development in the intestine. Hence the cat excretes *T.gondii* as oocysts which when ingested by other animals cause the disease. It may also result from the ingestion of contaminated uncooked meat.

Toxoplasmosis is found in all parts of the world, both in animals and Man. In Britain up to 50% of adults have antibodies to toxoplasma indicating previous infection even though the vast majority show no symptoms.

The primary infection rarely causes symptoms which are severe enough to be reported. In its acute form, the patient has fever and enlarged lymph glands. In immunocompromised individuals, primary infection can cause a much more severe illness affecting the brain, lungs and heart, invariably leading to death. Cerebral toxoplasmosis is recognized as a serious consequence of infection with the Human Immunodeficiency Virus. Congenital infection also occurs and is another important manifestation of this disease.

The incubation period is thought to lie somewhere between 10 and 23 days. Infection from person-to-person only occurs in the intrauterine infection. The oocysts excreted by cats become infective one to five days later and can remain viable in moist conditions for up to a year.

The definitive hosts are members of the cat family. The cat becomes infected by eating infected mammals like rodents and birds. The parasite then undergoes a complex process of development in the epithelial cells of the cat's intestine. For a short period of time the cat passes oocysts, a stage of the parasite that can remain potentially infective in the environment for long periods. However, despite the fact that two-thirds of the cat population have been infected, only 1% are likely to be passing oocysts at any one time. It is not known how often people become infested by these oocysts. It is thought that they acquire the infection either directly by injecting oocysts from soil (for example, during gardening) or by eating raw or insufficiently cooked pork, mutton or beef which contains the parasite. Transplacental infection also occurs in humans when the pregnant mother acquires a primary infection. The foetus can be affected at any stage of pregnancy, but is most at risk during the first trimester when infection can lead to fetal death. Congenital infection may also give rise to chorioretinitis, cerebral calcification and hydrocephalus in up to 60% of survivors. These severe consequences have led to a call for a national screening programme to combat this disease.

The most important means of preventing toxoplasmosis are the thorough cooking of meat and advising pregnant women to avoid handling cat litter, especially with bare hands.

Toxocara

Toxocara is a nematode (roundworm) and two species cause concern in the British Isles: *Toxocara canis* (adult form occurs in the small intestine of dogs) and *Toxocara cati* (found in the cat). Each has a complex but different life cycle. It is the minute larvae (about half-a-millimetre long) which invade the tissues of many vertebrates and cause symptoms in humans. Human infestation follows the ingestion of infected eggs from dog or cat faeces. The transfer may take place directly from hand to mouth (particularly in children) or possibly on salad vegetables. Surveys have shown that 5–25% of soil samples in garden, parks and sandpits are contaminated with toxocara eggs. After ingestion the eggs hatch into larvae in the intestine, penetrate the intestinal wall and reach various organs through the bloodstream. The larvae do not develop into adult worms in humans, but the wandering larvae can invade lungs, liver, the brain and eye. In the various tissues larvae produce an immune response and become the centre of an inflammatory reaction with subsequent fibrosis and granuloma formulation. In the great majority of cases, this gives rise to no symptoms but if the lesion is in a vital organ such as the eye it can lead to disturbance of vision or, in the brain, it can result in epilepsy.

It must be remembered that these are rare conditions. There are about 50 cases with ocular involvement reported in Britain each year, mostly children who have been in close contact with dogs. Nevertheless, it is a further reason to ban dogs from beaches, parks and playgrounds. At least 10% of dogs in Britain are infested and up to 35% of cats. Human infection is much more commonly associated with dogs.

Brucellosis

Brucellosis is caused by *Brucella abortus,* a small aerobic, Gram-negative coccobacillus which does not produce spores and induces abortion in cows; the carcasses and the milk both become infected. Other serological types are *Brucella melitensis* (which infects goats and sheep); *Brucella suis* (which infects pigs), and *Brucella canis* (which infects dogs) – none of which are endemic in Britain.

Brucellosis has a world-wide distribution but is more common in Mediterranean areas. By the beginning of the 1990s, following the introduction in Britain in 1971 of a compulsory scheme for eradication of brucella in cattle, the number of laboratory identifications had plummeted. When the disease does occur it is more often found in rural areas amongst workers (including veterinary surgeons) who are involved with cattle or their untreated milk, and also people who drink unpasteurised milk. Some infections are contracted abroad and imported with the traveller.

The illness is not sharply defined. Commonly it produces a so-called undulant fever with febrile periods followed by intervals with no increase in temperature. The fever often appears in the afternoons. The diagnosis should be considered in any pyrexia of unknown origin especially in groups with a potential occupational exposure. In about half the cases the organisms may be isolated in blood cultures taken from the patient in the acute stages of the illness. Otherwise the diagnosis is often made by serological tests which are of more value slightly later in the illness.

The incubation period is usually two to four weeks, but can often be several months. Person-to-person spread is virtually unknown. There are a number of animal reservoirs of the infection, but in Britain the only animal of importance was the cow. Direct contact with infected cattle – particularly the products of conception, and drinking unpasteurised milk from infected cows. The airborne route (inhalation of infected dust) in cattle sheds may occur.

Isolation and surveillance of cases is unnecessary. As human immunisation is not available, health education is important. Farmers should be taught how to avoid infection and the public made aware of the dangers of drinking untreated milk. Outbreaks have usually been traced to an infected herd if those working with it or drinking its milk become infected. The general measure of raising herds of cattle which are free from *Brucella abortus* infection and the pasteurising of milk could entirely eradicate the disease in humans. Whilst the eradication programme in Britain is very well advanced with most herds free from brucellosis, each year there are still a small number diagnosed. Close cooperation is required between the health and local authorities, together with the veterinary authorities, when cases or outbreaks occur.

Lyme Disease

First described in 1975 in Old Lyme, Connecticut, when several children developed acute arthritis, the causal agent, *Borrelia burgdorferi* (a spirochaete), was not identified until 1982. The organism is transmitted by the bite of the Ixodid group of ticks which live on wild animals (especially deer). It is not transmissible person-to-person. Susceptibility to infection is thought to be universal and the clinical manifestations are divided into two groups. Early symptoms include fever, malaise, headache, lymphadenopathy and a characteristic skin rash called erythema chronicum migrans. Present in about 7% of infected people, the rash develops after about five weeks and spreads slowly during the following months. Late manifestations, which may take years to appear, include arthritis, neurological abnormalities and heart problems.

Although it appears to be uncommon, cases of erythema chronicum migrans have been reported, mostly in the summer months, in Scotland and in the forests of East Anglia and Hampshire. Measures directed at combating this infection include covering exposed areas of skin, particularly legs and ankles, whilst out walking in the forest. If a tick should bite a person it should be removed promptly since transmission of the organism does not seem to occur until the tick has fed for a number of hours.

Orf

This is a common viral disease of sheep and goats and is transmitted to humans by occupational exposure. Farmers, shepherds and vets are usually affected by coming into direct contact with lesions on infected animals. The most common presentation is of a single lesion on the hands which develops into a weeping blister. The lesions, which can measure up to 3 cm in diameter, persist for three to six weeks and then disappear. Occurring mainly in rural communities, this self-limiting illness can be confused with anthrax (see below) or with malignancy.

Anthrax

Anthrax is caused by *Bacillus anthracis* is a large Gram-positive rod which occurs in short chains. The organism grows aerobically and forms heat-resistant spores capable of surviving for many years. It is exceedingly rare in Britain with only two cases having been notified in the last seven years. Patients are usually workers dealing with animal products such as carcasses, hides, hairs, wool and bonemeal. Sometimes, gardeners using unsterilised bonemeal have become infected. Although now very rare, the relevance of anthrax as a biological warfare weapon or bioterrorist weapon cannot be overlooked.

The skin is the organ principally affected in this disease. Although respiratory and intestinal forms are uncommon they may occur and are often fatal. In the cutaneous form, a skin lesion develops usually about two to four days after local infection. It becomes vesicular over a period of several days. After rupture of the vesicle, a deep-seated ulcer appears with swollen surrounding skin. It may then become covered by a scab: the characteristic eschar. If left untreated spread to the bloodstream will lead to a septicaemia which is fatal in as many as 20% of cases.

The diagnosis is usually confirmed by microscopy or isolation of the organism in culture of the skin lesion or blood.

The incubation period is between a few hours and seven days. Person-to-person infection has not been reported but, until the patient has received several days of treatment with antibiotics, it is wise to avoid handling the lesion which should be covered with an occlusive bandage.

Spores, often surviving for many years, are shed from the infected animal. Soil may also contain spores from the remains of dead animals. Transmission is by direct contact of the skin with either contaminated animal material or more rarely, inhalation of spores can produce the respiratory form of the disease. Ingestion of undercooked contaminated meat can result in the gastro-intestinal form.

Vaccination of workers in conditions where they are exposed to the risk of infection and the education of such workers in personal cleanliness, treatment of minor injuries and the hazards of handling potentially infected material are important control measures for anthrax. Protective clothing, dust reduction and medical supervision of those at risk at work are further preventive steps. Gardeners should take special care when using bonemeal known to be unsterilised. General environmental measures include the sterilisation of hair, wool, hides and bonemeal – particularly of imported products. Early diagnosis of affected animals or people and treatment with appropriate antibiotics is essential, as is the rapid identification of outbreaks in animals. The carcasses of animals dying from anthrax should be burnt or deeply buried in quicklime, with any contaminated material and equipment sterilised. Primary contacts (those in contact with the original animal source) should have daily medical surveillance for one week. Contacts of human cases do not require such medical surveillance. Close cooperation between health and local authority together with the veterinary authorities is necessary when cases or outbreaks occur.

Infections Rarely Occurring in Britain and Infections Acquired Abroad

Communicable disease associated with travel is a rapidly changing field and the account in this section must not be relied upon for the most up-to-date advice for travellers.

Malaria

Malaria is caused by a protozoan parasite, genus (family) name Plasmodium. Four species cause human malaria: two are common (*Plasmodium vivax* the cause of benign tertian malaria and *plasmodium falciparum* which causes malignant tertian malaria, a non-relapsing and serious disease with a high fatality rate) and two are uncommon (*Plasmodium malariae* and *Plasmodium ovale*).

Malaria is a very common disease in many parts of the tropics and subtropics: the vivax form in the Indian subcontinent, Central America and south-east Asia; the falciparum in Africa, South America and south-east Asia. Cases of malaria reported in Britain are virtually all imported. They increased steeply during the 1970s, then levelled off but increased again during the 1990s stabilising at roughly 2000 notified cases per year.

Early symptoms can be very non-specific and flu-like. After an initial period of general malaise, pyrexia, shivering and profuse sweating occur in cycles according to the stage of development of the parasite in the human body. These symptoms can vary both in type and severity according to the species of malaria. The diagnosis of malaria should be considered in any patient with a pyrexial illness who has recently been in an endemic area even if the individual has been taking antimalarial chemoprophylaxis. It is confirmed when the parasite is demonstrated microscopically in blood films.

The incubation period depends on the infecting strain: *P. falciparum* approximately seven to 14 days from the infected insect bite; *P. vivax* and *P. ovale* approximately eight to 14 days, and *P. malariae* seven to 30 days. The infection is not transmitted within Britain in the usual way by mosquitoes. The reservoir is Man. Transmission is by the bite of an infected female anopheline mosquito. The mosquito bites the person and ingests human blood containing gametocytes (the sexual stages of the parasite). In the mosquito's stomach these male and female stages join together to form sporozoites. These concentrate in the salivary glands of the mosquito and are injected into the person when the mosquito next feeds. They pass in the bloodstream to the liver where they develop into merozoites (pre-erythrocytic cycle).

The clinical attack begins when these are released into the bloodstream and invade the red cells, where they can undergo a complete cycle of development (erythrocytic cycle) resulting in further release of merozoites into the bloodstream and a further clinical attack. Some also develop into male and female gametocytes which can then be taken up by another mosquito. The life cycle in the mosquito spans eight to 35 days, depending upon the infecting species and the ambient temperature and the pre-erythrocytic cycle in the liver (six to nine days for *P. falciparum*, *vivax* and *ovale* and 12–16 days for *P. malariae*). The duration of the erythrocytic cycle varies with the species of parasite: 36–48 hours (*P. falciparum*); 48 hours (*P. vivax and P ovale*); and 74 hours (*P. malariae*), which accounts for the different periodicity of clinical attacks in the different forms. A proportion of the merozoites from the pre-erythrocytic cycles continue to develop in the liver (exo-erythrocytic cycle): this provides for the source of infection in relapses which may occur several months after a previous attack. Relapses are particularly common with *P. vivax* infections.

Isolation of cases is unnecessary and surveillance of contacts in Britain is only performed to ensure that fellow travellers have not also contracted the disease. However, it is important that a high index of clinical suspicion is maintained and malaria diagnosed and treated early when it does occur. Environmental measures are not required in Britain at the moment.

Travellers going to, or passing through, endemic areas should take appropriate precautions against malaria. Where this includes prophylactic antimalarial drugs these should be continued for four to six weeks after leaving the endemic area. Drug resistance is a problem and the most up-to-date advice must be given to travellers to particular endemic areas. The World Health Organization issues information annually about areas where drug-resistance occurs.

The most important groups for health education targeting are members of the ethnic minority populations within Britain, many of whom make relatively frequent trips to their countries of origin and who are not always aware of the risks of malaria and the importance of prophylaxis. Vigilance is also required in ensuring that aircraft do not import the mosquito (or expose passengers travelling between non-endemic areas in aircraft which have previously been used on tropical routes). Maintenance of high standards in screening potential blood donors is another vital control measure.

The four key elements of prevention are: awareness of risk, prevention of bites by sprays, bednets, chemoprophylaxis and early diagnosis if prevention fails.

Rabies

The rabies virus is a rhabdovirus. Found in many countries throughout the world, it causes primarily a disease of animals. The British Isles are at present rabies-free with only occasional imported cases in animals. Rabies has been detected in wildlife in various parts of Western Europe and progressively closer to ports along the English Channel in recent years, although the introduction of oral rabies vaccine into the animal population has led to a reduction in the number of cases overall. Bat rabies occurs in North America and to a lesser extent within the bat population of parts of Europe.

Rabies in man is characterised by an acute encephalitis that is virtually always fatal within a week of first symptoms. The victim is apprehensive, with headache, pyrexia and muscle spasms which progress to paralysis and death. The fear of water (more accurately of swallowing) has led to the name 'hydrophobia'. The laboratory diagnosis of the disease in the brain of a killed infected laboratory animal confirms the clinical manifestations in the patient.

The incubation period is normally three to eight weeks. It can be as short as nine days or as long as seven years. It depends on the dose of virus as well as the nerve supply of the area which is wounded and its proximity to the brain. The virus migrates along peripheral nerves from the site of the bite into the central nervous system. Person-to-person transmission has never been demonstrated, although it is a theoretical risk because human saliva does contain the virus in an infected individual. A rare mode of transmission is via corneal transplant from an infected person who died of the disease, but in whom it was not diagnosed.

Dogs and cats are usually infective from between three and 10 days before the onset of clinical illness and remain infectious throughout the course of the illness.

A variety of wild animals act as a reservoir: including foxes, wolves, dogs, cats and bats. However, for practical purposes the disease is transferred in the majority of cases by a dog bite (or less often a cat bite). Transmission is by the bite of an infected animal or more rarely by contact between infected animal saliva and the human mucous membrane. The virus cannot penetrate intact skin.

The main strategy for preventing rabies in Britain has been strict quarantine regulations coupled with legal penalties to prevent the disease being imported by animals. In 1999 the British Government introduced proposals for replacing rabies quarantine for pet cats and dogs with alternative arrangements including vaccination against rabies, blood testing for rabies antibodies and treatments for certain other exotic infestations, supported by appropriate documentation and certification. The new arrangements were introduced, initially in a pilot scheme, in early 2000.

Rabies vaccine is recommended for those working with the virus, who deal with imported animals, licenced bat handlers, those whose work may bring them into contact with rabid animals abroad, and long-stay travellers to rabies endemic areas where access to medical help may be delayed should they be bitten. Health education measures should be employed; firstly to encourage travellers to foreign countries to avoid all contact with animals, especially in those countries where rabies is endemic; and secondly, to warn them of the hazards of illegally smuggling animals into this country.

An individual who has been bitten by an animal (for example, a dog, a bat or other wild animal) in which there is a suspicion of rabies or in a foreign country where the disease is endemic should have the wound immediately washed and thoroughly cleansed under medical supervision. Post-exposure treatment with active and passive immunisation (vaccine plus human anti-rabies immunoglobulin) should be considered. The decision whether to proceed with vaccination depends on the likelihood that the animal is infected. If the animal was not captured and rabies is endemic in the particular country then it is prudent to proceed with post-exposure treatment.

Human diploid cell vaccine is given in a total of five doses either by deep subcutaneous or intramuscular injection over the deltoid region: the first immediately, the second on the third day after exposure, the third on the seventh day, the fourth on the fourteenth day and the fifth on the thirtieth day. Human rabies immunoglobulin is injected immediately around the site of the wound, and intramuscularly.

In the context of the British patient, all these measures depend on the quality and availability of medical services in the country which is being visited. An increasingly common occurrence as more people travel abroad, is a history of animal bite in a returning traveller. Medical care may not have been sought or may not have been available in the country concerned. Personal experience indicates that the public health physician often becomes involved in such a situation.

For example, a party of schoolchildren returning from a school trip abroad contained two members who gave a history of having been bitten by a dog which had exhibited aggressive behaviour towards them. It was only upon return to this country that parental concern led to the children presenting to the local accident and emergency department some four days after the bite. Through the Department of Health via its international links the animal was located and found to have remained healthy. Post-exposure treatment was not enforced but would have been commenced immediately if: there was no official record of the incident; the animal had escaped and could not be traced; or the dog had been killed and diagnosed as suffering from rabies.

Because dog bites are such a relatively common occurrence in Britain, it is easy to take a casual approach to a stray-dog bite sustained by someone returning from abroad (particularly if they appear fit and well). It is important that such cases are taken seriously. Advice can be obtained from the Public Health Laboratory on whether to instigate post-exposure rabies treatment in particular circumstances.

If an established case is diagnosed in Britain, rigid rules of isolation usually apply, although the risk of person-to-person transmission is very slight. Attendant medical and nursing staff, and all those potentially exposed to the patient's, saliva are offered immunisation. Health care professionals should wear protective gloves and gowns and concurrent and terminal disinfection should be practised.

Viral Haemorrhagic Fevers

Some haemorrhagic fevers caused by viruses such as yellow fever have been known from early times. However, since the mid-1950s, new haemorrhagic illnesses have been recognized in humans, although it is likely that they have been acquired from natural animal hosts. The main public health concern is that the viruses, having been transmitted from their natural host to Man, are then capable of producing person-to-person transmission. This risk is greatly minimised with strict isolation and meticulous medical and nursing procedures. Cases of this group of diseases are very rare in Britain and are almost exclusively imported by travellers from endemic areas.

- *Lassa fever* – caused by a member of the arena virus family. It was first isolated from an American missionary nurse in the Lassa township in Nigeria during 1969. Since then it has also occurred in Nigeria, Sierra Leone, Liberia and elsewhere in West Africa.
- *Marburg disease* – caused by a virus first described in Marburg in the Federal Republic of Germany in 1967 when 31 cases with seven deaths occurred in Germany and Yugoslavia due to direct contact with the blood, organs and tissues of a batch of African Green Monkeys originally trapped in Uganda. It is endemic in Central and Southern Africa.
- *Ebola fever* – a very large outbreak of viral haemorrhagic fever with high fatality rates occurred in the Southern Sudan and Zaire in 1976, where it still occurs. The causal virus was found to be morphologically identical to the Marburg virus but serologically distinct and the new strain was named the Ebola virus.
- *Hantaan virus* – produces a haemorrhagic fever with renal syndrome and is a major public health problem in China and Korea, where the case fatality rate reaches about 7%. A milder (but also sometimes fatal) disease occurring in Scandinavia and Eastern Europe is caused by an antigenic subtype: the Puumala virus.
- *Other haemorrhagic fevers* – other infections in this category are endemic in various parts of the World: for example *Dengue fever* (south-east Asia and the Caribbean), *Bolivian haemorrhagic fever* (rural areas of Northern Bolivia) and *Omsk haemorrhagic fever* (parts of Siberia).

A very small number of cases of haemorrhagic fever may be imported into Britain. The disease should be suspected in patients with unexplained pyrexia returning from endemic areas of the World, provided malaria has been excluded as a diagnosis. Symptoms vary but often there is an insidious onset with a variety of non-specific symptoms including general malaise, pyrexia, sore throat and enlarged lymph glands. Later, the patient's condition worsens with conjunctivitis, chest and abdominal pains, vomiting, and occasionally a mild maculopapular rash. Severe bleeding occurs between the fifth and seventh days most often into the gastro-intestinal tract and lung. Other features vary with the haemorrhagic fever concerned. For example, the severe form of Hantaan fever results in kidney symptoms and in some cases renal failure.

The incubation period varies according to the disease, for example:

- **Lassa fever** – usually six to 21 days;
- **Marburg disease** – three to nine days;
- **Ebola disease** – two to 21 days.

The surveillance period for these fevers is usually extended to 21 days as an added precaution.

Where person-to-person transmission occurs, diseases are infectious as long as blood and body secretions contain the virus, which can be several weeks after clinical recovery.

The reservoirs vary according to the disease:

- **Lassa fever** – a species of wild rodent (*Mastomys natalensis*) in rural West Africa;
- **Marburg** and **Ebola** disease – animal reservoir unknown;
- **Hantaan fever** – field rodents.

Routes of transmission are:

- **Lassa fever** – Man acquires the infection probably through contact with the rodent's urine. Person-to-person spread may occur via the upper respiratory tract in the acute phase but more often is due to contact with infected blood, urine or secretions of the patient.
- **Marburg and Ebola diseases** – although the original outbreak of Marburg disease occurred as a result of contact with African Green Monkeys, transmission of the disease from an animal to Man has not been demonstrated. Person-to-person spread has usually been due to very close contact with infected individuals. Many outbreaks have been related to hospitals in Africa where unsatisfactory practices have spread the disease amongst patients and staff. In some of these outbreaks the case fatality rate has been over 50%. Such hospitals acted as amplifiers of the infection with secondary cases occurring amongst staff and other patients. However, the introduction of adequate precautionary measures (care in handling a patient's blood, urine and other secretions) quickly brought the disease under control in one outbreak of Ebola fever. In the original outbreak of Marburg fever a number of secondary cases occurred amongst hospital staff who had been exposed to the patient's blood. In Britain, the main risk is to ward and laboratory staff involved in the care of patients with viral haemorrhagic fever.

When a suspected case of viral haemorrhagic fever occurs, an infectious diseases specialist must be contacted to exclude malaria as a diagnosis. Where there are good grounds for suspicion the Consultant in Communicable Disease Control is responsible for arranging the patient's admission to a high security isolation unit by a special ambulance crew wearing protective clothing and special respirators. The Department of Health and the Communicable Disease Surveillance Centre must be informed at the earliest opportunity. Close contacts of the patient, either those in the same household or workmates, are kept under strict daily surveillance for 21 days from the last date of exposure. A daily record is kept of temperature and, if a rise occurs or other signs or symptoms are evident, immediate isolation should be effected, and admission to a high security isolation unit considered.

Smallpox

Smallpox is caused by the Variola virus. Until the 1970s smallpox was one of the world's major killing infectious diseases and hence has been the subject of an active vaccination programme world-wide. In 1967 an eradication programme was launched by the World Health Organization. As a result of this action the last known natural case of smallpox occurred in Somalia on October 26, 1977. However, in 1978, a medical photographer in Birmingham University contracted the disease as a result of an escape of the virus from a laboratory. She died of smallpox but her mother, who was the only other case, survived. Since this accident, rigorous measures have been instituted to reduce the risk of future tragedies of this sort. Global eradication of the disease was pronounced by the World Health Assembly in 1980.

Sexually Transmitted Infections (STIs)

There were substantial increases (30% or more) of certain of the sexually transmitted infections (STIs) amongst teenagers in the mid-to-late 1990s; particularly gonorrhoea and genital chlamydia infection. This was despite the fact that these infections are both easily preventable and easily treatable.

Gonorrhoea

Gonorrhoea is a sexually transmitted disease which is found in all parts of the world. It is caused by a Gram-negative diplococcus – *Neisseria gonorrhoea*. The initial symptom in the male heterosexual is a urethritis with a purulent discharge. The disease may progress, particularly if treatment is delayed, to cause prostatitis or epididymitis. In women, the shorter female urethra means that symptoms sometimes pass unnoticed. Ascending infection of the female genital tract may cause salpingitis and (in the longer term) infertility. In either sex, rarely, joint inflammation or meningitis can occur. The gonococcus may affect the eyes of a baby born to an infected mother producing oph-thalmia neonatorum.

Gonococcal infection is much more common in homosexual than heterosexual men. They present with anorectal and pharyngeal gonorrhoea (both can also occur in heterosexuals but are much less common) as well as urethral infections.

The diagnosis is usually made clinically and confirmed by stained smears of the infective exudate and, subsequently, culture of the organism. Urethral swabs in heterosexual men and women are the usual clinical investigation. In addition, throat swabs and anorectal swabs (during proctoscopy) are important in homosexual men.

In both sexes the biggest reduction in incidence took place between 1985 and 1988 and was, at least in part, due a mass media safe sex campaign designed to reduce the risk of acquiring HIV infection. This rapid decline has, however, been short-lived and an upwards trend in the incidence of gonorrhoea has been observed during the 1990s.

Reported gonorrhoea rates are an important marker of unprotected sexual activity, particularly in the high-risk groups. This indicator is even more important given the advent of Human Immune Deficiency Virus (HIV) infection.

Genital Chlamydia Trachomatis Infection

Genital infection with *Chlamydia trachomatis* is difficult to distinguish on clinical grounds from gonorrhoea. There are a number of serotypes which cause diseases. The serotypes concerned cause symptoms similar to gonorrhoea but with much less prominent discharge. It can be complicated by epididymitis, salpingitis and can cause infertility. The majority of people infected have few or no symptoms and only become aware of the disease because of its late complications. Screening programmes which have been introduced in Sweden and America have led to significant reductions in both the level of infections and complications. Treatment is usually with tetracycline. Other serotypes of *Chlamydia trachomatis* cause *lymphogranuloma venereum*.

Trichomoniasis

The protozoan organism *Trichomonas vaginalis* is mainly an infection in women, though their male partners may be infected, remain asymptomatic or have mild symptoms. Women with this infection usually present with a strong smelling vaginal discharge, soreness of the external genitalia and pain during intercourse (dysparunia). A vaginal swab examined by microscopy and culture (and if necessary other more specialised tests) usually confirms the diagnosis. Antimicrobial treatment of both the woman and her partner is necessary to be sure of eradicating the infection.

Syphilis

Syphilis, one of the longest recognized sexually transmitted diseases, is caused by *Treponema pallidum*, a thin spiral organism (spirochaete) which does not stain well and is thus best seen with dark-field illumination microscopy.

It occurs in all parts of the world, and is mainly a disease of young adults. The 1960s and 1970s saw a large increase in the incidence of syphilis in part due to male homosexual spread of infection. The number of new cases is small in comparison with gonorrhoea, but it is more common in sea ports and large cities and there has been a number of recent, well-publicised outbreaks. A fall in the reported incidence of syphilis in male homosexuals occurred in the late 1980s, believed to be because of fear of AIDS, although heterosexually acquired infection in young adults rose.

Syphilis is invariably acquired by sexual contact. The spirochaete does not survive long outside the human body, hence indirect methods of transmission are not usually important. Congenital syphilis arises from prenatal infection via the placenta.

There are three stages of the acquired disease. The primary lesion (chancre) develops as a painless ulcer on the skin or mucous membrane at the site of entry of the spirochaete usually about three weeks after exposure. Even in untreated cases the primary lesion disappears and is followed within six to eight weeks by a generalised cutaneous rash heralding secondary syphilis. The tertiary stage develops after three to

20 years and can affect various parts of the body including bones, liver, cardiovascular system and the central nervous system, giving rise to classical tabes dorsalis and general paralysis of the insane. Early treatment with antibiotics has greatly reduced the occurrence of the secondary and tertiary stages.

In congenital syphilis, the foetus is frequently aborted or stillborn. If the child survives, handicapping conditions are the usual outcome. The organism may be seen in specimens under dark-field illumination microscopy or using immunofluorescent techniques. There are also a number of important serological tests which are used to help make the diagnosis.

The patient is infectious during the primary and secondary stages of the disease and may also be intermittently infectious during latent periods. Effective antibiotic treatment makes the patient non-infectious within one or two days.

Genital Herpes

Genital herpes is caused by the *Herpes simplex virus* (usually Type 2) which is transmitted by sexual intercourse. The Type 1 *Herpes simplex virus* is associated with lesions on the mouth and face ('cold sores') but can also cause the genital form of herpes.

Genital herpes is a relapsing condition. The skin heals and then can break down and ulcerate long after the primary infection. Symptoms of the primary infection include pain in the genitals and buttocks, sometimes fever followed by an eruption of vesicles on the skin and mucous membranes of the genital area which gradually break down to produce painful ulcers. Discharge and secondary bacterial infection are common.

Genital herpes occurs in male and female heterosexuals and male homosexuals (in whom it occurs on the penis, in the anorectal area and sometimes in the mouth). Treatment is symptomatic and sometimes antiviral drugs are effective.

The virus becomes latent in the dorsal root ganglia and can then recur at any time although the number and severity of recurrences varies greatly.

Anal and Genital Warts

Warts in the anal and genital areas are caused by viruses: mainly the *Human Papilloma Virus* (HPV) although another virus also causes a warty-type infection called *Molluscum contagiosum*. Reported cases of anogenital warts have increased in recent years in heterosexuals and homosexual men. It is likely that this represents a true increase in occurrence but greater awareness on the part of patients and clinicians has undoubtedly contributed to the increase. An important association is that between certain types of HPV and the development of cervical cancer.

Candidiasis

The yeast, *Candida albicans* is a relatively common cause of pruritus, severe vulval discomfort and vaginal discharge. In many cases, the infection is due to spread of the organism from the gastrointestinal tract where it exists as a commensal but, in some instances, it is sexually transmitted. Treatment with antimicrobial pessaries usually resolves the infection.

Other Diseases Transmitted Sexually

A number of other organisms can be transmitted sexually which are not thought of primarily as sexually transmitted diseases. These include *Hepatitis B, Hepatitis A, Scabies, Cytomegalovirus.*

Control of Sexually Transmitted Diseases

In the 1980s and 1990s the whole field of sexually transmitted diseases was transformed from a relatively quiet backwater of clinical and public health practice to one of major international importance by the emergence of the Human Immune Deficiency Virus (HIV) which causes the Acquired Immune Deficiency Syndrome (AIDS). This subject is covered in Chapter 3 but many of the control measures which apply to the control of its spread sexually, apply to other sexually transmitted diseases. Thus, HIV-directed health promotion and health education programmes aimed at modifying sexual behaviour and encouraging safer sexual practices, particularly in young people, are equally important to the prevention and control of these other diseases. Well designed and properly conducted sex education programmes have been demonstrated to bring about a measurable improvement in sexual attitudes and behaviour.

Traditionally, the focus for the prevention and control of sexually transmitted diseases has been the network of clinics provided around the country within the National Health Service. Prompt diagnosis and investigation of people presenting is vital and, in most diseases, the tracing of contacts of patients is a key control measure. Contact-tracing, or partner notification as it is now more commonly called, is a skilled exercise requiring considerable diplomacy and is often undertaken by specially trained nurses, health visitors or social workers. Many of the recent changes in sexually transmitted infection services have been stimulated by experiences of dealing with HIV infection in which it has been important to make sure that risk groups come forward for testing, advice and counselling. The spin-offs for the prevention and control of other sexually transmitted diseases have been important and beneficial.

Some Parasitic Diseases

Ectoparasites

Scabies

Scabies is caused by *Sarcoptes scabiei*, a small mite just visible to the naked eye. The disease occurs in most parts of the world. In Britain it appears to fluctuate over a 15-year cycle. 'The itch', as it was known, has a long history and it may have been the condition mentioned in the Old Testament for which the treatment advised was bathing in the River Jordan (now known to have a high sulphur content).

Skin lesions caused by burrowing of the mite are most commonly found between the fingers, on the anterior surfaces of the wrist and the soles of the feet. Symptoms occur when sensitisation develops with a papular rash which may spread to any part of the body except the face. Itching is intense, especially in bed at night. Scratching may result in secondary infection. The diagnosis is confirmed by extracting the female mite from the burrow and identifying it under the microscope.

The initial infestation passes unnoticed until sensitisation occurs about two months later. In people who have been previously infested the time is much shorter (one to four weeks). The affected person is infectious until effective treatment is carried out.

The reservoir is Man. Scabies in animals (such as dogs) does not transfer to Man. Transmission is by close personal contact such as holding hands or sexual intercourse. It has not been possible to demonstrate transfer by indirect means such as bed linen or clothing.

There is no need to isolate the patient after treatment but contacts should be examined and treated if necessary. It is helpful to treat all family contacts of the patient simultaneously to avoid reinfection. The maintenance of good personal hygiene standards should also be encouraged.

Lice

There are three types of human lice, all are members of the order *Anoplura* (sucking lice) and are parasites exclusively of mammals. All feed on the blood of the host and parasitize only one species, hence they are strongly host-specific. Moreover, many of the 500 known species of lice are so highly specialised that they only colonise one part of the body of their particular host.

Two genera of lice infest Man: *Phthirus* and *Pediculus*, although only one species of each is involved. When Man began to wear clothes and hair became restricted to the head, axilla and pubic areas, human lice themselves underwent modifications. The crab louse (*Phthirus pubis*) adapted to live on the hair around the human genitalia, whilst the body louse migrated to clothing, only returning to the host to feed. The head louse became a scalp dweller, and specialised to such a degree that its survival depends on being in almost continual contact with its source of food and warmth. There are two varieties of *Pediculus humanus* – *Pediculus humanus humanus* (the body louse) and *Pediculus humanus capitis* (the head louse).

The Body Louse (*Pediculus Humanus*)

This louse is different from the many species of *Anoplura* in that it lives on the host indirectly (on the clothing), laying its eggs on the seams, near the skin. It visits the body only long enough to obtain meals of human blood. The eggs are laid, attach to the fibres of clothing and, if the temperature is right, hatch within seven days. The young louse matures in about seven days and has an average life-span of 30 days. It is unusual for lice to remain on the body after the clothing has been removed. However, treatment usually consists of an appropriate topical application. A convenient way of delousing clothing is to put it dry into a tumble-drier for five minutes at the maximum temperature, a manoeuvre which kills both lice and eggs.

Crab Louse or Pubic Louse (*Phthirus Pubis*)

This parasite has preference for the coarse widely-spaced hair in the pubic area, though occasionally it may be found elsewhere on the hair of legs, beards or eye-lashes. The louse tends to feed from the same spot at the base of a hair. It is not easily visible since it blends in with the skin. The eggs are glued onto the hair and hatched in about eight days. The young louse is mature within a week. Spread is nearly always by sexual contact, and the appropriate current treatment should be chosen by consulting the British Pharmacopoeia.

The Head Louse (*Pediculus Humanus Capitis*)

This louse is strongly host-specific and for all practical purposes is found in only one place, the hair close to the scalp of human beings.

The eggs (nits) have been found on the hair of an Egyptian mummy and there are numerous references to the louse in literature from the time of the Greek classics. The head louse is about the size of a matchstick head and has a life-span of 30 days, but few survive in the natural state for so long. The eggs are laid in a glue-like medium which attaches them to a hair shaft, very close to the scalp. Usually they hatch within seven days into a nymph which becomes mature within about ten days. The sole food is human blood. The louse moves quickly but does not readily leave the host. The mode of transmission is almost certainly by the louse walking from one person's head to another when they are in close contact. Head louse infestation occurs throughout the world, but it appears to be more common in Western countries. Most infestations are light and the principal symptoms are itching of the scalp with consequent disturbances of sleep. Secondary infection may occur with scratching and, since lice can harbour in their intestines bacteria capable of causing impetigo, wounds may become infected in this way.

If someone, particularly a child or young person presents with an itchy scalp, impetigo or excoriation around the nape of the neck, head infestation must be ruled out. The eggs (nits) are firmly attached to the hair and hence can be distinguished from dandruff. The egg is laid on the hair shaft very close to the scalp and initially is greyish in colour and difficult to see. Later as the hair grows the nit becomes pearl white and easily visible. The eggs are frequently located behind the ears, although they may be found anywhere on the head. Eggs found more than a few centimetres from the scalp can be assumed to be dead. The live lice are difficult to see.

The insecticides most appropriate for the treatment of head infestation should be chosen by consulting the current edition of the British Pharmacopoeia. The reservoir of infestation is frequently the family so it is important that the whole family is treated at the same time.

Endoparasites

Enterobiasis (Threadworm Disease)

Threadworm is caused by *Enterobius vermicularis*, a small whitish thread-like nematode (roundworm) 5–12 mm long. The disease is found in most parts of the world and is the most common helminth infection affecting Man. Up to 15 million people may be infected in the United Kingdom and more often these are children.

The patient is often symptomless but may notice the threadlike worms on the surface of the stool. The most common symptom is itching around the anus which may lead to scratching and disturbed sleep. The worm may cause appendicitis or, by migration, vaginitis or salpingitis. These complications are however extremely rare and the majority of patients have very mild symptoms. Diagnosis by pressing 'Sellotape' on to perianal skin and then onto a microscope slide. Characteristic eggs are seen under the microscope.

The incubation period is two to six weeks, though it may take longer before symptoms appear, because the number of worms increases with continuous self-reinfections. The patient is infectious for as long as pregnant female worms remain in the gut. An individual worm lives for about two months. The reservoir is Man. Similar worms in other animals do not infect Man.

The adult worm lives in he caecum, small and large intestines. The gravid female migrates through the anal orifice and lays small sticky eggs on the skin of the peri-anal region. The eggs are then carried by the fingers to the mouth or indirectly to another individual. They are capable of survival for a few days on clothes, bed-linen or dust if conditions are cool and moist. However, person-to-person transmission is most common. The eggs when swallowed hatch out in the small intestine and the cycle recommences.

There is no need to isolate the patient but the family and other close contacts should be screened. Simultaneous treatment of all infected members of the family is essential to prevent reinfection. In addition, there should be education in personal hygiene, frequency washing of the peri-anal region and the need to keep fingernails short and clean. The most important general environmental control measures are frequent washing of personal clothing and bed-linen. The hot cycle of the domestic washing machine is sufficient to destroy the eggs. In institutions, the eggs may be present in dust so that a general clean-up should accompany treatment of patients.

Giardiasis

An increasing number of outbreaks of diarrhoeal disease have been reported due to *Giardia lamblia* (a flagellated protozoan), particularly in travellers from overseas. Although the incubation period is variable, symptoms usually occur within one to two weeks of the exposure. The main features of the clinical illness are nausea, abdominal pain and profuse watery diarrhoea. Travellers are infected from contaminated drinking water but infection may also be transmitted from person-to-person by the faecal–oral route.

Conclusions

Communicable disease surveillance and control remains a central component of public health practice. Despite the decline in the relative importance of communicable diseases as causes of death, they remain a major source of morbidity in the population. They can often produce distressing symptoms and complications. Whilst control of the acute outbreak of illness caused by a microorganism is vitally important and is the aspect of this field of work which keeps communicable diseases in the public eye, it is only one part of a comprehensive public health approach to communicable disease control. A detailed understanding of the nature, causes, modes of transmission and clinical features of communicable diseases is also essential to an overall strategy of population control of this group of diseases. So too, as in many other fields of public health, is the availability of accurate information and its proper analysis. There is also a need for clear policies for communicable disease control which place strong emphasis on prevention and on organisations working in partnership to address the problem.

Definitions of Terms used for Communicable Diseases and Parasites

Airborne transmission: This is due to the formation of droplet nuclei by evaporation; the particles are small and can be widely dispersed.

Carriers: People who intermittently or continuously harbour infective organisms without suffering the clinical manifestations of the disease. People who excrete the organisms only occasionally are referred to as intermittent carriers. Convalescent carriers are those who remain infective even after recovering from the illness and the term chronic carrier is applied if this condition persists over months or years. Typhoid carriers may excrete the organism for years usually because *Salmonella typhi* has infected the gallbladder. Some infections are carried by people who give no history of illness caused by the agent. This healthy carrier state occurs in diphtheria and meningococcal infection.

Commensals: Organisms which cause no harm to the host and one or both may gain benefit. If both gain benefit the state is symbiosis.

Communicable diseases: Synonymous with 'infectious diseases' and sometimes referred to as 'contagious diseases' or 'transmissable diseases', communicable diseases are caused by a living organism and transmitted from person-to-person or from animal or bird to Man either directly or indirectly.

Contact: A person who has the opportunity to acquire infection by virtue of having come into contact with an infected individual or animal, or contaminated environment.

Definitive or primary host: One in which a parasite reaches maturity or passes through its sexual stage.

Disinfection: The killing of an infectious agent outside the body by direct application of a chemical substance or by physical means such as heat. Concurrent disinfection is the application of disinfective measures to discharges, or excreta from the patient, as they occur. Terminal disinfection is the use of disinfective measures after the recovery or removal of the patient. It usually applies to rooms and furniture but is seldom necessary because thorough cleansing and good ventilation are equally effective.

Disinfestation: The removal or destruction of insects, their ova or larvae associated with an individual, his clothing or premises. It also applies to the destruction or removal of rodents.

Droplet transmission: Infection caused by a projection of small droplets from the nose or mouth due to sneezing, coughing, talking or exhaling. The range of spread is usually limited to a few feet.

Ectoparasites: These parasites live only on the surface of the host's body and are usually insects.

Endoparasites: These parasites live only inside the host's body; examples are worms and many protozoa.

Endemic: An endemic disease is one which is constantly present in a given geographical area, although it may temporarily increase its incidence to become an epidemic.

Endotoxins: Types of toxins (poisons) liberated only when the bacterial cell wall is broken and are important in causing shock.

Epidemic: An epidemic is an increase in the frequency of occurrence of a disease in a population above its baseline level for a specified period of time.

Exotic disease: An infectious condition which is not usually found in Britain but may be imported from overseas.

Exotoxins: Toxins produced by bacteria which pass into the tissues of the body. Examples of organisms which produce toxins resulting in illness are diphtheria and tetanus.

Facultative parasites: Parasites which are capable of an independent existence outside the host.

Hosts: Animals (including Man) which give support to, and provide a living environment for, an infectious agent. Some parasites pass through their stages of development in different hosts.

Incubation period: The time which elapses between the person becoming infected and the appearance of the first symptoms. Its length is mainly determined by the nature of the infecting organism but it is also influenced to some extent by the dose of the organism, the route of entry into the body and the susceptibility of the host.

Insect vector: An insect which carries the disease agent either mechanically (on its feet or other parts of its body) or within its body so that the agent is transmitted to the person being infected either by saliva (when the insect bites) or by faeces (deposited on the skin).

Intermediate or secondary host: One in which a parasite is in its larval or asexual stage

Medical parasitology: Although many viruses, bacteria and fungi which cause disease in a strictly biological sense are parasites, it is customary to restrict the term medical parasitology to that branch of medicine which deals with those parasites living in or on Man which are members of the animal kingdom. They fall into three main groups: protozoa (single cell organisms); helminths (worms); and arthropods (insects).

Nosocomial infection: An infection occurring in patients or staff which originated within the hospital or other institution.

Obligatory parasites: Parasites which cannot survive outside the host.

Pandemic: An epidemic of world-wide proportions.

Primary case: The first case which occurs in an outbreak, also referred to as the index case.

Reservoir of infection: Any animal, insect, plant or inanimate substance (for example, foodstuff) in which an infectious agent dwells and from which it is capable of being transmitted to a susceptible host.

Sporadic: A term used when cases of communicable diseases are not found to be linked to each other.

Subclinical: An infection by an agent which gives rise to no reported symptoms or signs in the host.

Vehicle: A contaminated, inanimate object (e.g., fomites such as toys, blankets, handkerchiefs, soiled linen) or material (e.g., food, water, milk, body fluids) allowing an infectious agent to gain entry to a suitable host. The organism might or might not have multiplied on the vehicle.

Zoonoses: Communicable diseases which are transmitted to Man from animals.

Chapter 10

Environment and Health

Introduction

Environmental issues are a prominent feature of society. They are raised in the classroom, in the media as well as in national and local politics. The relationship between human health and the environment is part of this wider debate. Partly this stems from a growing realisation that the physical environment is far more fragile and susceptible to human destructive influence than was previously believed. Partly it is because of the development of a much broader understanding of the determinants of health and ill-health, which include many environmental factors.

The concept of environment encompasses our physical surroundings; either natural or man-made, the air that we breathe, the pollution we create, the quality and availability of our water, the climate and natural life that make up our ecosystem, and the social, economic and political infrastructure which regulate and control our lives. It is together that these different facets of a complex environment exert their influence on health. This chapter, deals with that relationship.

Key Concepts

Humankind is part inheritor, part creator and part caretaker of the environment. In order both to maintain and promote good health, the environment in which we live must be supportive. It must be a healthy environment.

Sustainable Development

The interdependence of people and their environment is emphasised in the concept of sustainable development. In 1992, an Earth Summit was held in Rio de Janeiro which produced an action plan, Agenda 21, recommending the formulation of sustainable development strategies by every country. Sustainable development broadly means ensuring that policies and action which affect the environment meet the needs of the present without compromising future generations. Table 10.1 summarises the main components of the United Kingdom Sustainability Development Strategy and Table 10.2 shows the indicators used to monitor its success. This approach acknowledges that the earth and its atmosphere is a closed system. If all fossil fuels are allowed to burn, if noxious gases are pumped into the atmosphere, if raw sewage is poured into rivers and oceans and if population growth is allowed to continue unchecked, then it is future generations that will have to live with the consequences. The natural environment does have regenerative qualities but, if in the struggle to develop and survive they are destroyed, the result could be rapid degeneration to the point where the environment is no longer able to support human existence. This would not be sustainable development. At current rates of change this future state could possibly be only a few hundred years away.

Table 10.1   Sustainable development objectives

- Social progress which recognizes the needs of everyone
- Effective protection of the environment
- Prudent use of natural resources
- Maintenance of high and stable levels of economic growth

Source: A better quality of life: a strategy for sustainable development for the United Kingdom. London: The Stationery Office, 1999.

In the past, the reaction of people in many developed countries such as Britain has been to behave as if they had direct responsibility only for the environment in which they themselves live, effectively treating the environment as an open system. For example, provided that toxic waste is disposed of at sea or in other countries, as long as acid rain does not fall on its creators, as long as enough wealth is generated to obtain the resources needed and as long as population growth is contained, then a wider responsibility for the world's environment does not become a priority. This past approach ignored the irrefutable fact that the world's physical environment is one environment (a closed system), albeit a complex one. Pollution of the air and oceans does not recognize national boundaries; destruction of the ozone layer is a global problem; excessive use of natural resources in one part of the world deprives another; and population growth in one part of the world inevitably makes demands on the environment and its resources in other areas.

Table 10.2   Sustainable development indicators of progress

- Total output of the economy (GDP)
- Investment in public, business and private assets
- Proportion of people of working age who are in work
- Qualifications at age 19 years
- Expected years of healthy life
- Homes judged unfit to live in
- Level of crime
- Emissions of greenhouse gases
- Days when air pollution is moderate or high
- Road traffic
- Rivers of good or fair quality
- Populations of wild birds
- New homes built on previously developed land
- Waste arisings and management

Source: A better quality of life: a strategy for sustainable development for the United Kingdom. London: The Stationery Office, 1999.

The realisation of these fundamental principles leads inescapably to the conclusion that people within their own communities must start to look at their local environment as if it were a closed system. This means, for example, recycling waste wherever possible; using renewable rather than expendable resources; maintaining an optimum balance between resource use and population growth and maintaining the environment in a supportive state. In addition, the developed world has to start taking an interest in the management of the environment in less developed countries. If it tackles its own environmental problems without helping the developing world, then all that will be achieved is a shift of responsibility for the global environment on to those currently least able to do anything about it. Ultimately, the problem will be made worse, not better.

For most people, environment equates to their immediate home, neighbourhood, village, town or city. Different physical environments surround those who live in a large detached house with a garden compared to those living in a small flat in a high-rise block. Similarly, the environment of people living twenty miles from the nearest town is different from those living in the heart of a big city. World population continues to grow rapidly and it is clear that, if nothing else, we have to learn better how to accommodate such growth, live together and share a common future on this planet. The problems associated with such growth and development require a new environmental awareness. Charting the diversity of signs of environmental decline and improvement is important. For example, one of the indicators of progress in sustainable development is the population of wild birds (Figure 10.1). This is a good measure of wider environmental health and has showed material decline in the last three decades of the twentieth century. Developing good measures of the health of the environment is an essential step in assessing progress in the implementation of policies to improve it.

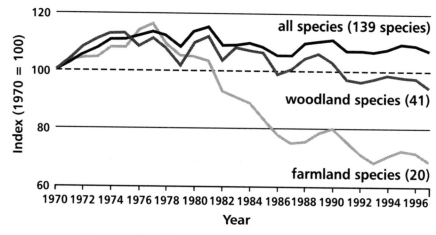

Figure 10.1 Populations of Wild Birds, United Kingdom.

Source: A better quality of life: a strategy for sustainable development for the United Kingdom. London: The Stationery Office, 1999.

Threats to the Environment

The twelve most important problems at an international level, which threaten future well-being have been called the Dirty Dozen (Table 10.3). These are all global issues which have major consequences for public health. The responsibility to tackle these issues is also a global one.

It is because people cannot see that addressing these problems will lead to immediate major local health benefits, that many continue to deny the need to act urgently, or indeed, at all. Such attitudes are widespread in society and pose one of the major threats to future human health. Much of the technology required to make industry, agriculture and transport less polluting; to harness renewable energy sources; to stabilise population growth; to provide sufficient food and to ensure global security, already exists. The problem is getting people to change their individual behaviour, policies and organisational practices.

Table 10.3 The Dirty Dozen of the ecological crisis – the 12 most important problems, at an international level, which threaten our future well-being

1.	Ozone depletion
2.	Global warming
3.	The energy crisis
4.	Air pollution
5.	Soil erosion
6.	Deforestation
7.	Water shortages
8.	Chemicals
9.	Toxic wastes
10.	Arms spending
11.	International debt
12.	Population growth

Source: Porritt J. *Where on Earth are We going?* London: BBC Books, 1990.

Policies for a Healthy Environment

Those working within the field of public health have an important role to play in keeping these issues constantly in the public mind. They can do this by, for example, focusing attention on those actions which can be taken by individuals and organisations within their localities or region which have a positive environmental impact and similarly, by influencing policy-makers.

In addition to its Sustainable Development Strategy, the United Kingdom government along with other countries in the European Region has produced a National Environmental Action Plan (NEHAP) which establishes a clear policy link between environment and health.

NEHAPs are intended as practical plans which will provide a stepwise approach to implementing change and clearly measurable outcomes. They are developed through assessing environmental health problems and risks and in wide consultation with all organisations – both public, private sector and non-governmental – in a partnership approach (Table 10.4). In many parts of the country this has led to the production of Local Environmental Health Action Plans (LEHAPs).

Local action might begin with all organisations embarking on a process of assessing the impact of their activities on both global and local environments and instituting, where possible, appropriate measures to lessen potentially damaging activities and encourage ones which are protective. Such a programme should be guided by a set of environmental principles. Actions like these, if taken by a majority of large organisations, will lead to the changes in infrastructure which are necessary to support widespread adoption of more environmentally-conscious lifestyles.

Table 10.4   Environmental health action plans

Address key environment and health interfaces: some examples

- *Housing* – good quality and well located
- *Community* – safe, accessible, environment – friendly leisure services and amenities
- *Transport* – affordable, safe walking and cycling routes, passenger safety, reduced traffic and pollutants from it
- *Air* – clean, risk-free indoor and outdoor air
- *Water* – sufficient, affordable, potable water
- *Waste* – minimise waste production
- *Noise* – low exposure to adverse effects of noise
- *Radiation* – minimise exposure to all forms of radiation
- *Industrial* – processes which minimise risks to health for production from chemicals and other by-products

Local Environmental Quality

The importance which people attach to their immediate environment is emphasised by a population survey carried out in one of Britain's larger cities. When people on Tyneside were asked: *'Do you have any ideas about how we could work towards making Newcastle a healthier city?'*, the most common comments related to improvement in the environment (Figure 10.2).

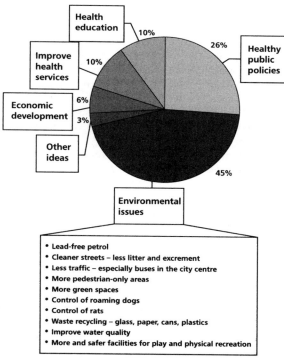

Figure 10.2   People's views (percentage of responses to the question) on what would make Newcastle upon Tyne a healthier city: showing the extent to which the public link health with environment.

Source: Newcastle Health & Lifestyle Survey, 1989.

The general public was making a clear and explicit link between their environment and health. Some of the issues raised related to making the environment more pleasant, with less litter, more green spaces and less traffic noise and pollution. Others were about making it safer, with less risk of ill-health from vermin, city centre traffic and unsafe play facilities.

This study provided a fascinating glimpse into people's perceptions of health. Aside from traditional notions of freedom from disease and positive lifestyles, experiencing a healthy environment was seen to be part of being healthy. It also places in a somewhat different light traditional environmental improvement activities at local level (control of dogs, litter, noise, and nuisances) which some have considered as unfashionable and having no place in a modern conceptualisation of public health.

The National Health Service is one of the largest users of energy, with expenditure representing some 1.6% of the total national consumption. Taken together, its staff, its facilities and the processes of care have a huge environmental impact. The consumption of fossil fuel is recognized as one of the most important causes of environmental damage, primarily through the generation of carbon dioxide emissions. However, since the first international oil crisis in the 1970s, energy consumption in the National Health Service has been reduced by approximately 30%. During the 1980s, savings of 10% were achieved despite major increases in clinical activity and the rapid growth of new technology. Energy savings have continued during the 1990s.

By focusing on the environmental impact of their work, organisations have the potential to produce major change. For example, the use of engineering techniques in the design and maintenance of buildings to increase the efficiency of energy use is of great importance. An illustration of the implication of such techniques in the health service is in the design of low-energy hospitals. These have incorporated high levels of insulation and glazing, efficient heat and light control systems and landscaping designed to help reduce heat loss. These features, together with the recycling of waste heat and the use of waste to generate heat and power, are all measures which can reduce energy consumption by up to 60%.

A holistic view is essential to a full consideration of the environment and health. Equally, the promotion of public health requires both a full understanding of these complex issues and a broadly-based approach to action programmes to create improvement.

In addition, public health is concerned with specific aspects of the physical environment which have the potential to influence health. The remaining sections of this chapter are concerned with some of these specific aspects, the threat which they can pose to human health together with measures required to prevent and protect health.

Health Impact Assessment

Decisions in many different fields taken at national governmental or local level may ultimately have an effect on the health of the population. For example, education has an important bearing on people's health and lifestyle in later life. So a national education policy, whilst primarily intended to improve an aspect of the education of school-age children, could secondarily have an influence on the health of the population in years to come. Similarly, a local plan to site a new young-people's centre alongside a busy dual carriageway whilst primarily intended to improve local leisure facilities, may have the secondary effect of increasing the rate of accidents (young people crossing the road) or asthma attacks amongst those attending from traffic fumes.

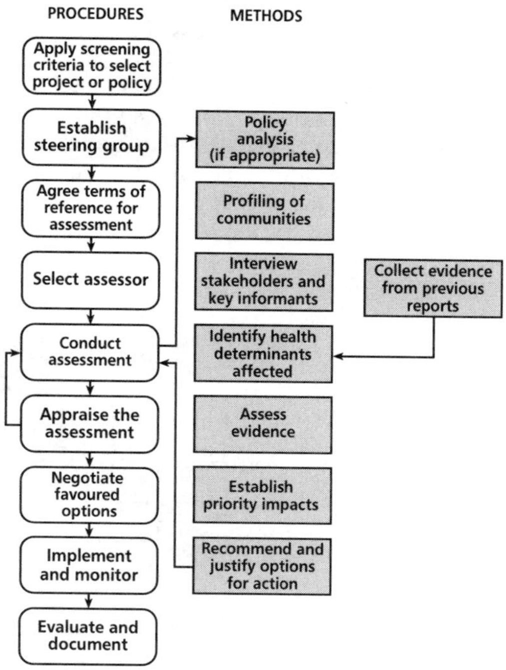

Figure 10.3 Stages in the health impact assessment process.

Source: Scott-Samuel A, Birley M, Ardern K. The Merseyside Guidelines for Health Impact Assessment. Liverpool: Merseyside Health Impact Assessment Steering Group, Liverpool Public Health Observatory, 1999.

The realisation that there may be health consequences to many aspects of policy-making has led to the development of methodologies to assess them.

Health Impact Assessment is a form of appraisal of policy in which the full health consequences of the policy can be explored (Figure 10.3). The methodology for Health Impact Assessment has been developed from a longer standing and similar approach used to assess the impact of planned new developments on the environment (Environmental Impact Assessment). The adaptation of such an approach to health has initially been applied to major projects: for example the proposed second runway at Manchester airport. However, in the late 1990s the British Government decided that major new government policies should be assessed for their impact on health and that local decisions makers must think about what the effects might be on health and in particular how they might reduce inequality.

Climate Change

There is strong evidence that the world is becoming warmer. The average annual temperature has increased during the twentieth century and it is predicted that average global temperatures will increase by 1 °C–3.5 °C by the year 2010.

Climate change can impact on human health in very diverse ways. Direct effects include those arising from exposure to higher temperatures (for example in heat waves) and those arising from depletion of the ozone layer (e.g., increase in skin cancer incidence). Indirect effects on health include an increase in the frequency of insect-borne disease, changes in the pattern of communicable diseases, more asthma and other respiratory illness because of greater atmospheric pollution, injury or death in storms and floods.

The production of greenhouse gases is a phenomenon of the lower atmosphere which leads to heating of the climate whilst depletion of ozone in the stratospheric, higher atmosphere leads to increased penetration of ultraviolet light. The two processes are closely linked (Figure 10.4).

Figure 10.4 Interaction between climate change, stratospheric ozone depletion and pollution.

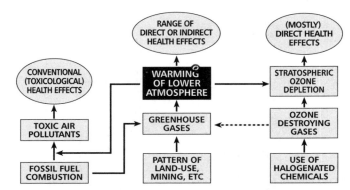

Source: Early human health effects of climate change and stratospheric ozone depletion in Europe. World Health Organization: Third Ministerial Conference on Environment and Health, London: 1999.

Water

Water is a resource. Looked at internationally, the provision of safe water to drink, to prepare food and for sanitation is an aspiration not a reality. The increased demand for water for domestic use with growing urbanisation for recreation and leisure, for industry and agriculture has meant that water is increasingly seen as a precious resource which cannot be taken for granted. The government issues guidance requiring water companies to agree with the Environment Agency, a water resource plan for the long term. Targets to reduce leakage from the water distribution system have also been set for each water company.

The quality as well as the availability of water is also an important public health issue. Microorganisms, chemicals and pesticides are all potential water pollutants which can affect human health.

Contamination of the water supply in the past has been a major cause of disease and death. It was the provision of a safe water supply, together with proper disposal of sewage, which constituted one of the triumphs of the public health pioneers of the last century.

Sources of Water

Water is an excellent solvent for most gases and many solids and also for carrying other substances in suspension. Surface water is the main source of public supply in Britain. Water flowing over the ground dissolves minerals and can carry suspended matter, as well as bacteria, viruses, protozoa, algae and various other plants and animals. Upland surface water in natural lakes and man-made reservoirs supplies about 35% of drinking water and is relatively free from contamination by human and animal waste. Lowland rivers, which supply about 30% of drinking water, become more polluted as they flow from their source to the sea. In some parts of Britain it is necessary to draw on sources from the lower reaches of rivers, and a full purification treatment may be necessary.

On the other hand, underground water from deep wells and boreholes requires only minimal treatment, being of good quality and almost free from contamination. This source contributes about one third of the public water supply. It may be 'hard' water because of the dissolved minerals but most people find it palatable.

Monitoring the Quality of Water

Water for human consumption undergoes regular physical, chemical and bacteriological tests. Physical properties, such as taste, colour and smell are high priorities in determining acceptability, although they may have little bearing on whether the water is safe to drink.

Chemical analysis to determine the type and importance of various chemicals present in water is well established. The decomposition of organic matter contributes to the presence of nitrogen compounds, either as inorganic ammonia, nitrate and nitrites or in its various organic forms. High concentrations of chlorides suggest contamination by sewage. Calcium and magnesium salts are an indication of the hardness of the water. The absence of dissolved oxygen is strong evidence of heavy pollution. In addition, chemical analysis may reveal the presence of small quantities of potentially dangerous substances – such as lead.

Bacteriological examination has been based mainly on isolating and quantifying faecal indicator organisms. *Escherichia coli* is an indicator of human or animal faecal pollution, and coliforms are a less specific indicator. Water companies will need to check for *cryptosporidium* oocysts in future.

Purification Treatment

The aim of purification is to remove pathogenic bacteria, harmful chemicals, suspended matter and any substance causing colour, odour or undesirable taste.

There are a number of methods of water purification, including coagulation filtration, disinfection with chlorine, the use of ozone and activated charcoal. The method most commonly used in Britain is described here. In general, underground water needs less treatment than river water.

Water is first coarse-filtered to remove solid objects and then stored in reservoirs to allow sedimentation. This storage system has the advantage of allowing the supply from the rivers to be cut off if excessive contamination occurs.

The next step in the purification process is filtration, through either slow or rapid filters. Slow sand-filters consist of sand resting on layers of graded gravel. The active part is the slime (containing bacteria, protozoa and other organisms) which forms on the surface, trapping fine suspended matter (including bacteria) and consumes and oxidises organic matter. Rapid sand-filters are more widely used and are made of coarser sand which allows the water to flow through more quickly. Salts of aluminium or iron are added to the water to form floccules, to help remove suspended matter, colour and organic substances. Some bacteria can pass through and their destruction depends on the next phase of purification which is disinfection.

Chlorine is the most widely-used disinfectant agent and is automatically delivered, by specialised equipment, at a sufficient concentration so that a residual concentration of 0.5 ppm (parts per million) remains after 30 minutes' contact with the water. Before the water is distributed, the level of chlorine is reduced by sulphur dioxide to 0.1–0.3 ppm so that at this residual level some disinfectant properties remain without causing complaints of chlorine taste or smell.

After purification, water is held in covered service reservoirs and delivered in main pipes sunk deep enough to avoid frosts.

Fluoride and Dental Health

The presence of fluoride in drinking water at about 1 ppm has been found to reduce dental decay in the population receiving it by some 30–50%.

Small amounts of fluoride occur naturally in water that is in contact with the Earth's rocks. In many countries, including parts of Britain, fluoride is also added to the water supply. Higher levels, which sometimes occur naturally, cause mottling of the dental enamel.

Such measures have been controversial with opponents claiming serious ill-effects following the consumption of fluoridated drinking water. However, most authorities have found no evidence to substantiate this claim. Other countries have introduced this well-health measure on a national basis. In Britain, the geographical distribution of fluoridated water is patchy, to the disadvantage of many children's dental health.

Nitrate

Agriculture is the main source of nitrate in the water. Nitrogen from the soil and from fertilisers is released into rivers and may seep into underground water. The amount which is leached from agricultural land depends on the farming activities as well as the climate. Nitrates in deep underground water may therefore be a reflection of agricultural activities in earlier years.

In parts of Britain the nitrate level in water sources is higher than the limit set by the European Council Directive on Drinking Water, but these waters are treated by water suppliers using denitrification plants to meet the limit before supply. In order to help overcome this problem the government has designated nitrate-sensitive areas, in which certain agricultural operations are regulated. In addition, farmers may qualify for payments to change their farming operations – such as switching from arable to grassland cultivation.

Lead

For centuries lead has been recognized as a poison. Lead in tap water is virtually always derived from the domestic plumbing system, particularly where the water is soft and acidic. Installation of lead pipework has been banned in houses since 1964.

A European Council Directive on Drinking Water introduced in 1998 reduced the maximum permitted level of lead in drinking water to 10 micrograms/litre (with an interim statement of 25 micrograms per litre to be met by 2003). There is evidence that lead can cause intellectual impairment in children and therefore levels of lead in drinking water should be as low as possible. This can be achieved by individuals flushing the pipes before consuming the water, and by water undertakings rendering the water more alkaline or adding orthophosphate. The replacement of lead pipes is the most satisfactory solution.

Aluminium

Acidic water sources, such as upland surface waters with substantial peat deposits, may contain relatively high concentrations of naturally-occurring aluminium. Aluminium sulphate and other aluminium compounds are also widely used in water treatment to improve the appearance and taste of the drinking water, and also aid the efficiency of disinfection. Most aluminium is removed in water treatment. If too much aluminium remains it causes colour and turbidity problems. The statutory limit is 200 parts per billion (micrograms per litre). Higher concentrations may be allowed when the aluminium is from the water source rather than from water treatment.

Research has investigated whether aluminium may be causal in Alzheimer's disease. There is no convincing evidence for this hypothesis thus far.

In the Camelford area of North Cornwall in 1988, extremely high concentrations of aluminium sulphate entered the water supply when a tanker driver delivered a supply to the wrong part of the Lowermoor water treatment works. Lead, copper and zinc dissolved from pipes by the highly acidic water made matters worse. People suffered from nausea, vomiting, abdominal pain, rashes and mouth ulcers. Concerns were expressed about late effects (e.g. memory loss, other cerebral damage, or fetal abnormalities). Studies so far have not established a firm association but follow-up work is continuing.

Sea Water

The possible effects on health of bathing in seawater contaminated by sewage are a matter of public concern. A number of studies world-wide have examined associations between bathing habits and infectious disease and there is general agreement that the risks to bathers of serious illness from bathing in UK waters are very small. Measures have been taken by the European Commission to set standards for the quality of bathing waters and for the treatment of sewage discharges. All significant coastal sewage discharges will have secondary treatment (see below). EC Directives lay down standards for sea bathing water expressed in total coliform organisms per 100 ml. Sampling is carried out on a regular basis.

Waste Management and Disposal

Households in Britain are responsible for some 26 million tonnes of waste each year – about 1 tonne of waste for each household. Industrial waste also accounts for about 26 million tonnes, commercial waste for about 17 million tonnes and construction and demolition waste for about 53 million tonnes, annually.

About 80% of waste in Britain is disposed of in some 4000 landfill sites and there are 11 municipal incinerators which recover energy by burning around 14% of waste. In addition, four specialised high-temperature incinerators deal with some of the most toxic waste.

Particular care must be taken in dealing with waste which is harmful to human health. So called 'hazardous waste' is waste with physical, chemical or biological characteristics with the potential to harm human health. It requires special handling on disposal so that it does not pose a risk to human health or to the environment. The categories of hazardous waste that routinely form part of municipal waste are very diverse. For example, batteries, part-empty paint tins, garden fertiliser and antifreeze can all be extremely toxic unless properly disposed of. Waste arising from health care (e.g., human tissues and organs, medicines, infected linen) pose an additional category of hazardous waste. So too does radioactive waste. In general there is a range of options for the management of hazardous waste (Figure 10.5). Ideally, much less waste, particularly hazardous waste, should be produced (avoidance). This involves investing in new designs for products, devising new low-waste processes for manufacturing and substituting less hazardous material for those that are toxic. Some forms of waste can serve as a raw material (reuse) whilst other types can be recycled into another manufacturing process to produce another material (recycling). Waste can be burned at high temperatures yielding energy from heat or treated chemically to degrade it. This aspect of waste management (recovery and treatment) is not suitable for all forms of waste. The final stage of waste management – for waste which cannot be treated in any of the above ways or for the residues of earlier steps – is disposal. This is skilled and specialised work and must be carefully managed and regulated if the process is not to produce short- or long-term damage to human health or to the environment.

Figure 10.5 A hazardous waste management hierarchy

Source: Hazardous Waste. Briefing pamphlet for local authorities No. 29. Copenhagen: WHO, Regional Office for Europe, 1998.

Municipal and Industrial Waste Disposed of to Landfill

Properly regulated landfill for the final disposal of both municipal and commercial wastes is a proven method of dealing with wastes safely. The environment is protected through both the planning and the waste-licensing regimes.

Local Authorities must take into account specific guidance when taking decisions in planning applications and appeals. This guidance covers the overall development of landfill sites – encompassing landfill design, construction and operational practice. The emphasis is on an engineering approach to landfill design and construction based on site-specific risk assessment, underpinned by quality management and good operational practice, to achieve a high standard of implementation and environmental protection.

Most landfill proposals require an environmental assessment before planning is determined. Environmental assessments consider the geological, hydrogeological and hydrological issues, as well as the assessment of traffic implications of a proposed development, amenity aspects, ecology, soils agriculture, landscape and cultural heritage.

In the United Kingdom, robust licensing legislation exists to control the disposal of waste to landfill. The purpose of a waste-management licensing system is to ensure that the recovery or disposal of controlled waste does not have an adverse impact on the environment, health or local amenities.

The Environment Agency administers and enforces the licensing system. The licence holder must ensure that these conditions are complied with at all times. The Agency is required, through statutory guidance, to inspect all licensed sites to check that this is done. Breach of the conditions of a waste management licence is a criminal offence.

Sewage Treatment

Domestic sewage contains a large number of intestinal organisms and is, therefore, potentially hazardous. The quantity is roughly equal to the amount of water used. A similar amount of industrial waste, which may contain toxic chemicals, runs into public sewers or directly into rivers as can agricultural waste water. About 80% of domestic refuse and industrial waste (some of it toxic) is disposed of in landfill sites, with precautions taken against effluent pollution of surface or underground water.

From an environmental and public health point of view, therefore, a main concern in the disposal of sewage and domestic and industrial waste is to prevent the contamination of the water environment through which, in the end, drinking water is derived.

Sewage treatment is made up of a number of stages. Standards for sewage treatment works are also determined and enforced by the Environment Agency.

Industrial Waste

Most chemicals in rivers are by-products of industrial processes but some, like pesticides, also come from agricultural activities. The government has compiled a 'Red List', which is drawn from a European Council Directive on Dangerous Substances in Water. These substances are persistent, toxic and liable to accumulate in living tissues. They include heavy metals, pesticides, chlorinated industrial chemicals and solvents. Renewed efforts are being made to reduce levels by applying environmental quality standards, by reviewing discharge consents and through government controls on the production and use of harmful substances.

Agricultural Waste

Farm slurry, because of the amount of organic matter it contains, is a hundred times more polluting than raw sewage. Silage effluent is even more polluting. Farm waste contains a wide variety of microorganisms, some of them pathogenic to man. In addition, it contains chemicals, particularly nitrates and phosphates. Some waste flows directly into streams and rivers. Much of it is returned to the land where it may be carried by erosion to ponds, lakes, streams and rivers. In lakes and ponds a problem known as eutrophication may occur. This is a process in which the water becomes richer and richer in nutrients, particularly phosphates and nitrates. There is then an accelerated growth of aquatic plants and algae, resulting in deoxygenation of the water, which becomes lifeless and foul-smelling. These nutrients also come from industrial and domestic waste. Detergents contribute up to half the phosphate content of domestic sewage.

Pesticides

The term pesticide encompasses a wide range of substances such as herbicides, fungicides, insecticides, rodenticides, soil-sterilants, wood preservatives and surface biocides. More precise definitions of specific substances and what controls govern their sale, storage and use are contained in United Kingdom and European legislation.

Pesticides can enter the human body by inhalation, ingestion or through the skin. Exposure can be through the environment, food, water, domestic or garden use and occupation. An essential step in protecting human health from the risk of pesticides is a formal process of approval which a manufacturer, importer and distributor must go through. Data on the substance must be provided for scrutiny.

Risk assessment requires the establishment of acceptable daily intakes (ADIs) for particular pesticides and maximum residue levels (MRLs). The levels of residue both in home-produced and imported food are monitored. In addition, surveys are carried out of residues in humans, wildlife and in the environment.

Statutory powers derived from both United Kingdom and Europe set out the controls that must be applied to protect people, animals and plants from the adverse effect of pesticides, to protect the environment and to make information available to the public.

A number of key bodies assist the government with regulation. The Advisory Committee on Pesticides gives expert advice and undertakes reviews of products and appraises product applications. The Pesticides Safety Directorate is responsible for registering certain categories of agricultural and horticultural pesticide whilst the Health and Safety Executive carries out the registration function of non-agricultural pesticides.

The Food Standards Agency, to be established by the government in the year 2000 (subject to Parliamentary approval), is expected to have a role in relation to food-related pesticides.

The health effects of acute exposure and acute poisoning by pesticides are well documented. Illnesses usually follow from either accidental or deliberate ingestion or skin contamination following careless handling. The symptoms occur shortly afterwards and, in the majority of cases, there is complete recovery without long-term complications.

The main interest to public health is the effect of small doses over a long period of time. Here the evidence is much less clear.

Nuisance

The term 'nuisance' has been used in legislation since the last century. Nuisances were thought to be responsible for ill-health at a time when it was believed that odours were the cause of disease. Nuisances are currently concerned with physical and psychological discomfort (for example, smoke, odours, noise). Local authorities have a legal obligation placed on them, by various Acts, to take action to abate 'statutory' nuisances.

Noise

Noise is an unwanted sound which causes discomfort to the listener. Sound is a form of energy which is transmitted through the air by rapid cyclic pressure changes. Noise in excess is regarded as a pollutant in the environment.

There is a wide range of literature on the effects of noise on hearing, sleep, communication, work and leisure, as well as other general physiological and psychological parameters. The evidence is not always convincing but some studies have found an association between noise and sleep disturbance, poor school performance and hypertension. There is ample evidence of very high degrees of annoyance caused by noise to sections of the population. Such factors are easy to identify but difficult to measure and thus, ultimately, also difficult to control. Noise may arise from many sources including in the environment (e.g., due to traffic, industry or recreation) or in the neighbourhood (e.g., domestic noise, human behaviour).

Workers have a high risk of noise-induced deafness if their environment has noise levels equivalent to a continuous level of 90 dBA or more. However, occupational deafness is the result of fairly lengthy exposure. Permanent deafness may also result from a single, loud explosive sound. Transient deafness (temporary threshold shift) may also be the sequel of exposure to a sudden loud noise or to prolonged intense noise.

Level, frequency, loudness and time are four characteristics of sound which are important when assessing noise.

Policies to control noise are one of the least well-developed aspects of environment and health.

Housing

Living accommodation is designed to provide shelter, security, privacy and comfort. Whether it be in the form of a house, a flat, a bed-sitting room, a caravan, a houseboat or a residential institution, all are covered by legislation.

The Industrial Revolution led to small houses and large tenements, crowding the centres of the new towns and cities, in narrow streets with little open space. Those dwellings were poorly ventilated, ill-lit, lacking in sanitary facilities and the practice of burning coal on open fires created a smoke-polluted environment.

The recognition of the association between poor housing and poor health was a main focus of the sanitary reformers of the last century. In the first half of this century, with the great improvements in sanitary conditions, emphasis changed to the link between inadequate housing and communicable diseases, particularly tuberculosis. Stress was placed on the design of houses to provide good ventilation, natural lighting, heating and the eradication of overcrowding. There is general acceptance that these measures contributed to the decline in tuberculosis and in other infectious diseases, prior to the advent of vaccination and effective therapeutic measures. By the 1950s, the great decline in communicable diseases lessened the emphasis on housing as a factor in ill health.

There has been a paucity of good research into the relationship between housing and health. However, it is now well established that there is a significant association between damp dwellings and respiratory symptoms in children. There is less convincing evidence for this as a cause of adults developing an excess of respiratory symptoms or for links between poor housing and other diseases. In studying this problem, it is difficult to eliminate the effect of confounding variables such as social deprivation which themselves are linked to poor health. However, taken together the relevance of housing to health is wide-ranging (Table 10.5).

Table 10.5 Health manifestations of poor housing

Feature of housing	*Example of health effect*
Homelessness (including temporary accommodation)	Increased risk of mental illness, alcohol and drug problems, tuberculosis
Quality of housing • Damp • Cold • Lacking amenities • Infestation • Overcrowding • Design • Noise insulation • Air quality	Asthma, bronchitis, hypothermia, fires, falls, stress, loss of sleep
Urban environment • High-rise • Access to services • Transport • Recreation • Fear of crime	Road traffic accidents, social isolation, violence, stress, poor access to health services

Source: The Health of Londoners, King's Fund Publishing, 1998.

The existing evidence points to cold homes being the primary health risk associated directly with the condition of the housing stock, contributing to a proportion of excess winter deaths each year.

In the past, the main process for dealing with unfit housing was slum clearance. This started in the 1930s and continued, with a break for World War II, until the mid-1970s. The emphasis then changed to renovation of existing houses with demolition of properties being an exceptional action. In 1979 there were 24,000 dwellings demolished in slum clearance areas but by the end of the 1980s this had fallen to 3500. On the other hand, the number of major renovations of dwellings doubled over the same time period. By the late 1990s there were 150 clearance areas remaining, containing fewer than 2100 dwellings.

The Local Government and Housing Act 1989 encouraged local housing authorities to assess the need for clearance and renovation on a systematic and area basis.

A new statutory concept of 'renewal areas' was introduced to allow a comprehensive approach covering renovation and development of housing alongside action on social, economic and environmental problems. It is envisaged that this activity would be spread over ten years. Thus, the authorities would have real scope to improve the housing, general amenities and to tackle environmental problems in an area.

Before declaring a renewal area authorities must carry out an assessment and consider various options. The assessment team will include, environmental health officers together with other officials, such as planners, valuers and accountants. In the late 1990s there were 114 renewal areas in 65 local authority areas in England. For areas of severe and multiple deprivation a comprehensive, area-based approach may be needed. This should aim to bring housing and regeneration spending together, extend economic opportunities for local people and improve neighbourhood management and the delivery of local services. It should tackle poor job prospects, high levels of crime, educational under-achievement and poor health.

Standards for housing are set through local and national legislation and enforced by local authorities. The statutory standard for fitness for human habitation includes: structural stability, freedom from dampness and serious disrepair, adequate lighting, heating and ventilation, satisfactory facilities for cooking food, piped supply of wholesome water, fixed bath or shower with hot and cold water, a toilet and effective drainage system. This standard is currently under review and a system of assessment of health and safety hazards in a home is proposed. This would include cold homes, radon, fire hazards and design of stairs.

All housing authorities are required, by law, to give priority, when allocating social housing, to people with a medical need for settled accommodation. Authorities have different methods of assessing medical priority, but most take decisions on advice of independent medical experts.

Rough Sleeping

During the 1970s, 1980s and 1990s the large cities of the world saw an increasing number of people sleeping rough. So called 'rough sleeping' is one of the strongest examples of social exclusion. Around 10,000 people are thought to sleep rough in England each year and something like 2000 each night.

Rough sleeping does not equate to homelessness. It accounts for a small proportion of homeless people. Homelessness is a person defined in legislation as a having no right to occupy a property as an owner or a tenant. People in temporary accommodation such as a hostel would be classified as homeless though they are not literally out on the streets as are rough sleepers. Many rough sleepers have mental health or alcohol problems and many have been in institutions (e.g., prison or local authority care). The key to reducing the number of people who sleep rough is a city-wide integrated approach involving local authorities, non-governmental agencies with expertise in this area and health services. Hostels, day centres and shelters can all play their part but the long-term aim should be to resettle the person in substantive accommodation. This means coordinating social housing policy with measures to tackle the individual's underlying needs (e.g., health, employment, life skills).

Atmospheric Pollution and Air Quality

In the eighteenth and nineteenth centuries, the Industrial Revolution brought increasing problems of atmospheric pollution from the chimneys of factories and houses in the new industrial towns. Legislation to control pollution at that time was directed mainly at industry. The zeal of the sanitary reformers, more than 100 years ago, in achieving safe drinking water and proper disposal of sewage, was not matched by an attack on the other environmental evil, air pollution, which had effectively turned the atmosphere over the large towns into a cloud of smoke. Over the years, the public showed little interest. Indeed, a major contributor to air pollution, the domestic open coal fire, was stoutly defended.

A dramatic turning point in attitudes to atmospheric pollution occurred in December 1952. A London 'smog' (the word 'smog' was coined in the early years of the twentieth century to describe fog filled with smoke) coincided with a steep rise in the number of deaths. Although excess deaths had been noted in other smog episodes, nothing quite as striking had occurred before. The matter received wide media coverage and a curious occurrence made the story even more sensational. A number of prime young cattle, at a show in London, also succumbed to the effects of pollution.

Legislation

The results of the events in the early 1950s in London led to the first Clean Air Act of 1956 and subsequent legislation. This set a framework for action and was enhanced by other factors, such as the trend towards the use of gas and electricity for domestic and central heating and the switch in the 1960s to natural gas, which is smoke-free and virtually sulphur-free.

A major feature of the legislation was to create smoke-control areas. In general in these areas it is an offence to emit smoke from a chimney. They are not 'smokeless zones' because controlled amounts of smoke from specific buildings are permitted, for example, as the result of lighting-up a furnace. The main thrust of the scheme was to reduce smoke from the domestic fire, which had been identified as contributing to 80% of pollution. Householders were provided with grants for conversion to smokeless fuel.

The result was a dramatic improvement. The average visibility on a winter's day in London increased from one to four miles. The concept in the legislation has been adopted by other countries and has been reinforced by air quality standards in European Commission Directives. By 1980, the perceived success of the reduction of atmospheric pollution led to the demise of the very bodies which helped to solve the problem: the Clean Air Council and the Medical Research Council's Air Pollution Unit. Furthermore, much of the monitoring network for air quality was dismantled. In recent years the network has expanded again. The consequence of these measures has been that the high quality of research into the effects of atmospheric pollution, which started at the time of the London smog, ceased in the 1980s in Britain and began again only in the early 1990s.

Gaps in knowledge about the association between current pollutants in the air and diseases of the lung remain. Comprehensive monitoring and high quality research is needed to assess the affects of atmospheric pollution on the population, especially the more vulnerable members.

Types of Pollutants

The British Government's National Air Quality Strategy aims to ensure that polluting emissions and ambient air quality do not harm human health and the environment. It does so by setting standards (taking account of European Commission Directives), extensively monitoring and implementing measures. In the strategy, eight pollutants in particular are targeted. These are briefly described in this section.

Sulphur Dioxide

In Britain, almost 70% of emissions of sulphur dioxide are from fossil-fuelled power stations and a substantial proportion also from industry. Reductions were achieved during the 1980s and early 1990s by reducing emissions arising from electricity generation. Further reductions depend on tight monitoring against standards and a particular focus on smaller power stations. Sulphur dioxide has effects on human health shortly after exposure so standards for outdoor levels are set as 15 minutes, 1 hour and 24 hour limits not to be exceeded a certain number of times per year.

Lead in the Air

Lead is a particularly dangerous heavy metal. During the 1980s, concern was expressed that the average blood-lead concentration of the population was high. A major contributor to lead in the atmosphere is the petrol engine. As a result, measures were taken, combined with tax incentives, to introduce unleaded petrol. Today, leaded petrol is declining in use rapidly and by 2000 leaded petrol will be available only on a very limited basis. The introduction of unleaded petrol has made possible the use of catalytic convertors, which remove a large part of the nitrogen oxides and volatile organic compounds from vehicle exhausts, and have been standard on all cars sold in the UK since 1993. Certain industrial processes, smelting in particular, also emit lead into the air. These remain a problem in some areas. The adverse health effects of lead include impaired brain development in children, abnormal synthesis of haemoglobin, and effects on certain other organs and systems (e.g., kidneys, reproductive).

Nitrogen Dioxide

Whereas sulphur dioxide gas is only produced when sulphur is present in the fuel being burnt, oxides of nitrogen are formed when any material is burned. The main sources of oxides of nitrogen are from power stations, large industrial plants and, in particular, motor vehicles, which contribute 80% of the nitrogen dioxide in urban environments.

During the latter part of the 1980s, with growing vehicle emission, levels of nitrogen dioxide were increasing, especially in urban centres. This is now being tackled in Europe through Vehicle Emission Standards.

Ozone is formed by the action of sunlight on nitrogen oxides and occurs in increased concentrations when hydrocarbons are present. Levels tend to be highest in southern Britain and recent research has shown that there are significant effects on health. Because of the trans-boundary nature of the photochemical chain reaction the ozone problem needs to be tackled on an international basis.

Nitrogen oxides and sulphur dioxide contribute to the formation of acid rain. The gases which are involved can be carried long distances by the wind and can cross national boundaries to affect neighbouring countries. Consequently, acidic air pollution can have a widespread effect on buildings, fish, wildlife and vegetation.

Particulates

Studies, in the United Kingdom, United States and Europe have shown that particulate air pollution, in particular small particles, is still an important cause of damage to health. In urban areas motor vehicles are a major source. Standards defined in term of the mass of particles (below a certain size) per volume of air have been introduced. Extensive monitoring of such particle concentrations is now undertaken in the United Kingdom and other developed countries.

Other Pollutants

Emissions of carbon monoxide, which is produced by incomplete combustion of fuel, have increased in the same way and for the same reasons as the oxides of nitrogen. In Britain, 85% of carbon monoxide emissions come from car exhausts. The application of European Commission standards should reduce this.

Carcinogenic air pollutants, including benzene, 1,3-butadiene and polycyclic aromatic hydrocarbons, are produced by vehicles and other fuel-burning processes. In the United Kingdom the National Air Quality Strategy has set standards for these pollutants. Incineration of waste has introduced the risk of dangerous pollutants, such as polychlorinated biphenyls and dioxins. European Commission Standards are set to control such pollutants.

Monitoring

Extensive monitoring of air pollutants is carried out by the UK Government. This allows the concentrations of pollutants to be assessed against EC Directive Limit Values and against the standards and objectives set out in the National Air Quality Strategy.

Key sites are connected directly to the Department of Environment so that information can be immediately available. This can be made public by weather bulletins to help people who might be affected by air pollution to take necessary steps.

Pollution from industry is the responsibility of the Environment Agency and of local authorities. They have responsibilities for ensuring air and water quality standards and that solid waste is properly disposed of. They also have enforcement powers to ensure that standards are met. The central government Department of Environment, Transport and the Regions has the responsibility to control pollution from vehicles. This is done by testing emissions from vehicles through MOT tests and roadside checks.

The Effects of Atmospheric Pollution on Health

There is wide agreement that patients with established respiratory or cardiac disease, particularly the elderly, suffer adverse effects of atmospheric pollution when it reaches peak levels. Recent research has shown that daily variations in levels of pollutants are associated with effects on health. The size of the effect is significantly larger than would have been predicted a decade ago. There is also accumulating evidence that long-term exposure to pollutants leads to impaired development of lung function and a reduction in life expectancy. There is also evidence of sulphur dioxide and ozone increasing the hypersensitivity of asthmatics. The acute effects of carbon monoxide are well known.

Indoor Air Quality

The population spends, on average, 90% of their time indoors and of that time 70% is in their own homes. Thus, air is breathed primarily in a closed environment and more attention is now directed at the microclimate.

Indoor pollution can arise from the activities of individuals (such as cigarette smoking), from combustion of fossil fuels, the growth of moulds in damp conditions from materials of which the building is constructed and emissions from the ground, such as radon, a naturally occurring radioactive gas. The increasingly recognized dangers from radon are discussed in the section on radiation.

Production of carbon monoxide can result through improper installation and maintenance of gas or solid fuel fires, where there is an inadequate supply of air. Lethal concentrations cause up to 70 deaths every year and at lower levels, the well documented, symptoms of chronic carbon monoxide poisoning occur.

Smoking tobacco can give rise to a variety of pollutants in the indoor climate. There is an increased incidence of respiratory illness in children and of lung cancer for non-smokers. It is estimated that several hundred lung cancer deaths a year in Britain can be attributed to passive smoking. In addition, smoking enhances the risk posed by radon, which is estimated to be ten times greater for the smoker than the non-smoker.

A wide variety of chemicals are found in modern building materials and household fittings. Their health impact has not been properly assessed but this is likely to be an important area of study in the future.

Reports of higher incidence of symptoms amongst people who work in certain buildings have given rise to the label 'sick building syndrome'. The type of symptoms reported relate to the eye, headaches, respiratory tract infections and sore throats. A variety of causes have been suggested, including poor air quality and the design of buildings. Research is continuing but has not yet established a specific link between any of the suggested causative factors and illness. However, improved ventilation seems to be helpful in reducing symptoms.

Transport

The transport system is responsible for major adverse impacts on health. Road traffic contributes to congestion, accidents, air pollution, and noise. Major roads can cause divisions and exclusion in communities, while planning decisions can mean that services, including health services, are sited so that access for some people is difficult, while for others car use is increased. The structure of transport systems can also make it difficult to choose healthy forms of transport; for example fear of accidents and crime means that far fewer children walk or cycle to school than a generation ago. While some of these effects can be tackled through 'technical fixes' such as catalytic converters or more fuel-efficient vehicles, it is obvious that in order to maximise benefits to health, transport systems need to be viewed as a whole, so that integrated and sustainable improvements can be made (Table 10.6).

Table 10.6   Some important elements of healthier policies on transport

- Reducing reliance on motorised transport
- Better coordination and integration of health, environment and transport at national and local level
- Enabling and encouraging forms of transport which support physical activity (e.g., walking and cycling)
- Increasing access to good public transport
- Targeting the reduction of health risks of transport on the most vulnerable (e.g., children, the elderly, the socially excluded)
- Reducing air pollution and noise arising from transport
- Minimising risks arising from transport pollutants and sources of injury

Radiation

Concern and attention in environmental and public health has centred primarily on ionising radiation, though reference will be made later to non-ionising radiation whose effects are the subject of increasing media scrutiny.

Most elements have stable forms. However, some natural elements such as radium and uranium, have no stable form and are said to be *radioactive* emitting *radiation* from their nuclei in moving towards a more stable configuration. Radioactive forms of stable elements can be produced artificially; for example, by bombardment with neutrons (widely used in medicine and industry).

Three types of radiation are emitted principally:

- *Alpha particles* – these particles are essentially identical to the helium nucleus; comprising two protons and two neutrons and consequently having a double positive charge and relatively large mass.
- *Beta particles* – these are identical to electrons but emitted from the nucleus after the internal transformation of a neutron into a proton and an electron.
- *Gamma rays* – like X-rays these are electromagnetic radiation and similar to light, but of much higher frequency. They may be regarded as quanta (or packets) of photons usually emitted during de-excitation of the nucleus – commonly after emission of a beta particle.

In passing through matter, including tissue, each form of radiation loses energy by *ionisation*: removing electrons from the orbital shells of atoms or molecules in the matter and leaving behind ions or free radicals as chemically-active species.

However, the alpha particle by its nature is densely ionising, depositing more energy per unit track length, having a high *linear energy transfer* (LET). Consequently, alpha particles have a relatively short range and greater propensity within the body for damaging cells. In contrast to alpha particles, which outside of the body are completely absorbed by a thin sheet of paper or the dead layers of skin, beta and gamma radiation have a lower LET and are more penetrating. Up to 1 cm of aluminium is required to absorb beta radiation and about 4 cm of lead to reduce the gamma ray intensity from, for example, a radium source by a factor of ten. Clearly, beta and gamma radiation can pose a potential risk outside of as well as inside the body.

Concepts of Radiation Dose to Individuals and Populations

The *absorbed dose* corresponds to the energy deposited per unit mass. Its unit is the gray (symbol Gy), named after a British scientist, and is equivalent to 1 joule per kilogram.

As might be expected, because of its high LET, 1 Gy of alpha radiation in tissue will cause more harm than 1 Gy of beta or gamma radiation. To provide a common measurement of potential harmfulness the *equivalent dose* is used which is equal to the absorbed dose multiplied by a factor to take account of the LET for that type of radiation. The unit of equivalent dose is called the sievert (symbol Sv), named after a Swedish scientist. For beta and gamma radiation the factor is 1 so that the absorbed dose and equivalent dose are numerically identical. In the case of alpha particles emitted within the body from inhaled or ingested material, the factor is 20 and an absorbed dose of 1 Gy corresponds to an equivalent dose of 20 Sv. Finally, it is necessary to recognize that the susceptibility of different tissues to the induction of malignancy is not the same. For example, the risk of fatal malignancy per Sv is greater for lung than the thyroid. To take account of these differences and the risk of serious hereditary effects, the equivalent dose is multiplied by a risk weighting factor for the different tissues, which can then be summed to give the *effective dose* (commonly abbreviated to 'dose'). A benefit of using the effective dose measure is that the risk to health for non-uniform distribution of equivalent dose in the body can be broadly expressed as a single number. For illustration, as will be seen shortly, the average annual effective dose from natural background radiation to inhabitants of the United Kingdom is 2200 microsieverts.

As the sievert is a relatively large dose of radiation, sub-multiples are commonly used. The microsievert is one-millionth of a sievert and the millisievert is one-thousandth of a sievert. The gray and sievert are Standard International (SI) units and earlier literature used the previous terminology of the rad (100 rad = 1 gray) for absorbed dose and the rem (100 rem = 1 sievert) for the equivalent dose.

Although radiation doses to individuals are generally of greatest interest, it is sometimes appropriate to have a measure of the total dose from a particular source to groups of people or a whole population. This total dose is expressed as the *collective effective dose* (commonly abbreviated to 'collective dose'). By analogy with man-hours, the collective dose is expressed in man sieverts (symbol man Sv) and is obtained by summing the average effective dose to each group multiplied by the number of people in that group.

As the population of the United Kingdom is about 56 million, the collective dose for the population is the product of this number and the average annual effective dose, that is about 124,000 man Sv. However, it is important to recognize that, although the collective dose would be the same for a population half this size and receiving twice the average dose, the personal risk to these individuals would obviously be doubled.

Effects of Ionising Radiation on Health

Soon after the discovery of X-rays by Röntgen in 1895 and of radioactivity by Becquerel in the following year, the harmful effects of radiation were noticed. The effects are dependent on the dose, dose-rate and tissues exposed, as summarised in Table 10.7.

Table 10.7   Principal harmful radiation effects: conditions for occurrence and sources of information

Health consequences	Circumstances of exposure	Sources of information
Early effects		
Death Erythema Sterility	High dose and dose-rate: • to much of the body • to area of skin • to testes and ovaries	Human data from various sources
Late effects		
Various cancers	Any dose or dose-rate Risk depends on dose Appear years later	Risk factors for human beings estimated from high doses and dose-rates in human health studies
Hereditary defects	Any dose or dose-rate Risk depends on dose Appear in offspring	Risk factors for human beings inferred from animal data and the absence of human evidence
Functional damage to organs and tissues	High dose at any rate Various times to appear	Human data from various sources
Learning disability	Dose in the womb Appears in the child	Limited human data

Source: Living with Radiation, The National Radiological Protection Board, 1998.

Early Effects

Early effects are associated with exposure to high dose and dose-rates. At the extreme, an absorbed dose of 5 Gy or more to the whole body delivered almost instantaneously is liable to be fatal because of acute damage to the gastro-intestinal, erythropoietic and central nervous systems. Brief exposure of a limited area of the body to a very large dose may be sub-lethal but some early effects may be generated. Whole-body doses of about 1 to 3 Gy may create the symptoms of Acute Radiation Sickness, including vomiting, diarrhoea and epilation but with a substantial probability of survival. Exposure of the skin to an almost instantaneous absorbed dose of 5 Gy would probably produce erythema within about a week and more serious damage would result with higher doses. Such doses to the testes or ovaries would be liable to cause sterility.

However, with whole-body doses rather less than 1 Gy or larger total doses received more protractedly, no early signs of injury may be apparent but may be manifested much later as malignancy or hereditary effects in offspring.

Late Effects

The two most important late effects of radiation are the induction of malignant disease and hereditary effects. In studies of groups of people, such as the Japanese survivors of atomic bombing and others exposed to ionising radiation, a greater incidence of various malignant disease was recorded in those exposed to relatively high doses of radiation some years previously. From these data, risk factors have been derived by UNSCEAR and the International Commission on Radiological Protection (ICRP), relating the excess of fatal cancers to the radiation dose received. Importantly, it is further assumed that there is no threshold below which fatal cancer might not be induced by radiation. The number of cancers increase with increasing radiation dose.

Clearly, these risk factors are based on relatively high doses received in a short period of time. Whereas, in the normal course of events, relatively small doses are received over longer periods. It would seem reasonable to expect reduced risks in the latter circumstances and indeed there is substantial evidence, at least for beta, X and gamma radiation that the risk is less at low doses and low dose rates. The risk factors, recently revised by ICRP, are expressed as a mathematical probability; for example, 1 in 20 per Sv (or $5 \times 10^{-2} Sv^{-1}$) and incorporating a dose and dose-rate effectiveness factor of 2 to make some allowance for this low dose-rate effect.

Similar considerations apply to hereditary effects. However, in human offspring there has been no conclusive evidence for hereditary defects attributable to exposure from natural or artificial radiation. The Japanese data failed to show statistically significant increases in hereditary defects but these negative findings, representing an upper estimate, together with animal data, were used by ICRP to estimate a risk factor for serious hereditary damage in humans. When all generations subsequent to a radiation exposure are taken into account, the value of the risk factor for severe hereditary effects is about 1 in 100 per Sv (or $1 \times 10^{-2} Sv^{-1}$).

To maintain proper perspectives it is important to recognize corollaries arising from the basic assumption of a proportional relationship between dose and risk, without a threshold. It implies that exposure to any dose of radiation, no matter how small, carries some risk. Consequently, even the smallest additional risks to a population will inevitably lead to a prediction of some associated deaths or hereditary effects which can be alarming. For example, a very small increase (of 20 microsieverts – about 1% of the average annual dose from natural background radiation) in the average dose to a population would give a calculated additional risk of only 1 in a million, but for the United Kingdom (population of 56 million) would lead to a prediction of 56 attributable cancer deaths and in other European countries (population 650 million) 650 attributable cancer deaths. It is sometimes necessary to remember that even for a fatal risk of 1 in 10,000, there is a probability of 99.99% that death will occur from some other cause (Table 10.8).

Table 10.8 Average annual risk of death in the UK from some common causes

Smoking 10 cigarettes a day	5.0×10^{-3}	1 in 200
Heart disease	3.3×10^{-3}	1 in 300
All cancers	2.5×10^{-3}	1 in 400
All causes, 40 years old	1.4×10^{-3}	1 in 700
All radiation (2.6 mSvy^{-1})	1.3×10^{-4}	1 in 7,700
Accident in the home	6.9×10^{-5}	1 in 15,000
Accident on the road	5.9×10^{-5}	1 in 17,000
Homicide	1.0×10^{-5}	1 in 100,000
Nuclear discharges (0.14 mSvy^{-1})	7.0×10^{-6}	1 in 140,000
Pregnancy, for mother	6.0×10^{-6}	1 in 170,000

Source: Living with Radiation, The National Radiological Protection Board, 1998.

Radiation Doses to the General Public in Perspective

The principal sources of radiation exposure to the general public include natural background radiation, medical exposures and discharges from the nuclear industry.

Natural background radiation arises from extra-terrestrial cosmic rays and through naturally radioactive elements in the earth's crust, notably uranium, thorium and potassium-40. Uranium occurs in soil and rock in concentrations varying from a few parts per million (ppm) to more than 1000 ppm. Uranium-238 is the parent of a long chain of radioactive daughters. The decay products include the alpha-emitting radioactive gas radon (radon-222), some of which escapes to the atmosphere, continuing to decay to radioactive daughters such as polonium-210 which is another natural alpha-emitting element that has a radiotoxicity similar to that of plutonium-239. Thorium is similarly distributed in the earth and radon-220 (called thoron) is akin to radon-222, being a daughter product of thorium-232. Potassium comprises 2.4% by weight of the earth's crust and naturally radioactive potassium-40 in turn constitutes 120 ppm of the stable element. Consequently, the public is exposed to *external radiation* from cosmic rays and gamma rays from radioactivity in the earth and to *internal radiation* through inhalation of radon, thoron and their daughter products and also through ingestion of foodstuffs and water incorporating natural radioactivity.

The primary source of medical exposures for the public as a whole is through diagnostic X-ray examinations, being much more common than radiotherapy procedures and outweighing the greater individual dose of the latter.

Figure 10.6, published by the National Radiological Protection Board (NRPB), shows that, for the general public, about 85% of the annual radiation dose is attributable to natural sources (primarily radon and its daughter products), about 14% is due to medical exposures and less than 0.1% is associated with nuclear discharges. This situation is clearly at variance with public perception. Expressed differently, the average annual dose due to natural background is about 2210 units (a unit being one micro-sievert), the corresponding dose from medical exposures is about 370 units and that from nuclear waste discharges less than 1 unit, giving a total of some 2581 units.

Figure 10.6 Annual radiation doses to UK population.

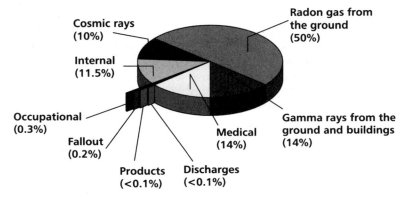

Source: Living with Radiation, The National Radiological Protection Board, 1998.

Non-ionising Radiation

Non-ionising radiation is radiation that does not produce ionisation in matter. Non-ionising radiation is broadly of two types: optical (ultraviolet, visible and infrared) and electromagnetic fields (EMF) (microwave, radio frequency and extremely low frequency). Radiations are described in terms of their wavelengths or frequency. For convenience optical and microwave radiations can be considered as packets of energy (photons) travelling through space. Radio frequency and extremely low frequency fields can be considered as time varying electric and magnetic fields moving through space in wave-like patterns. Optical sources of radiation include solar radiation (UV), infrared radiation and lasers. Electromagnetic fields are produced by electrical power-lines, electrical appliances at home and work, mobile phones and radio, television transmitters and phone base-stations.

Harmful Effects

The harmful effects of non-ionizing radiations are of three main types: photochemical, thermal and electrical effects. Photochemical effects result from chemical reactions in the body initiated by the absorption of photons and can be produced by radiations with short wavelengths such as solar ultraviolet radiation. However, optical radiation does not penetrate far into human tissue so the eyes and skin are the organs most at risk.

Examples of adverse photochemical effects are ultraviolet induced sunburn and snow blindness. There is good evidence that ultraviolet radiation especially can cause non-malignant skin cancer. Cutaneous malignant melanoma is much less common but of considerable public health concern, because of its serious nature and its rapid increase during the last few decades. Although direct evidence of a link with ultraviolet radiation is absent, there is epidemiological evidence that short-term, intermittent exposure to high levels of solar ultraviolet radiation, especially at an early age, may be a contributory factor in the causation of cutaneous malignant melanoma. There is a potential for risks to be increased through the effects of depletion of the ozone layer, although this is a winter phenomenon in the UK.

The longer wavelengths in infrared and microwave regions of the non-ionizing spectrum do not have enough energy to initiate photochemical reactions but can produce thermal injury resulting from the disruption of the molecular bonds of proteins and enzymes. Intense sources of optical and infrared radiations, such as lasers, can cause thermal burning. The lens of the eye lacks a direct blood supply and is therefore more susceptible to injury from heat. Hence, infrared and microwave radiation may increase the risk of cataracts.

At even longer wavelengths (which include the electric mains) electromagnetic fields can induce electric charge on the surface of the body and electric current within the body which can occasionally stimulate nerves. Direct contact with electric current will also lead to shock and burns. These immediate effects of human exposure to electromagnetic fields are well understood and restrictions are in place to avoid them.

There has, for some time, been much speculation about the possible delayed effects of electromagnetic fields on the body – in particular the risk of contracting cancer. Mobile telephones and their base stations have been a particular subject of concern.

Epidemiological studies of occupational and population exposures to various electrical and magnetic sources have not so far led to international consensus that there is consistent and persuasive evidence that EMF influence any of the stages of cancer development. Other effects such as brain function have also been scrutinised but the evidence here is even more limited. However, the science in this area is kept under review.

Environmental Protection

Measures to protect and improve the quality of the environment are contained in the Environmental Protection Act 1990 and in a number of other pieces of legislation, relating particularly to the role and responsibilities of the local authority.

The Department of Environment, Transport and the Regions is the government department with overall responsibility for coordinating and implementing environmental protection. There are a number of inspectorial and standards enforcement bodies (in particular, the Environment Agency the Health and Safety Executive and Local Authorities). The government is also advised by a the National Radiological Protection Board on the impact of natural and man-made radiation on human health.

The Environment Agency has overall responsibility for control of the most polluting industrial processes which may contaminate any aspect of the physical environment. It runs a control system known as the Integrated Pollution Prevention Control (IPPC).

The Environment Agency has powers and responsibility for managing water resources. It monitors water quality and assesses the extent to which water quality standards are being achieved, taking enforcement action where necessary.

Local authorities have wide-ranging powers and responsibilities concerning environmental protection. These relate to air quality, pollution control, toxic substances, waste, noise, nuisances, pests and vermin, dog control and litter. At a day-to-day level much of this work is carried out by environmental health officers who also have responsibilities in relation to communicable disease control and food hygiene.

With increased use of chemicals the chances of an industrial or transport accident causing chemical contamination of the environment and affecting human health have increased. Health Authorities have responsibility for dealing with the health aspects of such a chemical incident and should be involved with the Local Authority and the emergency services in maintaining a multi-agency plan, which will enable a coordinated and effective response.

Britain is now subject to a great deal of environmental protection legislation produced by the European Commission (EC). For example, and as has been mentioned, Directives cover drinking water, bathing water, air quality, larger combustion plants and hazardous waste.

Health Risks, Communication and Public Understanding

The last decade of the twentieth century saw a major growth in public concern about potential health hazards. This was reflected in widespread media coverage of scientific reports, government actions and human interest stories which appeared to suggest that a particular environmental or dietary agent carried a risk to human health. In Britain, the Bovine Spongiform Encephalopathy (BSE) epidemic in cattle, the use of genetically-modified crops and mobile telephones are all examples of issues which became the subject of media attention.

Certain issues where a risk is claimed to exist are more likely to frighten people than others (Table 10.9). Whilst understanding what underlies the public perception of risk is important, the greatest difficulty for public health policy makers relates to how a risk is assessed, when an intervention to reduce it should be taken and what should be communicated to the public.

Table 10.9 Fright factors

Risks are generally more worrying (and less acceptable) if perceived:

1. To be involuntary (e.g., exposure to pollution) rather than voluntary (e.g., dangerous sports or smoking)
2. As inequitably distributed (some benefit while others suffer the consequences)
3. As inescapable by taking personal precautions
4. To arise from an unfamiliar or novel source
5. To result from man-made, rather than natural sources
6. To cause hidden and irreversible damage; e.g., through onset of illness many years after exposure
7. To pose some particular danger to small children or pregnant women or more generally to future generations
8. To threaten a form of death (or illness/injury) arousing particular dread
9. To damage identifiable rather than anonymous victims
10. To be poorly understood by science
11. As subject to contradictory statements from responsible sources (or, even worse, from the same source)

Source: Communicating about Risks to Public Health: Pointers to Good Practice. London: Department of Health, 1997.

The most difficult areas to address are those in which an association is found (or claimed) between a risk factor and an adverse heath outcome yet it is not clear whether that association is causal. The question of establishing causality is discussed fully in Chapter 3 but it is a constantly recurring theme in this field of public health. Examples of issues which can be portrayed by the media as established 'cause and effect' include: a cluster of cases of childhood cancer around an industrial plant; people who take their stories to a tabloid newspaper with a claim that their illness is a result of exposure to a particular environmental hazard, and people who believe they are at risk from industrial pollutants.

The association may, or may not, be causal or the evidence may not be available to prove the case one way or the other. Yet, the public will usually expect an immediate response from the scientific community, government and the public health authorities. There are no easy answers to these questions.

Table 10.10 Determining public health policy in relation to a risk

- Assess the risk using the best scientific evidence
- Decide on whether an intervention should be made to reduce the risk
- Choose an appropriate intervention
- Communicate to those exposed to the risk or who perceive there is a risk
- Implement the intervention successfully or (if no intervention is taken) continue to research or monitor

As a first step (Table 10.10) a high-quality assessment of the scientific evidence is essential, sometimes coupled with a research investigation. At some point, a decision will have to be taken about whether it is appropriate to take an intervention to reduce the risk and what the nature of that intervention should be (e.g., legislative, providing public information or advice, altering a manufacturing or production process). Although it might be supposed that all the scientific evidence should be to hand before any intervention is contemplated, in practice public concern or media pressure may be so great that early action has to be considered.

This particular aspect of risk – when and how to intervene – became the focus of a great deal of debate in the 1990s in Britain as a result of the BSE crisis. The concept of the 'precautionary principle' has emerged. This has been defined in various ways but essentially is a judgement which must be applied in situations of scientific uncertainty where the postulated risk is serious and where action is being contemplated before the results of further research or investigation is to hand. Thus, the precautionary principle holds that action to protect the public health should be taken to reduce or control the risk 'in the meantime'.

In the whole area of health and risk it is essential that there is much openness and transparency about the issues and the scientific evidence as possible. The guiding principles must be based not only on a rigorous approach to evaluating the risk but also on sharing information with the public (Table 10.11). Without this there will be a breakdown of trust and the value of public health advice will be weakened.

Table 10.11   Guiding principles

- High quality assessment of science
- Full risk/benefit assessment
- Consistency of approach across risk areas
- Clear framework of interventions
- Approach should have integrity if judged in retrospect
- Protect the vulnerable
- Realistic sharing of uncertainty
- Information should provide insight
- Greater public participation in risk deliberations

Source: Saving Lives: Our Healthier Nation, The Stationery Office, London: 1999. (Cm 4386).

Conclusions

The importance of the relationship between the quality of the physical environment and people's health has long been recognized. Moreover, in recent years, there have been a number of major incidents around the world which have all too dramatically highlighted some of the contemporary threats and hazards both to the well-being of individuals and to the planet itself. With the current growth in interest and rapidly rising concerns about wider environmental issues, the future will see the current focus on environment and health evolving to the point when they become inextricably linked. One of the important roles of public health will be to promote this wider view of health as well as establishing measures to protect populations from the adverse impact of specific environmental hazards.

References

Chapter 1

Page 6: 1 Townsend P, Phillimore P, Beattie A. *Health and Deprivation: Inequality and the North*. London: Routledge, 1988.

2 Jarman B. *Identification of underprivileged areas*. BMJ, 1983; 286: 1705–9.

Page 29: 3 Hunt SM, McKenna SP, McEwan J, Backett EM, Williams J, Papp E. *A quantitative approach to perceived health status: a validation study*. Journal of Epidemiology and Community Health, 1990; 34: 281.

Chapter 3

Page 111: 1 Vallery Radot R. *The life of Pasteur*. London: Constable, 1902.

Page 113: 2 Lalonde M. *A new perspective on the health of Canadians. A working document*. Ottawa: Information Canada, 1974.

Page 114: 3 World Health Organization. *Targets for health for all: targets in support of the European regional strategy for health for all*. Copenhagen: World Health Organization, Regional Office for Europe, 1985.

4 Secretary of State for Health. *The Health of the Nation: a strategy for health in England*. London: HMSO, 1992 (Cm 1986).

5 Department of Health. *Saving Lives: Our Healthier Nation*. London: The Stationery Office, 1999 (Cm 4386).

Page 118: 6 National Screening Committee. *First report of the National Screening Committee*. London: Health Departments of the United Kingdom, 1998.

Page 119: 7 Wilson JMG, Jungner G. *The principles and practice of screening for disease*. Public Health Papers, 34. Geneva: World Health Organization, 1968.

Page 124: 8 Shapiro S. *Evidence of screening for breast cancer from a randomised trial*. Cancer, 1977; 39: 2772–82.

9 *Breast Cancer Screening*. Report to the Health Ministers of England, Wales, Scotland and Northern Ireland by a working group chaired by Sir Patrick Forrest. London: HMSO, 1987.

Page 132: 10 Department of Health and Social Security. *Inequalities in health: report of a research working group* (The Black Report). London: HMSO, 1980.

11 Townsend P, Phillimore P, Beattie A. *Deprivation and health: inequality and the north*. Beckenham: Croom Helm, 1987.

Page 133: 12 Wilkinson, R. *Unhealthy societies: the afflictions of inequality*. London: Routledge, 1996.

Page 134: 13 Acheson D. *Report of the Independent Inquiry into Inequalities in Health*. London: The Stationery Office, 1998. Chairman: Sir D Acheson.

Page 161: 14 Department of Health. Committee on Medical Aspects of Food Policy. Panel on Dietary Reference Values. *Dietary reference values for food energy and nutrients for the United Kingdom.* London: HMSO, 1991. (Reports on health and social subjects, 41). Chairman of COMA: Sir D Acheson.

Chapter 4

Page 178:   1   Department of Health. *The new NHS: modern, dependable.* London: The Stationery Office, 1997 (Cm 3807).

Page 192:   2   Donabedian A. *Evaluating the quality of medical care.* Milbank Memorial Fund Quarterly, 1966; 4: 166–206.

Page 195:   3   Deming WE. *Out of the crisis.* Cambridge: Cambridge University Press, 1986.

                4   Juran JM. *Managerial breakthrough.* New York: McGraw-Hill, 1964.

Page 197:   5   Liggins GC, Howie RN. *A controlled trial of antepartum glucocorticoid treatment for prevention of the respiratory distress syndrome in premature infants.* Paediatrics, 1972; 50: 515–525.

Page 211:   6   Gray AJG, Hoile RW, Ingram GS, Sherry KM, Tindall VR (eds). *The report of the National Confidential Enquiry into Perioperative Deaths 1996/1997 (1 April 1996 to 31 March 1997).* London: National Confidential Enquiry into Perioperative Deaths, 1998.

Chapter 5

Page 226:   1   World Health Organization. *International Classification of Impairments, Disabilities and Handicaps.* Geneva: World Health Organization, 1980.

Chapter 7

Page 291:   1   Faris REL, Dunham HW. *Mental disorders in urban areas: an ecological study of schizophrenia and other psychoses.* Chicago: University of Chicago Press, 1939.

                2   Hollingshead AB, Redlich FC. *Social class and mental illness.* New York: John Wiley, 1958.

Chapter 9

Page 392:   1   Salisbury DM, Begg NT (eds). *Immunisation against infectious disease.* London: HMSO, 1996.

Index